A history of the Hebrew langu

description of Hebrew from it[s] Semitic origins and the earliest settlement of the Israelite tribes in Canaan to the present day. Although Hebrew is an 'oriental' language, it is nonetheless closely associated with Western culture as the language of the Bible and was used in writing by the Jews of Europe throughout the Middle Ages. It has also been newly revived in modern times as the language of the State of Israel.

Professor Angel Sáenz-Badillos sets Hebrew in the context of the Northwest Semitic languages and examines the origins of Hebrew and its earliest manifestations in ancient biblical poetry, inscriptions, and prose written before the Babylonian exile. He looks at the different mediaeval traditions of pointing classical biblical Hebrew texts and the characteristic features of the post-exilic language, including the Hebrew of the Dead Sea Scrolls. He gives particular attention to Rabbinic and mediaeval Hebrew, especially as evidenced in writings from Spain. His survey concludes with the revival of the language this century in the form of Israeli Hebrew.

A history of the Hebrew language

A HISTORY OF THE HEBREW LANGUAGE

ANGEL SÁENZ-BADILLOS
Department of Hebrew and Aramaic Studies, Universidad Complutense, Madrid

Translated by
JOHN ELWOLDE
Department of Biblical Studies, University of Sheffield

CAMBRIDGE
UNIVERSITY PRESS

PUBLISHED BY THE PRESS SYNDICATE OF THE UNIVERSITY OF CAMBRIDGE
The Pitt Building, Trumpington Street, Cambridge, United Kingdom

CAMBRIDGE UNIVERSITY PRESS
The Edinburgh Building, Cambridge CB2 2RU, UK
40 West 20th Street, New York, NY 10011–4211, USA
477 Williamstown Road, Port Melbourne, VIC 3207, Australia
Ruiz de Alarcón 13, 28014 Madrid, Spain
Dock House, The Waterfront, Cape Town 8001, South Africa

http://www.cambridge.org

Originally published in Spanish as *Historia de la Lengua Hebrea* by Editorial AUSA, Sabadell 1988
© Angel Sáenz-Badillos and Editorial AUSA, Sabadell 1988
First published in English by Cambridge University Press 1993 as *A history of the Hebrew language*
First paperback edition 1996
Reprinted 1997, 2000, 2002, 2004

Printed in the United Kingdom at the University Press, Cambridge

A catalogue record for this book is available from the British Library

Library of Congress Cataloguing in Publication data
Sáenz-Badillos, Angel
[Historia de la lengua hebrea. English]
A history of the Hebrew language / Angel Sáenz-Badillos; translated by John Elwolde.
p. cm.
Translation of: Historia de la lengua hebrea.
Includes bibliographical references and index.
ISBN 0 521 43157 3 (hardback). ISBN 0 521 55634 1 (paperback)
1. Hebrew language–History. I. Title.
PJ4545.S2313 1993
492.4′09–dc20 93-20367 CIP

ISBN 0 521 43157 3 hardback
ISBN 0 521 55634 1 paperback

AU

Contents

Foreword

SHELOMO MORAG
Bialik Professor of Hebrew
The Hebrew University of Jerusalem

Originally written as a textbook for university students, A. Sáenz-Badillos's *Historia de la lengua hebrea* turned out to be the most comprehensive extant history of Hebrew.[1] The need for such a book has been felt not only among students and scholars but also among readers who, although not Hebraists, are, nonetheless, interested in the cultural history of the Jewish people. The translation of the book into English should, therefore, be welcomed – a wider circle of readers will now have access to the abundant mines of information it has to offer.

No history of the Hebrew language can be complete, not only because of the total length of the periods it has to cover – over 3,000 years – but also, and mainly, because the available sources do not provide all the data necessary for a continuous description. In tracing the history of Hebrew since its inception as a Canaanite dialect to present-day idiom, the author has exhaustively investigated the results of research carried out on the major chapters of this history. The rich bibliography the book includes – an asset in itself – bears evidence of the studies used in its preparation. It should be added that the author has made a point of presenting the conflicting views on a number of important

[1] Other modern scholarly works cover either a shorter period or the same period but with less detail: the *Histoire de la langue hébraïque* of M. Hadas-Lebel (1981), a fourth revised edition of which appeared in 1986, does not extend beyond the Mishnaic period; E.Y. Kutscher's posthumous *A history of the Hebrew language*, edited by R. Kutscher (E.Y. Kutscher 1982), suffers the limitations of an unfinished work; C. Rabin's *A short history of the Hebrew language*, which has been translated from Hebrew into English (Rabin 1973) and other languages, contains just eighty-six pages.

topics. Thus the book is also, to a considerable extent, a history of the scholarly study of Hebrew.

But the book is far from being an accumulation of research results and scholarly opinions – Professor Sáenz-Badillos has succeeded in achieving continuity in the description, portraying a clear picture of the language in its relationship with the history of the Jewish people.

A history of the Hebrew language is an important addition to the significant contributions to the study of Hebrew made by the Spanish school of Hebrew philology, and it has the merits to become an essential tool for teaching and research.

Acknowledgements

Dr J.F. Elwolde of the University of Sheffield undertook the burdensome task not only of translating the original but also of preparing camera-ready copy for publication. Moreover, he has been in regular contact with me during the last three years, with numerous recommendations for improving the original text to make it more useful to readers who are not specialists in Hebrew. He has also provided Hebrew and transcriptional equivalents for data presented originally in transliteration only,[1] substantially restructured the footnotes and Bibliography (which has been considerably expanded and updated for this version), and compiled an Index. All in all, the present volume may justifiably be regarded as a revised edition of the Spanish original.

We should like to express particular gratitude to Dr W.G.E. Watson, who regularly reviewed the translation as it

---

[1] The Hebrew forms and their associated transcriptions normally follow a traditional interpretation of Tiberian orthography and pronunciation (for example, *dagesh forte* is represented in transcription by the doubling of a consonant and *qameṣ gadol* by long *a*: ā), although tone-long and pure-long vowels are not distinguished from one another. Except where non-Tiberian orthography and/or pronunciation is clearly relevant (for example, at Qumran and in Samaritan and certain rabbinic forms), the great majority of Hebrew forms in this book, including those from Rabbinic, Mediaeval, and Israeli Hebrew, conform to Tiberian standards in consonant and vowel orthography and in pronunciation. Otherwise, unpointed forms are only used when quoting structures that appear in particular rabbinic or mediaeval works, although such forms are still transcribed in the normal way. Except in connexion with Samaritan Hebrew, the occasional use of 'pron.' before a transcription indicates the expected Tiberian pronunciation of an unvocalized form. In Chapter 6.5, 'Bab.' and 'Pal.' indicate Babylonian and Palestinian traditions of Rabbinic Hebrew. Where possible, the orthography of quotations has been checked against their original sources. In presenting Hebrew proper names, titles of publications, technical terms, and so on, this English edition generally follows *Encyclopaedia Judaica*.

progressed and prepared a preliminary version of the Index, and to Mr N.K. Bailey for his extensive assistance in proofreading. Thanks are also due to Dr N.R.M. de Lange and Dr D. Talshir for their help and encouragement in the early stages, to Mr J. Williams for his generous assistance with computing equipment and skills, and to Cambridge University Press for their alacrity in agreeing to undertake publication and their patience in seeing the work through to completion.

In the present reprint we have been able to incorporate various small changes and improvements arising in particular from the reviews of J. Blau, S. Bolozky, T. Muraoka, and S. Noegel.

ASB

Madrid

Chapter 1

HEBREW IN THE CONTEXT OF THE SEMITIC LANGUAGES

1.1 *Hebrew, a Semitic language*

Hebrew is a Semitic dialect or language which developed in the northwestern part of the Near East between the River Jordan and the Mediterranean Sea during the latter half of the second millennium BCE. The country comprising this area was known as Canaan, a name that is also associated with the language in its earliest written sources: שְׂפַת כְּנַעַן (śᵉp̄aṯ kᵉna'an) 'the language of Canaan' (Is 19:18). Elsewhere, the language is called יְהוּדִית (yᵉhūḏīṯ) 'Judaean, Judahite' (2 K 18:26, 28, etc.). In the Hellenistic period, writers refer to it by the Greek term *Hebraios, Hebraïsti* (Josephus, *Antiquities* I, 1:2 etc.),[1] and under the Roman Empire it was known as עִבְרִית ('iḇrīṯ) 'Hebrew' or לָשׁוֹן עִבְרִי(ת) (lāšōn 'iḇrī[ṯ]) 'Hebrew language' (Mishnah, Gittin 9:8, etc.), terms that recalled Eber (Gn 11:14), ancestor of the people that would become known, like Abraham (Gn 14:13), by the name 'Hebrew'.[2]

From a cultural perspective, this language was to play an extremely important rôle, not only in the history of the people who spoke it, but also within Western culture in general. It was to be

[1] However, G.H. Dalman (1905, 1) points out that Josephus and the author of John's Gospel use this term for both Hebrew and Aramaic.

[2] The origin of the name has still not been adequately explained. Understanding it as related to the root עבר ('br) 'pass', an allusion to a transition from the other side of the river, smacks of popular etymology. A more widespread modern view relates it to the Ḫabiru or Ḫapiru mentioned in numerous sources from Egypt and the Near East, although this implies that the name was originally an appellative and only later a gentilic. Clearly, such a theory would need to be specified in great detail. See Greenberg 1970; Loretz 1984.

the language of the Bible as well as the idiom in which the Jewish people would compose a large part of its literature, both prose and verse, a language which in spite of periods of obscurity has never completely disappeared, and survives in our own time with the cultural trappings of more than 3,000 years.[3]

A special aura soon developed around the language. For Jews it was לְשׁוֹן הַקֹּדֶשׁ (ləšōn haq-qōḏæš) 'the language of sanctity, the holy tongue'.[4] They also considered, like many Christians, that it was the very first language, the 'language of creation' in the words of the rabbis and the early Church Fathers: 'And all the inhabitants of the earth were (of) just one language and (of) just one speech, and they spoke in the language of the Temple, for through it the world was created, in the beginning.'[5] In a more rationalizing vein, this claim was justified by pointing out that only in Hebrew is the wordplay on אִישׁ ('īš) 'man' and אִשָּׁה ('iššā) 'woman' (Gn 2:23) possible – from this, the midrash concludes, the world must have been created through Hebrew.[6]

In the age of Rationalism, Hebrew was able to free itself from the reverential epithets it had accrued over centuries, and was viewed instead as simply another of the languages or dialects spoken in the extreme southeast of Asia, known from the eighteenth century

[3] See Chomsky 1969, 206ff.; Federbush 1967.

[4] Thus designated during the rabbinic era: Mishnah, Sotah 7:2, Targum Yerushalmi on Gn 31:11, etc. The name was widely used during the Middle Ages, and is standard in Hebrew literature. Sometimes it created conflicts in the realm of philology, so that certain mediaeval linguists, for example Menaḥem b. Saruq, refrained from comparing it with other languages.

[5] Targum Neofiti on Gn 11:1, according to the edition and translation of A. Díez Macho (Madrid/Barcelona, 1968), p. 56. A similar attitude is found in Targum Jonathan (see the translation of E. Levine in *Neofiti II: Exodus* (Barcelona, 1970), p. 550) and Pirke Rabbi Eleazar 24. See Díaz Esteban 1982.

[6] Bereshit Rabbah 18. The text was to be noted by Rashi in his commentary on the passage. However, alongside this tradition runs another, again widespread among Jews, Arabs, Syriac Christians, and the Church Fathers, according to which Aramaic or 'Syriac' is the oldest language and the language of creation. See Renan 1855, 223. For example, Theodoret of Cyrrhus claimed that the names of the earliest people were Aramaic, whereas Hebrew was the holy tongue given to Moses by God at the same time as the Torah, and was, thus, a taught rather than a natural language (*Quaestiones in Octateuchum*, in the edition of N. Fernández and A. Sáenz-Badillos (Madrid, 1979), pp. 56f.).

onwards as the 'Semitic' languages, a term first introduced by G.W. Leibniz and given wider currency by A.L. Schlözer on the basis of the list of Noah's descendants in Gn 10:21ff,[7] which itself reflects early ideas about the family relationship of Arabic, Hebrew, and Aramaic. Later, knowledge of new languages would lead to other names being added to the Semitic family, giving it a more appropriate position within the framework of the 'Afro-Asiatic' languages.

Nowadays, about seventy different languages or dialects are recognized as Semitic. They are spread unevenly in space and time, and vary greatly in their importance, from languages which have existed across large areas for centuries to small, scarcely documented, dialects, known only through recent epigraphic discoveries. But recognizable in all of them are common features of phonology, morphology, syntax, and vocabulary, at times considerably more significant than those shared by languages of other families, such as Indo-European.

In terms of geography, the Semitic languages are found throughout a large area, extending from Mesopotamia in the northeast down to southern Arabia and the coastlands of Ethiopia, and including the Syro-Palestinian region to the northwest.

Four and a half thousand years ago, in the northeast, Old Akkadian replaced Sumerian, a non-Semitic language which influenced Akkadian in a number of ways and from which Akkadian borrowed its system of cuneiform writing. In the northwest, in cities like Ebla, a Semitic language was also used during this period. In the second millennium BCE, while in the northeast Akkadian split into the Babylonian and Assyrian dialects, an area further to the west witnessed the rise of Amorite and, later, Ugaritic and other languages known through the Proto-Canaanite inscriptions, the inscriptions from Byblos and Sinai, and from the El-Amarna glosses. At the close of the second millennium, the

[7] See *Miscellanea Berolinensia* (Berlin, 1710), p. 4 and J.G. Eichhorn's *Repertorium für biblische und morgenländische Literatur*, VIII (Leipzig, 1781), p. 161.

differences between two families, Canaanite and Aramaic, became more pronounced, and both developed independently throughout the first millennium BCE. Hebrew, like Phoenician and some other less well-known languages, is a member of the Canaanite group. With its long and complicated history, it is, together with some minor Aramaic dialects, one of the few Northwest Semitic languages to survive to the present day.

In the southwest, from a later period, we find South Arabian, Arabic, and Ethiopic with their various dialects. The oldest inscriptions from this region may go back to the eighth century BCE. Historically, it is the most widespread of the groups, and has made the most noticeable impression right up to the present day.

The geographical area occupied by the Semitic languages is neither absolutely fixed nor completely sealed, as traces of non-Semitic languages are also found in it. Moreover, there are some extreme cases where it is difficult to decide whether or not a language should be regarded as Semitic. For example, some years ago it was argued that Libyan was Semitic,[8] although this has since been generally rejected – similar comments apply to other efforts to classify as Semitic the language of Mycenaean Linear A, Hittite, etc.

Following various attempts to describe the main characteristics of the Semitic languages, E. Ullendorff, in a well-known work,[9] reviewed the criteria which might be used in identifying a given language as Semitic. For Ullendorff, none of the principles standardly employed are by themselves conclusive. For example, the claim that in the Semitic languages there is a special relationship between consonants and vowels, with the consonants being predominant, often does not correspond with the statistical evidence. The claim that in the Semitic languages only the consonants convey meaning is not entirely true either, as the vowels can function as more than mere semantic 'modifiers' in

[8] See Rössler 1952; 1964.

[9] Ullendorff 1958.

connexion with nouns and particles, especially those that have a biliteral structure. Moreover, claims about the triliteralism of the Semitic root are clearly questionable, given that the phenomenon is known from other languages, and has not been proved to be of greater antiquity than the biconsonantalism preserved in various Semitic nouns and even verbs. The guttural and emphatic consonants, which are sometimes presented as typical of Semitic, are also found elsewhere, for example in the Cushitic languages. Parataxis, a characteristic of earlier stages of the Semitic languages, has lost its dominant rôle in a number of modern Semitic languages, and cannot therefore be regarded as a definite criterion.

Ullendorff's criticisms are offset by his positive suggestions. The Hamito-Semitic languages should be regarded as a single whole, in which the sharing of major linguistic features enables statements not merely of affinity among the languages but of 'genetic' relationship as well. Language identification and classification can be aided by, for example, examination of structural patterns, phonological incompatibilities, etc., cautious comparison of vocabulary, application of statistical analysis to various linguistic features, detection of isoglosses and bundles of isoglosses, and even investigation into whether speakers of Hamito-Semitic languages share a typical way of conceptualizing.

From the beginning of the tenth century, many Jewish scholars who lived in an Islamic cultural environment realized that comparison of Hebrew with other related languages, specifically Arabic and Aramaic, could assist in the understanding of the more obscure passages of the Bible and especially its *hapax legomena*. Thus began the study of Comparative Semitics, in which for various reasons Hebrew initially had a dominant rôle, but which was later to develop a more scientifically philological character.

In the Christian world, the polyglot Bibles of the sixteenth and seventeenth centuries as well as multilingual dictionaries like E. Castell's *Lexicon Heptaglotton* laid the foundations of comparative study, which was spurred on in the eighteenth century by the Dutchman A. Schultens.

In the nineteenth century, Comparative Semitics reached a peak with the important works of F.H.W. Gesenius, E. Renan, T. Nöldeke, A. Dillmann, C. Brockelmann, and others. This was the same period that saw the advance of Comparative Linguistics in general and the discovery of new Semitic languages thanks to archaeology and the laborious process of decipherment. Thus, due in large part to their efforts, it would nowadays be unthinkable to study any one of these languages without regard to the perspective offered by comparison with the structure and development of the rest.[10]

The present century witnessed the emergence of many famous Semitists, including most notably G. Bergsträsser, M. Cohen, W.F. Albright, G.R. Driver, and H.J. Polotsky, to whom we shall be referring later, as well as a number of outstanding scholars who are still alive today.[11]

1.2 *The Semitic languages*

Although interest in the Semitic languages started off as strictly linguistic, many investigators, including some of the best, have ventured into the fields of ethnic origins, anthropology, or culture, including religion. Thus, various modern scholars have argued that the linguistic unity of the different members of the Semitic family is explicable only as the result of a common origin.[12] According to them, there is sufficient evidence – for example, common geographical habitat and unity of language, history, and

[10] See Brockelmann 1944; Polotsky 1964; Hospers 1966; Ullendorff 1961; 1970. There is a bibliography in Hospers 1973, 365ff.

[11] See Hospers 1966; Sáenz-Badillos 1975.

[12] This has been defended by, for example, S. Moscati in numerous works, listed in the Bibliography. His view is shared by writers like E. Renan, G. Levi della Vida, W.R. Smith, and E. Nielsen.

culture – to regard speakers of the various Semitic languages as comprising a single people and perhaps even embodying a particular racial type.

Without entering too deeply into argument about these theories, we do not think it possible to progress beyond mere hypothesis in such matters, given that they refer to historically inaccessible times. And whether or not it is correct, this image of a Semitic people speaking the same language and living in the same culture is not the only possible one. Historical data can only take us back to a stage in which there is already more diversity than unity, with distinct peoples across a wide area speaking languages which have certain elements in common, sharing some aspects of culture, but also undergoing a number of independent developments as well.

Approaching the issue from a would-be 'historical' perspective, the ancient Semites' homeland or point of origin has long been debated. The plains of Central Asia, Mesopotamia, Syria-Palestine, North Africa, and finally and most commonly, Arabia, have all received support in this kind of study.[13] A quite widespread view would identify the ancient Semites with the nomads of the Arabian desert – from here there would have been a number of migrations towards the periphery, with various groups gradually settling in neighbouring cultivatable lands. Some experts have claimed that groups of Semites had established themselves in the area of Syria before the third millennium BCE.[14] And given the notion of Hamito-Semitic unity, it is hardly surprising that various scholars have argued that the first speakers of Semitic came from the north of Africa, and that they then could have settled in a single place or immediately spread out across the Near East.[15]

The difficulties associated with this historical problem have left their mark on strictly linguistic issues – supporters of the 'historical' approach have to assume the existence of a series of

13 The different theories are listed in Hadas-Lebel 1981, 10f.

14 See R. Meyer 1966–72, I, 13f.

15 See Rabin 1982, 339f. The thesis of a possible African origin had already been formulated by T. Nöldeke (1899, 11).

proto-languages (Proto-Northwest Semitic, etc.), for which we have no documentation at all, while attempting to draw up a precise 'family tree' of the Semitic languages. In contrast, a more sober and objective approach to the comparative data offers an image of distinct Semitic languages sharing a range of features.

The diversity of the Semitic languages is especially problematic for supporters of the 'historical' theory, and has led to various versions of the hypothesis, widespread for several decades now, that successive waves ('Invasionswellen') of Semites proceeded from the Arabian desert to the surrounding territories, imposing their particular dialects in these places. Thus, between 2000 and 1700 BCE there would have been an Amorite (early West Semitic) wave, and between 1400 and 900 an Aramaean (late West Semitic) wave; finally, in the eighth century CE, there was an Arab wave.[16] The historical basis for the first two 'invasions' is not as clear as that of the last one, leading some authors,[17] in more recent studies, to develop a theory of 'infiltration' which is less rigid than the 'wave' theory.

Even if it is clear that the migration of Semitic-speaking groups did play a part in spreading the various languages, it is difficult to account in this way for the origins of the substantial differences that can exist between one Semitic language and another. As emphasized some time ago,[18] there are no clearly defined boundaries between the languages of the different 'waves' and no inherited features shared between distant areas, which we should expect if the 'wave' theory were correct.

The actual situation is better explained by reference to, for example, dialect geography, according to which the spread of linguistic features generally moves from the centre outward towards the margins, resulting in clear differences between the dialects of one zone and another as well as clear and consistent isoglosses. Thus, for example, when a feature which is not the

16 See R. Meyer 1966–72, I, 14f.
17 S. Moscati and others.
18 See Rabin 1963, 106.

result of internal development within the language is found in areas far apart from one another, it should be regarded as a preserved common, primitive, element, whereas novel linguistic features have succeeded in diffusing themselves in the territory between such areas.

Using this method we can distinguish a central zone in the Semitic area, namely the Arabian peninsula, and two peripheral regions, first, from Palestine to Mesopotamia including Ugarit, and second, Ethiopia. In the northern periphery, circumstances led to major cultural development which turned the area into the least conservative zone and the most important centre of innovations. In this way, the divisions among the Semitic languages are explicable in terms of diffusion of such innovations within the region from a conglomeration of homogeneous dialects, geographically located from the beginning in the same situation as that in which they are historically attested. Isoglosses and bundles of isoglosses separate some Semitic languages from others, while other equally important isoglosses pass through the various language groups.

However, the 'wave' theory has recently been defended less controversially,[19] not by assuming migration of ethnic groups but by reference to the existence of *linguae francae*, like Akkadian in the second millennium BCE or Aramaic in the first, which would have fostered cultural contacts and parallel developments in different Semitic dialects. Phenomena regarded by proponents of dialect geography as evidence for the spread of innovations can also be explained by contacts among languages and parallel developments.

The classification of the Semitic languages has been the object of long debate and continuous revision because of new discoveries. The traditional view which distinguished five principal languages, Akkadian, Canaanite, Aramaic, Arabic, and Ethiopic, is clearly inadequate today. And if, thanks to dialect geography or a highly

[19] See Blau 1978.

modified version of the 'wave' theory, we can explain why Akkadian and Ethiopic or Arabic and Ugaritic share certain features, there remain problems concerning the grouping and classification of dialects about which there is still no basic agreement.

A common view is that the first division within the Semitic area happened before 3000 BCE, separating Northeast Semitic (Akkadian) from the rest. It seems likely that before 2000 BCE West Semitic had already split into two branches, Northern and Southern. At the end of the second millennium the Canaanite and Aramaic groups emerged within Northwest Semitic. In the south, differences developed among Arabic (North Arabian), South Arabian, and Ethiopic. Each one of these branches eventually evolved into the languages and dialects we know today.

C. Rabin, from the viewpoint of dialect geography, divides the Semitic languages into two marginal areas, Northern and Southern, and a Central area stretching from the Mediterranean to Arabia.[20] I.M. Diakonoff prefers to speak of the Northern Peripheral (Akkadian) and Northern Central (Northwest Semitic) zones as distinct from the Southern Central (Arabic) and Southern Peripheral (South Arabian and Ethiopic) zones.[21]

However, there remain many problems within each of these areas. In Northwest Semitic, for example, the correct identification and characterization of the language of Ebla, which was only discovered in 1974, has still not been properly resolved. One of its discoverers, G. Pettinato, proposed that Eblaite be regarded as a third group within Northwest Semitic.[22] But there have also been many other suggestions – a notable one argues for the relative independence of Eblaite from East and Northwest Semitic, labelling it as Northeast, or simply Northern, Semitic.[23]

20 See Rabin 1963, 107.

21 See Diakonoff 1965, 11f.

22 See Pettinato 1975.

23 See, for example, Hecker 1982, 8. A sign of growing interest aroused in the language of Ebla are the international congresses dedicated to it, in which very diverse opinions have

Furthermore, the traditional distinction between Canaanite and Aramaic dialects is in crisis. The evidence of languages like Amorite, Ugaritic, Ya'udic, Nabataean, and Palmyrene have also considerably disrupted earlier classifications.[24]

Our knowledge of Amorite, attested solely in proper names which appear on cuneiform tablets and which display features of Northwest Semitic, is far from adequate, and recent studies have complicated the issue further by suggesting that languages as far apart as, for example, Ya'udic, the Aramaic dialects, Hebrew, Phoenician, and North Arabian, may be regarded as dialects of Amorite.[25]

The discovery of Ugaritic in 1929 also required a revision of traditional theories. In the first years following its decipherment, C. Virolleaud, Z.S. Harris, C.H. Gordon, and others placed it among the Canaanite dialects.[26] M. Cohen assigned it an intermediate position between West and East Semitic,[27] N.H. Ṭur-Sinai concluded that it was a branch of South Semitic,[28] and A. Goetze, J. Cantineau, and, in later studies, C.H. Gordon, emphasized Ugaritic's special characteristics and advocated its autonomy.[29] M.J. Dahood insisted in numerous works on a close relationship with Hebrew.[30] Nowadays Ugaritic is regarded as a Northwest Semitic language, but it is a matter of debate as to whether it should be considered as a special subgroup having a more or less close relationship with Eblaite and forming a type of 'North Semitic', or whether it should be placed within the

been expressed – see Cagni 1981; 1984; Fronzaroli 1984. I.M. Diakonoff (1990) suggests that Eblaite was a part of the Common Proto-Semitic dialect continuum, positioned between East and West Semitic. C.H. Gordon (1990) calls it a 'border language'.

24 See, for example, Moscati 1956; Friedrich 1965; Ginsberg 1970.

25 Following G. Garbini (1972, 43f.), who also proposes a new classification of the Semitic languages: (1) Canaanite, (2) Akkadian, (3) the Amorite group, (4) South Arabian, (5) Ethiopic (155ff.). See von Soden 1960.

26 See Virolleaud 1931; Harris 1939, 97ff.; Gordon 1940a, 88.

27 See M. Cohen 1952, 104ff.

28 See Ṭur-Sinai 1951–52.

29 See Goetze 1941; Cantineau 1932–40; 1950; Gordon 1947a, etc.

30 See Dahood 1959, etc.

Canaanite group, as suggested by, for example, H.L. Ginsberg,[31] who attempted to class it with Phoenician in contrast to the subgroup formed by Hebrew and Moabite.

The differences between Aramaic on the one hand and the Canaanite languages and Ugaritic on the other seem to have gained general acceptance nowadays. However, the distinction between these two major groups is not valid before the end of the second millennium, as in the earliest stage of the Northwest Semitic languages they had not yet diverged.[32] Moreover, the traditional unity of the Aramaic dialects has been threatened by attempts to include Ya'udic, attested in the north of Syria from perhaps the close of the second millennium BCE, with archaic features similar to those of the Canaanite dialects.[33] Also in connexion with the Aramaic group, there is debate about the nature of the Palmyrene and Nabataean dialects, which use an Aramaic script and which are usually included within the Aramaic group, but which in the opinion of some experts might really be dialects of Arabic.[34]

The validity of the Southern Semitic group is still often disputed. Certain scholars have claimed, somewhat uncovincingly,[35] that Arabic is genetically related to Canaanite, Ugaritic and Aramaic,[36] while others believe that South Arabian and Ethiopic have special ties with Northeast Semitic.[37]

In the northeast, Old Akkadian (*c.* 2800–1950 BCE) was replaced by the Babylonian and Assyrian dialects in the second millennium; Akkadian spread over a vast area, until finally conceding entirely to Aramaic around the sixth century BCE. The influence of its

31 1970, 105.
32 See Garbini 1960, 9ff.; Moscati 1969, 4ff.
33 See Dion 1974.
34 See Hecker 1982, 9.
35 See Blau 1978, 31ff.
36 R. Hetzron (1974, 191) proposes a new Central Semitic group which would include Arabic, Canaanite, and Aramaic, in contrast to a Southern Semitic group comprising South Arabian and Ethiopic.
37 See Hetzron 1974, 183f.

Sumerian substratum is obvious not only in the use of a cuneiform system of writing, but also in the weakness of the laryngeal and pharyngeal consonants in Akkadian. In contrast to the other Semitic languages, Akkadian does not use, except as a stative, the verbal pattern *qatala*, known throughout the western area, or the internal passive pattern *qutila*.[38]. It is not certain whether its second prefix-conjugation of the verb, *iparras* (= *yaqattal*), represents a special new formation, or whether, as many specialists believe, it is a Proto-Semitic or even Hamito-Semitic form.[39] The spread of Akkadian as the language of administration throughout the Near East led to contacts with Indo-European languages and also facilitated the borrowing of hundreds of its lexical items by languages like Hebrew.

The results of recent investigations into Eblaite are still not sufficiently clear to permit an adequate classification. The almost 15,000 tablets that were uncovered in 1974–1975 were written between 2500 and 2300 BCE and contain numerous proper names of a Northwest Semitic type along with many words and phrases in a language that is still the object of much debate.[40]

Amorite, again a language under dispute, is attested in Syria and Mesopotamia between 2250 and 1000 BCE, and is known mainly because of the proper names and some common nouns found in the tablets from Mari and other places nearby. Despite the many difficulties connected with Amorite, the common view is that it is the oldest Northwest Semitic language yet discovered.

Contrary to the Northeast variety, West Semitic presents as a characteristic innovation the use of *qatala* as a verbal form; regarding the form *yaqtulu*, opinions are divided, with the majority

38 See Blau 1978, 25.

39 See von Soden 1952, 126ff., and, on this specific problem, Polotsky 1964, 110f.

40 See Pettinato 1975. Studies about Ebla have since multiplied. Apart from the works cited in note 23, see, for example: Pettinato 1981; Dahood 1982; H.-P. Müller 1984, etc. The Missione Archeologica Italiana in Syria has begun to publish the series *Archivi reali di Ebla: testi*, of which volumes I (Archi 1985), II (Edzard 1981), III (Archi and Biga 1982), and V (Edzard 1984) have appeared. See also Beld, Hallo, and Michalowski 1984; Gordon, Rendsburg, and Winter 1990. There is a regularly appearing journal dedicated to Ebla.

of Semitists viewing it as Proto-Semitic or Hamito-Semitic, while others claim that it is a western innovation.[41]

Among the peculiarities of the Northwest Semitic languages as a whole, which we shall examine in greater detail in Chapter 2, particularly noteworthy is the change of initial *w* to *y*, which cannot very easily be explained on phonetic grounds, as well as the complete assimilation of unvocalized *nun* to the following consonant (although this feature is not unique to the Northwest area). Some experts would also include the development of 'segolate' vocalization of certain monosyllabic nouns.[42]

Arabic clearly shares certain features with Northwest Semitic, like the verbal form *yaqtulu*, suffix-conjugation suffixes in *-t* (as opposed to *-k* in Southern Semitic), the development *-at* > *-ah* in the pausal form of the feminine noun (which did not occur in, for example, Ugaritic or Phoenician), the interrogative *mah*, etc. However, it does not appear that Arabic should be included in the same 'Central' group to which Canaanite and Aramaic belong,[43] given that such similarities might be due to parallel development, while on the other hand features shared by Arabic with other languages of the Southern group are much more decisive – notable among these are the broken plurals[44] and the special development of the verbal form *qatala*, which are innovations in morphology that distinguish this group from other branches of Semitic. It has been accepted for some time that South Arabian and Ethiopic should be regarded as a single unit distinct from Arabic.[45]

Within the Southern area, the earliest South Arabian inscriptions are usually dated between the eighth and fifth centuries BCE.[46] Ancient dialects include Sabaean, Minaean, and Ḥaḍrami, which

41 See Blau 1978, 27ff., with its bibliography on this subject.

42 See Ginsberg 1970, 103.

43 As suggested in Hetzron 1974, 191.

44 See Blau 1978, 29f.

45 See, for example, Cantineau 1932.

46 See Hecker 1982, 9f.

disappeared around 1000 CE. The present-day languages of Meḥri, Shḫawri, etc. represent a branch of the same language family.

The coastlands of East Africa were colonized from South Arabia, leading to the development of Ethiopic dialects like Ge'ez (third to twelfth centuries CE), from which, in the north, Tigriña and Tigre are descended; in the south we should note Amharic (first attested in the fourteenth century CE) as well as other dialects like Harari and Gurage, the origins of which are uncertain.[47]

To the north, the North Arabian inscriptions from Thamud, Liḥyan, etc., date from between the fifth century BCE and the fifth century CE, with Classical Arabic appearing relatively late – the inscription of King Mar'alqais, found south of Damascus and dated at 328 CE, is usually said to be the first document in Arabic.[48] Of the various dialects of the Arabian peninsula, Classical Arabic arose as a potential *lingua franca* halfway through the first millennium CE, progressing from its earliest literary manifestations in the pre-Islamic poetry of the sixth century CE and especially in the Koran to extend its dominion in spectacular fashion with the conquests of the Caliphate, and continuing alive and active in a great variety of dialects until the present day.

1.3 *Common or Proto-Semitic*

Consistent with the idea that the Semitic peoples have a single ethnic origin, the tendency has been to regard Common Semitic as a proto-language with particular characteristics which can be reconstructed, on the basis of features held to be primitive in the various historically-documented Semitic languages.[49]

Nowadays, however, the validity of the family-tree image and the idea often associated with this that one or more languages can

47 An important attempt at genealogical classification, especially of the Ethiopic languages, is Hetzron 1974.

48 See Hecker 1982; Altheim and Stiel 1965, 313ff., 357ff.

49 See, for example, Moscati 1960.

'give birth' to another tend to be regarded with suspicion as they go beyond the evidence of the extant linguistic data. Various attempts to reconstruct this alleged common language have not met with scholarly acceptance.[50]

If, nonetheless, the term 'Proto-Semitic' is still to be used, it simply refers to the totality of common features – isoglosses – exhibited by the historically-observable Semitic languages, which might have been shared by this group of dialects at its earliest period.[51] Thus, 'Proto-Semitic' is more a postulate or linguistic convention than an actual ancient language spoken by a recognizable group.

The ancient Semitic languages have no common system of writing, and the sorts of writing that exist do not correspond exactly with the classification of the Semitic languages by other criteria. In the northeast, Akkadian adopted cuneiform from the non-Semitic Sumerians, and this was to have a major influence on the language. In the northwest and south a new system evolved, later to be passed on to Greek, Latin, and other Indo-European languages. During the second millennium BCE, however, certain languages in the northwest still used the Akkadian writing system or a cuneiform alphabet, like the one at Ugarit.

According to J. Naveh,[52] the Semitic alphabets originated with Proto-Canaanite (eighteenth to seventeenth centuries BCE), from which there was derived around 1300 BCE the Proto-Arabic script, the ancestor of the systems used in the South Arabian and Ethiopic scripts. Phoenician writing is a continuation of the Proto-Canaanite system, and from these developed the Palaeo-Hebrew script (*c.* 800 BCE) and the Aramaic script (*c.* 700 BCE), which was adopted by Hebrew after the Babylonian exile. Around 200 BCE there emerged

50 See R. Meyer 1966–72, I, 17, etc., and Garbini 1972, 162f.: 'una lingua comune alla base del semitico, e ancora più alla base del semitico-camitico, mi sembra che sia assolutamente da escludere.'

51 See Ullendorff 1961; 1970; Moscati 1969, 15.

52 1982, 9ff.

a variety of Aramaic script known as Nabataean, from which the system used by Arabic would later develop.

These genuinely Semitic writing systems are historically later than Mesopotamian cuneiform and Egyptian hieroglyphics, and more or less contemporary with Hittite and Cretan pictographic writing. A further system is attested in the inscriptions from Byblos and Balu'ah, both in the Syria-Palestine region, which probably date from the second millennium BCE. Although these texts have still not been deciphered, they seem to represent an attempt at a syllabic script that was later abandoned.[53]

The Proto-Canaanite pictographic texts from Shechem, Gezer, and Lachish (seventeenth to sixteenth centuries BCE), like the Proto-Sinaitic inscriptions from Serabit el-Khadem (*c.* 1500 BCE), again pictographic, are the oldest examples of alphabetic writing in the Northwest Semitic area. The signs used are often acrophonic, and it is clear that the inventors were acquainted with Egyptian hieroglyphic texts. In its origins, the system was exclusively consonantal, and seems to have employed twenty-seven different characters. The Ugaritic alphabet from around the fourteenth century BCE uses thirty characters – at Ugarit, and to a lesser extent at other sites in Palestine, the techniques of cuneiform writing have been adapted to an alphabetic principle.

Generally, a writing system was adapted to the phonemics of a particular language – in this respect, it is noteworthy that the system employed by Phoenician, the ancestor of the Hebrew and Aramaic scripts, had by the twelfth century BCE already dropped five characters, reflecting the fact that Phoenician has just twenty-two consonantal phonemes.[54]

Although vowels are indicated in the cuneiform syllabaries, they are lacking from the alphabetic scripts of the northwest and south. Ugaritic has three different characters to represent *alef* with the vowels *a*, *i*, and *u*. Other alphabets gradually introduced a system

53 See Naveh 1982, 21f.
54 See Naveh 1982, 31ff.

of *matres lectionis* to indicate vocalization, at first only at the end of a word, later on within the word as well. The introduction of special vowel signs came much later, employing a wide range of systems, frequently of a very limited character.

The Proto-Semitic phonological system contains perhaps twenty-nine consonantal phonemes,[55] which despite certain modifications have been conserved with great fidelity in languages like Arabic.

According to their point of articulation, the Proto-Semitic consonants can be bilabial (/p b m/), high alveolar, that is, interdental or predorsal (/ṯ ḏ ṯ̣ ḏ̣/), low alveolar or dental (/t d ṭ/), liquid (/r l n/), sibilant (/s z ṣ/),[56] prepalatal (/š/), lateralized (/ś/), dorsopalatal or mediodorsal (/k g q/), velar or postdorsal (/ḫ ġ/), pharyngeal (/ḥ ʿ/), or laryngeal (/ʾ h/). There are also the semiconsonants /w/ and /y/.

According to manner of articulation, seven pairs are distinguished as voiced : voiceless – /p/ : /b/, /ṯ/ : /ḏ/, /t/ : /d/, /s/ : /z/, /k/ : /g/, /ḫ/ : /ġ/, /ḥ/ : /ʿ/. Other pairs exhibit the contrast normal : emphatic – /t/ : /ṭ/, /ṯ/ : /ṯ̣/, /s/ : /ṣ/, /k/ : /q/. The exact nature of the emphatic phonemes is, however, a matter of debate. It is unclear whether they represent glottal occlusion as in Ethiopic or, instead, velarization as in Arabic, although the sort of glottal ejective found in Ethiopic seems to be older.[57] In diagrammatic representation, part of the system is occasionally displayed as a triangular pyramid, in accordance with the opposition voiceless : voiced : emphatic.[58]

According to their degree of aperture, the Proto-Semitic consonants can be plosive (/p b t d ṭ k q g ʾ/), fricative

55 The most important study of the Semitic consonantal system must be that of J. Cantineau (1951), which was followed by the works of A. Martinet (1953) and S. Moscati (1954).

56 Regarding the affricate realization of *ṣade* in the Semitic languages, see the important work by R.C. Steiner (1982). On the sibilants in general there is a large bibliography. See Faber 1984 and the references there.

57 See Moscati 1969, 23f.

58 Thus, Cantineau 1951, although A. Martinet disagreed with this model.

(/ṯ ḏ ṯ̣ s z ṣ š ḫ ġ ḥ h/), lateral (/l/) or lateralized (/ḍ ś/), vibrant (/r/), or nasal (/m n/).

THE PROTO-SEMITIC CONSONANTAL PHONEMES

Point of articulation	Voiceless	Voiced	Emphatic	Degree of aperture
Bilabial	p	b		Plosive
		m		Nasal
Interdental	ṯ	ḏ	ṯ̣	Fricative
			ḏ̣	Lateralized
Dental	t	d	ṭ	Plosive
	s	z	ṣ	Fricative
		l		Lateral
	ś			Lateralized
		r		Vibrant
		n		Nasal
Prepalatal	š			Fricative
Dorsopalatal	k	g	q	Plosive
Velar	ḫ	ġ		Fricative
Pharyngeal	ḥ	ʿ		Fricative
Laryngeal	ʾ			Plosive
		h		Fricative

Proto-Semitic also possessed two semiconsonantal (or semivocalic) constrictive phonemes, bilabial /w/ and prepalatal /y/, which underwent a number of changes in the various languages. Of particular significance is the development of /w/ to /y/ in initial position in the northwest – thus, Akkadian, Arabic, Ethiopic *wld*; Ugaritic, Hebrew, Aramaic *yld*.

The Proto-Semitic vowel phonemes are /a/ (open, velar), /i/ (closed, front palatal), and /u/ (closed, back velar), each of which has short and long forms.

From a diachronic perspective, among the more notable changes in the Proto-Semitic consonantal phonemes are the replacement of the voiceless bilabial plosive /p/ by the fricative /f/ in the south and, in the northwest, the spirantization of the series /b g d k p t/ and weakening of the pharnygeals and laryngeals, from the second half of the first millennium BCE. It is also clear that the interdentals /ṯ ḏ ṭ ḍ/ underwent a particularly large number of modifications, especially from the first millennium BCE – thus, in Hebrew /ṯ/ shifts to /š/ (cf. Ugaritic *ṯr*, Hebrew *šor*), /ḏ/ to /z/ (Ugaritic *'ḫḏ*, Hebrew *'ḥz*), /ṭ/ to /ṣ/ (Ugaritic *ṭl*, Hebrew *ṣel*), and, similarly, /ḍ/ shifts to /ṣ/ (South Arabian *'rḍ*, Hebrew *'ereṣ*). The sibilants, which number at least five distinct phonemes (a sixth has been proposed),[59] have also evolved in an odd way – this is particularly true of /s/, /ś/, and /š/, in respect of which, in most of the languages, there has been a reduction from a ternary to a binary system of contrasts, with the neutralized contrast varying from one language to another (cf. Akkadian *ešir*, Hebrew *'eśer*; Hebrew *ḥameš*, Arabic *ḫams*).[60] The velars also underwent significant changes, especially in Hebrew and Aramaic, where the contrast with the pharyngeals was neutralized (Akkadian *aḫu*, Hebrew *'aḥ*; Ugaritic *ġlm*, Hebrew *'elem*).

59 See Goetze 1958.
60 See Rabin 1963, 107f.

In morphology, the (synchronic) study of the compatibility of consonants within the Semitic triconsonantal root has been of particular significance, and has been conducted with great precision in various modern works.[61] Among the conclusions are the following: identical or homorganic consonants do not appear in first and second positions; even though identical consonants can appear there, homorganic consonants do not appear in second and third positions (although this rule is not as strictly followed as the preceding one); similarly, with regard to positions one and three, homorganic consonants are not so rigorously excluded.

Most words in the Semitic languages can be completely defined in terms of root and pattern.[62] Although in their historically-documented forms, the Semitic languages generally use triliteral morphological roots, various studies have stressed the importance of biliteralism in Proto-Semitic, including its Hamito-Semitic phase.[63] The existence of biliteral roots, especially in certain classes of nouns and in the 'weak' verbs, and of semantic connexions which hold among various triliteral roots that have two radicals in common is now regarded as clear proof of the importance of biconsonantalism in the earlier stages of Semitic, although there is perhaps insufficient evidence to claim that all Hamito-Semitic roots were originally biconsonantal, with the Semitic languages evolving later in the direction of triconsonantalism.

In contrast to the traditional idea that the consonants are the basic and most typical elements of the Semitic root and have a unique position in the expression of meaning, several recent works have emphasized the considerable importance of the vowels. J. Kuryłowicz has tried to apply to the Semitic languages the same methods that have produced excellent results in connexion with

61 See J.H. Greenberg 1950. Although this study is based mainly on the analysis of some 4,000 Arabic roots, its conclusions apply equally to Proto-Semitic, at least in respect of verb morphemes. See the notes and the additional material of J. Kuryłowicz (1972, 9ff.).

62 As emphasized in Cantineau 1949.

63 See Moscati 1947, Botterweck 1952, and the refinements of Kuryłowicz 1972, 6ff.

the Indo-European language family,[64] attempting to explain the Semitic verbal system as a function of apophony. In a similar way, P. Fronzaroli has stressed the rôle of the vowels in Proto-Semitic, suggesting that they might be present in the lexeme, as well as having morphological and semantic functions.[65]

A detailed study of internal inflexion in the Semitic languages was conducted by K. Petráček.[66] Using Prague School methods, he paid special attention to the origin and development of infixed grammatical morphemes in noun and verb in the different Semitic languages. In his discussion of the noun, particular consideration is given to the internal or 'broken' plurals which have been much debated in recent years and for which many explanations exist:[67] singular collective (C. Brockelmann and others), abstract (T. Nöldeke), a function of apophony (J. Kuryłowicz), etc. A. Murtonen provides a detailed analysis of these plurals and the singular forms with which they are associated. Petráček's view was that in the plural two independent lexical units are combined, one singular, the other collective or abstract, and between these two a formal relationship is established of such stability that it eventually develops into a paradigm, with the formal relationship becoming a morphological marker of plurality. Thus emerged a formal, more or less mechanical, system of marking the plural in which plural forms which were originally purely lexical (collectives) have evolved into the basis for regular, morphological, marking of the plural.

F. Corriente questioned whether this type of construction occurs outside South Semitic, as similar instances from other areas lack the characteristic apophony of the South Semitic broken plurals. Nonetheless, he argued for the antiquity of the phenomenon and its possible Hamito-Semitic origin. Synchronically, he regarded the broken plurals as exemplifying apophony, although diachronically

64 See Kuryłowicz 1957–58; 1972, 32ff.

65 See Fronzaroli 1963.

66 1960–1964.

67 See especially Murtonen 1964 and Corriente 1971.

they represent a type of external inflection which only appears to be internal.

The case endings have also given rise to a variety of arguments. Many specialists accept that Proto-Semitic has a declension system of sorts, using cases parallel to those of Indo-European: nominative (sg. *-u*, pl. *-ū*, du. *-ā*), genitive (sg. *-i*, pl. *-ī*, du. *-ay*), accusative (sg. *-a*, pl. *-ī*, du. *-ay*).[68] However, C. Rabin is dubious of this widespread view and approaches the function of these endings in a different way.[69] The main purpose, he believes, is not the same as that of the Indo-European case endings, but rather reflects a peculiarly Semitic system of 'states' (absolute, emphatic, predicative, governed).

A striking phenomenon of a different kind is the similar development within many different Semitic languages, albeit by various routes and at different times, of the feminine ending *-at*, so that the *-t* is dropped in the absolute state but retained in the construct. J. Blau has demonstrated that in the various languages this process reflects parallel developments from a very similar basic structure.[70]

The Semitic verb remains controversial, with the problems raised by H. Bauer's classic 1910 study still unresolved. According to Bauer, the oldest form of the verb is the imperfect, which does not indicate 'subjective' or 'objective' time but rather 'every possible moment', since it is completely atemporal. The 'apocopated' form *yaqtul* is actually the more original, being lengthened later to *yaqtulu*.

In contrast to Bauer's defence of the old idea that the Semitic tenses refer to points in time, S.R. Driver, partly on the basis of Indo-European studies, such as G. Curtius's grammar of Greek, had earlier argued for an 'aspectual' theory of tenses in Hebrew.[71]

68 See Moscati 1969, 94ff.
69 See Rabin 1969.
70 See Blau 1980.
71 See S.R. Driver 1892.

For C. Brockelmann,[72] the 'tenses' are subjective aspects whereby a speaker refers to a process as having occurred (perfect) or as in the process of unfolding (cursive, imperfect). F. Rundgren,[73] while warning of the danger of employing the concept of 'aspects', drawn from a very different linguistic context, accepts that in the Semitic verb there are two aspects, stative/fientive or cursive/constative, which can only be understood in relationship to one another.

Nowadays, it is generally accepted that the verb form *qatala* (and its variants *qatila, qatula*) existed in Proto-Semitic, although in the light of Akkadian this is thought to have originally been a nominal form with suffixes; in West Semitic it developed into a truly verbal form which expressed a state or a condition that had been brought to completion. The number of prefix-conjugations in existence at this stage is a matter of debate – while some argue for a single conjugation, of the type *yaqtulu,* which would have indicated an action without specifying whether or not it had been completed (and which became specialized in West Semitic to express incomplete action in particular), others claim a second prefix-conjugation *yaqattal,* a durative present corresponding to the Akkadian *iparras* and attested as well, according to them, in other West Semitic dialects.[74] It is very likely that these conjugations would have expressed through their affixes different moods of the verb (indicative, subjunctive, jussive, energic), as seems to be indicated by Arabic on the one hand and Ugaritic on the other.[75]

[72] 1951.
[73] 1963.
[74] See Goetze 1938, Rössler 1961; R. Meyer 1966–72; Friedrich and Röllig 1970; Blau 1978. An opposing view is taken in Goshen-Gottstein 1969 and T.L. Fenton 1970.
[75] See Moscati *et al* 1969, 134f.

1.4 *The Hamito-Semitic or Afro-Asiatic group*

The Semitic languages are not an isolated language family, but are closely related to other groups of languages found throughout northern Africa. These African language families differ not only from the Semitic group, but from one another as well. The idea of a possible 'family relationship' among Semitic and African languages appeared in the eighteenth century,[76] and pioneering studies were conducted by, for example, Volney and the Spanish Jesuit Hervás y Panduro. During the nineteenth and twentieth centuries this idea gradually gained strength,[77] eventually being developed in a fully scientific fashion.

The publication of M. Cohen's classic 1947 study, *Essai comparatif sur le vocabulaire et la phonétique du chamito-sémitique,* opened a new era in the comparative study of the Hamito-Semitic languages, the existence of which as a definite language community is now virtually beyond doubt. The name Hamito-Semitic, derived from the Bible, is deliberately vague. Its greatest disadvantage is that it suggests the existence of two large groups of languages, Semitic and Hamitic, which is inappropriate given that there are many groups within Hamitic itself. Apart from other names which have not fared any better,[78] the designation that today enjoys general acceptance is 'Afro-Asiatic', which was first proposed by J.H. Greenberg[79] and is now widely used in the English-speaking world.[80]

76 A detailed bibliography can be found in M. Cohen 1947.

77 Thanks to the sometimes controversial studies of specialists like T. Benfey, J.C. Adelung and J.S. Vater, U.F. Kopp, M.G. Schwartze, T.N. Newman, E. Renan, J.G. Müller, M. Schultze, F. Müller, F. Praetorius, H. Zimmern, T. Nöldeke, and, in the twentieth century, C. Brockelmann, H. Möller, W. Schmidt, J. Pedersen, and especially the members of the Hamito-Semitic linguistic groups that were founded in Paris and Leningrad in 1931 and 1934 respectively.

78 Such as 'Eritrean' proposed by M.A. Bryan (1947) and A.N. Tucker (1967).

79 1952.

80 See, for example, Hodge 1970.

The most representative Hamitic groups are Egypto-Coptic (documented from the fourth millennium BCE), Libyco-Berber (with an inscription from the second century CE),[81] Cushitic (from East Africa), and, according to some, Chadic.[82] The problems of classification of the almost 200 different languages which make up this *phylum* have been examined in important studies by J.H. Greenberg, who used statistical methods, A.N. Tucker, and, in particular, I.M. Diakonoff.[83]

Comparative study raises many difficult issues mainly because of the vast differences in time among the various languages, almost 6,000 years in some instances, and because many African languages were not properly documented until the last or even the present century. In addition, comparative methods themselves, based primarily on morphology, phonetics, and vocabulary, are under constant review.[84] Interference arising from contact between different groups, like Cushitic and Semitic in Ethiopia, makes this kind of study even more complicated.

In the field of phonology, there has been some agreement since the appearance of Cohen's work that the Hamito-Semitic system of consonant and vowel phonemes differs little from that proposed for Proto-Semitic, although I.M. Diakonoff has suggested the existence of two new phonemes, a glottalized voiceless bilabial, /p'/, and a further sibilant, /s̠/.[85]

In comparative morphology, special attention has been given to the Hamito-Semitic root, verb, noun, and pronoun,[86] all of which

81 Included in this group is Guanche, spoken in the Canary Islands until the seventeenth century.

82 See D. Cohen 1968.

83 See J.H. Greenberg 1952; Diakonoff 1965; Tucker 1967. A good description of the development of the issue from its beginnings can be found in Hodge 1970.

84 See, for example, von Soden 1965. Not so long ago, linguists like H. Möller and V. Christian were still concerned with the problem of where and when the putative ancestors of the Hamito-Semites settled after their various migratory movements (cf. A. Cuny 1946), although this kind of issue is now regarded as outdated.

85 See Diakonoff 1965; see as well D. Cohen's general study (1968, 1300ff.) of Hamito-Semitic phonology.

86 See Hodge 1970, 243ff. Cf. D. Cohen 1968, 1307ff.

are still under discussion. However, despite differences in emphasis and presentation, it is generally accepted that a biconsonantal root predominated in the Hamito-Semitic languages, and it is also argued that there was at least one prefix-conjugation, and that there may have been a further conjugation with duplicated second radical. The existence of a suffix-conjugation, although defended by, for example, O. Rössler,[87] is regarded by others as very doubtful.[88]

Because of the greater difficulty involved, syntactic analysis has made much slower progress. Comparative lexicology continues to depend on the relevant material in Cohen, although there are also some more recent studies, especially on the relationship of Egyptian to the Semitic languages.[89]

The vitality of the Groupe Linguistique d'Études Chamito-Sémitiques in Paris, reflected in its *Comptes rendues*, and the conferences devoted specifically to the field of Hamito-Semitic studies, are an indication of continuing scholarly interest and of the many tasks which still lie ahead.

1.5 *Hamito-Semitic and Indo-European*

Starting with the publications of H. Möller at the beginning of the twentieth century,[90] there have been a number of studies on the relationship of the Afro-Asiatic *phylum* and Indo-European, despite the problems associated with this kind of study. Although the lexical comparisons of Möller and M. Honnorat[91] did not seem particularly compelling, pioneering studies of comparative phonetics and morphology, such as those of A. Cuny,[92] have

87 1950.
88 See D. Cohen 1968, 1307ff.; Hodge 1970, 247ff.
89 For example, Lacau 1970.
90 See, for example, Möller 1906; 1911.
91 1933.
92 1943; 1946.

helped clarify the relationship. However, as a result of assumptions about racial history then prevalent, Cuny, and other scholars like H. Pedersen and G.I. Ascoli, went beyond the evidence of shared linguistic features in developing the hypothesis of a proto-language which was the common ancestor of both Indo-European and Hamito-Semitic. Ascoli called this putative language 'Aryo-Semitic', whereas Pedersen and Cuny preferred 'Nostratic'. Other scholars, such as P. Meriggi, also came to support this idea, which, however, should not be regarded as well-founded.

In this type of analysis the methods used are of primary importance, and nowadays the approach of Möller and Cuny is rightly viewed with suspicion. But there are difficulties as well with the more recent analysis by S. Levin, who, basing himself primarily on vocalized texts, concluded that there are many common features among Hebrew, 'an aberrant Semitic language',[93] Greek, and Sanskrit. Other studies, like that of M. Fraenkel,[94] which follow in the path laid down by Möller, are excessively simplistic, limited to a rather crude, unscientific, comparison of vocabulary.

Much more acceptable is the work of M.L. Mayer,[95] who, without employing the image of a family tree, examined the zones of contact between the two language groups, drawing attention to Akkadian-Hittite and Ugaritic-Hittite isoglosses, Semitic loanwords in Greek, and so on. We agree with his conclusion that it is becoming ever more likely that in prehistoric times groups of Indo-European and Semitic languages co-existed or at least existed in close proximity to one another, and that perhaps, after the completion of the necessary investigations, it might be possible to speak not of a 'mother language' (in the sense intended by Ascoli, Möller, Pedersen, or Cuny), but of a range of isoglosses across the Indo-European and Semitic languages.

93 S. Levin 1971, 704. The work is reviewed in von Soden 1974.

94 1970. See Sáenz-Badillos 1974.

95 1960.

Chapter 2

HEBREW, A NORTHWEST SEMITIC LANGUAGE

2.1 *The Northwest Semitic languages*

The geographical and historical facts of Hebrew place it within the Northwest Semitic group of languages. Recent archaeological and epigraphic discoveries have been of critical importance in increasing our knowledge about the linguistic geography of this group, although on occasions the scarcity of evidence still prohibits a precise evaluation of the characteristics and peculiarities of these languages or dialects and of the relationships they have with one another.[1]

As against the traditional classification of Northwest Semitic into two subgroups, Canaanite and Aramaic, the tendency nowadays is to accept the proposition of S. Moscati and G. Garbini that before the first millennium BCE one cannot speak of a contrast between Canaanite and Aramaic, but rather of a group of languages with various features in common.[2] Less disputable is the exclusion from Northwest Semitic of Eblaite, attested in the north roughly halfway through the third millennium BCE, as already noted in Chapter 1.

The end of the third millennium saw the arrival in the east of Amorite. This language was spoken by a nomadic group called in cuneiform texts *Amurru*,[3] who settled west of the Euphrates around Mari and used Akkadian in writing. A large number of proper names as well as some common nouns are virtually the sole

[1] A good recent study is Garr 1985.

[2] See Moscati 1956, etc.; Garbini 1960, 11f.

[3] On the meaning of the name, see Altman 1980.

remains of this Northwest Semitic language. The documents containing them were found mainly in Syria (Mari, Alalakh), and also in Mesopotamia (Ur). Following the early work of T. Bauer,[4] who was the first to investigate the people he called 'the East Canaanites', there have been studies of some of the names, which date from 2300 to 1600 BCE.[5] The application of modern methods of analysis to these names, which are far more numerous than was thought a few years ago (6,662 according to the most recent works), offers the promise of much more precise results.[6]

The cuneiform transcriptions do not provide exact details about the consonants of Amorite, but they do yield important information about the vowels. The original Semitic case-ending vowels are preserved, there is contraction of vowels separated by ', *h*, *w*, or *y*, giving rise to long vowels, the diphthongs *aw* and *ay* are retained, and initial *w* changes to *y*.[7] Morphological features include two first-person suffixed pronouns, *-na* and *-ni*, as well as two passive participles, *qatilum* and *qatulum*.[8]

In the northwest, following the excavations at Ras Shamra begun in 1929, we have also become familiar with a large number of Ugaritic documents. These are written in a cuneiform alphabet, and include archaic poems, letters, legal texts and other official prose documents, as well as other texts in a less official prose, dating from the fourteenth to thirteenth centuries BCE. The texts were officially published in *Mission de Ras Shamra*,[9] and led

4 1926.

5 Information about this language has been considerably improved by, for example, the following studies: Jean 1946; 1950; Finet 1956; Gelb 1958; 1968; Goetze 1959; Huffmon 1965; Bucellati 1966; Greenfield 1969; Krahmalkov 1969; Priebatsch 1977.

6 See Gelb 1980.

7 See Beyer 1969, 17ff.

8 See Garbini 1960, 175ff.

9 Eighteen volumes (Paris, 1936–78), incorporating *Le Palais royal d'Ugarit* and *Ugaritica*, I–VII, and including both texts and studies, produced by C.F.A. Schaeffer, C. Virolleaud, J. Nougayrol, E. Laroche, A. Herdner, and others. Many other editions and translations into various languages have also appeared. See, for example, Caquot, Sznycer, and Herdner 1974, Caquot, de Tarragon, and Cunchillos 1989, and especially Dietrich, Loretz, and Sanmartín

immediately to a lengthy debate about the character of Ugaritic and its relationship with the other Semitic languages.[10] Further texts in Ugaritic have appeared in the last few decades at Ras Ibn Hani, close to Ras Shamra, and at other sites along the Mediterranean.[11]

Some of the more outstanding features of Ugaritic are its preservation of most of the Proto-Semitic consonantal phonemes, including the velars and interdental fricatives, and its use of a cuneiform alphabet which employs three graphemes for *alef* in combination with each of the three basic vowels, *a*, *i*, and *u*. The diphthongs *aw* and *ay* are usually reduced to *o* and *e*. Initial *w* is converted to *y*, as generally in Northwest Semitic. On the other hand, *ā́* has not changed to *ṓ*, against the general trend. There is usually assimilation of *n* to a following consonant, and vowel assimilation is also common, with *a-i* changing to *i-i*, and *a-u* to *u-u*.

A causative conjugation with *š-* is found in Ugaritic (with parallels in Akkadian, the Proto-Sinaitic inscriptions, and parts of Southern Semitic). The language also preserves case-ending vowels in the noun, the feminine termination *-t* in nouns and verbs, the dual suffixes *-am* (nominative) and *-em* (oblique) and the

1976. There is a vast literature on the language collected in four volumes in Dietrich, Loretz, Berger, and Sanmartín 1973 and in Dietrich, Loretz, and Delsman 1986.

10 Among the numerous studies of Ugaritic, Gordon 1965 stands out as a basic work, as do the studies of J. Cantineau (1932–40; 1950), A. Goetze (1938), C. Brockelmann (1941), E. Hammershaimb (1941), A. Jirku (1953, etc.), J. Aistleitner (1954; 1967), P. Fronzaroli (1955), H. Goeseke (1958), T.L. Fenton (1963), F. Grøndahl (1967), M. Dietrich and O. Loretz (1968), S. Segert (1968; 1983), D. Marcus (1968, etc.), J. Sanmartín (1971), K. Aartun (1974–78), and E. Verreet (1984–85). There is a concordance to the Ugaritic texts by R.E. Whitaker (1971). Segert 1984 is a well-arranged and up-to-date grammar of Ugaritic. See also the bibliographic resources cited in the previous note. Special mention should be made of the many lexicographic studies of Ugaritic in relation to Hebrew produced by M.J. Dahood from 1952 onward – see Martínez 1967. Proof of the interest which Ugaritic continues to arouse is to be found in the two periodical publications devoted solely to it, *Ugarit-Forschungen* (Neukirchen-Vluyn) and the *Newsletter for Ugaritic studies* (Saskatoon), and also in the attention it receives in many other specialist journals on Oriental studies.

11 See the bibliography about these discoveries in Cunchillos 1982; 1985; del Olmo 1986, 36, n. 24.

adverbial suffixes *-h, -t, -ny,* and *-m.* There are independent oblique personal pronouns, *hwt, hyt, hmt* '(of) him, her, them', an adverb *p,* as well as a conjunction of the same form. In contrast to later Canaanite languages, there is no article.[12] Clearly some of these features have to be classed as conservative, and can be explained in terms of their antiquity and Ugarit's geographically peripheral location.[13]

Especially noteworthy is the richness of the derived conjugations and verb moods. The use of the verb has received special attention, and remains controversial. In the archaic and poetic texts it is possible that the prefix- and suffix-conjugations primarily express aspect (cursive/constative), whereas in later prose texts their main function is temporal.[14] According to some experts, Ugaritic has two prefix-conjugations, a narrative 'imperfect', *yaqtulu,* and a 'present-future', *yaqattalu,* alongside the 'perfect' stative, *qatila,* restricted to a specific group of verbs.[15] But there is argument about whether, as defended by many experts, there exists a form *qatala,*[16] or whether *qtl* should be read only as *qatila* or *qatula.*[17] There is also argument concerning a possible 'present-future'. C.H. Gordon, who rejects it, regards *yqtl* as a 'universal tense', the standard form in narrative, which can be used for the past, present, or future, and which can express different moods through changes in the vocalization. Alongside the indicative, *yaqtulu,* there is a subjunctive, *yaqtula,* and possibly two forms of the energic mood, using the suffix *-an* or *-anna.*

The *waw*-consecutive is found, as in Hebrew, in prose but not poetry. It is likely that internal passives existed for all the active conjugations, of which the *Shaf'el* and *Hishtaf'el* are noteworthy.

12 See Garbini 1960, 178ff.; Beyer 1969, 20; Ginsberg 1970, 106ff.

13 See Segert 1984, 14.

14 See Segert 1984, 56, 88f.

15 See Goetze 1938; Hammershaimb 1941; Gordon 1965, 67ff.

16 Thus, Dahood 1965, 20; Segert 1984, 58.

17 Thus, Gordon 1965, 68.

The prefix *t-* is often used instead of *y-* in the third person plural masculine.

The use of the prepositions and particles, studied especially by M.J. Dahood and his school, has shed light on possible archaic usages and previously overlooked senses in Biblical Hebrew. The interest of many Hebraists in Ugaritic has helped to establish very clear parallels and points of linguistic, literary, and cultural contact between Ugarit and Israel, resulting in a significant improvement in our understanding of biblical literature in general.[18]

The language of the central area of Northwest Semitic during the second millennium BCE is known indirectly through a number of ancient Egyptian sources, especially the so-called Execration Texts from the twentieth to nineteenth centuries BCE,[19] some Proto-Canaanite inscriptions and seals from the eighteenth century BCE onward,[20] the El-Amarna letters from the fourteenth century BCE, and the pseudo-hieroglyphic texts from Byblos, from the first half of the second millennium BCE.

The 379 letters from Tell el-Amarna began to be discovered in 1887 – they are cuneiform tablets through which the lords of the Mesopotamian states and the vassals of the Egyptians in Syria and Palestine communicated with the rulers of Egypt. Many of them have come from the central and southern areas of Byblos, Gezer, Jerusalem, and Megiddo. They date from around 1385-1355 BCE and usually include Canaanite glosses and other signs of influence from the scribes' mother tongue on the Akkadian which they wrote. Initial studies and publication were undertaken at the end of the last century, subsequently attracting much attention.[21] They

[18] See especially Dahood and Penar 1972 and Schoors 1982 on literary and lexical parallels.

[19] Studied by, for example, M. Burchardt (1909–10), K. Sethe (1926), J. Simons (1937), G. Posener (1940), W.F. Albright (1941), and W.L. Moran (1957).

[20] See the bibliography in Suder 1984, 96ff., Israel 1986, and Lemaire 1988.

[21] Of particular importance is Knudtzon 1907–1915, with the supplement by A.F. Rainey (1978), and the works of F. Thureau-Dangin (1922), G. Dossin (1934), C.H. Gordon (1947), R. Borger (1967), P. Artzi (1968), and A. F. Rainey (1975).

have been examined from a linguistic standpoint by, for example, F.M.T. Böhl, E. Ebeling, and E. Dhorme.[22]

The vowel system of the glosses shows signs of development, with widespread use of *e*; reduction of diphthongs, omission of short unstressed vowels, and shift of *ā́* to *ṓ* (as in the later Canaanite languages, but not in Ugaritic). The old system of case-ending vowels has probably been preserved, as is, for example, the adverbial suffix *-um*. There is a relative particle, *ašar*, as well as a first-person singular pronoun, *anuki*, with the first-person pronominal suffix *-ya* for the singular and *-nu* for the plural. Other features are a *Qal* passive, a causative conjugation *hiqtil*, and a passive participle *qatul*.[23] The tense system includes a perfect, *qatala*, jussive, *yaqtul*, 'indicative', *yaqtulu*, and also a form *yaqtula*, which can be regarded as a kind of subjunctive used to express wishes, orders, intentions, etc., and a possible forerunner of the Hebrew cohortative.[24]

One of the scholars at the forefront of attempts to decipher the pseudo-hieroglyphic texts from Byblos was E. Dhorme,[25] although his views did not gain complete acceptance at the time,[26] and are still regarded as not fully confirmed. Difficulties of interpretation prevent a proper understanding of the language, which is usually considered to be an ancestor of Phoenician or of Canaanite in general.

The southern area is represented by the forty-five Proto-Sinaitic inscriptions, which were first discovered at the beginning of the century near the mines of Serabit el-Khadem, in the west of the Sinai peninsula, and which probably date from the middle of the

[22] See Böhl 1909; Ebeling 1910; Dhorme 1913–14.
[23] See Beyer 1969, 23ff.; Garbini 1960, 180f.
[24] See Moran 1960; Rainey 1973.
[25] 1946–48.
[26] See the reservations of R. de Langhe (1948), and the subsequent attempts at decipherment by G. Janssens (1957), M. Martin (1961; 1962), and H. Sobelman (1961).

second millennium BCE.[27] Despite repeated attempts by W.F. Albright, who devoted a number of works to deciphering these texts,[28] they still present difficulties. The suggestion that the inscriptions might be of a proto-Arabic character is probably not correct.[29] Much more likely is Albright's theory that they are examples of a Northwest Semitic dialect spoken by the miners.[30]

Notwithstanding the difficulties in interpretation, it appears that the phonemes /ḏ/, /ṯ/, /ḫ/, and /ġ/ are attested, along with, for example, partial assimilation of *nun* to the following consonant, contraction of the diphthongs *aw* and *ay*, the feminine ending *-t*, the masculine dual and plural *-m*, and causative š-.[31]

Some names and other words from the southern area are also found in the Egyptian Execration Texts, already mentioned, and in El-Amarna letters from places like Megiddo and Jerusalem.

The end of the second millennium BCE sees the appearance in writing of some of the languages which would later be classed as Canaanite or Aramaic. The oldest parts of the Bible, like the Song of Deborah (Jg 5) and other archaic passages, might originally have been written in the twelfth to thirteenth centuries BCE. The oldest Phoenician inscriptions date from around 1100 BCE. According to some scholars, after 1400 BCE the languages which would later develop into Ya'udic and Aramaic separated from those of the future Canaanite group. Although Aramaic and Ya'udic shared the same pattern of development for some time, Ya'udic began to emerge clearly as a language in its own right from the start of the first millennium BCE.[32]

27 Controversy about dating continues. See Puech 1986, 187.

28 See Albright 1948; 1966.

29 See van den Branden 1958; 1962; 1962a; 1979.

30 In recent years new inscriptions have been discovered in the same area. See Beit-Arieh 1981; 1981a; 1982.

31 See Beyer 1969, 27.

32 See Dion 1974, 338ff.

From the viewpoint of dialect geography,[33] one can speak of Northwest Semitic as a dialect continuum, with Phoenician at one end and Aramaic at the other. These and the intervening languages form a chain of dialects within which, nonetheless, two groups are clearly visible, Canaanite and Aramaic.

Geographical distance or proximity from the two main centres of linguistic innovation, for Phoenician and for Aramaic, as well as political, economic, military, cultural, and religious circumstances would all have been determining factors in the linguistic unity and diversity of the Levant in the first half of the first millennium BCE.

The Canaanite group clearly differs from the Aramaic, as shown by the isoglosses of each group. Some are of a phonological or phonetic nature, for example the Canaanite languages share a series of innovations, such as the shifts of /ḍ/ and /ṭ/ to /ṣ/ and /ḏ/ to /z/, and of *ā́* to *ṓ*, as well as the almost wholesale reduction of diphthongs, loss of intervocalic *he*, and assimilation of word-initial and -medial *nun* to the following consonant (in Aramaic this only occurs in certain areas and under specific conditions).[34] Typical of the Aramaic group is the shift of /ḍ/ to /q/ in the oldest inscriptions.

There are also lexical isoglosses,[35] such as, in the Canaanite group, a secondary form of *hlk*, namely *ylk*, used in the prefix-conjugation, or the words for 'roof' (Hebrew *gag*), 'table' (Hebrew *šulḥan*), 'window' (Hebrew *ḥallon*), 'old', of things (Hebrew *yašan*) or of persons (Hebrew *zaqen*), 'expel' (Hebrew *grš*), etc. The Aramaic group, on the other hand, has its own words for 'truth' (*qušṭ*), 'son' (*baru/bir*, in contrast to *banu*), and 'lord' (*mari*), for example.

Other isoglosses are morphological in character: in the Canaanite group, for example, the masculine plural suffix is *-m* (except in Moabite, which, like the Aramaic dialects, uses *-n*), the first person singular pronoun is *'anaku* (as against Aramaic and Common

33 Such as that developed recently by W.R. Garr (1985, 229ff.).

34 See Harris 1939, 9ff.

35 See Ginsberg 1959; 1970, 103.

Semitic *'ana*), the interrogative personal pronoun is *mi*, and the article is a vocalized form of *h*. In the verb, the prefix *t-* is found instead of *y-* in the third person plural feminine, hollow verbs use the derived conjugations *Po'lel* and *Hithpo'lel* instead of *Pi'el* and *Hithpa'el*, and the active participle of hollow verbs and most stative verbs is the same as the base-form of the suffix-conjugation. The vocalization of the verb prefixes and attenuation of *a* in the first syllable of suffixed forms in the derived conjugations are other features shared by members of the Canaanite group.

Some characteristic innovations of the Aramaic dialects are: the suffixed definite article -', the relative particle *di*, the numeral *ḥad*, *ḥadah* 'one' (masc. and fem., instead of *'aḥad*, *'aḥadah*), *-awh(i)* as the third-person singular masculine possessive suffix for plural nouns, *qatil* as the *Pe'al* passive participle, the vowel pattern *a-i*, and assimilation of initial *y-* to the following consonant in certain roots.

A number of languages still present difficulties of classification. For example, debate continues regarding the Deir 'Allā inscription from around 700 BCE. The fragments were found in 1967 in the eastern part of the Jordan Valley,[36] and the complete text was published in 1976.[37] At first the language was viewed as a previously unknown Aramaic dialect, but there has been a tendency in recent years to emphasize its proximity to the Canaanite dialects.[38] Given that it shares significant isoglosses with

36 See Franken 1967, which assigns them to the Persian period.

37 By J. Hoftijzer and G. van der Kooij.

38 See Hoftijzer and van der Kooij 1976, 300. J.A. Fitzmyer (1978) regards the language as a type of Old Aramaic. The same position is taken by A. Caquot and A. Lemaire (1977, 208) and by P.K. McCarter (1980, 50f.). A. Rofé (1979) attempts a new approach, suggesting it is an example of the Midianite language, but this has aroused little interest. S.A. Kaufman (1980, 73) is unwilling to regard the language as Aramaic. A 1980 Harvard doctoral thesis by J.A. Hackett (Carlton) presented a new reading of the fragments without many of the traditional 'Aramaisms', concluding that the text represents a Canaanite dialect. The published version (Hackett 1984), an exhaustive study of the text, develops the same argument – the dialect has Aramaic isoglosses, but is nearer to Southern Canaanite (p. 124). Other works that discuss the inscription include Naveh 1967; Cross 1969; 1973; 1975; Lapp 1970; Hammershaimb 1977; Ringgren 1977; H.-P. Müller 1978; 1982; Garbini 1979; Lemaire

Old Aramaic on the one hand (such as the shift of */ḏ/ > /q/ and the use of the pronominal suffix *-wh*) and with the Canaanite languages on the other (especially, for example, in its verbal system and lexicon and its use of the relative particle *'š*), it is probably best to regard the Deir 'Allā inscription as representative of a dialect intermediate between these two groups of languages.[39]

Within the Canaanite group, and very close to Hebrew in terms of geography and linguistic characteristics, are Phoenician, in the middle of the Northwest Semitic area, and Ammonite, Edomite, and Moabite to the south and east, all known from the beginning of the first millennium BCE.

Epigraphic evidence for Phoenician (or Phoenicio-Punic) comes from thousands of inscriptions, dating from the tenth century BCE to the fifth century CE,[40] from ancient Lebanese coastal cities like Tyre, Sidon, and Arvad, as well as from Cyprus and throughout the eastern Mediterranean. It spread later from Iraq to the Atlantic, and especially, in the form of Punic, to North Africa, where it continued as a written language until the second century CE, surviving a few more centuries as a spoken dialect.[41] Until the fifth century BCE it employed a purely consonantal script, although afterwards under the influence of Aramaic and Latin it represented vowels by way of graphemes for semiconsonants and laryngeals. The language spoken at Byblos may be regarded as a special dialect of Phoenician,[42] as may Ashdodite, the language of the

1979–84; 1985; B.A. Levine 1981; Weinfeld 1981–82; Weippert and Weippert 1982; Hackett 1984a. E. Puech (1985, 10ff.) thinks the inscription is an example of Ammonite, a theory also defended in his review (Puech 1986a) of Hackett 1984. The most recent views of various scholars are recorded in Hoftijzer and van der Kooij 1991.

39 See Garr 1985, 229ff.

40 See Herr 1978, 171f.

41 Among the more important studies of Phoenician are Harris 1936; Sznycer 1967; Friedrich and Röllig 1970 (1st ed. by Friedrich, 1951); Segert 1976. Phoenician vocabulary has been studied by R.S. Tomback (1978) and M.J. Fuentes (1980). See the collection of articles on Phoenician language and culture by G. del Olmo and M.E. Aubet (1986). On the Phoenician inscriptions in Spain, see Fuentes 1986.

42 See Ginsberg 1970, 108ff.

Philistines, which seems to be more closely related to Phoenician than to other Canaanite languages.[43]

In terms of geography, history, and culture, Phoenician clearly has a close affinity with Ugaritic, as recently emphasized,[44] and their shared isoglosses in phonology, morphology, syntax, and vocabulary demonstrate that this extends to language as well. Nonetheless, Ugaritic and Phoenician each retains its individual character, and the similarities of the two languages are not sufficient to establish a 'genetic' relationship.

In Phoenicio-Punic there are, as in Hebrew, twenty-two consonantal graphemes corresponding to a similar number of phonemes. The Proto-Semitic interdentals have evolved in the same direction as in Hebrew, and, similarly, the differences between velars and pharyngeals have been neutralized; at a later date there has been weakening and merger of the pharyngeals and laryngeals. There are signs of a dual pronunciation of the *bgdkpt* consonants, *nun* is usually assimilated to a following consonant, *w* shifts to *y* in initial position, as throughout the Northwest Semitic area, *ā́* changes to *ṓ*, as in other Canaanite dialects, and later to *u*, and intervocalic *w* and *y* are usually elided. Diphthongs are generally contracted, *aw* to *o* and *ay* to *e*, and short accented vowels tend to be lengthened.[45]

In morphology there are many points of contact with Hebrew. For example, Phoenician uses the article *h-*, retains the first person singular pronoun *'nk*, and, later on at least, it introduces a *nota accusativi*. In the noun, the old feminine ending *-t* is used. The third person masculine singular pronominal suffix is archaic *-h*, reduced later to *-y* (-' in Punic), with *-nm* in the plural. As in pre-exilic Hebrew, the pattern **qatl* is retained for monosyllabic nouns. The genitive suffix *-i* is preserved along with some modal endings in

43 See Ginsberg 1970, 110f.
44 See del Olmo 1986.
45 See Beyer 1969, 25; Garr 1985, 23ff.

the verb. The causative *yiqtil*, relative *'š*, and negative *bl* (alongside *'y*) are characteristics of Phoenician.[46]

In vocabulary, there are some differences from Hebrew, such as the use of the verb *kwn* instead of *hyh* 'be', *p'l* instead of *'śh* 'do, make', and *ḥrṣ* instead of *zhb* 'gold'.[47] It is noticeable that the Phoenician terms are often shared with Ugaritic.[48]

Ammonite has been known for only a relatively short time from a number of seals and fragmentary inscriptions from the seventh to sixth centuries BCE.[49] Over the last few decades a fragmentary inscription dating from the middle of the ninth century BCE has been found in the citadel of Amman,[50] along with an inscribed statue,[51] a fragment from the theatre of Amman,[52] and a bronze bottle with a complete inscription from Tell Sirān from around 600 BCE,[53] as well some ostraca from Tell Ḥisbān (Heshbon),[54] and an ostracon from Nimrud.[55] In addition, more than sixty-one Ammonite seals from around the seventh century BCE have been

46 See Beyer 1969, 25ff.; Ginsberg 1970, 109; Garr 1985, 79ff.

47 See Harris 1939, 52; Segert 1976, 23.

48 See del Olmo 1986, 45–49.

49 See Diringer 1934, nos. 98, 103; Vattioni 1969, nos. 98, 115–117, 157, 165, 166, 194, 225, 229; Donner and Röllig 1971–76, III, 78f.

50 Published by S.H. Horn (1967–68; 1969), and studied by F.M. Cross (1969), W.F. Albright (1970), and G. Garbini (1970); see as well Garbini 1972, 97ff.; Palmaitis 1971; R. Kutscher 1972; Veenhof 1972; Puech and Rofé 1973; Dion 1975; van Selms 1975. W.J. Fulco (1978) attempted a new reading of the inscription. See also Shea 1979; 1981; Sasson 1979; D. Sivan 1982, 219; Jackson 1983, 9ff.

51 See Aharoni 1950–51; Barnett 1951; Puech 1985.

52 See Dajani 1967–68; Oded 1971; Cross 1975; Fulco 1979; Jackson 1983, 45ff.

53 Published and studied by F. Zayadine and H.O. Thompson (1973; 1973a); H.O. Thompson (1973); H.O. Thompson and F. Zayadine 1974; F.M. Cross (1973); K.R. Veenhof (1973); P.-E. Dion (1975); C.R. Krahmalkov (1976); O. Loretz (1977); W.H. Shea (1978); R.B. Coote (1980); M. Baldacci (1981); B.E.J.H. Becking (1981); K.P. Jackson (1983, 35ff.).

54 Published by F.M. Cross (1969a; 1973a; 1975; 1976; 1986); see Jackson 1983, 51ff.

55 Published by J.B. Segal (1957), and studied by W.F. Albright (1958), who attributed it to exiles from the northern kingdom, but reinterpreted as Ammonite by J. Naveh (1980); see Jackson 1983, 63ff.

found.[56] These discoveries have led to a rather better understanding of Ammonite.[57] The language is characterized by, for example, plural constructs in *-e* (rather than *-ey*, just as in early Phoenician), a masculine plural suffix *-m*, assimilation of *nun* to a following consonant, the occasional use of prosthetic *alef* before sibilants, contraction of the diphthong *ay*, but not *aw*, elision of intervocalic *y*, the feminine suffix *-t*, the relative *'š/š*,[58] the article *h-*,[59] regular use of final *nun* in the third person plural masculine of the prefix-conjugation,[60] pronominal suffixes *-k* and *-h* for the second and third persons singular, and, possibly, an accusative particle *t-*.[61] Some have even seen Arabic influence, but this is rather implausible.[62]

Edomite is known from various seals and short inscriptions on jugs and ostraca from the seventh to sixth centuries BCE,[63] an ostracon from Umm el-Biyāra,[64] at least six (probably eight) seals,[65] as well as some names in cuneiform writing and Greek.[66] Possibly the Lachish incense-altar inscription from the fifth century BCE is a further example of this language.[67] The transcription of the Edomite divine name *Qauš* in cuneiform texts from the eighth and seventh centuries BCE seems to indicate that the diphthong *aw*

56 See Heltzer 1976; Avigad 1977; Israel 1977; 1987; Herr 1978, 58ff.; Jackson 1983, 69ff.; Abbadi 1985.

57 On the Ammonite language in general, see D. Sivan 1982; Jackson 1983; Aufrecht 1983.

58 The second of these is doubtful, occurring just once in a seal of uncertain origin. See Jackson 1983, 77ff.

59 See Israel 1979; Jackson 1983, 41; Garr 1985, 223.

60 See Jackson 1983, 33.

61 See D. Sivan 1982, 228. K.P. Jackson (1983, 21f.) thinks it highly unlikely that the initial *taw* of *tdltbdlt* in the Amman citadel inscription should be interpreted as the *nota accusativi*.

62 See, for example, Landes 1962, 109. G. Garbini (1972, 107ff.) concluded that it is a North Arabian dialect; cf. Garbini 1974.

63 See Glueck 1938, etc.

64 See M. Bennet 1966; Israel 1979a.

65 See Herr 1978, 161ff.; Beit-Arieh and Cresson 1985.

66 See Geraty 1972.

67 See Cross 1969a; Naveh 1971, 27.

remained uncontracted for a considerable time, with the form *Quš* first appearing only in texts from the fifth century BCE.[68] Also attested is assimilation of *nun* to a following consonant, the article *h-*, and syncope of *y* in *bd* 'in the hand' (from *ba-yad*).[69]

Moabite is preserved mainly in the inscription of King Mesha (*c.* 835 BCE),[70] as well as in various small fragments, such as the text from Kerak,[71] and seven (possibly nine) seals.[72] Its similarity to Hebrew in many respects is so striking that it has even been suggested that the Mesha inscription was the work of an Israelite scribe.[73]

It is possible that Moabite has retained mimation in the singular, contrasting with nunation in the plural and dual, as in Proto-Semitic.[74] *Nun* is assimilated to a following consonant, the diphthongs *aw* and *ay* are usually contracted (cf. *lelah* 'night'), there is probably an *ā́* > *ṓ* shift,[75] and there is evidence of prosthetic *alef* before a sibilant. The masculine plural construct terminates in *-ay*[76] and the feminine singular marker is *-t* (*bmt* for Hebrew *bamah* 'high place, shrine').[77] In the suffix-conjugation the first person singular ends in *-ti*. The feminine demonstrative pronoun is, as in Hebrew, *z't*, which might also imply the use of *alef* as a *mater lectionis*.[78] The relative particle is *'šr* and the article *h-*, as in Hebrew. There is no elision of the *h* in the prefix-conjugation of the verb *hlk*. The particle *'t* is used with the direct object as in Hebrew (cf. *'yt* in early

68 See Beyer 1969, 29.
69 See Garr 1985, 225.
70 See Donner and Röllig 1971–76, I, 33; II, 168–79; B. Mazar (Maisler) and Rabin 1970.
71 See Murphy 1952; Reed and Winnett 1963; Freedman 1964; J.C.L. Gibson 1971, 83f.; Swiggers 1982.
72 See Avigad 1970; 1977; Herr 1978, 154ff.
73 See Segert 1961. The inscription's syntax is analyzed in Andersen 1966.
74 See Blau 1979–80, 143f.
75 See Blau 1979–80, 147f.
76 See Garr 1985, 224f.
77 See Beyer 1969, 29.
78 See Blau 1979–80, 148.

Phoenician),[79] but only, it seems, when the object is the name of a person or place.[80]

Within the Canaanite group, Hebrew has a special place, almost half-way between Phoenician and Old Aramaic, and, in its turn, a centre of innovations which spread throughout the neighbouring areas.[81] Although revised over the following centuries, the oldest biblical texts contain sections dating from the twelfth century BCE. Despite its size, however, the Hebrew Bible does not include every Hebrew word from biblical times. The earliest inscriptions in Hebrew date from the tenth century BCE.

The language adopted various structures on the analogy of other elements already in the system, such as the first person singular pronoun *'ani* alongside the archaic *'anoki,* the plural and dual masculine suffix *-m,* the first person singular suffix *-ti* in the suffix-conjugation, and the prefix *t-* in the third person plural feminine of the prefix-conjugation. Other characteristic features include frequent non-assimilation of *nun* when it occurs as the third radical of a verb, elision of postvocalic *alef,* and loss of the suffix *-t* in the absolute state of the feminine noun and of case-ending vowels generally in the noun (both with certain exceptions).

Hebrew shares with other Northwest Semitic dialects such innovations as the masculine plural construct suffix *-ay,* syncope of intervocalic *yod,* and of intervocalic *he* in the third person pronominal suffixes and in prefix forms of the causative conjugation, the masculine singular demonstrative *zeh* (sometimes functioning as a relative particle), the personal interrogative pronoun *mi,* the article *ha-,* the accusative particle *'et,* the relative particle *'ašer* (otherwise known only from Moabite), the adverbial suffix *-ah,* and loss of final syllable in a number of jussive and *waw-*

[79] Probably derived from **iyyat,* as J. Blau (1979–80, 150f.) has demonstrated.

[80] See Blau 1979–80, 151ff.

[81] See Garr 1985, 229f. For H.L. Ginsberg (1970), it is even possible to speak of two contrasting groups, one 'Hebraic' the other 'Phoenic', with the former including Moabite and possibly Ammonite and Edomite as well.

consecutive forms of the verb.[82] In the northern dialect, with very few exceptions, the diphthongs *aw* and *ay* undergo contraction (thus, *yen* < **yayn* 'wine', and *qeṣ* < **qayṣ* 'summer'). This occurs in medial as well as final position, and continues a trend found in Ugaritic, the El-Amarna letters, and Phoenician. In the southern dialect, on the other hand, this contraction does not occur, and an anaptyctic vowel, added halfway through the first millennium BCE, is found after the diphthong (*bayit* 'house', *yayin* 'wine'), as in Old Aramaic and at Deir 'Allā.[83]

Similarly, the various usages associated with such particles as *l-* and *ki* and the use of the infinitive absolute in place of a finite verb are also found in other Northwest Semitic languages.[84] There are occasional instances of the third person singular masculine pronominal suffix in *-i(y)*, feminine singular nouns in *-ot*, *Shaf'el* and *Ishtaf'el* derived conjugations of the verb, new uses of the particles, suffixed constructs, double-duty suffixes, and verbs derived from nouns denoting numerals or parts of the body, as well as traces of the old case-ending vowels and of the *Qal* passive.[85]

Special to Hebrew are such features as the archaic third person plural pronominal suffix *-mo*, demonstrative pronouns augmented by *hall-*, the development of *yēš* as an independent existential particle, the adverbial suffix *-am*, the uses of jussive and cohortative forms, the form of the third person feminine of the suffix-conjugation of verbs with third radical *y*, and the loss of the suffix *-t* in the third person feminine of the suffix-conjugation.[86]

82 See Garr 1985, 225ff.

83 See Garr 1985, 38f.

84 See W.L. Moran's excellent article (1961).

85 These and other features have been highlighted since the 1960's by M.J. Dahood and his followers, who have published important studies about the relationship of Hebrew to the other Northwest Semitic languages, especially Phoenician and Ugaritic: see, for example, van Dijk 1968; Tromp 1969; Blommerde 1969; Dahood and Penar 1970; van der Weiden 1970; Sabottka 1972; Cathcart 1973, etc. However, Dahood's more extreme claims are largely rejected nowadays.

86 See Garbini 1960, 186.

2.2 *Dialect development and its consequences*

The classic study of the development of the various Northwest Semitic dialects is Z.S. Harris's *Development of the Canaanite dialects,* published in 1939. Although its principal concern is diachronic, it also offers a synchronic perspective on the results of the developments described. Certain questionable aspects of the work reflect the state of knowledge at the time. For example, his inclusion of Ugaritic, the language of Hatra, and Ya'udic as Canaanite dialects significantly mars an otherwise magisterial treatment.[87] In the work, Harris tries to establish as far as possible an absolute chronology, or failing that a relative one, for the various linguistic changes that occurred in the Northwest Semitic area, although this is one of the study's most controversial features.[88]

Changes that may have taken place before the second half of the second millennium BCE include the reduction of diphthongs, the disappearance of mimation in the singular noun, the evolution of the interdentals, the neutralization of certain sibilants, and the assimilation of *nun* to a following consonant. Before 1365 BCE (the time of the El-Amarna letters) the following changes occurred: disappearance of case-ending vowels, *ā́* > *ṓ* shift, development of the verb pattern *qatala,* and abandonment of the preterite form *yaqtulu.*

Before the thirteenth century BCE, there was a change in the position of the accent along with, for example, abandonment of the *yaqatalu* verb pattern, development of specialized lexical forms, and augmenting of biradical roots. Syncope of intervocalic *h* and of *w* and *y* between short unaccented vowels took place prior to the ninth century BCE, along with the loss of word-final short vowels

87 In Garbini 1960, the various Northwest Semitic dialects are examined from a synchronic perspective, although a few pages (173–192) are devoted to their development. The work has some very valuable features to match its many weak points, shown up by E.Y. Kutscher (1965) in a painstaking review.

88 See, for example, the review in Ginsberg 1940a, and the judgement of W.R. Garr (1985, 4f.).

and, in some dialects, of the ending *-t* in the third person feminine singular of the suffix-conjugation, and there was also a lengthening of accented vowels. Around the ninth century BCE, the contrast between velars and pharyngeals was neutralized. Changes that would have occurred before 700 BCE include the reduction of pre- and post-tonic vowels, spirantization of the *bgdkpt* consonants, disappearance of the suffix *-t* in feminine nouns in the absolute state, replacement of the relative *zu* by *('a)š* / *'ašer*, and the decline of the first person singular pronoun *'anoki* in favour of *'ani*. Other late changes, such as the weakening of pharyngeal and laryngeal consonants and the introduction of anaptyctic vowels in nouns to prevent a word-final sequence of two consonants, would have taken place in Hebrew and Phoenician after the exile.[89] As one might expect, not all scholars accepted Harris's chronology without demur,[90] and there are various specific dates that can be substantially revised, something we shall return to later.

Harris thinks that the Canaanite dialects can be grouped into two categories, Coast and Inland, with the former being more innovative and the latter more conservative.[91] With regard to their origin and diffusion, linguistic changes correspond to the absence or presence of foreigners and to the extent of commercial and political relations between the different areas. Some changes, however, took place independently in different dialects.

We have deliberately avoided speaking about the reconstruction of 'Proto-Canaanite' or 'Proto-Northwest Semitic', as if the features shared by the dialects in the area were all derived from a common ancestor, for this would be to overlook the effects of parallel developments[92] and of contacts among the different dialects and their possible intermingling.[93] Within an overall evolutionary

89 See Harris 1939, 29ff.

90 Contrast, for example, the quite different chronologies proposed in Bergsträsser (1918–29, I, 163ff.) and in Birkeland (1940, 49ff.). A synopsis is presented in Rabin 1971a, 67f.

91 See Harris 1939, 98.

92 See Meillet 1921, 36ff.

93 See U. Weinreich 1953, 31ff.

framework, it has been suggested that if such parallel developments and contacts are taken into account, the differences among the various Canaanite dialects might actually have been greater originally than they were later on.[94]

As a result of the developments undergone by the Northwest Semitic languages, in particular the Canaanite dialects, the following picture emerges.

With regard to the consonants, the Proto-Semitic bilabials, which had been preserved in the northwest during the first half of the second millennium BCE, suffered a double crisis in the second half, due to the trend toward spirantization of /p/ and /b/ and because of a measure of instability which sometimes led to the replacement of voiceless phonemes by their voiced counterparts. In the interdentals, as previously noted, there was a major change in Phoenician and Hebrew, contrasting with the different developments that took place in the more conservative Aramaic dialects. There was a high degree of stability in the dorsopalatals and, generally, in the dentals, with the exception of the sibilants which were reduced in number. The velar consonants, which had shown some instability in the second millennium BCE, were neutralized with the pharyngeals throughout the first millennium. The pharyngeals and laryngeals, well-preserved in the second millennium BCE, were reduced and progressively weakened in the first millennium.[95]

Regarding the semivowels, the transition of word-initial *w* to *y* is typical of Northwest Semitic. In the first millennium BCE the semivowels weaken and even disappear from intervocalic positions in some dialects. The vowel system tended to become richer with distinctions in vowel quality taking precedence over differences of quantity. Older vowels were progressively displaced by newer ones. A large part of the Northwest Semitic area

[94] See Blau 1968, 36.
[95] See Harris 1939, 81ff.; Garbini 1960, 19ff.

experienced a shift from *ā* to *ō*, with diphthongs normally being reduced throughout the region, although retained in specific environments in some dialects. In the first millennium BCE, *shewa* appears in a number of Canaanite dialects.

It is difficult to state with certainty the position of the accent, although it is possible that penultimate stress predominated. When final short vowels disappeared, the accent often remained on what had become the final syllable. The shift of accent led to the loss of vowels that were further away from the accent and the lengthening of others nearer to it.

In morphology, independent (non-suffixed) pronouns appear in the various dialects in very similar forms, and never with *š*-, as occurs in Akkadian and South Arabian. There are some archaic forms in Ugaritic, Phoenician, and Hebrew, such as *naḥnu* 'we'. The pronominal suffixes include a first person singular in *-i* and later *-ya*. Commonly, *n* precedes various suffixes of this kind. The demonstrative pronouns have very different forms in the various dialects. In the relative pronoun, both *š* and *d* occur, with the latter being perhaps the older and certainly the more widespread. For the interrogative and indefinite pronoun, *mn* is used throughout the area, although in some dialects a new form, *my*, has been introduced.

In the noun, the feminine singular suffix *-t* is often omitted in Hebrew and Aramaic. Case endings are retained in the second millennium BCE only to disappear almost completely thereafter. Mimation has ceased in the singular noun, being retained in some instances in the plural. In the second millennium BCE there are no clear markers of determination, with the prefixed definite article appearing in most of the Canaanite dialects in the next millennium.

The verb shows a greater wealth of patterns and moods in the second millennium, which later became progressively more simple. Particularly difficult is the problem of the 'tenses'. The suffix-conjugation, *qatala*, developed rapidly, with a punctual value of 'preterite', thus differing from its East Semitic equivalent. The prefix-conjugation, *yaqtulu*, underwent a slower, although clear, development, taking on a durative function of present-future.[96] The existence of the form *yaqattalu* in Northwest Semitic is a matter of debate. The subjunctive, *yaqtula*, and the energic, *yaqtulan(na)*, alongside a contracted form, *yaqtul*, are attested in practically the whole area. In the prefixes of the prefix-conjugation there is a gradual shift from *a* to *i*. Other changes affected only certain dialects, such as the disappearance of the suffix *-t* in the third person singular feminine in Phoenician and Hebrew. The infinitive construct might be an innovation of Northwest Semitic, originating probably as a verbal noun.[97]

With regard to the particles, certain innovations are common to the whole area, with local variations in the different dialects. There is a gradual trend toward an increasing number of more narrowly defined particles. In vocabulary as well there are parallel developments, with shared changes in the forms of certain roots or other elements, utilization of new morphological patterns, and fluctuation in the frequency of various forms.[98]

96 See R. Meyer 1966–72, I, 26f.
97 See Harris 1939, 83ff.; Garbini 1960, 85ff. Garr's treatment (1985, 79ff.) is substantially different.
98 See Harris 1939, 85f.; Garbini 1960, 161ff.

Chapter 3

PRE-EXILIC HEBREW

3.1 *The historical unity and development of Hebrew*

Hebrew has a long history. It has persisted as a written language for more than 3,000 years. As a spoken language, it has had to survive in many different situations, following the complicated historical course of the Jewish people, which has spent more than half its existence in a bilingual setting, adapting to a wide range of cultural and linguistic environments. Such a history has left obvious and important marks on the language.

Nonetheless, from one perspective, especially if we concentrate on the written language, it is possible to speak of the historical unity of Hebrew throughout its existence. The language has remained substantially the same down the years, undergoing changes that have appreciably affected its vocabulary but not, on the whole, its essential morphological, phonological, or even syntactic structure. The truth of this statement even extends to the Hebrew spoken and written today, following a fascinating process of revival. The fundamental unity of Hebrew, both its language and its literature, is beyond doubt.

Not only have the basic structures of the language, its morphological system, and especially its verbal morphology, been preserved without major changes over the centuries, but it is also possible to claim that the vocabulary of the Bible has been the basis for all later periods, despite the numerous innovations of each era.[1]

Nonetheless, we cannot ignore the deep differences that also characterize each stage of the language, and the many factors that

[1] See especially Ben-Ḥayyim 1985.

have led historically to its diversification. It might be said that diversity and unity have been constant companions during the language's 3,000-year life. However, when attempts are made to establish a clear division of this history into different periods, it is difficult to reach a general consensus, as the criteria used can differ greatly.

We definitely have to take into consideration the main language spoken by a writer, be it Hebrew (during the centuries it survived both as a spoken and as a written language), Aramaic, Arabic, or the vernacular of the various peoples among whom the Jews lived in the diaspora.[2] We might also include, in addition to purely linguistic criteria, other socio-historical considerations which have had a substantial bearing on the various stages of the language, leading to distinctive 'consolidations of the language'.[3] There are also other factors that have left their mark on the language and most definitely have to be taken into account if an adequate classification of Hebrew in its various stages and traditions is to be achieved. These include such matters as differences of dialect, historical changes that led to the dominance of one dialect over others, and the diversity of different groups and communities who continued to make use of Hebrew.

In the rest of this book, mainly for practical reasons, Hebrew will be divided into four periods corresponding to four quite different linguistic corpuses: Biblical Hebrew (BH), Rabbinic Hebrew (RH), and Mediaeval Hebrew (MH), as well as Modern or Israeli Hebrew (IH), which is only afforded summary treatment in this work. However conventional and unadventurous this classification might seem, it does serve as a framework for our goal of providing a diachronic view of the language, while at the same time implying acceptance of the argument that RH is clearly distinguished from BH by many factors, especially in morphology and lexis. We also recognize that the status of MH is much less clearly defined than

[2] This is the basic criterion established by Z. Ben-Ḥayyim (1985).
[3] Thus, C. Rabin (1985).

that of either of the two earlier stages, given that it frequently uses both BH and RH in varying degrees for its basic elements. As an example of the revitalization of a language in almost complete disuse, IH is an extremely interesting phenomenon. However, it breaks the pattern of the language's natural development and lies outside the main scope of the present work.

Within BH itself, subdivisions can be made according to the period or stage of the language. The earliest Hebrew texts that have reached us date from the end of the second millennium BCE. The Israelite tribes that settled in Canaan from the fourteenth to thirteenth centuries BCE, regardless of what their language might have been before they established themselves there, used Hebrew as a spoken and a literary language until the fall of Jerusalem in 587 BCE. It is quite likely that during the First Temple period there would have been significant differences between the spoken and the written language, although this is hardly something about which we can be exact. What we know as BH is without doubt basically a literary language, which until the Babylonian exile existed alongside living, spoken, dialects. The exile marks the disappearance of this language from everyday life and its subsequent use for literary and liturgical purposes only during the Second Temple period. The latest biblical texts date from the second century BCE if we disregard BH's survival in a more or less artificial way in the Dead Sea Scrolls, for example, and in certain kinds of mediaeval literature.

The Hebrew of the poetic sections of the Bible, some of which are very old despite possible post-exilic revision, as well as the oldest epigraphic material in inscriptions dating from the tenth to sixth centuries BCE, we call Archaic Hebrew, although we realize that there is no general agreement among scholars regarding this term. The language used in the prose sections of the Pentateuch and in the Prophets and the Writings before the exile, we call Classical Biblical Hebrew, or BH proper. Late Biblical Hebrew (LBH) refers to the language of the books of the Bible written after the exile.

It has often been stated that BH is not a language in the full sense of the word but merely a 'fragment of language',[4] only a part of the language actually used by the Israelites prior to the exile. This is without doubt one of the most serious limitations for an adequate study of its history. Ten centuries ago, the Jews of Spain were fully conscious of this, as demonstrated by the words of some Cordoban scholars: 'Had we not left our country as exiles, we should today possess the whole of our language as in former times.'[5] The approximately 8,000 lexical items preserved in the books of the Bible would not have been enough to meet the needs of a living language.

3.2 *The origins of Hebrew*

The historical problem of the origins of Hebrew, sometimes raised as a question of the kind 'What was the language spoken by the Patriarchs?' or 'What was the language of the conquerors of Canaan?' is beyond the scope of this study, which is concerned only with more narrowly linguistic issues. Whatever the truth of the matter, we have to recognize that the exact beginnings of the Hebrew language are still surrounded by mystery.[6]

From the moment of its appearance in a documented written form, Hebrew offers, as we saw in the previous chapter, clear evidence that it belongs to the Canaanite group of languages, with certain peculiarities of its own. Possibly this means that when the Israelite tribes settled in Canaan they adopted the language of that country, at least for their written documents. Ancient, and certainly anachronistic, traditions about these semi-nomads allude to Aramaean ancestors (see Dt 26:5), but inferences of a linguistic nature should not, in principle, be drawn from this. In the passage where Jacob and his descendants are portrayed as making a final

[4] See Ullendorff 1971.

[5] S. Benavente, *Tešubot de los discípulos de Menaḥem contra Dunaš ben Labraṭ* (Granada, 1986), 20.

[6] See Rabin 1979, 71.

break from Laban (Gn 31:47), various writers have seen an allusion to the time when the Israelites abandoned Aramaic and adopted the Canaanite language of the country they were living in. In any case, there is a clear continuity between Hebrew as it is historically attested and the language of the El-Amarna letters, which date from before the settlement of the Israelites in Canaan. This is not to deny that Israel's monotheism could have had clear implications for particular semantic fields, thus distinguishing Hebrew from the languages of other Canaanite peoples.[7]

Combining historical and linguistic issues, it was suggested in the first decades of this century that Hebrew is not a homogeneous linguistic system but a '*Mischsprache*',[8] in which it is possible to distinguish an early Canaanite layer, very close to Akkadian, and another more recent layer, closer to Aramaic and Southern Semitic. The clearest evidence for this theory, it was argued, was the existence of forms like קָם (qām) 'he arose' and רָם (rām) 'he was raised', in which the transition *á* > *ó* had not taken place as it had in the other Canaanite dialects, and which contrasted with other forms like נָקוֹם (nāqōm) 'we shall arise' and מָרוֹם (mārōm) 'height', where the change has occurred. In the noun צאן (ṣōn) 'flock', it is possible that the same transition has taken place, with the consonantal form צאן (ṣ'n) reflecting an earlier pronunciation with an *a* vowel rather than an *o*.

This theory aroused fierce debate. Its opponents believed that the data adduced in its favour could be explained either as resulting from an unaccented *a* or as dialect forms, without needing to accept the notion of two levels of morphological structure in the hollow verb (of which the verbal forms cited above are examples). Moreover, the kind of linguistic borrowing

7 See Morag 1985.

8 The first to formulate this theory was H. Bauer who in 1910 (23ff.) was already arguing that some elements of Hebrew, such as the consecutive tenses, had a close relationship with Akkadian. In the *Historische Grammatik* (H. Bauer and Leander 1922, 16ff.), the hypothesis is developed in the clearest terms.

proposed would be more probable in connexion with words closely related by meaning (due to socio-cultural factors) rather than, as was the case in Hebrew, by morphology – for example, nouns of the type *qaṭṭāl* denoting profession or ending in ָן (-ān). Neither could it simply be admitted that the consecutive tenses of the verb belonged to the earlier stratum and the other forms to the later.[9]

As well as modified versions of the *'Mischsprache'* hypothesis which continued to receive a measure of support until recently,[10] there have also been claims by various scholars, often led by considerations of an allegedly historical nature, that clear traces of Aramaic can be found in the origins of Hebrew.[11] However, the various rebuttals of the *'Mischsprache'* theory[12] have ensured that it is no longer generally regarded as very plausible nowadays, and a different kind of approach to the problems which fuelled the theory is favoured.

Various recent studies[13] have emphasized that Aramaic might have influenced Hebrew very strongly, not when Hebrew first emerged but many centuries later, in the second half of the first millennium BCE up to the beginnings of the Common Era. Thus, it is generally accepted that in the phonology, morphology, and lexicon of LBH, as well as in RH, there is a significant Aramaic component. Similarly, in the linguistic system of the Masoretes features of Aramaic pronunciation have been superimposed on Hebrew.

9 See Bergsträsser 1923, 253ff. Bauer's response (1924) presents no substantially new arguments in favour of his theory.

10 Thus, for example, G.R. Driver (1936, 151) claims 'Clearly the two main strands of which Hebrew is woven are Accadian and Aramean'; in G.R. Driver 1953 he lays great emphasis on the influence of Aramaic on Hebrew poetry, although he also accepts that some 'Aramaisms' might go back to Common Semitic.

11 See, for example, Birkeland 1940; Baumgartner 1959, 222–25. R. Meyer (1966–72, I, 29) appears to offer some support to these claims, but in his 1957 article, Meyer clearly distanced himself from them, even though he recognized the existence of various levels, from old Canaanite, through an intermediate Amorite stage, to Israelite Hebrew.

12 See Landsberger 1926; Harris 1939, 11, n.; Beyer 1969, 12ff.

13 For example, Beyer 1969; Vogt 1971.

If, in various ways, we recognize in Hebrew elements that differentiate it from the neighbouring Canaanite dialects, we do not believe that these are derived from the Aramaic or Amorite that the Israelites might perhaps have spoken before they settled in Canaan, but instead that they result, for example, from linguistic conservativism, from independent linguistic developments within Hebrew, and from dialect diversity (about which we are acquiring ever more evidence). Increasingly it is believed that whereas BH was the language of literature and administration, the spoken language even before the exile might have been an early version of what would later become RH.[14] There are notable differences between the type of language used for poetry (which seems to be closer to the languages found in neighbouring countries) and that employed by classical prose,[15] as well as differences between the northern and southern or Jerusalemite dialects. A further significant feature is the influence of various foreign languages on Hebrew over the centuries.[16]

3.3 *The language of archaic biblical poetry*

The poetry of the Bible, like that of other Northwest Semitic literatures, employs a language which differs in various ways from the language of prose, reflecting, in general, an earlier stage of Hebrew and with a closer affinity in language, style, and content with neighbouring dialects, especially those to the north.

Notable among the biblical passages that best reflect Archaic Hebrew are the Song of Moses (Ex 15), the Song of Deborah (Jg 5), the Blessings of Jacob (Gn 49) and of Moses (Dt 33), the Oracles of

[14] See M.H. Segal 1936, 7; Bendavid 1951, 69ff.; Rendsburg 1980.

[15] See G.R. Driver 1953.

[16] Thus, for example, C. Rabin: 'It is ... possible to surmise that some of the fusional character of Hebrew may be due to interdialectal borrowing and to continuous exposure to outside influence, rather than to what happened at the very moment the local Canaanite language was adopted by the Israelite settlers.' (1970, 313)

Balaam (Nm 23–24), and the Poem of Moses (Dt 32), as well as Ps 68 and other early psalms. The written corpus is relatively small, and has been altered over the centuries to accommodate changes in orthographic practice, although it still clearly preserves certain archaic features. In recent decades the consonantal text has been the object of many studies, based on analysis of its metrical structure and on the spelling reflected in contemporary inscriptions, in an attempt to clarify these documents and to restore archaic forms that the Masoretes failed to recognize.[17]

Included among these is the widespread use of the third person pronominal suffix מוֹ- (-mō), for example יְכַסְיֻמוֹ (yᵉkasyūmū) 'they cover them' (Ex 15:5), with preservation of the original י (y) of the root, and יֹאכְלֵמוֹ (yōklēmō) 'it consumes them' (Ex 15:7), the second person feminine suffix כִי- (-ky), the third person singular masculine suffix ה- (-h) instead of ו- (-w), as in עירה ('yrh, pron. 'īrō) 'his donkey' (Gn 49:11), and with הוּ- (-hw), for example יְהוּ- (-yhw, pron. -ēhū), instead of יו- (-yw, pron. -āw) in the plural, the infinitive absolute with temporal value, as in *ne'dori* for Masoretic נֶאְדָּרִי (næ'dārī) '(is) glorious' (Ex 15:6), energic forms of the kind וַאֲרֹמְמֶנְהוּ (wa-'ᵃrommænᵉhū) 'I shall exalt him' (Ex 15:2) and תִּשְׁלַחְנָה (tišlaḥnā) 'she extends' (Jg 5:26), as well as זֶה (zæ), זוֹ (zō), and זוּ (zū) used as relative particles (Ex 15:13; Jg 5:5), and the relative -שֶׁ (šæ-) or -שַׁ (ša-), as in שַׁקַּמְתִּי (šaq-qamtī) '(the time) that you arose' (Jg 5:7), which also exemplifies the use of the second person feminine in תִי- (-ty). Other archaic features include the negative בַּל (bal) instead of לֹא (lō'), the indefinite or interrogative pronoun מן (mn) in מִן־יְקוּמוּן (min yᵉqūmūn) 'whoever rises up', (Dt 33:11), the verbal suffix ת- (-ṯ) in the third person feminine, as

---

[17] In this connexion, the works of W.F. Albright and his school stand out. Examples include Albright on the Balaam Oracles (1944), the Psalm of Habakkuk (1950), and Ps 68 (1950–51), F.M. Cross and D.N. Freedman on the Blessings of Moses (1948), Ps 18 (1953), and the Song of Miriam (1955), and B. Vawter on Gn 49 (1955). Among general studies are Albright 1945, Cross and Freedman 1952, Freedman 1960, 1972, 1980, and Hummel 1957. See, however, D.W. Goodwin's criticisms (1969) about the methods employed in this type of work. There is a good presentation of the issues raised by the Song of Deborah in Soggin 1981.

in אָזְלַת ('āzelat̲) 'she went' (Dt 32:36), and the adverbial use of enclitic *mem* in *motne-m qamaw* for Masoretic מָתְנַיִם קָמָיו (mot̲nayim qāmāw) 'the loins of his opponents' (Dt 33:11). There are also possible traces of the old case endings in nouns suffixed by *i* or *o* in the construct state, for example בְּנִי אֲתֹנוֹ (benī 'at̲ōnō) 'the son of his she-ass' (Gn 49:11) and בְּנוֹ צִפֹּר (benō ṣippōr) 'the son of Zippor' (Nm 23:18), and in such forms as אֵימָתָה ('ēmāt̲ā) 'terror' (Ex 15:16), which, in an earlier form of the text we now have, may have been analysable as אֵימָה ('ēmā) with accusative suffix.

Attempts have also been made to reconstruct forms that are not clearly attested but which probably existed at this stage, such as the *Qal* passive, for example יֻלַּד (yullād̲) 'he was born', or instances of verbs with infixed *-t-*, for example, at Dt 33:3, *himtakkū* 'they prostrated themselves', from the root מוך (mwk) or מכך (mkk), for הֵם תֻּכּוּ (hēm tukkū) (meaning uncertain) in the Masoretic Text. Only rarely can the article be regarded as part of a poem's original text, but when used it has a special demonstrative force, as with הַגֶּבֶר (hag-gæb̲ær) 'that man' (Nm 24:3), a reminder of the article's original rôle as a deictic particle (cf. Ugaritic *hn*).

The use of the prefix-conjugation to express the preterite, even when unaccompanied by *waw*-consecutive, the variety of usages of the particles, such as vocative -לְ (l-), as in לָרֹכֵב (lā-rōk̲ēb̲) 'o, rider' (Ps 68:34), 'adjectival' clauses without relative pronoun, and the widespread use of paratactic and hypotactic asyndeton are some of the more noticeable syntactic features of early biblical poetry.[18]

In archaic poetry there are hardly any adjectives or nouns used as adjectives, although there are genitive constructions (sometimes comprising three members) that fulfil the same function, for example זִבְחֵי־צֶדֶק (zib̲ḥē ṣæd̲æq) 'righteous sacrifices' (lit. 'sacrifices of righteousness'; Dt 33:19). The accusative particle אֵת ('ēt̲) is used very rarely, and it is possible that when it does occur it too has a special demonstrative force. The relative אֲשֶׁר ('ašær) is

[18] See Freedman 1960; Moran 1961, 59ff.; E.Y. Kutscher 1982, 79f.; Hadas-Lebel 1981, 64ff.

nearly always replaced by an asyndetic attributive clause, or, on occasions, by such particles as -שֶׁ (šæ-), זֶה (zǣ), or זוֹ (zō), already noted, or -הַ (ha-) followed by a participle.

In respect of the verb, there is overall a measure of fluctuation and inconsistency, to be expected of a system at a transitional stage. The suffix-conjugation seems solidly established as the means of expressing the past, being the most widely-used form in narrative, and usually conveying a punctual aspect with regard to an already completed action. There are also some instances of stative verbs. The prefix-conjugation usually conveys a durative aspect, referring to an action that the speaker regards as unfinished; its temporal significance cannot be clearly defined, seeing that is found both with its old preterite value, especially with *waw*-consecutive or with אָז ('āz) 'then', and in reference to the present or future. It is very often used modally, as a volitive or desiderative, retaining in part, along with the cohortative, the function of the old subjunctive. Sequences in which the prefix-conjugation is followed or preceded by the suffix-conjugation or, occasionally, the participle are commonly encountered, although there seems to be no motive for this usage, beyond, perhaps, one of style.

The active participle can be used as a noun or a verb, often having a narrative function in respect of the past or the present. At other times it functions as an adjective, like the passive participle. The infinitive absolute expresses emphasis when accompanied by a finite form of the same root. Occasionally, though, it refers to past or present time. The infinitive construct with prefixed preposition is often used to introduce temporal and other clauses.

The use of the particles is particularly interesting. There are far fewer of them than in later stages of Hebrew, and their usage is similar to that found in other Northwest Semitic languages. Thus, for example, we have good evidence for -לְ (l^e-) as an asseverative particle, as in לַי״ (la-Y.) 'truly, Y. is ...' (Ps 89:19) or as a vocative (Ps 68:34; see above), for כִּי (kī) and perhaps even -וְ (w^e-) as emphatic particles, for enclitic *mem*, with no particular meaning, and for the deictic value of particles like -הַ (ha-) and הֵם (hēm).

In the syntax of the sentence, there is a noticeably widespread use of nominal clauses, and of asyndeton in both paratactic and hypotactic structures. It is common to find logical subordination under the guise of a formally paratactic structure. Hypotactic constructions are normally introduced by a restricted number of particles some of which, -וְ (we-) for example, have a variety of functions. There are various sorts of possible *'casus pendens'* in which the subject is usually strongly emphasized. Although the normal order is subject-predicate in noun clauses and predicate-subject in verb clauses, there are many variations, usually, perhaps, for the sake of emphasis.

A specialized vocabulary is also well attested. Certain lexical items are only used in the poetic texts, with different terms employed for prose. Thus, for example, we find in archaic biblical poetry חזה (ḥzh) 'see' for prose ראה (r'h), אזן ('zn) hi. 'listen' for שמע (šm'), הוה (hwh) 'be' for היה (hyh), אתה ('th) 'come' for בוא (bw'), חוה (ḥwh) pi. 'tell' for אמר ('mr), שתל (štl) 'plant' for נטע (nṭ'), פעל (p'l) 'do, make' for עשה ('śh), צעד (ṣ'd) 'walk' for הלך (hlk), נגה (ngh) 'shine' for אור ('wr), שער (ś'r) 'know' for ידע (yd'), קנה (qnh) 'create' for ברא (br'), דין (dyn) 'judge' for שפט (špṭ), זעם (z'm) 'become angry' for כעס (k's), מחץ (mḥṣ) 'strike' for נכה (nkh) hi., אֹמֶר ('ōmær) 'word' for דָּבָר (dāḇār), אֹרַח ('ōraḥ) 'way' for דֶּרֶךְ (dæræḵ), גֶּבֶר (gæḇær) and אֱנוֹשׁ ('ænōš) 'man' for אָדָם ('āḏām), חֶמֶר (ḥæmær) 'wine' for יַיִן (yayin), חָרוּץ (ḥārūṣ) and פָּז (paz) 'gold' for זָהָב (zāhāḇ), טֶרֶף (ṭæræp̄) 'food' for אֹכֶל ('ōḵæl), כַּבִּיר (kabbīr) 'great' for גָּדוֹל (gāḏōl), and רֹזְנִים (rōzenīm) 'princes' for שָׂרִים (śārīm).[19] The noun in סוּתֹה (sūṯō) 'his robe' (Gn 49:11) is a *hapax legomenon* in the Bible, but is found in other Northwest Semitic languages.[20] שָׂדַי

[19] See G.R. Driver 1953; Rabin 1971a, 66; E.Y. Kutscher 1982, 80.
[20] See E.Y. Kutscher 1982, 80.

(śāḏay) at Dt 32:13 is equivalent to שָׂדֶה (śāḏæ) 'field' elsewhere in the Bible.

Expressions used almost exclusively in poetry include *hapax legomena* and other rare words, which tend to be concentrated in the oldest biblical texts. Generally, it may be said that these items existed during the archaic period of the language, later disappearing from normal use. Thus, in the Oracles of Balaam (Nm 23:7ff.) we encounter, for example, רֹבַע (rōḇa') 'dust', attested in other Semitic languages like Akkadian, צֻרִים (ṣūrīm), which means 'mountains' only in this passage, נְחָלִים (neḥālīm) 'palms', as distinct from its homophone 'currents (of water)', שְׁתֻם (šeṯūm) 'pierced', from a root used in RH, עָדַי ('āḏay), probably from עַד ('aḏ) 'promise', דרך (drk) possibly in the sense of 'govern', and כּוֹכָב (kōḵāḇ) perhaps meaning 'descendant'. The occurrence of so many lexical items of this kind in a single passage is evidence of its antiquity.[21]

Some of the roots peculiar to archaic poetry are also found in other Northwest Semitic dialects. Thus, for example, פעל (p'l) 'do, make', מחץ (mḥṣ) 'strike', and חָרוּץ (ḥārūṣ) 'gold' are common in Canaanite and Ugaritic texts, whereas יְתַנּוּ (yeṯannū) 'let them recount' (Jg 5:11) and מָחֲקָה (māḥaqā) 'she destroyed' (Jg 5:26) correspond phonologically more to Aramaic than to Hebrew, which uses instead the cognate roots שנה (šnh) and מחץ (mḥṣ). Probably this situation arises not so much from any direct influence of other languages on Hebrew as from the existence of isoglosses shared by the dialects of the area at the time these texts were written, or from the sort of evident literary contact attested in the well-known example of common word pairs.[22]

The characteristic language of archaic Hebrew poetry could be due to the poems' great antiquity and also to their possible provenance in the north, an area which was more exposed to the cultural preferences and innovations of neighbouring peoples and

21 See Morag 1980–81.

22 See Avishur 1974, etc.

which had more contact with their literature. But it is unlikely that this language is simply the dialect spoken by the northern tribes in contrast to the southern dialect which later became dominant. Comparison with the situation in the Northwest Semitic area would seem to suggest that these poems reflect a literary language which we lack the data to describe in full, but which should, nonetheless, be clearly distinguished from the everyday spoken language.

3.4 *The language of the inscriptions*

Although we possess relatively few inscriptions in Hebrew, they constitute an extremely important source of information for our knowledge of Archaic Hebrew. With the earliest inscriptions dating as far back as the close of the second millennium BCE, the inscriptional material as a whole is contemporary with a substantial portion of the Bible, with the advantage of not having undergone revision over the centuries.

Pre-exilic Hebrew epigraphic material is listed in general works like those of D. Diringer, S. Moscati, and, in particular, those of H. Donner and W. Röllig, J.C.L. Gibson, and most recently and comprehensively, G.I. Davies.[23]

It is still not certain that the twelfth-century alphabet, which follows some obscure lines on an ostracon from ʻIzbet Ṣarṭah, can be classed as a Hebrew inscription.[24] From the tenth century comes

[23] Diringer 1934; Moscati 1951; Donner and Röllig 1971–76 (especially II, 180–201); J.C.L. Gibson 1971; Davies 1991; also Hestrin, Israeli, Meshorer, and A. Eitan 1973; Avigad 1979; Naveh 1982, 65ff. Studies of wider Semitic epigraphy include: Académie des Inscriptions et Belles-Lettres 1881–83; 1900–33; Lidzbarski 1898; 1902–15; Cooke 1903; Degen, W.W. Müller, and Röllig 1972–78; Teixidor 1986 (first published in *Syria* from 1967). See the classified bibliography of R.W. Suder (1984).

[24] See Kochavi 1977; Demsky 1977; Garbini 1978a; Naveh 1978a; Cross 1980; Dotan 1981; E.Y. Kutscher 1982, 64; Puech 1986, 170ff. A. Dotan proposed some interesting readings for this ostracon, the first four lines of which might contain a number of short phrases in Hebrew.

the so-called Gezer calendar.[25] The inscription on a bowl from northern Sinai is from the ninth century BCE,[26] and the two ostraca from Tell Qasile,[27] the votive inscriptions from Kuntillet 'Ajrud,[28] and the short texts from Hazor[29] might also be dated to the ninth century or the beginning of the eighth to which belong as well the ostraca from Samaria[30] and the Ophel,[31] the ivory inscriptions from Nimrud,[32] and various seals. From around 700 BCE, we have the Siloam tunnel inscription,[33] two inscriptions on the tomb of Shebna, a high-ranking royal official, also from Siloam,[34] the Kadesh-Barnea ostraca,[35] and inscribed jar handles from Gibeon.[36] The six ostraca from Meṣad Ḥashavyahu, near Yavneh Yam,[37] three funerary inscriptions from Khirbet-el-Qom,[38] and some seals and inscribed jar handles are from the eighth century BCE. The twenty-one ostraca from Lachish,[39] many of the hundred or so

25 See Albright 1943; Février 1948; Cross and Freedman 1952, 45ff. The syntax of the Gezer calendar is examined in Honeyman 1953.

26 See Meshel and Meyers 1976.

27 See B. Maisler (Mazar) 1950–51, 208–10; 1951.

28 See Meshel 1978; Chase 1982; Weinfeld 1984; Lemaire 1984; Hadley 1987a.

29 See Yadin 1960; S. Yeivin 1969; J.C.L. Gibson 1971, 18f.

30 See Reisner, Fisher, and Lyon 1924; Albright 1936; B. Maisler (Mazar) 1948; Yadin 1959; 1961; 1962; 1968; Aharoni 1962; 1966a; I.T. Kaufman 1966; Shea 1977. On the ostraca in general, see Lemaire 1977a.

31 See Cook 1924; Y. Sukenik (Yadin) 1946–47; Prignaud 1970; J.C.L. Gibson 1971, 25f.; Lemaire 1978; Naveh 1982a; Shiloh 1984.

32 See Barnett 1957; Millard 1962; J.C.L. Gibson 1971, 19f.; Röllig 1974, 44f.

33 See J.C.L. Gibson 1971, 21ff. and Puech 1974, where mention is made of more than 220 studies of the inscription since its discovery in 1880.

34 See Avigad 1953a; 1955; 1979, 23f.; Ussishkin 1968–69; 1969; J.C.L. Gibson 1971, 23f.

35 See Lemaire and Vernus 1980; 1983; R. Cohen 1985.

36 See Pritchard 1956; Avigad 1959; J.C.L. Gibson 1971, 54ff.; Frick 1974.

37 See Naveh 1960; 1961; 1962; 1964; Amusin and Heltzer 1964; J.C.L. Gibson 1971, 26ff.; Lemaire 1977a, 259ff.; Pardee 1978; Suzuki 1982; Sasson 1984.

38 See Dever 1969–70; Lemaire 1977; Avigad 1979, 24; Zevit 1984; Catastini 1984; Hadley 1987; O'Connor 1987; Margalit 1989.

39 See Torczyner, Harding, Lewis, and Starkey 1938; Ginsberg 1935; 1938; 1940; Albright 1938; de Vaux 1939; Tufnell 1953; J.C.L. Gibson 1971, 32ff.; Lemaire 1977a, 83ff.; Ussishkin 1978; 1983; Cross 1985.

documents from Arad,[40] the funerary cave graffiti from Khirbet Beit Lei,[41] and a jar from the cemetery at Azor[42] date from the sixth century BCE. More than 160 seals from various periods have been preserved.[43] Recent archaeological excavations have continued to uncover new inscriptions of various sizes from a wide range of places.[44] In the Hinnom Valley two small silver amulets dating from the seventh century BCE have been found – one of these contains the Priestly Blessing from Nm 6:24–26.[45] An ivory pomegranate bearing a short inscription in Hebrew was recently acquired by the Israel Museum, Jerusalem.[46]

The Murabba'at palimpsest (Mur 17),[47] the oldest surviving Hebrew papyrus, is also dated from around the eighth to seventh centuries BCE, with a fragment of a letter and a text of an economic nature. The contents of all these inscriptions and documents are quite brief and hardly facilitate a detailed linguistic analysis of the region in pre-exilic times.

Without doubt, one of the most widely analysed and discussed texts is that of the Gezer tablet, which was discovered in 1908, and believed by some to represent an older dialect than Hebrew,[48] although in fact it employs forms characteristic of northern Hebrew. Particular difficulty attaches to the interpretation of the form *yrḥw* which occurs four times in this 'agricultural calendar' or

40 See Aharoni 1966; 1968a; 1970; 1981; J.C.L. Gibson 1971, 49ff.; Rainey 1971; 1977; Lemaire 1977a, 145ff.; Pardee 1978a; van Dyke Parunak 1978; Sasson 1982.

41 See Naveh 1963; Cross 1970; Lemaire 1976; P.D. Miller 1981.

42 See Dothan 1961.

43 See Vattioni 1969; 1971; 1978; Herr 1978, 80ff.; Hestrin and Dayagi-Mendeles 1978–79; Garbini 1982.

44 For example: Ramat Raḥel (Aharoni 1961; Lemaire 1977a, 257f.); Beth Shean (Tzori 1961); En Shemesh (Grant and G.E. Wright 1939); Khirbet Raddana (Aharoni 1971; Cross 1971); Tell al-Rimaḥ (Cody 1970); Giv'at ha-Mivtar (Naveh 1970); Beer Sheba (Lemaire 1977a, 271ff.); Khirbet el-Meshash (Lemaire 1977a, 275); Aroer (Lemaire 1980); Tell 'Ira (Beit-Arieh 1983; Garfunkel 1988).

45 The excavation was directed by G. Barkay in 1975; see Barkay 1984.

46 See Lemaire 1981a; 1984a.

47 Published by J.T. Milik (1961, 93–100); see J.C.L. Gibson 1971, 31f.

48 See Garbini 1954–56.

'votive tablet', and is generally understood as a dual with third person singular suffix: *yaṙḥayhū > yarḥēhū > yarḥēw* 'his two months'.[49] A feature of this text is the reduction of what were once diphthongs, a characteristic of the northern dialect as opposed to its Jerusalemite counterpart – thus, *kl* 'measuring' for expected BH *kyl* (*kayil*) and *qṣ* for BH *qyṣ* (*qayiṣ*) 'summer (harvest)'.

Reduced diphthongs are also found in the Samaria ostraca, with, for example, *yn* for BH *yyn* (*yayin*) 'wine' (cf. *yyn* on an ostracon from Arad). On an ostracon from Tell Qasile a non-reduced diphthong, *byt* 'house (of)', appears next to a contracted one, *ḥrn* 'Horon' (i.e. *ḥoron* < **ḥawran*).[50] Another distinctive feature of the Samaria ostraca is the form *b-št* instead of BH *b- šnh* (*ba-šanah*) 'in the year', with assimilation of *nun* as in Phoenician and Moabite and conservation of the old feminine marker. The third person singular masculine pronominal suffix with *-h* occurs in the Lachish letters and at Yavneh Yam,[51] where we also find the first person singular suffix-conjugation form *klt* 'I measured'.[52] A letter from Lachish has the possibly colloquial form *'t* in place of BH *'th* (*'attah*) 'now'.[53] In theophoric names of the southern dialect the element *-yhw* is the norm, for example *'ḥyhw* 'Ahijah' in the Ophel ostracon, while in the north the *-h-* disappears, leaving the reduced form *-yw*.[54] The particle *l-*, which accompanies personal

49 As suggested by W.F. Albright (1943). Previously he had accepted H.L. Ginsberg's interpretation (1936a) that it was a nominative dual construct, *yarḥa*, which had undergone the Northwest Semitic change to *yarḥo*. Albright rejected this view as the orthography of Archaic Hebrew, which did not employ *matres lectionis*, became better known. G. Garbini (1954–56) raised the possibility that the form is a nominative plural construct in *-u*, similar to that of Ugaritic, a solution accepted by J.C.L. Gibson (1971, 3) as well. P. Skehan (noted in Cross and Freedman 1952, 46f., n.11) analyzed the construction as 'involving a prospective suffix, in apposition with the following noun.' J.B. Segal (1962) advanced the hypothesis that the final *waw* is actually the hieratic numeral 2, which has a similar form to the letter *w* in the palaeo–Hebrew script.

50 See Cross and Freedman 1952, 48; J.C.L. Gibson 1971, 15ff.

51 See Donner and Röllig 1971–76, II, 191, 200.

52 See J.C.L. Gibson 1971, 30.

53 Also conserved in the *ketiv* of Ezk 23:43 and Ps 74:6. See Cross and Freedman 1952, 52f.

54 See Cross and Freedman 1952, 51; Ṣarfatti 1982, 81f.

names on many seals, jars, and other inscriptions, has been interpreted in various ways, but is probably simply the *lamed* of ownership.[55]

The inscriptions tend to employ a defective orthography, although occasionally we find forms with *y* or *w* in medial position which do not merely reflect uncontracted diphthongs, for example *'rwr* (*'arur*) 'cursed' in the eighth-century BCE Siloam tomb inscription, as against *'wd* 'still' and *mwṣ'* 'source' from the Siloam tunnel, which might have preserved the diphthong: *'awd, mawṣa'*. Orthographic analysis of the inscriptions[56] clearly demonstrates that before the tenth century Hebrew writing, like Phoenician, was purely consonantal, and that it was halfway though the ninth century BCE, under the influence of Aramaic, that the *matres lectionis* began to be introduced, at first only at the end of a word, but later in medial positions as well. A form like *r'w* 'his fellow' in the Siloam tunnel inscription was read as *re'ew* (< *re'ehu*, without the later development, frequently attested in BH, to *re'o*). We do not know whether, in line with this interpretation, a form like *hyt* 'she was', which appears in the same inscription, should be read as *hayat*, as in RH, or *hayata*, which would be closer to classical BH.[57] In the Lachish ostraca from the sixth century BCE there are various medial *matres lectionis*. In the ostraca from Arad, from more or less the same time, *w* is already commonly used for *u*, with *y* often representing *i*. However, there are no other medial *matres lectionis*, and *h* at the end of a word can stand for *e*, *a*, or *o*.[58]

55 Thus, for example, N. Avigad (1979, 27ff.). Y. Yadin (1959; 1962; 1968) argued that it introduces names of important landowners or producers of wine, oil, and grain, who were paying taxes, sending gifts, etc. A.F. Rainey (1962; 1967; 1970; 1971; 1982), on the other hand, believes it refers to the recipient of produce. Cf. Lemaire 1981; Mommsen, Perlman, and J. Yellin 1984.

56 See especially Cross and Freedman 1952, 45ff., although some of the authors' opinions, regarding, for example, the late development of medial *matres lectionis*, are usually accepted only in modified form today. Cf. Zevit 1980; Ṣarfatti 1982, 60f.

57 See Puech 1974, 201.

58 See van Dyke Parunak 1978.

Quite often the epigraphic forms coincide with biblical readings preserved only as *ketiv*, although the Masoretes have tried to standardize them through *qere*. Examples are the third person singular masculine suffix *-w* instead of *-yw* with plural nouns, as in *'nšw* 'his men', or *-h* with nouns in the singular, and instances of haplography, as with *ḥyhwh* instead of *ḥy yhwh* '(as) Y. lives', or of *scriptio defectiva*, as in *'t* for *'th* 'now' or *ktym* for *ktyym* 'Kittim'.[59]

In the Lachish ostraca the second person singular verb suffix is *-th*, but at Arad it alternates with *-t*. It seems clear that in the longer form the *he* functions, as throughout most of the Bible, as a word-final *mater lectionis*. In the inscriptions the second person masculine pronominal suffix is regularly *-k*, for example, *bytk* 'your house', and this has been explained in various ways.[60]

There are some interesting examples of the omission of the article, although this is not systematic. Thus, *l-śr 'r* 'to/for (the) governor of (the) city' at Kuntillet 'Ajrud as against *śr h-'r* '(the) governor of the city' in two seventh-century *bullae* – and the expected biblical form – might reflect a colloquialism.[61]

The vocabulary of the inscriptions corresponds in the main to that of BH, although there are some unknown words such as *'ṣd* in the Gezer calendar, which is clearly related to מַעֲצָד (ma'ᵃṣāḏ) 'sickle' in BH. One of the most debated items is *zdh* in the Siloam tunnel inscription, which has been understood in many ways – 'fissure', 'narrow place', 'ardour', 'resonance', 'drilling', etc.[62] Analysis of the epigraphic material has also uncovered the names of two weights, *nṣp* and *pym*.[63] The term *klb*, which frequently ocurs in the Lachish letters and is attested both at El-Amarna and in the Bible, might be a synonym of the standard word for 'slave'.[64]

59 See Ṣarfatti 1982, 65ff.

60 See Ṣarfatti 1982, 68f.

61 See Ṣarfatti 1982, 71ff.

62 See Puech 1974, 201ff.; Görg 1980.

63 See E.Y. Kutscher 1982, 67f; Hadas-Lebel 1981, 75f.; Ṣarfatti 1982, 73.

64 See Margalith 1983 and Sasson 1979a, a doctoral dissertation which examines various words from the inscriptions.

The noun *'mh*, found in a number of funerary inscriptions, might be the title of a high-ranking female courtier.

Some words are used in a different sense from that attested in the Bible. Thus, at Arad *'wd* is a noun, 'residue', while in BH it functions as an adverb, 'still'. The readings of some words are doubtful: *šmn rḥṣ* in the Samaria ostraca can be interpreted as *šemen* 'oil' that is *raḥuṣ*, 'washed, refined', or *raḥaṣ* 'of ablution'. The formulas of greeting which begin the Lachish letters do not occur in the Bible and seem to derive from a different social environment.[65]

3.5 *Pre-exilic Hebrew prose*

When we consider that the cultural and religious centre at the time of the Judges was in the north of Israel, in the mountains of Ephraim and Benjamin, it is not surprising that the language of archaic biblical poetry has obvious connexions with the poetry of the Canaanite north. In contrast, classical Hebrew prose is clearly linked to the reigns of David and Solomon and their successors in Jerusalem. This does not necessarily mean that the advent of the Davidic monarchy saw a replacement of the northern language by the southern – rather, an 'official' language was created, which was used at court and in educated circles in Jerusalem, and which was intended to be as understandable in the north as in the south, although, clearly, southern features would have predominated.[66] The language of prophetic and liturgical poetry from this period is not markedly different from that of the prose writings.

Pre-exilic Hebrew, as we saw in the last chapter, evolved alongside other Northwest Semitic languages, developing many features that distinguish it from Proto-Semitic, for example, the transition of initial *w* to *y* and of *ā́* to *ṓ*, reduction of diphthongs

65 See Pardee 1982; Ṣarfatti 1982, 74ff.
66 See Rabin 1979.

(although not in every instance), disappearance of final short vowels, elision of the feminine marker *-t* in the noun and the verb, conversion of the interdental consonants to sibilants, assimilation of *nun* to a following consonant (with some exceptions), loss of preterite value in the prefix-conjugation (except when preceded by *waw*-consecutive, which was extended, by analogy, to the suffix-conjugation), development of the cohortative, virtual disappearance of the *Shaf'el*, the suffix *-ti* for the first person singular, and the use of the article.[67]

On the assumption that the consonantal system of pre-exilic Hebrew has in general been satisfactorily preserved, there have been various attempts to reconstruct the vocalization and pronunciation of classical BH, which certainly differs considerably from that established by the Masoretes fifteen centuries later. Basing themselves primarily on comparative grammar, scholars have tried to highlight the most important changes, mainly phonetic, which can be detected in Hebrew after 600 BCE.[68]

Among the most significant of these, including some which had already begun to take place before the exile, are the following: elision of syllable- or word-final *alef*, which probably occurred quite early,[69] spirantization of the *bgdkpt* consonants, which resulted originally in their dual realization as plosives or fricatives, with fricative realization clearly dominant later, neutralization of velar and pharyngeal phonemes (/ḫ/>/ḥ/, /ġ/>/'/), the exact date of which is unclear,[70] neutralization of /ś/ and /s/, 'segolatization' which introduced anaptyctic vowels to avoid sequences of two consonants (**kalbu* > *keleb*, **sipru* > *seper*),[71] pretonic vowel lengthening and consonant reduplication, perhaps

67 See Rabin 1971a, 58f.

68 See especially Bergsträsser 1918–29, I, 11ff., 163ff.; Harris 1941; Beyer 1969, 37f. Birkeland 1940, 59ff. concentrates on the changes introduced by the Tiberian Masoretes.

69 See Blau 1976, 22f.

70 See Wevers 1970 and Blau 1982, which show that at the time of the Greek translation of the Pentateuch (around the third century BCE), the difference between these two groups of phonemes was still felt.

71 See Blau 1976, 34.

with displacement of the accent to the final syllable,[72] Philippi's law, by which short /i/ changes to /a/ in closed accented syllables (*ḥapiḍta > ḥapaṣta)[73] and the law of attenuation by which /a/ in certain environments changes to /i/ (*massima > missim), reduction of certain vowels to *shewa* or, in the environment of a laryngeal consonant, to another ultrashort vowel, reduction of final doubled consonants, vowel changes before and after the laryngeals, reduction of double laryngeals and of double /r/,[74] disappearance of intervocalic /h/, weakening of the pharyngeal and laryngeal consonants, possibly a further contraction of diphthongs or the use of anaptyctic vowels (**baytu* > *bayit*, **mawtu* > *mawet*), etc.[75]

Other phenomena are even later and affect only specific Hebrew traditions, such as the Tiberian, in which *qameṣ*, which often corresponds to Proto-Semitic /ā/, is pronounced as /å/. There are also noticeable differences among the various traditions in the pronunciation of *ṣere* and *segol* (which, like *pathaḥ* and *qameṣ*, are undifferentiated in the Palestinian tradition), *ḥolem*, *resh*, etc.[76]

It is not always easy to determine the precise date of each of these events. But it is certain that they occurred between the time when Hebrew was still a living language and the era of the Masoretes. In addition to recording the actual changes in language, which in many instances were not confined to Hebrew, the Masoretic pointing system also reflects the linguistic views of the Masoretes in a variety of ways, with evidence of Aramaic influence and of unduly subjective reconstruction.[77] Approaching the matter from the opposite direction, that is, by eliminating from Masoretic

72 See Bergsträsser 1918–29, I, 165.

73 J. Blau (1981) has examined in great detail the relative chronology of this well-known law, demonstrating that, although it began operating later than vowel lengthening due to pause, it was still functioning after the change to syllable-final accent in pausal forms ending with a closed syllable.

74 See Harris 1941, 145; Blau 1976, 31f.

75 See Beyer 1969, 38f.; Rabin 1971a, 59.

76 See Rabin 1971a, 59.

77 Note the judgement of K. Beyer (1969, 33), as well as the well-known view of P.E. Kahle, about which we shall have cause to comment later, and which we do not share in every detail.

Hebrew whatever has resulted from the processes listed above, various attempts have been made, with differing degrees of success, to reconstruct pre-exilic Hebrew, including its morphology.[78]

From a completely different perspective, the language of pre-exilic prose differs from that of archaic poetry in possessing a greater stability in its use of the article and *nota accusativi* and in its distinction between simple and *waw*-consecutive forms of the verb. Particles like אֲשֶׁר ('ᵃšær) and כִּי (kī) are used much more often, reducing the number of asyndetic structures.[79]

Although they certainly existed, there are no clear traces of different pre-exilic dialects, beyond a few variations in the treatment of diphthongs and the well-known text at Jg 12:1ff. regarding the pronunciation of *shibboleth*.[80] Some prophetic books, like Hosea, reflect the linguistic environment of the northern kingdom, and may contain several specific dialect features, which would explain why they have so many parallels to the constructions and vocabulary of other Canaanite or Northwest Semitic languages.[81] In the remaining pre-exilic prose books and in non-archaic poetic texts, there are notable differences of style and, in some instances, linguistic traces of different periods of composition, even though the language used in all such works remains basically the same, and may properly be called classical BH.

All traditions of Hebrew agree that in BH there are twenty-one consonantal and two semiconsonantal phonemes, represented by twenty-two graphemes. One of these stands for two different phonemes, /š/ and /ś/, while a further six at least are polyvalent – these are the graphemes corresponding to the *bgdkpt* series, each member of which has a dual realization as plosive or fricative

78 A particularly good example is that of K. Beyer (1969).

79 See Rabin 1971a, 66.

80 See E.Y. Kutscher 1982, 14f.

81 See Kuhnigk 1974.

depending on its phonetic environment, the two variants having the status not of distinct phonemes, but rather of allophones.[82] Of the twenty-nine supposed Proto-Semitic consonantal phonemes, the interdentals have been neutralized with the dental fricatives and the velars with the corresponding pharyngeals. The number of vowel phonemes varies according to the different Masoretic traditions.

In the language as represented by the Tiberian tradition the accent usually falls on the final or, less often, penultimate syllable. But the accent in Hebrew has a complicated history within which various stages can probably be identified.[83] If originally the accent fell mainly on the penultimate syllable (or occasionally on the antepenultimate), the loss of final short vowels would have resulted in the accent tending to be left on what was now the final syllable. Pausal forms and certain suffixed forms preserve the accent and vocalization of an earlier period. Closely connected to developments in the accent is the lengthening of some pretonic vowels, the reduction to ultrashort vowels of vowels in open syllables positioned relatively far from the accent, and the appearance of anaptyctic vowels to avoid sequences of two final consonants in some word patterns. All these changes probably occurred after the exile.[84]

According to all Masoretic traditions, the verb has a prefix- and a suffix-conjugation. The prefix-conjugation, originally expressing actions (rather than states), is used to denote the durative or cursive aspect of an action or process taking place now or in the future. The suffix-conjugation, originally expressing the stative, denotes a state of being that has arisen in the past, and conveys a

82 See Cantineau 1950b; M.H. Segal 1928; Schramm 1964; Blau 1976, 5ff.

83 See Blau 1976, 30ff.

84 See Grimme 1896; Brockelmann 1904; Hommel 1917; Cantineau 1931; 1932a; Artom 1931–32; Goetze 1939; Poebel 1939; 1939a; Rabin 1960; J.C.L. Gibson 1966; Blau 1978a; 1979; 1979a; 1981.

punctual or constative aspect.[85] In addition, the preterite function of the Proto-Semitic prefix-conjugation has been preserved in BH's 'consecutive' (or 'conversive') tenses, the origins and significance of which are still not absolutely clear.[86]

Verbal moods are significantly reduced in BH, although it is still possible to recognize remains of the old narrative-indicative, final, preterite-jussive, imperative, and energic moods.[87] It has even been claimed that there is a durative (**yaqqattalu*) form.[88] In the prefix-conjugation, shortened (jussive) forms as well as lengthened forms with final *-n* (*nun paragogicum*), or, in the first person, final *-ah*, (cohortative), are also used, albeit infrequently. The infinitive absolute has a much reduced narrative or emphatic function whereas a new form, the infinitive construct, normally with pronominal suffix and/or prefixed particle, is widespread.

There are also fewer derived conjugations of the verb in BH, although nowadays there is a tendency to recognize forms not identified by the Masoretes, such as the passive of *Qal*,[89] the causative *Shaf'el*,[90] and *Nuf'al* and *Hothpa'el* as the passives of

85 The tense system and the possibly aspectual function of the Hebrew verb has been the object of numerous studies over the last century. S.R. Driver (1892) tried to apply to Hebrew the categories used for Greek by G. Curtius, arguing that the Hebrew verb indicates the character of an action, not the time it takes place. Thus, the imperfect expresses incipient action, the participle, continuing action, and the perfect, completed action. Many Hebraists accepted Driver's theory. See A.B. Davidson 1901; Williams 1967, etc. Others, like H. Bauer (1910), rejected such a view outright, arguing that in Hebrew the tenses also express different points in time. See Bergsträsser 1918–29, II, 9–14; G.R. Driver 1936; Blake 1951a; Hughes 1970. On the other hand, C. Brockelmann (1956), D. Michel (1960), F. Rundgren (1959; 1961; 1963), E. Jenni (1968), R. Meyer (1966–72, III, 39ff.), P. Kustár (1972), J. Kuryłowicz (1972; 1973), and others have defended in different ways the hypothesis that the Hebrew verb expresses aspect. Cf. Mettinger 1974; McFall 1982; Zuber 1986; Niccacci 1990 (originally published in Italian, 1986). A. Torres (1982) presents an assessment of the different views on this issue.

86 See Lambert 1893; Gordon 1938a; Cazelles 1947; Hartom 1950–51; Schramm 1957; Sheehan 1970; T.L. Fenton 1973. O.L. Barnes (1965) reinterprets the Hebrew tense system in an attempt to demonstrate that a return to the theory of consecutive tenses is not necessary.

87 See R. Meyer 1966–72, II, 96ff.

88 See Rössler 1961; 1962; R. Meyer 1966–72, II, 97. Contrast Bloch 1963.

89 See Williams 1970; Blau 1976, 51; E.Y. Kutscher 1982, 36.

90 See, for example, Rabin 1969a; Wächter 1971.

respectively, *Nif'al* and *Hithpa'el*.[91] The rôle of some of these has merited special attention in the last few years.[92]

In the suffix-conjugation, the third person feminine singular suffix loses its original *taw*: *-at* > *-ah*. The specifically feminine form of the third person plural disappears, leaving a trace only in certain *ketiv* readings.[93] However, in the prefix-conjugation, although there are also a few examples to indicate that the third person plural feminine could occur with the masculine prefix *y-*, a peculiarity of BH is its use of a special feminine form, identical to that used for the second person plural.[94]

Almost a quarter of the nouns in BH are originally monosyllables, in which a sequence of two consonants at the end has been avoided by the inclusion of an anaptyctic vowel (an infrequent phenomenon in the Palestinian and Palestino-Tiberian traditions, and different from Babylonian anaptyxis), which also appears in forms containing a diphthong, for example **baytu* > *bayit* and **mawtu* > *mawet*; this diphthong is usually reduced in construct forms, as with **baytahu* > *beto*. Some *qeṭāl* forms may be due to Aramaic influence.[95] The prefix *ma-* changes to *mi-*, in accordance with the phonetic laws operative in the Tiberian tradition, resulting in such forms as מִשְׁפָּט (mišpāṭ) 'judgement'.[96] There are no special morphological patterns for adjectives.[97]

It has been pointed out that although the vocabulary of BH is very small compared to that of a living language, due to its particular circumstances, it is especially rich in certain areas relevant to the lives of farmers or shepherds, to mountains, clouds, every kind of naturally-occurring water and the places in which it

91 See Qimron 1988.

92 See especially the study by E. Jenni (1968) on the *Pi'el*, which functions as a factitive in intransitive verbs and as a resultative in transitive verbs. See the review in Blau 1970b.

93 See E.Y. Kutscher 1982, 39f.

94 See E.Y. Kutscher 1982, 41f.

95 See Malone 1971.

96 See Baumgartner 1953.

97 See de Lagarde 1889; Barth 1894. F. Werner (1983) conducted an extensive study of adjectives based on nouns and participles or which share some common semantic element (colour, possibility of action, infirmity or defect, etc.). However, the data are drawn from RH and even IH as well as BH.

collects, the desert, thorns, etc.[98] Some names of places[99] and persons[100] preserve interesting grammatical and lexical features which have not survived in other sorts of written text.[101]

Over a quarter of the words in the Bible appear just once, and of these no less than 289 belong to roots used only once in BH. From a very early period they have attracted the attention of philologists, who have had to resort to RH or Comparative Semitics to explain them. Despite every effort, in certain instances it is only the context that enables the researcher to uncover the approximate meaning of such a word.[102]

There is a quite large number of borrowings from other languages, both Semitic and non-Semitic, especially those which, historically, have had a significant cultural influence in the region. This is true of Sumerian, Akkadian,[103] and Egyptian,[104] which left their mark on Canaan before the Hebrew language as we know it came into existence. Ugaritic and Phoenician, on the one hand, and the Southern Semitic dialects, on the other, have also given rise to many loanwords in BH.[105] There was a very considerable Aramaic influence during the exile and Second Temple period, although this had previously been much more limited.[106] There is also influence, though to a much lesser extent, from Persian and Greek. Some Hebrew words derive from Anatolian languages, such as Hittite,[107] or even from Sanskrit.[108] The greater part of these borrowings are names of plants, metals and precious stones, utensils and vestments, measures, and technical terms from agriculture, navigation, and architecture, as well as, for example, vocabulary for military and political administration.[109]

98 See E.Y. Kutscher 1982, 53ff.
99 See especially Borée 1930.
100 See Noth 1928.
101 See E.Y. Kutscher 1982, 57ff.
102 See Rabin 1962; Greenspahn 1984.
103 See Theis 1912; Landersdorfer 1916; Zimmern 1917.
104 See Yahuda 1933 (originally published in German, 1929); Lambdin 1953.
105 See Ullendorff 1956; Leslau 1958; Guillaume 1965.
106 See Kautzsch 1902; Wagner 1966; E.Y. Kutscher 1982, 75ff.
107 See Rabin 1963a.
108 See Rabin 1962a.
109 See Ellenbogen 1962.

Chapter 4

BIBLICAL HEBREW IN ITS VARIOUS TRADITIONS

4.1 *The transmission of Biblical Hebrew*

The preservation of classical Hebrew is inseparably connected with how the text of the Bible was transmitted down the centuries. After a long period of formation in which the various texts were expanded, modified, and, after the exile, adjusted in a variety of ways,[1] and in which the palaeo-Hebrew script gradually gave way to Aramaic square characters, the text of each book began to stabilize. Originally, this was not a totally uniform process, as is evident from the variants found in early manuscripts and the versions, but it did become more obvious and thoroughgoing, especially in the Tannaitic period.

By the end of the first or the beginning of the second century CE,[2] the consonantal text seems to have become completely stable, bringing to an end a period of textual diversity, which had arisen due perhaps to the existence of various local texts[3] or more probably to the use of particular versions within different religious or other groups.[4]

Within the Jewish community, awareness of the sacred character of the biblical text, ultimately extending to its smallest details, helped to guarantee its transmission from one generation to

[1] See, for example, Eissfeldt 1965, 562ff.; Fohrer 1968, 488ff.; McCarthy 1981.

[2] See M. Greenberg 1956; Barthélemy 1978, 341ff.

[3] Following a theory first stated by W.F. Albright (1955), F.M. Cross (1958; 1964; 1966) became a notable advocate of this view, which, however, has found little favour in more recent scholarship.

[4] See Talmon 1970; Cross and Talmon 1975, 321ff.

another in the home and especially among the community's teachers and religious officers. Long before precise notes about the conservation of the text had been set down in writing, a much older oral tradition had developed in order to ensure the transmission in exact detail of the text, which could not be modified or undergo addition or deletion of a single letter.[5]

The *soferim* or professional scribes played a major rôle in the careful conservation of the text and in determining the precise form in which it was to be read and pronounced. The rabbinic writings allude to the painstaking work of the *kotvanim* and *lavlarim*, copyists and clerks charged with reproducing the text in every detail, while other specialists worked out the exact significance of more obscure features.[6]

In the era of the *Amoraim*, the *halakhah* had already established precise guidelines about how the text of the Bible was to be read and written. Without touching the received consonantal text at all, certain indications and signs were introduced into copies of the text to make it easier to understand. The rules about pauses and accents, which enable a correct melodic recitation of the text, also seem to date from this time.[7]

The first Masoretic observations to help establish the use of *scriptio plena* or *defectiva* in the text were listed in manuscript form before the eighth century CE. Vocalization systems and various traditions of reading the biblical text had been fixed and then transmitted orally many centuries before it was felt necessary to embody it in graphic notation. The various systems of accentuation and vocalization introduced into the text of the Bible by the Masoretes had started to develop by about the sixth or seventh century CE.[8] As is well known, from the tenth century one such system eventually imposed its authority over the others, spreading from Tiberias to the entire Jewish world. This was the system

[5] See the words of Josephus in *Contra Apionem* 1:42.

[6] See Dotan 1971, 1405.

[7] See Dotan 1971, 1412f.

[8] See Morag 1974; Chiesa 1979, 37; Dotan 1981a.

devised by the Masoretic family of Ben-Asher in the wake of painstaking scholarly analysis, which essentially reflected a highly-developed tradition of pronunciation and synagogue reading handed down over the centuries. The most important editions of the Hebrew Bible, from that of Jacob b. Ḥayyim[9] to those of the present day, have been based on the various codices that preserve the Ben-Asher system of pointing. And it is on the basis of these texts, reproducing more or less exactly the Ben-Asher tradition, that analysis of BH has been conducted, albeit with some attention being paid to other traditions.

There can be little doubt about the general trustworthiness of the process of transmission as outlined. Even apparently heterogeneous or 'anomalous' forms in the biblical text are actually reflections of phenomena known from LBH, of dialect-forms, or of obvious influence by cognate languages.[10] Nonetheless, there was a long period between the editing and canonization of the biblical texts and their pointing by the Masoretes. Over many centuries it was possible for the original vocalization, transmitted only in oral form within a multilingual environment, to alter considerably. Partly this was due to developments within Hebrew itself and partly because of the influence of dominant languages, particularly Aramaic and, later, Arabic. The formation of a unified standard text probably also involved the elimination of terms and structures that were too archaic to be understood so many centuries after the material had first been composed.

According to Paul Kahle's well-known thesis,[11] the Masoretic, especially the Tiberian, system of punctuation is not simply a representation of how Hebrew was actually pronounced in the sixth to eighth centuries; it also bears witness to the active intervention of the Masoretes, who deliberately introduced various corrections or reconstructions intended to guarantee that Hebrew

[9] Published by Daniel Bomberg in Venice, 1524/25. It represents a text that embodies a variety of Masoretic traditions.

[10] See Morag 1972a; 1974.

[11] First formulated in Kahle 1921; see Kahle 1959 (1st ed., 1947), 164ff.

would be 'pronounced as it should be', and not as it actually had been during the previous centuries, influenced by Aramaic.[12] The Masoretic innovation or reconstruction of a phonological system that had fallen into disuse had been of particular relevance to the pronunciation of the gutturals (reconstructed on the basis of Arabic), the dual pronunciation of the *bgdkpt* consonants, the pronominal suffix ךָ- (-ḵā), and the verb suffix תָּה- (-tā). Although reflected in other studies,[13] such an image of Masoretic activity is generally rejected nowadays.[14] However, it is possible, independently of Kahle's thesis, to accept that there might be important differences between Masoretic Hebrew and the language of the pre-exilic writings.

Before examining how BH has been handed down by the various Masoretic traditions – Palestinian, Babylonian, and Tiberian – it is worth viewing the process of transmission from the other end, by looking at material which takes us as near as possible to the pre-exilic period and which represents traditions of a 'pre-Masoretic' type. Apart from making comparisons with, for example, the Qumran and Samaritan traditions (see Chapter 5), or, as we have done in earlier chapters, comparing phenomena and processes in Hebrew with those of other Northwest Semitic languages, additional information about pre-Masoretic Hebrew can also be obtained by analysis of the many Greek and Latin transcriptions from the third century BCE to the fourth century CE.

12 In Kahle 1921, 1927–30, 25ff., and 1959, 156ff., Kahle based his theory on examination of, for example, the Palestinian and Samaritan traditions, the Greek transcriptions in A. Sperber 1937–38, and *piyyuṭ* rhymes.

13 See Leander 1936; R. Meyer 1951; Murtonen 1968a.

14 The response of eminent Semitists was diametrically opposed to Kahle's theory; see, for example, Bergsträsser 1924, and, more recently, Brønno 1940, etc., E.Y. Kutscher 1949–52, III, 43f., 1982, 19ff., Ben-Ḥayyim 1954, 63f., 97ff., and Dietrich 1968, 124ff.

4.2 *The testimony of the Greek and Latin transcriptions*

The numerous Greek and Latin transcriptions of Hebrew names and other expressions, which date mainly from the third century BCE to the fourth century CE, undoubtedly provide first-hand information about pre-Masoretic BH.[15] Because we know far more about the phonology and pronunciation of Greek and Latin than of the Semitic languages, these transcriptions represent an invaluable witness to the Hebrew of this period. On the other hand, it has to be recognized as well that there are considerable difficulties involved. In the first place, the phonology of Greek and Latin is very different from that of Hebrew, and these languages do not possess graphemes that can exactly represent the sounds of Hebrew. And although we do not know what judgements were actually made when transcribing so different a language, the authors of the transcriptions would certainly have approached Hebrew from the phonological perspective of their own language. The variation of place and time is also a problem, as we cannot simply accept that BH, which had already ceased to be a living language, underwent a unified development in places as diverse as Alexandria and Palestine. Neither do we know if the data afforded by the transcriptions correspond to the standard, more or less official, pronunciation of Hebrew in this period or to dialect or substandard forms. On top of all these difficulties is the fact that the transcriptions have to be studied in manuscripts that are frequently late and defective, presenting many variants and corruptions in names that the copyists found completely alien.

The transcriptions in the Septuagint, which reflect the intellectual and linguistic climate of Alexandria in the third to second

15 Examples of the many studies on this subject are: Frankel 1841; Siegfried 1884; Könnecke 1885; Mercati 1895–96, etc.; Růžička 1908; Margolis 1909–10; 1925–26; Schlatter 1913; Wutz 1925, etc.; Speiser 1925–34; Pretzl 1932; A. Sperber 1937–38; Staples 1939; Lisowsky 1940; Brønno 1940, etc.; Sutcliffe 1948; Kahle 1961; 1962; Barr 1966–67; 1967; 1967a; Emerton 1970; Wevers 1970; Sáenz-Badillos 1975a; Harviainen 1977; Janssens 1982; Murtonen 1981–82; 1986.

centuries BCE, might cast some light on the neutralization of the Proto-Semitic velar phonemes /ḫ/ and /ġ/ with their corresponding pharyngeals, a process which still does not seem to have been fully completed by the time that the Greek translation of the Pentateuch was made. According to one modern study,[16] whereas in almost all instances of names that include an original /ḥ/ this phoneme is transcribed by zero or by vowel mutation, in the majority of names with an original /ḫ/, the usual transcription is *kappa* or *chi*. Thus, there was still a perceived difference between the two Hebrew phonemes, even though both were represented by a single grapheme. Somewhat similar comments apply to /ġ/: except in the last books of the Bible /ʿ/ is transcribed in a fairly systematic way by zero or vowel mutation, whereas original /ġ/ is represented by *gamma*.[17] Thus, when the Greek translation of the Pentateuch was made, /ġ/ was still a distinct phoneme, but when the remaining books were translated, it may no longer have been pronounced, surviving exclusively in public reading of the Bible before finally disappearing completely.[18]

Paul Kahle and his followers, in particular A. Sperber,[19] assessed the evidence in a quite different way. According to Sperber, at the time the Septuagint was composed the gutturals did not have real consonantal value,[20] and were normally transcribed as vowels. The *bgdkpt* consonants had just one realization in Greek,[21] namely, as fricatives. Analysis of the Greek transcriptions in Origen's *Secunda*

16 See Wevers 1970. Although in this study Wevers clearly distances himself from earlier positions, like that of Růžička (1908), his conclusions have generally been well received (see, for example, Steiner 1977, 120, n. 28), and have also been further developed and refined, particularly in J. Blau's decisive 1982 article (pp. 146ff.).

17 See Blau 1982, 113ff.

18 See Blau 1982, 143f.

19 1937–38.

20 Even though /ḥ/, according to Sperber, was transcribed in an earlier period by *chi* (but see Wevers 1970).

21 Occasionally, however, *kappa* appears in place of *chi*, and where there is gemination, sequences like *tau-theta* are found in the Septuagint.

(third century CE)[22] and of the Latin transcriptions of Jerome (fourth century CE) corroborated for Sperber Kahle's theory concerning the gutturals and the *bgdkpt* consonants.

Both gutturals and *bgdkpt* aroused great controversy. In the first place, the transcription data are not entirely unequivocal, and, in any case, they do not have to be interpreted in the way proposed by Kahle's followers. Regarding the *bgdkpt* consonants, in the second-century CE transcriptions of Aquila, Symmachus, and Theodotion, 'the Three',[23] the tendency is for just one transcriptional equivalent for each consonant, but there are also clear signs of a dual realization, especially when the consonants have *dagesh*. A more uniform system of transcription is found in the *Secunda*, which systematically uses *chi*, *phi*, and *theta*, and in Jerome's transcriptions, which employ *ch*, *ph*, and *th*.[24] However, as various scholars have pointed out,[25] it cannot be inferred from this type of data alone that the relevant Hebrew consonants were realized only as fricatives. The fact that in the transcriptions of the Septuagint or of 'the Three' we can also find *kappa*, *pi*, and *tau*, which have always had exclusively plosive value in Greek, is evidence of a dual, plosive/fricative, pronunciation of *kaf*, *pe*, and *taw* at the time. The examples from the *Secunda* or Jerome are more difficult to evaluate. Here, a single series of Greek or Latin graphemes, corresponding to an aspirated or fricative pronunciation, is used. But again, there is no reason to assume that the absence of overt indications of allophonic differences in these transcriptions means that the only realization of the Hebrew phonemes was fricative.[26]

Looking at the problem from a wider perspective, we find that the data cited correspond to information provided by Greek

22 On the second column of Origen's *Hexapla*, see Jellicoe 1968, 106ff. and Fernández 1979, 191ff.

23 See Sáenz-Badillos 1975a.

24 With the well-known exception of *appadno* at Dn 11:45.

25 Especially E. Brønno (1943, etc.) in respect of the *Secunda* and J. Barr (1967) for Jerome.

26 See, for example, Brønno 1968, 195f.; Barr 1967, 1ff.

transcriptions of other Semitic languages from the same era. Although throughout the region from the sixth century BCE the *bgdkpt* consonants first underwent a process of aspiration, followed later by spirantization of those occurring after a vowel, there are clear signs of dual realization in the majority of contemporary Aramaic dialects and in every tradition of Hebrew. There is no proof that the plosive realization ever ceased, or that Hebrew suffered significant phonological changes, and this means that the Masoretes' intervention could not have been as radical as Kahle and his school claimed.

In the laryngeals and pharyngeals, there is again a gradual process of weakening and merger. Although in the Septuagint consonantal graphemes are used to indicate the presence of /ḥ/, /ḫ/, or /ʻ/, in 'the Three' this occurs rarely, and only in connexion with /ḥ/, while in the *Secunda* just one example of the same procedure has been detected. The standard technique of 'the Three' and the *Secunda* is to retain only the vowel following a laryngeal or pharyngeal. Jerome systematically employs *h* to reproduce the *adspiratio* of /h/ or the *adspiratio duplex* of /ḥ/, and he indicates that the laryngeals and pharyngeals were each pronounced as an *adspiratio* or with *rasura gulae,* pointing out that the Jews of this period were amused by the inability of Christians to pronounce correctly the gutturals and various other letters. Other statements of Jerome are less clear. For example, when he indicates that /ʻ/ is merely a *vocalis littera,* this probably has to be understood in the context of an attempt by Jerome to prevent /ʻ/ being read as a *g*.[27]

It seems then that we may not infer from Origen (the *Secunda*) or Jerome that the laryngeals and pharyngeals were no longer pronounced at all in their time. To begin with, it has to be remembered that the Greek alphabet cannot adequately express

27 See Barr 1967. Barr believes that the statement that the gutturals were 'adspirationes suas vocesque conmutant' (*De nominibus hebraicis*, PL 23, 773) should not be understood to mean that they were confused with one another, but that each was pronounced differently in Hebrew.

the pronunciation of these consonants.[28] Moreover, throughout the transcriptions there are at least indications that the sounds had not entirely disappeared from pronunciation. It should be pointed out, however, that a process of weakening affecting these consonants can be detected from the second half of the first millennium BCE up to the beginnings of the Common Era in many Canaanite and Aramaic dialects close to Hebrew, as well as in every tradition of Hebrew, even though in some areas their values were better preserved. It is possible to determine two centres from which the phenomenon of guttural-weakening spread out, an eastern (Babylonian Talmud, Mandaean) and a western (Samaria, Qumran, various sites in Galilee). The existence of an Akkadian substratum in the east and a Greek in the west would also have played a part.[29] But it is difficult to find support from the material cited for the theory of the complete disappearance of the gutturals and their restoration by the Masoretes, as held by Kahle and his school.[30]

The transcriptions offer us substantial information about many other aspects of contemporary Hebrew phonology and morphology. Vocalization does not always coincide with that established later by the Tiberian Masoretes, but occasionally comes closer to what is found in other Hebrew traditions. Tiberian *qameṣ* is sometimes represented by *alpha*, sometimes by *omicron*, *pathaḥ* and *segol* by *alpha* and *epsilon*, and occasionally *omicron*, *ṣere* generally by *eta*, and *ḥireq* by *iota*, although at times for various reasons this is replaced by *alpha* (where the 'law of attenuation' has not operated) or *epsilon*. *Ḥireq gadol* is represented by *epsilon-iota* or simply *iota*, *ḥolem* by *omicron* or *omega*, and *qibbuṣ* and *shureq* normally by *omicron-upsilon*. *Shewa mobile* is usually expressed by zero, less often by *epsilon*, and rarely by *alpha* or another vowel. Like the *ḥaṭef*s or ultrashort vowels, *shewa quiescens* is sometimes represented by a full vowel, but again it is zero that predominates.

28 See Brønno 1968, 193.

29 See Sáenz-Badillos 1975a.

30 See Janssens 1982, 41ff.

This material and similar data also suggest that penultimate stress was dominant, as in other Hebrew traditions. 'Philippi's law' did not operate, at least in the transcriptions of the *Secunda*.[31]

At the start of a word, *waw* is usually transcribed as *omicron-upsilon*, with this sequence or *omega* in non-initial positions. At an early period, *zayin*, like the other sibilants, was represented by *sigma*, but later by *zeta*.

Morphological developments did not always proceed in a straightforward way. For example, in connexion with segolate nouns, whereas in the Septuagint and 'the Three' the vocalization *a-e* predominates, forming a bisyllabic word with anaptyctic vowel, the *Secunda* better reflects their originally monosyllabic shape. There is a more uniform transcription of nouns of the type *maqṭāl*, which did not shift to *miqṭāl* as in the Tiberian tradition.[32] The article is reproduced as *a-*, with gemination of the following consonant indicated in the *Secunda* and later works. The prefixed particles have the form *ba-*, *cha-*, *la-*, although they can also appear with *e-* or without a vowel.[33] The second person singular masculine pronominal suffix is *-ach*. As in other traditions of Hebrew, verbs, including suffixed forms, retain both vowels in the stem. The second person singular masculine of the suffix-conjugation normally ends in *theta*; in the prefix-conjugation, the prefix usually takes *a* or *e*.[34] The first vowel of the *Pi'el* and *Hif'il* is *e*.[35]

There are, of course, problems in interpreting the different data, even setting aside the position of Kahle and his followers. E. Brønno believed that the *Secunda* confirms the reliability of the Tiberian tradition, although he recognized that certain developments had taken place in the interim.[36] For E.Y. Kutscher,

[31] See Brønno 1943, 448. But cf. Ben-Ḥayyim 1988–89, 119f.
[32] See A. Sperber 1937–38, 135ff., 191f.; Brønno 1943, 451.
[33] See A. Sperber 1937–38, 194f.; Brønno 1943, 452.
[34] See A. Sperber 1937–38, 156f.
[35] See A. Sperber 1937–38, 164ff.; Brønno 1943, 448.
[36] See Brønno 1943, 462f.

on the other hand, the transcriptional material differs from Tiberian Hebrew because it does not correspond to the official or standard version of Hebrew, represented exclusively by synagogue readings of the Bible, but rather to dialect or 'substandard' forms.[37] But given that we have no information whatever about the tradition of synagogue reading, Kutscher's distinction is difficult to prove. The Greek and Latin transcriptions represent an earlier stage of Hebrew than do the Masoretic traditions, and they coincide in several ways with conservative features found in various traditions of Hebrew. The nature of the data we possess suggests we value each and every tradition rather than creating a dichotomy between the normative tradition and the others. The wide range of features we have noted indicates that linguistic development was far from uniform. Even though they share a number of common tendencies, a variety of Hebrew traditions is seen to have co-existed during this period.

4.3 *Biblical Hebrew according to the Palestinian tradition*

In 1839, S.D. Luzzatto first drew attention to the *Maḥzor Vitry*'s use of the expression נקוד ארץ ישראל (niqqūḏ 'æræṣ yiśrā'ēl) 'the pointing of the Land of Israel, Palestinian pointing',[38] in contrast to the Tiberian system and to 'our pointing'.[39] From that time, even though texts with this kind of vocalization were unknown, the

[37] See E.Y. Kutscher 1974, 61–71.

[38] In the edition of S. Hurwitz (Berlin, 1889–93), p. 462.

[39] See *Kerem Ḥemed*, IV (1839), 203. After long debate, this passage is today interpreted in very different ways: M. Friedländer (1896, 94f.) believed that 'our pointing' refers to the Babylonian system, a view accepted by P.E. Kahle (e.g. 1927–30, 24). N. Allony (1964) thought it referred to the Palestino-Tiberian pronunciation. I. Eldar (1978, I, 172ff.) showed that the supralinear Palestinian pointing system was not known at the time in Europe, and that the author used the expression 'Palestinian pointing' with reference to the type of pronunciation that Allony called Palestino-Tiberian, widespread in central Europe during the Middle Ages – 'our pointing' would, therefore, have been another system found only in France and parts of Germany.

term 'Palestinian pointing' started to gain currency, with reference to the supralinear notation of one of the three most important Masoretic traditions and reflecting a Hebrew dialect or group of dialects from Palestine dating from at least the seventh century CE. From the end of the last century, thanks to the momentous discovery of the Cairo Genizah documents, various biblical and *piyyūṭ* texts which employ at least a partial Palestinian system became known.

The first Palestinian texts were published by A. Neubauer.[40] Shortly afterwards, M. Friedländer wrote two studies of the pointing system employed,[41] and C. Levias edited a number of liturgical texts.[42] The beginning of the twentieth century saw the appearance of Paul Kahle's first study on the subject to which he would later make so decisive a contribution.[43] His great work *Masoreten des Westens*[44] contains important analyses of the Palestinian system as well as editions of liturgical and biblical texts which use it. Kahle's views were developed in his contribution to Bauer and Leander's *Historische Grammatik*[45] and, later, in *The Cairo Genizah*.[46] For him the pronunciation underlying the Palestinian system is that used by official circles in Palestine in the sixth to eighth centuries CE. It constitutes an early, rather impractical, stage of Tiberian pointing, which in turn represents no more than a correction of the earlier system on the basis of an idealized model of a form of language that never actually existed.[47]

Over the decades, other scholars have continued the work of editing and studying new fragments.[48] Works of particular

40 1894–95.

41 Friedländer 1894–95; 1896.

42 See Levias 1898–99.

43 Kahle 1901. See also Kahle 1901a; 1925.

44 Kahle 1927–30.

45 Kahle 1922, 98ff.

46 Kahle 1959 (1st ed., 1947), 66ff., 336ff.

47 See Kahle 1921; 1922, 84.

48 See, for example, Spanier 1929; Kober 1929; Edelmann 1934; Ormann 1934; Leander 1936; Bar 1936; Murtonen 1958; Weil 1961–62. See also Dotan 1971, 1433ff.; Morag 1972, 34ff.

importance are those by A. Díez Macho,[49] N. Allony,[50] M. Dietrich,[51] E.J. Revell,[52] Y. Yahalom,[53] and B. Chiesa,[54] which have made available a greater number of fragments of text with Palestinian vocalization, and advanced our knowledge about this tradition and its development.

Although there are quite significant differences among the various manuscripts, the most widespread Palestinian system used in biblical texts employs seven graphemes to represent the vowel phonemes: ˉ for Tiberian *pathaḥ*, ˈ for *qameṣ* (sometimes represented by the previous grapheme), ˙˙ for *segol*, ˙˙ for *ṣere*, ˙ for *ḥireq*, ˙˙ for *ḥolem*, and ¨ for *shureq* and *qibbuṣ*;[55] *shewa* is marked in various ways.[56] All vowel phonemes are indicated, but not allophones. Non-phonemic entities are expressed, inconsistently, through multivalent signs.[57] There is fluctuation in the use of graphemes corresponding to Tiberian *pathaḥ* and *qameṣ* and *ṣere* and *segol*, for which some early manuscripts employ just one sign. Various explanations for this inconsistency have been attempted. It has, for example, been attributed to a lack of expertise on the part of the *nakdanim*,[58] to reasons of calligraphy,[59] to differences in

49 1954; 1957; 1963a; 1967; 1971; in Díez Macho 1971a, 61–77 there is a general survey of problems associated with the Palestinian system.

50 With A. Díez Macho: 1958; 1958a; 1959; 1959a. An important work is Allony's 1973–74 edition of rabbinic texts with Palestinian pointing.

51 1968.

52 1969; 1970; 1970a; 1972; 1977 (in which Revell provides a list of all known biblical texts which use a Palestinian system).

53 1969–70

54 1978.

55 This at least is the traditional interpretation, which can be seen, for example, in the works of Kahle and in Morag 1972. A. Dotan (1971, 1434f.), however, believes that the seven Palestinian signs correspond to no more than the five basic vowels.

56 However, some scholars, for example M. Dietrich (1968, 119ff.), argue that in its pure form the Palestinian system uses only five vowels in the biblical manuscripts. On the use of other Palestinian signs, see Fassberg 1987.

57 See Morag 1972, 37f.

58 Thus, Díez Macho 1971a, 73, following A. Bendavid.

59 Thus, Dietrich 1968.

manuscripts from different periods,[60] or to an earlier stage of traditional pronunciation in which more vowel phonemes were distinguished.[61]

Of particular relevance to the development of this system are the Palestinian *piyyuṭim*, which appear to be older than most of the known biblical fragments. Y. Yahalom,[62] who studied this type of text from various Genizah fragments, concluded that the oldest ones, from the eighth to ninth centuries, use a more limited system of vocalization in which just six graphemes, for five vowels and *shewa*, represent a type of pronunciation that does not distinguish *pathaḥ* from *qameṣ* or *ṣere* from *segol* and which may be regarded as close to what would become traditional Sephardi pronunciation.[63] In later manuscripts a seventh grapheme, ⁘, is used specifically for *shewa*, and in some manuscripts for *ṣere*. Leaving aside a small group of manuscripts, there seems to be a recognizable development toward a progressively more differentiated vowel structure that gradually grew closer to the Tiberian system. In the light of Yahalom's important study earlier interpretation of Palestinian biblical fragments needs to be examined very carefully.

There is general agreement that the differences between the Palestinian and Tiberian traditions are so great that they may even reflect separate dialects. Despite the lack of uniformity within the Palestinian system, it is worth mentioning, for example, its different use of *shewa* and of graphemes corresponding to *a* and *e* vowels, the many occasions on which one vowel is replaced by another, especially one of similar quality, its vocalization of conjunctive *waw*,[64] and the insertion of the vowel *e* to avoid word-final sequences of two consonants.[65] Kahle's opinion

60 Thus, for example, Yahalom 1988, 121ff.

61 Thus, Morag 1972, 37.

62 1988.

63 The relationship with Sephardi pronunciation had already been argued by P. Mordell (1928–29), although he considered the Palestinian to be the most recent of the three vocalization systems.

64 See Revell 1970, 61ff.

65 See Dietrich 1968, 124ff.

notwithstanding, it cannot be demonstrated that the gutturals had ceased to exist in Palestinian pronunciation.

E.J. Revell has tried to establish a typological classification of biblical manuscripts, distinguishing up to twelve different sorts of vocalization on the basis of their level of agreement with the Tiberian tradition.[66] In contrast to the view of most earlier researchers, Revell thinks that the oldest Palestinian manuscripts are those that employ one sign for each phoneme. In addition to his external classification, based on the use of the graphemes, Revell further divides the manuscripts into two basic types which he claims are representative of two layers of Hebrew pronunciation – two dialect groups, one of which might have been used in Palestine, the other in Egypt. This aspect of his work is perhaps especially controversial.[67] In a later work, biblical texts are classified according to the accents used, with Revell eventually concluding that there are no essential differences from the Tiberian system of accents.[68]

A basic issue, and one that has given rise to a wide range of theories, concerns the relationship of the Palestinian and Tiberian system. The most common view is that the Palestinian system is older than the Tiberian, but that under the latter's influence it became ever more similar to the tradition imposed by the school of Ben-Asher.[69]

Revell, on the other hand, argues that the Palestinian tradition represents a more developed and, therefore, later form of language than the Tiberian, although they share a common origin.[70] In his view, the consistent use of different graphemes for the *a* and *e*

66 See Revell 1970a, 32ff.

67 See Díez Macho 1971, 550f.

68 See Revell 1977, 37ff.

69 This is the position of most specialists. See Kahle 1927–30, 24; Bendavid 1958; Dietrich 1968; Allony 1973–74, etc. It also appears to have been adopted by A. Dotan (1971, 1436), though in his view we do not possess the original Palestinian system, which would have been closer to (though not identical with) Tiberian pronunciation rather than Sephardi. Thus, Tiberian influence on later Palestinian texts has restored the original situation to some extent.

70 See Revell 1970a, 104ff.; 1972, 34ff.

vowels is a feature of an earlier period, which tended to disappear later on. Vowel changes within the Palestinian system, according to Revell, correspond to processes known from a less developed stage of the Tiberian tradition, and sometimes represent the end-point of a process begun there. The Tiberian tradition has adopted a well-preserved, archaic, pronunciation, whereas the Palestinian is based on 'vulgar' biblical texts and expresses a less well-preserved form of the language that has been more affected by outside influences and colloquialisms. As a system of pointing, the Palestinian must have have been created before, or in isolation from, the Tiberian. However, there was a time when the systems co-existed, with the Tiberian exerting influence on the Palestinian, eventually becoming totally dominant, even over those who continued to use a Palestinian pronunciation.

However, there are few scholars who accept Revell's chronology or his view that the Palestinian system did not develop from having a lesser to a greater number of signs.[71] Thus, the prevailing hypothesis continues to be that the Palestinian tradition is earlier than the Tiberian, although, under the influence of the latter, it developed forms that were closer to Tiberian ones. Both systems co-existed for a time, reflecting two or more traditions of pronunciation.[72]

Equally difficult to accept is the theory of B. Chiesa,[73] who developed a complicated historical and linguistic backdrop to prove that the bearers of the Palestinian tradition came from the priestly families of Jerusalem who had re-established themselves in northern Arabia after the Roman conquest (thus explaining a possible Arabic influence in the Palestinian system) and returned to Palestine during the Caliphate of Omar. It is indeed possible

71 See Díez Macho 1971, 564; Yahalom 1988, 122ff.

72 For the history of relations between the two traditions a special value attaches to MS 594 Box B, Env. 12 of the Jewish Theological Seminary of America in New York, studied by P.E. Kahle (1959, 336ff.) and by A. Díez Macho (1957e, 28f.). In Kahle's opinion, Tiberian punctuation has replaced Palestinian in this manuscript. For Díez Macho it represents a transitional stage between the two systems of pointing.

73 1978.

that a geographical setting away from the main Galilaean centres should be sought, probably in the south of Palestine,[74] but it is almost impossible to be more precise.

It is not easy to determine the exact place of this tradition in the development of Hebrew. In certain ways it appears to be close to Samaritan Hebrew.[75] Other aspects coincide with the simple Babylonian system of vocalization,[76] although there are very important differences as well. Its relationship to the Tiberian tradition remains, as we have said, subject to debate. Furthermore, it is not yet generally accepted that the tradition employs five basic vowels, in which respect it would coincide with Sephardi pronunciation. Many issues still need to be resolved.

We now turn to a special system of punctuation which shares Palestinian and Tiberian features and corresponds to a different pronunciation of Hebrew and to a different use of the Tiberian graphemes. Of the many names used to describe this system, we prefer to follow N. Allony in calling it Palestino-Tiberian.

Kahle, who was familiar with some codices of this type, classified them as belonging to the Ben-Naphtali manuscript tradition,[77] even though the actual relationship with the Ben-Naphtali school of Tiberian Masoretes is relatively limited. A. Díez Macho pointed out the origins of this type of manuscript in the Palestinian system, designating the resulting system 'proto-Masoretic'.[78] Subsequently, he proposed the name 'pseudo-Ben-Naphtali', established various subdivisions, and published the fullest lists so far of manuscripts of this kind.[79]

A. Sperber, in his study of Hebrew biblical manuscripts, came across four codices with a type of vocalization that he called 'pre-

74 See M. Weinreich 1963–64, 142ff.

75 See Morag 1972, 35f. Kahle had already indicated that there was a close relationship.

76 See Kahle, 1927–30, 32ff.

77 See Kahle 1927–30, 45*

78 See Díez Macho 1956, 204ff.

79 See especially Díez Macho 1963a, 18ff.; 1971a, 79ff., 199ff.

Masoretic': Codex Reuchlinianus (from 1105/06), Parma MSS 1848 and 2808, and the London Bible. Believing that they could make a significant contribution to our understanding of a very early stage of Hebrew, Sperber undertook the task of editing them.[80] However, his views regarding these problematic texts were fiercely contested. For S. Morag,[81] there are indications that the pointing system used in the manuscripts represents a late development of the Palestinian tradition, and so can hardly be called 'pre-Masoretic' when in fact it is 'post-Masoretic'. In a later work,[82] Morag describes the system as 'fuller Palestinian', emphasizing the fact that the signs employed are identical with Tiberian ones, although they reflect a Palestinian tradition.

I. Yeivin preferred to call these manuscripts 'non-Masoretic',[83] whereas M.H. Goshen-Gottstein speaks of a Tiberian '*non-receptus*' tradition. Thus, he avoids any implication of chronological priority or connexion with the Palestinian tradition. Instead, Goshen-Gottstein emphasizes that it is basically similar to the ancestor of the Ben-Asher and Ben-Naphtali traditions, even though it uses a different graphic system.[84] A little later, N. Allony coined the term 'Palestino-Tiberian',[85] now widely accepted in scholarly circles.[86]

The origins of this type of pointing should be sought in the east, most probably in Palestine. However, it also spread into central Europe in particular, where it became closely connected with the activity of Ashkenazi scribes from the middle of the twelfth century.[87] It seems certain that when the Ashkenazi Jews felt the need to vocalize their texts they had a choice of two systems still extant in the east, the Tiberian and the Palestino-Tiberian. Because the latter conformed better to Ashkenazi pronunciation, they often

80 See A. Sperber 1956–59; 1970.

81 1959.

82 Morag 1972, 38ff.

83 See I. Yeivin 1959–60.

84 See Goshen–Gottstein 1963, 108ff.

85 See Allony 1964.

86 It is already adopted, for example, in Morag 1968, 842f.

87 See Eldar 1978, I, xviff.

opted for it, although they also introduced significant modifications. After a period in which both forms of pointing were used in biblical and liturgical texts, the Tiberian system became more and more dominant until it completely ousted its Palestino-Tiberian counterpart around the middle of the fourteenth century.[88]

Although the Palestino-Tiberian tradition does not exhibit a uniform system of pointing, and it is not possible to establish clear subdivisions,[89] the following basic features have been identified: differentiation of consonantal and non-consonantal י (y), ו (w), א ('), and ה (h) by means of a sign above or within the character, indication of syllable boundaries, vocalization of all consonants in whatever position, including the use of *shewa* in final position in the case of א ('), ח (ḥ), and ו (w), the use of *dagesh* in all consonants except ה (h), ח (ḥ), ע ('), and ר (r), and a redundancy feature whereby, as in the Palestinian system, *pathaḥ* interchanges with *qameṣ* and *ṣere* with *segol*, so that in any given text either one sign or two signs can be found. It therefore represents the most complete system of pointing, which attempts to resolve, first, the problem of letters which can have a consonantal or a non-consonantal value, and secondly, by its indication of syllable boundaries, the difficulties caused by the use of a bivalent *shewa* sign.[90] Peculiarities of the system include the vocalization *wi-*, *bi-*, *ki-*, and *li-* for the clitics, and *yi* for *y*^{e}, when these forms are prefixed to words beginning with י (y).

4.4 *Biblical Hebrew according to the Babylonian tradition*

From the end of the ninth century there is evidence of a special Babylonian dialect of Hebrew. Its existence is affirmed, for

88 See Eldar 1978, I, xviiiff.

89 See Díez Macho 1963a; 1971a.

90 See Morag 1972, 38f.

example, in a *responsum* of Mar Ṣemaḥ b. Ḥayyim Gaon.[91] Of particular importance is Al-Kirkisānī's statement of 937 declaring that the Jews of Babylonia have their own pronunciation.[92] Various mediaeval writers also confirm the spread of this tradition,[93] and there are frequent references in the mediaeval literature to differences between eastern (*madneḥa'e*) and western (*ma'arava'e*) readings of consonants, particles, and *qere/ketiv* variants. Lists of such differences exist in a variety of recensions.[94]

In 1839, in the synagogue at Chufut-Kale, the Karaite scholar A. Firkowich found a codex containing the text of the Prophets. It was dated 916 and used a hitherto unknown supralinear system of vocalization. Firkowich presented the manuscript to the Society of History and Antiquities in Odessa, from where, in 1863, it passed to the Imperial Public Library in St Petersburg, which had recently acquired another of Firkowich's collections that included three similar documents from Kaffa.[95] Other manuscripts with the same kind of pointing were also found in the Second Firkowich Collection left by him after he died in 1874, and later acquired by the Russian government. It is very likely that these fragments had been discovered by Firkowich some years before in the synagogue of Old Cairo on a journey to the east.

Initial information about the Babylonian manuscripts reached the world of scholarship through E.M. Pinner's *Prospectus*.[96] After various studies by S.D. Luzzatto,[97] H. Ewald,[98] and A. Geiger,[99] we owe the first extensive analysis of the Babylonian tradition to S. Pinsker,[100] who worked out the details of this system of

91 See I. Yeivin 1985, 28.
92 See Klar 1953–54, 320–28.
93 See I. Yeivin 1985, 29ff.
94 See Chiesa 1979, 15ff.
95 See Kahle 1913, xxvif.
96 Pinner 1845.
97 See G. Falk, *Sefer halikhot kedem*, II (Amsterdam, 1847), pp. 22f.
98 1848.
99 1857, 484–90.
100 1863.

pronunciation from a study of the Prophets Codex (Kb 13) which was published a little later by H.L. Strack[101] and appeared in the *Catalog* of A. Harkavy and Strack.[102] At the same time, Strack provided details about the Second Firkowich Collection and announced that six new fragments with Babylonian punctuation had been found.[103] W. Wickes, in his study of Hebrew accents,[104] discussed the system represented by the Prophets Codex (Kb 13). Several studies over the following years contributed in various ways to a better understanding of the system.[105]

The most influential figure involved in clarifying the Babylonian pointing system was without doubt Paul Kahle, who in 1902 wrote a study of a manuscript he had found in Berlin (Or qu 680) and which he correctly classified as Yemenite-Babylonian. But it was above all his *Masoreten des Ostens*[106] that was to become the basic work of reference for this tradition. The book includes *Textproben* from sixty Babylonian manuscripts, which are also described, photographic reproductions of seventeen fragments, an analysis of Babylonian pointing, an attempt at classification of the manuscripts, which was later universally accepted, and a grammatical overview of Hebrew and the Aramaic of the Targums according to the Babylonian tradition. Most of the documents brought together by Kahle are from the Cairo Genizah texts held at Cambridge, with some manuscripts from Leningrad, Berlin, and London. In later works, he was to increase substantially the number of manuscripts with this vocalization, which had reached around 130 by 1937.[107]

From 1954, A. Díez Macho discovered and published various manuscripts and fragments of Babylonian or Yemenite origin, many of which were housed at the Jewish Theological Seminary of

[101] 1876.
[102] 1875.
[103] See Strack 1875.
[104] Wickes 1970, II (originally published, 1887), 143ff.
[105] See Margoliouth 1893; Friedländer 1896; Praetorius 1899; Weerts 1906.
[106] Kahle 1913.
[107] See Kahle 1928; 1937.

America in New York.[108] Important studies of the Babylonian pointing system include those by G.E. Weil, H.P. Rüger, F. Díaz Esteban, S. Morag, L. Díez Merino, A. Navarro,[109] and, most notably, I. Yeivin, whose *The Hebrew language tradition as reflected in the Babylonian vocalization*[110] marks the most significant contribution to our understanding of this tradition since it was first discovered.

After Kahle's initial studies, it was recognized that in Babylonia two distinct systems of vocalization had developed: a simple (*einfach*, 'E') and a complex (*kompliziert*, 'K'). The simple system used the following vowel graphemes: ʸ for /a/, ᵛ for /ā/, ¨ for /e/, ˙ for /i/, ⁚ for /o/, and ′ for /u/, as well as ´ for *shewa mobile*, thus representing six basic vowel sounds. This 'simple' system does not represent any allophones, nor does it have signs corresponding to Tiberian *segol* or *qameṣ ḥaṭuf*. It uses special signs comparable to Tiberian *dagesh* and *rafeh*, although they are employed somewhat differently. *Shewa quiescens* (zero) is not marked. Many Babylonian texts are pointed defectively.[111] Some manuscripts use a similar system patterned only from points, which affects the graphic form of three of the vowels.[112]

Complex Babylonian employs a number of vocalization systems, most significantly the 'perfect' and the 'imperfect'. The first of these has special signs for each kind of syllable and uses them consistently, which cannot be said of the imperfect system.[113] Usually it also incorporates special signs for allophones of /a/, /e/, /i/, and /u/, although various interpretations are possible

108 See Díez Macho 1954a; 1954b; 1955; 1956a; 1957a; 1957b; 1957c; 1957d; 1958; 1959; 1959a; 1959b; 1960a; 1971a.

109 Weil 1963; Rüger 1963; 1966; Díaz Esteban 1966; Morag 1972; 1973; Díez Merino 1975; Navarro 1976.

110 I. Yeivin 1985; see as well earlier works by the same author: 1962; 1962a; 1964; 1965; 1968; 1972.

111 See Morag 1972, 30ff.

112 See I. Yeivin 1985, 61ff.

113 See I. Yeivin 1985, 64ff.

here.[114] Gemination is marked by a univalent sign (a small horizontal bar over the preceding vowel), and the plosive values of the *bgdkpt* phonemes are indicated just as they are in the 'simple' system. *Shewa mobile* and *quiescens* are represented by a single sign. Vocalic and consonantal values of *alef* and *he* are carefully distinguished, and a single, bivalent, sign represents /i/ when it occurs before a doubled consonant or within an unstressed closed syllable.

Historically, it seems certain that the simple system is earlier. Its origins are to be sought in the sixth to seventh centuries, after which it developed into the more comprehensive complex system, which is as accurate and all-embracing as its Tiberian counterpart. For a time both systems, Babylonian and Tiberian, existed independently. Testimonies like that of Al-Kirkisānī demonstrate that the Babylonian system was widespread in the first half of the tenth century.[115] But probably in association with the decline of the Jewish communities of Babylonia, it gave way more and more to pressure from the Tiberian system, finally being replaced by it. Alongside manuscripts that use a simple or complex system of Babylonian pointing there are many other intermediate ones, as well as some in which a second hand has added complex or Tiberian signs to originally 'simple' texts. At an even earlier stage, no doubt under the influence of the Syriac grammarians, an exclusively point-based graphic system was being used.

Kahle was the first to propose a system of manuscript classification according to the type of vocalization used (E, K) and the portion of the Bible covered (a: Torah, b: Prophets, c: Writings), thus: Ea, Eb, Ec, Ka, Kb, Kc. This system is still in use today, although I. Yeivin has complemented it by grouping manuscripts into five categories on the basis of the kind of pronunciation they reflect:

114 See Morag 1972, 33, n. 55.
115 See Chiesa 1979, 44.

(1) Totally Tiberian pronunciation with slight traces of Babylonian pronunciation;
(2) Basically Tiberian pronunciation with some Babylonian grammatical features;
(3) Intermediate or recent Babylonian pronunciation but with inconsistent treatment of the gutturals;
(4) Intermediate or early Babylonian pronunciation with the gutturals consistently vocalized with a vowel or *shewa*;
(5) Early Babylonian pronunciation with full vowels for the gutturals, etc.[116]
Occasionally a manuscript does not fully conform to any of these categories and so should be classed as intermediate. From another perspective, three phases in the development of the Babylonian tradition can be distinguished: Old (OB, Type 5), Middle (MB, Types 3–4), and Young (YB, Types 1–2).[117]

OB uses a simple, more or less *defectiva*, system of pointing. If vocalized, *alef* and *'ayin* take a full vowel. *Ḥireq* is written after consonantal *yod*, and *pathaḥ* after *'ayin* at the end of a word. *Shewa mobile* is indicated, as sometimes is *shewa quiescens*. Auxiliary vowels are also used.

MB generally employs a *plene* orthography, and its pointing is more systematic. The gutturals sometimes take a full vowel, at other times *shewa*. Consonantal *yod* at the beginning of a word normally takes *shewa*, auxiliary vowels are rarely used, and changes of vowel are common. According to some scholars, the phonetics of this stage could not have evolved from OB, and may even be earlier.[118]

Among the representative documents of YB are many Yemenite manuscripts, vocalized according to both simple and complex systems. Tiberian influence varies greatly. Occasionally, they display typically Yemenite features, such as the interchange of *ṣere* and *ḥolem* and of *pathaḥ* and *shewa*.

116 See I. Yeivin 1985, 91.
117 See I. Yeivin 1985, 92.
118 See Díez Macho 1971a, 53f.

In fact, Yeivin believes that we can only speak of two real phases in the language, an earlier (OB) and a later (MB), with YB representing a mixture of language traditions rather than constituting a stage of the language in its own right. OB and MB differ most sharply in their use of the vowel signs. OB employs an incomplete, relatively limited, system of vocalization, whereas MB vocalizes fully. In OB, the *shewa* sign is used somewhat inconsistently, sometimes representing *shewa quiescens*, whereas in MB it only expresses *shewa mobile*. Differences in the vocalization of the gutturals, the use of anaptyctic vowels and of *ḥireq* after consonantal *yod*, etc. indicate that there would also have been differences in pronunciation. OB and MB would, thus, reflect the Babylonian dialect of Hebrew at two stages. Yeivin goes so far as to suggest a possible geographical difference – Persia and Yemen. While our oldest MB texts are from 950, there are YB manuscripts dating from 900 down to 1450. The earliest sources of OB are from around 800. We also find that the Rabbinic Hebrew of OB manuscripts shares certain phonetic features with the Biblical Hebrew represented by MB.

Clearly, then, there are difficulties involved in regarding the Babylonian tradition as a single or homogeneous phenomenon following just one line of development. If, despite this, we continue to speak of a Babylonian Hebrew tradition or dialect, we have to add many provisos to our statements. However, Yeivin believed that the evidence is indeed sufficient to claim that Tiberian and Babylonian are two Hebrew dialects which diverged relatively late and which share the same basic laws of phonetic development, differing with regard only to relatively recent grammatical features. Thus, for example, the law of attenuation, the use of auxiliary vowels for the gutturals, and the shortening of *ṣere* and *ḥolem* in closed unstressed syllables are features shared by both dialects, whereas morphological differences that cannot be viewed as the result of phonetic changes are very scarce.

The Babylonian system of accents is similar to the Tiberian, with some small variations. In OB, unlike the complex system (which follows Tiberian), the accent is not written over the tone-bearing syllable, only disjunctive accents are shown, not conjunctives, and *mappiq* is not indicated, for example.[119]

A characteristic feature is the insertion of *ḥireq* after consonantal *yod*, which occurs in OB at the beginning and, quite often, at the end of a word, but is rare in the middle. On the other hand, *ḥireq* is not found before consonantal *yod* in the Babylonian tradition.[120]

The gutturals are especially noteworthy, with a number of clear differences from the Tiberian tradition. In Babylonian, there is a tendency to treat *he* and *ḥet* more and more like non-gutturals. On the other hand, the short vowel that follows *alef* and *'ayin* is retained as a full vowel, whereas the one that precedes them is reduced to a murmured vowel. Due to this and because of the insertion of certain auxiliary vowels, there are many small differences between the two traditions. Nonetheless, the Babylonian tradition has more similarities than differences with respect to Tiberian, although the special treatment afforded to the gutturals is more striking in the latter.[121]

The rules governing *dagesh* and *rafeh* are similar in the two traditions, although *dagesh* occurs more frequently at the end of a word in Babylonian. In OB it is also found with *resh*, as well as in other circumstances that the Tiberian Masoretes would have considered inappropriate.[122]

In the vowels there are several differences between the two systems. Babylonian pointing, in its simple form, uses six vowels, with one sign only for Tiberian *pathaḥ* and *segol*, and indicates nothing about vowel length. Historically long vowels have undergone few changes (occurring mainly in YB and in Yemen), but the short vowels more. Short vowels in open unstressed syllables are more common in Babylonian than in Tiberian, due to the retention of short vowels after gutturals in the Babylonian

[119] See I. Yeivin 1985, 243ff.
[120] See I. Yeivin 1985, 269.
[121] See I. Yeivin 1985, 283ff.
[122] See I. Yeivin 1985, 333ff.

tradition, *ḥireq* is found after consonantal *yod*, and anaptyctic vowels are also employed. Because of the tendency to use *pathaḥ* in the final syllable of verbs, and because Philippi's law has had a greater effect and the law of attenuation a lesser, short *pathaḥ* is more widespread than *ḥireq* in Babylonian.

Anaptyctic vowels are very common in OB (though rare in YB), particularly when following the gutturals *alef* and *'ayin*, in the middle of a word, and when preceding nasal, vibrant, and lateral consonants. The rules governing anaptyctic vowels in segolate nouns are similar to the Tiberian ones. The equivalent of *pathaḥ* is the most commonly used of these regardless of whether or not the preceding consonant is a guttural. In the jussive, some verbs use *ṣere* as an auxiliary vowel.[123]

Although the use of *shewa* is similar to that found in Tiberian, the Babylonian tradition has many different ways of indicating it. In OB it is not certain that *shewa mobile* and *quiescens* were distinguished, although they clearly are in MB and YB. This might lie at the root of certain features of OB, such as the use of *ḥireq* after consonantal *yod* and of various anaptyctic vowels that do not occur in MB or YB, and the fact that *shewa mobile* and *pathaḥ* are not interchangeable.[124]

Verb forms are basically the same as in Tiberian, although with certain differences, for example, in the vocalization of the final radical with *pathaḥ* or *ṣere* or in changes due to the gutturals. The second person singular feminine of the suffix-conjugation often has a *dagesh* in the final *-t*. In the prefix-conjugation, the *alef* prefix of the first person singular is regularly vocalized with *ḥireq*. Both prefix- and suffix-conjugations of the *Pi'el* are vocalized with *pathaḥ* in the second syllable. In the *Hof'al*, the first syllable is normally vocalized with *shureq* instead of Tiberian *ḥolem*. The *Hithpa'el* usually takes *pathaḥ* in the final syllable.[125]

[123] See I. Yeivin 1985, 364ff.

[124] See I. Yeivin 1985, 398ff.

[125] See I. Yeivin 1985, 419ff.; Kahle 1902, 51ff.; 1913, 183ff.

In the noun, the most notable differences from Tiberian are found in the vocalization of gutturals, in forms corresponding to Tiberian segolates, and in the use of *pathaḥ* or *ḥireq* in closed unstressed syllables. Most nouns with preformative *m-* are vocalized with *pathaḥ* and not, as in the Tiberian tradition, with *ḥireq*.[126] In contrast with the situation in Tiberian, *waw copulativum* is normally vocalized with *shewa*, even when it precedes labial consonants, only taking *ḥireq* when the following consonant has *shewa*, or, occasionally, if the consonant is a guttural, *pathaḥ*.[127]

Many of the manuscripts that represent YB come from Yemen. Although at first the Jewish communities of Yemen must have had their own diverse traditions of pronunciation,[128] their textual tradition and phonetic system are intimately connected to the Babylonian tradition, and are therefore discussed here. During its peak in the eighth to ninth centuries, the Babylonian version of Hebrew extended from Persia to Yemen. It declined in the tenth century with the disappearance of the main academies under the weight of Muslim power, and was replaced by the Tiberian system. However, the origins of the Yemenite system are still relatively obscure.

Halfway through the last century, J. Sappir informed the West about a manuscript with Yemenite vocalization.[129] From the end of the nineteenth century, and especially after the mass exodus of the Jews of Yemen, scholars have had an abundance of texts with Yemenite supralinear vocalization. According to A. Díez Macho, who was one of the main participants in the discovery and examination of Yemenite manuscripts,[130] there are three main types:

[126] See I. Yeivin 1985, 745ff.

[127] See I. Yeivin 1985, 1152ff.

[128] See Morag 1983a, 146.

[129] See Sappir 1866–74, which details Sappir's contacts with the Jews of Yemen on his travels there in 1857–1858.

[130] See Díez Macho 1957c and, most importantly, 1971a, 22ff.

(1) Yemenite-Babylonian, representative of the Babylonian tradition and pointing. But because Tiberian pronunciation gradually became dominant in Yemen even though a Babylonian notation was still preserved, there are many more surviving Yemenite-Tiberian than Yemenite-Babylonian manuscripts;
(2) Yemenite-Tiberian, represented by most manuscripts and the only ones to have been written in Yemen after the thirteenth to fourteenth centuries. Babylonian signs are still used, but there is a gradual introduction of Tiberian forms;
(3) Mixed Yemenite: in addition to the supralinear signs, these manuscripts retain a mixture of Babylonian and Tiberian features. There are still many unresolved questions about the origins of the mixed system and about the absence of complex Babylonian pointing in Yemenite manuscripts.

Studies of Yemenite pronunciation are centred, as might be expected, on the present-day state of the language, which, however, is regarded as having derived from a dialect represented by Babylonian vocalization. The most important analyses were conducted by the great pioneer Ḥ. Yalon,[131] and, in particular, by S. Morag.[132] Habbani, one of the five sub-dialects distinguished by Morag, preserves archaic forms which might reflect the early pronunciation of Hebrew in this area, for example, the Babylonian vocalization of *waw copulativum* before *shewa*, the pronunciation of *qameṣ* as *a* (rather than *å*) and the conservation of certain phonemes not found in neighbouring languages, such as /v/ and /p/. E.Y. Kutscher interpreted as archaisms a number of features that Morag regards as late innovations.[133]

131 1963–64a.

132 See especially the extensive study in Morag 1963, as well as Morag's works from 1955–57 and 1973.

133 See E.Y. Kutscher 1966.

4.5 *Biblical Hebrew according to the Tiberian tradition*

The third and most important Masoretic Hebrew tradition is the Tiberian. Because of the difficulties in dating the various traditions, 'third' should not be understood as having any chronological significance. Neither can the tradition be dealt with as monolithic or homogeneous, seeing that it is represented by a variety of different Masoretic schools. None, though, ever acquired the prestige attained by the family of Ben-Asher (bA), the primacy of which was challenged only briefly by Moses b. David Ben-Naphtali (bN). In the *masorah magna* written in the margins of Codex Leningradensis B 19a, mention is made of the 'masters of Tiberias', who were probably a group of Masoretes earlier even than Moses Ben-Asher and not to be identified with either bA or bN. The 'men of Tiberias', also mentioned in these marginal notes, might have been the same or a different group of Masoretes.[134]

Our direct information about bN is very limited. The name has been preserved only in relation to his dispute with the bA school, and Elijah Levita himself presents it in an incorrect form. Of the bA family we know the names of five generations:[135] Rabbi Asher and his son Nehemiah, Asher b. Nehemiah, Moses Ben-Asher, and Aaron b. Moses Ben-Asher. The last two are certainly the most important members of the family, and their work represents the culmination of a long process.

Whereas we know today some manuscripts that claim the honour of having been vocalized by the bA school, no extant manuscript reproduces the bN tradition in a pure form.[136] Numerous mediaeval lists note the differences between the two schools,[137] but they are full of contradictions and their value is

[134] See Díaz Esteban 1968, 65.

[135] From a treatise on the *shewa* which exists in various copies. See Oxford, Bib. Bodl., MS heb. e. 74, ff. 59–60.

[136] See Pérez Castro 1956, 140ff. The nearest to bN is without doubt the Prophets Codex from Cairo, but this is hardly pure bN.

[137] Some of these were catalogued by C.D. Ginsburg in his 1880–1905 edition of the Masorah. See Bendavid 1956–57; 1957–58.

limited.[138] Such lists tell us where the differences lie, given that the basic frameworks are normally the same, but we cannot be certain of the precise nature of these differences.

Mishael b. 'Uzziel, who was certainly active at the same time as, or just a little later than, Aaron Ben-Asher, wrote a treatise in Arabic on the differences between the two schools, the *Kitāb al-Ḫulaf*, which became the principal document of many scholars studying the characteristics of bA and bN.[139] Although some investigators have cast doubt on the antiquity and genuineness of Ben 'Uzziel's list, it still provides an important means of determining the nature of a particular reading.[140] Much of this Arabic treatise, including the list of differences, is reproduced in the Hebrew work *'Adat Devorim*, by Joseph ha-Qostandini, one of many adaptations of *Hidāyat al-Qāri*, written in the second half of the eleventh century.[141] Other written compositions of the Masoretes, such as Aaron Ben-Asher's *Dikdukei ha-Ṭe'amim*,[142] or treatises like *Sefer Okhlah we-Okhlah*,[143] can be of considerable help in determining the character of different readings,[144] although specialists are aware that in any mediaeval list of this kind there can be many errors.[145]

138 See Díaz Esteban 1968, 73; already noted by Ginsburg (1880–1905, IV, 414).

139 For example, P.E. Kahle. One of Kahle's pupils, L. Lipschütz (1962), prepared a critical edition of Ben 'Uzziel's treatise from the seven known manuscripts. See Pérez Castro and Azcárraga 1968.

140 Regarding these lists, very different views are held. For example, F. Pérez Castro, discussing the corrections introduced into MS Leningrad B 19a, remarks: 'The correspondence of these corrections with the readings that Ben 'Uzziel gives as belonging to Ben-Asher shows that Ben 'Uzziel was well informed about Ben-Asher's punctuation' (1965, 314). In a much less positive vein, M.H. Goshen-Gottstein believes this list of differences to be 'a copy of a secondary compilation' (1963, 100). F. Díaz Esteban observes that there are often discrepancies between the marginal notes of B 19a and Ben 'Uzziel's lists (1968, 73f.).

141 See Dotan 1971, 1474.

142 Dotan 1967.

143 Díaz Esteban 1975.

144 See Pérez Castro, 1955a, 4.

145 See Bendavid 1956–57; 1957–58; Pérez Castro 1955a; 1956; L. Lipschütz 1962; 1965; Pérez Castro and Azcárraga 1968; Goshen-Gottstein 1963; I. Yeivin 1980, 141ff. Goshen-Gottstein (1963, 99), in his enthusiastic commendation of the Aleppo Codex, argues

However, for some time now a more direct approach to the issue has been available, namely, analysis of the Aleppo Codex, which uniquely and perfectly represents the bA tradition, having been vocalized by Aaron Ben-Asher himself.[146] For a while, it was thought that the codex had been destroyed when the synagogue where it was kept was burnt in 1948, but four-fifths were recovered, and it is housed today in the Ben-Zvi Institute, Jerusalem. Although not all specialists agree in assigning such absolute pre-eminence to the Aleppo Codex,[147] the prevailing tendency today is to accept it as the basic standard for checking to what extent other manuscripts and lists have preserved genuine features of the bA tradition.[148]

To Maimonides we owe definitive confirmation of the outstanding value of the codex vocalized by Aaron Ben-Asher, who was probably already regarded in Maimonides's time as a great authority. Maimonides's words of praise are mainly concerned with the way in which open and closed sections and poetic passages are displayed within the codex; he also emphasizes the great care with which Ben-Asher had checked the work.[149]

The Aleppo Codex is the earliest manuscript to contain the whole Bible with its corresponding *masorah*, and is the prototype of

that this document on its own provides sufficient information for determining whether readings are really attributable to bA, and, indeed, for judging whether or not the text of Ben 'Uzziel is correct (see below, note 148).

146 One of the staunchest defenders of the Codex's authenticity is Goshen-Gottstein (1960; 1960a, 1ff.; 1963, 112ff.). The following is one of his most direct statements (emphasized throughout by Goshen-Gottstein): 'The Aleppo Codex is not only the oldest complete codex of the Tiberian Bible text known to us, but it is altogether the earliest complete codex of that Masoretic subsystem which had been perfected by the Ben-Ashers.' (1963, 88) See also Löwinger 1960; Ben-Zvi 1960.

147 For example, G.E. Weil (1963a, especially p. 197) expressed doubts about whether this manuscript was really the best of those written at Tiberias. A. Dotan (1965) concludes that it was not really vocalized by Aaron Ben-Asher.

148 Thus, M.H. Goshen-Gottstein: 'Since the character of the Aleppo Codex has been established, the procedure must be reversed. It is the Aleppo Codex that is now our yardstick for judging the character of other manuscripts – and for judging Mishael.' (1963, 99) Cf. Menachem Cohen 1983–84.

149 *Mishneh Torah*, Sefer Ahavah, Hilkhot Sefer Torah, 8:4.

the Tiberian biblical text.[150] Painstaking analysis by I. Yeivin[151] shows conclusively that, even though it does not always coincide with features indicated in the lists of *ḥillufim* or in the *Dikdukei ha-Ṭe'amim*, it is without doubt the manuscript that most closely approximates to them. Nonetheless, the codex does have some oddities as well, like the use of *ḥaṭef ḥireq* or of murmured vowels after non-guttural consonants, and it represents an earlier stage of vocalization and accents than the one which became widespread years later, following a process of systematization and simplification. Its Tiberian character and its relationship to the subsystem developed by the most important of the Tiberian Masoretes, Aaron Ben-Asher, is obvious. The codex is more complete than any other from the bA school, and tends toward a detailed vocalization which indicates exactly how the text is to be pronounced. Moreover, the manuscript is virtually free of scribal errors and there are hardly any differences between text and *masorah*. It reflects in a very pure form old features of accentuation which are absent from more recent manuscripts.

There are also some other important codices which are regarded as closely related to the bA family or which at least were written in the tenth century when the family flourished:

(1) Codex Leningradensis B 19a, used by R. Kittel and P.E. Kahle as the basis for the third edition of *Biblia Hebraica* and for the edition by A. Dotan.[152] It has been corrected by a second hand, responsible for many erasures and changes in order to make the text conform more closely to bA,[153] although it still preserves some bN readings. Its colophon bears the date 1008/09, and according to the scribe it was a copy of a manuscript vocalized by Aaron Ben-Asher, who also provided the *masorah*. It is the manuscript which approximates most closely to the Aleppo Codex, although it differs occasionally

150 See Goshen-Gottstein 1963, 86ff.
151 1968.
152 1973.
153 As shown by F. Pérez Castro (1955a).

in vocalization and accents. Its *masorah* is later and sometimes contradicts the text;[154]
(2) British Museum Codex Or. 4445 of the Pentateuch.[155] Two hands can be distinguished. In the first, bA readings greatly outnumber bN ones, whereas in the second the ratio is much more even.[156] It appears to have been written in the same period as the Aleppo Codex, around 925, although with rather less care. In some respects it can be regarded as belonging to a less developed stage of the tradition than that represented by the Aleppo Codex;[157]
(3) Codex Cairensis of the Prophets, prepared, according to its colophon, by Moses Ben-Asher in 895.[158] It is written with great care, but has a very small *masorah magna*. It differs in many ways from the Aleppo Codex and often corresponds to bN readings, although it cannot be regarded as a pure representative of this type of text either. The differences between the work of father and son in the same family of Masoretes[159] may be interpreted as a reflection of older traditions – two Masoretic subgroups or subsystems – with Moses Ben-Naphtali, who was also a disciple of Moses Ben-Asher, staying faithful to the tradition of his master, while Aaron developed another subsystem to perfection;[160]
(4) MS Heb. 24, 5702 (formerly MS Sassoon 507), in the National and University Library of Jerusalem, is probably from the tenth century. Although carefully written, it often disagrees with bA readings and displays other features which reflect a mixed

[154] See I. Yeivin 1980, 18ff. The manuscript was published in facsimile by D.S. Löwinger (1970).
[155] Dated by C.D. Ginsburg between 820 and 850 and by P.E. Kahle in the tenth century.
[156] See Pérez Castro 1955a.
[157] See I. Yeivin 1980, 19ff. Kahle (1959, 117f.) suggested that the manuscript was the work of Aaron Ben-Asher in his early period, with the Leningrad codex being a copy of his definitive text. F. Díaz Esteban believes that the lack of any eulogy for Aaron Ben-Asher in the manuscript is not proof that it must have been written during his own lifetime.
[158] Published in facsimile by D.S. Löwinger (1971), and in a critical edition by F. Pérez Castro (1979–88) and his collaborators as part of the groundwork for the *Biblia Poliglota Matritense* (an eighth volume, containing an alphabetic index to the *masorah*'s, has been announced).
[159] Emphasized by F. Pérez Castro (1955a, 26).
[160] See Goshen-Gottstein 1963, 105ff.

tradition. Similar comments apply to MS Sassoon 1053, from the same period, which is even less consonant with the bA tradition,[161] as well as to other manuscripts from the Second Firkowich Collection, kept in the St Petersburg Public Library.[162]

According to Mishael b. 'Uzziel, the differences between bA and bN relate to a number of general matters and to 867 specific passages, although in other instances the two schools share readings not found in other Masoretes. There are a few examples of minor variants in the text, such as על־מות ('l-mwt) for עלמות ('lmwt) at Ps 48:15, and some well-known differences in vocalization, such as bA לְיִשְׂרָאֵל (le-yiśrā'ēl) for bN לִישְׂרָאֵל (l-īśrā'ēl) 'to Israel', in the forms of proper names like 'Issachar' and the divine name, and in *qere/ketiv* variants. There are also differences in vocalization and in the use of the murmured vowels and of *dagesh, rafeh, maqqef,* and the various accents, particularly *ga'ya,* which reflect distinct traditions and, on occasions, different subsystems.[163]

Tiberian vocalization employs univalent signs to represent seven basic vowel phonemes, namely /a/, /æ/,[164] /e/, /i/, /å/, /o/, u/ (of which two use the same sign), and certain of their ultrashort, normally allophonic, counterparts.[165] The Tiberian system only indicates the quality or timbre of a vowel, not, unless it is ultrashort, its length. It also has two bivalent signs, one (*shewa*) for /^{e}/ and zero,[166] probably with phonemic value, the other (*dagesh*) for two non-phonemic features – gemination of non-guttural

161 See I. Yeivin 1980, 21f.

162 See I. Yeivin 1980, 22ff.

163 See I. Yeivin 1980, 141ff.

164 J. Cantineau (1950b, 114) and other linguists believe that this may be in fact an allophone of /a/ and not a true phoneme.

165 Of the ultrashort vowels, only the one corresponding to /å/ has a clearly phonemic character, although its functional load is very light; see Morag 1983, 1095. However, it is also possible to attribute phonemic value to the opposition of *shewa quiescens* and *mobile,* and to the contrasts between the remaining ultrashort vowels and their full equivalents; see Blau 1976, 11.

166 As also in the complex Babylonian system.

consonants and plosive (as opposed to fricative) realization of the *bgdkpt* consonants.[167] The system also indicates whether י (y), ו (w), א ('), and ה (h) have vocalic or consonantal value.

The Tiberian Masoretes must have faced many orthographic problems, due in part to the *defectiva* character of the old Hebrew writing system and the uneven but gradual introduction of *matres lectionis*,[168] and in part to the simultaneous existence of various traditions of pronunciation leading in some instances to so-called 'mixed forms' in the text of the Bible.[169] The resulting system is quite comprehensive, faithfully reproducing the phonological structure of the language while also providing sufficient phonetic information to read it correctly. The pronunciation of Hebrew reflected in this system is characterized by its use of seven vowel sounds – in addition to the five basic ones, two others have been added: *qameṣ* is either realized as /å/, intermediate between /a/ and /o/, or, instead, represents an open /o/; *segol* is realized as /æ/, intermediate between /a/ and /e/, or is, instead, best characterized as an open /e/.[170] This range of vowels with its clear distinction between *pathaḥ* and *qameṣ* and *ṣere* and *segol* has not been preserved in any contemporary pronunciation of Hebrew.

Tiberian vocalization, like the other traditions of Hebrew, does not indicate accents, which are represented by a special system of notation that also marks cantillation for liturgical reading as well as syntactic conjunction and disjunction. By applying a series of disjunctive binary divisions right down to the minimal rhythmic units, the Masoretes were able to develop, through their system of accents, a logico-syntactic analysis of the verses of the Bible, in addition to indicating where the accent fell and establishing a guide to recitation.[171]

167 The system is thus defined by S. Morag (1972, 22ff., 69ff.) and further revised in Morag 1983.

168 See Cross and Freedman 1952, 65ff.

169 See Morag 1974; R. Meyer 1966–72, I, 79f.

170 In contrast to the Tiberian system, the Babylonian has just six qualitatively different vowels, lacking an equivalent to Tiberian *segol*, and the Palestinian tradition, according to our presentation has, in its earliest phase, only the five basic vowels.

171 See Wickes 1970 (a reprint of works from 1881 and 1887, with an introduction by A. Dotan); Spanier 1927; M.B. Cohen 1972; Dotan 1971.

Chapter 5

HEBREW IN THE PERIOD OF THE SECOND TEMPLE

5.1 *Post-exilic Biblical Hebrew*

The Babylonian exile marks the beginning of a new stage in the development of Hebrew. The spoken and written languages had been drifting apart before the exile, and the social and political turmoil brought about by the fall of Jerusalem and the destruction of the First Temple produced a significant change in the linguistic *status quo* to the detriment of Biblical Hebrew, a compromise literary language. Returning exiles from the upper and better-educated classes, who had been exposed for several decades to an Aramaic cultural and linguistic environment, would have preferred Aramaic, which had spread throughout the Assyrian empire as the language of administration, commerce, and diplomacy. Quite probably, though, their contemporaries from the lower classes, who had remained in Judah, would still not have been able to understand Aramaic, just as they had been unable to understand it a century and a half before.[1]

During the period of Persian domination, from the edict of Cyrus (538 BCE) up to the victory of Alexander (332 BCE), due to historical and political circumstances the Jewish community experienced a degree of multilingualism. Aramaic became standard for communication with the outside world and in certain kinds of literature, although at the same time a late form of Biblical Hebrew (LBH) was often used in literary composition, maintaining

[1] Cf. 2 K 18:26=Is 36:11.

a style found in earlier works of scripture. In addition, it is very likely, at least in the south, that people continued to speak a vernacular form of Hebrew which some centuries later would be written down and receive the name of Rabbinic Hebrew (RH).[2]

LBH is the language of most of the books of the Bible written after the exile. Right up to the time of the destruction of the First Temple, classical Hebrew had continued in use, as demonstrated by biblical texts and, especially, by inscriptions and ostraca reflecting contemporary usage. The exile, which meant an end to the monarchy and led to the breakdown of social structures, signalled a time of profound change which also significantly affected the Hebrew language. In the writings that followed this event an attempt was made at first to imitate pre-exilic works, repeating their formulas and vocabulary. A degree of modernization, though, was unavoidable. The impact of the colloquial language is very obvious, as is the growing influence of Imperial Aramaic. In Galilee and Samaria, Aramaic dialects became the day-to-day means of communication, whereas Judah held on to Hebrew. It is likely that by this time square Aramaic characters had already begun to replace the palaeo-Hebrew script, although the process was not completed until the Hellenistic period, and remnants of the old system were maintained right down to the Bar-Kochba revolt.[3] The continued use of Hebrew as a literary idiom despite all these changes resulted principally from a sense of veneration which compelled authors of religious works to look for models in the pre-exilic language. During half a millennium LBH was used for the closing books of the canon, most of the deutero-canonical literature, a number of pseudepigraphic and apocalyptic compositions, and the Qumran documents. The Pharisees deliberately avoided LBH, presenting their teaching in the language of the spoken vernacular. Due to their labours, this

[2] See Rabin 1958; 1976; Naveh and Greenfield 1984.
[3] See M. Wagner 1966, 7; Naveh and Greenfield 1984, 125ff.

form of Hebrew would soon develop into a literary language (RH), which later replaced LBH.[4]

There are, however, obvious differences of language and style in the various books composed in LBH. In some, great efforts have been made to reproduce the earlier biblical language faithfully, whereas in others we can see clear traces of the colloquial idiom, an early form of RH. In the majority of works, though, the most outstanding feature is the dominating influence of Aramaic.[5] LBH did not develop in a straightforward way. As an exclusively literary language, isolated from the real world, nothing prevented the authors of later works, like Esther and Daniel or some of the Dead Sea Scrolls, from trying to adhere more closely than earlier, exilic, works, like Chronicles and Ezra, to the language of the Torah.

The researcher's first major difficulty is to establish exactly what the LBH 'corpus' is. Of course, textual criticism is of great help in ascertaining which books may be regarded as post-exilic, but there are often serious disagreements among the experts. On the other hand, arguments from linguistic analysis can also be problematic – if a large number of Aramaisms within a book were to be accepted as a criterion for its lateness, this would lead to the grouping together of archaic poetic texts, which retain vestiges of an early shared vocabulary, and later texts, which have been influenced by Imperial Aramaic. Aramaisms of themselves cannot be used as proof that a work is post-exilic.[6]

4 See Rabin 1976, 1015.

5 See Bendavid 1967, 60ff.

6 A very similar position was adopted by, for example, E. Kautzsch (1902, 104), whose study of Aramaisms was standard for many years. In our view, though, a much more precise and valid analysis is that of A. Hurvitz (1968, 235ff.), who agrees with the remarks directed at Kautzsch by T. Nöldeke (1903) and establishes the rule that an Aramaism may be used as evidence that a work is late only if it occurs with some regularity in late Hebrew. Furthermore, such a form ought not to be isolated, but should be found in the context of other Aramaisms, and there should be no other explanation for its presence within a text – for example, the Aramaisms of Job or Proverbs may derive from Old Aramaic, and are, therefore,

Practically every biblical book in its present state has some trace of Aramaic, in vocabulary, morphology, or syntax. In certain instances, this may be due to late reworking of material or to the activity of the Masoretes, but often Aramaisms are also found in the original form of a book. Aside from ancient poetic texts, the works in which Aramaisms are relatively abundant are Esther, Koheleth, Song of Songs, Ezra, Job, Daniel, Nehemiah, and 1 & 2 Chronicles.[7] Job is peculiar in that archaic elements appear alongside features that are late and perhaps dialectal, and so it is advisable at present to set this book apart from other works that are clearly post-exilic. We should bear in mind, though, that some books written after the exile, like Ruth and Lamentations, contain hardly any Aramaisms, and that a number of the Psalms, as well as some other post-exilic sapiential and prophetic works, are not especially affected by them.

Of special interest for the linguistic study of this period are post-exilic loanwords from Persian and Greek, taken into Hebrew indirectly *via* Aramaic.[8]

Various scholars have tried to show that the original language of a number of books from the Persian and Hellenistic periods was Aramaic, and that they were later translated into Hebrew. This view has been defended, although never entirely convincingly, in connexion with Job, Koheleth, Daniel, Esther, 1 & 2 Chronicles, Proverbs, and even Ezekiel.[9] The same issue is met in respect of pseudepigrapha from the Hellenistic, Hasmonaean, and Roman periods.[10]

Work in this field demands precise methods. If we begin by comparing writings that we know for certain to be post-exilic, such as 1 & 2 Chronicles and Ezra-Nehemiah, with parallel pre-exilic

very different from post-exilic Aramaisms, whereas the language of the Song of Songs may appear to have Aramaic features because of its origins in the northern kingdom.

7 See M. Wagner 1966, 145.

8 See M. Wagner 1966, 152f.

9 See the list of attempts in M. Wagner 1966, 146ff.

10 See Rost 1971, 22ff.

texts, like Samuel-Kings (which runs parallel to Chronicles), we can discover many differences between the two periods. Analysis should then be extended to passages which do not have parallels but are independent compositions of the Chronicler and linguistically more representative, seeing that they do not rely on other sources.[11] Without needing to assume that they are all completely homogeneous, it then becomes possible to examine other books that might be post-exilic for characteristics shared with the definitely post-exilic material, for late features, and for Aramaisms, so that we can draw firm conclusions about a given work's date of composition. Comparison with the Dead Sea Scrolls, Ben Sira, liturgical texts, Samaritan Hebrew, and RH then allows us to identify the main features of this stage of the Hebrew language.[12] Ultimately, though, it is difficult to arrive at a completely secure analysis, as there is always the possibility that what appear to be late features, akin to those of the spoken vernacular, might be interpreted as dialectal, originating in the north, for example.[13] Only by detailed study, using both literary and linguistic criteria, can a fair degree of certainty sometimes be achieved.

The Book of (1 & 2) Chronicles is especially instructive about the nature of LBH, as on many occasions it rewrites passages from Samuel-Kings, bringing the language up to date and adapting it to post-exilic usage. Regarding orthography, we see in Chronicles a tendency to employ a more *plene* form of writing, with *matres lectionis* more widespread than in BH. There are also changes in

[11] Whereas A. Kropat's classic study (1909) is based on an analysis of the parallel texts in Chronicles and Samuel-Kings, R. Polzin's more recent work (1976) argues that it is the non-parallel texts of 1 & 2 Chronicles that more genuinely represent the essential characteristics of post-exilic Hebrew. We believe that the two approaches are complementary rather than contradictory, although, from a methodological perspective, it is easier to begin by using Kropat's technique.

[12] The fullest and most convincing study of this subject is undoubtedly that of A. Hurvitz (1972).

[13] See Gordon 1955a.

noun patterns, with archaic forms replaced by late ones[14] – for example, מַמְלָכָה (mamlāḵā) 'kingdom' is systematically replaced by מַלְכוּת (malḵūṯ). Another difference is that instead of the usual form דַּמֶּשֶׂק (dammæśæq) 'Damascus', found in Kings and other writings from the earlier period, the Chronicler uses on six occasions the form דַּרְמֶשֶׂק (darmæśæq).[15] Some archaic particles which had been used almost exclusively to express emphasis, such as אַךְ ('aḵ) 'surely' and נָא (nā') 'pray', have been eliminated from the parallel texts in Chronicles, and many expressions regarded as archaic have been replaced by more modern equivalents.[16] Particularly widespread are changes in pronouns and particles, so that, for example, אָנֹכִי ('ānōḵī) 'I' is systematically replaced by אֲנִי ('ᵃnī), with אֶל ('æl) 'to' being replaced by לְ- (le-), מִפְּנֵי (mip-pene) 'from before' by מִלִּפְנֵי (mil-li-p̄nē), and אֵיךְ ('ēḵ) 'how' by הֵיךְ (hēḵ). There are also differences in more general vocabulary, with, for example, גְּוִיֹּת (gewīyyōṯ) 'bodies' being replaced by גופת (gūp̄ōṯ) and אֶשֶׁל ('ēšæl) 'tamarisk' by אֵלָה ('ēlā) 'terebinth' at 1 C 10:12.[17]

Certain morphological features clearly reflect late usage, such as the 'double plural' בִּירָנִיּוֹת (bīrānīyyōṯ) 'fortresses' (2 C 17:12; 27:4) formed from בִּירָה (bīrā), itself a late term.[18] Some nouns, like חֶדְוָה (ḥæḏwā) 'joy' (Ne 8:10; 1 C 16:27), אִגֶּרֶת ('iggæræṯ) 'letter', and פֶּחָה (pæḥā) 'governor', only, or nearly only, appear in post-exilic books. This is also true of expressions like טוֹב עַל (ṭōḇ 'al) '(be) acceptable to'[19] and of the use of certain particles, such as עַל ('al) for אֶל ('æl) 'to'. All the above features are characteristic of LBH. The replacement of some singular forms by plurals in parallel texts, for example פְּסָחִים (pesāḥīm) for פֶּסַח (pæsaḥ) 'Passover' and

14 See E.Y. Kutscher 1982, 81.
15 See Hurvitz 1972, 17f.
16 See Bendavid 1967, 67ff.
17 On vocabulary, see Polzin 1976, 123ff., a study of 84 expressions from Chronicles which might be regarded as representative of LBH because of meaning or usage.
18 See Hurvitz 1972, 18f.
19 See Hurvitz 1972, 22ff.

דָּמִים (dāmīm) for דָּם (dām) 'blood', or the use of double plurals in genitive constructions, such as חָרָשֵׁי עֵצִים (ḥārāšē 'ēṣīm) 'workers of woods' (1 C 14:1) and אַנְשֵׁי שֵׁמוֹת ('anšē šēmōṯ) 'persons of reputes' (1 C 12:31), foreshadow similar developments in RH.[20]

The syntax of Chronicles contains a number of features that are clearly late. Some are due to Aramaic, others to natural developments within Hebrew.[21] The author systematically avoids impersonal constructions of the sort -וַיִּקְרָא לְ (way-yiqrā' le-) 'and one named (the city)' (i.e. 'and [the city] was named'; 2 S 5:9), replacing this by -קָרְאוּ לְ (qāre'ū le-) lit. 'and they named (the city)' (1 C 11:7), or עַד בּוֹאֲךָ ('aḏ bō'aḵā) 'until you come' (lit. 'until your coming'), as well as the passive of *Qal*, so that, for example, יֻלַּד (yullaḏ) 'he was born' is replaced by the *Nif'al* form נוֹלַד (nōlaḏ). Instead of compound expressions of the sort בְּנֵי יִשְׂרָאֵל (benē yiśrā'ēl) 'children of Israel' or בֵּית יִשְׂרָאֵל (bēṯ yiśrā'ēl) 'house of Israel', the Chronicler simply writes יִשְׂרָאֵל (yiśrā'ēl) 'Israel'. The infinitive absolute is not employed for expressing orders and its use as an emphatic, in conjunction with finite forms, is also avoided. Lengthened forms of the verb, ending in ן- (-n) or cohortatives, for example, are hardly used at all.

Plural forms generally replace archaic collectives and other grammatically singular items from BH. When a word is repeated, the resulting phrase has the distributive value of Latin *quivis* or 'each one of': compare BH גֵּבִים גֵּבִים (gēḇīm gēḇīm) 'many pools' (lit. 'pools, pools') at 2 K 3:16 with LBH לַבֹּקֶר לַבֹּקֶר (lab-bōqær lab-bōqær) 'each morning' (lit. 'in the morning, in the morning') at 1 C 9:27. Transitive forms are preferred to intransitives and the infinitive construct with proclitic -לְ (le-) 'to' has almost completely replaced its simple equivalent and is used in preference to the prefix-conjugation or participle. The infinitive construct preceded

20 See Bendavid 1967, 70f.

21 Although it has been severely criticized in certain respects, the classic study of the syntax of Chronicles is that of A. Kropat (1909). See also the more recent analysis by R. Polzin (1976, 28ff.), which distinguishes thirteen 'grammatical and/or syntactic features' that are clearly late and not due to Aramaic influence and another six that may be Aramaisms.

by the proclitic particles -בְּ (be-) 'in, when' or -כְּ (ke-) 'as, when' is found less often, as is עִם ('im) 'with' followed by a verbal noun, etc., and there is also a marked reduction in the use of the narrative formula וַיְהִי (wa-yehī) 'and it came to pass' at the beginning of a sentence.

Certain particles acquire different uses – אֲבָל ('abāl) is no longer asseverative ('indeed'), but adversative ('but'), אַךְ ('ak) has almost disappeared, and when it is used its value is adversative or restrictive ('only'), not asseverative, the use of כִּי אִם (kī 'im) as a restrictive ('but only, except') is more widespread, and אָז ('āz) 'then' is nearly always used with the suffix-conjugation (cf. 1 C 16:7). Nouns denoting materials are usually placed in front of numerals, not after them, and they are normally in the plural. Asyndetic juxtaposition has already become a rarity. Various forms of conjunction are used, sometimes with -וְ (we-) 'and' preceding the first element. There are many elliptical sentences, lacking an explicit subject or verb, and the infinitive construct with preposition is preferred to subordinate clauses introduced by a conjunction. Pronominal suffixes with accusative function are more often attached directly to the verb than to the object-marker אֵת ('ēt), the use of which progressively diminishes. Second and third person plural feminine suffixes are replaced by their masculine equivalents in the verb and the noun. In some cases, proleptic pronouns are used to express possession. As in Aramaic, names of weights and measures come before expressions of quantity, in appositional relationship. Also perhaps of Aramaic origin is the use of רַבִּים/וֹת (rabbīm/ōt) 'many' (masc., fem.) as an attributive adjective before the noun (Ne 9:28; 1 C 28:5, etc.) and of the particle -עַד לְ ('ad le-) 'until' before a noun, as well as the non-assimilation of *nun* when the preposition מִן (min) 'from' precedes a noun without the definite article.[22]

Sometimes the particles אֵת ('ēt), as in RH, and -לְ (le-), as in Biblical Aramaic, are used to emphasize the subject of a sentence or

[22] See Polzin 1976, 61ff.

the final expression in a sequence. *Waw*-consecutives are frequently replaced by copulative forms and *waw apodosis* has disappeared. As in Aramaic, -לְ (le-) often functions as object-marker. Occasionally, an attributive adjective precedes a noun, and there are instances of unusual word order within sentences, so that, for example, a noun in the accusative can precede an infinitive verb. An attributive clause may be joined in asyndetic parataxis to a noun preceded by the article. Genitive relationships are sometimes constructed asyndetically, especially after כֹּל (kōl) 'all' or a preposition, and the article can occasionally introduce a noun clause or a verb in the suffix-conjugation (1 C 29:8, 17, etc.).[23] The uses of the particle עַל ('al) to indicate direction, of -לְ (le-) '(in order) to' in final clauses, and of מִקְצָת (mi-qṣāṯ) instead of מִן (min) 'from' may be regarded as Aramaisms. Significant differences in vocabulary, especially technical terms, in style, and in the use of particles endow the work with a quality which clearly distinguishes it from pre-exilic compositions.

Some of the language used when Chronicles was written might have been influenced by RH, for example the use of the preposition אֵצֶל ('ēṣæl) 'beside' with the verb ישב (yšb) 'sit, dwell', instead of בְּקֶרֶב (be-qæræḇ) or בְּתוֹךְ (be-ṯōḵ) 'in the midst of', or with the verb בוא (bw') 'come', instead of אֶל ('æl) 'to'. The same is true of word order, for example שְׁלֹמֹה הַמֶּלֶךְ (šelōmō ham-mælæḵ) 'Solomon, the King' at 2 C 10:2 instead of הַמֶּלֶךְ שְׁלֹמֹה (ham-mælæḵ šelōmō) 'the King, Solomon' at 1 K 12:2. Sometimes there is a significant correspondence with liturgical usage, as in the accumulation of virtually synonymous verbs or nouns (cf. 1 C 16:4; 29:11), marking a major departure from the norms of pre-exilic Hebrew.[24]

Although it is commonly held that Ezra and Nehemiah should be grouped together with 1 & 2 Chronicles in a single 'Work of the Chronicler', there is considerable divergence in language and style

23 See Kropat 1909, 72ff.
24 See Hurvitz 1972, 45ff.

between these two sets of books.[25] Not only do the Aramaic sections of Ezra (4:8–6:18; 7:22–26) and 'the Nehemiah memoirs' (Ne 1:1–7:5; 12:27–13:31) clearly differ from the other material, but there are also notable differences from Chronicles in the rest of Ezra-Nehemiah as well. Although contemporary works tended to dispense with shortened forms of the verb, 1 & 2 Chronicles always use these in consecutive tenses. Whereas Ezra-Nehemiah and Daniel frequently employ a form analogous to the cohortative preceded by -וְ (we-) 'and' – וְנֹאכְלָה (we-nōkelā) 'and we shall eat' (Dn 1:12), for example – such constructions are normally avoided in 1 & 2 Chronicles. Ezra-Nehemiah systematically employs the contracted form יָה (yā) in theophoric names, whereas Chronicles alternates this with the older form יָהוּ (yāhū), as, for example, in יְשַׁעְיָהוּ (yešaʻyāhū) 'Isaiah'. There are also striking differences in vocabulary, especially of a technical nature, and in style. Although Chronicles might present linguistic features that are later than those found in Ezra-Nehemiah, the author often diverges, intentionally it would seem, from the general tendencies of his time. Nonetheless, Ezra-Nehemiah and 1 & 2 Chronicles share so many linguistic features that a similar origin for all four books is at least a reasonable possibility.[26]

In the Book of Nehemiah, and particularly in 'the Nehemiah memoirs', already mentioned, the influence of Aramaic is clear. It is found in vocabulary, like אחז ('ḥz) 'shut', זְמָן (zemān) 'appointed time', as well as in longer expressions, which are really calques – הַמֶּלֶךְ לְעוֹלָם יִחְיֶה (ham-mælæk le-'ōlām yiḥyæ) 'may the king live forever' (2:3), אִם־עַל־הַמֶּלֶךְ טוֹב ('im 'al ham-mælæk ṭōb) 'if it please the king' (2:7), נִשְׁמַע לְ- (nišma' le-) 'it was heard by', etc. As in Chronicles and Ezra, cardinal numbers come after the noun. There might also be some examples of influence by the spoken vernacular, coinciding with later RH usage, for example הָיוּ אֹמְרִים (hāyū 'ōmerīm) 'they used to say' (6:19), אֶצְלָם ('æṣlām) 'among

[25] See Japhet 1968; Williamson 1977; Braun 1979; Throntveit 1982; Talshir 1988.
[26] See Talshir 1988.

them' (4:6), וַיִּכְעַס הַרְבֵּה (way-yik̲'as harbē) 'and he became very angry' (3:33), and the use of the relative particle אֲשֶׁר ('ᵃšær) in a way that corresponds to RH -שֶׁ (šæ-) and Aramaic דִּי (dī).

The same is true of Ezra which has similar linguistic features, with Aramaic calques like הַהֵרִימוּ (ha-hērīmū) 'which they raised' (8:25) for אֲשֶׁר הֵרִימוּ ('ᵃšær hērīmū) or לִירוּשְׁלָם (l-īrūšālayim) '(bring) to Jerusalem' (8:30) for יְרוּשָׁלַיְמָה (yᵉrūšālaymā), as well as RH-type expressions such as עַד לַשָּׁמַיִם ('ad̲ laš-šāmayim) 'up to heaven' (9:6), כֵּלִים לַזָּהָב (kēlīm laz-zāhāb̲) 'vessels of gold' (1:11), and תַּעֲנִית (ta'ᵃnīt̲) 'fast' (9:5).[27]

Turning to Daniel, the central issue is no longer the very obvious influence of Aramaic, but the possibility that those sections that have reached us in Hebrew were also originally written in Aramaic, and then translated.[28] Such a thesis has not, however, been proved beyond doubt. Whatever the case, in their present form these sections display an attempt to imitate BH.[29]

Certain of the Psalms present clear examples of late usage, containing a considerable number of words and longer expressions that only occur in the post-exilic books, RH, or Aramaic. This is not to say that other compositions within Psalms are not representative of pure BH.[30]

More difficult to place, from a linguistic perspective, is the short Book of Jonah, which is generally agreed to be post-exilic.[31] For some, the book exemplifies a fundamentally biblical type of Hebrew, although it also displays a number of RH features, especially in vocabulary.[32] In contrast, other scholars have emphasized Aramaisms like עשת ('št) htp. 'think' (1:6), זַעַף (za'ap̄) 'rage' (1:15), and טַעַם (ṭa'am) 'decree' (3:7). They have also pointed

27 See Bendavid 1967, 64ff.

28 See Rowley 1932; Zimmermann 1938; 1939; 1960–61; Ginsberg 1948.

29 See Archer 1974.

30 See the magnificent study by A. Hurvitz (1972), which may be regarded as one of the most important contributions to our knowledge of LBH. His analysis shows that Psalms 103, 117, 119, 124, 125, 133, 144, and 145 contain post-exilic linguistic features.

31 See Fohrer 1968, 442.

32 Thus, Bendavid 1967, 60f.

to other late items of vocabulary, such as סְפִינָה (sepīnā) 'ship' (1:5), טול (ṭwl) hi. 'hurl' (1:4), שתק (štq) 'be quiet' (1:11), and מנה (mnh) pi. 'appoint' (2:1; 4:7),[33] and to some grammatical usages similar to those already noted in Chronicles. The author's habit of switching between אֲנִי ('anī) and אָנֹכִי ('ānōḵī) 'I' (1:9) and אֲשֶׁר ('ašær) and -שֶׁ (šæ-) 'who, which' (4:10-11), together with his use of such obvious Aramaisms as בְּשֶׁלְּמִי (be-šæl-le-mī) or בַּאֲשֶׁר לְמִי (ba-'ašær le-mī) 'on account of whom' (1:7-8), contribute to the idiosyncratic character of this book.

In the Song of Songs, the popular spoken language is for the first time given literary and poetic representation.[34] It is a post-exilic collection of poems celebrating love and marriage, containing words from Aramaic, like עֶרֶשׂ ('æræś) 'couch' (1:16), Persian, for example פַּרְדֵּס (pardēs) 'orchard' (4:13),[35] and Greek, for example אַפִּרְיוֹן ('appiryōn) 'palanquin' (3:9), from *phoreion*. There are clear differences from BH: *waw*-consecutive is avoided, the relative -שֶׁ (šæ-) is used instead of אֲשֶׁר ('ašær), and the infinitive construct with proclitic particle is hardly found at all. Some BH expressions are employed, however, if only for rhetorical effect. Sometimes BH forms are used alongside others that would later be found in RH – compare, for example, the conjunctions כִּי (kī) and -שֶׁ (šæ-) 'that' at 2:5 and 5:8. There are numerous instances of vocabulary lacking in BH but known from RH – שׁוּק (šūq) 'marketplace' (3:2), אָמָּן ('ommān) 'craftsman' (7:2), כֹּתֶל (kōṯæl) 'wall' (2:9), מֶזֶג (mæzæḡ) 'mixture' (7:3), קְוֻצּוֹת (qewuṣṣōṯ) 'locks of hair' (4:2), and תאם (t'm) hi. 'bear twins' (4:2) are examples of forms that occur only in the Song of Songs and the rabbinic literature; furthermore, such expressions give the impression of being living words, not the results of archaic or artificial usage. There are also longer phrases typical of RH, such as כִּמְעַט שֶׁעָבַרְתִּי ... עַד שֶׁמָּצָאתִי (ki-m'aṭ šæ-'āḇartī ... 'aḏ šæm-māṣāṯī) 'I had scarcely passed ...

33 See A. Werner 1979; Qimron 1980.

34 See Bendavid 1967, 74ff.

35 See Jepsen 1958.

when I found' at 3:4, or with a very different word order from that of the classical language, exemplified in אַל־תִּרְאוּנִי שֶׁאֲנִי שְׁחַרְחֹרֶת ('al tir'ūnī šæ-'ᵃnī šᵉḥarḥōræṯ) 'do not look at me because I am dark' (1:6).

The Book of Koheleth (Ecclesiastes), probably from the second half of the third century BCE, has its own peculiarities combined with a language very close to RH and a degree of Aramaic influence. Thus, it uses noun patterns in וֹן- (-ōn), such as חֶסְרוֹן (ḥæsrōn) 'lack' at 1:15 and שִׁלְטוֹן (šilṭōn) 'dominance' at 8:4, and in וּת- (-ūṯ), as in סִכְלוּת (siḵlūṯ) 'folly' at 2:3, both characteristic of RH (the latter possibly under Aramaic influence), and others that are clearly Aramaic – כְּבָר (kᵉḇār) 'already' (1:10), קְרָב (qᵉrāḇ) 'war' (9:18). As in other late works, the article is not elided after a particle, for example כְּהֶחָכָם (kᵉ-hæ-ḥāḵām) 'like the sage' (8:1), and the pronoun אָנֹכִי ('ānōḵī) 'I' is never used. זֹה (zō) is sometimes found for the demonstrative pronoun זאת (zōṯ) 'this' (2:2, etc.). Other features of Koheleth include the use of the particles עֲדֶן ('ᵃḏæn) and עֲדֶנָה ('ᵃḏænā) 'still' (4:2, 3), quite alien to BH but well known in RH, and a tendency to create compounds by the elision of word-initial and word-final consonants. Similar RH-type features are the accumulating of particles, for example, בְּשֶׁכְּבָר (bᵉ-šæk-kᵉḇār) 'given that already' (2:16), and the use of אִי ('ī) instead of אוֹי ('ōy) 'alas' (4:10; 10:16). The use of the relative particle is also striking – although there are slightly more instances of BH אֲשֶׁר ('ᵃšær), RH -שֶׁ (šæ-) is very common too, especially with new roots that are not used in BH. As in RH, -שֶׁ (šæ-) also attracts other particles, for example כְּשֶׁבָּא (kᵉ-šæb-bā) 'as he came' (5:14) and מִשֶּׁתִּדּוֹר (miš-šæt-tiddōr) 'than that you should vow' (5:4), and verbs with final א (') are not distinguished from those with final ה (h).

We might say that in Koheleth there has been a conscious blending of BH and RH, with the latter perhaps predominating. Koheleth avoids using *waw*-consecutive and introduces a late usage of the participle as present tense, negated by אֵין ('ēn) 'not'. It is not unusual to find a form of expression from one period of the language alongside its equivalent from another, in the case of the demonstratives or the relative particle, for example. At times the writer attempts to give a veneer of BH to typically RH expressions, as with אֲשֶׁר־רָאִיתִי אָנִי טוֹב ('ᵃšær rā'īṯī 'ānī ṭōḇ) 'that which I have seen to be good' at 5:17, טוֹב אֲשֶׁר תֶּאֱחֹז בָּזֶה (ṭōḇ 'ᵃšær tæ'ᵆḥōz bā-zǽ) 'it is good that you hold onto this' at 7:18, or, at 12:1, עַד אֲשֶׁר לֹא ('aḏ 'ᵃšær lō') 'before (something does) not (happen)' instead of עַד שֶׁלֹּא ('aḏ šæl-lō'). Elsewhere, the impact of RH is very clear, for example וְיֹתֵר שֶׁהָיָה (wᵉ-yōṯēr šæ-hāyā) 'and in addition to being', at 12:9, has no parallel in BH.[36] It has been claimed that the language of Koheleth was influenced by the northern dialect,[37] or by Phoenician or Canaanite.[38] Although these possibilities cannot be excluded, they do not sufficiently account for the book's linguistic peculiarities.

A number of factors supports the view that other biblical works were also written during or after the exile, although their late features are not so clear. Ezekiel,[39] Haggai, Zechariah, Malachi,[40] Isaiah 55–66, Proverbs, parts of Job,[41] Lamentations,[42] Ruth,[43] etc.[44] come into this category.

Although uncertainties remain about whether the Book of Esther was composed in the Maccabaean or Hasmonaean periods, it is, in

36 See Bendavid 1967, 77ff.; du Plessis 1971.

37 Thus, Gordon 1955a.

38 See Dahood 1952; 1952a; 1962.

39 See Hurvitz 1982. In this exilic book there are still no clear features from LBH, although it does provide evidence of the beginning of processes that would reach full development in the Persian period.

40 A.E. Hill (1981) places Malachi around 500 BCE, but points out that its language does not contain many grammatical or lexical features from LBH.

41 See Hurvitz 1975, where it is shown that at least the narrative sections at the beginning and end of the book contain linguistic features that are clearly late.

42 See Löhr 1894.

43 Many Aramaisms have been found in the text of Ruth, for example לָהֵן (lāhēn) 'therefore' (1:13) and לְקַיֵּם (lᵉ-qayyēm) 'to establish' (4:7). See Eissfeldt 1965, 483.

44 Although since the time of Wellhausen, the priestly redaction of the Pentateuch – the 'Priestly Codex' (P) – has been included in the same category, the linguistic analysis by A. Hurvitz (1974) shows that in its present state the work is better regarded as a product of the pre-exilic period.

any case, one of the latest biblical writings. Linguistic features may point to a date well into the second century BCE, although the fine points of this judgement are open to debate. There are those who regard the book as written in a fundamentally biblical idiom, with RH-type modifications,[45] and others who view it as a RH text with influence from BH.[46]

In Esther, new elements from the period are found alongside others typical of the older language and representative of pure BH. There are instances of BH usage in connexion with, for example, the tenses of the verb, *waw*-consecutive, the infinitive construct preceded by proclitic particle, the infinitive absolute, the narrative formula וַיְהִי (wa-yᵉhī) 'and it came to pass', the genitive construction, interrogative *he*, the relative אֲשֶׁר ('ᵃšær), and basic sentence syntax. A deliberate imitation of classical biblical style can be perceived, although it is not carried out in an absolutely consistent way. Many of Esther's linguistic features correspond to usages noted in Chronicles. These include repetition of a noun to signal distributive value, pluralization of collective nouns, frequent use of the infinitive construct preceded by -לְ (lᵉ-) 'to' in structures that replace the imperative or other finite forms of the verb, disuse of the infinitive absolute in commands, direct attachment of accusative suffixes to the verb, and overlapping uses of the particles.

Nonetheless, in other respects, beyond those already noted, the language is closer to BH than to that of Chronicles. For example, Esther does not employ the particles -לְ (lᵉ-) or אֵת (ēṯ) before a subject for emphasis, retains the feminine form of the third person plural suffix, and places cardinal numbers before the noun.[47] Such features indicate to what extent we are dealing here with an artificial literary language. On the other hand, there are also some important features that are shared with RH. These include word

45 Thus Bendavid 1967, 61.
46 See Rabin 1958, 152f.
47 See Striedl 1937.

order, for example אֲשֶׁר־הוּא יְהוּדִי ('ᵃšær hū' yᵉhūḏī) 'that he was a Jew' at 3:4, the substitution of עמד ('md) 'stand up' for קום (qwm), the periphrastic use of היה (hyh) 'be' with the participle, and the employment of the relative particle אֲשֶׁר ('ᵃšær) on the analogy of RH -שֶׁ (šæ-), as in יוֹדְעִים אֲשֶׁר (yōḏᵉ'īm 'ᵃšær) 'knowing that' at 4:11. Sometimes a different preposition is preferred, as in בֵּין הָעַמִּים (bēn hā-'ammīm) 'among the peoples' at 3:8; the same verse also witnesses to the use of אֵין ('ēn) 'not' negating a participle. There are also several late items of vocabulary not used in BH, for example, עָתִיד ('āṯīḏ) 'ready' (3:14), רָצוֹן (rāṣōn) 'desire' (1:8), כשר (kšr) 'be right' (8:5), and אִלּוּ ('illū) 'if only' (7:4), as well as words from Aramaic, such as יְקָר (yᵉqār) 'honour' (1:20) and אנס ('ns) 'compel' (1:8), and from Persian – דָּת (dāṯ) 'law' (1:13) and אֲחַשְׁתְּרָן ('ᵃḥašᵗᵉrān) 'royal' (8:10), for example.[48]

From the second to first centuries BCE come the Hebrew fragments of Ben Sira, Jubilees, and the Testaments of the Twelve Patriarchs, most of which were discovered in caves near the Dead Sea. For Ben Sira we also have some mediaeval fragments preserved in the Cairo Genizah. In Ben Sira, the main tendency is to imitate BH, although clear traces of RH are also recognizable.[49] Its orthography attempts to follow the BH model, although occasionally it accords with the practice of contemporary works, as with מזנים (mznym) for BH מאזנים (m'znym, pron. mōzᵉnayim) 'scales' in the Massada manuscript of Ben Sira, 42:4. The relative pronoun can be אֲשֶׁר ('ᵃšær) or -שֶׁ (šæ-), and Ben Sira's vocabulary contains BH elements, including both archaisms and terms from LBH, as well as components from RH and Aramaic.[50]

48 See Bendavid 1967, 62ff. In a doctoral thesis, R.L. Bergey (1983) analysed a total of fifty-eight late features in the phonology, morphology, syntax, and vocabulary of Esther, pointing out, for example, that at least seventeen do not occur in the other post-exilic books but are found in RH. In its language, then, Esther would come closer than any other book of the Bible to RH.

49 See Strauss 1900; M.H. Segal 1958; Torrey 1950; Ackroyd 1953; Rabin 1958, 152. T. Penar (1975) tries to shed light on the Hebrew text of Ben Sira from parallels in Northwest Semitic, along the lines established by M.J. Dahood. His approach complements our own.

50 See E.Y. Kutscher 1982, 87ff.

It has been shown that in the last half of the second century BCE, still within the Second Temple period, there emerged another literary language as a rival to LBH. This language, although of short duration, seems to have been well established, incorporating features from both BH and RH, and to have been used in the composition of historical works relating to the Hasmonaean period and in early liturgical texts.[51] These synagogue texts are very similar in their language, with sentences constructed according to the rules of RH, the tense system of BH (including consecutive tenses and the infinitive absolute), and a mixed vocabulary, with terms from BH (many of them *hapax legomena*), RH, and Aramaic, as well as novel creations.

From the Persian period, there remains a small amount of epigraphic material written in Hebrew – some coins from Tell Jemmeh and Beth Zur, with legends in palaeo-Hebrew characters,[52] two seal-impressions on *bullae* from a cave in Wadi Daliyeh,[53] a seal from Tell Mikhal, etc.[54] In comparison, the surviving Aramaic material is much more abundant. From the Hellenistic period, there are also some inscribed jug handles, as well as coins from the time of the Hasmonaean monarchy until the Bar-Kochba revolt (in palaeo-Hebrew characters). Various funerary inscriptions from Jerusalem and a number of early synagogues clearly date from the end of this period, and alternate in their language between Hebrew, Aramaic, and Greek.[55] The data they provide about linguistic conditions in the area are quite limited.[56] However, they are sufficient to indicate, for example, preference

51 According to C. Rabin (1958, 153ff.; 1970, 319f.; 1976, 1015ff.), the historical works have been lost, but some fragments have been preserved within rabbinic literature, such as the account of King Yannai in the Babylonian Talmud, Kiddushin 66a, of Simeon the Just in *Sifre* to Nm 22 and the Babylonian Talmud, Nedarim 9b, and of the sons of Levi at Zoar, in the Mishnah, Yebamoth 16:7.

52 See Rahmani 1971.

53 See Cross 1969d; Avigad 1976a.

54 See Naveh and Greenfield 1984, 122f.

55 See Naveh 1981.

56 See E.Y. Kutscher 1956a.

for *scriptio plena*, use of both ה (h) and א (') to represent final /ā/ and of word-final ן- (-n) rather than ם- (-m), elision of initial א (') in proper names, and weakening of the laryngeals, pharyngeals, and ר (r). They also confirm that Hebrew continued to be spoken and understood in Jerusalem and Judaea.

One of the most noteworthy features of the LBH corpus as a whole is a far-reaching series of changes in the verbal system. The suffix-conjugation is used only for the past and the prefix-conjugation for the future. The participle used on its own marks the present, whereas in periphrasis it indicates frequentative action, as in RH. We can also see, for example, the loss of shortened and lengthened forms of the verb, changes in the infinitive, the disappearance of modal distinctions, and a decrease in use, or abandonment, of consecutive tenses. Apart from a noticeable increase in the number of particles, there are also differences with respect to BH both in the usage of particles and in verb-preposition combinations. Lexical changes, for example the abandoning of words regarded as old-fashioned, the extension and significant modification of semantic fields, and the use of new words from dialects of Hebrew, other Semitic languages, Persian, and Greek have given this phase of the language a quite distinctive character.[57] Most of the changes noted witness to an evolution from BH and the adoption of new elements, frequently Aramaic in origin, that represent a process of development which would find full expression in RH. But LBH is not to be regarded simply as an intermediate stage with no real character of its own – not all of its words or structures were retained by RH, and these are sufficiently noteworthy to warrant the study of LBH in its own right.

[57] See Hadas-Lebel 1981, 101ff.; E.Y. Kutscher 1982, 82ff.

5.2 *The language of the Dead Sea Scrolls*

The story of the discovery of the Dead Sea Scrolls is well known. Dating from the second century BCE to the second century CE, they were largely composed by members of Jewish groups or sects that had established themselves along the Dead Sea.[58] Here, we need only mention that the most important discoveries include biblical manuscripts, most notably 1QIsa[a] (a complete scroll of Isaiah in an updated, 'vulgar', text), and fragments of biblical texts (Isaiah, Exodus, Psalms, etc.), as well as a variety of non-biblical manuscripts, such as the Manual of Discipline or Rule of the Community (1QS), the Rule of the Congregation (1QSa) and Blessings (1QSb), Hymns or *Hodayot* (1QH), the *Pesher* (Commentary) on Habakkuk (1QpHab), the War Scroll (1QM/4QM[a-e]), the Temple Scroll (11QT), and, in Aramaic, the Genesis Apocryphon (1QapGen). There are also some letters from Bar-Kochba. The language of the Copper Scroll (3QTr) differs from that used in the other writings, and may be classed as colloquial or Mishnaic Hebrew.[59] The same is true of some other shorter documents including a letter of a legal nature, the complete text of which still awaits publication.[60]

It would be difficult to exaggerate the significance of these discoveries for our knowledge of linguistic conditions at the time. They fill what had previously been a gap in our knowledge of Hebrew that had prevented a proper description of its development. Nonetheless, it has to be remembered that these documents cover a considerable period, some 300 years in fact, and are not, therefore, of a homogeneous character. The writings originated in various different environments, and the language

58 General studies of the Scrolls include those of F. Pérez Castro (1951–52), J.A. Sanders (1967), G. Vermes (1982; 1987), and M. Delcor and F. García Martínez (1982). The most recent bibliography of the numerous investigations into this material is contained in Fitzmyer 1990; cf. LaSor 1958; Burchard 1959–65; Jongeling 1971; 1973.

59 Thus, Milik 1962, 221ff. Cf. Thorion 1985–86a.

60 See Qimron and Strugnell 1985.

employed in a document also depends to a considerable extent on the type of literature being composed. The material exhibits varying levels of dialect influence, colloquialism, Aramaizing, etc. It is, therefore, essential as far as possible to avoid generalization and to refrain from attempting to incorporate into the overall description of the language the idiosyncracies of a given manuscript, no matter how important that document appears to be.[61]

Nor would it be correct simply to assume that the linguistic features of these writings are representative of all the Hebrew that was written and spoken in Palestine at the time. Although, logically, the Dead Sea Scrolls should reflect more generally prevailing linguistic phenomena, the sociological and historical contexts from which they derive must not be forgotten. It is quite possible that members of the Qumran sect reacted against the general tendencies of their time. The *Ḥasidim*, who were forerunners of both the Essenes and the Pharisees, had adopted as their literary language a mixture of BH and RH, already noted in the previous section, with RH clearly predominating. The Pharisees, who emerged from the common people, taught in a vernacular Hebrew which they later elevated to the status of a literary language (RH). The members of the Qumran sect, on the other hand, consciously tried to eliminate colloquial elements from the literary language, symbolizing by this search for a purely biblical form of language their 'return' to the pure religion of the desert.[62] It has been argued that instead of independently reviving BH, the sectarians chose to continue using LBH, which still existed as a literary language, combining it with distinctive linguistic

61 See Goshen-Gottstein 1958, especially the important observations (pp. 130ff.) on the differences displayed by the major documents from Qumran in their most significant linguistic features.
62 See Rabin 1958, 144.

features of their own.[63] But in spite of its stylistic proximity to LBH and the use of BH archaisms, the Qumran dialect, like Samaritan Hebrew, has particular traits which connect it with, and distinguish it from, other forms of Hebrew known from the period. Moreover, it is probable that Qumran Hebrew was used not just in writing but also as a living spoken language. It would not, therefore, be merely a continuation of LBH.[64]

Many different elements combined to form the language of the sectarians. It is also possible that more than one language was spoken at Qumran, depending on where particular sectarians had originated. Some literary works would have been written in Aramaic, and we have clear proof of the use of the vernacular language, RH, in the Copper Scroll, the language of which differs little from that of the Bar-Kochba letters. Greek was also known, as indicated by the Greek fragments discovered.[65] Reflections of different traditions of Hebrew have been identified in the writings of the group, with some features corresponding to what would become Babylonian Hebrew and others to the Samaritan dialect. The Scrolls also contain, for example, terms taken from BH but invested with completely new meanings, as well as archaisms and traces of other Semitic dialects such as Edomite.[66] Between the earliest and latest documents an evolutionary process has undoubtedly taken place,[67] so that the language has become gradually more distant from BH and more under the influence of Aramaic and RH.

The great diversity of features in the literary Hebrew of the Dead Sea Scrolls has led to a variety of theories regarding the existence of different dialects that were used simultaneously by members of

63 See the remarks of A. Hurvitz cited in Morag 1988, 148, n. 1. R. Polzin (1976, 6ff.) underlines the archaic character of the language of Qumran which is sometimes closer to that of the Pentateuch than to that of Chronicles.

64 As emphasized by S. Morag (1988).

65 See Segert 1963.

66 See E.Y. Kutscher 1972, 1583ff.

67 As clearly illustrated in Murtonen 1963–64.

the sect, culminating in the claim that we should not speak of a uniform pronunciation, but rather of a juxtaposition of different traditions.[68] But providing evidence for such a mixture of dialects is difficult. From an analysis of the pronominal suffixes, E.Y. Kutscher concluded that in the text of 1QIsa[a], and at Qumran generally, there are traces of two Hebrew dialects. One was 'standard', more traditional, and used for Bible readings in the synagogue, whereas the other was 'substandard', used in other spheres of life as a colloquial language, and eventually acquired definitive form in Mishnaic Hebrew.[69] However, on occasions this division involves some violence to the linguistic data.

Without doubt the language used at Qumran has a number of close parallels with Samaritan Hebrew, as demonstrated in numerous studies, of which those by Z. Ben-Ḥayyim are of particular importance.[70] In certain respects the Samaritan dialect seems to be later than the language of Qumran: short *u*, which is sometimes represented at Qumran by *waw*, shifts towards *e/a* in Samaritan, the second person singular masculine suffix which often has the form כה- (-kh) at Qumran is only found in this form three times in the Samaritan Pentateuch.

In sum, the prevailing view is that the Dead Sea Scrolls represent a fundamentally biblical form of language in a late stage of development. Despite religiously-motivated opposition, at least in the sect's beginnings, this continuation of LBH moved progressively closer to RH and also fell under the influence of

68 This is the view of R. Meyer (1957a). Although he does not venture to pinpoint the origin of each dialect, Meyer suggests that the tendency to vocalize with *o* might have come from Galilee, while in the area around Shechem a more archaizing form of language was probably used. But see Goshen-Gottstein 1958, 135.

69 See E.Y. Kutscher 1952 (31 October); 1971, 1583ff.; 1974, 61ff.; 1982, 93ff.

70 See, for example, Ben-Ḥayyim 1958a, 207: 'The linguistic tradition emerging from the DSS is on the whole identical with that of the Samaritans. There being no reason to believe that the DS Sect belonged to the Samaritan community, it follows that the said tradition was current in Palestine outside the Samaritan community as well as within its ranks.' On the whole, this was also the view of Ḥ. Yalon, A. Sperber, and P.E. Kahle.

Aramaic. At the same time, as already stated, Qumran Hebrew has certain features characteristic of a living, spoken, dialect.[71]

Linguistic studies of Qumran have tended to display a partial, often 'atomistic',[72] character, frequently concentrating on the language of a single document. Without doubt, the most important of such studies is E.Y. Kutscher's exhaustive analysis of 1QIsa[a],[73] which describes one of the most remarkable manuscripts to be found there, and represents the most complete work on the language of Qumran.

For Kutscher, this text represents a popular version of Isaiah, reflecting in its language the situation in Palestine in the centuries just before the Common Era. The proper names used in the scroll reveal a late stage of the language, for example, the form, noted in the previous section, דרמשק (Tib. darmæśæq) as opposed to the more common MT version דַּמֶּשֶׂק (dammæśæq) 'Damascus'. In theophoric names, short forms like חזקיה (Tib. ḥizqīyyā) 'Hezekiah' and ישעיה (Tib. yᵉšaʻyā) 'Isaiah', are used instead of the longer and older MT variants: חִזְקִיָּהוּ (ḥizqīyyāhū) and יְשַׁעְיָהוּ (yᵉšaʻyāhū). The use of *scriptio plena* is also characteristic of a late stage of the language.

Overall, the language of the manuscript has been 'modernized'. BH had ceased to exist as a spoken language centuries before, and ordinary people, who spoke in RH or Aramaic dialects, could barely understand it or even read it correctly. The only BH they understood consisted of elements retained within RH or forms familiar from Aramaic. Archaic expressions and *hapax legomena* had become unintelligible, and words which were written the same in Hebrew and Aramaic tended to be pronounced as though they were Aramaic. For all of these reasons a 'vernacular text' developed, which attempted to make its contents understandable, while protecting itself against Aramaic pronunciation by means of

71 See, for example, Mansoor 1958; Schreiden 1959; Segert 1963; 1968; E.Y. Kutscher 1971; 1982, 93ff.; Morag 1988.

72 To use an expression from Goshen-Gottstein 1958, 102.

73 E.Y. Kutscher 1974, originally published in Hebrew in 1959.

matres lectionis, as with לוא (lw') for MT לא (l') 'not', רואש (rw'š) for MT ראש (r'š) 'head', etc., and by replacing some words and archaic expressions by others which were, presumably, more familiar, for example שוליך (Tib. šūlayiḵ) 'your skirts' (also found in RH) in place of MT שֹׁבֶל (šōḇæl) at Is 47:2. We should not discount the possibility, however, that 1QIsa[a] has occasionally preserved readings that are superior to those of MT. There is an abundance of every kind of Aramaism, and a tendency to modernize can be seen at all levels of the language: MT נִחֻמִים (niḥūmīm) 'comforts' at Is 57:18 is replaced by תנחומים (Tib. tanḥūmīm) and the archaic חַיְתוֹ (ḥayᵉṯō) 'beasts of' at Is 56:9 by חית (Tib. ḥayyaṯ), כּוֹס (kōs) 'cup' is treated as masculine, as in RH, etc.

A somewhat different situation is found in connexion with the pronouns and pronominal suffixes. הואה (hw'h) 'he' and היאה (hy'h) 'she' might reflect earlier forms, whereas the second person plural אתמה ('tmh) seems to have arisen on the analogy of other pronouns. The singular feminine suffix of the verb in תי- (-ty) and of the noun in כי- (-ky) are more likely to be Aramaisms than archaisms, whereas כה- (-kh) is the old form of the second person masculine pronominal suffix.[74] Perhaps forms of this type are the results of penultimate stress, as evidenced in other traditions of Hebrew.

In Kutscher's view, the dialect of the person who wrote the Isaiah Scroll corresponds to a large degree with the vernacular language that was soon to develop into RH, although it is not to be equated with this or with the official tradition of synagogue liturgical reading, from which it differs even more strikingly. Thus, the text represents a distinct, probably regional, dialect, which should not be regarded as an intermediate link between an earlier form of BH and the Tiberian tradition.[75] Nonetheless, the scroll does preserve some archaic elements. For example, there are

74 This is further evidence to refute Paul Kahle's claims about Masoretic reconstruction.

75 See E.Y. Kutscher 1974, 61f.

indications that the language used was less subject to dissimilation, with שולח (šlwḥ) being used for MT שִׁלֹחַ (šīlōaḥ) 'Shiloah' and עוזוז ('wzwz) for MT עִזּוּז ('izzūz) 'mighty'; nouns of the pattern *quṭl*, which in Tiberian often change to *qiṭl* or *qaṭl* when the vowel is in a closed unstressed syllable, for example אִמְרָה ('imrā) 'word', are preserved as *quṭl* in the Isaiah Scroll, as they are in the Babylonian tradition of Hebrew – רונה (rwnh) as opposed to MT רִנָּה (rinnā) 'cry', etc.

Studies like this, as well as many others that have concentrated on particular texts[76] or that attempt a more wide-ranging analysis,[77] in particular the surveys of Kutscher[78] and his pupil E. Qimron (which presents data from all of the Scrolls),[79] have led to a clearer picture of the nature of Qumran Hebrew.

The orthography of this variety of Hebrew is characterized by the use of *scriptio plena*, which is found in every document and reflects the general tendency of the time. Although the various *matres lectionis* are used somewhat inconsistently even within a single document, a striking feature is the frequent employment of *waw* to indicate any vowel of timbre *o* or *u*, including the Tiberian ultrashort vowels, for example חודשים (ḥwdšym; Tib. ḥᵒḏāšīm) 'months'. *Yod* occurs less often, representing in particular the long vowels, as in יקים (yqym; Tib. yāqīm) 'he will establish', although it can also come at the end of a word instead of *he* to indicate an *e* vowel, as in יעני (y'ny) for MT יענה (y'nh, pron. ya'ᵃnæ) 'he will answer', particularly in the construct of nouns with *he* as their third consonant – שדי (śdy) for MT שדה (śdh, pron. śᵉḏē) 'field of'. When *waw* or *yod* has consonantal value, it may be repeated, as with ישתחווה (yšthwwh; Tib. yištaḥᵃwæ) 'he will bow down' and

[76] For example, Leahy 1957 and Revell 1962 on the Manual of Discipline, Wallenstein 1959, de Vries 1964–66, Hurvitz 1964–66 and 1967, and Qimron 1970–71 on *Hodayot*, and Silbermann 1961–62 on the Habakkuk *pesher*.

[77] See R. Meyer 1950; Ben-Ḥayyim 1958; Goshen-Gottstein 1958; 1960a; Mansoor 1958; Schreiden 1959; Murtonen 1963–64; G.R. Driver 1965; Morag 1988, etc.

[78] 1971.

[79] See E.Y. Kutscher 1971; Qimron 1986 (originally a 1976 doctoral thesis, written in Hebrew).

והייה (w-hyyh; Tib. wᵉ-hāyā) 'and it will be', or it can be written with a following *alef*, as in עואר ('w'r) instead of MT עִוֵּר ('iwwēr) 'blind'. In instances of *scriptio defectiva*, we have to bear in mind the possibility that such forms might often correspond to patterns of vocalization peculiar to Qumran, so that, for example, חמר (ḥmr) 'clay' might have been pronounced as 'ḥemar' rather than (Tib.) 'ḥōmær'. Particularly noticeable is the use of pairs of *matres lectionis* to represent a single vowel, especially *alef-waw* or *waw-alef* for *o*, for example לוא (lw'; Tib. lō') 'not' and ראוש (r'wš; Tib. rōš) 'head'. Note as well ראישון (r'yšwn; Tib. rīšōn) 'first', כיא (ky'; Tib. kī) 'because', and מיא (my'; Tib. mī) 'who?', and פרעוה (pr'wh; Tib. par'ō) 'Pharaoh' and כוה (kwh; Tib. kō) 'thus'. This phenomenon is widespread in 1QIsaᵃ and other biblical texts, apparently diminishing over time.[80] Occasionally, *samekh* is used instead of *sin*. Kutscher wisely prefers to view such features not as phonological innovations but as orthographic customs peculiar to the time, attested to a greater or lesser extent in other contemporary epigraphic and literary sources.[81] It is also possible that an important rôle was played by practical, pedagogical, attempts to ensure the correct, non-Aramaizing, pronunciation of certain words.[82]

Phonologically, the language of Qumran represents a period of transition and fluctuation, during which, as is true of other texts from this time, Aramaic and perhaps Greek were able to exert a marked influence. Weakening, merger, and loss of the laryngeals and pharyngeals is typical. Attempts have been made to distinguish two phases in this process, the first one pertaining to the writers of the original documents, who still pronounced the four phonemes distinctly, and the second belonging to copyists,

[80] Thus, Murtonen 1963–64, 71f.

[81] See E.Y. Kutscher 1974, 186.

[82] A different explanation is proposed by E. Qimron (1986, 22) who claims that the additional *waw* (and *yod*) is 'a means to indicate the sound *o* (or *i/e*)'. He also mentions the 'desire to lengthen short words'.

who could no longer differentiate them.[83] From a different perspective, formal, especially biblical, texts can be treated separately from the others. In the former, particularly in the Isaiah Scroll, there are many instances of merger and interchange of gutturals: חמר (ḥmr) for MT אָמַר ('āmar) 'he said', אסיר ('syr) for הָסֵר (hāsēr) 'to remove', שעיס (ś'ys) for שָׂחִיס (śāḥīs) 'uncultivated crops', אתה ('th) for עַתָּה ('attā) 'now'.[84] In the second group of texts, on the other hand, it is elision, albeit of a very unsystematic kind, that is the dominant feature. The confusion of the gutturals may not always simply be a matter of phonology – occasionally it also has a lexical dimension, as when the preposition על (Tib. 'al) replaces MT אֶל ('æl) for example,[85] or it can involve morphological change, as with להוב (lhwb) for MT לַהַב (lahab̠) 'flame'. In addition, non-initial *alef* is always quiescent, and is often found in places where its presence is difficult to explain. Overall, it can be said that the treatment of laryngeals and pharyngeals at Qumran does not differ substantially from that found in other traditions of Hebrew and in Aramaic dialects of the period.[86]

Of particular interest is the retention of original short *u*, which from the second half of the second millennium BCE had tended to shift to *i* in Hebrew.[87] In some varieties of Hebrew, such as Samaritan, a complete transformation occurred, whereas in others, Babylonian for example, there was some resistance to this tendency. But the situation at Qumran is quite remarkable. Not only are archaic forms preserved, as in the Babylonian tradition, as with רונה (rwnh) for MT רִנָּה (rinnā) 'cry', but ו (w) also appears in many environments where other traditions of Hebrew have *i* or a murmured vowel: שולח (šwlḥ) for MT שִׁלֹחַ (šīlōaḥ) 'Shiloah',

[83] See Murtonen 1963–64.
[84] See E.Y. Kutscher 1974, 505ff.
[85] See Goshen-Gottstein 1958, 108.
[86] See Sáenz-Badillos 1975, 124ff.
[87] For example, חוּץ (ḥūṣ) 'outside' > חִיצוֹן (ḥīṣōn) 'outer', תּוֹךְ (tōk̠) 'midst of' > תִּיכוֹן (tīk̠ōn) 'middle'; cf. אֹמֶר ('ōmær) and אִמְרָה ('imrā) 'word', etc. See E.Y. Kutscher 1974, 452ff.; Qimron 1986, 35ff.

גודפים (gwdpym) for גִּדּוּפִים (giddūpīm) 'revilings', קובציך (qwbṣyk) for קִבּוּצַיִךְ (qibbūṣayik̲) 'your collections', פותאים (pwt'ym) for פְּתָאִים (p^e^t̲ā'īm) 'simple people', אוהול ('whwl) for אֹהֶל ('ōhæl) 'tent', יכתובהו (yktwbhw) for Tib. יִכְתְּבוּהוּ (yik̲t^e^b̲ūhū) 'he will enlist him', etc. It is difficult to accept that this *waw* represents a murmured vowel (the existence of which at Qumran has not been proved) or that it could have been read as *a* or *e*.[88] Thus, we have to turn to another sort of explanation, based on morphology, which claims that at Qumran the Proto-Semitic pattern *qutl* occurs as *qwṭl*, *qṭwl*, or *qwṭwl* in the construct, with *qwṭl* as the standard form of the absolute. As in the Greek transcriptions, the auxiliary vowel in these forms probably does not conform to the Tiberian model.[89]

Although stress is still a matter of debate, it is quite likely that the orthography of some of the forms already noted and of the so-called 'pausal forms in context', such as ידרושהו (ydrwšhw) 'they will seek him' and התקדישו (htqdyšw) 'they sanctified themselves' for Tiberian contextual (non-pausal) forms יִדְרְשׁוּהוּ (yid̲r^e^šūhū) and הִתְקַדְּשׁוּ (hit̲qadd^e^šū), indicate that at Qumran stress was often penultimate, contrary to the Tiberian tradition, but consistent with Samaritan Hebrew and, perhaps, the Greek transcriptions.[90]

Other interesting phonetic features are attested in the Dead Sea Scrolls. There is a tendency to omit *resh*, and perhaps to pronounce it less forcefully. Weakening of the laryngeals might be the cause of the appearance of new semivowels – for example מאיות (m'ywt) 'hundreds' for MT מֵאוֹת (mē'ōt). Occasionally the *nun* is not assimilated, as in מי ינתן (my yntn) for MT מִי יִתֵּן (mī yittēn) 'who will give?'. The labials and *resh* influence the quality of a preceding vowel, as in קוברך (qwbrk) 'your grave' for MT קִבְרְךָ (qib̲r^e^k̲ā), even when that vowel would be *shewa* in the Tiberian tradition, for example שובי (šwby) for שְׁבִי (š^e^b̲ī) 'captivity'.

88 See R. Meyer 1957a; 1958. Meyer emphasizes the comparison with Phoenician, and ascribes its origin to dialect.
89 See Qimron 1986, 36ff.
90 See Qimron 1986, 40ff.; Morag 1988, 155ff.

Something similar occurs with the laryngeals and pharyngeals: compare מואד (mw'd) for מְאֹד (me'ōḏ) 'very'. The Qumran documents frequently employ ו (w) or א (') for Tiberian *shewa mobile,* as in סודום (swdwm) for סְדֹם (seḏōm) 'Sodom' and כלאיות (kl'ywt) for כִּלְיוֹת (kilyōṯ) 'kidneys of', for example. There are some instances of consonantal assimilation, such as אגזרי ('gzry) for MT אַכְזָרִי ('akzārī) 'cruel', or of interchange of homorganic voiced and voiceless consonants, for example גד (gd) for MT גַּת (gaṯ) 'wine-press'. As in RH, final *mem* and *nun* are interchangeable.[91] The orthography of words like בנו (bnw) for MT בניו (bnyw, pron. bānāw) 'his sons' demonstrates contraction of the diphthong *aw* in final position, possibly an old dialect feature.[92]

In terms of morphology, the language of Qumran contains some striking features. The third person singular personal pronouns הואה (hw'h) and היאה (hy'h)[93] alternate with the classical forms without final *he,* as do the second and third person plural pronouns אתמה ('tmh) and המה (hmh) (this last form is also found in BH). The second person singular feminine אתי ('ty) and the first person plural אנו ('nw) are perhaps Aramaisms. Similarly, the pronominal suffixes with final *he,* כה- (-kh) 'your (sg.)', כמה- (-kmh) 'your (pl.)', and מה- (-mh) 'their', occur alongside others without it. It has been argued that these data are explicable in terms of the existence of two alternative paradigms arising from internal processes within Hebrew, comparable in some ways to the situation in Samaritan Hebrew.[94] It has not been proven that the alternation of ך- (-k) and כה- (-kh) corresponds to a dual pronunciation '-aḵ' and '-ḵa', in the way that Paul Kahle understood it, as though the second form were a reaction against

91 See E.Y. Kutscher 1974, 496ff.; Qimron 1986, 25ff.

92 See Qimron 1986, 33f.; Morag 1988, 152f.

93 These have been much debated, and interpreted as, for example, archaic or dialect forms, analogical formations, or simply instances of *scriptio plena.* See E.Y. Kutscher 1974, 433ff.; Qimron 1986, 57f.; Morag 1988, 156f.

94 Thus, Goshen-Gottstein 1958, 118f.; 1958a, 103ff.

an Aramaizing pronunciation.[95] In the second person singular feminine, the forms ךְ- (-k) and כי- (-ky) are found. A similar alternation is found among the third person singular masculine suffixes: ו- (-w), יו- (-yw), and יהו- (-yhw). The last of these, which is also found in the Samaritan and Babylonian traditions and possibly reflects an old dialect feature, is the furthest removed from Tiberian Hebrew, as it has not undergone elision of intervocalic ה- (-h-) or contraction of the ensuing diphthong.[96] The third person singular feminine suffix, in MT הָ- (-hā), is sometimes written הא- (-h') or הה (-hh). Suffixed forms of the kind אבותם (Tib. 'ᵃḇōṯām) 'their fathers' are preferred to those of the kind אבותיהם (Tib. 'ᵃḇōṯēhæm), and, as in BH, there is a marked preference for the relative particle אשר (Tib. 'ᵃšær) rather than -ש (Tib. šæ-).[97]

In the noun there are few basic divergences from the Tiberian tradition, once we discount those items already noted, which result from the particular style of orthography used at Qumran and which might occasionally correspond to distinctive noun patterns. Sometimes an Aramaic influence is possible, as in בסור (bswr) for MT בֹּסֶר (bōsær) 'sour grapes', or in the widespread use of the pattern *qṭwl* for construct nouns, as already noted, for example רחוב נפש (rḥwb npš) for Tiberian רֹחַב נֶפֶשׁ (rōḥaḇ næp̄æš) 'breadth of soul' and שפול ידים (špwl ydym) for שֵׁפֶל יָדַיִם (šēp̄æl yāḏayim) 'sinking of hands'. Further evidence of a change in noun patterns at Qumran could be provided by forms like לוהב (lwhb) for לַהַב (lahaḇ) 'flame', רוקמה (rwqmh) for רִקְמָה (riqmā) 'embroidery', גמול (gmwl) for גֹּמֶל (gōmēl) 'ripening', and חוזיר (ḥwzyr) for חֲזִיר (ḥᵃzīr) 'pig', while אגמן ('gmn) instead of אַגְמוֹן ('aḡmōn) 'bulrush' probably indicates a preference for the Aramaic suffix in ָן (-ān).[98] There are many nouns with prefixed *mem*, although it is unclear whether the pronunciation of this had shifted to *mi-*, as in Tiberian, or whether it was retained as *ma-*, as in other traditions. Certain

95 See Martin 1957; Wernberg-Møller 1957; E.Y. Kutscher 1974, 446ff.

96 See Morag 1988, 156f.

97 See Qimron 1986, 77ff.; Morag 1988, 160f.

98 See E.Y. Kutscher 1974, 365ff.; Qimron 1986, 65.

plural forms, such as נגועים (ngw'ym) for נְגָעִים (negā'īm) 'blows', differ from BH, following a tendency already evidenced by LBH and quite common in RH.

In the verb, we may note the presence of the archaic second person singular feminine suffix תי- (-ty), as in LBH and Samaritan, perhaps due to Aramaic influence. The lengthened suffix תמה- (-tmh) of the second person plural masculine, represented by אכלתמה ('kltmh) for Tiberian אֲכַלְתֶּם ('akaltæm) 'you ate', also found in Samaritan Hebrew, appears to be a recent innovation.[99] The second person singular masculine suffix written as תה- (-th) is also found occasionally in MT for תָּ- (-tā). Forms of the third person singular feminine such as ונתרת (w-ntrt) for ונותרה (w-nwtrh, pron. we-nōterā) 'and she was left' are clearly of Aramaic origin, as is the third person plural feminine ending in ה- (-h).

Forms like ישפול (yšpwl) for יִשְׁפַּל (yišpal) 'he will fall' suggest that there might have been a prefix-conjugation vocalized with *o*: compare Qumran שלוח (šlwḥ) with MT שְׁלַח (šelaḥ) '(to) send' at Is 58:9. Although at times this feature contrasts very obviously with the situation in Tiberian Hebrew, it is consistent with other traditions of Hebrew and Aramaic. The final *nun* of lengthened forms of the verb is dropped as in LBH. A conspicuous feature is the first person ending in ה- (-h), for example ואכתובה (w-'ktwbh) for Tiberian וָאֶכְתֹּב (wā-'æktōb) 'and I wrote', which alternates with other forms without it. In a number of LBH writings, this pattern is used as a simple indicative, but the Dead Sea Scrolls are the only documents to employ it in consecutive forms of the verb, thus distinguishing the first person from the second and third persons which use short forms of the verb.[100]

Another striking feature of Qumran Hebrew is the use of 'pausal forms in context', with or without suffixed pronouns, for example יכתובו (yktwbw) 'they will write' and ידרושהו (ydrwšhw) 'they will seek him' for non-pausal Tiberian forms יִכְתְּבוּ (yiktebū) and

[99] See Qimron 1986, 43.
[100] See Qimron 1986, 43ff.

יִדְרְשֻׁהוּ (yiḏrᵉšūhū), as well as with structures of the pattern *yqwṭl*, including suffixed forms, such as וישומעוני (w-yšwm'w-ny) for Tiberian וַיִּשְׁמְעוּנִי (way-yišmᵉ'ū-nī) 'and they heard me'. The orthography here clearly indicates a tradition at variance with the Tiberian but with certain similarities to Samaritan Hebrew and to the Greek transcriptions. The phenomenon could be due, at least in part, to penultimate stress, as we have already noted.[101] An explanation is also required for imperatives like עוברי ('wbry) for Tiberian עִבְרוּ ('iḇrū) 'pass!' and דרושו (drwšw) for דִּרְשׁוּ (diršū) 'seek!', which might have a similar origin or reflect Aramaic influence. The claim that in the Scrolls, as in Samaritan, there is a present-future of the type *yaqaṭṭal* is probably not correct.[102] The infinitive construct occurs commonly, as in the other later traditions of Hebrew, whereas clear instances of the infinitive absolute are quite scarce.[103]

The *Hithpa'el* is very common in the Dead Sea Scrolls, extending its rôle as a passive and replacing other less frequent passive structures, just as in RH and Aramaic.[104] In verbs having third radical *yod*, shortened and standard forms alternate, with preference being given to the former, at least in biblical manuscripts.

In the particles there is a noticeable Aramaic influence, in orthography, for example תחות (tḥwt) for MT תַּחַת (taḥaṯ) 'instead of', in non-assimilation, as in ומן בנות (w-mn bnwt) for MT וּמִבָּנוֹת (ū-mib-bānōṯ) 'and (better) than daughters', and in the interchangeable use of certain prepositions – אֶל ('æl) and עַל ('al) for example. Elsewhere there are similarities with RH – אילי ('y-ly)

101 See I. Yeivin 1972a; E.Y. Kutscher 1974, 332ff. In his discussion of this issue, E. Qimron (1986, 50ff.) chooses a morphological solution: to the old form יקטולני (yqṭwlny), a new one, יקוטלני (yqwṭlny), has been added.

102 See R. Meyer 1961a.

103 See Qimron 1986, 47f. In contrast, J. Carmignac (1985–86) believes that the use of the infinitive absolute at Qumran closely mirrors biblical usage.

104 See Qimron 1986, 48f.

for אוי־לי ('wy ly, pron. 'ōy lī) 'woe to me', ממעלה (m-m'lh) for מִמַּעַל (mim-ma'al) 'from above', etc.[105]

In syntax, although the material is not very uniform, it is possible to see quite clearly how Hebrew was evolving, given that the Scrolls represent an intermediate stage between BH and RH, and contain elements of each.[106] Despite their relatively late composition, the documents are representative of LBH and are in many ways very close to the post-exilic books of the Bible, albeit with a number of archaic features and a distinctive style. Although the Scrolls are closer to the traditions represented by Samaritan and Babylonian Hebrew and the Greek transcriptions than to Tiberian Hebrew, the significance of this should not be overstated.

The use of tenses does not differ essentially from that found in BH[107] – the suffix-conjugation is used for completed past action whereas the prefix-conjugation denotes action continuing in the present or the future, and the indicative voice of the prefix-conjugation and the old energic are employed as narrative moods, thus diverging from RH usage. However, the large number of variations from MT in biblical manuscripts indicates that the tense system was undergoing a transformation.[108] In the non-biblical texts, there are various periphrastic constructions of היה (hyh) 'be' with the participle.[109] Although these do appear in LBH, they are more typical of RH. The continued use of *waw*-consecutive with the prefix-conjugation (less often with the suffix-conjugation) lends an air of antiquity. The BH introductory formula וַיְהִי (wa-yehī) 'and it came to pass' is no longer found. The infinitive absolute used for emphasis and the infinitive construct with prefixed

105 See E.Y. Kutscher 1974, 214f., 389ff.

106 See G.R. Driver 1965, 436ff.

107 See A. Rubinstein 1953; 1955; 1956; 1957; R. Meyer 1957a; Leahy 1957; 1960; Revell 1961–62; 1964–66; Carmignac 1964–66; 1972–75; 1977–78; 1985–86. S.J. de Vries (1964–66) studied the tense system of *Hodayot*. J.C. Kesterson (1984) examines the longer, more representative, Qumran documents. See also Thorion-Vardi (Vardi) 1985–86 on the Damascus Covenant (CD) from the Cairo Genizah.

108 See E.Y. Kutscher 1974, 324ff.

109 See Goshen-Gottstein 1958, 129.

particle are disappearing, being replaced, as in LBH and RH, by finite forms of the verb.[110]

Changes in conjugation or in the form of verbs, which are very common in 1QIsa[a], indicate the abandonment of less common structures and their replacement by other, better-known, ones – thus, for example, the passive of *Qal* in the Isaiah Scroll is replaced by the *Nif'al*.[111] As in LBH the impersonal use of the passive is replaced by the active verb in the third person plural,[112] and the infinitive preceded by the particle -לְ (le-) 'to' is used in orders, with negation effected by the particle לֹא (lō') 'not', as in לוא לצעוד (Tib. lō' li-ṣ'ōḏ) '(they are) not to walk'. The use of the infinitive construct preceded by -לְ (le-) 'to' has become standard, as in all subsequent stages of the language.

The personal pronoun is found in various positions.[113] In biblical texts there is a slight tendency to smooth out the syntax by adding the accusative particle in places where it does not occur in MT.[114] The object-marker אֵת ('ēṯ) is also used with subjects for emphasis,[115] although there is a complementary tendency, as also in LBH, not to attach it to the pronominal suffixes. Occasionally it is replaced by a preposition such as עַל ('al). If an attributive adjective has the article, the article may be omitted from the noun.[116]

In the syntax of the sentence, a clear predominance of verbal over nominal clauses is detectable,[117] with active clauses preferred to passive,[118] and subordinate clauses to co-ordinate ones. Following the standard practice of LBH, asyndetic relative clauses are avoided, with the relative particles אֲשֶׁר ('ᵃšær) and -שֶׁ (šæ-) or

110 See E.Y. Kutscher 1974, 346ff.; Carmignac 1985–86.
111 See E.Y. Kutscher 1974, 358ff.
112 See E.Y. Kutscher 1974, 401ff.
113 See Mansoor 1958.
114 See Goshen-Gottstein 1958, 130.
115 See Nebe 1972–75a.
116 See G.R. Driver 1965, 436ff.
117 See Revell 1964–66.
118 See Mansoor 1958; G.R. Driver 1965, 436ff.

some other means being employed instead. In non-biblical texts, as in RH, we find the relative and negative particles together, אֲשֶׁר לֹא ('a̮šær lō'), introducing prohibitions.

The vocabulary of the Dead Sea Scrolls has been the object of many limited studies which have helped to shed light on the lexicon of the time.[119] However, we lack an overall statement drawing together the results of such analyses. Kutscher divides this vocabulary into native and foreign elements.[120] Native components are drawn from the various stages of BH – archaic, for example אזן ('zn) hi. 'listen', standard, and late, for example מִדְרָשׁ (midrāš) 'study', from RH, for example כְּנֶסֶת (kenæsæṯ) 'assembly', and from other dialects of Hebrew. There are some notable examples of lexical specialization of terms from BH – קֵץ (qēṣ) 'time', גּוֹרָל (gōrāl) 'group', דֶּשֶׁא (dæšæ') 'Spring', etc. Non-Hebrew components include loans and loan-translations from Aramaic, as in the case of סֶרֶךְ (særæḵ) 'rule, order', from Persian, for example רָז (rāz) 'secret', and also from Greek and Latin, for instance מִגְדָּל (miḡdāl) 'tower' in the military sense of Greek *purgos,* Latin *turris,* although the number of words of similar origin is very small, probably for ideological reasons. There are also some words of uncertain provenance. It is obvious that the vocabulary of Qumran was more extensive than that of BH, and was open to morphological and semantic innovation. It has all the characteristics of a language in a changing, multilingual, environment, wanting to stay faithful to tradition but often forced to accept change.

119 Among the many works worthy of mention, that of M.Z. Kaddari (1968) stands out. It provides an extensive and rigorous analysis of the semantic field of obligation, building up a dictionary of the various terms and their relationships with one another.

120 See E.Y. Kutscher 1971, 1588ff.; 1982, 100ff.

5.3 *Samaritan Hebrew*

It is difficult to ascertain at what period the Hebrew spoken by the Samaritan community began to develop as an independent dialect. Attempts to connect it directly with the pre-exilic northern dialect seem rather extreme, given the length of time involved. After the conquest of Samaria, the introduction of foreign colonies there must have influenced the local language.[121] However, the indigenous population did not experience the kind of exile that affected Judah, and so there was no interruption in the natural development of their spoken language. Although this is not the view held by the Samaritans themselves, the emergence of the community as a sect distinct from official Judaism, and the definitive formation of the Samaritan Pentateuch (SP), took place much later, after John Hyrcanus had destroyed Shechem and the shrine on Mt Gerizim in the Hasmonaean period.[122] Thus, it is not until the latter part of the second century BCE that we can begin to talk of a specifically Samaritan tradition of Hebrew (SH), although its roots may be considerably earlier.

Before the exile the same language was spoken in Samaria as in the south of the country, albeit with certain peculiarities of dialect. Similarly, in the Persian period the language of Samaria suffered the same vicissitudes as that of Judah. The SP often displays differences, sometimes intentional, from the standard text of the Torah, and exhibits characteristics of Second Temple Hebrew (LBH). At the time the Samaritan split occurred, the Samaritans, like their contemporaries in the south, probably used Hebrew only as a literary language, employed subsequently at different periods for composing various prayers and *piyyuṭim*. The clearest representation of the Samaritan tradition is, rather, its liturgical reading of the Bible, zealously transmitted down the generations.

121 R. Macuch (1969, 132ff.) finds in this event an origin for the loss of the laryngeals in Samaritan phonology.

122 As convincingly demonstrated by J.D. Purvis (1968, 98ff.).

The history of SH as a literary language is short. Already at the start of the Common Era we find SH gradually being replaced in religious literature by Samaritan Aramaic, with the former being reserved for liturgical reading and coming under varying degrees of phonetic influence from Aramaic. In the Middle Ages, Arabic became the dominant spoken and written language and also left its mark on the liturgical reading of SH. Around the fourteenth century there was a revival of the language, evidenced by *piyyuṭim* of the period. The SH tradition of liturgical reading of the Torah has been retained up to the present day, although it is not easy to differentiate genuinely archaic elements, reflecting a pre-Masoretic Hebrew dialect (and forming an important link in the history of the language), from secondary accretions that over the centuries have attached themselves to older traditions.[123]

Sources for the study of SH include:[124]

(1) The SP, known in the West from the time that Pietro della Valle purchased and brought back the first Samaritan manuscripts at the beginning of the seventeenth century. It displays more than 6,000 variants of every kind in respect of MT; There are considerable problems in establishing the text of the SP, which has undoubtedly added to the difficulties facing linguistic analysis;[125]

(2) A number of old, partially-vocalized, manuscripts, such as British Museum MS Or. 6461 (1339/40) and Trinity College, Cambridge R. 16/41 (1482?). Some of the signs are late and we cannot always be sure of their exact value;

(3) Samaritan grammatical works written in Arabic from the tenth to eleventh centuries, published by Z. Ben-Ḥayyim;[126]

[123] See Ben-Ḥayyim 1958–62, 89ff.; 1989, 517.

[124] Following Ben-Ḥayyim 1971.

[125] The scholarly edition of A. von Gall (1918) is still the most reliable, although as yet there is no standard text of the SP. Certainly the popular version prepared by A. and R. Sadaqa (1962–66) has no such pretensions. F. Pérez Castro (1959) reproduced the text of *Sefer Avisha*, which is without doubt the oldest extant manuscript of the SP. L. Girón (1976) published a good critical edition of Genesis.

[126] 1957–77, I.

(4) First-hand information about the pronunciation of the present-day Samaritan community. The most important works in this field are the transcriptions of J.H. Petermann (1868), H. Ritter and A. Schaade, collected in 1917 and later edited by A. Murtonen,[127] further transcriptions also by Murtonen (1960), as well as those published by Z. Ben-Ḥayyim.[128] The material is rather uneven, having been transcribed according to a variety of methods and resulting from work of varying quality. In the case of Petermann, who was the first to approach the living pronunciation of Samaritan in a scientific way, the system used is confusing, especially with regard to the precise quality and length of the vowels and the position of the accent. The transcriptions of Schaade and Ritter are much more accurate, and mark accent and quantity satisfactorily. However, their material is extremely limited and tends to be overburdened with secondary or incidental features. The arbitrary mixture of correct and erroneous transcriptions in Murtonen's dictionary makes it extremely difficult to use. A general criticism of this kind of study is that what are presented as 'variants' often result from mistakes in recording, informant error, or misinterpretation by the researcher.[129]

The first attempts to describe the Samaritan language were made by members of the community itself, influenced, like Saadiah and the other Jewish grammarians, by Arab philologists. In the tenth century, Ibn Darta circulated a number of rules for the reading of Samaritan Hebrew.[130] A century later, in his *Qawānīn al-Maqra*,[131] Abū Sa'īd analysed various aspects of the verb, the suffixes, the

[127] Ritter and Schaade 1959.

[128] 1957–77, III

[129] See Ben-Ḥayyim 1971.

[130] See Ben-Ḥayyim 1957–77, I, 305ff.

[131] See Ben-Ḥayyim 1957–77, I, 129–71.

article, etc. Muryān b. As'ad did the same in his *Mulḥaq bi-Mukhtaṣar al-Tawṭi'a*.[132]

The first important attempt at the systematic description of Samaritan Hebrew is the thirteenth-century *Kitāb al-Tawṭi'a* by Abū Isḥāq b. Ibrāhīm b. Faraj b. Mārūth Shams al-Ḥukamā',[133] with fourteen sections devoted to the parts of speech in general, proper names and nouns, pronouns, the construct state, verbal nouns, the classification of the forms of the verb, the *Qal, Pi'el, Pa'el, Hif'il, Nif'al,* and *Hithpa'el,* the imperative, transitive and intransitive verbs, and the particles. Nowadays this work's interest is more historical than linguistic.[134] In the fourteenth century Eleazar b. Phineḥas b. Joseph made an abridged version under the title *Mukhtaṣar al-Tawṭi'a*.[135]

In the West, scholarly curiosity was aroused when della Valle's manuscript became known, and from the middle of the seventeenth century grammatical and linguistic studies of varying quality, and based on wholly inadequate data, began to appear.[136] A new era, in terms of quality, began only after the publication of the first-hand studies by Petermann, the first scholar to make contact with contemporary Samaritans and to present a scientific analysis of their pronunciation. Despite the limitations already mentioned, the *Versuch* and *Grammatica*[137] of Petermann marked a completely new and much more insightful approach to the study of SH. The *Grammatica* follows a traditional pattern, detailing the system of writing and all the parts of speech. It also includes an analysis of a small section of the SP, a chrestomathy, and a

132 See Ben-Ḥayyim 1957–77, I, 249–75.

133 See Ben-Ḥayyim 1957–77, I, 3–127.

134 See Macuch 1969, 235ff.

135 See Ben-Ḥayyim 1957–77, I, 173–221.

136 For example, Ravis 1648–50; Morin 1657; Beveridge 1658; Hilliger 1679; Keller 1683; 1705 (1st ed., Cize, 1682); T. Bennet 1732; Boberg 1733; 1734; Masclef 1743; J. Robertson 1758; Stöhr 1796; Gesenius 1815; Marcel 1819; Uhlemann 1837; Kirchheim 1851; Nichols 1858; Nöldeke 1862; 1868 (Nöldeke first brought to scholarly attention the existence of Samaritan grammatical works composed in Arabic); Geiger 1863; Kohn 1865; 1876.

137 Petermann 1868; 1873.

glossary. Studies that appeared in the immediately following years[138] simply rely on the information gathered by Petermann.

Paul Kahle gave new impetus to the study of SH with his own works[139] and those of his pupils – F. Diening, for example, concentrated on the pronoun and verb, basing himself on the transcriptions of Petermann and Ritter and Schaade and on four early vocalized manuscripts.[140] F. Pérez Castro edited and provided a highly competent analysis of the oldest Samaritan biblical manuscript, the *Sefer Avisha*.[141] A. Murtonen has also devoted a number of works to Samaritan Hebrew which have presented important new material, even though Murtonen's methods have met with resistance within the scholarly community.[142]

One of the most ambitious ventures in SH grammar was that of R. Macuch.[143] Using recordings obtained from personal contact with informants among the present-day Samaritan community, Macuch collected and analysed all the various features that have characterized SH throughout its history, in an attempt to explain their origins. Despite its undeniable merits, the work was not received very favourably by other specialists, who all pointed out that Macuch had not clearly enough distinguished contemporary pronunciation from traditional, nor provided criteria for determining the antiquity of the former. He was also criticized for attempting an overall statement before all the underlying issues had received adequate treatment.[144]

138 Such as those of M. Heidenheim (1884–96), J. Rosenberg (1901), and J.A. Montgomery (1907).

139 Kahle 1898; 1950.

140 Diening 1938.

141 Pérez Castro 1959.

142 See Murtonen 1960–64, characterized by R. Macuch (1969, 237f.) as virtually unreadable ('indigesta moles')!

143 1969.

144 See the reviews by G. Fohrer (1970), E. Ullendorff (1970a), D. Winton Thomas (1974), R. Degen (1971, 63ff.), and, in particular, Z. Ben-Ḥayyim (1971).

The most knowledgeable expert in the field of SH today is Prof. Ze'ev Ben-Ḥayyim, whose work started to appear in 1938. Apart from analyses of specific issues and a meticulous study of the relationship of SH with the other traditions of Hebrew, especially the language of Qumran, Ben-Ḥayyim also wrote a five-volume work, *The literary and oral tradition of Hebrew and Aramaic amongst the Samaritans*. This provides material of inestimable value for our knowledge of the Samaritan tradition, and concludes (Vol. V) with Ben-Ḥayyim's definitive grammar of SH, which is without doubt the most important contribution yet made to our understanding of SH.

It appears that the earliest Samaritan vocalization system employed only a diacritical point in order to distinguish homographs, to indicate consonantal as opposed to vocalic values, to differentiate the two phonemes represented by *waw*, /w/ and /b/, and, sometimes, to indicate the plosive and fricative allophones of /p b t d/.[145] Although we cannot be sure of the exact date, at some point in the Middle Ages, and definitely after the spread of the Tiberian system, various signs for representing the vowels started to be introduced. However, this was never carried out in a complete and systematic way but was always partial and haphazard, designed either to prevent mistakes in reading or for teaching purposes. This supralinear system of vocalization is not easy to interpret. It uses five signs for the vowels (ˈ, ˉ, and ˇ, all called *pathaḥ*, ‘ for *i*, and ^ for *u* and *o*) and another for *dagesh* (-:), as well as various other signs with different functions. How the three kinds of *pathaḥ* are distinguished from one another is not clear, and cannot be determined with certainty from the comments of the mediaeval grammarians.[146] In some later manuscripts there

145 See Ibn Darta's rules of pronunciation in Ben-Ḥayyim 1957–77, I, 305ff., as well as Ben-Ḥayyim 1954a and Morag 1972, 41ff.

146 P.E. Kahle (1950) identified ˈ as *ā*, ˉ as *a*, and ˇ as *æ*. Ben-Ḥayyim has progressively altered his views about the correct interpretation, originally (1954a) suggesting that ˉ corresponds to *'a*, ˈ to *a*, and ˇ to *e*, but arguing more recently (1971) that ˈ corresponds to *å* and ˉ to *a*.

are fewer signs, with a single point being used for two distinct vowels. The value of some of these signs is still a matter of debate. There is no special grapheme for *shewa*, which was not used in the early pronunciation of SH. Allophones are not marked either.[147]

In SH orthography, the weakening of the gutturals is prominently reflected, giving rise to confusion of the letters that originally represented them, so that they are exchanged with great ease and sometimes omitted entirely. Occasionally, *alef* and *he* are replaced as *matres lectionis* by *yod* and *waw*. The Samaritans tried to effect a thoroughgoing *scriptio plena*, although fluctuations in the phonetic system have sometimes prevented this from being carried out in a consistent way. Gutturals are sometimes inserted unnecessarily. Doubling of consonants, which affects *resh* as well, is more common than in the Tiberian tradition. It is clear, however, that a standard text needs to be established before any definitive study of Samaritan orthography can take place.[148]

The more important features of Samaritan phonetics include an indistinct pronunciation of *u* and *o*, absence of *shewa*, spirantization of some plosives, weakening and disappearance of gutturals, reduction or elision of certain vowels, and the development of auxiliary vowels. SH has been influenced by the Palestinian Arabic process of *imāla*, whereby *a* is realized as *æ*. There is also a tendency to obscure the quality of vowels.[149]

The transformations undergone by the laryngeals and pharyngeals merit special attention, since they cannot simply be equated with those which took place in other traditions of Hebrew that also experienced a weakening of these sounds. In SH, the distinctive pronunciation of all these consonants was lost, with a neutralization of /h/ and /'/ on the one hand and of /ḥ/ and /ʻ/ on the other, the tendency being to pronounce them only as א (') or ע (ʻ). They are omitted between identical vowels, as for example in

147 See Macuch 1969, 67ff.; Ben-Ḥayyim 1957–77, V, 4ff.; 1989, 517.

148 See Macuch 1969, 28ff.; Ben-Ḥayyim 1957–77, V, 7ff., 53ff., 65ff.

149 See Murtonen 1960–64, II, 322ff.; Ben-Ḥayyim 1989, 518ff.

לחם (Tib. læḥæm; SH lēm) 'bread'. Between *i* and another vowel they are pronounced as double *y*, thus מאדם (Tib. mē-'āḏām; SH miy-yådåm) 'from Adam', etc. Between *u* or *o* and another vowel they are pronounced as double *w*, as in כחי (Tib. kōḥī; SH kuwwi) 'my strength'. Between a vowel and a consonant they drop out entirely. In this situation, the non-guttural consonant is usually duplicated and the vowel lengthened, as in מחמצת (Tib. maḥmæṣæṯ; SH māmmēṣ^{e}t) 'leavened produce'. ח (ḥ), ע ('), and sometimes also א (') at the start of a word, under certain conditions are pronounced as ע ('), for example אָח (Tib. 'āḥ; SH 'ā) 'brother'. א (') and ע (') disappear after the proclitic particles -ב (b-) 'in', -ו (w-) 'and', and -ל (l-) 'to'. א (') is not pronounced at the end of a word, and at the end of a syllable it is coloured by the following vowel.[150] Macuch and Ben-Ḥayyim diverge in their interpretation of these changes. According to Macuch, they are due to foreign influence, although the language in question is not Aramaic (since, in his opinion, Aramaic developed in a quite different way) but Akkadian, that is, the language spoken by the Assyrian colonists who settled in Israel in the seventh to sixth centuries BCE. For Ben-Ḥayyim, on the other hand, the changes in SH are explicable against a background of parallel developments within Palestinian Aramaic and Samaritan Aramaic.

In contrast to the views of Paul Kahle which have already been presented (Chapter 4.2), E. Brønno rightly pointed out that the disappearance of the laryngeals in SH is not really comparable to what we see in the Greek transcriptions of the *Secunda*, but has resulted from a quite different linguistic process. In the transcriptions, the loss of these consonants derived from the inability of the Greek alphabet to represent the guttural sounds of Hebrew, and, in contrast to the situation in SH, their disappearance left no mark on accompanying vowels or consonants.[151]

150 See Macuch 1969, 132ff.; 1989, 544ff.; Ben-Ḥayyim 1971, 248ff.; 1957–77, V, 25ff.; 1989, 518f.
151 See Brønno 1968, 193ff.

The influence of Aramaic and Arabic is also felt in other changes in the consonantal system, for example, secondary phenomena in the pronunciation of labials and dentals, replacement of the voiceless palatal by its voiced counterpart, and neutralization of the phonemes /ś/ and /š/ and of final /m/ and /n/.[152] Although Ibn Darta was able to remark on the continued existence in his own time of the dual pronunciation of /b d p t/ (providing, incidentally, a further reason for doubting Kahle's theory about this issue), it is not preserved today, where we find *pe* always, and *bet* in certain conditions, pronounced as a fricative, with *gimel*, *dalet*, *kaf*, and *taw* always plosive. *Waw*, as already noted, represents two phonemes. Once again, Brønno was right to emphasize the difference between the Samaritan tradition and that represented by the Greek transcriptions.[153]

All of this serves to highlight the difficulty of reconstructing ancient Samaritan pronunciation. The theory of Paul Kahle and F. Diening that Samaritan pronunciation has changed little since its earliest stages cannot be accepted in full. Even though there is agreement in essential points between the mediaeval vocalized manuscripts and the modern reading tradition, there are also considerable differences; in addition, it has been noted that individual informants can differ markedly from one another in their reading of the text.[154] This is not to deny the possibility, of course, that contemporary Samaritan pronunciation might conserve many archaic features that could bring us significantly closer to the pre-Masoretic stage of the Hebrew language.

As a consequence of the neutralization of the laryngeals *he* and *ḥet* and of the sibilants *sin* and *shin*, the Samaritan consonantal system was reduced to twenty phonemes.[155] It does not exhibit the

[152] See Macuch 1969, 83ff.; Ben-Ḥayyim 1957–77, V, 20ff., 68; 1989, 518ff.

[153] See Brønno 1968; cf. Ben-Ḥayyim 1954, 97ff.; 1989, 518.

[154] See Macuch 1969, 83ff.; Ben-Ḥayyim 1971.

[155] See Ben-Ḥayyim 1957–77, V, 20ff. R. Macuch (1969, 97ff.) thinks that there are only eighteen consonantal phonemes, due to the disappearance of all the laryngeals and pharyngeals.

allophonic variation of *bgdkpt* found in other Hebrew traditions. Doubling of consonants, which also affects *resh*, and is often found in connexion with the disappearance of gutturals, is more widespread than in the Tiberian tradition.[156]

As noted previously, SH vocalization raises special difficulties of interpretation. There are five vowel phonemes: /å/, /a/, /e/, /i/, and /o, u/, but it is virtually impossible to ascertain their exact phonetic realization without having recourse to data from contemporary pronunciation, which is analysed very differently in the various transcription systems. According to Ben-Ḥayyim, they are realized by seven different vowels: *u, o, å, a, e, ᵉ*, and *i*, all of which, apart from ᵉ, have from two to four different lengths. Of the seven Tiberian vowels, six are also found in Samaritan Hebrew.[157]

Some of the more important differences from the Tiberian tradition in respect of vowels are frequent conservation of original *ā*,[158] shift of *ay* to *ī* (in Tiberian, *ay* > *ē*), lack of attenuation (*a* > *i*) in initial closed syllables, even though Philippi's law applies in a fairly regular way, and retention of full vowels in places where the Tiberian tradition has *shewa mobile* (where there was originally a long vowel in an open syllable or a short vowel in a closed syllable).[159] There is a shift *i* > *ē* shift in open syllables and short *u* > *ā*/*ē* in closed ones, as in קדש (Tib. qōḏæš; SH qådᵉš) 'holiness'. Other phenomena are the absence of *pathaḥ furtivum*, a preference for dissimilation rather than assimilation of vowels, contraction of sequences of similar vowels when an intervening guttural disappears, use of secondary vowels to break up consonant clusters, and of prosthetic vowels, as in שפה (Tib. śāp̄ā; SH ašfa) 'lip', pronunciation of *waw* as a consonant (*w*), where in Tiberian it

156 See Macuch 1969, 148ff.; Ben-Ḥayyim 1957–77, V, 20ff.

157 See Ben-Ḥayyim 1957–77, V, 29ff. Macuch (1969, 151ff.) distinguishes the following vowels: central (short a, æ; long ā, ǣ), front (short e, i, ö, ᵉ; long ē, ī), and back (short o, u, å; long ō, ū, å̄; ultralong â).

158 This shifts to *o* in Tiberian; see Brønno 1968, 199ff.

159 However, Ben-Ḥayyim (1957–77, V, 37ff.) has shown that the absence of *shewa* cannot be regarded as a primitive feature of SH, in view of the Samaritans' evident familiarity with the *shewa* before the modern period.

might be realized as a vowel (*u*, etc.), and retention of rising diphthongs and introduction of new diphthongs.[160] There is a general tendency to use syllables containing a long vowel, and there may be a preference for penultimate stress as in other varieties of Hebrew and in Aramaic.[161]

Noteworthy features of SH morphology are, for example, the retention of the archaic form of the first person singular pronoun, אנכי ('nky, pron. ånåki), the second person feminine singular אתי ('ty, pron. åtti), the first person plural אנחנו ('nḥnw, pron. ånånnu), the second masculine plural אתם ('tm, pron. attimma), and the third masculine plural המה (hmh, pron. imma). The demonstrative pronouns are used more often than in Tiberian.[162]

In the verb, new roots arise from metathesis and various phonetic changes. The system of verbs differs in certain ways from that of Tiberian, and is more recent. Vowel changes and the introduction of secondary vowels have created a number of new forms. The internal passive, specifically as represented by the *Hof'al* and *Pu'al*, has almost completely disappeared, being replaced by active structures or by external passives. As at Qumran and in LBH, the Qal passive is replaced by the *Nif'al*.[163] In the suffix-conjugation only the pattern *qåṭål* is employed, as, for example, in כבד (Tib. kāḇēḏ; SH kåbåd) 'he was heavy'; in the prefix-conjugation the difference between *yiqṭōl* and *yiqṭal* forms is ignored, with *yiqṭål* being the only form used. Two types of *Pi'el* are found, one with reduplication of the second radical, the other without – similar remarks apply to the *Nif'al*. Some old forms of the verb, such as the infinitive absolute, have disappeared – normally just one structure, identical with the suffix-conjugation form, *qåṭål*, is used for both absolute and construct states of the infinitive, and where distinct forms are found, their usage does not

160 See Macuch 1969, 164ff.; Ben-Ḥayyim 1957–77, V, 37ff., 56ff. Cf. Murtonen 1959.
161 See Ben-Ḥayyim 1957–77, V, 48ff.
162 See Macuch 1969, 240ff.; Ben-Ḥayyim 1957–77, V, 167ff.
163 See Ben-Ḥayyim 1957–77, V, 131ff.

correspond to that of the Tiberian tradition.[164] Aramaic influence is observable in *Ethp'el* structures.

Overall, there is a higher degree of uniformity than in Tiberian, and secondary changes mean that SH in fact represents an even greater departure from Hebrew in its early stages. Nonetheless, certain archaic elements have been preserved. These include the suffix ת- (-t, pron. -ti), in the second person singular feminine of the suffix-conjugation, and, in the prefix-conjugation, the suffixes י- (-y, pron. -i) or ין- (-yn, pron. -ᵉn) for the second person singular feminine and ון- (-wn, pron. -on) and נה- (-nh, pron. -inna) for the second and third person plural masculine and feminine, respectively. Cohortatives and shortened forms of the imperfect are avoided, as in LBH, and consecutive and copulative tenses are not formally distinguished. Phonetic developments have resulted in up to six different forms of the active participle.[165]

In the morphology of the noun, the Tiberian pattern is generally followed, although there are several instances of developments on the basis of false analogy. Due to the different position of the accent and the absence of *shewa*, SH, unlike Tiberian, retains the same vocalization in both construct and absolute forms of the masculine singular noun; elsewhere, absolute and construct states are only differentiated by their endings, not by stress. There are some examples of changes in gender and of adjectives taking the feminine plural suffix if modifying a masculine noun inflected as a feminine in the plural, and *vice-versa*. Only a few remnants of the dual persist. The masculine plural ending is ים- (-ym, pron. -ᵉm). The most frequent vocalization patterns for the segolates are represented by *må̊lᵉk* and *ʿābᵉd*. The Tiberian *ma* > *mi* shift in *maqṭāl* structures does not occur. Certain archaizing features of the biblical text, such as the adverbial suffix ם- (-m), have been

164 See Ben-Ḥayyim 1957–77, V, 152ff.; 1989, 518f.
165 See Macuch 1969, 256ff.; Ben-Ḥayyim 1957–77, V, 69ff.; 1989, 523ff.

eliminated. Some relics of the accusative ending, absent from Tiberian, can be noted.[166]

Reconstructing the syntax of SH in its early stages is no easy matter. Because of the difficulties involved in establishing rules of grammar on the basis of a corpus such as the SP, for which there is still no scientifically established definitive text, grammatical analysis has concentrated instead on the present-day Samaritan tradition. Comparison of SP with MT reveals an attempt to make the text conform to later usage, known from LBH. There are some minor syntactic differences in, for example, the use of the relative in places where it is lacking in MT and in noun number – for instance the singular is used for dual parts of the body. The article is used differently, but is not governed by any fixed rules. Different usages attach to the *he* of direction and the various derived forms of the verb, and there are also changes in the system of tenses. *Waw*-consecutive with the suffix-conjugation is avoided. The infinitive construct with proclitic particle is replaced by the prefix-conjugation, and the infinitive absolute by finite forms. There are also changes in verb government, and various Arabisms have been incorporated.[167] In the syntax of the sentence, there are few changes with respect to MT, although the conjunction is sometimes added or removed.

In the vocabulary of the SP we can also see a tendency to eliminate unknown roots, *hapax legomena,* and so on, replacing them by more familiar expressions. In some instances the changes have clearly taken place under Aramaic influence.[168]

The practical impossibility of making a detailed and scientifically valid diachronic study of SH, which would separate those elements that reflect the earliest phase of the language from additions introduced from the Middle Ages onward, poses a great difficulty in assessing the Samaritan tradition and its contribution

[166] See Macuch 1969, 376ff.; Ben-Ḥayyim 1957–77, V, 179ff.

[167] See Macuch 1969, 467ff.; Ben-Ḥayyim 1957–77, V, 245ff.

[168] See E.Y. Kutscher 1982, 110f. However, the influence of Aramaic on other aspects of SH should not be exaggerated, as Ben-Ḥayyim has shown (1957–77, V, 256ff.; 1989, 526ff.).

to our understanding of the historical development of Hebrew, and in defining its relationship to other varieties of Hebrew. At all events, it is important not to view the tradition in isolation, as a marginal dialect, but rather as having a close relationship with other forms of Hebrew, especially that of the Dead Sea Scrolls, on the one hand, and RH, on the other.[169] Many of the special features of SH to which we have drawn attention are not far removed from those of other Hebrew traditions of the period. The use of full vowels instead of Tiberian *shewa* and of penultimate stress (if correctly identified) is also found in the Dead Sea Scrolls, for example, and seems to reflect what was happening in Hebrew as a whole at the time rather than processes specific to particular dialects.[170]

169 See Ben-Ḥayyim 1958–62, 90ff., 252ff.; 1989, 522ff. In Ben-Ḥayyim's opinion, SH stands closer to RH than to BH, especially in its morphology of the verb and pronoun.
170 See Ben-Ḥayyim (1958–62, 99ff.). Ben-Ḥayyim regards the Samaritan tradition as later than that represented at Qumran.

Chapter 6

RABBINIC HEBREW

6.1 *Early studies*

For many centuries the language of rabbinic literature as a subject in its own right aroused little interest. The tendency among Jewish and Christian grammarians was to neglect Rabbinic Hebrew (RH) in favour of BH, although they were aware of differences between them.

The mediaeval Jewish philologists held widely differing attitudes to the character and importance of RH, as well as to its use in practice. It is even possible that the Karaite-Rabbanite controversy is reflected in such differences. Writers like Saadiah held RH in great esteem, utilizing it particularly in the interpretation of biblical *hapax legomena* – for Saadiah, the Bible includes only part of the vocabulary of its time, with the rest of the language being conserved in popular tradition recorded by rabbinic literature. Menaḥem b. Saruq, on the other hand, considered RH to be a completely different language from the Hebrew of the Bible, and he only rarely used it for solving linguistic problems. However, this stance was not adopted by the majority of grammarians,[1] whereas the much more positive attitude of Ibn Janaḥ, with his frequent use of comparisons from RH, was to influence other scholars who used this author's works either in the original Arabic or in translation. Nonetheless, the Jewish philologists of Spain hardly ever considered RH as worthy of study in its own right, and included it only marginally in their grammars and dictionaries.

[1] See Netzer 1983.

So far as the use of RH is concerned, even though it undeniably formed a component of Mediaeval Hebrew, purists looked askance at its employment in poetry. However, in certain types of prose, especially in law and science, RH began to be regarded as more appropriate than BH for the topics under consideration.

The most important mediaeval work on RH is without doubt the *'Arukh* of Nathan b. Yeḥiel of Rome, an extensive dictionary of the Talmud, *midrashim*, and Gaonic literature, compiled in the first half of the twelfth century.[2] The dictionaries of Tanḥum Yerushalmi (thirteenth century), dealing exclusively with the *Mishneh Torah* of Maimonides, and Elijah Levita's *Tishbi* (sixteenth century) also contain valuable material for the study of RH.[3]

However, critical study of RH did not really begin until the nineteenth century, with the first issue under consideration one of identity – what is Mishnaic Hebrew? The question was asked by, for example, S. Löwisohn in 1812,[4] and became more pressing with the appearance in 1845 of the first scientific grammar of RH, A. Geiger's *Lehr- und Lesebuch zur Sprache der Mischnah*. Taking up a widely-held view, Geiger argued that the spoken language of the rabbinic period was Aramaic and that RH was simply an artificial language which had been developed by the rabbis using components from BH and, more importantly, Aramaic, as a nationalistic reaction against the use of a foreign language. Thus, RH was commonly spoken of at this time as being nothing more than a 'Hebraized Aramaic'. Geiger's attitude was possibly influenced by his rôle as a leader of the Reform movement, with its tendency to assimilation. C. Siegfried and H.L. Strack, M. Friedmann, and G.H. Dalman adopted similar positions,[5] insisting that RH was merely 'Hebraized Aramaic'. This in turn

2 Published and revised on many occasions since the fifteenth century. The most accessible contemporary edition is A. Kohut's *Sefer he-'Arukh ha-shalem* (*'Aruch completum*) in 9 vols. (Vienna, 1878–92; reprinted New York, 1950).

3 See Téné 1971, 1362.

4 Chapter 18.

5 See Siegfried and Strack 1884, 5; M. Friedmann 1896; Dalman 1905 (1st ed., 1894), 10.

provoked a heated reaction from various conservative Jewish scholars throughout the nineteenth century. Significant dissenting voices were those of H.L. Graetz, S.D. Luzzatto, and T. Nöldeke,[6] and, from 1908, M.H. Segal,[7] who became the principal defender of an opposing thesis, which emphasized the character of RH as a living language.

Segal highlighted RH's peculiarities of vocabulary, grammar, style, and diction, claiming that it differed greatly from BH and that it had only a limited similarity to Aramaic. The fundamental question for him was whether RH represented a 'genuine and natural' language, albeit somewhat coloured or disfigured by the influence of Aramaic, or whether it was artificial and contrived, with Aramaic, a living language, being subordinated to a lifeless Hebrew. Was it a development of BH, intensified and accelerated by Aramaic, or an artificial mixture of dead Hebrew with living Aramaic, neither one thing nor the other?

To resolve this issue, Segal conducted an analysis of RH morphology and syntax, making thorough comparisons with BH and Aramaic. He concluded that in terms of grammar RH is completely independent of Aramaic and basically the same as BH. The origins of the differences from BH that do exist are to be sought in an earlier stage of the language from which new forms have developed in a spontaneous and regular way. Many of these forms bear the stamp of colloquial usage in a naturally evolving language. Some syntactic features which might appear to be Aramaic are, in fact, common to all the Canaanite dialects. Aramaic influence is, therefore, very restricted in syntax, although much more evident in vocabulary, leaving RH as a natural, living, vernacular dialect, which has evolved in a gradual and orderly way from BH.

Although Segal's analysis would not prove acceptable in every detail, his basic thesis has received general acceptance, and clearly

6 See Graetz 1844–45; Luzzatto 1846–47; Nöldeke 1899, 25.

7 1908–09; 1910; 1927, §§ 6–27; 1936, 4–17.

represents the standard position today. It has been further strengthened in recent years by direct evidence of RH provided by the Dead Sea Scrolls (the Copper Scroll and the Bar-Kochba letters) and by synagogue inscriptions.[8] This material demonstrates that the language was used in daily life in matters unrelated to rabbinic activity, and that it cannot be viewed merely as a scholarly creation.[9] Although there has still not been a thorough study of possible RH influence in the Septuagint, in the Greek of the New Testament (where it is common to speak of 'Aramaisms') and the early Christian writers, in the language of Qumran or of the Samaritan community, or in Aramaic dialects of the time, no-one today would be so rash as to address the issue in the same way as Geiger.[10]

However, as a reaction against Segal's more extreme positions, certain highly-respected scholars, including E.Y. Kutscher, have claimed that Segal understated the influence of Aramaic on RH, especially in phonology, syntax, and vocabulary.[11] Thus, Kutscher raised the possibility that RH should be viewed as a 'mixed language', a fusion of Hebrew and Aramaic.[12] In a refinement of this suggestion, J. Fellman has proposed that because RH is relatively free of Aramaic morphological influence, a more appropriate designation would be 'langue mélangée', applied in similar situations in the field of Romance languages.[13]

Among the tools for the study of RH, we should begin by mentioning the major nineteenth-century grammars, even though today their interest is mainly historical. After the appearance in 1845 of the first complete and systematic grammar, by A. Geiger,

[8] See, for example, Yadin 1961a; E.Y. Kutscher 1961–62.

[9] See Milik 1961, 70. Rabin 1958 assembles the most compelling arguments. Regarding the epigraphic evidence, see Naveh 1978; 1981; 1981a, 137.

[10] See, for example, Chomsky 1951–52; Cavalletti 1957; E.Y. Kutscher 1960; Grintz 1960; Díez Macho 1963b; Ott 1967; Fitzmyer 1970; Rabin 1970; 1976; Fellman 1977.

[11] See especially E.Y. Kutscher 1971a; 1972a.

[12] See E.Y. Kutscher 1972a, 74.

[13] See Fellman 1977, 22.

came the works of L. Dukes, J.H. Weiss, and C. Siegfried and H.L. Strack,[14] as well as a number of other important studies.[15]

The twentieth century saw the publication of K. Albrecht's grammar[16] and, most significantly, that of M.H. Segal.[17] Although it can be criticized in many respects, and despite serious flaws in its method, Segal's work is still the most complete analysis of rabbinic morphology and syntax. E. Porath wrote an important study of RH in the Babylonian tradition,[18] while the Palestinian tradition has been examined by N. Allony,[19] the Yemenite by I. Shivtiel,[20] and the Italian by M. Bar-Asher.[21] C. Albeck devoted a chapter of his introduction to the Mishnah[22] to a study of RH. A major contributor to the study of RH later in the twentieth century was E.Y. Kutscher, and his article in *Encyclopaedia Judaica* is one of the best summaries of the current state of knowledge about RH, as is an earlier work in Hebrew, which also offers a detailed account of rabbinic grammar.[23]

In addition to Nathan b. Yeḥiel's dictionary, already noted, and that of A.T. Hartmann,[24] mention must be made of J. Levy's magnificent *Wörterbuch*[25] and the smaller dictionary of M. Jastrow,[26] as well as of other less exhaustive works like that of G.H. Dalman,[27] although it has to be said that all of these have

[14] Dukes 1846; Weiss 1867; Siegfried and Strack 1884.
[15] For example, Stein 1888; Hillel 1891; Sachs 1897; Siegfried 1897.
[16] Albrecht 1913.
[17] 1927. M.H. Segal 1936 is a substantially revised Hebrew edition.
[18] Porath 1938.
[19] 1973–74.
[20] 1937–39; 1963.
[21] 1980.
[22] Albeck 1971, the Hebrew original of which appeared in 1959 (Jerusalem).
[23] See E.Y. Kutscher 1971a; 1963.
[24] 1825–26.
[25] J. Levy 1924 (1st ed., 1876).
[26] 1886–1903.
[27] 1938.

numerous limitations and deficiencies, especially in connexion with etymology and the provenance of particular words.[28]

The concordances prepared by various members of the Kosovsky family for the text of the Mishnah, the Talmuds, and the Tannaitic literature are, likewise, an indispensable tool for philological work. The Academy of the Hebrew Language has prepared a microfiche concordance of all the Tannaitic writings, which opens up the posibility of a much more exact analysis of RH as it really was.

6.2 *Origins and classification of Rabbinic Hebrew*

Now that controversy about the character of RH has faded, there is some measure of agreement regarding its origins. BH, which was always basically a literary idiom, ceased to be a living language in the period following the Babylonian exile. Even though it survived in the form of LBH, in the later books of the Bible, this was no more than an imitation of pre-exilic style. In Jerusalem and Judaea the daily language after the return from exile (538 BCE) was no longer BH but, instead, a spoken, more demotic, dialect. Whether this was an existing, possibly pre-exilic, Hebrew dialect, a late version of BH developed under the influence of Aramaic, or a type of 'new common language', as suggested by C. Rabin,[29] is much more difficult to ascertain, although recent research favours the first possibility.

For several centuries RH remained an exclusively spoken language. From the second century BCE, it was used by the Pharisees for delivering their lessons, and it was the medium in which the teachings of the rabbis were transmitted until they finally attained written form. This is when RH also became a literary language, in the first or second century CE. Some of the

28 See the harsh criticism in E.Y. Kutscher 1972, 6ff.
29 1973, 39.

Dead Sea Scrolls, like the Copper Scroll, which is difficult to date, or the Bar-Kochba letters, from around 135 CE,[30] are the oldest written examples of RH known to us. Earlier testimony from Qumran speaks of a 'blasphemous' and 'uncircumcised' tongue, which very probably refers to the language of the sect's Pharisaic adversaries, namely RH.[31]

The formation and evolution of RH should be viewed against the background of the languages spoken in Palestine in the post-exilic and intertestamental periods. In the last chapter we noted the multilingualism that was associated with Persian and Hellenistic domination of the region. The succeeding Maccabaean, Hasmonaean, and Roman administrations saw no fundamental changes in the linguistic situation, although with the Romans Latin was introduced into various aspects of public life.

In connexion with the situation at the beginning of the common era, many New Testament scholars have considered the issue in terms of the well-known question 'What language was spoken at the time of Jesus?' or 'What was the language of Jesus and the first Christians?' Looking at this from a purely linguistic perspective, it is generally agreed that the inhabitants of Palestine at the time were acquainted in varying degrees with Hebrew, Aramaic, Greek, and Latin. Differences emerge, though, regarding the geographical and chronological limits of each language, its level of penetration within those limits, and its local characteristics.

The thesis that Jesus spoke in Greek is not new and was defended as long ago as the seventeenth century by Vosius, by D. Diodati in the eighteenth century, and in the nineteenth century by Paulus, Hug, and Credner.[32] More recently, A.W. Argyle aroused controversy by arguing in effect that Jesus spoke Greek and that his audience understood it as easily as they did

30 See E.Y. Kutscher 1961–62.

31 See Rabin 1976, 1018f.

32 See Díez Macho 1963b; Fitzmyer 1970.

Aramaic.[33] Although the claim was welcomed by some, others were in forthright opposition to it.[34]

Indisputable evidence of the forceful impact of Hellenism is furnished by numerous Greek inscriptions, graffiti, and correspondence, Greek pseudepigrapha written in Palestine, second-century CE Greek translations of the Bible ('the Three'), the Greek fragments of the Dead Sea Scrolls, and the Graecisms found throughout rabbinic literature.

Studies by S. Lieberman, G. Zuntz, J.T. Milik, E.R. Goodenough, R.H. Gundry, J.N. Sevenster, and D. Sperber[35] on a wide range of Greek influence have continued the classic early work of scholars like S. Krauss,[36] and have made absolutely clear the importance and pervasiveness of Hellenistic language and culture in Palestine. It should be noted, though, that in certain places Judaism seems to have offered greater resistance to Hellenism and that urban centres were much more Hellenized than rural areas, although with the suppression of the Bar-Kochba revolt (135 CE) the process of Hellenization and Romanization was greatly intensified.

Various writers have, in similar fashion, stressed the rôle of Latin, the language of Roman administration,[37] which left its mark in a number of public inscriptions as well as in a few of the Dead Sea Scrolls. Its influence is noticeable in specific aspects of RH semantics.

No one doubts the extent to which Aramaic had spread throughout the Levant from the middle of the first millennium BCE until it was supplanted by Arabic in the seventh century CE. A more difficult question, which has led to significant scholarly

33 See Argyle 1955–56.

34 See the responses of J.K. Russel (1955–56), H.M. Draper (1955–56), and R.M. Wilson (1956–57).

35 Lieberman 1942; 1950; Goodenough 1953–65; Zuntz 1956; Milik 1957; Gundry 1964; Sevenster 1968; D. Sperber 1975, etc.

36 1898–1900.

37 See Fitzmyer 1970, 504ff.

disagreement, concerns differences among, and classification of, the various dialects of Aramaic.

The most extreme thesis is that during the exile the Jews exchanged their language for Aramaic, reserving Hebrew, already a dead language, for literature. This was Saadiah's view, and also, in various forms, that of a number of nineteenth- and twentieth-century scholars, including A. Geiger (whose attitude was discussed in the preceding section), A. Meyer, G.H. Dalman, A. Dupont-Sommer, and F. Altheim and R. Stiehl.

Meyer[38] argued that Jesus's mother tongue was Aramaic, and that most of the intertestamental writings were originally written in Aramaic and later translated. Although Dalman believed that the case for Aramaic as the spoken language of the Jews in New Testament times was already proven, he presented concisely the weightiest evidence, concluding that Jesus grew up in an Aramaic environment, and that he had to use Aramaic in order to be understood by his disciples and the people.[39]

More recently too, this claim has been made with equal forthrightness. Dupont-Sommer argued that Aramaic was the only language current among ordinary people at the time of Jesus and that it was the language spoken by Jesus and the Apostles.[40] Similarly, Altheim and Stiehl[41] argued that from the beginning of the Hellenistic era Aramaic had completely supplanted Hebrew as a spoken language.

A more sophisticated approach to the problem distinguishes Middle Aramaic (from 300 BCE) and Late Aramaic dialects. In the first group, E.Y. Kutscher placed Targum Onkelos and the Aramaic translations from the Dead Sea Scrolls as well as inscriptions from around Jerusalem and Aramaic expressions in the New Testament. The later dialects, which belong to Western Aramaic, are classified

38 1896.

39 See Dalman 1902 (originally published in German, 1898; 2nd German ed., 1930), 11f.

40 See Dupont-Sommer 1949a, 99.

41 1966.

as Galilaean, Samaritan, and Christian-Palestinian Aramaic.[42] Of these, the Galilaean dialect is of particular interest because it was used, for example, in the Aramaic sections of the Palestinian Talmud, the Palestinian targums, numerous *midrashim*, synagogue inscriptions, and various Gaonic works. However, neither the terminology nor the classification itself have received universal consent. From another perspective, it is possible to distinguish literary Aramaic, Aramaic *koinē*, and various spoken dialects.[43]

Nowadays, there are few scholars who would disagree that in Galilee and Samaria the spoken language of the time was basically Aramaic. More controversial, though, is the extent of the use of Aramaic in Judaea in this period. The discovery of Aramaic texts among the Dead Sea Scrolls, as well as earlier evidence from, for example, names of persons and places, have demonstrated conclusively that the use of Aramaic was well established, albeit not completely dominant, in Judaea.[44]

There are also some uncompromising defenders of the theory that a form of BH was still used. Thus, it is argued that at the time of Jesus the lower classes in Palestine mainly spoke Hebrew, in the form not of RH (a literary language fused from BH and popular dialects), but of vernacular dialects which had been evolving in a natural way from BH. This was the view of, for example, H. Birkeland,[45] praised by some, but severely criticized by most.[46]

Nowadays, the most extreme positions have been abandoned and it is almost unanimously agreed that RH, Aramaic, and, to some extent, Greek were spoken in this period by large sections of the population of Palestine, although there are differences in the geographical distribution of each language and its importance.

Simplifying matters, we can say that the most widely-spoken language was Galilaean Aramaic in Galilee, Samaritan Aramaic in

42 See E.Y. Kutscher 1970.

43 See, for example, Díez Macho 1963c, 50f.

44 See Lapide 1972–75.

45 1954.

46 See, for example, R. Meyer 1957b; Segert 1957.

Samaria, and Rabbinic Hebrew in Judaea, although, as we have already indicated, at certain times and places more than one language may have been used.

Controversy about the use of RH is, in practice, limited to the period preceding the destruction of the Second Temple, because thereafter it is well documented in rabbinic literature as a written language.[47]

There is general agreement that two main periods of RH can be distinguished. The first, which lasted until the close of the Tannaitic era (around 200 CE), is characterized by RH as a spoken language gradually developing into a literary medium in which the Mishnah, Tosefta, *baraitot* and Tannaitic *midrashim* would be composed. The second stage begins with the *Amoraim*, and sees RH being replaced by Aramaic as the spoken vernacular, surviving only as a literary language. Thus it continued to be used in later rabbinic writings until the tenth century in, for example, the Hebrew portions of the two Talmuds and in midrashic and haggadic literature. During both periods, it is possible to distinguish a Palestinian and a Babylonian tradition.[48]

Without doubt, the decisive incident separating these two periods is the collapse of the Bar-Kochba revolt in 135 CE, which led to the dispersal of the people of Judaea. Although it is possible that the lower-class, rural, population stayed put and continued using Hebrew, the more educated sections of society had to leave the area and settle in Galilee, where after a few generations they spoke only Aramaic, employing RH just occasionally in writing. However, there are various indications from the fourth century to indicate that Hebrew did not die out entirely as a spoken language in Judaea, although it is difficult to ascertain how widely it was used.[49]

47 See Rabin 1970, 320f.

48 See Rabin 1970, 320f.; E.Y. Kutscher 1971a, 1591; 1982, 116f., 141f.

49 Of relevance is the testimony of R. Jonathan of Bet Guvrin in Judaea, in the fourth century, and of Jerome, who made his Latin translation of the Bible in the same area, using Jewish informants. See E.Y. Kutscher 1972a, 57ff.

In the Amoraic period, therefore, RH is almost exclusively a literary language, characterized in general terms by the incorporation of new elements from BH and Aramaic.[50] As in the Tannaitic era, Babylonian texts differ substantially from Palestinian ones.[51]

In Chapter 5.1, we mentioned the language of synagogue prayers composed in the main during the last centuries BCE or in the Tannaitic period – their special characteristics and their ample use of BH mixed with RH are best studied separately.[52]

An important issue concerns the origins of RH and the components it borrowed right from the beginning. The first point is difficult to answer, given that although in certain respects RH may be viewed as deriving naturally from the latest form of BH, it also possesses many features that have not necessarily evolved from BH, and some that are actually earlier.[53]

The well-known dictum of R. Joḥanan, 'The language of the Torah by itself and the language of the sages by itself',[54] is open to various interpretations, and it may be that by the second century CE there was not yet a full awareness of the differences between the two types of Hebrew. Nowadays, though, the tendency among various distinguished Israeli linguists is to emphasize the total unity of Hebrew throughout its history, stressing that a sense of the historical identity of the language has never ceased from the rabbinic era to the present day.[55] This, however, should not be taken to imply a denial of the clear differences that exist, from a synchronic perspective, between BH and RH, nor an affirmation of a direct 'genetic' dependency of the latter on the former.

The differences from BH are clear. RH evidences a weakening in the gutturals found in all the languages of the region and it also

50 See E.Y. Kutscher 1972a, 54ff.; Sokolof 1969.

51 See Porath 1938; E.Y. Kutscher 1972a, 61ff.; Moreshet 1972; 1974; S. Abramson 1974.

52 See Rabin 1976, 1015ff.; E.Y. Kutscher 1972a, 53ff.

53 See, for example, Bar-Asher 1985, 86ff.

54 Babylonian Talmud, 'Avodah Zarah 58b.

55 As a representative example of this position, see Ben-Ḥayyim 1985.

employs final *mem* and *nun* interchangeably. Like LBH, it avoids *waw*-consecutive, the infinitive absolute expressing emphasis, and the infinitive construct with proclitic particles, for which it employs instead nouns derived from verbs. It makes substantial changes to the tense system, regularly employing participles to express the present and, in conjunction with the verb היה (hyh) 'be', frequentative action. It has its own way of expressing the passive, dispensing with internal passives. It only makes a distinction of gender in the third person singular. It uses -שֶׁ (šæ-) instead of various BH conjunctions and the BH relative אֲשֶׁר (ʼ^{a}šær) 'who, which', although, in general, RH employs more conjunctions than BH. It uses regular patterns for forming a greatly increased number of nouns derived from verbs, as well as adjectives. It prefers the particle שֶׁל (šæl) 'of' to express the genitive, and employs a distinctive vocabulary, with numerous expressions taken from Aramaic and Greek.[56]

Loanwords in RH clearly result very often from its proximity to Aramaic. However, C. Rabin rightly points out that we need to investigate which of them are due to the influence of fully-formed Aramaic on a fully-formed Hebrew, which ones could have derived from a northern parent-dialect of RH (with isoglosses shared by Aramaic), and which ones result from parallel developments in Middle Aramaic and Hebrew of the same period.[57] It is also possible that in certain instances it was RH which affected Aramaic, as we know that some Aramaic dialects have been influenced by Hebrew.

56 See Rabin 1976, 1020ff.
57 See Rabin 1970, 322f.

6.3 *New approaches to the study of Rabbinic Hebrew*

Serious difficulties are encountered in studying RH, as E.Y. Kutscher and C. Rabin pointed out some years ago.[58] The text of the Mishnah and other rabbinic writings was transmitted in a basically consonantal form, and even after vocalization had been introduced it was not felt necessary to do for these texts what the Masoretes did for the Bible. There are very few early manuscripts, and apart from some fragments the texts generally date from the first half of the second millennium CE. In more recent manuscripts, vocalization has usually been adjusted to Tiberian norms, and it was this that provided the basis of nearly all printed texts in, and grammars of, RH.

Thus, Kutscher emphasized, over the centuries the language of the Mishnah was modified, especially, consciously or unconsciously, under the influence of BH, until many of its distinctive features were almost completely lost. Most work on RH from the nineteenth century and the first half of the twentieth century was flawed because it did not take into account this process of modification, but accepted the printed editions in an uncritical fashion and treated RH as a single corpus, without distinguishing sufficiently the various phases of the language that we have previously noted.

Trying today to reconstruct early or original forms of RH is not an easy task, even for those who regard it as necessary. It is made more difficult by the scarcity of epigraphic material from the period and by the absence of closely-related dialects. The discovery from the beginning of this century of good manuscripts of rabbinic literature in general and of the Mishnah in particular, with a much more reliable vocalization, has led to a fundamental change of perspective. Scholars have emphasized the high quality of the vocalization evidenced in, for example, MS Kaufmann A 50 from

58 See E.Y. Kutscher 1964; 1971a; 1972; 1972a; Rabin 1970, 321ff.

Budapest,[59] the pointed part of Parma MS De Rossi 138, and especially the many rabbinic fragments from the Cairo Genizah. W.H. Lowe's edition of the Cambridge codex of the Mishnah[60] is regarded as a further important contribution to the study of RH.

Examination of this new material, of a much greater value than anything previously known, served to convince the experts that in the majority of manuscripts, and especially in the numerous printed editions published from 1492 onwards, characteristic features of RH had been eliminated and replaced by better-known ones from BH. Basing themselves to a greater or lesser extent on the new material, a number of scholars began to develop new ways of approaching RH. J.N. Epstein analysed the text of the Mishnah,[61] C. Albeck prepared two good introductions to rabbinic literature[62] as well as the Mosad Bialik edition of the Mishnah,[63] and Ḥ. Yalon was responsible for the vocalization of the same work and for numerous studies of RH, as well as for a 'school' dedicated to the restoration of original rabbinic forms.[64]

The person who did most to promote this type of enquiry was without doubt E.Y. Kutscher, who tried to establish criteria for judging the reliability of a rabbinic manuscript's vocalization.[65] For Kutscher, the quality of a manuscript can be measured by its orthography, so that documents which display orthographic features similar to those of good Galilaean Aramaic texts or of contemporary Hebrew and Aramaic inscriptions are considered to be more reliable, whereas a text is suspect if it shows a tendency to assimilate to BH or Babylonian Aramaic. Proper names serve as a touchstone, as inscriptions and transcriptions from the period show which linguistic forms were actually in use. Sometimes they

59 Published in facsimile by G. Beer (The Hague, 1929; repr. Jerusalem, 1968).
60 Cambridge, 1883.
61 See J.N. Epstein 1964 (1st ed., 1948).
62 Albeck 1969; 1971 (Hebrew original, Jerusalem, 1959).
63 Jerusalem, 1952.
64 However, the vocalization is still a compromise between BH-influenced pointing and the results of recent research into RH.
65 See E.Y. Kutscher 1963, 248ff.; 1964, 38ff.

can also indicate the trustworthiness of a particular vocalizer (often not identical with the person who wrote out the consonantal text), and to what extent he has normalized a rabbinic text to biblical forms.

Kutscher found the greatest signs of reliability in the text of Budapest MS Kaufmann A 50, written in Italy before 1150.[66] The text is vocalized throughout, and Kutscher showed that in its orthography, its personal and possessive pronouns, particles, nouns, and verbs, it reflects a very old tradition, uninfluenced by BH. Although Kutscher also regarded the Parma and Cambridge texts and the Genizah fragments as reliable, he based his outline of rabbinic grammar in the main on MS Kaufmann. Nowadays the notion of a 'best manuscript' does not usually find favour with textual critics, but the special nature of the rabbinic texts and the difficulties involved in determining their textual classification provide at least some justification of Kutscher's view of the correct way to study RH.

In a number of recent works, Prof. M. Bar-Asher has specified two distinct linguistic traditions within MS Kaufmann A 50, one belonging to the scribe who copied the consonantal text from earlier codices, and who is very reliable, another belonging to the vocalizer, who probably carried out his work in Italy in the eleventh or twelfth century.[67] This second tradition is also an old and very respectable one, but it contains later features, such as corrections on the basis of BH or the Babylonian Talmud and elimination of rare forms in favour of more common and better-known ones. Errors like these occur especially in certain sections for which it seems the vocalizer could not depend on an entirely reliable direct tradition.

Subsequent to Kutscher's work, there have been important studies on other representative manuscripts of the Mishnah, which also have to be taken into account. G. Haneman analysed Parma

66 See Beit-Arié 1980.
67 See Bar–Asher 1976; 1983; 1984a.

MS De Rossi 138,[68] written in southern Italy at the end of the eleventh century, and some forty per-cent of which is vocalized, and M. Bar-Asher has devoted a number of studies to Parma MS De Rossi 497, Paris MS BN h. 328-29, written in northern Italy between 1399 and 1401, and Florence MS NA 209, by the same copyist in 1402.[69] There is also an unpublished analysis of a manuscript in the Antonin collection in Leningrad (MS 262).[70] These studies have demonstrated that Kutscher's assessment has to be modified significantly, and that the study of RH needs to utilize not just one manuscript but detailed and contrastive analysis of the various traditions. In spite of this, Kutscher's main point has been thoroughly confirmed, namely that even given the differences among the manuscripts, their vocalized text comes much closer than any of the later printed editions to the living language of the Mishnah.

Although many aspects of RH and its dialects have still not been clarified, modern analyses of the language emphasize the clear differences it displays between one time and place and another. Thus, the language of the Bar-Kochba letters differs in obvious and important ways from that of the Mishnah, for example, its apparent use of a proclitic -ת (t-), probably equivalent to the object-marker אֵת (’ēṯ), or of the genitive particle שֶׁל (šæl) separated from a following noun with article: של הגואין (šæl hag-gō’īn) ‘of the heathens’.[71] Even within Palestine itself, there may have been differences of dialect. This is suggested by forms such as הימנו (hymnw, pron. hēmennū) and הימנה (hymnh, pron. hēmennā), instead of Tiberian מִמֶּנּוּ (mim-mænnū) ‘from him’ and מִמֶּנָּה (mim-mænnā) ‘from her’, which are found in the south of the country and reappear later on in the Babylonian branch of RH.[72]

68 Published in facsimile, Jerusalem, 1970. See Haneman 1974a; 1980.
69 See Bar–Asher 1971, 1–20; 1980.
70 See Netan’el 1972.
71 See E.Y. Kutscher 1961–62.
72 See Bar-Asher 1984, 213f.

As well as a number of features connected to the particular ways in which texts were transmitted, vocalized, and pronounced, mediaeval and later traditions of Hebrew have retained some important archaic features of rabbinic language.[73] Some decades ago, Ḥ. Yalon began inquiring into this, and the work has been continued by a number of his students. Thus, I. Shivtiel produced various studies on the Yemenite tradition of RH,[74] and M. Bar-Asher an analysis of the mediaeval Italian tradition of RH,[75] while S. Morag, director of the Hebrew University language traditions project, has pointed out that we need to take into account not only Babylonian and Yemenite traditions, but also those of Syria and the West.[76]

Standardly, RH is described as it appeared during the Tannaitic period, particularly in Palestine. However, the tradition is not uniform. As M. Bar-Asher has made clear,[77] those manuscripts that contain the oldest texts of the Mishnah, without the Babylonian Talmud, represent the Palestinian branch of RH, and clearly differ from Mishnaic texts incorporated within the Babylonian Talmud, which belong to the Babylonian branch. Although there are some indications that the Babylonian branch originated from the Palestinian, as they stand there are important differences – in the consonantal writing system: Palestinian פניי (pnyy), עקיבה (‘qybh), כן (kn), for Babylonian פנאי (pn’y), עקיבא (‘qyb’), כאן (k’n), etc.; in pronunciation: Palestinian משם (miš-šēm) ‘because of’, מגמר (migmār) ‘perfume’, דחיו (dᵉḥāyō) ‘he pushed him’, for Babylonian משום (mi-šum), מוגמר (mugmār), דחאו (dᵉḥā’ō); in morphology: Palestinian מלכיות (malkīyyōṯ) ‘kingdoms’ for Babylonian מלכויות (malkūyyōṯ), and even in syntax and vocabulary.

Within the Palestinian branch, Bar-Asher distinguishes a western and an eastern variety, with the former represented by the

73 See Morag 1956–57.
74 See, for example, Shivtiel 1937–39; 1963.
75 Bar-Asher 1980.
76 See Morag 1956–57, 8ff.
77 See Bar-Asher 1984, 187ff.; 1987 (especially pp. 26f.).

text of some of the earliest vocalized manuscripts, like Budapest MS Kaufmann A 50 (in its consonantal text and in its vocalization), Parma MS De Rossi 138, Cambridge MS Add. 470, 1, and Paris MS BN h. 328-29, and by the oral tradition of Italian RH. The eastern version is found in some Genizah fragments with Babylonian vocalization, and, for example, in Parma MS De Rossi 497 and Leningrad MS Antonin 262, as well as in the oral tradition of communities living for many years under Islam, in Persia, Yemen, Syria, Iraq, and North Africa (although these traditions sometimes tend toward the Babylonian branch). The differences between the two types are significant, especially in connexion with phonology and morphology, to such an extent that we can speak of two distinct traditions of pronunciation, both Palestinian in origin. For example, the western variety does not exhibit the reduplication of ר (r) seen in the east, which has סַרָּגִין (sarrāgīn) for western סָרָגִין (sārāgīn) 'weavers', and it vocalizes the relative particle -שׁ (š-) with *segol* (šæ-) instead of *shewa*, which is used in the east, as in שְׁהוּא (šᵉ-hū') 'which he'. Eastern short *u* is realized in the west as *o* (*qameṣ* or *ḥolem*), for example זוּגִּין (zuggīn) for זָגִּין (zoggīn) 'bells'. In the east, the definite article is vocalized as -הֶ (hæ-) when it precedes a word beginning with אָ ('ā). In the west, in the noun pattern *qall*, *pathaḥ* is preferred to eastern *qameṣ*, whereas the western noun pattern exemplified by גוזלן (gozlān) 'robber' is found in the east as גזלן (gazlān). Other differences include western צִפֹּרֶן (ṣippōræn) for eastern צְפֹרֶן (ṣᵉpōræn) 'claw', and western אַחְיוֹת ('aḥyōṯ) or אַחֲיוֹת ('aḥᵃyōṯ) for eastern אֲחָיוֹת ('ᵃḥāyōṯ) 'sisters'.

6.4 *Orthography, phonetics, and phononology of Rabbinic Hebrew*

In RH we see a significant increase, compared to BH, in the use of *matres lectionis*. In this respect RH continues a process already evidenced in, for example, the Dead Sea Scrolls. In particular, it employs *waw* for any *o* or *u* vowel, including *qameṣ ḥaṭuf,* as with כותב (kwtb, pron. kōṯēḇ) 'writing' or עומרים ('wmrym, pron. 'ºmārīm), 'sheaves'; similarly, *yod* is used for *i* or *e* vowels – ליכתוב (lyktwb, pron. liḵtōḇ) 'to write'. Sometimes an *a* vowel is represented by *alef,* for example שיארה (šy'rh, pron. šᵉyārā) 'caravan'.[78]

Waw and *yod* are often doubled when they have consonantal value. A final *e* may be indicated by *yod*. Sometimes we also find the combination *alef-waw,* typical of Qumran orthography. Only in Babylonia can the word-final diphthong *ay* be represented by *alef-yod,* בנאי (bn'y, pron. bānay) 'my sons', for example – in Palestinian manuscripts, as in epigraphic material from Palestine and Qumran,[79] it is written as *yod* or *yod-yod*: בניי (bnyy).

As Segal has noted,[80] our knowledge of the pronunciation of RH derives from both external and internal sources. Among the former are transcriptions of Greek and Latin words in rabbinic writings and of Hebrew words in certain Greek and Latin works, the traditions of pronunciation preserved by Jewish communities, and manuscripts with at least some vocalization. Internal evidence is drawn from examination of *matres lectionis* and consonant mutation in rabbinic writings and of explicit linguistic comments found there, as well as from comparison with BH as preserved by the Masoretic tradition. Today, given the changes that have taken place in the subject this century, it is accepted that each of these two types of evidence has to be assessed quite differently.

The phonological system of RH is difficult to describe exactly, but it does not seem to have altered very significantly from that of BH. The consonantal phonemes are essentially the same, with the exception that certain classes of consonants have undergone changes that affected most languages in the region at the close of the first millennium BCE and the beginning of the Common Era.

78 See E.Y. Kutscher 1971a, 1595.

79 See E.Y. Kutscher 1964, 39f.

80 M.H. Segal 1927, §§ 29–35.

There does not appear to be sufficient evidence to back the argument advanced by Paul Kahle and his followers that the distinction between laryngeals and pharyngeals had been completely neutralized, and that they had virtually dropped out of use in the rabbinic period.[81] If we examine the Greek transcriptions of Hebrew by Aquila, Symmachus, and Theodotion, which are contemporary with the Tannaitic period, we find that they do not entirely eliminate laryngeal and pharyngeal phonemes, although, it must be said, reproduction of these sounds by Greek consonants is rare. Compared to more ancient transcriptions, like those of the Septuagint, we can agree that the consonantal value of these phonemes had become weaker, but it is certainly not correct to speak of their virtual disappearance.

The data provided by other sources of information, such as rabbinic literature[82] and other Hebrew and Aramaic dialects of the period, point to the same basic conclusion – that there was a weakening of these two groups of consonants, spreading out from two main centres of diffusion, one in the east (the Babylonian Talmud, Mandaean), the other in the west (Samaria, Qumran, certain parts of Galilee). This process continued for some centuries, although never to the extent that we might speak of a complete neutralization of the two series. Greek influence, especially in large urban centres, doubtless played a part in the process,[83] but it should perhaps not be regarded as the only, or even the most important, factor.

Interchange and confusion of laryngeal and pharyngeal graphemes is quite common and clearly testifies to the same phenomenon.[84] Examples of confusion between *ḥet* and *kaf*, as in לִחְלוּחַ (liḥlūaḥ) for לִכְלוּךְ (liklūk) 'soiling', show beyond doubt that

81 On this issue and the different attitudes towards it, see Sáenz-Badillos 1975.

82 For example, in the Mishnah: Shabbat 8:1; 23:5; 'Eruvin 5:1, 'Avodah Zarah 1:1; in the Babylonian Talmud: Megillah 24b, Berakhot 32a, 'Eruvin 53a, b, Pesaḥim 75b, 'Avodah Zarah 2a.

83 See, for example, E.Y. Kutscher 1971a, 1595

84 See M.H. Segal 1927, §43 and 1936, 32ff., and, more recently, Sharvit 1989.

perceptions of their consonantal value had not entirely disappeared, and further evidence is provided by the reproduction of various Greek words adopted into rabbinic vocabulary, such as חֲטִיטוֹס (ḥᵃṭīṭōs), from *kataitux* 'helmet', and חֲלַף סִדְרָה (ḥᵃlāp̄ sid̠rā),[85] from *klepsudra* 'bowl'. It has even been claimed that there was a shift from *ḥet* to *'ayin*,[86] as in Galilaean Aramaic and Samaritan Hebrew, but we feel there is insufficient evidence to support this.

With regard to its treatment of the *bgdkpt* sounds, RH certainly took part in the generally prevailing process of spirantization, although our sources of information, in particular the Greek transcriptions of Aquila, Symmachus, and Theodotion, do not justify the claim that the plosive realization of these consonants had completely disappeared, as argued by Kahle and his followers.[87] On the contrary, there is abundant evidence in the transcriptions and in other dialects of the region that during this period the dual realization of these consonants (originally, non-emphatic plosives) was retained. Indeed, in RH the interchange of *bet* and *pe*, on the one hand, and of *bet* and *waw*, on the other, clearly bears witness to a dual realization. In any case, it should be recognized that spirantization was a more general phenomenon, which did not develop a clear phonemic function or alter the phonological system of RH with respect to BH.

Of the other groups of phonemes, the sibilants are especially interesting (for example, in the transcriptions of 'the Three', only two equivalents are used, *zeta* for *zayin*, and *sigma* for the rest), as are the nasals, *m* and *n*, the neutralization of which is frequently attested.

The vowel phonemes do not appear to have changed, although there are some alterations in the realization of certain vowels. Instead of *ḥireq* (*i*), a type of *e* (*segol*) was pronounced, and in place of *qibbuṣ* (*u*), a type of *o* (*qameṣ ḥaṭuf* or *ḥolem*), as indicated by the

85 See D. Sperber 1975, 168ff.
86 See E.Y. Kutscher 1971a, 1595.
87 See Sáenz-Badillos 1975.

writing of the name הֶלֵּיל (hællēl), for הִלֵּל (hillēl) 'Hillel', in MS Kaufmann, or חוֹצְפָּה (ḥoṣpā) for חֻצְפָּה (ḥuṣpā) 'impudence', etc.[88] Assimilation of vowel to nasal consonant probably accounts for forms like אוּם ('um) instead of BH אֵם ('ēm) 'mother' in certain contexts, שׁוּם (šum) instead of BH שֵׁם (šēm) 'name' in particles like מִשּׁוּם (mi-šum) and עַל שׁוּם ('al šum) 'because', at least in Babylonia,[89] and מְסֻבִּין (mesubbīn) instead of מְסִבִּין (mesibbīn) 'reclining'. Assimilation is also found in connexion with ר (r), as in קוֹרְדּוֹם (qordōm) for BH קַרְדֹּם (qardōm) 'spade'.[90] All these examples have parallels in the Greek transcriptions of the period. A rare case of vowel harmony is that of בִּיסִיד (bī-sīḏ) for בְּסִיד (be-sīḏ) 'with lime'.

Consonant assimilation and dissimilation occur in the same circumstances as in BH. There are some very significant cases of interchange among various groups of consonants.[91] Especially common is the interchange of *sin* and *samekh*, with the latter predominating in RH, for example, סֵבֶר (sēḇær) 'hope', חֶרֶס (ḥæræs) 'shard', and פרס (prs) 'split'. In contrast to the tendency of Northwest Semitic, RH increases the number of forms beginning with *waw*, for example וָלָד (wālāḏ) 'child' and וַעַד (wa'aḏ) 'meeting'. *Bet* and *waw* are sometimes used interchangeably, for example יווני (yawnæ), יבנה (yaḇnæ) 'Jabneh'.

Dissimilation of consonants is encountered in words like מַרְגָּלִית (margālīṯ) 'pearl' (Greek *margarites*), and vowel dissimilation in forms like נִימוֹס (nīmōs) 'law' (Greek *nomos*). Metathesis can be seen in, for example, מַלְגֵּז (malgēz) instead of BH מַזְלֵג (mazlēḡ) 'fork'. Word-initial laryngeals are sometimes omitted, as in כָּרֵת (kārēṯ) for BH הִכָּרֵת (hikkārēṯ) '(to) be cut'. In the same way, initial *mem* is not found in forms like חוּתָּךְ (ḥuttāḵ) for מְחֻתָּךְ (meḥuttāḵ) 'being cut up'. Within the word, certain consonants can be elided, particularly in a number of characteristic

88 See E.Y. Kutscher 1971a, 1595.

89 See M.H. Segal 1927, § 37; Bar-Asher 1987, 26.

90 See E.Y. Kutscher 1971a, 1596.

91 See M.H. Segal 1927, §§ 45–59; 1936, 35ff.

compound structures, for example אִלְמָלֵא ('ilmālē') 'if not', from אִלּוּ ('illū) 'if only', אִם ('im) 'if', and לֹא (lō') 'not', and הֲרֵינִי (hªrēnī) 'it is I', from הֲרֵי (hªrē) 'behold', and אֲנִי ('ªnī) 'I'. Word-final elision occurs in אֵי ('ē), for BH אֵין ('ēn) 'not', and יוֹסֵי (yōsē) 'Yose', for BH יוֹסֵף (yōsēp̄) 'Joseph'. Prosthetic *alef* is often found in native words, for example אֲגוּדָל ('ªgūdāl) for גּוּדָל (gūdāl) 'thumb', as well as in transcribed Greek forms, for example אַכְסַנְיָא ('ak̲sanyā) 'hostel' (Greek *xenia*).[92]

6.5 *Morphology of Rabbinic Hebrew*

The morphological system of RH has elements in common with BH alongside others that owe their presence to the influence of Aramaic, as well as forms which are clearly the result of internal developments within Hebrew, or which derive from different BH dialects.

In connexion with the personal pronouns, the form אָנֹכִי ('ānōk̲ī) 'I', which is hardly used at all in LBH, has been completely replaced by אֲנִי ('ªnī). Segal's opinion that the second person singular pronoun אַתְּ ('att), of Aramaic origin, is only used very rarely for the masculine[93] has had to be revised in the light of the use of this form by MS Kaufmann in twenty per-cent of instances,[94] despite a general tendency in the manuscripts to adjust the text to the norms of BH. In the first person plural, in contrast to the majority of dialects of the time, which use forms related to BH אֲנַחְנוּ ('ªnaḥnū), RH has אָנוּ ('ānū), probably formed by analogy with the first person singular pronoun and the suffixed form of the plural pronoun, for example קְטָלָנוּ (qᵉṭāl-ānū) 'he killed us', and certainly a reflection of an internal development within Hebrew itself.[95] With the second and third person plural pronouns,

92 See M.H. Segal 1927, §§ 61–65.

93 See M.H. Segal 1908–09, 657; 1927, § 69; 1936, 45f.

94 See E.Y. Kutscher 1964, 41.

95 The form appears just once in BH, as a *ketiv* at Jr 42:6.

הֵם/הֵן/אַתֶּם/אַתֶּן ('attæm/'attæn) 'you' (masc./fem.) and הֵם/הֵן (hēm/hēn) 'they' (masc./fem.), the neutralization of final *mem* and *nun* has led to the interchangeable use of masculine and feminine forms in contrast to BH.[96]

Among the suffixed pronouns are Aramaizing forms of the second person singular, ־ָךְ (-āk̲) in the masculine, ־ִיךְ (-īk̲) in the feminine.[97] Although it has been argued that the first of these might be an ancient form within BH, earlier even than the regular ־ךָ (–k̲ā), it is unlikely that in the context of RH it is actually an archaic element.[98] The first person singular suffix can be attached to a participle, for example חוֹשְׁשָׁנִי (ḥōšešanī) 'I apprehend'.[99] In the second and third person plural pronominal suffixes, we find the same phenomenon already noted in connexion with the independent forms of these pronouns; also evidenced in some manuscripts are forms of these suffixes in ־ים (-ym) – these have often been corrected to better known forms.[100] In the third person feminine, there is some confusion between singular and plural forms.[101]

To express possession, proclitic and independent forms of the particle שֶׁל (šæl) 'of', or, with the article, שֶׁלָּ- (šæl-lā-) have developed, providing a parallel to the biblical expression אֲשֶׁר לְ- ('ᵃšær le-) 'which (belongs) to' and similar formations in other Semitic languages.

The most typical demonstrative pronouns are זוֹ (zō) 'this' for the feminine, already found in LBH, and the new form אֵלּוּ ('ēllū) 'these' for the plural, probably the result of internal analogical development. To point out distant objects, third person pronouns are used, for example חמורך הוא (ḥᵃmōrek̲ā hū') 'that donkey of

[96] See E.Y. Kutscher 1964, 42f.

[97] As noted by Ḥ. Yalon in his introduction to C. Albeck's edition of the Mishnah (Jerusalem, 1952), pp. 15ff. Contrast M.H. Segal 1927, § 71.

[98] See Ben-Ḥayyim 1954, 63f.

[99] Mishnah, Shabbat 22:3; see Albeck 1971, 193.

[100] See E.Y. Kutscher 1971a, 1596.

[101] See Nathan 1984.

yours' (lit. 'your donkey he'), alongside the intensive forms הַלָּז (hallāz) and הַלָּה (hallā) (masc.) and הַלֵּזוּ (hallēzū) (fem.) in the singular, and הַלָּלוּ (hallālū), הָאֵילוּ (hā-'ellū) in the plural. The object-marker אֵת ('ēt) with suffix can also have demonstrative value, for example, אותו איש ('ōtō 'īš) 'that man'; when followed by the relative particle, the resulting combination, אֶת שֶׁ- ('æt šæ-), forms an indefinite pronoun, 'who(m)ever'. For the reflexive, RH prefers a semantically fossilized construction based on עֶצֶם ('æṣæm) 'bone', as in קונה את עצמו (qōnæ 'ēt 'aṣmō) 'he acquires himself (i.e. his freedom)'. A special kind of reflexive construction uses the preposition עַל ('al) 'upon', for example קיבל עליו (qibbēl 'ālāw) 'he took upon himself'.

Alongside the BH interrogative pronouns מִי (mī) 'who?' and מָה (mā) 'what?', RH also employs the interrogative particle אֵי ('ē), derived from Proto-Semitic *'ay and attested in BH – it is normally found with the demonstrative: אֵיזֶה ('ē-zæ), אֵיזוֹ ('ē-zō), אֵי אֵלּוּ ('ē 'ēllū) 'which?' (sg. masc. and fem., pl.). New to RH is כְּלוּם (kelūm) used in negative contexts as an indefinite pronoun or interrogative particle, for example לא עשה כלום (lō' āśā klūm) 'he hasn't done anything' and כלום יש עבד (kelūm yēš 'æbæd) 'is there a slave?'.

The relative is expressed by שֶׁ- (šæ-) 'who, which', also found in other Hebrew dialects, even appearing in ancient BH poetic texts like the Song of Deborah (Jg 5), and with parallels in Amorite and Akkadian. Its many and varied uses are similar to those of אֲשֶׁר ('ašær) in BH, although some new usages also develop, so that, for example, it can be employed pleonastically before לֹא (lō') 'not', as in בפניו ושלא בפניו (be-pānāw we-šæl-lō' be-pānāw) 'in his presence and (which is) not in his presence'.

Noun patterns do not differ greatly from those of BH, although certain kinds of BH formation are used much more often. Thus, the type *qeṭīlā* (based on the *Qal* conjugation), exemplified by שְׂרֵיפָה (śerīpā) 'conflagration' and by קִרְיָה (qiryā) 'reading' and בִּרְיָה (biryā) 'creature', both from roots with original final א (') or י (y), is used for *nomina actionis* and, especially, for abstract nouns like בְּדִיקָה (bedīqā) 'verification'. There are also the rarer *Qal*-based patterns *qᵉṭēlā* and *qᵉṭālā*, for example כְּנֵסָה (kᵉnēsā) 'entrance' and צְוָחָה (ṣᵉwāḥā) 'shout', new patterns, such as *qāṭēl*, which have given rise to forms like גָּזֵל (gāzēl) 'robbery', forms ending in וֹן- (-ōn), for example פִּדָּיוֹן (piddāyōn) 'redemption', and segolate patterns of an Aramaic kind, like *qᵉṭāl*, exemplified by כְּלָל (kᵉlāl) 'rule'.

Very frequent is the *Pi'el*-based pattern *qiṭṭūl*, also known from the Bible, used mainly for abstract nouns, for example, בִּטּוּל (biṭṭūl) 'annulment' and אִסּוּר ('issūr) 'prohibition'. The pattern *qaṭṭālā*, exemplified by כַּוָּנָה (kawwānā) 'intention', is borrowed from Aramaic. In nouns derived from the *Hif'il*, there is increased use of the pattern *haqṭālā*, for example הַדְלָקָה (hadlāqā) 'lighting up' and הוֹרָאָה (hōrā'ā) (Bab.) or הוֹרָיָה (hōrāyā) (Pal.) 'instruction', although the pattern *hæqṭēl* is also found in nouns like הֶקְטֵר (hæqṭēr) 'burning' – in Babylonian RH, as in BH, the pattern sometimes has the form *haqṭēl*. The passive and reflexive derived conjugations do not develop nominal structures of their own, using instead patterns, or variations on patterns, already mentioned.

A feature of RH is the use of the noun suffix ָן- (-ān) to express the agent of an action, for example גַּזְלָן (gozlān) 'robber' or רָצְחָן (roṣḥān) (Pal.), רַצְחָן (raṣḥān) (Bab.) 'murderer'. The same sense can also be expressed through the *Qal* infinitive absolute, *qāṭōl*, as, for example, in the Aramaism לָקוֹחַ (lāqōᵃḥ) 'purchaser'. Another characteristic pattern is *qᵉṭīlā* expressing the result of an action, for example חֲתִיכָה (ḥᵃṯīḵā) 'piece'.[102]

There was little Aramaic influence in the formation of nouns,[103] despite the need to compensate for the absence of BH infinitive constructs used as nouns. On the other hand, in an attempt to express new shades of meaning, there is an abundance of derivational patterns involving reduplication, affixation, and so on, as seen, for example, in the formation of diminutives.

[102] See E.Y. Kutscher 1969a, 51ff.; 1971a, 1601.
[103] Thus, M.H. Segal 1927, § 217; 1936, 66ff.

The Hebraization of loanwords, from Greek and Latin in particular, led to new morphological patterns, as with אַכְסַנְיָא ('aḵsanyā) 'hostel' (Greek *xenia*), although in general loanwords were adjusted to patterns already extant in RH, as in the case of קָרוֹן (qārōn) 'wagon' (Latin *carrus*).

There are many different reduplicative structures. Some have gemination of the third root consonant, as with דַּבְלוּל (daḇlūl) 'excrescence', עַרְבּוּבְיָא ('arbūḇᵉyā) 'confusion' (feminine form), and אַדְמוּמִית ('aḏmūmīṯ) 'redness' (suffixed form), others duplicate both second and third radicals, for example יְרַקְרַק (yᵉraqrāq) 'yellow', and yet others, derived from hollow and geminating roots, reduplicate the entire root, as with גַּלְגַּל (galgal) 'wheel', שַׁלְשֶׁלֶת (šalšælæṯ) 'chain' (feminine form), and דִּקְדּוּק (diqdūq) 'detailed analysis'.[104]

There are also many different ways of forming diminutives. They can be derived by reduplication, as in גַּנּוּנִית (gannūnīṯ) 'little garden', with suffixes like וֹן- (-ōn) and ִית- (-īṯ), as in זֵרְעוֹנִים (zērᵉ'ōnīm) 'seeds' or גְּדוּדִית (gᵉḏūḏīṯ) 'small group', through insertion of a vowel, as in סְלִילָה (sᵉlīlā) 'small basket', or by paraphrase, for example בֶּן־גָּמָל (bæn gāmāl) 'young camel' (lit. 'son of a camel').[105]

RH does not differ greatly from BH in its inflection of the noun, although the neutralization of final *mem* and *nun* means that the masculine plural is often, as in Aramaic, ִין- (-īn). Apart from its more frequent use of the archaic feminine suffix ַת- (-aṯ), as in כֹּהֶנֶת (kōhænæṯ) 'priest's wife' and אִלֶּמֶת ('illæmæṯ) 'dumb woman', RH also employs the suffixes ִית- (-īṯ) and וּת- (-ūṯ), for example אֲרָמִית ('ᵃrāmīṯ) 'Aramaic' and עַבְדוּת ('aḇḏūṯ) 'servitude'. RH developed distinctive feminine plural suffixes in ָאוֹת- (-ā'ōṯ) (Bab.) or ָיוֹת- (-āyōṯ) (Pal.), for example מַרְחֲצָאוֹת/מַרְחֲצָיוֹת (marḥᵃṣā'ōṯ/marḥᵃṣāyōṯ) 'bath-houses', and ִיּוֹת- (-īyyōṯ), as in מַלְכִּיּוֹת (malkīyyōṯ) 'kingdoms' for BH מַלְכֻיוֹת (malḵūyōṯ), for

104 See M.H. Segal 1927, §§ 244–48.
105 See M.H. Segal 1927, § 276.

nouns ending in וּת- (-ūṯ) in the singular.[106] Masculine plural forms sometimes differ from those that would be expected, or are normally found, in BH, for example, נְזִקִין (neziqīn) from נֶזֶק (nēzæq) 'damage', שְׁוָרִים (šewārīm) from שׁוֹר (šōr) ox', שְׁוָקִים (šewāqīm) from שׁוּק (šūq) 'market', צְדָדִים (ṣedāḏīm) from צַד (ṣaḏ) 'side', חֲצָאִין (ḥaṣā'īn) from חֲצִי (ḥaṣī) 'half', and שְׁלוּחִין (šelūḥīn) from שָׁלִיחַ (šālīaḥ) 'envoy'. The same is true of feminine nouns, for example אוֹתִיּוֹת ('ōṯīyyōṯ) from אוֹת ('ōṯ) 'letter (of alphabet)', בְּרִיתוֹת (berīṯōṯ) from בְּרִית (berīṯ) 'covenant' (without plural in BH), and אִמָּהוֹת ('immāhōṯ) from אֵם ('ēm) 'mother'.

Some masculine nouns take the feminine plural suffix וֹת- (-ōṯ), for example חִנּוֹת (ḥinnōṯ) from חֵן (ḥēn) 'favour', כְּלָלוֹת (kelālōṯ) from כְּלָל (kelāl) 'rule', תִּינוֹקוֹת (tīnōqōṯ) from תִּינוֹק (tīnōq) 'baby', חֲיָלוֹת (ḥayālōṯ) from חַיִל (ḥayil) 'army', עֲיָרוֹת ('ayārōṯ) from עִיר ('īr) 'city', and מֵימוֹת (mēmōṯ) from מַיִם (mayim) 'water'. Similarly, there are some feminine nouns which take the masculine plural suffix ים- (-īm) – יוֹנִים (yōnīm) from יוֹנָה (yōnā) 'dove', נְמָלִים (nemālīm) from נְמָלָה (nemālā) 'ant', and בֵּיצִים (bēṣīm) from בֵּיצָה (bēṣā) 'egg', for example. Occasionally, both types of plural are evidenced, as with יָמִים/יָמוֹת (yāmīm/yāmōṯ) from יוֹם (yōm) 'day' or שָׁנִים/שָׁנוֹת (šānīm/šānōṯ) from שָׁנָה (šānā) 'year', with each form having a slightly different shade of meaning and the 'feminine' variant only used with suffixes. In RH we sometimes find plurals of nouns only attested in the singular in BH, for example אֲבָרִים ('aḇārīm) from אֵבֶר ('ēḇær) 'limb', דְּשָׁאִין (dešā'īn) from דֶּשֶׁא (dæšæ') 'grass', and תְּמִידִים (temīḏīm) from תָּמִיד (tāmīḏ) 'daily sacrifice'. Likewise, there are singular forms of nouns only attested in the plural in BH, for example אַלְמוּג ('almūg) 'coral-wood', בֵּיצָה (bēṣā) 'egg', and בָּצָל (bāṣāl) 'onion'.[107] The dual is used more than in BH, with existing forms retained and new ones created, for example מַסְפָּרַיִם (maspārayim) 'scissors' and בֵּינְתַיִם (bēntayim) 'meanwhile'.

106 See E.Y. Kutscher 1982, 129.
107 See M.H. Segal 1927, §§ 281–91.

Of the BH derived conjugations, the *Pu'al* has almost completely disappeared, except in the participle. In the suffix-conjugation the *Hithpa'el* has been replaced by a new paradigm, the *Nithpa'al*, expressing a reflexive-passive sense. Some scholars have argued for the existence of a *Nuf'al* alongside the *Nif'al*, and this is well attested in good RH manuscripts, for example נוּגְאֲלוּ (nuḡ'ᵃlū) 'they were redeemed' and נוּצַּר (nuṣṣār) 'formed'.[108] In verbs with first radical *waw* or *yod*, an *Ettap'al* conjugation is sometimes used, under the influence of Aramaic. The *Shaf'el*, the provenance of which is a matter of debate, is sometimes used as a causative alongside the *Hif'il*. In verbs having *nun* as first radical, there are traces of a possible *Qal* passive (not necessarily archaic), as in נֻטַּל (nuṭṭal) 'it was taken'.[109] The number of quadriliteral paradigms has been increased through reduplication or affixation (*Pi'lel, Pilpel, Pir'el*, etc.). However, other paradigms that had not been greatly used in BH, such as *Po'el* and *Po'lel*, disappear completely in RH, with hollow verbs able to develop regular *Pi'el* forms, for example, כִּוֵּן (kiwwēn) for BH כּוֹנֵן (kōnēn) 'he confirmed' and נִתְכַּוֵּן (niṯkawwan) for BH הִתְכּוֹנֵן (hiṯkōnēn) 'it was confirmed'. This continues a trend already encountered in LBH, for example קִיֵּם (qīyyam) 'he established' (Est 9:31) for קוֹמֵם (qōmēm).

There are some minor changes in the semantic values of the derived conjugations. *Qal* continues to express simple action, and is sometimes used as a denominative, for example פרה חולבת (pārā ḥōlæḇæṯ) 'milch cow'. In intransitive verbs, the RH *Qal* no longer signifies a state (being old, fat, etc.) but only the process by which such a state is achieved. As in BH, the *Nif'al* can make a verb reflexive or reciprocative, or, most commonly, passive. It is also used as an inchoative. The *Pi'el* is used as an intensive in connexion with repeated actions or actions performed on many objects or by many subjects – it can also function as a denominative, causative, inchoative, and so on, sometimes

108 See Yalon 1963–64, 152ff.; Moreshet 1980a.

109 The significance of this form is questionable – see Kutscher 1982, 127 and the associated bibliography.

displacing the simple *Qal* form. The *Hif'il*, as in BH, can be causative, denominative, or inchoative, sharing the first of these functions with the *Shaf'el*, although it is also used as an equivalent of the *Qal*.[110] Its passive is the *Hof'al*. The *Hithpa'el* and *Nithpa'al* paradigms are used for reflexive, inchoative, reciprocal, and, occasionally, passive relationships (the last of which is only rarely thus expressed in BH), but they have lost the denominative function that is possibly attested in BH, expressing instead the result of verbal action.

In the suffix-conjugation, there is a tendency to treat masculine and feminine forms alike through the neutralization of final *mem* and *nun*. The feminine forms of the prefix-conjugation disappear (continuing a trend already started in BH), as do forms ending with *nun*, for example תִּשְׁמְרוּן (tišmerūn) 'you will keep'. As at Qumran, pausal forms, especially those of the *Hof'al*, are often used in non-pausal environments, for example, הֻקְדָּשׁוּ (huqdāšū) for הֻקְדְּשׁוּ (huqdešū) 'they were dedicated'. Feminine participles usually take the termination ־ֶת (-æt̲), for example כּוֹתֶבֶת (kōt̲æb̲æt̲) 'writing', although this is not true for hollow verbs and verbs with final radical *alef* or *yod*. Masculine plurals end with ־ִין (-īn). In the imperative, feminine plural forms are replaced by their masculine equivalents. The participle can be negated through לֹא (lō') 'not', and the infinitive through שֶׁלֹּא לְ- (šæl-lō' le-) 'so as not to'.

In the regular verb, the suffix-conjugation of *Qal* retains only the patterns *qāṭal* and *qāṭēl*, although all three BH patterns of *Qal* participle are found. In the prefix-conjugation, there is a tendency for verbs with second vowel in *a* to be replaced by forms with *o* (which extends even to verbs with a pharyngeal as third radical), for example יִשְׁחוֹט (yišḥōṭ) for BH יִשְׁחַט (yišḥaṭ) 'he will slaughter'. The only surviving form of the *Pu'al*, the participle, sometimes drops its preformative ־ְמ (me-), yielding, for example, חוּתָּךְ (ḥuttāk̲) for BH מְחֻתָּךְ (meḥuttāk̲) 'being cut up'. Assimilation of ־ת־ (-t̲-) in the *Hithpa'el* and *Nithpa'al* is more common than in

[110] See Moreshet 1976.

BH: e.g. מְקַדְּשִׁין (miqqaddᵉšīn) for BH מִתְקַדְּשִׁים (mit̲qaddᵉšīm) 'sanctifying themselves'. The *Hif'il* sometimes takes a preformative א (') instead of ה (h), and elision of the -ה- (-h-) of the infinitive can also occur, as in לַרְבּוֹת (larbōt̲) for BH לְהַרְבּוֹת (lᵉ-harbōt̲) 'to increase', a common phenomenon in the *Nif'al* – לִיבָּטֵל (libbāṭēl) for BH לְהִבָּטֵל (lᵉ-hib-bāṭēl) 'to cease'. In the *Hof'al*, the vowel of the preformative is normally *u* (for BH *o*).

Of the irregular verbs, those with third radical *alef* are treated like those with final *yod*, as in Aramaic, for example קָרִיתִי (qārīt̲ī) for BH קָרָאתִי (qārāt̲ī) 'I called' – these verbs usually have ־ָת (-āt̲) as the third person singular feminine marker, for example הָיָת (hāyāt̲) 'she was', regarded as archaic or dialectal in BH (although its real nature and provenance is a matter of debate),[111] instead of the normal BH form הָיְתָה (hāyᵉt̲ā). The *Qal* masculine participle can be of the same pattern as קֹנֶה (qōnæ) 'buying' or זָכֶה (zāk̲æ) 'obtaining privilege', while in the *Nif'al* the feminine participle can be of the type נִכְוַת (nik̲wat̲) 'being burned' or נִטְמֵת (niṭmēt̲) 'becoming unclean'.

In verbs with first radical *yod* or *nun*, the infinitive is based on the pattern of the prefix-conjugation: e.g. לֵירֵד (lērēd̲) for BH רֶדֶת (rædæt̲) '(to) go down', לִתֵּן (littēn) for BH תֵּת (tēt̲) '(to) give', לֵידַע (lēd̲a') for BH דַּעַת (da'at̲) '(to) know'. Some of these verbs have developed secondary roots, for example ועד (w'd) for BH יעד (y'd), giving rise to the *Pi'el* form וִעֵד (wi'ēd̲) 'he designated' and ותר (wtr) for BH יתר (ytr) 'be plentiful'. Examples of *Qal* infinitives of verbs with initial radical *alef* are לוֹמַר (lōmar) for BH לֵאמֹר (lēmōr) 'to say' and לוֹכַל (lōk̲al) for BH לֶאֱכֹל (læ'ᵆk̲ōl) 'to eat'.

Verbs with second radical *yod* take *waw* instead, for example דון (dwn) for BH דין (dyn) 'judge', which in the *Nif'al* suffix-conjugation has the form נָדוֹן (nād̲ōn) (as BH) or נִדּוֹן (niddōn) 'he was judged', with the latter also used for the participle. In the *Pi'el*,

[111] E.Y. Kutscher (1982, 128) suggested that it could have survived, for phonological reasons, as a dialect form, passing into RH from the dialect. This is very different from the view of J. Blau (1983a), who considers such forms to be not archaic but pausal.

Pu'al, and *Hithpa'el* derived conjugations, the BH patterns are replaced by structures similar to those used by the regular verb. In geminate verbs, the *Qal* suffix-conjugation and participle is formed on the analogy of regular verbs, for example, גֹּשֶׁשֶׁת (gōšæšæṯ) 'touching'. This is true as well in the *Nif'al, Pi'el, Pu'al,* and *Hithpa'el*, but in the *Hif'il* geminate verbs retain a biliteral structure.

In the system of tenses we again observe major changes, already noticed in LBH. Lengthened (cohortative) and shortened (jussive) forms of the prefix-conjugation are no longer used. *Waw*-consecutive forms and the infinitive absolute have also fallen into disuse. The infinitive construct is usually prefixed by the particle -לְ (le-) 'to' or, in appropriate syntactic environments, -מִלְ (mil-le-) lit. 'from to', but it does not take the prepositions כְּ (ke-) 'as, when' or בְּ (be-) 'in, when', as in BH, this type of construction being replaced by finite forms of the verb preceded by the relative particle.

With regard to the resulting system, scholarly opinion has undergone significant change since the appearance of the first nineteenth-century grammars, which spoke only of 'tenses'. As Kutscher and his school have claimed, in RH there are two forms of the verb which have as their primary function the expression of time, namely the suffix-conjugation, used for the past, and the active participle, used for the present and the future. On the other hand, the prefix-conjugation tends to have a more modal function, expressing, for example, desires, intentions, and commands (which can be conveyed in association with either the imperative or the relative particle -שֶׁ [šæ-] followed by a subjunctive). The active participle is also found in periphrastic constructions with the verb היה (hyh) 'be' to express actions that are repeated, habitual, or concurrent (a rare usage in LBH); it can be used as well to indicate such nuances as necessity or obligation, or to express axiomatic truths. The passive participle is sometimes employed as a 'present perfect', and on occasions it can also replace the active participle, for example, מקובל אני (mequbbāl 'anī) 'I have (lit. 'am') received'.[112] Other periphrastic constructions, like the infinitive preceded by -עָתִיד לְ ('ātīd le-) '(he is) ready to', -צָרִיךְ לְ (ṣārīḵ le-) '(he is) needing to', and -סֹפוֹ לְ (sōpō le-) 'his end is to', can be used to express the future. The imperative has been retained in its traditional function.[113]

However, in his 1983 doctoral thesis, M. Mishor adopted a significantly different approach to the RH verb, arriving at the following conclusions: the suffix-conjugation, more than any other form of the verb, functions as a narrative tense, even though it can be used in other ways as well. For example, it can describe a state of being (the rôle it originally fulfilled), express logical relations, indicate, like the participle, a performative sense in legal texts, or formulate a hypothetical or metaphorical condition. The prefix-conjugation expresses a subjective or distant perspective removed from reality, and is employed in wishes, requests, rhetorical questions, and expressions of emotional states, as well as, occasionally, to present an action in an abstract, atemporal, way. The imperative is used for orders and requests, but not for wishes.

The function of the participle is to express acts in a concrete, descriptive, way. The active participle tends to be used in connexion with the present and future tenses, whereas the passive participle is used for the past. In statements of a didactic or halakhic nature, as well as in the expression of actions for which time is irrelevant, the participle is the form most commonly used. It is also employed to express states of being (especially in the past), and continuity or repetition of actions, either on its own or in combination with various parts of the verb היה (hyh) 'be', in collocation with which the participle functions (as does the infinitive preceded by -לְ (le-) 'to, for') like a noun. The infinitive is, in reality, an abstract noun, which in its verbal applications expresses finality or intended goal, or serves as a modal complement.

112 See J. Blau 1953.

113 See E.Y. Kutscher 1971a, 1600f.; in a more recent work by one of Kutscher's students, S. Sharvit (1980), verbal aspect in RH is also examined.

Certain nominal expressions are employed as auxiliaries: עָתִיד ('āṯīḏ) '(he is) ready (to)' and סֹפוֹ (sōpō) 'his end (is to)' express the future, דַּרְכּוֹ (darkō) 'his custom (is to)', וְהֹלֵךְ (we-hōlēḵ) 'and (he is) going', וּבָא (ū-ḇā) 'and (he is) coming', and וְעֹמֵד (we-'ōmēḏ) 'and (he is) standing', before or after a participle, all express continuous action, and -הֹלֵךְ וְ (hōlēḵ we-) '(he is) going and' indicates a progressive change in a state or quality signified by a following participle.

In respect of vocabulary, there are significant differences from BH if we accept Segal's figures. According to him, of the 1,350 verbs in BH, 250 are not used in RH, which has, however, incorporated 300 new verbs and has assigned new meanings to many others.[114] Verbs from ancient poetic texts, as well as roots that BH uses only rarely, are not found in RH, but neither are some very common BH verbs, like איב ('yb) 'be an enemy' (especially as a participle: 'enemy'), בגד (bgd) 'betray', and גור (gwr) 'reside temporarily', or certain denominative verbs like לחם (lḥm) 'eat' and גבל (gbl) 'border'. In place of these, RH occasionally uses cognate roots, or, commonly, unrelated verbs, for example רצה (rṣh) instead of אבה ('bh) 'like' and למד (lmd) instead of אלף ('lp) 'learn'. New verbs in RH are sometimes of archaic or dialectal origin or are based on biblical forms, as in the case of certain denominatives. Many of the words shared by BH and RH have different relative frequencies, and have very often undergone changes in meaning.

6.6 *Grammar and vocabulary of Rabbinic Hebrew*

Although we now possess a number of detailed studies on specific topics, Segal's work, with its comprehensive analysis of RH

114 Scc M.H. Segal 1927, §§ 83–102; 1936, 104ff.

syntax,[115] still supplies most of our information on this subject, despite the known limitations of his sources.

Personal pronouns are generally used less than in BH, and when they are they normally have emphatic value, for example אַף הוא עשה ('ap̄ hū' 'āśā) 'he was the one who did it' (lit. 'indeed he did'). The possessive pronoun שֶׁל (šæl) 'which (belongs) to, of' is often associated with a proleptic use of the pronominal suffix, as in שורו של בעל הבית (šōr-ō šæl ba'al hab-bayit̲) 'the ox (lit. 'his ox') of the master of the house'. A similar phenomenon is seen in structures like אין מלוין לו לאדם ('ēn malwīn lō lā-'ād̲ām) 'they do not accompany man' (lit. 'they do not join to him – to man').

The demonstrative adjective follows the noun, with the article, as in BH, for example בעולם הזה (bā-'ōlām haz-zæ) 'in this world', or without it, as in ככר זו (kikkār zō) 'this loaf'. As a pronoun it precedes its complement, for example, זו מידה (zō middā) 'this is a characteristic'. The particle אֵת ('ēt̲) may also be used as a demonstrative: אותו היום ואותו האיש ('ōt̲ō hay-yōm we-'ōt̲ō hā-'īš) 'that day and that man'. אֵיזֶהוּ ('ēzæhū) 'who?, which?' is used as an interrogative alongside מָה (mā) 'what?', as in איזהו חכם ('ēzæhū ḥāk̲ām) 'who is wise?' and מה קול שמעת (mā qōl šāma'tā) 'what voice did you hear?'.

The most common way of expressing the reflexive is through עֶצֶם ('æṣæm) 'oneself' (lit. 'bone'), as in גורם רעה על עצמו (gōrēm rā'ā 'al 'aṣmō) 'causing harm to himself'. There are many ways of expressing an indefinite subject, particularly in the language of halakhic case-law, for example שואל אדם (šō'ēl 'ād̲ām) 'if someone asks' (lit. 'a person asking'), כל השכיח (kol haš-šōk̲ēaḥ) 'whoever forgets', and מי שאכל ושכח (mī šæ-'āk̲al we-šāk̲aḥ) 'whoever ate and forgot'.[116]

Rules of gender are broadly similar to those of BH, although there are some new feminine formations, generally in late texts, for example זְאֵבָה (ze'ēb̲ā) and כַּלְבָּה (kalbā) for a female wolf and dog

[115] See M.H. Segal 1927, §§ 306–517; 1936, 173ff.
[116] See M.H. Segal 1927, §§ 404–39.

respectively. Occasionally the same word is found in masculine and feminine variants, each associated with a different meaning – גַּן (gan) 'garden' and גִּנָּה (ginnā) 'vegetable garden' or חוֹב (ḥōḇ) 'debt' and חוֹבָה (ḥōḇā) 'offence', for example.

RH does not differ greatly from BH in its use of the article, although omission is more frequent, as with שַׁעַר הָעֶלְיוֹן (ša'ar hā-'ælyōn) for הַשַּׁעַר הָעֶלְיוֹן (haš-ša'ar hā-'ælyōn) 'the Upper Gate' or הַמַּעֲרָכָה גְדוֹלָה (ham-ma'ᵃrāḵā ḡᵉḏōlā) for הַמַּעֲרָכָה הַגְּדוֹלָה (ham-ma'ᵃrāḵā hag-gᵉḏōlā) 'the great pile'. Genitives are most commonly expressed through the construct chain, as in BH, although there is greater flexibility in RH. For example, constructions like בָּתֵּי הַבַּדִּים (bāttē hab-baddīm) 'olive-presses', with *rectum* in plural, for BH בָּתֵּי הַבַּד (bāttē hab-baḏ), with *rectum* in singular, and בֵּית הַגִּתּוֹת (bēṯ hag-gittōṯ) 'wine-presses', with *regens* in singular, *rectum* in plural, for BH בָּתֵּי הַגַּת (bāttē hag-gaṯ), with *regens* in plural, *rectum* in singular, exist alongside normal BH patterns of the type חוּטֵי צֶמֶר (ḥūṭē ṣæmær) 'threads of wool'. In preference to this kind of structure, RH will sometime use forms like הַבַּיִת שֶׁלַּמֶּלֶךְ (hab-bayiṯ šæl-lam-mælæḵ) 'the palace' (lit. 'the house which is to the king') or בֵּיתוֹ שֶׁלַּמֶּלֶךְ (bēṯō šæl-lam-mælæḵ) (lit. 'his house which is to the king'). Other features include the use of יֶתֶר עַל כֵּן (yæṯær 'al kēn) 'more than that' or יוֹתֵר (yōṯēr) 'more' in the comparative, and of -שֶׁ (šæ-) 'who, which' in the superlative, as in היפה שבהן (hay-yāp̄ā šæb-bā-hæn) 'the most beautiful of all' (lit. 'the beautiful one which is among them').[117]

In addition to its characteristic use of tenses, noted in the preceding section, RH also employs a number of auxiliary verbs: דחק (dḥq) 'press', חזר (ḥzr) 'go back', מהר (mhr) pi. 'hasten', שכם (škm) hi. 'do early', שנה (šnh) 'repeat', שקד (šqd) 'be diligent', בוא (bw') 'come', הלך (hlk) 'go', ירד (yrd) 'go down', עלה ('lh) 'go up', יצא (yṣ') 'go out,' etc.[118]

[117] See M.H. Segal 1927, §§ 366–93.
[118] See M.H. Segal 1927, §§ 364–65.

RH syntax contains various traces of the spoken language in, for instance, the use in vows of the asseverative particle קוֹנָם (qōnām), for example קונם אם לא נמניתי (qōnām 'im lō' nimnēṯī) 'truly, if I had not been numbered' (i.e. 'I swear that I was numbered'), or in the occasional use of prayerlike, wishful, statements of the type יהי רצון ש- (yehī rāṣōn šæ-) 'God would that' (lit. 'may it be (God's) will that'). Other characteristic RH devices include disjunctive sentences with פְּעָמִים (pe'āmīm) 'sometimes', as in פעמים שהוא איש פעמים שהוא אשה (pe'āmīm šæ-hū' 'īš pe'āmīm šæ-hū' 'iššā) 'sometimes it is a man, sometimes a woman', antithetic statements with אֶלָּא ('ællā') 'but', as in לא כי אלא בסלע לקה (lō' kē 'ællā' ḇe-sæla' lāqā) 'not so, but he struck against a stone', and interrogatives with שֶׁמָּא (šæmmā') 'perhaps', or with כְּלוּם (kelūm) 'anything, anyone' when a negative response is expected. Relative clauses are more widespread than in BH, often replacing the infinitive construct with particle, as in כְּשֶׁאָמַר (ke-šæ-'āmar) 'when he said' for BH בְּאָמְרוֹ (be-'omrō) (lit. 'in his saying').

Adverbial or circumstantial clauses are typically construed with a wide range of particles. Frequently these are new formations, fossilized nouns, or compound structures with the relative -שֶׁ (šæ-), expressing, for example, cause, as in בשביל שאני זכר הפסדתי (bišḇīl šæ-'anī zāḵār hip̄sadṯī) 'because I am a male, have I lost?', or concession, as in אף כשאמרו ('ap̄ ke-šæ-'āmerū) 'even though they were to say'. Comparison is often expressed by כַּיּוֹצֵא בוֹ (kay-yōṣē' bō) 'likewise' (lit. 'like that which goes out with it'). Final clauses may be construed with, for example, עַל מְנָת ('al menāṯ) 'on condition that, for the sake of', as in שלא על מנת לקבל פרס (šæl-lō' 'al menāṯ le-qabbēl perās) 'which is not for the sake of receiving a reward', or שֶׁמָּא (šæmmā') 'lest', as in שמא יקלקלו (šæmmā' yeqalqelū) 'lest they become corrupt'. Temporal clauses use a large number of particles nearly always compounded with the relative -שֶׁ (šæ-), for example -מִשֶּׁ (miš-šæ-) 'after' (lit. 'from [the time] that'), -כָּל־זְמַן שֶׁ (kol-zeman šæ-) 'while' (lit. 'all the time that'), and -עַד שֶׁ ('aḏ šæ-) 'until'. Although conditional clauses are generally similar to those of BH, RH also uses וְאִם לָאו (wᵉ-'im lāw) 'and if not' to introduce a negative alternative and אִלְמָלֵא ('ilmālē'), אִלְמָלֵא לֹא ('ilmālē' lō'), or אִלּוּלֵי ('illūlē) 'if (only)' to introduce a hypothetical condition.[119]

RH vocabulary has been studied in particular by E.Y. Kutscher, who provided the real impetus for this kind of analysis and was working towards the production of a new dictionary of rabbinic literature, as yet incomplete.[120] Kutscher's analysis indicates that roughly half the vocabulary of RH is shared by BH. The remainder is made up of BH material which has undergone various changes of a morphological or semantic nature, of Hebrew words from outside the Bible, and of loans from other languages, especially Aramaic, Akkadian, Persian, Greek, and Latin.[121]

Among elements common to RH and BH are the more resilient expressions of the Semitic languages, such as numerals, names of parts of the body, kinship terms, and nouns expressing time, dress, food, and basic human actions. But there are some notable changes even in these areas: for example, חֹטֶם (ḥōṭæm) 'nose' for BH אַף ('ap̄), אַבָּא ('abbā) 'father' for BH אָב ('āḇ), אִמָּא ('immā) 'mother' for BH אֵם ('ēm), שַׁחֲרִית (šaḥᵃrīṯ) 'morning' for BH בֹּקֶר (bōqær), עַרְבִית ('arḇīṯ) 'evening' for BH עֶרֶב ('æræḇ), שָׁעָה (šā'ā) 'hour', כנס (kns) ni. 'enter', צָרִיךְ (ṣārīḵ) '(it is) necessary', and לָקוֹחַ (lāqōᵃḥ)

[119] See M.H. Segal 1927, §§ 440–517.

[120] The intention was that this dictionary would incorporate the most important results of modern scholarship, drawing on the work undertaken by such figures as Ḥ. Yalon, J.N. Epstein, I. Löw, G.H. Dalman, and S. Lieberman, which has led to a significantly different appreciation of the rabbinic material from that evidenced by earlier lexica. See Volumes I and II of the *Archive of the new dictionary of rabbinical literature*, produced at Bar-Ilan University. Volume I (1972) was edited by E.Y. Kutscher, although it only appeared after his death, and Volume II (1974), by M.Z. Kaddari.

[121] See E.Y. Kutscher 1971a, 1603ff. Albeck 1971, 199ff. is a listing of all the words in the Mishnah that do not appear in the Bible or are used there in a different sense, classified as 'new words, words from the Bible, or foreign words'. But this compilation dates from 1920, as the writer makes clear. In connexion with the verbs, there appeared in 1980, a little after the death of its author, an important study by M. Moreshet, *A lexicon of the new verbs in Tannaitic Hebrew*, which showed that 241 of these items are based on BH, 210 are taken from Aramaic, 23 from Akkadian, 4 from Persian, 30 from Greek and Latin, and another 96 from various other sources.

'purchaser', are all typical RH words. In certain areas such as dress, business, and craft, there is very little similarity between RH and BH, whereas in others, farming for example, the vocabulary is practically identical.[122]

Although there are only a few vestiges of Archaic Hebrew vocabulary in RH, there are numerous instances of vocabulary shared by RH and LBH, probably because of the influence of vernacular Hebrew on the last manifestations of the biblical language. Because of the incomplete nature of BH as it has come to us, it is not surprising that RH is familiar with words which are very likely of Hebrew origin but are simply not found in our corpus of BH, for example חזר (ḥzr) 'go back', מסק (msq) 'gather olives', and שְׂרָף (śᵉrāp̄) 'resin'.

Some BH words have undergone changes of meaning in RH, for example עוֹלָם ('ōlām) 'world' (BH: 'eternity'), מַעֲשֶׂה (ma'ᵃśæ) 'event' (BH: 'action'), נהג (nhg) 'behave' (BH: 'lead'), and גזר (gzr) 'decide' (BH: 'cut'). Elsewhere there are changes of form, with, for example, BH מַשְׂאֵת (maś'ēṯ) 'smoke signal' converting to מַשּׂוּאָה (maśśū'ā) in RH. Certain plural forms in RH, such as שְׁמִטִּים (šᵉmiṭṭīm) 'sabbatical years' or פֵּרוֹת (pērōṯ) 'fruits', are found as collective singulars in BH, while some nouns which only occur in the plural in BH are met in RH as singulars also, for example בָּטְנָה (boṭnā) 'pistachio'. In the rabbinic literature there are also various innovations based on BH roots, much debated by the mediaeval grammarians. For example, we find 'raise' expressed not by the *Hif'il* (causative) form of the verb רום (rwm) 'be high', but instead by a new verb, תרם (trm), a back-formation from תְּרוּמָה (tᵉrūmā) 'wave offering', itself derived from רום (rwm). There are also some characteristic nouns derived from verbs, for example, וַעַד (wa'aḏ) 'meeting-place' and וִדּוּי (widdūy) 'confession', with initial *waw*, for *yod* in BH.

The largest number of loanwords consists of those borrowed directly or indirectly from Aramaic. These include many verbs, such as ארע ('r') 'occur', מחה (mḥh) pi. 'protest', and חטא (ḥṭ') htp. 'ingratiate', as well as nouns like כְּלָל (kᵉlāl) 'rule', שָׁעָה (šā'ā)

122 See E.Y. Kutscher 1961, 73ff.

'hour', and אֶמְצַע ('æmṣa') 'middle' (which entered Hebrew from Greek *via* Aramaic). Loan-translations are also common, for example אחז ('ḥz) meaning 'shut', like Aramaic אחד ('ḥd). כּוֹס (kōs) 'cup' is treated as masculine and שָׂדֶה (śāḏæ) 'field' as masculine or feminine, as in Aramaic.[123]

Akkadian loanwords often came to RH by way of Aramaic. Sometimes they are of Sumerian origin, as with גֵּט (gēṭ) 'bill of divorce'. Originally Akkadian words are תַּגָּר (taggār) 'merchant', תַּרְגּוּם (targūm) 'translation', דַּף (dap̄) 'page', זוז (zwz) 'move away', etc. Persian loanwords include גִּזְבָּר (gizbār) 'treasurer' and וֶרֶד (wæræḏ) 'rose'.

RH also has hundreds of expressions derived from Greek, which can be administrative in nature, as with בּוּלֵי (būlē) 'town council' (from *boulē*), religious, as with לִיטוּרְגְיָה (līṭūrgᵉyā) 'service' (from *leitourgia*), or legal, as with קָטֵיגוֹר (qāṭēgōr) 'prosecutor' (from *katēgoros*) and פָּרַקְלֵיט (pāraqlēṭ) 'defence lawyer' (from *paraklētos*), and there are also terms from, for example, material culture, like אֲוִיר ('ᵃwēr) 'air' (from *aēr*) and זוֹג (zōḡ) 'pair (of animals)' (from *zeugos*), or from business, as with פִּנְקֵס (pinqēs) 'account book' (from *pinax*).[124] Borrowing is sometimes associated with metathesis, as in the case of נָמֵל (nāmēl), the Babylonian RH version of לְמֵן (lᵉmēn) 'port' (from Greek *limēn*).[125] There are also some recognizable calques from Greek, like יפה אמרת (yāp̄æ 'āmartā) 'you have spoken well' (cf. *kalos* 'beautiful, good'). Terms of Latin provenance are less frequent, and have generally come to RH through Greek. They tend to derive from such areas as adminstration, as with יוּדְקֵי (yūḏiqē) 'judge' (from *judex*) and לִיבְלָר (liḇlār) 'scribe' (from *librarius*), or military life, for example לִגְיוֹן (liḡyōn) 'legion' (from *legio*).[126]

123 See Gluska 1983.

124 These were studied in S. Krauss's classic work (1898–1900), which was immediately heavily criticized – of the approximately 1,500 expressions exposed to etymological analysis, the status of more than half was reckoned to be seriously in doubt. More recently, D. Sperber, of Bar-Ilan University, has published many works (especially 1977–79; 1982), as well as vocabularies for specific areas of the language (1984; 1986), which may be regarded as the basis of a potential new comprehensive dictionary.

125 See E.Y. Kutscher 1972c, 96.

126 See E.Y. Kutscher 1982, 137ff.

Chapter 7

MEDIAEVAL HEBREW

7.1 *Historical and geographical background*

It is not easy to establish precise boundaries for that stage of the Hebrew language generally known as Mediaeval Hebrew (MH). We have already said that RH stopped being used as a living vernacular around the end of the second century CE, surviving for several centuries, however, alongside Aramaic, as a literary language.[1] Although the transition to MH cannot be clearly defined, sometime during the sixth to seventh centuries and with the advent of Arab domination, there was a first movement towards the revitalization of Hebrew which may be considered as marking the beginnings of MH, even though the language remained deeply rooted in its past. This was the heyday of the Palestinian *payṭanim,* liturgical poets who employed a highly idiosyncratic, prayerlike language pervaded by biblical allusion and neologism.[2] The same period sees the redaction of some late *midrashim* and the beginning of Masoretic activity.

The new vitality was limited to Hebrew as a literary language, but this does not mean that the language had disappeared entirely from daily use. Even though across the world Jewish communities tended to adopt the language of the host country for normal communication, they continued to pray and to read the Bible in Hebrew. This means as well that Hebrew must still have been

[1] See Rabin 1970, 324ff.

[2] However, the beginnings of *piyyuṭ* are to be found several centuries earlier, as shown by Ḥ. Schirmann (1953, 123).

taught in Jewish schools, and the testimonies of various mediaeval travellers show us that the use of the language in conversation had not ceased completely, as there were some communities, admittedly few in number, that used Hebrew in everyday life. We now possess a considerably greater quantity of financial documents written in Hebrew, including, for example, merchants' notes and papers concerning trade, taxation, and loans and other commercial transactions. From the same period there are also numerous Hebrew inscriptions, especially on gravestones.[3] Sending letters in Hebrew to people or communities in distant countries was a standard practice, and travellers from other countries arriving in a Jewish community would normally employ the language for purposes of communication. Although certain writers made efforts to 'revive' Hebrew, there are many indications that it had never completely died out as a spoken language.[4]

A new phase in the revival of Hebrew as a literary language began in the tenth century. Starting in the east, it very soon reached the western limits of the Islamic world, and, in particular, Andalusia. Advances in Arabic grammar which awoke interest in the philological study of Hebrew, as well as Karaite concentration on BH and Rabbanite efforts not to be outpaced, contributed to this linguistic renaissance.[5]

Thus, we see that MH was not simply an artificial, derivative continuation of such traditional genres as *piyyuṭ*, which had gained new strength in ninth-century Italy. The Hebrew used by the Jews of Al-Andalus developed a previously unknown vitality both in poetry – a new secular verse inspired by Arabic genres as well as a different brand of religious poetry – and in prose – philological studies, commentaries on Bible and Talmud, and works of a theological, philosophical, polemical, scientific, and medical nature. However, Hebrew was not the only language used in these

[3] See, for example, Cantera and Millás 1956.

[4] See Chomsky 1969, 206ff.

[5] See Allony 1973; 1974a; 1975; 1979; Roth 1983.

fields, as Jewish writers also employed Arabic, occasionally for poetry, but much more often in prose.

The overall picture is complex and lacks a single clear pattern of development. Closely connected with the historical and social milieu in which the literature was produced and the formation of a distinctive tradition which very soon imposed limits on the various genres, there is a more or less marked tendency for writers to fall back on the linguistic inheritance of BH and RH. Thus, they transform the senses of old words, create new ones by analogy, expand grammatical forms in order to adapt them to new requirements of expression, and accept some degree of modification of Hebrew under the influence of such languages as Arabic, Aramaic, Latin and other members of the Romance family, and German.

MH is not, properly speaking, a 'language' comparable to BH or RH. It did not possess sufficient vitality in daily life or even in literature to develop into a reasonably complete and homogeneous system. MH written works display many differences, but not enough to speak of different dialects. This is because MH was never a language in the full sense, but rather a revival of linguistic usages and traditions, developed according to each writer's judgement, depending on his particular social and cultural background, and in line with his own ideas about the language.

It is clear that throughout this revival a major rôle was played by the rise of philology, originating in the east and encouraged on the authority of Saadiah and other scholars from North Africa, which developed with incredible vigour in Andalusia in the tenth and eleventh centuries. Nonetheless, it should be remembered that all the resulting studies were primarily concerned with BH and do not necessarily attempt to encourage the use of Hebrew as a living language, but rather to describe its grammar and vocabulary in the best way possible. Only passing reference is made to RH, and philologists do not usually discuss the revitalization of the language that was taking place before their eyes. It is not surprising, then, that these works are often written in Arabic, not

Hebrew. However, there were some powerful personalities, including Solomon ibn Gabirol, who felt a sort of divine calling impelling them to rescue their people from its blindness and to serve it with a tongue which spoke the worthiest of languages.[6]

It has been correctly pointed out that Jews in the Middle Ages held a variety of attitudes towards Hebrew.[7] Those who lived under Islam approached the issue very differently from those in Christian lands. The latter, although sometimes employing Romance languages, preferred Hebrew for their literary works, even though this was often only achieved by means of poor style, dubious morphology, and questionable syntax. Jews living under Islam, in contrast, had tended since the beginning of the tenth century to use Arabic for prose but Hebrew for poetry in an obvious attempt to distinguish this from contemporary Arabic poetry, written in the language of the Koran. This could have had an ideological basis, expressly stated by certain writers as an attempt to promote their own linguistic heritage, BH, as no less aesthetically pleasing than the language of the Koran. There was also a religious factor – a scrupulously orthodox Jew would have found it difficult to express his feelings in the sacred language of another religion. However, an additional important factor relates to the level of competence in Arabic itself – whereas authors and readers had no difficulty in writing and understanding standard Arabic prose, Arabic poetry, based much more closely on the language of the Koran, was considerably more demanding.

Many voices were raised throughout the Middle Ages in defence of the use of Hebrew. Among others, Saadiah, Solomon ibn Gabirol, Moses ibn Ezra, Judah al-Ḥarizi, Judah ibn Tibbon, and Profiaṭ Duran lamented in one way or another the abandonment of the language. Some connected it directly with the sad situation of the Jewish people in exile. At one point in his life, we find Maimonides regretting that he had written most of his

[6] Thus, in Ibn Gabirol's *Sefer ha-'Anak*, vv. 14–22. See Sáenz-Badillos 1980, 16.
[7] See Halkin 1963.

work in Arabic, perhaps because he had become increasingly aware that many European readers had no access to his works.[8] Nevertheless, when dealing with particular philosophical or scientific topics, most Jews living in Muslim countries resorted to Arabic (generally written with Hebrew characters),[9] which remained during this period the language of scholars, both Jewish and Muslim.

In Christian territories, certain translators, like those of the Ibn Tibbon family, who felt keenly the problem of using both languages, complained that Hebrew had an excessively limited vocabulary in comparison with Arabic. However, Al-Ḥarizi and Profiaṭ Duran countered by blaming the situation on the ignorance of those using the language. While the Jews of central Europe were taking great liberties with the rules of Hebrew grammar, authorities like Ibn Janaḥ and Moses and Abraham ibn Ezra exerted themselves in a variety of ways in order to recover the language in its full purity. The legitimacy of RH as a means of expression, on its own or mixed with BH, was doubted by the most extreme purists, although Ibn Janaḥ, like Tanḥum b. Joseph Yerushalmi and others, defended it.

The point at which MH ends is as uncertain as its beginnings. Setting aside the part played by some Jews in the Renaissance, Judaism as such, after the expulsion from Spain in 1492 and the difficulties experienced by Jewish communities elsewhere, did not undergo any significant major social or cultural changes until the second half of the eighteenth century. For many historians, the Jewish 'Middle Ages', and thus, in some sense, MH as well, did not end until then. It is only with the *Haskalah* (Jewish Enlightenment) that genuine modernization begins, although in respect of language this was just as much tied to the past as was the Hasidic literature of the time.[10]

[8] See his letter to the Jewish community of Lunel in A. Lichtenberg, *Koveṣ teshuvot ha-RaMBaM we-iggerotaw* (Leipzig, 1859, repr. 1969), pp. 44 a–b. See Halkin 1963, 238f.

[9] See Baron 1958, 3ff.

[10] See Rabin 1973, 57ff.

MH spread as extensively as Jewish communities themselves, throughout the civilized world. With regard to MH literature, we should distinguish an eastern area which includes Palestine, Babylonia, and Egypt, a western area including North Africa and Spain, and a central European, or Ashkenazi, area from Italy to England and from France to eastern Europe.

The study of MH has only begun relatively recently. In the West, until the nineteenth century, primarily theological motives ensured an almost exclusive concentration on BH, and, occasionally, particularly among Jewish grammarians and lexicographers, on RH as well. From the middle of the last century, some basic works of mediaeval Hebrew literature started to appear in the West, along with a number of important studies on MH literary and linguistic features due to the labours of, for example, M. Sachs, W. Bacher, L. Zunz, J. Derenbourg, A. Neubauer, S.G. Stern, P. Kokowtzow, and M. Jastrow. The manuscripts of the Cairo Genizah, now housed in libraries throughout the world, have enormously increased our knowledge of this literature.

Even so, it still has to be said that the systematic and rigorous study of MH began only a few decades ago, and our present improved state of knowledge owes much to work undertaken in recent years in Israel and by Jewish scholars from other countries. Thus, we are still in the initial phase of a new discipline, where we lack as yet the necessary detailed studies of MH writers and works to develop a complete picture of the various linguistic forms which are included under the general name of MH.

For the language of the *payṭanim,* we rely on the listings of L. Zunz,[11] the embryonic dictionary of J. Kena'ani,[12] studies by M. Zulay, S. Lieberman, A. Mirsky, S. Spiegel, and most importantly in recent years, Y. Yahalom.[13] The language of Saadiah

[11] 1920 (1st ed., 1855), 116ff., 367ff.

[12] 1930–31.

[13] See Zulay 1936, etc.; Lieberman 1939; Spiegel 1963; Mirsky 1965–66; Yahalom 1974, etc., especially 1985.

has received the attention of, among others, C. Rabin, Z. Ben-Ḥayyim, S.L. Skoss, M. Zulay, and Y. Ṭovi.[14]

The language of the Jewish poets of Spain has been studied by, for example, B. Klar, S. Abramson, N. Allony, M. Medan, A. Mirsky, Ḥ. Schirmann, Y. Ratzabi, S. Spiegel, and Y. Ṭovi.[15] The language of translations from the Arabic was the subject of M.H. Goshen-Gottstein's 1951 doctoral thesis and other works.[16] Various studies by I. Efros, C. Rabin, G.B. Ṣarfatti, M.Z. Kaddari, A. Sáenz-Badillos,[17] and others have analysed the language of prose writings, in particular those of a scientific, philological, and mystical character. W. Bacher, D.H. Baneth, Y.A. Zeidmann, M.H. Goshen-Gottstein, and F.D. Fink are among those who have contributed to the study of the language of Maimonides.[18] The language of Rashi has been analysed by, for example, I. Avinery.[19] The *Sefer Ḥasidim* has been the subject of two doctoral theses, by M. Azar and S. Kogut, at the Hebrew University, Jerusalem. A. Novel and C. Rabin have published various works on the language of Ashkenazi Jews.[20]

Also of importance are the many mediaeval inscriptions that have reached us. Limiting ourselves to Spain, after the initial work undertaken primarily by F. Fita, A.S. Yahuda, and M. Gaspar Remiro, F. Cantera and J.M. Millás finally brought to fruition a magnificent catalogue of a quite remarkable number of funerary and monumental texts, as well as short inscriptions written on, for example, seals and precious objects.[21]

[14] See Rabin 1943; Skoss 1942; 1952; Ben-Ḥayyim 1952–53a; Zulay 1964; Ṭovi 1982.

[15] See S. Abramson 1941–43; Allony 1941–43; 1960; 1974; 1976, etc.; Medan 1951; Mirsky 1952–53; Klar 1953–54; Schirmann 1954; 1965–66; 1979; Ratzabi 1956–57, etc; Spiegel 1974; Ṭovi 1972–73; 1982.

[16] Gottstein (Goshen-Gottstein) 1947; 1951; 1953a; Goshen-Gottstein 1957; 1961; 1968.

[17] See Efros 1926–27; 1929–30; Rabin 1943; 1945; Ṣarfatti 1968; Kaddari 1970; Sáenz-Badillos 1982; 1985.

[18] See Bacher 1903; 1914; Baneth 1935–36; 1952; Zeidmann 1943; Gottstein (Goshen-Gottstein) 1947; Fink 1980.

[19] 1940–60.

[20] See Novel 1958–59; Rabin 1968b.

[21] See Cantera and Millás 1956.

A broader view of the language is found in analyses of MH phonology, such as I. Garbell's article on the pronunciation of Hebrew in Spain,[22] vocabulary, for example, J. Klatzkin's dictionary,[23] and syntax, for example, C. Rabin's doctoral thesis.[24] An overall treatment of the language must remain a desideratum until many more detailed studies have been completed. There does exist a typewritten version of the classes of Prof. N. Allony in the University of Beer Sheba,[25] which, however, does not reflect the depth of his learning in the field of MH, as he never revised it with a view to publication. Meanwhile, E. Goldenberg's article in *Encyclopaedia Judaica* is the best available general description of MH.[26]

7.2 *The language of the* payṭanim

The Hebrew of the *payṭanim* may be regarded as a continuation of Palestinian RH, as used in public prayer. Early *piyyuṭ* originated and developed in the synagogues of Palestine as part of the *ḥazzan*'s repertoire, offering him an opportunity for variety and innovation that was absent from the fixed format of traditional prayers and Bible readings.

From the time of L. Zunz,[27] it has been usual to describe the language of the *payṭanim* as a mixture of BH and RH, with the former predominating, although it also contains some characteristic new forms, usually coined by the *payṭanim* themselves. The resulting language was well-suited to a religious and highly nationalistic poetry which had many similarities to midrashic homily.

22 Garbell 1954.
23 Klatzkin 1928–33.
24 Rabin 1943a.
25 Allony 1974 (105 pages).
26 E. Goldenberg 1971.
27 1920 (1st ed., 1855), 116ff.

BH elements are obvious in vocabulary and morphology. The *payṭanim* use verbal forms found in BH, not RH, including the *Pu'al* (preferring internal to external passives), *waw*-consecutive, long and short forms of the verb, and the infinitive absolute. However, there is significant variation in the use of BH among writers from different periods. Thus, in the poems of Yose b. Yose we find consecutive forms of the verb, the prefix-conjugation rather than the RH participle, and even archaic suffixes in imitation of ancient poetry. The first generations, up to the time of Yannai, stayed basically faithful to BH, using a simple and intelligible style, but this is rarely true of the later *payṭanim*. With Kallir we reach the ultimate in complexity and obscurity, and his successors try to return to a more straightforward BH.[28]

Most *piyyuṭ* uses features typical of RH, such as the *Nithpa'al* or the infinitive preceded by the double particle -מִלְּ (mil-le-) 'from (doing)' (lit. 'from to [do]'). In rhymes from the time of Yannai, laryngeals and gutturals are freely exchanged, as in RH and other Hebrew dialects of the period. Also, as in RH, we find, for example, that the second person masculine pronominal suffix is -ָךְ (-āḵ) , verbs with final *alef* are treated like those with final *he*, and there is interchange of *sin* and *samekh* and of final *mem* and *nun*. Orthography is generally *plene*, the third person singular feminine of verbs ending in *he* does not take a final -ה (-h) in the suffix-conjugation, thus, לָקָת (lāqāṯ) 'she was struck' for BH לָקְתָה (lāqeṯā), contextual forms of the verb are sometimes replaced by pausal ones, geminate verbs are conjugated as if regular, היה (hyh) 'be' with the participle is used to express frequentative action, and -עָתִיד לְ ('āṯīḏ le-) '(be) ready to' is employed for the future.[29]

But the *payṭanim* sometimes also develop distinctive usages of their own, for example the infinitive with prefixed particle -מִ (mi-) 'from', not found in either RH or BH but probably constructed from both. There are some notable changes in the verb, such as the

[28] See Rabinovitz 1985, 33.
[29] See Rabinovitz 1985, 33ff.

replacement of passive forms by reflexives, perhaps on stylistic grounds. Although *piyyuṭ* was significantly influenced by Aramaic, especially the Aramaic of the Targums, it maintained a more biblical form of expression than that found in the *midrashim*, with which *piyyuṭ* has undoubted points of contact, preferring to develop new usages rather than employing special midrashic terms. It has a strongly nationalistic tone, extending to a scrupulous selection of vocabulary, in which foreign words are discarded in favour of Hebrew ones. In contrast to the standard midrashic technique, Greek terms are not simply transliterated but are translated by Hebrew equivalents. Often though, the *payṭanim* chose Hebrew words which sounded similar to the Greek originals, altering the meaning of the Hebrew as necessary, for example, גֶּיא (gǣ') 'valley' is often employed to denote Greek *gē* 'earth' and מְכִירָה (mᵉḵīrā) is used for Greek *machaira* 'sword'.[30]

The language of *piyyuṭ* also contains many apparently deliberate innovations. The oddity of its vocabulary comes not only from its many complicated allusions, but also from the use of rare biblical words and the introduction of Aramaisms or new expressions with little regard for what is normal in Hebrew. The *payṭanim* created numerous forms of the verb by conjugating every kind of irregular verb as if it were a hollow verb, eliminating any weak first or third radical, especially in the suffix-conjugation. Thus, for example, סָע (sā') is used for נָסַע (nāsa') 'he set out', as though the root were סוע (sw'). In some noun patterns as well, the final consonant is dropped, leading to such forms as מַעַשׂ (ma'aś) for מַעֲשֶׂה (ma'ᵃśæ) 'action' and תַּאַו (ta'aw) for תַּאֲוָה (ta'ᵃwā) 'desire'.

Through analogical formation, every possible form of a verb and its derived conjugations is used, even if it does not exist in BH, and new forms of nouns and verbs are created by the addition of suffixes and prefixes, and so on. Thus, for example, from the nouns בֶּטֶן (bæṭæn) 'womb' and תְּרוּעָה (tᵉrū'ā) 'shofar-blast', we find the verb forms הבטין (hiḇṭīn) 'he made pregnant' and התריע

30 See Yahalom 1985, 41ff.

(hiṯrīaʻ) 'he sounded the *shofar*' (similar formations are known from RH), from the particles טֶרֶם (ṭæræm) 'before' and בִּלְעֲדֵי (bilʻadē) 'except for', we have the verb forms טרמני (ṭēremanī) 'he preceded me' and בלעד (bilʻēḏ) 'he made an exception', and from the verb עתר ('tr) 'pray', the noun עֶתֶר ('æṯær) 'prayer'. In genitive constructions, abstract nouns frequently have adjectival significance. A device that enjoyed great popularity among contemporary audiences consisted in the creation of endless unnecessary synonyms through the arbitrary shortening or lengthening of words, for example אַו ('aw) instead of תַּאֲוָה (ta'awā) 'desire' and פַּחְדּוֹן (paḥdōn) alongside פַּחַד (paḥaḏ) 'fear'. The *payṭanim* are quite liberal in their use of gender and number in the noun, and use distinctive morphological patterns, among which *qæṭæl*, *qiṭṭūl*, *qeṭīlā*, and *qiṭlōn* stand out. In verbs, they replace the suffix ה- (-h) by ת- (-t), and add the proclitics -כְּ (ke-), -בְּ (be-), -לְ (le-), and -מִ (mi-) to finite forms of the verb, seen especially in the construction of -כְּ (ke-) 'as, when' with the suffix-conjugation, for example, כהלכו (ke-hālekū) for כַּאֲשֶׁר הָלְכוּ (ka-ašær hālekū) 'when they went'.[31] Often, such features are not innovations of the *payṭanim* but forms of expression taken over from midrashic literature or the spoken language, continuing the tendency in RH to mix grammatically acceptable forms with novel kinds of derivation.[32]

Frequently, the names of biblical characters and places are replaced by allegorical, periphrastic, or allusive expressions. Often, the source of such nouns is *midrash*, at other times, the poet's own imagination. Yose b. Yose seems to have been the instigator of this custom in Hebrew liturgical poetry, which is even more accentuated in later poets.[33] The generally high level of use of midrashic material by the *payṭanim* means that *piyyuṭ* might be very broadly defined as poetic *haggadah* – it is certainly true that *piyyuṭ* cannot be understood without reference to *midrash*.

31 See Zunz 1920, 116ff.; E. Goldenberg 1971, 1609ff.

32 See Mirsky 1965–66.

33 See Mirsky 1977, 61ff., for a list of the allusive nouns in Yose b. Yose.

The character of *piyyuṭ* meant that it was very difficult to understand and appreciate. Criticism of classical *piyyuṭ*, and in particular the compositions of Eleazar birebbi Kallir, is well known from the work of Abraham ibn Ezra.[34] According to the latter, most of these compositions constitute riddles or parables laden with difficult allusions, in contrast with the simplicity and clarity of prayers found in Scripture itself. Many terms have been borrowed from the Talmud, the language of which is not suitable for prayer, complains Ibn Ezra – the daily prayers are composed in the language of the Bible, and it is not appropriate to pray in a language other than this. The BH vocabulary used by *piyyuṭ* is full of errors, with changes of gender and so on. Finally, the *payṭanim* interpret Scripture fancifully, according to *derash* and *haggadah*, and not, as they should, literally, in accordance with the *peshaṭ*. Ibn Ezra contrasts *piyyuṭ* and all its deficiencies with the flawless poetry of Saadiah. Although his criticisms are not of a purely linguistic nature, they represent traditional objections to *piyyuṭ* which survived until quite recently and which are characterized by a lack of understanding of the social and historical background of the genre. It is not unusual to see exaggerated attacks on the obscurity and difficulty of *piyyuṭ*, dismisssed as *aṣ koṣeṣ*,[35] full of allusion and code, abounding in wordplay and at times a barely intelligible conciseness of expression.

The attitude of literary and linguistic scholars to *piyyuṭ* has altered greatly in the last two centuries. In contrast to the censures of mediaeval purists as well as a variety of later writers, scholars of the stature of F. Delitzsch, S.D. Luzzato, L. Zunz, S. Spiegel, M. Zulay, and Y. Yahalom have defended the fundamental validity of the genre and the positive qualities of its language and style. Because of this change in attitude and the new insights offered by the large number of *piyyuṭ* compositions discovered in the Cairo

34 In his commentary to Ec 5:1. See the edition of this text and comments in Yahalom 1985, 183ff.

35 Literally 'the wicked one ran', the initial words of a *kerovah* by Kallir which have become a rather pejorative term for the stylistic oddity of *piyyuṭ*.

Genizah, a very diferent appreciation of the language of *piyyuṭ* has developed. Instead of considering it as a contrived, artificial product, the tendency nowadays is to see in *piyyuṭ* and its survival over more than six centuries a continuation of the spoken language of Palestine before its demise – a reflection of a living language, despite being couched in a peculiar style. While prose-composition on other topics employed the dominant language, either Aramaic or Arabic, synagogue poetry continued to use Hebrew, albeit in a different literary form, with a distinctive style that merged RH elements with a large BH component and afforded the *payṭanim* considerable freedom for innovation.[36] As a whole, then, *piyyuṭ* comprises a specific variety of Hebrew with its own clear characteristics, halfway between the language of the *Amoraim* and the *midrashim* and MH proper.

7.3 *The language of Saadiah Gaon*

In common with many later Jewish writers, Saadiah wrote his poetry in Hebrew but employed Arabic for virtually all his prose writing. Although Arabic dominates his work, Saadiah's Hebrew compositions, and in particular his poetry, the first to be written in Babylonia, mark the start of a vigorous revival of Hebrew from the beginning of the tenth century. Furthermore, Saadiah's attempts to promote a better knowledge of Hebrew, through important works of grammar and lexicography, left a deep impression on subsequent philology. Nonetheless, it is not unusual to find certain contradictions between Saadiah's linguistic theory and the language he actually uses in his Hebrew writings. There are also noticeable differences between the language employed in his poems and that found in his prose compositions, which are generally much closer to the Hebrew of the Bible.

[36] See especially Yahalom 1985, 20ff.

Saadiah's poetry, like that of Hai Gaon which has a very similar style, is in some ways a continuation of the language of *piyyuṭ*, although Saadiah consciously rejects the excessive obscurity and linguistic anomalies of this genre. M. Zulay argues that Saadiah is an intermediate link between the *payṭanim* and the Jewish poets of Spain in the following centuries.[37] That the language employed by Saadiah and his school is not as biblical as the Hebrew of the later poets is demonstrated, for example, by the liberality shown by Saadiah and his followers in creating new nouns and verbs. In this connexion, they exploit every morphological pattern and root which appears in the Bible, without limiting themselves to forms actually attested there. On the other hand, Saadiah and his school also defend the ideal of the 'purity of the language', in terms of clarity, correctness, and beauty, producing material free from errors and from irregularities in the derivation of new forms.

Certain features of Saadiah's poetry echo those of the *payṭanim*. An example is the creation of secondary forms of all kinds of words merely for the sake of novelty, as in אֱמִימָה ('ēmīmā) 'horror', using לִפְנִימָה (li-p̄nīmā) 'inwards' as a model, תְּמֹרֶת (t^e^mōræṯ) 'exchange', on the analogy of קְטֹרֶת (q^e^ṭōræṯ) 'incense', and גִּשְׁמָה (gišmā) 'rain', following שִׂמְלָה (śimlā) 'mantle'. Members of different classes of irregular verb are frequently treated as hollow verbs, the -נ- (-n-) of the first person singular pronominal suffix is omitted, giving rise to forms like להצילי (l^e^-haṣṣīl-ī) for לְהַצִּילֵנִי (l^e^-haṣṣīl-ēnī) 'to save me', the particle -כְּ (k^e^-) 'as, when' is used before finite forms of the verb, as in כנכתבה (k^e^-nikt^e^ḇā) for כַּאֲשֶׁר נִכְתְּבָה (ka-^a^šær-nikt^e^ḇā) 'when it was written', new verbs are formed from nouns, for example, from תְּהוֹם (t^e^hōm) 'abyss, התהים (hiṯhīm) 'he threw into the abyss', and *vice versa*. There are numerous synonyms with different forms, and arbitrary derivations from certain roots, so that we find, for example, סדסד (siḏsēḏ) instead of יָסַד (yāsaḏ) 'he laid a foundation', affecting the imperative, infinitive, and prefix-conjugation forms of the verb as

[37] See Zulay 1964.

well. Basing himself on forms found only very rarely in BH, Saadiah quite often utilizes patterns like *pe'altāhū*.[38] He omits root letters, so developing new shortened forms, and, on the analogy of doublets found in the Bible, he constructs his own alternative terms without any recognizable difference in sense.[39] As occasionally in BH, the article is sometimes not elided, for example בהשמים (be-haš-šāmayim) 'in the heavens', and Saadiah also uses the typically LBH construction of הַ- (ha-) as relative particle before finite forms of the verb, as in ההלכו (hæ-hāleḵū) 'who went', and even before whole clauses. In some genitive constructions the article is attached to the *nomen regens*. Saadiah uses numerous feminine forms of nouns found in BH only in the masculine, employs new noun patterns, and so on.[40] Neither does he hesitate to exploit RH, regarding it as a continuation and logical development of BH. In its frequent use of allusion, Saadiah's idiom again coincides with that of the *payṭanim* who preceded him.

In other respects Saadiah's language is entirely biblical: for example, he uses the *waw*-consecutive and the negative particles בַּל (bal) 'not' and פֶּן (pæn) 'lest', his treatment of geminate roots is consistent with BH, and he uses the infinitive absolute to express emphasis.[41] Biblical features are especially noticeable in certain kinds of poetry, such as the *bakkashot* (supplications). But even when assiduously imitating biblical style, Saadiah moves in a distinctive way, adding a final *he* to certain forms and inserting the same consonant in the *Hif'il*, for example, תהחים (tahaḥayām) for תְּחַיֵּם (taḥayām) 'you will revive them', neglecting number and gender concord, and, in general, introducing, by analogy, striking innovations in every aspect of the language.[42] Other features were later to be found in the Jewish poets of Spain, including faithfulness to the rules of grammar, a critical attitude toward the

38 See Zulay 1964, 31f.
39 See E. Goldenberg 1971, 1612ff.
40 See Zulay 1964, 32.
41 See Zulay 1964, 33f.
42 See Ṭovi 1982, 270ff.

payṭanim and only a cautious use of their methods, frequent use of participles, and the employment of long and short forms of the verb without implying differences of mood. In Saadiah, we find the same word being used in many different senses, the incorporation of *hapax legomena* into standard BH vocabulary, and the use of calques, especially from Arabic, which had a considerable influence on Saadiah's vocabulary and on his ideas about grammar.[43]

A few of Saadiah's poems are written in RH, and sometimes he uses words or whole phrases from rabbinic literature or typically RH forms, for example ילבוש (yilbōš) for יִלְבַּשׁ (yilbaš) 'he will dress', as well as rabbinic metaphors. Although he wrote no poems in Aramaic, Saadiah does not baulk at taking words from Biblical or Rabbinic Aramaic.[44]

Saadiah's Hebrew prose works are not very numerous – his *Reply* to Ḥiwi al-Balkhi[45] and the *Essa Meshali*[46] are really polemics in verse form. In prose, properly speaking, we have the Hebrew prologue to the *Egron*,[47] fragments of the *Sefer ha-Galuy*[48] (in rhymed prose), a halakhic work about the calendar, *Sefer ha-Mo'adim*,[49] other works of doubtful authenticity, and various *responsa* and epistles.[50] Saadiah's prose, which directly imitates biblical style and is quite different from the language used in his poetry, would serve as a model for the Jewish poets of Spain.[51] As seems to be implied by Saadiah's own words, one of his intentions in compiling a dictionary was to facilitate the use of Hebrew in

43 See E. Goldenberg 1971, 1612ff.

44 See Ṭovi 1982, 274ff.

45 See I. Davidson, *Saadia's polemic against Hiwi Al-Balkhi: a fragment edited from a Genizah ms.* (New York, 1915); S. Poznanski, *Teshuvot RaSaG 'al she'elot Ḥiwi ha-Balkhi* (Warsaw, 1916); S.A. Wertheimer, *Sefer teshuvot Rabbenu Se'adya Ga'on le-Ḥiwi ha-Balkhi* (Jerusalem, 1930–31).

46 See Lewin 1932; 1943; Mann 1932; Zucker 1964.

47 See N. Allony, *Ha-'Egron: Kitāb 'uṣul al-shir al-'Ibrani* (Jerusalem, 1969).

48 See Schechter 1902; Chapira 1914.

49 See Ḥ.Y. Bornstein 1904.

50 See Schechter 1903.

51 See Allony, *Ha-'Egron*, 117.

poetry, while at the same time giving it back its character as a living, spoken, language, appropriate to the Jewish people's every situation.[52] Like his opponents, Saadiah employs a revitalized form of BH, which is purer and clearer than that found in his poetry, replete with biblical citations and generally free of anomalous biliteral forms of the verb or of the use of prepositions as conjunctions without the relative particle אֲשֶׁר ('ᵃšær). Although Saadiah employs a number of innovations from RH and *piyyuṭ*,[53] his principal source of material and ideas is BH, as found in both prose and poetic books of the Bible, with a preference for lexical and grammatical *hapax legomena*. He uses the *waw*-consecutive, the relative particle אֲשֶׁר ('ᵃšær), and forms from archaic biblical poetry, such as the suffix מוֹ- (-mō), alongside expressions taken from rabbinic literature, and numerous calques and loanwords from Arabic.[54]

But divergences from BH are not uncommon either. Saadiah employs the *nomen actionis* *qᵉṭīlā* of RH and *piyyuṭ*, and *Hithpa'el* is used as a passive of *Pi'el*, unusual in BH but standard in RH. The locative suffix is joined to the *nomen rectum*, not *regens*, and adjectives and participles are used as adverbs. Saadiah has a mixed system of tenses, so that, for example, while he does not use the BH consecutive tenses, neither does he use the participle to express the present, as in RH. Occasionally he employs *waw copulativum* in a way reminiscent more of Arabic than of Hebrew, infinitive constructs with -לְ (lᵉ-) 'to' or -מִלְּ (mil-lᵉ-) lit. 'from to', and the RH expression הָיָה לוֹ לֵאמֹר (hāyā lō lēmōr) 'he might have said' (lit. 'it was to him to say'). The adjective רָאוּי (rā'ūy) '(it is) proper' is used as an impersonal predicate, as in Hebrew prose from Spain.

There is an increase in modal and auxiliary verbs, for example הקדים תת (hiqdīm teṯ) 'he was first to give', the infinitive preceded by -לְ (lᵉ-) 'to' can take a subject other than that of the main verb, and the particle יֵשׁ (yēš) 'there is' is found introducing the subject

52 See Allony, *Ha-'Egron*, 391.
53 See Rabin 1943, 127ff.
54 See Allony, *Ha-'Egron*, 117ff.

of a nominal clause. The government of prepositions differs notably from BH and is closer to Arabic. The auxiliary היה (hyh) 'be' can be followed by the prefix-conjugation rather than the participle, genders are often switched, perhaps due to the demands of rhyme, and the definite article is frequently omitted. An adjective may precede a noun for the sake of emphasis, as in רבים עבדים (rabbīm ʿabāḏīm) 'many slaves', and an adverbial expression or object can be placed before the predicate, as in יש בדתו בוגדים (yēš be-ḏāṯō bōḡeḏīm) 'some betray his faith' (lit. 'there are against his faith traitors'). The third person pronominal suffix is sometimes used demonstratively as in RH, for example בם בלשונות (bām bi-lšōnōṯ) 'in those same languages' (lit. 'in them, in languages'), מָה (mā) 'what?' is used in the sense of 'which?', and unreal conditions can be expressed through the particle לוּ (lū), as in BH, or with אִלּוּ ('illū), as in LBH and RH. Temporal clauses are sometimes followed by אָז ('āz) 'then', as in Arabic.[55] As a whole, Saadiah's prose language may be characterized as more archaizing and less innovative than that of the Hebrew literature of Spain. His vocabulary comes from various sources, with an emphasis on biblical *hapax legomena*, although there are also expressions from RH and new forms that are sometimes found in Saadiah's poetic works as well.

7.4 *The language of the Hebrew poetry of Spain*

From the middle of the tenth century, the Jews of Muslim Spain enjoyed a period of remarkable cultural development which contributed to the renaissance of Hebrew, at least in its literary expression. Both language and literature were significantly affected by the great historical and social changes which overtook the Jews of Andalusia. The Andalusian court poet, earning a living by his work, was a new figure in Jewish society. Such a person was

[55] See Rabin 1943, 130ff.

erudite, usually familiar with the techniques and themes of Arabic poetry, and aware of contemporary tastes as well as of the Jewish poetic tradition. His product was necessarily very different from that of a Palestinian *ḥazzan* of the Byzantine period.

In addition, the activity of language scholars and their interest in BH, which developed gradually in the context of the Karaite controversy, critically influenced the nature of Hebrew poetry in Spain. The fact that the rôle of poet and philologist was often combined also helped to give the language a greater purity, a grammatical correctness previously unknown in poetry, and a distinctively biblical style which heralded an approach quite different from that of the *payṭanim* or Saadiah. On the other hand, prose composition, sometimes in Hebrew, more often in Arabic, was governed by considerations of an entirely different nature.

A very important aspect of Hebrew poetry in Spain, especially with regard to technical aspects of prosody (the number of syllables) and to rhyme, is its use of a contemporary pronunciation of Hebrew. Poetic rhyme, in turn, adds to a considerable body of knowledge about the pronunciation of Hebrew in Muslim and Christian territories, alongside material from Hebrew grammatical works and transcriptions from one language to another.[56] It is also certain that there were local influences on Hebrew from Arabic, Castilian Spanish, and Catalan. Arabic influence is particularly evident in laryngeals and gutturals, which have a much weaker pronunciation in the Christian territories, as well as in emphatics. In Castile and Catalonia, final nasals tended to weaken or disappear, and the various sibilants were sometimes confused with one another. Rhyming patterns attest that in the Iberian peninsula neither *pathaḥ* and *qameṣ* nor *ṣere* and *segol* were distinguished in pronunciation – the resulting system, with just five vowel phonemes, was probably similar to that of the earliest stage of the Palestinian tradition.

[56] An excellent analysis was conducted by I. Garbell (1954); see also Klar 1951.

Shewa mobile is transcribed in older texts as *a*, with *e* predominating in later ones. There does not appear to be any linguistic reason regarding differences in the realization of *shewa* to explain why in the quantitative metrical system it forms an essential component of the *yated*,[57] whereas in the syllabic system it is practically disregarded. The fact that both phenomena can appear in the work of a single poet suggests that what we have here is a difference in prosodic technique, not a reflection of two pronunciations of *shewa*.

There are striking differences among the various kinds of poetry. Liturgical verse began by using traditional forms, including some known from *piyyuṭ*. However, the special place held by Andalusian poets in society, the social pressures they faced, and the changing preferences of their public gradually altered the character of the idiom, which resisted significant Arabic influence and became closer than its oriental predecessors to BH.

In Al-Andalus, there were two clearly defined types of liturgical poets, with some, like Joseph ibn Abitur and Isaac ibn Ghayyat, holding positions as spiritual leaders of the community and rabbinic scholars, while others, such as Solomon ibn Gabirol and Judah Halevi, were genuine court poets – secular scholars or professionals who received the backing of patrons.[58] The poetic output of these two types was necessarily very different, with that of the second being more personal and innovative, whereas a more communal ethos and a continuation of the earlier Palestinian *piyyuṭ* tradition prevails in the first group. In fact, all Hebrew liturgical poetry from Spain retains some connexion with *piyyuṭ*, however striking the differences. But there are also very clear changes of structure, with liturgical poetry subjected to contemporary aesthetic norms instead of resulting from the improvisation of a *ḥazzan*.[59] Often, a single poet would write

57 Metrical unit composed of a consonant with murmured vowel followed by a syllable containing a normal vowel. See below, n. 79.

58 See Schirmann 1954a.

59 See Fleischer 1975, 413ff.

liturgical and secular verse, generally attempting to distinguish them very carefully by imposing upon himself two distinct disciplines, to the extent that the resulting poetry can appear to be the work of different writers.[60]

Piyyuṭ forms and other features characteristic of the era of the *payṭanim* are even seen in the most typical poetry of the classical period, at the height of the eleventh century. Sometimes they give the impression of being used deliberately, in order to add an archaic flavour to a text. There were, in fact, at this time many different currents that had a direct bearing on the liturgical poetry of Spain. Thus, it was decisively influenced by the abandoning of traditional structures, the introduction of new subjects, styles, and aesthetic categories, the use, on occasions, of Arabic metrical verse alongside rare types of syllable-based poetry, the influence of *muwashshaḥ* and *zajal* structures, and, above all, by a new awareness about the proper use of Hebrew in a climate of opinion which demanded linguistic purity. But there were also reactionary tendencies, finding expression, for example, in the development of a syllable-based verse that was regarded as more in keeping with the character of Hebrew, in opposition to the growing dominance of quantitative metre, which only found limited acceptance in liturgical poetry. There was also a clear resistance to the influence of Arabic, given the religious context of Hebrew poetry, and it is very likely that it was in reaction to such influence that the *payṭanim* came to be viewed as a source of inspiration.

Although a return to BH is characteristic of all Andalusian liturgical poetry, seen even in the earliest preserved material from the tenth century, such as the writings of Dunash b. Labraṭ, the retention of *piyyuṭ* forms is a striking feature, especially of the first generations of poets. For example, Joseph ibn Abitur finds no difficulty in continuing to employ the biliteral forms of weak verbs typical of *piyyuṭ*, such as בָּט (bāṭ) for BH בָּטָא (bāṭā') 'he uttered', צָר (ṣār) for BH יָצַר (yāṣar) 'he formed', and טָף (ṭāp̄) for BH תִּטֹּף

[60] D. Yellin (1975, 203) comments thus in connexion with Ibn Gabirol.

(tiṭṭōp̄) 'she dripped', as well as allusive names like מְצֻלֹלִים (miṣlōlīm) 'depths' for 'waters' and אֶרֶץ ('æræṣ) 'land' for 'heaven', distinctive *piyyuṭ* meanings, such as מצפצפים (meṣap̄ṣep̄īm) '(they are) singing (lit. 'chirping')' and פָּץ (pāṣ) 'he spoke (lit. 'he split')', new morphological patterns, like מִזְמָר (mizmār) for BH מִזְמוֹר (mizmōr) 'psalm', and masculine plural suffixes with feminine nouns. On the other hand, Ibn Abitur also employs rabbinic devices, like the periphrastic use of participles with the verb היה (hyh) 'be', as well as other constructions typical of mediaeval Spain, such as לְמַעַן (le-ma'an) expressing cause. In the *kinah* (lament) *Bekhu Aḥay*, the only one of his poems to use quantitative metre, Ibn Abitur manages to employ no less than fifteen *Pu'al* participles (masculine and feminine) as well as some *Nif'al*s. These do not always occur simply because of metrical considerations, and they produce a remarkable stylistic effect. The subject of the composition is such as to discount any notion that Ibn Abitur was attempting to ridicule the technique that he had deliberately set out to avoid in the rest of his work.

Solomon ibn Gabirol's preoccupation – almost a vocation, according to his own words – with the Hebrew language is very obvious in his didactic poem *Ha-'Anak*.[61] Yet even he, at the height of the classical period, often adopts the methods of the *payṭanim* in his liturgical poems and distances himself from BH with many innovations and changes, similar to those for which Abraham ibn Ezra would later criticize Kallir and his followers. Thus, for example, Ibn Gabirol's word order can sometimes turn a work into a linguistic puzzle, he mixes Talmudic and biblical vocabulary,[62] and he commonly uses biliteral forms of irregular verbs, such as כָּס (kās) for כָּסָה (kāsā) 'he covered' and טָו (ṭāw) for טָוָה (ṭāwā) 'he spun', and the suffix-conjugation preceded by -כְּ (ke-) 'as, when', as in כנס (ke-nās) 'when he fled' or כראו (ke-rā'ū) 'when they saw'. As in *piyyuṭ*, terms from *haggadah* and *midrash* abound (the 'seven

61 See Sáenz-Badillos 1980.

62 See Yellin 1975, 228ff.

heavens', the *middot*, or 'attributes' of God, etc.), although, as is common in the Hebrew poetry of Spain, often subjects drawn from philosophy, science, and, occasionally, mysticism replace the topics of the *payṭanim*.[63] Ibn Gabirol also uses allusive or symbolic names such as צִיר (ṣīr) 'messenger' for Moses or שָׂטָן (śāṭān) 'adversary, Satan' for Esau.[64] It is not necessity but desire for novelty that leads him to create new nouns from patterns like *qæṭæl*, for example כֶּמֶס (kæmæs) 'mystery' and פֶּלֶל (pælæl) 'prayer', *qiṭṭūl*, for example, עִקּוּל ('iqqūl) 'tortuousness', and *qeṭīlā*, for example בְּהִיקָה (behīqā) 'splendour', affixed forms like בְּרִיחוּת (berīḥūṯ) 'flight' and מַבָּע (mabba') 'utterance',[65] as well as forms of verbs absent from BH, for example בֹּהֵק (bōhēq) 'shining', הָדוּךְ (hāḏūḵ) 'submissive', and many other participles, in addition to verbs derived from nouns, rare roots, or particles, such as להג (lhg) 'say, prattle' (used in *Qal* and *Nif'al*), and anomalous structures like לתתן (le-ṯittēn),[66] for standard BH לָתֵת (lā-ṯēṯ) 'to give', and שכינו (šeḵīnō) instead of שְׁכִינָתוֹ (šeḵīnāṯō) 'his abode'.[67]

It has been claimed that Isaac ibn Ghayyat was one of the last Hebrew poets in Spain to be influenced by the *payṭanim*,[68] although his numerous works also display clear differences from one another. Ibn Ghayyat's *ma'amad* for the Day of Atonement is a large and particularly obscure composition with close connexions to earlier *piyyuṭ*, although generally his language is much nearer to BH than is normal in the Palestinian *payṭanim*, with less use of allusion and midrashic concepts, and the introduction of new terms in keeping with contemporary interests in technical matters. As is customary in Hebrew poetry from Spain, Ibn Ghayyat often quotes whole passages from the Bible, though frequently in a context and for a purpose completely different from those of the

63 See Fleischer 1975, 413ff.; I. Levin 1986.
64 See Yellin 1975, 228ff.
65 See Yellin 1975, 218ff.
66 As at 1 K 6:19.
67 On the language of Ibn Gabirol's liturgical poetry, see Yellin 1975, 203ff.; Yarden 1977–79, 635ff.
68 See Schirmann 1954, 303.

original text. Most of the words and morphological forms he uses are entirely biblical, although he also employs RH from time to time, particularly when describing the structure of the body in his *'Avodah* and in some of the *zulatot*. *Piyyuṭ* forms are also found, for example the infinitive after finite forms of the verb, as in **ויצא יצא** (way-yēṣē' yāṣō') 'and he kept on going out', and the use of a great many nouns in morphological patterns unknown to BH but attested in the *payṭanim*, as with לַעַן (la'an) and טֶנֶף (ṭænæp̄) for לַעֲנָה (la'ᵃnā) 'wormwood' and טִנֹּפֶת (ṭinnōp̄æṯ) 'dirtiness'. Alongside such elements, there are also other characteristically mediaeval linguistic features, due mainly to the influence of Arabic, for example זְמָן (zᵉmān) 'time' and יָמִים (yāmīm) 'days' to imply 'fate', עֵין הַלֵּב ('ēn hal-lēḇ) 'eye of the heart' meaning 'inner vision', and וְאִם (we-'im) 'and if' in the sense of 'even though'. Ibn Ghayyat also uses various scientific or philosophical terms invented by himself or taken from contemporary writers.[69]

The generation of Moses ibn Ezra and Judah Halevi is typified by a vigorous quest for biblical purity, which extended to poetry intended for public prayer. The standards of purity listed by Ibn Ezra in his *Kitāb al-Muḥāḍara wal-Mudākara* are valid in principle for both liturgical and secular poetry:

> everything you find in it [the text of the Bible], use, and when you cannot find something, do not apply analogy. Go where the language goes and stop where it stops, as an imitator, not a creator, a follower, not an inventor ... If you find one of the many roots that are only conjugated in the *Infi'al* and *Itfi'al* or a verb the subject of which is not specified, do not conjugate it except in the forms in which you have found it. Be careful about plurals and singulars, except where you already know of a similar form or where it is actually attested [in the Bible]. The poets consider it admissible to put luminaries in the plural ... and they have done the same with stones and gems ... but the

[69] See Schmelczer 1965, 52ff., 142.

greatest mistake is made by those who decline these nouns as if they were verbs.[70]

However, these rules were never fully obeyed, not even in the work of Ibn Ezra himself, who recognizes his youthful waywardness by citing the words of a certain ascetic: 'if the only person who is going to reprove you has to be completely free of fault, no-one will ever do it'.[71] In fact, in his liturgical poetry Ibn Ezra often uses non-BH forms taken from the *payṭanim* or inventions of his own, for example nouns like אֶצֶר ('æṣær) 'group', בִּקּוּשׁ (biqqūš) 'supplication', and מִשְׁבֶּרֶת (mišbæræṯ) 'breakage', verb forms like זוֹרֵר (zōrēr) 'scattering', and denominatives like שבל (šbl) 'travel', from שְׁבִיל (šebīl) 'path'.[72]

The same may be said of Judah Halevi, whose deserved fame as a language purist did not stop him, for example, creating new forms of verbs additional to those found in BH, deriving singulars from plurals and *vice versa,* such as אֹם ('ōm) from אֻמִּים ('ummīm) 'peoples' and הוֹנִים (hōnīm) from הוֹן (hōn) 'wealth', or from employing many passive participles, like בָּחוּן (bāḥūn) 'tested' and בָּרוּא (bārū') 'created', unattested in BH but some of which are common in RH and the *payṭanim*. Typical BH constructions, such as the *waw*-consecutive, are hardly used, and the meanings of BH words are sometimes closer to mediaeval than to biblical usage. Halevi's use of RH is limited but clear. Thus, in a small number of didactic or halakhic poems and in the *azharot* he deliberately employs RH, although in general its influence is restricted to, for example, the use of the second person singular masculine suffix ָךְ- (-āḵ) and certain nouns and forms of the verb, such as כַּפָּרָה (kappārā) 'expiation', שְׁכִינָה (šekīnā) 'divine presence', and טבע (ṭb') in the *Nif'al*, 'be sunk'. Halevi also retains a number of *piyyuṭ* features, such as -כְּ (ke-) 'as, when' before the suffix-conjugation, as in כלקח (ke-lāqaḥ) 'as he took', shortened forms, like בִּין (bīn) for

70 107 v. ff., according to the translation of M. Abumalham, *Moše ibn Ezra, Kitāb al-muḥāḍara wal-mudākara. Edición y traducción* (2 vols., Madrid, 1985–86), II, 225ff.

71 *Kitāb al-muḥāḍara wal-mudākara,* 116 r. (Abumalham, II, 247).

72 See Ratzaby 1959.

בִּינָה (bīnā) 'understanding', and new morphological patterns, as with תַּעְדּוּד (ta'dūḏ) for עֲדִי ('ᵃḏī) 'jewellery'. Occasionally, he will also use an Arabic calque, such as פֶּלֶךְ (pælæḵ) 'whirl (of spindle)' in the sense of 'the heavens', or other kinds of mediaeval expression commonly found in literature from Spain, for example תְּרוּמָה (tᵉrūmā), 'heave-offering' in BH, in the sense of 'raising'. Overall, though, it may be said that the language of Halevi's liturgical poetry is further from *piyyuṭ* and nearer to BH than may be said of the previous generation of poets.[73]

We have already noted (Chapter 7.2) the decidedly critical attitude of Abraham ibn Ezra towards what he regarded as the excesses of the *payṭanim*, and so it is not surprising that his language tends to approximate closely to BH. It is in his era, during the twelfth century, that the liturgical poetry of Spain begins to diverge noticeably from that of the earlier, Palestinian, *payṭanim*.

Secular poetry, which was free of existing Jewish traditions, emerged in the atmosphere of the Muslim court and adopted the traditional metre of Arabic literature as well as its themes, images, and conventions. Nonetheless, despite accepting this foreign influence, Hebrew poetry also reacted against contemporary trends in an attempt to establish an identity of its own, and its quest for biblical purity at any cost is, alongside the influence of Arabic, its most distinctive characteristic.

The new metre set conditions on the poet's choice of words and subjected him to a series of restraints or 'exigencies of metre'[74] which lie behind several new features of this poetry, such as changes in the forms of words and the use of rare words, different morphological patterns, and lengthened or shortened forms purely on the basis of metrical requirement, without reference to established usage. Thus, the poet will select the relative particle

73 See Hazan 1980, 119ff.

74 See E. Goldenberg 1983.

אֲשֶׁר ('ᵃšær) or -שֶׁ (šæ-) or the first person singular pronoun אֲנִי ('ᵃnī) or אָנֹכִי ('ānōḵī) according to metrical convenience and not because of fidelity to BH or RH. Similarly, the requirements of the *yated* have led to the standard employment of the particle לְמַעַן (le-ma'an) to express cause ('because') rather than purpose ('so that') and to the disuse of the causal particle יַעַן (ya'an). The first critics of the new technique, the followers of Menaḥem, pointed out, in harsh rebuttal of Dunash, that to employ Arabic metre in Hebrew poetry means that consonants not normally followed by vowels have to accept them and, conversely, vowels that would normally follow gutturals have to be suppressed. *Qameṣ ḥaṭuf* has to be eliminated or must appear in inappropriate contexts, and the position of the accent has to be altered, leading to changes in the morphological pattern of certain words. All of this, in their opinion, contributed to the 'destruction of the language'.[75] The reply of Yehudi b. Sheshet, a pupil of Dunash, who tries to find precedents for these features in Scripture and who emphasizes the importance of the new method introduced by his master,[76] is not particularly convincing, although it represents the pragmatic consensus which, in fact, prevailed among the poets of Spain, who accepted Dunash's new techniques without hesitation and used them for centuries to come.

The 'exigencies of metre', which had already been debated by the Arab grammarians and accepted by some of their schools, could lead even linguists as outstanding as Jonah ibn Janaḥ to justify certain quite controversial poetic usages. These were, of course, exceptional, and restricted to poetry, which was regarded as being subject to rules different from those governing the normal language. Thus, in Ibn Janaḥ's *Sefer ha-Rikmah*[77] and *Sefer ha-*

[75] See S. Benavente, *Tešubot de los discípulos de Menaḥem contra Dunaš ben Labraṭ* (Granada, 1986), *12ff., 15ff.

[76] See M.E. Varela, *Tešubot de Yehudi ben Šešet. Edición, traducción y comentario* (Granada, 1981), *17ff., 34ff.

[77] See M. Wilensky, *Sefer ha-rikmah (Kitāb al-luma') le-R. Yonah ibn Janaḥ mi-targumo ha-'Ivri shel R. Yehudah ibn Tibbon*, 2nd ed. (2 vols) by D. Téné (Jerusalem, 1964), 43.

Shorashim,[78] it is accepted, despite the protests of the followers of Menaḥem, that because of the demands of the *yated*, Dunash had to use the form עֲבוּר (ʻᵃḇūr)[79] in place of בַּעֲבוּר (ba-ʻᵃḇūr) 'because of' – at the end of the day, in Ibn Janaḥ's view, the -בּ (b-) here is simply an extra particle, and he notes that the Arabs make the same sort of allowances in their poetry. Similar comments apply to Dunash's use of כשקט (kᵉ-šāqaṭ) 'while he rested', which had also been censured by the followers of Menaḥem.[80] Even though Ibn Janaḥ views as incorrect the use of the particle -כְּ (kᵉ-) 'as, when' before the suffix-conjugation, he claims that it is justified here on metrical grounds, and he displays a similarly permissive attitude to various nouns, the morphological patterns of which have been changed by the poets. However, there are some innovations that Ibn Janaḥ sees as excessive, including, for example, the use of בֵּין ... וְ (bēn ... wᵉ-) 'between (x) and (y)' instead of בֵּין ... וּבֵין (bēn ... ū-ḇēn) lit. 'between (x) and between (y)'.[81] Rarely, a particular rhyming pattern will justify the use of an unusual form.[82]

Moses ibn Ezra, despite his stand against the use of forms of the verb that do not appear as such in the Bible, is more lenient in his attitude to poetic innovation resulting from metrical constraints and to certain usages of the article and adjective. However, he is less tolerant than Ibn Janaḥ of changes in the gender or number of nouns.[83]

78 See the entry for the root *'BR*.

79 This form, with a murmured vowel in the first syllable, fulfils the conditions of a *yated*. See above, n. 57.

80 In my *Tešubot de Dunash ben Labrat. Edición crítica y traducción española* (Granada, 1980), I accepted the reading כשוקט (kᵉ-šōqēṭ) 'while resting' in accordance with the oldest manuscript, British Library MS Add. 27214, which contains a text of very high quality. However, the indirect tradition regarding this passage shows that at the time of the followers of Menaḥem the most widespread reading was כשקט (kᵉšāqaṭ) 'while he rested', and they criticized this form as inadmissible according to BH. Cf. Benavente, *Tešubot de los discípulos de Menaḥem*, *25, 37.

81 See Wilensky, *Sefer ha-rikmah*, 306.

82 See E. Goldenberg 1983, 133ff.

83 See E. Goldenberg 1983, 135ff.

In general, though, the ideal defended by contemporary scholars was that of a pure biblical language, a theme that recurs in the works of, among others, Moses ibn Ezra, Judah Halevi, and Abraham ibn Ezra, who probably had in mind the excesses of Saadiah and his school in the creation of new linguistic forms. Thus, they claimed, it is essential that a poet always employ grammatically correct forms, without attempting to create new ones by the arbitrary use of analogy. A verb should only be used in the derived conjugations in which it is actually found in Scripture, not others that are theoretically possible. In nouns, the number and gender of the classical language have to be respected and nouns must only be used in the morphological patterns attested in BH – only in the infinitive are some new formations admissible.[84]

In most secular poetry, BH provides the major and most characteristic linguistic component. Most of the vocabulary is taken from the Bible, and BH grammar is normally employed. This is true even of the earliest poems from the tenth century, such as the letters in the form of verse written by Menaḥem b. Saruq for Ḥasdai ibn Shapruṭ, and for subsequent Hebrew poetry from Spain. It is the use of BH which distinguishes this poetry very clearly from that of other times and places.

The Jewish poets of Spain often intersperse their works with whole phrases from the Bible, either word-for-word or with slight modifications, radically altering original meanings to suit new contexts and topics, sometimes converting a poem into a patchwork of quotation and allusion. This so-called 'mosaic' (*iqtibās*) style, although characteristic of all Hebrew poetry from Spain, is most common in the postclassical, mannerist, period, from the middle of the twelfth century, and especially in the *maqāmāt*. For rhetorical effect, poets deliberately exploited the contrast between the original meaning of a biblical text, which would be well-known to listeners and readers, and its new sense in the secular context of a poem. The use of biblical words and texts

84 See E. Goldenberg 1971, 1618.

can simply be a general feature of poetic style, but occasionally it represents a calculated attempt to give a passage a particular undercurrent of meaning. Although the Arabs were aware of similar techniques, Hebrew poetry has probably developed independently in this respect, through its own dynamic. Disrespect and irreverence are generally avoided.[85]

Even where such explicit use of scripture is absent, the poet will try to restrict himself to BH, except on a few occasions where Arabic, Aramaic, or RH are deliberately used in compositions of a specific character. In secular poetry, it is nearly always the tense system of BH rather than RH that is employed, with such features as *waw*-consecutive, the infinitive absolute, the infinitive construct with proclitic particle, and long and short forms of the verb. The present-future is usually expressed by the prefix-conjugation and the past by the suffix-conjugation. Secular poetry also conforms to BH in its use of the article, relative pronoun, and, especially, particles. It generally avoids the archaisms of ancient biblical poetry as well as features characteristic of LBH or RH. However, in the search for a select vocabulary and elevated style, rare biblical words and *hapax legomena* are often used.

Nonetheless, however much a poet might have wanted to limit himself to the Hebrew of the Bible, he also had to be able to increase his means of expression. Therefore, to a greater or lesser extent, he would fall back on analogy to form new words. This does not represent a mere desire for novelty, as was perhaps true in respect of the *payṭanim* and Saadiah, but a genuine linguistic need. It was exactly this sort of analogical innovation, and the limits to which it should be allowed to extend, that most exercised the prescriptivists and defenders of linguistic purity. But even during periods when the purist ethos was at its height, a certain degree of controlled expansion of the language was tolerated.[86]

85 See Schirmann 1954, 31ff.; Ratzaby 1970; Pagis 1976, 70ff.

86 See Klar 1953–54, 31ff.

On the other hand, cultural pressures, including the dominance of Arabic, also left their mark, especially in various aspects of syntax and in vocabulary. Divergence from BH in the sphere of vocabulary is particularly striking, influenced both by new developments in lexicography and biblical exegesis and by the widespread use of calques from Arabic. Poets were well aware of contemporary arguments regarding the interpretation of particular words, and chose the meanings that best suited their purposes. For example, for Moses ibn Ezra, חֹלֶה (ḥōlæ) means '(he is) falling', in accordance with Ibn Janaḥ's interpretation of Ec 5:12, and, according to Dunash and his followers, ערג ('rg) means 'cry out'.[87] With varying degrees of justification, old expressions were given new meanings which generally could be deduced from their contexts, so that, for example, פֶּגֶר (pægær) and גְוִיָּה (gᵉwiyyā) were used to mean 'body', and not just 'corpse'. Arabic was responsible for many new senses of BH words, influencing Hebrew more in this way than through direct loanwords.[88] Consistent with contemporary aesthetic norms, a poet would demonstrate his ability by composing rhymes of the same word with different senses. These are not always based solely on scriptural usage, so that, for example, צִיר (ṣīr) can mean 'pain', 'messenger', and 'door-hinge'.[89]

As is only to be expected, in secular poetry as elsewhere principles and ideals are one thing, reality is another, and virtually every poet introduced linguistic innovations into his work. Thus, we sometimes find non-biblical words or the use of allusions reminiscent of the *payṭanim*, as with יְחִידָה (yᵉḥīḏā) 'unique (one)' for 'soul' (although on occasions such features represent a new method of comparison and metaphor), the particle -כְּ (kᵉ-) 'as, when' before the suffix-conjugation, and biliteral forms of the verb. Derived conjugations of the verb that are uncommon in BH, such

87 See Klar 1953–54, 174ff.

88 D. Pagis (1976, 169) calculated that in Moses ibn Ezra's secular poetry there are more than 700 new meanings of biblical words.

89 Thus, Moses ibn Ezra in *Ha-'Anak* and, occasionally, Judah al-Ḥarizi in the *Taḥkemoni*.

as the passives *Pu'al* and *Hof'al*, are overused due to the influence of Arabic, verbal nouns are created, new adjectives are formed from participles, and new singular nouns are derived from plurals and *vice versa*. By the close of the thirteenth century, fidelity to BH had declined markedly, especially in poetry composed in the Christian kingdoms of Spain.

The rabbinic component is another feature of this poetry that should not be overlooked. Andalusian poetry uses many RH expressions, although the number varies from one writer and period to another. The extent to which RH was accepted also had, at least partially, an ideological basis, in the controversy between Rabbanites and Karaites over the legitimacy of accepting the language of rabbinic literature as 'pure' or 'correct'. Following the example set by Saadiah, most Spanish writers, with the exception of Menaḥem b. Saruq and some of his followers, considered it legitimate to treat RH as a close continuation of BH, and of help in interpreting difficult biblical texts. The generation of Ibn Khalfon and Samuel ha-Nagid found no difficulty in making generous use of RH or in forming new words according to RH models, and once the era of linguistic purism, in the eleventh and twelfth centuries, ended RH was again used with little hesitation. It has been noticed that RH words are vocalized according to a variety of traditions, not only Tiberian, but also Babylonian and sometimes Palestinian, giving the impression that the Andalusian poets were aware of all of these traditions and used whichever seemed most suitable to a particular metre.[90]

Indeed, most poets accepted rabbinic forms with remarkable freedom, and not even purists were completely opposed to the use of RH, be it for by then indispensable technical terms or for words and phrases that had become widespread or with no BH equivalents, for example צָרִיךְ (ṣārīḵ) 'needing (to)', -מִלְּ (mil-le-) 'from (doing)' (lit. 'from to [do]'), אוֹקְיָנוֹס ('ōqyānōs) 'ocean', and וֶרֶד (wæræḏ) 'rose'. It only required a particular word, meaning, or

90 See Ṭovi 1972–73; Ratzaby 1967; 1972–73.

morphological pattern to be found but once in the Bible for its use to be accepted as entirely valid by philologists. Similarly, it was not unusual for biblical texts to be given a forced or extravagant interpretation in order to justify a form or meaning that had come into common use.

The same phenomenon of accepting and justifying new meanings is also seen in connexion with terms employed according to their meaning in Arabic, as, for example, וְאִם (wᵉ-'im) in the sense of 'nonetheless' (lit. 'and if'; cf. *wa'in*). Generally, though, calques from Arabic are less frequent in Hebrew poetry than in the prose of mediaeval translations into Hebrew. They are found in particular in technical expressions and in literary and symbolic figures. Thus, for example, בַּיִת (bayiṯ) lit. 'house' is a 'verse', צְבִי (ṣᵉḇī) 'gazelle' and עֹפֶר ('ōp̄ær) 'doe' are the Arabic *ẓaby* or *ġazāl* 'beloved', זְמָן (zᵉmān) 'time' and יָמִים (yāmīm) 'days' take on the same sense as *az-zamān* 'fate', תֶּבֶל (tæḇæl) is the 'world' as the enemy of mankind, בְּנוֹת הַיָּמִים (bᵉnōṯ hay-yāmīm) lit. 'daughters of the days' means 'misfortunes, forces of destiny',[91] and מְרִיב (mᵉrīḇ) 'antagonist' is used in the sense of *al-'uḏḏāl* 'the one who chides a lover'. Meanings attested only rarely in BH became standard through the influence of Arabic equivalents, as with שָׁב (šāḇ) in the sense of 'he became, turned into' (normally 'he went back'; cf. *'āda*) and מַעֲנֶה (ma'ᵃnæ) in the sense of 'meaning' (usually 'answer'; cf. *ma'nā*). Compounds with אֲחִי ('ᵃḥī), אֲבִי ('ᵃḇī), בֶּן (bæn), and בַּעַל (ba'al) 'brother, father, son, master of' are often calqued from Arabic, for example אֲחִי בִין ('ᵃḥī ḇīn) 'intelligent person' (lit. 'brother of understanding'), אֲבִי שִׁיר ('ᵃḇī šīr) 'the greatest poet' (lit. 'father of poetry'), and בַּעַל מַדָּע (ba'al maddā') 'educated person' (lit. 'master of knowledge').

Purely phonetic considerations can lie behind the adoption by a Hebrew word of the meaning of an Arabic homophone, as, for example, with אֲבָל ('ᵃḇāl) 'but' in the sense of *bal* 'even more' and שָׁם (šām) 'there' used like *thamma* 'afterwards'. The relatively rare

91 See I. Levin 1962.

BH verb חָשַׁק (ḥāšaq) 'he loved' became more widespread due to its similarity to *'ašaqa* in the same sense, דִּין (dīn) 'judgement' took on the sense of *dīn* 'religion', and יְתוֹמָה (yetōmā) 'orphan girl' that of *yatīmah* 'unique'.

Although some of the resulting structures can also have a basis in BH, significant Arabic influence is seen as well in combinations of verb and preposition, for example, נשא בְּ- (nś' be-) 'transport' (lit. 'carry with'), בוא בְּ- (bw' be-) 'bring' (lit. 'come with'), ירד בְּ- (yrd be-) 'take down' (lit. 'go down with'), and תמה מִן (tmh min) 'be surprised at (lit. 'from')'. An Arabic origin again lies behind a number of changes in gender that became more frequent in prose, leading to structures like דְּמוּת נִמְשָׁל (demūṯ nimšāl), 'comparable image', where a feminine noun takes a masculine adjective.[92]

Notwithstanding the overall features we have described, each poet used the language in his own distinctive way. Thus, Menaḥem b. Saruq, whose work is the oldest surviving material we possess from the poet-grammarians of Spain, in the middle of the tenth century, already employs a predominantly biblical style, with archaic pronominal suffixes like למו (lā-mō) 'to them', infinitive absolutes like היה היה (hāyō hāyā) 'he really was', lengthened forms of the verb such as ישובון (yešūḇūn) 'they will return', and parallelism. However, the same writer also uses rabbinic forms, so that, for example, the relative particle -שֶׁ (šæ-) is found alongside BH אֲשֶׁר ('ašær), and RH זְמָן (zemān) alongside BH עֵת ('ēṯ) 'time'. Menaḥem uses rabbinic phrases like יֵשׁ עַל (yēš 'al) 'there is (obligation) upon, must', and accepts rabbinic meanings of words, for example חמץ (ḥmṣ) in the sense of 'delay, mature'. Like the *payṭanim*, he treats the noun אֹם ('ōm) 'nation' as feminine and has recourse to allusive expressions like ארץ משואה ('æræṣ mešō'ā) 'land of desolation', in the sense of 'exile'. Menaḥem expands the language with new forms based on MH usage, like שִׂבָּרוֹן (śibbārōn) 'hope' (as in Arabic), עִצָּרוֹן ('iṣṣārōn) 'detention', סֵפֶד (sēp̄æḏ) 'lament', סכות (sekōṯ) '(to) see, listen',

[92] See E. Goldenberg 1971, 1621f.; Pagis 1976, 68ff.

האניני (ha'ᵃnīnī) 'pity me!', and מצחצח (mᵉṣaḥṣēᵃḥ) 'speaking with purity'. However, due no doubt to his ideological stance, Menaḥem hardly ever succumbs to the influence of Arabic.

Dunash b. Labraṭ also uses a mainly biblical style in his poetry, with a clear preference for BH over RH forms. Thus, although on one occasion he utilizes the form בשל (bᵉ-šæl) 'in which', Dunash normally employs the BH relative אֲשֶׁר (ᵃšær). He also uses conjunctions typical of BH, and, frequently, the infinitive construct with proclitic particle. However, we hardly ever find archaisms or features like *waw*-consecutive or the infinitive absolute in his writing, even though elements typical of LBH do occur, for example the use of -לְ (lᵉ-) as object-marker or preceding an infinitive but without expressing purpose, and other forms of expression taken from the later books of the Bible. His tense system is closer to that of RH, with the participle used as the main means of expressing present action and, in conjunction with היה (hyh) 'be', in a number of periphrastic constructions that express repeated action. Other features also reflect RH, for example the second person singular masculine pronoun אַתְּ ('att) and a few instances of the *Nithpa'al* conjugation, although these are not sufficient to permit us to claim that RH is a major element in Dunash's poetry. *Piyyuṭ* influence is seen in the use of עֲבוּר ('ᵃḇūr) expressing purpose ('so that') and of the particle -כְּ (kᵉ-) 'as, when' before the suffix-conjugation, as in כנהפך (kᵉ-næhpaḵ) 'as he turned' and, perhaps, כשקט (kᵉ-šāqaṭ) 'while he rested' (but see above, n. 80), although Dunash's work is in other respects very different from that of the eastern *payṭanim*. Dunash was not a strict purist with regard to mediaeval features either, creating through analogy new forms of the verb, deriving new plurals from nouns found only in the singular in BH, for example names of animals and precious stones, and employing a large number of passive participles, especially *Nif'al*s. Arabic influence is not particularly evident, although it is visible in demonstrative constructions, for example זה הפרץ (zǣ hap-pæræṣ) 'this breach', and in changes in various verb-preposition combinations, such as -זעף בְּ (z'p bᵉ-) for

זעף עַל (z'p 'al) 'be angry with', as well as in a number of other expressions, for example הניב אסף (han-nīḇ 'āsap̄) 'he gathered together the language', בספרים (bi-sp̄ārīm) 'in (great) numbers', טַעַם (ṭa'am) 'meaning', מְפֹּרָד (mepōrāḏ) '(in) prose', אדות ('ōḏōṯ) 'circumstances', מוּסָר (mūsār) 'culture', גַּרְסָן (garsān) 'student', and עֲרוּגָה ('arūgā) 'garden'.[93]

Isaac ibn Khalfon, at the beginning of the eleventh century, employs a fundamentally biblical form of expression, although there are also many traces of RH and *piyyuṭ*. Often he will use the morphological pattern *qeṭīlā*, as in בְּלִיעָה (belī'ā) 'swallowing', זְכִירָה (zekīrā) 'remembering', and פְּשִׁיעָה (pešī'ā) 'sinning', as well as other rabbinic expressions like עִתּוֹת וְשָׁעוֹת ('ittōṯ we-šā'ōṯ) '(at) times and hours, always' and מְאוֹר עֵינַי (me'ōr 'ēnāy) 'light of my eyes', allusive names such as עֲלוּקָה ('alūqā) 'leech' for 'hell', and Aramaic expressions like צְפִירָה (ṣepīrā) 'crown' and נֶאֱצָלוֹת (næ'æṣālōṯ) 'pressed'. In Ibn Khalfon's secular poetry we can recognize a number of typically *piyyuṭ* features, such as the particle -כְּ (ke-) 'as, when' before the suffix-conjugation, for example כשם (ke-śām) 'when he placed' and כצוה (ke-ṣiwwā) 'when he ordered', shortened forms like מַעַשׂ (ma'aś) for מַעֲשֶׂה (ma'aśæ) 'action' and לַעַן (la'an) for לַעֲנָה (la'anā) 'wormwood', as well as other expressions like הורך (hōrāḵ) for אָבִיךָ ('āḇīḵā) 'your father', עתר ('æṯær) for עֲתִירָה ('aṯīrā) 'supplication', and להסביבי (le-hasbīḇī) instead of the predicted BH form לְהַסְבֵּנִי (le-hasbēnī) 'to surround me'. Standards of linguistic purity had still not been defined in Ibn Khalfon's day, and he found little difficulty in creating new forms such as עֲנִיקָה ('anīqā) 'donation' and רָפוּת (rāp̄ūṯ) 'weakness'. His use of the particles also often differs from BH, so that we find, for instance, -בְּ (be-) used as a causal conjunction alongside עֲבוּר ('aḇūr) for בַּעֲבוּר (ba-'aḇūr). There are also very clear traces of Arabic in Ibn Khalfon's poetry, and we find most of the calques already noted as well as others like חֹשֵׁק (ḥōšēq) 'lover',

[93] See Allony 1947; Sáenz-Badillos 1982.

לֵבָב (lēḇāḇ) 'essence' (lit. 'heart'), מוּסָר (mūsār) 'culture', and פֵּרוּד (pērūḏ) 'separation'.[94]

Samuel ibn Nagrel'a ha-Nagid played an important rôle in developing the new style of Hebrew that emerged halfway through the eleventh century. The importance of this complex figure, a pupil of Judah Ḥayyuj and a linguist in his own right, who also held high position in society, gives particular significance to his use of the language and his linguistic innovations. However, he did not escape criticism in this respect, and his tendency to create new words turned him into a prominent target of the purists. Naturally, the Bible is the principal source of his words and structures, but he also makes liberal use of analogical formation in order to expand his linguistic resources, and practically all the excesses criticized by Moses ibn Ezra are to be found in his work. Thus, for example, he breaks up set-expressions in order to yield such new words as קָט (qāṭ) 'almost' from כִּמְעַט קָט (ki-m'aṭ qāṭ) 'hardly anything' at Ezk 16:47, בָּבוֹת (bāḇōṯ) 'pupils' from בְּבַת עֵינוֹ (beḇaṯ 'ēnō) 'the pupil of his eye' at Zc 2:12, and מוֹרָשִׁים (mōrāšīm) 'thoughts' from מוֹרָשֵׁי לְבָבִי (mōrāšē leḇāḇī) 'possessions of my heart' at Jb 17:11. The same writer derives new plurals from singulars, especially names of luminaries and precious stones, for example חֲרָסִים (ḥarāsīm) 'suns', זְהָבִים (zehāḇīm) 'golds', and לְשָׁמִים (lešāmīm) 'opals', singulars from plurals, as with אַף ('ap̄) 'face' and כִּפּוּר (kippūr) 'atonement', absolutes from constructs, as with עֲפָרוֹת ('ap̄ārōṯ) 'dusts', and verbs from nouns, as with מְסֻפֶּרֶת (mesuppæræṯ) 'surrounded by sapphires'. Masculine nouns like גַּן (gan) 'garden', דָּבָר (dāḇār) 'word', and מַזָּל (mazzāl) 'fortune' are treated as though they were feminine, and feminine nouns like חֶרֶב (ḥæræḇ) 'sword' and חָצֵר (ḥāṣēr) 'court' as masculine, and many BH words are given meanings quite different from those they usually have in the Bible, so that, for example, אוֹר ('ōr) can mean 'rain', 'sun', or 'plant', אֵת

94 See Mirsky 1961, 40ff.

(ʾēṯ), 'axe', חוּג (ḥūḡ), 'sky', הִפָּזוֹן (ḥippāzōn), 'fear', and the verb חמד (ḥmd), 'envy'.[95]

There is also a significant rabbinic component in the poetry of Samuel ha-Nagid. Apart from two compositions in which his son, who compiled his father's *Diwan*, notes that he had deliberately employed the language of the Talmud, there is noticeable influence from rabbinic language and motifs as well as quotations from rabbinic works and the liturgy. Indeed, many passages, especially in *Ben Mishlei* and *Ben Kohelet*, cannot be understood except against their rabbinic background. Conversely, there is very little influence from *piyyuṭ*, other than a few forms like מַעַשׂ (maʿaś) for מַעֲשֶׂה (maʿaśǣ) 'action' and גַּשְׁתִּי (gaštī) for נָגַשְׁתִּי (nāḡaštī) 'I approached', and Samuel ha-Nagid refrains from using other *piyyuṭ* expressions common among his contemporaries. His poetry's typically mediaeval character is seen in its innovations with regard to BH, as already noted, in its use of many new noun patterns, exemplified by נוּם (nūm) for תְּנוּמָה (tenūmā) 'sleep', פֶּלֶד (pælæḏ) for פְּלָדָה (pelāḏā) 'steel', חֲרִיזָה (ḥarīzā) ' rhyming', and נְדִידָה (neḏīḏā) 'wandering', as well as in its use of the derived conjugations, so that we find, for example, the verb אזן (ʾzn) in the *Qal* ('hear'), שפל (špl) in the *Nifʿal* ('be laid low'), and שיב (śyb) in the *Hifʿil* ('cause to age').[96]

Arabic influence is also a marked feature of Samuel ha-Nagid's poetry, which includes many calques apart from those already mentioned, for example אָחֵר (āḥēr) '(the) hereafter', רְבִיעָה (re bīʿā) 'Spring', חָבֵר (ḥāḇēr) 'owner', אֵצֶל (ʾēṣæl) 'in the opinion of', אָן (ʾān) 'where?', כַּמָּה (kammā) 'how often?', גזר (gzr) 'pass', and חתך (ḥtk) 'derive', as well as the use of כְּבָר (keḇār) 'already' with the suffix-conjugation, like the Arabic *qad*, and Arabic-influenced prepositional usages, such as קָרוֹב מִן (qārōḇ min) 'near to (lit. 'from')', תמה מִן (tmh min) 'be surprised at (lit. 'from')', and דמה כְּ (dmh [pi.] ke-) 'compare with (lit. 'as')'.[97]

[95] See Yarden 1958–62; 1966, 14ff., 400ff. Cf. Yellin 1975, 150ff.
[96] See Yarden 1966, 18ff.; Ratzaby 1967.
[97] See Yarden 1966, 24ff.; Ratzaby 1967.

The three great figures of Hebrew poetry's Golden Age, Solomon ibn Gabirol, and in particular, Moses ibn Ezra and Judah Halevi, are the most eminent representatives of biblical purism. This is not to deny, however, that they also expanded forms found in the Bible with greater or lesser freedom, or that their work contains clear examples of the effects of metre and rhyme and of changes in meaning due to Arabic influence. Of the three, Ibn Gabirol is the least constrained in his use of BH, for which he often earned the censure of Moses ibn Ezra, as in the following well-known passage:

> But the greatest error is committed by those who decline these nouns as if they were verbs: שהיא משוהמת (šæ-hīʾ mᵉšūhæmæṯ) ['which is covered in onyx, "onyxed"'], כלה מיושפה (kullāh mᵉyuššāp̄ā) ['all of it covered in agates, "agated"'], extracting these declensions from שהם (šōham) ['onyx'] and ישפה (yāšᵉp̄ē) ['jasper'].
>
> One said, ונפש פניניה (wᵉ-næp̄æš pᵉnīnīyyā) ['and pearly soul'], taken from אדמו עצם מפנינים ('āḏᵉmū 'æṣæm mip-pᵉnīnīm) ['in body they were redder than corals' (Lm 4:7)], for which [noun] there exists no singular, and what he wanted to say is 'a soul like a jewel', but this is untenably arbitrary.[98]

Here, as often elsewhere, there is direct allusion to Ibn Gabirol, who, despite using BH as his primary source and employing such features as lengthened forms of the verb, archaic suffixes, and *hapax legomena*, also has recourse to a number of characteristically RH usages, like the infinitive introduced by -לְ (lᵉ-) not expressing purpose and noun patterns of the type *qᵉṭīlā*, *qiṭlōn*, etc., as well as to elements known from *piyyuṭ*, as, for example, in his use of כבשל (kᵉ-ḇāšal) 'when it was cooked' and כערף (kᵉ-'ārap̄) 'when he beheaded'. Moreover, Ibn Gabirol does not always respect the gender of nouns, and he uses numerous calques from Arabic in his

98 See Abumalham, *Kitāb al-muḥāḍara wal-muḏākara*, 111 r.

vocabulary as well as many passive formations from the same source.[99]

Even in the poetry of Moses ibn Ezra himself it is not uncommon to find additional particles, such as גַּם (gam) 'also', וְאַף (we-'ap̄) 'and indeed', and הֵן (hēn) 'lo', which are not required on semantic grounds and the use of which can only be justified because of metre. The same applies to various unnecessary pronominal suffixes, which simply help to maintain the rhyme. Ibn Ezra also changes the word order of sentences, uses pausal forms in context and contextual forms in pause, and even employs construct forms at the end of a verse. The syllabic constraints in his metre lead him to insert a *he* in forms like יהבין (yehāb̲īn) for יָבִין (yāb̲īn) 'he will understand' and תהשלים (tehašlīm) for תַּשְׁלִים (tašlīm) 'she will complete', and to use expressions in a different form or meaning from those with which they are found in BH, for example, אֱנוֹשׁ ('ænōš) instead of אִישׁ ('īš) 'person', מְתֵי (me tē) instead of אַנְשֵׁי ('anšē) 'persons of', and בְּלִי (belī) instead of לֹא (lō') 'not'.[100] Although to a much lesser extent than poets of earlier generations, Ibn Ezra has recourse to new morphological patterns for nouns, as with אֲבָרִים ('ab̲ārīm) instead of the collective אֶבְרָה ('æb̲rā) 'wing(s)' and מַעֲצָבוֹ (ma'aṣāb̲ō) instead of עָצְבּוֹ ('oṣbō) 'his pain', and to new derived conjugations of verbs, like שמר (šmr) in the *Pi'el* ('guard') and גשם (gšm) in the *Hif'il* ('let rain fall'). He also uses a number of lengthened forms of the verb, such as וְאֶצְעָדָה (we-'æṣ'ād̲ā) 'and I shall march', as well as abbreviated forms of nouns, for example אַהַב ('ahab̲) for אַהֲבָה ('ahab̲ā) 'love' and אֲפֵל ('apēl) for אֲפֵלָה ('apēlā) 'darkness'. Mixed in with such biblical features as the collective singular with plural verb, we also find in Ibn Ezra elements from RH, like the use of לְ (le-) as object-marker, and other forms typical of MH, for example גזלני (gezālanī) 'he plundered me' in place of גָּזַל מִמֶּנִּי (gāzal mim-mænnī) 'he plundered from me', הָעֵת (hā-'ēt̲) 'the time' in the sense of בָּעֵת (bā-

[99] See Cano 1978.
[100] See Yellin 1935–36.

'ēṯ) 'at the time', and עִתִּים ('ittīm) 'at times' (lit. 'times'). Ibn Ezra also treats עֵינַיִם ('ēnayim) '(pair of) eyes' on one occasion as though it were masculine. Typically mediaeval as well are the senses attached to, for example, כִּנּוֹר (kinnōr) 'lute', שוב (šwb) 'turn into', עולם הַנְּפָשִׁים ('ōlām han-nᵉp̄āšīm) 'the world of spirits', and בְּנֵי עולם (bᵉnē 'ōlām) 'the people of (this) world'.

Of all the poets of Spain, Judah Halevi is without doubt the most rigorous in his adherence to BH, although this does not prevent him from also employing some typically mediaeval features. For example, formulas of adjuration are based on Arabic models, the negative particles בַּל (bal) and בְּלִי (bᵉlī) are used with the prefix-conjugation and participle, respectively, nouns in the absolute rather than the construct state are used for reasons of metre, as in יפי תארה (yop̄ī ṯo'ᵒrāh) 'the beauty (of) her form', plurals with new technical meanings are derived from singular nouns, for example פְּלָכִים (pᵉlāḵīm) 'heavenly bodies', and suffixed forms of the verb that are not normal in BH, such as יפחדני (yip̄ḥaḏ-nī) 'he will frighten me' and יריבוני בך (yᵉrīḇū-nī ḇᵉ-ḵā) 'they will argue with me because of you' are found, as are calques from Arabic like מְתֵי אַהֲבָה (mᵉṯē 'āhᵃḇā) 'lovers' (lit. 'men of love').

It is in the vocabulary of the Golden Age of Hebrew poetry in Spain that the greatest real differences from BH are to be found, due primarily to the influence of Arabic. In addition to the widespread use of calques already listed, many new meanings of words also appear for the first time during this period, to be absorbed into the language of following generations. These include אַךְ ('aḵ) 'even more', עֲדֵי ('ᵃḏē) 'even', צָעִיר (ṣā'īr) 'small', גּוּשׁ (g ūš) 'worms', חִידָה (ḥīḏā) 'conversation, composition', זֶכֶר (zækær) 'smell', עָלוּם ('ālūm) 'hidden sin', רַקָּה (raqqā) 'cheek', גִּיל (gīl) 'generation, era', מִדְבָּר (miḏbār) 'cemetery', גבר (gbr) 'calculate' (like its Arabic cognate), אמר ('mr) hi. 'name as emir, governor',

בלל (bll) 'moisten', שחר (šḥr) 'rise at dawn', and חקר (ḥqr) 'scorn'.[101]

The Hebrew of later poetry, especially from the Christian kingdoms, has still not been properly examined, although in general it conforms to the features already described, with different aspects predominating in different writers.[102] Changes of taste, mannerism, fondness for processes of a more or less eccentric kind,[103] the introduction into poetry of popular philosophical and mystical motifs, as well as the occasional influence of Romance have all left clear marks on the language of the generations that followed the great classical period.

Although in the works of Abraham ibn Ezra BH and Arabic are still the major influences, we can also see the first signs of a new era. Thus, for example, the expression נולד בלי כוכב (nōlāḏ bᵉlī kōḵāḇ) 'born without a star' probably translates a popular Romance figure of the time, although it is also known in Arabic and other languages. In Ibn Ezra's poetry we also encounter nouns shortened because of metre, for example מַחְשָׁב (maḥšāḇ) and מַעֲמָס (ma'ᵃmās) for מַחֲשָׁבָה (maḥᵃšāḇā) 'thought' and מַעֲמָסָה (ma'ᵃmāsā) 'burden', as well as a number of allusive names reminiscent of the *payṭanim*, such as חָמוּד (ḥāmūḏ) 'beloved', with reference to Isaac, 'the beloved son'. On occasions, Ibn Ezra will modify the gender of a noun, writing כחרבים (ka-ḥᵃrāḇīm) for כַּחֲרָבוֹת (ka-ḥᵃrāḇōṯ) 'like swords' and treating כְּנָפַיִם (kᵉnāp̄ayim) '(pair of) wings' as masculine. Because of the metre he will sometimes replace an absolute form with a construct, as with בין (bᵉ-yēn) for בְּיַיִן (bᵉ-yayin) 'with wine', occasionally coupling this with a change in word order: ליל באישון (lēl bᵉ-'īšōn) for בְּאִישׁוֹן לַיְלָה (bᵉ-'īšōn laylā) 'in the depths of night' (Pr 7:9). Some

101 See S. Abramson 1941–43; Medan 1951; Mirsky 1952–53; Klar 1953–54; Ratzaby 1956–57; 1965; 1969; Allony 1959; 1960; 1964a; 1966; 1969; 1975; 1976.

102 It is interesting that D. Yellin's study of the language of Todros b. Judah ha-Levi Abulafia, which employs a similar framework to one used for describing the language of Moses ibn Ezra (Yellin 1975, 241ff., 262ff.), shows no appreciable differences of substance between the two writers.

103 See, for example, I. Davidson 1914.

biblical words take on new meanings, as with מִבְרָח (miḇrāḥ) 'escape', for example.

Judah al-Ḥarizi uses the 'mosaic' style in his *maqāmāt*, with numerous biblical passages taken completely out of context. In other respects, his work is one of the last representatives of pure BH, both in his rhymed prose and in his translations from Arabic in the form of poetry or of prose. Nonetheless, he employs many rabbinic expressions, for example כְּנוּסָה (kᵉnūsā), a Talmudic term meaning 'married woman', and, just like his predecessors in the classical period, he departs from the norms of strict purism, as well as displaying very clear examples of Arabic influence in vocabulary and verb-preposition combinations.[104] In subsequent writers, the Arabic component, retained solely in an attempt to imitate the great classical poets of Andalusia, gradually gave way to different influences, notably from RH and Aramaic, with the occasional use of calques from the Romance languages.[105] Thus, Meshullam b. Solomon da Piera, who lived in Gerona halfway through the thirteenth century, imitates the Andalusian style, with, for example, Arabisms like מְתֵי אֹמֶן (mᵉtē 'ōmæn) 'faithful ones' (lit. 'men of faith'), changes of gender, so that עֵינַיִם ('ēnayim) '(pair of) eyes' is treated as though it were masculine, and various changes to accommodate quantitative metre. At the same time he also employs expressions from RH or Aramaic, for example עֲגִילֵי ('ᵃḡīlē) 'shields of'.

Probably the last of Spain's Hebrew poets was Saadiah ibn Danan, who left Granada at the end of the fifteenth century. Although his poems are few and not at all well-known,[106] they follow the pattern of Andalusian poetry, with a language that is fundamentally biblical, albeit in an obscure style and a stilted syntax. Ibn Danan's work also contains various traces of RH, such as the use of -לְ (lᵉ-) as object-marker and the second person singular masculine pronominal suffix in ךָ- (-āḵ), as well as a

---

[104] See Schirmann 1930, 10ff.
[105] See Pagis 1976, 182ff.
[106] See Targarona 1986.

number of Arabisms, related to vocabulary and to the use of passives and auxiliary verbs, for example.

7.5 *The language of the Hebrew prose of Spain*

A major part of mediaeval Hebrew prose, particularly from Spain and Provence, has been strongly influenced by Arabic language and literature. But the importance of this general feature cannot hide the very clear linguistic differences that also exist among the various writings. To begin with, we can distinguish original Hebrew works from translations, especially of Arabic and Latin texts. Within the first group (Hebrew originals), we have to discriminate between works written in Muslim-dominated areas, which evidence varying degrees of Arabic influence, and others composed in Christian territories, which are generally less subject to such influence. Additionally, each literary genre raises its own linguistic problems that have to be solved in different ways, which means that we need to distinguish further, at the very least, narrative or literary works, compositions of a philological, philosophical, or mystical character, and works of science. In the second group (translations), although translations from Arabic, particularly those undertaken by the Ibn Tibbon family from Granada, are the most typical of the period, they do not, of course, represent the only activity in this field, and are very different from, for example, the translations from Latin made in northeastern Spain and Provence.[107]

We do not know the individual circumstances that motivated some Jewish writers to choose Middle Arabic and others to choose Hebrew for their prose composition. Probably the main reason would be personal, depending on the writer's familiarity with, and

[107] M.H. Goshen-Gottstein, to whom we owe a number of very important studies in this area, proposed (1968) a classification into six periods, corresponding, in practice, to the different levels of Arabic influence on Hebrew prose. Unfortunately, the study of each of these periods has virtually ceased in recent years.

competence in, a particular language. Another consideration would be his intended readership's knowledge of a given language. In any case, if a writer did elect to write in Hebrew, be it on a literary, philosophical, or scientific topic, he had a great deal of freedom about the type of language to be employed given the scarcity of existing models to imitate. The standards of poetic language were of little importance here, and linguistic purism was never imposed or even really considered as a guide to writing prose. Thus, whereas some writers used a form of language near to RH for scientific composition, others employed something closer to BH. Whatever the choice, the language of all these original prose writings contains biblical and rabbinic elements and evidences a varying but very significant level of Arabic influence, especially in syntax and vocabulary.

The use of Hebrew by the tenth-century Andalusian philologists for their lexical and syntactic studies signifies a decisive step forward in the development of Hebrew technical writing in the Middle Ages. By writing his dictionary (the *Maḥberet*) in Hebrew, Menaḥem b. Saruq was clearly distancing himself from his closest antecedents in the east and in North Africa. Hebrew was also to be the language used in the controversy following the appearance of Menaḥem's work and in all tenth-century grammatical studies from Spain, until the great linguists of the eleventh century (who were to define the path that Hebrew philology would take), decided to start using Arabic again.

For Menaḥem, the decision to write about the language of the Bible in Hebrew did not force him to use a strictly biblical form of language. The 'purity of the language' was a concept that did not gain ground extensively until several generations later, only really applying then to secular poetry, and Menaḥem neither defends purism as a theory nor is governed by it in practice. He limits himself to avoiding what he considers to be errors, bad usages, or words created out of ignorance of the language, so that, for example, he criticizes such derivations as תָּרַמְתִּי (tāramtī) 'I contributed (an offering)' from תְּרוּמָה (terūmā) 'heave-offering.[108] But the Hebrew Menaḥem uses is, nonetheless, typical of the period, with a strong BH component mixed with a large number of rabbinic and mediaeval structures.

The preference for BH in the *Maḥberet* is exhibited above all in its use of the relative and demonstrative pronouns and of the particles, which are normally well known from BH. Apart, perhaps, from the occasional use of *nun paragogicum*, there are hardly any archaisms, *waw*-consecutive is not used and the infinitive absolute followed by finite verb is rare. Conversely, the infinitive construct with proclitic particle occurs frequently, and the system of tenses also coincides with BH (without the lengthened or shortened forms of the verb found in other kinds of text), although the participle is occasionally used as a present tense when expressing a generalization or norm, in accordance with rabbinic usage. Genitive relationships are usually represented by the construct chain, with the particle שֶׁל (šæl) 'of' found but rarely. The LBH conditional particle אִלּוּ ('illū) is common.

Other much less significant rabbinic elements in Menaḥem's language include the plural in ־ִין (-īn), particularly common in names of letters of the alphabet, for example, certain particles, the occasional use of the feminine demonstrative זוֹ (zō) 'this' or the placing of the demonstrative adjective after a noun and without the article, periphrastic constructions of the participle with the verb היה (hyh) 'be', and a few instances of the *Nithpa'al*. He rarely uses devices typical of the *payṭanim*.

Menaḥem's language contains many elements of mediaeval origin, although they are not so great as to alter its fundamentally biblical character. Although opposed in principle to the free expansion of forms found in the Bible, Menaḥem, nonetheless, employs analogy to increase his linguistic resources when his subject matter is far removed from that of the Bible. Moreover, because he is the first writer to use Hebrew to present particular

108 See my edition of Menaḥem's *Maḥberet* (Granada, 1986), *20.

linguistic issues, his need to innovate is, in fact, quite considerable. Although Menaḥem himself does not recognize it, he is also substantially indebted to Arabic, especially in the area of linguistic terminology.

Several types of analogical formation later criticized by Moses ibn Ezra can be found in Menaḥem's work, although their extent varies greatly – whereas changes in BH gender and number are not very common, Menaḥem will often use a BH verb in a derived conjugation in which it is not attested in the Bible, and will also frequently employ passive structures probably of Arabic origin. In the meanings given by the *Maḥberet* we also often find new nominal forms, especially of the type *q^e^ṭilā*, although these do not normally occur in the other prose sections. Sometimes, the demonstrative adjective, without article, precedes the noun, as in mediaeval usage.

There are noticeable changes in the syntax of the verb, and it is not unusual to find a verb used in a modal or auxiliary capacity as well as a number of stereotyped expressions which probably result from Arabic influence, and various constructions of the passive participle with היה (hyh) 'be'.

Menaḥem's vocabulary is, again, mainly of biblical origin, with no noteworthy innovations other than the many new and unusual usages found in his technical vocabulary. Although in this respect Menaḥem was not starting out afresh, given that earlier writers had already coined a considerable number of linguistic terms, he still makes his own very personal and characteristic contribution. In contrast with the tradition of accepting loanwords or calques from Arabic, Menaḥem prefers to create new terms, although he does not entirely reject expressions already in existence, and, in fact, we can recognize in his work many technical terms of Arabic provenance.[109]

Much of Menaḥem's linguistic terminology is taken from daily life, extending the semantic range of everyday nouns and verbs

[109] See Bacher 1974 (originally published 1895), 90f.; Sáenz-Badillos 1976, 18ff.

like יצא (yṣʾ) 'go out' and נפל (npl) 'fall' in order to give them a specialized linguistic sense. Particularly striking is the use of physiological and anthropomorphic terms, which give the language the appearance of a living being. At the same time, Menaḥem borrows many words from the sphere of law and religion, for example חק (ḥōq) 'statute', דָּת (dāṯ) 'law', and מִשְׁפָּט (mišpāṭ) 'judgement', as well as from the semantic fields of truth, correctness, and measurement.

Overall, despite the fact that it has been influenced to some extent by Arabic, especially in more technical areas, the *Maḥberet* cannot simply be regarded as an 'Arabizing' composition, but should be included among those writings which use a predominantly biblical form of Hebrew.[110]

Dunash b. Labraṭ had as the model for his Hebrew prose-composition various works by his teacher Saadiah (see Chapter 7.3), although it has to be recognized that while Dunash's language stays basically faithful to BH, it differs greatly from the mosaic of biblical phrases so typical of Saadiah's writings. In morphology, syntax, and vocabulary, Dunash's prose is fundamentally biblical, although without archaisms or the *waw*-consecutive. While there is just one isolated instance of the infinitive absolute, the infinitive construct preceded by preposition is frequent, and sometimes introduces a circumstantial clause. The particles are almost entirely biblical and only rarely rabbinic, although there are also some typically mediaeval, Arabic-influenced, usages. With respect to the demonstratives, a further characteristic feature, seventy-six per-cent of the examples attested are biblical and the remainder mediaeval. In its use of plural forms and the article, Dunash's language is again consistent with biblical usage, and there are no structures characteristic of the *payṭanim*.

In the verb, there is rather greater RH influence. The use of the participle to express the present or, with היה (hyh) 'be', to indicate repetitive action, is quite common, though less so than in Dunash's

110 See Sáenz-Badillos 1985.

poetry. Rabbinic influence may also be evidenced in a number of demonstratives and particles compounded with -שֶׁ (šæ-) 'who, which', although the dominance of the BH relative אֲשֶׁר ('ašær) is almost total. Noun structures of the type *qᵉṭīlā* and *qiṭṭūl* are found quite often in the *Teshuvot*, and also perhaps of rabbinic origin are the expressions -עלי ל ('ālay lᵉ-) 'I have to' (lit. '[it is] upon me to') and היה ראוי להיות (hāyā rā'ūy li-hyōṯ) 'it should have been' (lit. 'it was fitting to be'), although in the latter example Arabic influence is also possible.

Direct Arabic influence is seen in various uses of the particles, for example על שלושה שערים ('al šᵉlōšā šᵉ'ārīm) 'in (lit. 'on') three sections' and ואם יתכן להיות פתרונם אחד (wᵉ-'im yittāḵēn li-hyōṯ piṯrōnām 'eḥāḏ) 'even though (lit. 'and if') their meaning might be the same', and there are also some changes in verb-preposition combinations, as exemplified by ואתמה ממך (wᵉ-'æṯmāh mimmæḵā) 'and I was surprised at (lit. 'from') you'. As well as the many calques in technical vocabulary, the meanings of more common words have also been influenced by Arabic, as with אחי חכמה ('aḥī ḥoḵmā) 'erudite person' (lit. 'brother of wisdom'), יאגור (yæ'æḡōr) 'he gathers', עד ('ēḏ) 'proof', and שם נופל על (šēm nōpēl 'al) 'name applied to (lit. 'falling upon')'. Other instances of Arabic influence include the use of certain verbs as modal auxiliaries, for example אבוא לבאר ('āḇō' lᵉ-ḇā'ēr) 'I am going to explain', the employment of participles as object-noun complements, as in מצאנו מסותר (māṣānū mᵉsuttār) 'we found hidden', as well as changes in the normal sequence of tenses.

Assessing Dunash's work as a whole, even though the type of language he uses is primarily biblical, with a number of RH elements added, the influence of Arabic is much more obvious than in the work of Menaḥem.[111] The rest of the tenth-century linguistic debate between the supporters of Menaḥem and Dunash, proceeded along the lines set by these two basic works. Moreover, the Hebrew employed in philosophical compositions of the period

111 See Sáenz-Badillos 1982.

does not differ substantially from this standard, despite their special vocabulary and numerous Arabic calques.[112]

The language of the *maqāmāt* and other kinds of mediaeval narrative composition takes a variety of different directions. Works that inherited the motifs and topics of traditional *midrash* also retained linguistic features of later RH, typical of haggadic literature. In the *maqāmāt* and in collections of stories and fables of Arab origin, the influence of Arabic is very clear, although notable writers like Al-Ḥarizi also endeavoured to employ a language that approximated closely to BH, incorporating extensive mosaics of quotations from the Bible. Halakhic compositions followed a different path, characterized by closer continuity with RH, whereas writers of historical works, like Abraham ibn Daud, or of travel chronicles, notably Benjamin of Tudela, used a form of Hebrew akin to BH, although with a number of RH particles, such as אֶלָּא ('ællā') 'but rather', -שֶׁ (šæ-) 'who, which', -עַד שֶׁ ('aḏ šæ-) 'until', and -מִפְּנֵי שֶׁ (mip-pᵉnē šæ-) 'because', as well as some mediaeval expressions possibly of Arabic origin, for example קָרוֹב מִן (qārōḇ min) 'near to (lit. 'from')'.

A very different form of expression was employed in the scientific writings of Abraham bar Ḥiyya, who lived in a Christian environment from the close of the eleventh century until about 1136. His personal situation as astronomer and high functionary in the court of Barcelona (which extended its influence to Provence, at that time united politically and culturally with Catalonia) played an important part in his decision to engage in scientific writing. In the introduction to his encyclopaedic work *Yesodei ha-Tevunah*, he sets forth his motives: 'I have not entered this subject of my own will nor to gain glory, but because many illustrious figures of my generation, whose advice I am obliged to follow, have urged me to do so, for in all the land of Ṣarfat [Christendom] there is no book in Hebrew that is devoted to these sciences.'[113]

112 See Klatzkin 1928–33.

113 See J.M. Millás, *La obra enciclopédica Yesodé ha-Tebuná u-Migdal ha-'Emuná de R. Abraham bar Ḥiyya ha-Bargeloní* (Madrid/Barcelona, 1952), 37.

Thus it was, in consideration of the Jewish communities of Europe that did not understand Arabic, that Bar Ḥiyya came not only to translate various works into Romance and Latin but also to compose the first works of science and philosophy written in Hebrew, contributing to the creation of a technical vocabulary for these subjects while maintaining a coherent language and style. Even when he is not actually translating, his data are taken from Arabic works, and Bar Ḥiyya's first problem was to coin Hebrew expressions which would reproduce with sufficient accuracy scientific categories that had not previously been discussed in Hebrew.

Bar Ḥiyya's linguistic standard is RH, although he includes elements from every stage of Hebrew. It has been noted that his language derives, above all, from the Mishnah, giving it a more archaic flavour than Rashi's, for example, despite the numerous innovations in terminology.[114] Most of the expressions Bar Ḥiyya uses already existed in Hebrew, but he gives them different senses, adapting them to their new contexts by borrowing meanings from Arabic. Thus, for example, מַאֲמָרוֹת (ma'ªmārōṯ) 'words' and יְסוֹדוֹת (yᵉsōḏōṯ) 'foundations' are 'categories', אוֹפָן ('ōpān) 'wheel' is 'orbit' or 'horizon', and גָּדֵר (gāḏēr) 'wall' is 'definition' or, like its Arabic homophone, 'square-root'. דִּבּוּק (dibbūq) 'cleaving' and חִבּוּר (ḥibbūr) 'joining' signify '(planetary) conjunction', הִיּוּלִי (hīyyūlī) '*hyle*' is חֹמֶר רִאשׁוֹן (ḥōmær rīšōn) 'primordial matter', חִדּוּשׁ (ḥiddūš) is, like its Arabic homophone, 'creation', and יְצִירָה (yᵉṣīrā) 'formation' takes on an additional meaning of 'essence, nature'. כּוֹכַב הַזָּנָב (kōḵāḇ haz-zānāḇ) is 'comet' (lit. 'star of the tail'), מַזָּל צוֹמֵחַ (mazzāl ṣōmēªḥ) is 'ascendant (lit. 'sprouting') sign', מַעְתִּיקִים (ma'tīqīm) are 'believers in metempsychosis' (lit. 'shifters'), תִּשְׁבֹּרֶת (tišbōræṯ) is 'geometry', and תִּקּוּן (tiqqūn) may signify not only 'improvement' but also '"regulation" (of the year)'

114 See Efros 1926–27; 1929–30; Ṣarfatti 1968, 61ff., especially 111ff., where Ṣarfatti carefully distinguishes Hebrew words that have taken on new meanings due to their similarity in sense or pronunciation to Arabic terms, those that have taken on meanings 'independently', where no such similarity exists, calques, and loanwords proper.

or 'correct location (of a star)' by geometrical method.[115] Loanwords proper, such as מֶרְכָּז (mærkāz) 'centre' and קֹטֶב (qōṭæḇ) '(celestial) pole', are far fewer.

Although he also employs biblical vocabulary, the great majority of Bar Ḥiyya's terms are drawn from RH, for example בְּשָׁעָה שֶׁ- (bᵉ-šā'ā šæ-) 'at the hour that, when', כְּלוֹמַר (kᵉ-lōmar) 'that is to say', רָאוּי (rā'ūy) 'fitting', עָתִיד לְ- ('āṯīḏ lᵉ-) '(be) about to', and אֲפִלּוּ ('ᵃpillū) 'even if'. Commenting on various biblical texts, he replaces BH words by RH ones, but at the same time, in a typically mediaeval manner, Bar Ḥiyya also uses the BH particles אֲשֶׁר ('ᵃšær) 'who, which' and כִּי (kī) 'that' much more than their rabbinic equivalent, שֶׁ- (šæ-), and displays his eclecticism by employing both RH אֶלָּא ('ællā') and BH כִּי אִם (kī 'im) to express 'but rather', often followed, as in RH, by לְבַד (lᵉḇaḏ) 'only'.

In Bar Ḥiyya's grammar, Arabic influence is more obvious in various ways. For example, he changes the gender of nouns, as with בגלות הזה (bag-gālūṯ haz-zǣ) 'in this [masc.] exile [fem.]', modifies the position of the demonstrative, as in אלו החכמות ('ēllū ha-ḥoḵmōṯ) 'these sciences', and employs זֶה (zǣ) 'this' as a neuter pronoun. Bar Ḥiyya also uses the verb היה (hyh) 'be' as an auxiliary with the prefix-conjugation, for example היה יעשה (hāyā ya'ᵃśǣ) 'he used to do' (lit. 'he was, he will do'), employs the collocation יֵשׁ שָׁם (yēš šām) 'there is (there)', and does not repeat particles before a second, co-ordinate, noun.

A generation later, Abraham ibn Ezra, who was similarly concerned with transmitting Muslim culture to the Jewish communities of Europe, wrote in a language based mainly on BH. His familiarity with Arabic, demonstrated in his translation of Ḥayyuj into Hebrew, is reflected in the Hebrew he uses, and especially in his technical vocabulary. Curiously, while being very demanding about the accurate use of words, even censuring Dunash for using the verb פתר (ptr) instead of פרש (prš) pi. 'interpret', he is not entirely systematic in his own choice of words,

115 See Efros 1926–27; 1929–30.

often employing such synonyms as בֵּינוֹנִי (bēnōnī) 'participle' and שֵׁם הַפֹּעַל (šēm hap-pō'al) 'verbal noun' or מָקוֹם (māqōm) '(in) place (of)' and תְּמוּרָה (tᵉmūrā) '(in) exchange (for)' apparently for no other reason than a desire for variety. However, he scrupulously avoids using certain contemporary grammatical terms, replacing, for example, תֵּבָה (tēḇā) 'word' by מִלָּה (millā), מָקוֹר (māqōr) 'infinitive' by שֵׁם הַפְּעֻלָּה (šēm hap-pᵉ'ullā) lit. 'noun of action', and שמש (šmš) pi. 'function as a servile' by שרת (šrt) pi. Ibn Ezra also borrows expressions from, in particular, the Masoretes and Menaḥem b. Saruq, although he often invests them with new meanings, as with הֵא הַתֵּמָהּ (hē' hat-tēmāh) 'interrogative *he*' and הַמְתָּנָה (hamtānā) 'pause', and, in connexion with *shewa*, he uses שֹׁקֵט (šōqēṭ) 'resting' in the sense of נָח (nāḥ) 'quiescent'. Sometimes the same word can be used in very different senses, for example סְמִיכוּת (sᵉmīḵūṯ) 'construct state', 'suffixation', 'non-pausal form', 'suffixed verb'.[116]

In the realm of mathematics, Abraham ibn Ezra's scientific terminology is similar to that of Bar Ḥiyya and influenced by him, although he avoids the use of certain loanwords, preferring, for example, נְקֻדָּה (nᵉquddā) or מוּצָק (mūṣāq) to מֶרְכָּז (mærkāz) 'centre', and introducing new words of Hebrew provenance which have meanings suited to his needs, such as מְכוֹנָה (mᵉḵōnā) 'stand' and כְּלִי נְחֹשֶׁת (kᵉlī nᵉḥōšæṯ) 'astrolabe' (lit. 'instrument of bronze'). Ibn Ezra's interpretation of such expressions in his biblical commentaries is often reflected in their use as technical terms.[117] In his non-technical writing, Ibn Ezra prefers a purist style close to that of the Bible, and he tends to choose particles typical of BH rather than of RH.

In many respects, the most representative Hebrew prose of the period is that of the translations from Arabic, which would be imitated by later writers, including those from territories free of Muslim domination. From the eleventh and, especially, the twelfth,

116 See L. Prijs 1950.
117 See Ṣarfatti 1968, 130ff.

century, there was a growing interest in giving Jews from the rest of Europe access to the great Arabic works of their oriental and Andalusian co-religionists, as well as to other outstanding studies in science and philosophy from the Islamic world. Over some 600 years, about a thousand works were translated into Hebrew, the most important ones several times.[118] The translators, led for two centuries by the Ibn Tibbon family, felt that Hebrew was not entirely adequate for translating Arabic works, and despite advocating, at least in theory, the use of a grammatically correct language free of foreign influence,[119] they never fully succeeded in this.

In their endeavour to reproduce the original texts faithfully, the translators were often obliged to neglect style and to commit grammatical irregularities, mixing genders and changing prepositions. When Hebrew could offer no immediate solution, they often resorted to calquing from Arabic vocabulary and syntax. They were influenced less by the classical language than by Middle Arabic as it had developed in Spain.[120]

The first attempts at translation, such as the Hebrew versions of a number of Ḥayyuj's works by Moses ibn Chiquatilla in the eleventh century, are rather unusual in that they represent a translation that is not literal but more free and periphrastic, with greater importance given to clarity and linguistic purity than to strict verbal fidelity.[121] There is even some additional material where the sense of the original text could have been unclear to his readers, as well as omissions or alterations where Ibn Chiquatilla disagrees with the original author. In its much closer proximity to BH, his language clearly contrasts with that of the tenth-century grammarians. Abraham ibn Ezra's translations a century later also try to be faithful to BH, although they show more respect for the

118 See Steinschneider 1893.

119 See Judah ibn Tibbon's will to his son, in I. Abrahams, *Hebrew ethical wills* (Philadelphia, 1926), 68.

120 See Blau 1985.

121 See Poznanski 1895, 71ff.

literal sense of the original text. However, it was not this kind of translation that was to become the dominant model, but that represented by the work of the Ibn Tibbons.

This family's most illustrious member, Judah ibn Tibbon, explains in the introduction to his translation of *Ḥovot ha-Levavot* that the *geonim* used Arabic in those countries dominated by Islam

> because all the people understood that language. Moreover, this is a rich and diversified language meeting the various requirements of speakers and authors. Its phraseology is precise, lucid, and presents the substance of each subject matter far more penetratingly than is possible in Hebrew. For all we possess of the Hebrew language is what we find in the Bible, which is not adaequate for the needs of every speaking person. They [the eastern scholars] also intended to benefit through their works the uneducated populace unfamiliar with the holy language.[122]

This statement can be seen as representing a summary explanation of why Judah ibn Tibbon and the rest of his family undertook their work of translation.

The vocabulary of this type of Hebrew employs various technical expressions taken directly from Arabic as loanwords, for example תַּאֲרִיךְ (ta'ᵃrīḵ) 'history', הַנְדָּסָה (handāsā) 'geometry', מֶרְכָּז (mærkāz) 'centre', אֹפֶק ('ōp̄æq) 'horizon', and אַקְלִים ('aqlīm) 'region' (of Greek origin), although some writers, like Samuel ibn Tibbon and Judah al-Ḥarizi, struggled to use existing Hebrew words. In fact, the adoption of loanwords was already a centuries-old procedure, and even authors like Menaḥem b. Saruq, who had avoided the use of Arabic on ideological grounds, employed it in the creation of numerous technical terms. In translations of dietary, medical, and pharmacological works, names for medicines, foods, and plants sometimes simply appear in Hebrew transcription, as with אַשְׁרוֹב ('ašrōḇ) 'syrup'. The translators also use words that sound like their Arabic counterparts, even when there is no

122 For the text of the original, see A. Zifroni, *Sefer Ḥovot ha-levavot le-R. Baḥya ben Yosef ibn Paquda be-targumo shel R. Yehudah ibn Tibbon* (Jerusalem, 1928), 2. The translation is taken from Baron 1958, 6.

etymological connexion whatsoever, for example לָכֵן (lāḵēn), usually 'therefore', is used in the sense of Arabic *lakin* 'but', צֵרוּף (ṣērūp̄) 'combination' in the sense of *tasrīf* 'inflection', and פֶּרֶק (pæræq) 'parting' in the sense of *farq* 'difference'.

However, the most frequent means of forming new words is by loan-translation, where the content of an Arabic technical or scientific term is expressed through an existing Hebrew word or through a new morphological inflection of a known Hebrew root. In this way, Hebrew acquired hundreds of new words in each subject in which translations were undertaken, with a vastly increased number of contexts in which words could now be used. Thus, for example, in philology, we find מִלִּים נִרְדָּפוֹת (millīm nirdāp̄ōṯ) 'synonyms' (lit. 'chased words'; cf. *mutarādifāt*), בִּנְיָן (binyān) 'verb conjugation, *binyan*' (lit. 'structure'; cf. *binā*), מִשְׁקָל (mišqāl) 'morphological pattern' (lit. 'weight'; cf. *wazn*), שֹׁרֶשׁ (šōræš) '(morphological) root' (cf. *aṣl*), and מָקוֹר (māqōr) 'infinitive' (lit. 'source'; cf. *maṣdar*), and in philosophy, בְּכֹחַ (be-ḵōaḥ) 'potential' (lit. 'with power') and בְּפֹעַל (be-p̄ō'al) 'actual' (lit. 'with action'), as well as a large number of abstracts in וּת-(-ūṯ), for example מְצִיאוּת (meṣī'ūṯ) 'existence', אֵיכוּת ('ēḵūṯ) 'quality', and כַּמּוּת (kammūṯ) 'quantity'. Hebrew words from earlier stages of the language gain new meanings under the influence of Arabic so that, for example, עִנְיָן ('inyān) 'concern' and פָּנִים (pānīm) 'faces' come to indicate 'meaning' and 'senses', and דִּין (dīn) 'judgement', 'religion', while שֶׁבֶר (šæḇær) 'breach' is used for the vowel name *hireq*.

The type of language used in the original work also played a part in the choice and frequency of Hebrew vocabulary, producing striking effects by attaching unusual senses to common words. For example ראה (r'h) 'see' can mean 'think', based on Arabic usage, חִדּוּשׁ (ḥiddūš) in the sense of 'accident' is used in preference to other Hebrew terms because of its similarity to Arabic *ḥadaṯ*, and the frequency of כִּמְעַט קָט (ki-m'aṭ qāṭ) 'hardly anything' is due more to the use of *qaṭ* in Arabic than to any biblical influence.[123] A Hebrew word could also take on the homonymy of its Arabic equivalent or develop homonymy under the influence of related Arabic expressions. Thus, שַׁעַר (ša'ar) means not only 'gate' but also 'chapter (of a book)' and 'explanation', just like Arabic *bāb*, and מַאֲמָר (ma'ᵃmār) is used to express the meanings of both *maqāla* 'essay' and *maqūla* 'category'.[124]

Of particular note in morphology is the frequency of adjectives formed by suffixing ִי- (-ī), for example גַּשְׁמִי (gasmī) 'corporeal', as in Arabic, which are replaced by words corresponding to the morphological pattern *qaṭlān* in literature that approximates more closely to RH. Common as well are abstracts in וּת- (-ūṯ) which, like those ending in ִית- (-īṯ), are usually treated as masculine, as in Arabic. There are many other examples of changes in gender due to Arabic, for example דַּעַת (da'aṯ) 'knowledge' and אֱמֶת ('æmæṯ) 'truth' become masculine, and טֶבַע (ṭæḇa') 'nature' feminine, with the adjective sometimes agreeing simply with the superficial form of the noun it is qualifying, for example המקומות הרחוקות (ham-mᵉqōmōṯ hā-rᵉḥōqōṯ) 'the distant [fem.] places [masc.]'. Infinitives can take the article, as with ההעשות (ha-hē'āśōṯ) lit. 'the to-be-done'. Construct chains are frequently used instead of שֶׁל (šæl) 'of', and the construct noun can take the article, for example הבעלי דינים (hab-ba'ᵃlē dīnīm) lit. 'the possessors of judgements' instead of בַּעֲלֵי הַדִּינִים (ba'ᵃlē had-dīnīm) lit. 'possessors of the judgements' (i.e. 'litigants'), as can a comparative adjective, for example היותר חשוב (hay-yōṯēr ḥāšūḇ) 'the most important'.

In the verb, the translations mark a significant departure from BH, eliminating consecutive, lengthened, and shortened forms and no longer distinguishing different moods. Verbs often take prepositions on the analogy of Arabic, for example פלא מִן (pl' [ni.] min) 'be amazed at (lit. 'from')' (also found in the Bible), and

123 See Blau 1985, 248f.
124 See E. Goldenberg 1971, 1625ff.

resulting combinations sometimes acquire the idiomatic meanings of their Arabic equivalents, as with אמר בְּ ('mr b^e-) 'believe (lit. 'say') in' (cf. *qāla bi-*). Various intransitive verbs of motion are able to express transitive relationships when followed by the preposition -בְּ (b^e-) denoting cause, as in Arabic.

Similarly, through the influence of original Arabic texts the various derived conjugations of the verb are used in a distinctive way. The *Qal* sometimes has the value of the *Hif'il* and *vice versa*, as with זכר (zkr) 'remind' (usually 'remember') and רמז (rmz) hi. 'give a signal' (usually 'cause a signal to be given'), the *Nif'al* is used impersonally, for example ישפט (yiššāpēṭ) 'it will be judged', and the *Hithpa'el* is frequently employed, as in Arabic, to express passive or reciprocal relationships, although internal passives of the *Pu'al* and *Hof'al* type are also used. Passive participles are created for certain intransitive verbs, expressions of the sort ולו היה יכולנו (w^e-lū hāyā yāḵōlnū) 'and if we had been able' are found, and there are also other structures, known from Arabic but absent from BH, which employ an auxiliary verb, for example היה יחייב (hāyā y^eḥayyēḇ) 'he had to' or לא היה יהיה (lō' hāyā yihyǣ) 'he had not been', or which use the particle כְּבָר (k^ebār) 'already' like the Arabic *qad* to form compound past tenses, as in היה כבר עושה (hāyā ḵ^eḇār 'ōśǣ) 'he had done' (lit. 'he was already doing'), or, with the prefix-conjugation, to express possibility. The infinitive and the verbal noun are employed interchangeably, and there is frequent use of the expression לִהְיוֹתוֹ (li-hyōṯō), lit. 'for his being', to express cause, 'because he is'.[125]

A feature of the noun in this kind of Hebrew is the use of an undetermined demonstrative adjective before a determined noun, for example זה האיש (zǣ hā-'īš) 'this man', as in Arabic, in preference to the biblical structure of determined noun followed by determined demonstrative. Genitive constructions in which an absolute noun is associated with two construct nouns joined by -וְ (w^e-) 'and', as in Middle Arabic, are also found, and there are

125 See E. Goldenberg 1971, 1628ff.; Allony 1974, 77ff.

changes of gender, with, for example, כֹּחַ (kōaḥ) 'strength', עֵץ ('ēṣ) 'tree', and מָקוֹם (māqōm) 'place' treated as feminine and פַּעַם (pa'am) 'occasion'as masculine. Again as in Middle Arabic, there is a change in the gender of the numerals three to ten, and plurals are formed from words normally occurring only in the singular and *vice versa*, for example בְּשָׂרִים (bᵉśārīm) from בָּשָׂר (bāśār) 'flesh' and פָּן (pān) from פָּנִים (pānīm) 'face'. The use of the article, for instance before a construct, is different from that found in BH and is more consistent with Arabic. Particles like כֹּל (kōl) 'all' and גַּם (gam) 'also' are found between nouns and adjectives, and the use of comparatives and superlatives also follows the Arabic model, for example היותר משובח (hay-yōṯēr mᵉšubbāḥ) 'the most praiseworthy' and יותר מצליח האנשים (yōṯēr maṣlīaḥ hā-'anāšīm) 'the most successful of persons'. Similarly, constructions with numbers differ from those found in BH, for example השלוש רוחות (haš-šālōš rūḥōṯ) instead of the expected BH form שְׁלוֹשׁ הָרוּחוֹת (šᵉlōš hā-rūḥōṯ) 'the three spirits'.

The object-marker is frequently omitted, and secondary complements, from an adjective to an entire clause, are common. Nouns are sometimes used circumstantially, expressing cause, time, place, and so on. Adverbial expressions can take pronominal suffixes, as with כאתמולך (kᵉ-'æṯmōlᵉḵā) 'as your yesterday'. In the use of particles, Arabic is the dominant model and there are numerous differences from every previous stage of the language, with many changes of meaning and new structures, so that, for example, כֹּל (kōl) 'all' followed by a noun means 'each one (of)', and קְצָת (qᵉṣāṯ) and מִקְצָת (miqṣāṯ) mean 'one of, some of', with מִן (min) 'from' and מָה (mā) 'what?' functioning as partitives, as in סוד מן הסודות (sōḏ min has-sōḏōṯ) 'one of the secrets' (lit. 'a secret from the secrets') and יש לו סבה מה (yēš lō sibbā mā) 'there is some reason to it' (lit. 'there is to it reason what'). Suffixed pronouns are widely used, sometimes reinforced by independent personal pronouns, for example ויש לנו ואנחנו בו מאמר (wᵉ-yēš lā-nū wa-'anaḥnū ḇō ma'amār) 'there is a declaration in it for us, precisely for us'.

Arabic and Archaic Hebrew practice coincides in the frequent use of an asyndetic relative clause following an indefinite antecedent; on the other hand, the article and relative pronoun are often used in contexts in which they would also occur in BH or RH, but not in Arabic. Object-noun complements are frequently used in place of the infinitive, as in נרצה שנדע (nirṣæ šæn-nēḏa') lit. 'we shall want that we shall know' or צריך שנתבונן (ṣārīḵ šæn-niṯbōnēn) 'it is essential that we understand', while, in contrast, infinitive constructions often replace adverbial expressions of time, purpose, cause, or comparison, for example לִהְיוֹתוֹ (li-hyōṯō) 'because he is' (lit. 'for his being'). There is an increase in the frequency of cognate objects, and the particles -מִ (mi-), כְּגוֹן (kᵉgōn) 'for example', and כְּמוֹ (kᵉmō) '(such) as' are used in enumerating items. אָמְנָם ('omnām) is often employed like the Arabic *ammā* to emphasize a subject ('as for'), and verbs expressing fear or prevention sometimes take a redundant negative particle. Arabic influence is also particularly obvious in subordinate clauses, especially in the choice of particles and in the use of tenses.[126]

A rare dissenting voice among the translators belongs to Judah al-Ḥarizi, who made a second Hebrew version of Maimonides's *Guide to the Perplexed*, shortly after the appearance of the edition by Samuel ibn Tibbon, in the first decade of the thirteenth century. Although his translation technique, previously seen in the work of Moses ibn Chiquatilla and Abraham ibn Ezra, was not to gain favour, Al-Ḥarizi's endeavours to avoid Arabisms and to present his translation in a simple and understandable form of BH are very significant.[127] This procedure applied even to philosophical and scientific technical terms, which differ greatly from those used by the Tibbonid school, and for which, in general, Al-Ḥarizi, like Abraham ibn Ezra before him, tried to employ BH. His glossary of terms, corresponding to that of Samuel ibn Tibbon, was directed not to a small group of specialists, but to the public at large. It is

126 Gottstein 1951, M.H. Goshen-Gottstein's doctoral thesis, remains a basic text for the syntactic analysis of the translations from Arabic. See also E. Goldenberg 1971, 1631f.
127 See Steinschneider 1893, 428ff.

strikingly different from Ibn Tibbon's glossary, explaining meanings in an easy way and containing hardly any direct loanwords from Arabic. Nonetheless, later translators moved decisively towards the Tibbonid model, and Al-Ḥarizi's rôle as translator was quickly forgotten.[128]

So great was the impact and spread of 'Tibbonid Hebrew' that nearly all writers after the twelfth century, including kabbalists, halakhists, and biblical commentators, use words and phrases taken from the translators, albeit in different ways. Thus, in the Kabbalah there is a large number of neologisms, introduced in an attempt to adapt the language to new mystical concepts. The usual procedure was to give existing words new semantic content, so that, for example, סְפִירוֹת (sᵉp̄īrōṯ) 'ciphers' becomes the *'sefirot'* or divine emanations, with כֶּתֶר (kæṯær) 'crown' as the name of the first of these. תִּקּוּן (tiqqūn) 'correction', דְּבֵקוּת (dᵉḇēqūṯ) 'cleaving', כַּוָּנָה (kawwānā) 'intention', and צִמְצוּם (ṣimṣūm) 'contraction' are all examples of words which were to express fundamental mystical ideas, having undergone a process of 'sacralization'.[129] The language of the kabbalists is usually Hebrew mixed with Aramaic, close to that used in earlier midrashic literature but also with expressions created by the translators for philosophical subjects. In the Zohar, the Aramaic is frequently artificial, incorporating quite discordant dialect features, with limited influence from Arabic but various traces of Romance, for example גַּרְדִּינִים (gardīnīm) 'guardians' and אֵשׁ נֹגַהּ ('ēš nōḡah) 'synagogue'.[130]

Although Maimonides composed most of his work in Arabic, he does use, in the *Mishneh Torah*, for example, a form of Hebrew close to RH, with a significant BH component and relatively few Arabisms. Overall, his language is less affected by Arabic and more elegant than that of the translators, even though his forms quite often originate in the Hebrew used in translations. Many set-phrases in Maimonides are pure RH, for example כמו שנאמר (kᵉmō

128 See Ṣarfatti 1968, 182ff.

129 See Kaddari 1970.

130 See Scholem 1971, 1203ff.

šæn-næ'ᵆmar) 'as it was said' and בענין שנאמר (bᵉ-'inyān šæn-næ'ᵆmar) 'concerning what was said'. Similarly, in Maimonides we see characteristically RH uses of, for example, the infinitive construct, *Nithpa'al*, and proleptic pronouns, although many of the features he employs reflect later usage, as, for example, his use of the pattern *pā'ēl* for *pō'ēl* in the participle and of *yif'ōl* instead of *yif'al* in the prefix-conjugation, as in יחפוץ (yaḥpōṣ) 'he will desire'. As Maimonides explains in the introduction to the *Sefer ha-Mitzvot*, he deliberately chose the Mishnah as his model so that his language would be clear, accurate, and intelligible to every reader. Maimonides intersperses his work with numerous words and brief quotations from the Bible, and he translates Aramaic expressions from the Talmud, for example בן מצר (bæn mæṣær) for *bar miṣra* 'neighbour' (lit. 'son of a border'). Although Maimonides carefully avoids many of the Arabisms that the translators had introduced in various fields, Arabic, as his native language, has, nonetheless, left its mark in both grammar and vocabulary. Thus, for example, he will frequently use the infinitive construct, places the article before a noun in the construct state, as in העבדי אלילים (hā-'ōḇᵉḏē 'ᵆlīlīm) 'idolaters' (lit. 'the worshippers of idols'), and employs such expressions as עִקָּר ('iqqār) 'principle' and צוּרָה (ṣūrā) 'form'.[131]

Quite different are the Hebrew translations of Latin works, which began to be produced in the thirteenth century, especially in Provence. The translators responsible for these later compositions were not usually endowed with great knowledge of Hebrew, with the need to produce workable translations overriding considerations of linguistic quality. Such translations were limited to reproducing the most notable scientific and medical literature of the time, using a characteristically mediaeval mixture of biblical, rabbinic, and contemporary features, with the occasional Arabic calque taken from existing works. Direct influence from Latin in

131 See Bacher 1903; 1914; Baneth 1935–36; 1952; Zeidmann 1943; 1955; Goshen-Gottstein 1957; Dienstag 1969; Fink 1980.

the form of loanwords is quite small, with paraphrase being employed for expressions regarded as otherwise untranslatable.[132]

7.6 *Mediaeval Hebrew in Italy and central Europe*

The social and cultural environment in which the Jewish communities of Italy and other parts of Europe lived was very different from that of the Iberian peninsula. Relations with Palestine were particularly strong at important periods, for example during the flowering of Hebrew literature in Italy in the ninth and tenth centuries. The influence of the *payṭanim* is especially noticeable in the poetry of this early period from Italy. Solomon b. Judah ha-Bavli, who was born in the east but had settled in northern Italy, was one of the first Hebrew poets in Europe, and played a significant rôle in the future development of liturgical poetry in Italy and central Europe. He was heir to the ancient tradition of *piyyuṭ* of the school of Kallir and his followers, and his language was cast in its mould, containing not only biblical, rabbinic, and Aramaic elements, but also, especially, numerous features typical of the *payṭanim*, such as new forms of nouns and verbs and the introduction of servile letters into the root.[133] In contrast to the Spanish tradition, which was undergoing development at this time, the Hebrew poetry of Italy remained faithful to the Palestinian standard for several centuries. In the thirteenth century, and especially with the work of Immanuel of Rome, an important change took place, with an acceptance of the BH model used by the poets of Spain, albeit with a number of distinctive features, ranging from the incorporation of rabbinic elements and Arabic calques to the direct influence of Italian, exemplified by הַשֶּׁלּוֹ (haš-šæl-lō) 'his' (lit. 'the which-is-to-him').[134]

132 See Ferre 1987.
133 See Fleischer 1973, 95ff.
134 See E. Goldenberg 1971, 1633f.

In his prose, the tenth-century Italian physician Shabbetai Donnolo mixes RH and BH, with additional components from Greek, Latin, and spoken Italian.[135] Halfway through the eleventh century, Aḥimaaz b. Palṭiel wrote *Megillat Aḥimaaz* using a type of Hebrew close to that of the *payṭanim*, but also with traces of Italian influence.

In Provence, Judaism maintained an unmistakably Spanish character, and, strengthened by the arrival of important groups of Andalusian Jews, the Provençal community played an extremely important rôle in the translation of Arabic works and their dissemination to the Jews of northern France and the rest of Europe. 'Tibbonid Hebrew' was, in reality, a Provençal creation.

In all other parts of Europe, Hebrew prose was composed using a late form of RH in which, alongside the dominant rabbinic component, there are BH and Aramaic elements, as well as Arabisms emanating from Spain or Provence. It was also influenced to varying degrees by the spoken languages of the period – French, Middle High German, and Yiddish. The proportions in which all these elements are found differs according to writer, time, and place.

Rashi and the Tosafists employed this type of Hebrew, which in their case shows French influence, for example the use of עשה ('śh) 'do, make' in the various senses of *faire*, changes in gender, etc. RH is clearly dominant, although there are also some BH words and constructions. In his commentary on the Talmud, Rashi often uses Aramaic as well, and he frequently employs neologisms. His easy and intelligible style would become a model for generations.[136]

In the *Sefer Ḥasidim*, written in central Europe during the twelfth to thirteenth centuries, there is noticeable influence from Middle High German and Yiddish in, for example, the use of prepositions, everyday vocabulary, and various calques, and in the frequent extension of the meanings of words so that they correspond to

135 See Muntner 1949; 1971.
136 See Avinery 1940–60.

their German equivalents. This last feature is particularly striking, and occurs elsewhere in Ashkenazi Hebrew, so that, for example, עשה ('śh) 'do, make' functions like *machen*. Forms that do not have a German equivalent, such as the object-marker, are used less often, as is the article. The participle is used indicatively to refer to the present and the future, with the prefix-conjugation employed as a subjunctive, expressing doubt and possibility, for example, and היה (hyh) 'be' with the participle functioning like the German preterite. The sequence of tenses also often reflects that of German. Although RH forms the main component in *Sefer Ḥasidim*, there are some notable oddities, such as the use of the *Nuf'al* derived conjugation. Consecutive tenses, lengthened forms of the verb, and other constructions typical of BH are also found.

Relations with the Jews of Spain and Provence led to the Arabizing style of earlier Spanish writers making its mark on the type of prose used, for example, in Poland during the sixteenth and seventeenth centuries. The kabbalistic and philosophical works of the *Ḥasidim* in the eighteenth century also employ a version of Hebrew quite similar to that found in Spain. In later Ashkenazi writings there is an increased use of words and phrases from Aramaic.[137]

137 See E. Goldenberg 1971, 1635ff.

Chapter 8

MODERN HEBREW

8.1 *The period of transition*

The transition from Mediaeval to Modern or Israeli Hebrew (IH) came about slowly, over several decades. According to some experts, a new phase of the language had already begun in the sixteenth century. Among its earliest manifestations were A. dei Rossi's *Me'or Einayim* (1574), the first Hebrew play by J. Sommo (1527–92), and the first Yiddish–Hebrew dictionary by Elijah Levita (1468–1549).[1] Hebrew continued to be used in writing, and attempts were made to adapt it to modern needs. The eighteenth century saw the first examples of Hebrew newspapers, in connexion with which I. Lampronti (1679–1756) at Ferrara and, from 1750, M. Mendelssohn at Dessau were pioneers. From 1784 until 1829 the quarterly review *Ha-Me'assef* appeared fairly regularly. Edited by the 'Society of Friends of the Hebrew Language', it received contributions from important figures of the *Haskalah*. The first regular weekly, *Ha-Maggid*, began publication in Russia in 1856.

In the second half of the eighteenth century, the *Haskalah* made a significant impact on the language. The new 'illuminati' or *maskilim* viewed Rabbinic Hebrew with disdain, believing it to be full of Aramaisms and replete with grammatical errors, and they lamented the sorry state of Hebrew in the diaspora. According to them, the blame lay with the *payṭanim*, the influence of Arabic in mediaeval philosophy, the use of the 'corrupt' Yiddish language, and with the inadequacies of Hebrew itself in comparison with

[1] See Rabin 1970, 326f.

other languages.[2] The most important representatives of this cultural movement tried to restore Hebrew as a living language. Not only did they attempt to purify the language and to promote correct usage, but they also increased its powers of expression, and showed little aversion to calquing modern terms from German and other western languages.[3]

Although certain figures, such as I. Saṭanow, regarded RH as a legitimate component of the new language, the majority settled on a pure form of Biblical Hebrew for poetry and on an Andalusian style of prose, similar to that used by the Ibn Tibbons. Poets like A.D. Lebensohn and J.L. Gordon, writers like M. Mendelssohn, N.H. Wessely, I. Saṭanow, and J.L. Ben-Ze'ev, dramatists like D. Zamoscz (who wrote the first modern play, in 1851), novelists like A. Mapu (who, in 1853, composed the first work to use this new style), and even translators of Yiddish like S.J. Abramowitsch (Mendele Mokher Seforim, at the close of the nineteenth century) all helped in important ways to lay the foundations of Modern Hebrew.[4]

Although some nineteenth-century writers tried to use a fundamentally biblical form of language, they often introduced structures that were alien to its spirit and frequently made grammatical errors, incorrectly employing the article with nouns in the construct state, treating intransitive verbs as transitives, confusing particles, and so on. Also, they frequently had recourse to turgid paraphrase in a desperate attempt not to stray from the limited vocabulary of the Bible for expressing contemporary referents, thus endowing many biblical expressions with new content. A. Mapu, whom we have already mentioned, emphasized

[2] See Pelli 1974.

[3] For S. Spiegel (1930), the revitalization of Hebrew by the *maskilim* was not an end in itself, but rather an instrument in their ultimate objectives of assimilation and absorption within European culture. Given their disparagement of Yiddish, the reformers turned to Hebrew as the language that could be best understood by all the Jews of eastern Europe.

[4] The language of the *Haskalah* has been studied in particular by J. Kena'ani (1932–33) and Y. Yitshaki (1969–71). D. Patterson (1962) examined the language of nineteenth-century novelists.

the inadequacy of BH for the demands of literature and advocated the use of post-biblical sources.

This tendency is clearly seen in the work of Mendele Mokher Seforim (1835–1917), whom many regard as the real creator of Modern Hebrew.[5] Jewish culture underwent a marked change at the end of the nineteenth century, with the abandonment of the ideal of assimilation and its replacement by the nationalist and Zionist programme of the *Hibbat Zion*. Mendele, who wrote in both Yiddish and Hebrew, accepted into his language the most varied elements not only from BH but also from all the later stages of the language, as well as from Yiddish. J.Ḥ. Alkalai, A.J. Schlesinger, Y.M. Pines, and others also made successful contributions to the task of ensuring that Hebrew would once more possess the character of a spoken language.

8.2 *The revival of Hebrew*

A new era opened with the publication in 1879 of Eliezer Ben-Yehuda's article entitled 'A burning question'. The use of Hebrew as a spoken language was to be for Ben-Yehuda one of the most important aspects of the new plan for settlement in Palestine. From 1881 Ben-Yehuda lived in Jerusalem, and, starting with his own family, forged ahead with his objective of changing Hebrew into a language suitable for daily use. With enthusiastic backing from such supporters of the nationalist cause as Y.M. Pines and D. Yellin, he struggled to give new life to the language. One of his greatest endeavours was to develop an appropriate vocabulary, in which Ben-Yehuda incorporated material from ancient and mediaeval literature and created new words eventually to be included in his monumental *Thesaurus* (continued after Ben-Yehuda's death by M.H. Segal and N.H. Ṭur-Sinai).

[5] See Pattterson 1962; Díaz Esteban 1970; E.Y. Kutscher 1982, 190ff.

Although the Jews who were already established in Palestine had previously used Hebrew as a *lingua franca*, it was not employed more generally, and the various immigrant communities continued to speak their native languages. Among the factors that helped turn Ben-Yehuda's dream into reality were the lack of a national language in the region, a desire on the part of successive waves of immigrants from central and eastern Europe to renew Jewish culture, and memories of the centuries of ancient grandeur that the Jews had once experienced in the very place they now lived. Many other personalities played a part in this undertaking, which at the beginning appeared little less than impossible. Among them were important groups of teachers who adopted the cause of teaching Hebrew *via* Hebrew.[6]

During this first stage of the revival, which lasted up to 1918, consideration was given to a number of problems in phonology (adaptation of Hebrew to the pronunciation of foreign names, resulting in the introduction of some graphemes that are followed by an apostrophe), orthography (adoption of *scriptio defectiva*), and morphology and syntax (no deliberate major changes). However, the process did not follow just one path – at the end of the nineteenth century, for example, I. Epstein and other leading teachers cultivated a separate pronunciation in Galilee, that continued to gain ground until 1920 before eventually disappearing completely.[7]

But the most pressing issue was the creation of new words, the basic task of Ben-Yehuda and the *Va'ad ha-Lashon*, which began to operate in 1890. In the introduction to Ben-Yehuda's *Thesaurus*, the methods employed for adapting the language to everyday needs are explained. These include a return to the scientific and technical Hebrew vocabulary of the Tibbonid translations and the introduction of Arabic loanwords on the basis of semantic proximity to Hebrew, with their forms adapted to Hebrew

6 See Parfitt 1972; A. Bar-Adon 1975, 18ff.; Ornan 1986.
7 See A. Bar-Adon 1975.

patterns, as in מַחְסָן (maḥsān) 'store' from Arabic *makhsan*. From the Mishnah, Talmud, and *midrashim*, Ben-Yehuda adopted any potentially useful Hebrew and Aramaic expressions, and even Greek and Latin loanwords. Aramaic morphological patterns and suffixes were employed, and precise senses established for infrequent biblical words, especially *hapax legomena*, the meanings of which are not evident from context. Roots attested in BH were exploited to derive additional vocabulary according to traditional morphological patterns. The end result of this was an immense and thoroughgoing enhancement of the expressive potential of the language.[8]

It should not be forgotten, however, that several thousand words thus created would later fall into disuse because they did not enjoy the favour of language users, and eventually disappeared completely. The waves of immigrants who arrived from 1905 did not take easily to some of the innovations, preferring foreign words, especially those considered to be of universal usage, and resisted the use of the newly revived language. The same fate awaited other attempts at the creation of new words, such as those of M. Schulbaum and I. Avinery, and the endeavours of many others who tried in one way or another to plan the development of the language. The dissemination of such neologisms could not always be easy or rapid, as their acceptance by speakers depended on a variety of social factors not of a purely linguistic nature.[9]

A new stage was reached with the British Mandate in Palestine (1918–48), under which Hebrew was accepted as one of the country's official languages in 1922. The number of speakers quickly grew, and at the same time various cultural institutions (including the Hebrew University of Jerusalem), helped to increase considerably the technical vocabulary of the new language.

[8] See D. Cohen and Zafrani 1968, 14ff.
[9] See Blanc 1957; Morag 1959a, 259ff.; Fainberg (Allony-Fainberg) 1977.

After the creation of the State of Israel in 1948, Hebrew was fully consolidated as the country's principal language, developing its own characteristics with unusual vitality. New immigrants from east and west, speaking every kind of language, quickly learned the new Hebrew in special centres (*ulpanim*), while a fresh generation of strongly nationalistic native-born Israelis developed novel linguistic usages and even took pride in distancing themselves from those who regarded Hebrew as a Semitic language. In 1953 the Academy of the Hebrew Language replaced the *Va'ad ha-Lashon* in its task of looking after the interests of the language and increasing its powers of expression without sacrificing purity.

8.3 *Israeli Hebrew*

The relatively brief life of this new language, which is nowadays usually referred to as 'Israeli Hebrew',[10] has often been accompanied by controversy. Its relationship to earlier stages of Hebrew, its status as an independent language with a distinctive character of its own, and differences between academic prescription and popular usage have often been the cause of dispute.[11]

The rebirth of Hebrew as a spoken language was associated from the beginning with a series of normative measures to direct the language and to conserve it intact. For some time, attempts were made to impose a prescriptive or 'normative' grammar – a typical representative of this approach would be I. Epstein (1862–1943), whose work was to some extent continued by I. Pereṣ and I. Avinery.

After a period of discussion, BH was accepted as the basis of the new language, omitting a number of archaisms and obsolete

[10] See Rosén 1958.
[11] See Morag 1959a; Díaz Esteban 1970.

structures, such as the consecutive forms of the verb, cohortatives, and the infinitive absolute with emphatic function. Some components, like the basic system of tenses, were incorporated from RH, although this was modified by the employment of BH structures in certain areas. In general, the terminology of the mediaeval grammarians was adopted. The usual standard for writing and pronunciation was to be the Tiberian system of vocalization, in combination with various *matres lectionis* to facilitate the reading of unpointed texts. The aspect of BH regarded as least appropriate for contemporary needs was its syntax, with preference being given here to RH, albeit heavily influenced by western languages. In vocabulary, a greater openness was shown to all the previous stages of Hebrew, and items were also accepted from Aramaic, Arabic, and the non-Semitic Jewish languages. In everyday usage, homophonous and homonymous forms were avoided, in order to minimize the risk of ambiguity, and there was a tendency to use standard morphological patterns.[12]

The most important controversy about the nature of IH began in 1930, when the issue of the co-existence of BH and RH underwent scholarly review. Some specialists claimed that they were not so easily reconcilable as had been thought and that their uncontrolled merger could produce structural disorders, given that BH and RH were associated with different ways of expressing the same content. Against this background, J. Klausner wrote the first ever grammar of Modern Hebrew (1933–34),[13] which he presented from an entirely RH perspective. This is because Klausner believed that RH should be the only basis of IH, and by attempting to describe Hebrew in strict conformity to RH usage, he hoped to prevent it from developing into an arbitrary mixture of traditions.[14]

A. Bendavid opted for a greater variety of possible means of expression. In *Leshon ha-Mikra 'o Leshon Ḥakhamim?* ('Biblical

[12] See E.Y. Kutscher 1982, 198ff.

[13] Klausner 1938 (2nd ed.).

[14] A few years later (1942–43), Klausner also published the Book of Amos in his version of IH.

Hebrew or Rabbinic Hebrew?'),[15] Bendavid examined the agreements and antagonisms between the two systems. He stressed that IH can express the same thing in two different ways, and rejected the possibility of returning to a uniform language. Nonetheless, Bendavid proposed that norms be established in order to prevent the process of merger occurring in an unsystematic or uncontrolled way. The exclusive 'or' of the book's title is nowadays viewed as quite unnecessary, especially when it is realized that Hebrew, in its revitalized form, exploits many elements common to both BH and RH, which had co-existed in the language throughout the rabbinic and mediaeval periods.[16]

Z. Ben-Ḥayyim, who for a long time was president of the Academy of the Hebrew Language, was a leading figure in an important war of words against H.B. Rosén and others in the 'anti-normativist' camp. According to Ben-Ḥayyim, the struggle between BH and RH in the modern language meant that it was impossible to speak of a 'system' in a Saussurian sense, and that it would be pointless to devote structural analyses to this phase of the language. In his view, the process of development was still continuing, and only at the end of it would the competing elements be restructured in a new system. Linguistic specialists should guide the process towards a successful conclusion. Meanwhile, the traditional rules were to be observed, and both types of language could be used.[17]

H.B. Rosén, who promoted a descriptive linguistic approach, devoted a chapter of his *Ha-'Ivrit Shellanu* ('Our Hebrew') to the topic 'Elements in conflict'.[18] For Rosén, the supposed struggle of systems did not actually exist, since restructuring had already occurred. Israeli Hebrew is a new *état de langue*, as structurally autonomous as BH or RH. Thus, structural description is fully

[15] Bendavid 1951. The revised edition of 1967 makes some important changes, extending to the title in which 'or' is replaced by 'and'.

[16] See Rabin 1985b.

[17] See Ben-Ḥayyim 1952–53.

[18] Rosén 1955, 83ff.

justified, and it is to this that Rosén dedicated the most important part of his book.[19] He argued strongly for the acceptance of contemporary linguistic usage, including recent colloquialisms and the vocabulary of young native-born Israelis, or 'sabras'. Rosén's work provoked fierce reactions, both in favour and against, especially among writers and language teachers. Rosén advocated the acceptance of IH as a written language, without the need to conform to rules taken from ancient sources which had by then become virtually meaningless.

In another important book, *'Ivrit Ṭovah* ('Good Hebrew'),[20] Rosén described the syntactic restructuring that had taken place in IH, which represented 'good Hebrew', even if prescriptive grammarians were largely unaware of this. In an article published around the same time,[21] Rosén emphasized some of his basic ideas: IH is not an artificial construct but an active system of language and the principal means of communication among members of a territorially-defined social group, and fulfils the requirements of a living language. In the short but swift history of this language, which had come into existence just a few years before, it had broken away from its traditional written sources in order to transform itself into a complete system of language, able to express every nuance of expression required of a language or which a speaker might wish for. IH's categories differ from those of previous stages in the language, but in Saussurian terms they represent a 'system' that is both complete and 'closed'.

According to Rosén, in IH the various traditions of reading Hebrew have come together to form a *koinē* from different dialects, in accordance with well-known rules of language. Thus, the most discordant non-common elements have been eliminated, and a compromise has been reached among the various competing tendencies. A new system has come into being in which there are two sometimes different stylistic levels, with BH and RH elements

19 Rosén 1955, 138–245.
20 Rosén 1977 (1st ed., 1958).
21 Rosén 1958.

which are often used alongside one another. A non-Hebrew substratum has had an additional influence on the internal development of the language. Also, compared with the classical period, contemporary Hebrew does not have an unduly large amount of contact with the Hebrew of scripture and liturgy. Ordinary speakers have laid down their own grammatical rules, in spite of official teaching. What traditional grammar would regard as 'errors' or 'mistakes' in daily language are, in reality, the linguistic innovations of a new stage in the language which has displaced previous forms of Hebrew.

Along similar lines, from 1952 to 1954 H. Blanc wrote two dozen articles in the literary review *Massa* with the revealing title *Leshon Benei 'Adam* ('Language as people speak it'), in an attack on excessive prescriptivism. According to Blanc, a modern linguistic approach must be adopted if we are to discover what is really taking place in IH. Blanc provided transcriptions of Israeli speech, and in his course on spoken Hebrew he attempted a comprehensive description of IH as it is actually spoken.[22]

Rosén tried something similar with his teaching grammar, *A Textbook of Israeli Hebrew*.[23] An acceptance of IH on its own terms is also the basis of the many other grammars of contemporary Hebrew published in Israel and elsewhere over the last decades, such as those of C. Rabin, D. Cohen and Ḥ. Zafrani, G. Alster and B.M. Mossel, and H. Simon.[24] Over the last forty years IH has become accepted as a proper object of independent linguistic inquiry, and academic study of the language has begun with numerous doctoral theses from universities in Israel and other western countries devoted to providing a more detailed analysis of this stage of the Hebrew language.[25]

22 See Blanc 1960.

23 Rosén 1969 (1st ed., 1966).

24 Rabin 1948a (1st ed., 1943); D. Cohen and Zafrani 1968; Alster and Mossel 1969; Simon 1970.

25 See Rosén 1977a, 30ff.

In the light of all we have said, it is natural to ask whether there is a point at which IH ceases to be a Semitic language. Some linguists have emphasized the high level of 'Indo-Europeanization' of the language, despite the fact that most of its components are BH and RH in origin. For such scholars, although externally IH still appears to be a Semitic language, its semantic relationships are Indo-European and its conceptual approach is western.[26] Corresponding to the various stages of its revival, Hebrew was first influenced predominantly by the Slavic languages, replaced later by German, and eventually, and more decisively, English, though we should not forget the rôle played by French and Spanish, the native languages of many of the Jews now living in Israel. The aspects of IH that have probably been most affected by such influences are syntax and vocabulary, and it is these that have changed the most in comparison with the classical language.[27] Nonetheless, it needs to be emphasized that the means of expression inherited by IH, as well as the basic nucleus of its morphology and syntax, are clearly Semitic in origin.[28]

8.4 *Studies in Israeli Hebrew*

Given the size of the bibliography available, we have to limit ourselves to some of the more outstanding works on various

26 See Ullendorff 1957; Díaz Esteban 1970. In a recent study, P. Wexler (1990) makes a detailed argument for the thesis that IH is a Slavic language: 'Both Yiddish and Modern Hebrew are dialects of Judeo-Sorbian – a West Slavic language' (p. 99). For Wexler, language revival, including the resurrection of a genuine Northwest Semitic language, is an impossibility, and Modern Hebrew was the creation of 'native speakers of a Slavic language – Yiddish – by means of a partial language shift' (p. 100). But although some of Wexler's claims cannot be faulted, his thesis is unlikely to attract much scholarly support.

27 There is an extensive bibliography on this issue. See, for example, Spiegel 1930; Plessner 1931; Rieger 1935; Aeshcoly 1937; Yalon 1937–39, I, 62–78; II, 70–76; Weiman 1950; Gottstein (Goshen-Gottstein) 1953–54; Bachi 1956; Tubielewicz 1956; Livni 1957; Morag 1959a; 1972b; Ben-Asher 1960; 1965; Ṭur-Sinai 1960; Téné 1961; 1969; 1969a; Chomsky 1962; Eisenstadt 1967; E. Eitan and Ornan 1971; Kaddari 1976; Schwarzwald 1981; E.Y. Kutscher 1982, 196ff.

28 See Rosén 1977a, 24ff.

aspects of IH. The phonology and phonetics of IH were examined many years ago by D. Yellin, A.Z. Idelsohn, and Z. Jabotinsky.[29] More recent general studies include those of H. Klarberg, J. Mansour, W. Weinberg, I. Garbell, and M.J. Chayen.[30] S. Morag has undertaken important work on the pronunciation of different Jewish communities, R. Patai examined the pronunciation of Israeli 'sabras',[31] C. Rabin the phonetics of the colloquial language,[32] and N. Peladah the frequency of particular sounds in present-day Hebrew.[33] E.S. Artom investigated the pronunciation of Italian Jews,[34] and A.S. Corré that of the Anglo-Sephardis.[35] I. Garbell devoted various studies to the pronunciations found in Iran, Asia, and Africa,[36] whereas Ḥ. Zafrani concentrated on the Arabic speakers of North Africa.[37] S. Morag examined the different linguistic regions of Yemen,[38] and P. Enoch compared the phonetics of Modern Hebrew and French.[39]

In morphology, most attention has been focused on the innovations of IH, such as the introduction of nominal and adjectival compounds to a Semitic language characterized by the absence of compounding.[40] R. Mirkin has examined the new suffixes employed in the formation of nouns,[41] M. Masson investigated IH diminutives,[42] and I. Yannay multi-radical verbs.[43]

29 See Yellin 1905; Idelsohn 1913; 1917; Jabotinsky 1930.

30 Chanoch (Garbell) 1930; Garbell 1955; Mansour 1959–60; Weinberg 1966; 1973; Klarberg 1970–71; Chayen 1971–72; 1973.

31 See Patai 1953–54

32 See Rabin 1938.

33 See Peladah 1958–59

34 See Artom 1946–47.

35 See Corré 1956.

36 See Garbell 1946–47; 1968.

37 See Zafrani 1963–66.

38 See Morag 1963

39 See Enoch 1965.

40 See, for example, Altbauer 1964; Kaddari 1964–65a; Mirkin 1957–58; 1961–62.

41 See Mirkin 1961–62.

42 See M. Masson 1974.

43 See Yannay 1973–74.

A. Bar-Adon showed that the imperative was being replaced by the future tense,[44] and R. Sivan studied the exploitation of verbal forms for the creation of new words.[45] The different morphological types of IH noun have been examined by M. Ben-Asher,[46] and the passive participle with intensifying function, by R. Mirkin.[47] Various scholars have applied structural techniques to IH as a linguistic system.[48]

Apart from general analyses of IH syntax,[49] there have also been more specialized studies, for example those of M. Altbauer on negation,[50] S. Ariel on the derived conjugations of the verb,[51] A. Bar-Adon on new imperative and jussive forms with the particle -שֶׁ (šæ-),[52] H.B. Rosén on determination,[53] and H. Maschler on modality.[54] The syntax of the sentence has been examined in various works by, for example, U. Ornan and E. Rubinstein on the noun clause,[55] I. Pereṣ and S. Bahaṭ on the relative clause,[56] M. Ben-Asher on conditional sentences,[57] and T. Vardi on concessive clauses.[58]

In the field of lexis, the increase in vocabulary following the revival of Hebrew is represented by modern dictionaries, especially the *Thesaurus* of E. Ben-Yehuda and the *Millon Ḥadash* of

44 See A. Bar-Adon 1966.
45 See R. Sivan 1968.
46 1960.
47 1957–58.
48 See, for example, Harris 1948; 1954; Weiman 1950; Rosén 1955; Shapiro and Shvika 1963–64; G. Fraenkel 1966; Chayen and Dror 1976; Cole 1976; Sadka n.d.
49 See, for example, Pereṣ 1943; Nahir 1946–47; Yo'eli 1953–54; Rosén 1961a; Ornan 1965; Levenston 1965; 1966; 1967–68; Blau 1966; D. Cohen and Zafrani 1968; Azar 1971–72.
50 Altbauer 1964.
51 Ariel 1973.
52 A. Bar-Adon 1966.
53 Rosén 1961a.
54 Maschler 1966.
55 See Ornan 1964a; E. Rubinstein 1965; 1968.
56 See S. Bahaṭ 1964; Pereṣ 1967.
57 See Ben-Asher 1965
58 See Vardi (Thorion-Vardi) 1967.

A. Even-Shoshan.[59] A major new work is J. Kena'ani's *Oṣar ha-Lashon ha-'Ivrit li-Tkufoteha ha-Shonot*, the eighteenth volume of which appeared in 1988. A special kind of contribution to this field has been made by the Historical Dictionary of the Hebrew Language project, still in progress, and there are also many works dealing with specific aspects of IH vocabulary.[60] A list of a thousand words considered essential for learning IH was compiled by I. Mehlmann, H.B. Rosén, and J. Shaked,[61] the language of children was examined by A. Bar-Adon,[62] and that of sailors and fishermen, by M. Altbauer and by S. Morag and R. Sapan.[63] Slang has been investigated by M. Fraenkel, R. Sapan, and C. Rabin,[64] and loanwords from Palestinian Arabic by H. Blanc.[65] Yiddish influence on IH vocabulary was also examined by Blanc,[66] and the influence of English and other languages by I. Garbell.[67] The creation of new words in IH has been analysed by M. Masson.[68] Semantic analysis is still in a process of development, although some significant contributions have been made.[69]

[59] 7 vols., Jerusalem, 1979–80. The work first appeared in 1966.

[60] See for example, Chanoch (Garbell) 1930; Rieger 1935; Avinery 1935–36; Rivkai 1938; Altbauer 1947–48; 1953–54; Avrunin 1953–54; A. Bar-Adon 1959; E.Y. Kutscher 1961; Gan 1961–62; Rabin 1963–66a; Adar 1965; Morag and Sapan 1966–67; Nir 1967; R. Sivan 1968; Berggrün 1970; Kaddari 1970.

[61] 1960.

[62] 1959.

[63] See Altbauer 1953–54; Morag and Sapan 1966–67.

[64] See M. Fraenkel 1949; Sapan 1963; 1965; Rabin 1963–66a.

[65] 1954–55.

[66] 1965.

[67] Chanoch (Garbell) 1930.

[68] 1976; 1989.

[69] See, for example, Altbauer 1947–48; Gan 1961–62; Moreshet 1966–67a; Nir 1967; Téné 1969; Kaddari 1970.

8.5 *Phonology, morphology, and syntax of Israeli Hebrew*

This is not the place to offer a detailed account of these topics, as the task has already been accomplished very competently in works dedicated to them – Rosén's *Contemporary Hebrew*,[70] for example, as well as other books of more limited scope.[71] We shall restrict ourselves to giving a very brief presentation of the most outstanding relevant features of Modern Hebrew.

One of the most sensitive issues faced by linguists during the regeneration of Hebrew was that of pronunciation. The Jews who had come together in Israel were from very disparate communities, each one of which had its own phonetic traits. Leaving aside the Samaritan pronunciation, which had no influence whatever on the new phase of the language, there were at least three basic and quite distinct traditions that had to be reckoned with (apart from many other less important features associated with specific communities, generally as a result of influence from the indigenous languages of their various host-countries). The Jews of Yemen, under the influence of Arabic, pronounced *gimel* with *dagesh* as a velar, affricate, or prepalatal *g*, differentiating it thus from fricative *gimel*; the remaining *bgdkpt* phonemes were also associated with plosive and fricative allophones. In the vowel system, the influence of the ancient Babylonian tradition was still noticeable, with a complete loss of discrimination between *pathaḥ* and *segol*; in the south-west and in Aden, *ḥolem* and *ṣere* have the same realization. In an outstanding study of this subject, S. Morag carefully distinguished the different pronunciations of the various regions of the Yemen.[72]

Sephardi pronunciation displays great regional variety, although all versions have certain general features in common, for example the non-differentiation of *pathaḥ* and *qameṣ* (unless *qameṣ* occurs in

70 Rosén 1977a.

71 A good summary of IH, extending over more than fifty pages, is provided in E.Y. Kutscher 1982, 247ff.

72 See Morag 1963.

a closed unstressed syllable) and of *ṣere* and *segol.* The *bgdkpt* consonants do not have a uniform pronunciation, although the prevailing tendency is to omit the dual realization of *g, d,* and *t,* but to retain it for the others. In Arabic-speaking countries, as in the Yemenite tradition, the gutturals are enunciated very carefully.

In the Ashkenazi tradition the gutturals, especially *alef* and *'ayin* are no longer pronounced, fricative *taw* is realized as *s,* while *ṭet* and *taw* with *dagesh* are both pronounced as *t. Bet, kaf,* and *pe* retain a dual realization. There is no uniform system of vowel pronunciation, with *ḥolem* being pronounced regionally as *ey, y, oy, aw,* or *ow. Qameṣ,* pronounced as *o* or *u,* is distinguished from *pathaḥ,* and *ṣere,* realized as *ey* or *ay,* from *segol.*[73]

Although the need for uniformity has been recognized since the final decades of the nineteenth century, in practice it has not been easy to achieve, and has depended to some extent on the social predominance of particular groups. From a theoretical perspective, linguists tended to favour the retention of features from oriental pronunciation, which were regarded as being closer to the original Semitic character of the language. In 1923, the *Va'ad ha-Lashon* intervened in an attempt to standardize the pronunciation of *bet* as *v, waw* as *w,ḥet* as *ḥ* (not *ḵ*), *ṭet* as *ṭ, 'ayin* as *',* *ṣade* as *ts, kof* as velar emphatic *q,* and *taw* as *t.* The system, had it been adopted, would have been similar in many respects to the Sephardi tradition, particularly with regard to the vowels. However, popular pronunciation followed its own course and, in practice, rejected such rules.

The actual development of IH is comparable to the pattern found generally in the formation of *koinē* languages, characterized by the abandonment of any excessively idiosyncratic features in the various dialects.[74] In fact, the present-day pronunciation of IH is only a more or less informal and spontaneous compromise among the competing tendencies. In the phonological system of

73 See Morag 1971.
74 See Rosén 1969a.

the 'sabras' or native-born Israelis, nineteen consonantal and five vocalic phonemes have been found, all of which are shared by the Ashkenazi and Sephardi traditions. But given that six characteristically Sephardi phonemes have been rejected, we may justifiably say that the Ashkenazi tradition is dominant.[75] S. Morag has claimed that in the spoken language there is a sixth vowel phoneme, *á*, which can be traced back to the historical *o* found in the sequence *a'a*.[76]

In practice ע (') has become identical with א ('), ק (q) with כּ (k), ח (ḥ) with כ (k̲), and ט (ṭ) with ת (t). A dual pronunciation of *bet*, *kaf*, and *pe* has been retained as has the distinction between *samekh* and *ṣade*. In vowel pronunciation, the Sephardi tradition has prevailed. Thus, *pathaḥ* and *qameṣ* are pronounced the same, *ḥolem* is realized as *o*, and *ṣere* can be pronounced as either *e* or *ey*. In contrast to this popular pronunciation, academic Hebrew, supported by its use within official organizations and institutions and on Israeli radio and television, tries to maintain, for example, the 'oriental' pronunciation of *ḥet* and *'ayin*, the gemination of consonants containing *dagesh forte*, and the enunciation of *shewa mobile* (which is virtually always omitted in colloquial Hebrew). The standard pattern of accentuation is Sephardi, although the Ashkenazi tradition of penultimate stress has left its mark on some proper names.[77]

Similarly, the correct way to write IH has been the object of scholarly debate from the beginning. In 1905, D. Yellin proposed a system of 'grammatical' writing without vowels, similar to the consonantal orthography of the standard version of the Bible. In 1929, the *Va'ad ha-Lashon* adopted this system, allowing the use of *matres lectionis* where ambiguity might arise. While arguments about these measures lasted many years, writers and ordinary members of the public followed a different, more flexible, procedure. In practice, the official method presupposed too good a

[75] See Patai 1953–54.
[76] See Morag 1971.
[77] See E. Eitan and Ornan 1971, 1645ff.

knowledge of grammar and was too complicated for new immigrants. The use of *yod* for *i* and *e*, *waw* for *o* and *u*, and even *alef* for *a*, as well as the use of *waw-waw* and *yod-yod* to indicate the consonantal realization of the semivowels has gradually become the norm in non-academic situations.

In 1948, the official rules of the *Va'ad ha-Lashon* appeared in *Leshonenu*.[78] These are practically the same as those accepted by the Academy of the Hebrew Language in 1969.[79] The use of *alef* and *'ayin* as vowel-letters and of *waw* for *qameṣ qaṭan* and *ḥaṭef qameṣ* was rejected, even though this went against a number of prevailing trends. The use of a diacritic point inside the ו (w) to signify *u*, or over it to represent *o*, was retained, as were the forms of *bet*, *kaf*, *pe*, and final *he* with *dagesh*. Consonantal *waw* was to be indicated by the use of a single ו (w).[80]

IH morphology does not differ fundamentally from that of earlier stages of the language, although in this area too popular usage diverges from academic prescription. From 1905, attempts were made to impose biblical morphology, as used by the writers of the *Haskalah*. In the wake of a notorious controversy in 1910, the *Va'ad ha-Lashon* adopted D. Yellin's proposal that whenever a BH grammatical form or item of vocabulary exists, it should be retained, if necessary supplemented by elements taken from the Mishnah, Talmud, or midrashic literature, with any Aramaic expressions being recast in Hebrew form. This was the approach officially adopted in textbooks and in the teaching of Hebrew at school. However, in other areas post-biblical usages have become equally widespread, and writers, journalists, and ordinary users of the language tend to follow their own rules. The Academy of the Hebrew Language tries to make decisions about the use of various forms attested in BH and RH.

As we have already mentioned, it is in syntax that IH has been most exposed to outside influence, especially from the indigenous

[78] 16, 82–83.
[79] See *Leshonenu le-Am* 206 (1970).
[80] See Weinberg 1971–72.

languages of the countries of origin of the various groups that make up the new State of Israel. But because of the fluctuating nature of the language and the problems of distinguishing between personal style and more generalized linguistic structure, it is difficult to undertake comprehensive analyses of newly introduced features of syntax. Only a few innovations have been noticed, such as the frequency of non-restrictive relative clauses, especially in the language of journalism, as well as jussive sentences or commands with the particle -שֶׁ (šæ-) followed by the prefix-conjugation. More than ever, it is ordinary people who accept or reject forms of expression that fall just outside the prescribed structures of the Academy of the Hebrew Language. For example the traditional form אֵינֶנִּי רוֹצֶה (ʾēnænnī rōṣæ) 'I do not want' (lit. 'not-I wanting') has fallen into disuse in the day-to-day language which uses instead אֲנִי לֹא רוֹצֶה (ʾanī lōʾ rōṣæ) (lit. 'I not wanting'). The vernacular language has also converted originally impersonal and intransitive structures into transitive ones, for example יֵשׁ לִי אֶת הַסּוּס (yēš lī ʾēṯ has-sūs) 'I have the horse' (lit. 'there is to me the horse'), where the object-marker אֵת (ʾēṯ) is inserted contrary to the standard rules of grammar.[81]

IH displays a certain arbitrariness in its use of components from earlier periods. For example, the BH way of expressing the genitive relationship by the use of a noun in the construct state followed by another in the absolute exists alongside the RH genitive with שֶׁל (šæl) 'which is to, of'. The incorporation of these two types of structure into the language has led to some interesting distinctions. For example, the BH form פִּנְקַס חָבֵר (pinqas ḥāḇēr) means 'membership card', whereas the RH structure פִּנְקָס שֶׁל חָבֵר (pinqās šæl ḥāḇēr) means 'card of a colleague', הַבָּשָׂר שֶׁלִּי (hab-bāśār šæl-lī) is 'my meat' and בְּשָׂרִי (bᵉśār-ī) 'my flesh', thus introducing a contrast between nouns of alienable and inalienable possession. There are also instances of morphological suppletion, with the root אמר (ʾmr) 'say' being replaced in the infinitive, future, and

81 See Díaz Esteban 1970.

imperative by *Hif'il* forms of the root נגד (ngd), which in BH has a distinctive meaning of its own. The confusing homophony of מִמֶּנּוּ (mim-mænnū), both 'from him' and 'from us', is avoided by using a separate prepositional form מֵאִתָּנוּ (mē-'ittānū) 'from us'.[82]

Without doubt, one of the areas most open to innovation has been that of vocabulary. As we have already noticed, it was from the beginning one of the main preoccupations of Ben-Yehuda and many other specialists, as well as the *Va'ad ha-Lashon* and the Academy of the Hebrew Language. At first, this was a matter of incorporating the rich heritage of Hebrew literature through the ages, and especially from the mediaeval period. Ḥ.N. Bialik, one of the early pillars of the movement to regenerate Hebrew, argued that all existing Hebrew expressions should first be garnered in a comprehensive dictionary, before turning to the creation of new items of vocabulary. However, expressions were sometimes constructed from other sources for concepts that could have been expressed by words from earlier stages of Hebrew. Ben-Yehuda favoured making substantial use of the rich lexicon of Arabic, with the specific aim of conserving Hebrew's Semitic character. However, this trend did not last.

Although initially there was great resistance to the inclusion of words deriving from western languages, with the preference being instead for new words based on Semitic roots, a significant part of modern international vocabulary, especially of a technical nature, has established itself within IH. At present, it has been calculated that some ten per-cent of the words in Hebrew dictionaries might be of foreign, usually western, origin. In addition to loanwords, there are also many loan-translations, which often have a transparently European origin, as with גַּן יְלָדִים (gan yelādīm) 'kindergarten' (lit. 'children's garden'), for example.

E. Eitan and U. Ornan arrived at the following classification of new elements in IH vocabulary: (1) nouns and adjectives formed by the addition of suffixes such as ָן- (-ān), וֹן- (-ōn), and וּת- (-ūṯ);

[82] See Rosén 1958.

(2) compounds of existing words, for example קוֹלְנוֹעַ (qōl-nōaʻ) 'cinema' (lit. 'voice-movement'), which represent a striking innovation in Hebrew morphology; (3) denominative verbs; (4) verbs formed by adding a prefix or suffix to a root; (5) items derived from acronyms or other morphological blends, for example תַּנָ״כִי (tanāḵī) 'biblical', derived from תַּנַ״ךְ (tanaḵ), an acronym of *Torah, Nevi'im, Ketuvim,* the three divisions of the Hebrew Bible; (6) new causative structures with prefixed -שִׁ (ši-); (7) passive verbal adjectives in ā-ī, such as קָרִיא (qārī') 'readable'.[83]

The rebirth of Hebrew this century has without doubt been the most exciting of events for linguists because of the many unique features involved. Conceived and brought to reality by the determination of a people wanting to recapture its own identity, IH is not the result of natural evolution but of a process without parallel in the development of any other language. Thus, it represents the final link in a never completely broken chain, connecting it across more than 3,000 years to the earliest passages of the Bible. The continuity of Hebrew's literary heritage and the historical unity of the language are undeniable facts that run through the richly varied stages and forms we have tried to reflect in this book.

[83] See E. Eitan and Ornan 1971, 1651ff.

Bibliography

Abbreviations

AAL=Afroasiatic Linguistics; AcOr=Acta Orientalia; ADAJ=Annual of the Department of Antiquities of Jordan; AfO=Archiv für Orientforschung; AION=Annali dell'Istituto Orientale di Napoli; AJBI=*Annual of the Japanese Biblical Institute;* AJSL=*American Journal of Semitic Languages and Literatures; ALUOS=The Annual of Leeds University Oriental Society; ANDRL=Archive of the New Dictionary of Rabbinic Literature* (Vol. I ed. by E.Y. Kutscher, Vol. II ed. by M.Z. Kaddari; Ramat-Gan); *APCI=Actes du Premier Congrès International de Linguistique Sémitique et Chamito-Sémitique, Paris 16–19 juillet 1969* (ed. by A. Caquot and D. Cohen; The Hague/Paris); *ArOr=Archiv Orientální; AuOr=Aula Orientalis; ASTI=Annual of the Swedish Theological Institute; AUSS=Andrews University Seminary Studies; BA=The Biblical Archaeologist; BASOR=Bulletin of the American Schools of Oriental Research; BeO=Bibbia e Oriente; BEOIFD=Bulletin d'Etudes Orientales de l'Institut Français de Damas; BFAC=Bulletin of the Faculty of Arts, Université Egyptienne, Cairo; BibOr=Biblica et Orientalia; BIES=Bulletin of the Israel Exploration Society; BIJS=Bulletin of the Institute of Jewish Studies; BJES=Bulletin of the Jewish Exploration Society; BJRL=Bulletin of the John Rylands Library; BM=Beth Mikra; BO=Bibliotheca Orientalis; BSLP=Bulletin de la Société de Linguistique [de Paris]; BSOAS=Bulletin of the School of Oriental and African Studies; BZ=Biblische Zeitschrift; BZAW=Beihefte zur Zeitschrift für die alttestamentliche Wissenschaft; CBQ=The Catholic Biblical Quarterly; EB=Encyclopaedia Biblica (Enṣiklopedyah Mikra'it); EI=Eretz-Israel; EJ=Encyclopaedia Judaica; EstBib=Estudios Bíblicos;* ET=*The Expository Times; FolOr=Folia Orientalia; FrancLA=Studii Biblici Franciscani, Liber Annuus; GLECS=Comptes rendus du Groupe Linguistique d'Etudes Chamito-Sémitiques; HA=Hebrew Abstracts; HAR=Hebrew Annual Review; HCL=Hebrew Computational Linguistics; HS=Hebrew Studies; HTR=Harvard Theological Review; HUCA=Hebrew Union College Annual; IEJ=Israel Exploration Journal; IJAL=International Journal of American Linguistics; IOS=Israel Oriental Studies; JA=Journal Asiatique; JANES=Journal of the Ancient Near Eastern Society; JAOS=Journal of the American Oriental Society; JBL=Journal of Biblical Literature; JCS=Journal of Cuneiform Studies; JEOL=Jaarbericht van het Vooraziatisch-Egyptisch Genootschap 'Ex Oriente Lux'; JJS=Journal of Jewish Studies; JKF=Jahrbuch für kleinasiatische Forschung; JNES=Journal of Near Eastern Studies; JNSL=Journal of the Northwest Semitic Languages; JPOS=Journal of the Palestine Oriental Society; JQR=Jewish Quarterly Review; JRAS=Journal of the Royal Asiatic Society of Great Britain and Ireland; JSS=Journal of Semitic Studies; JTS=The Journal of Theological Studies; KirSef=Kiryat Sefer; LBdOr=Literatur-Blatt des Orients; LeshLA=Leshonenu la-'Am; MasSt=Masoretic Studies; LSWANA=Linguistics in South West Asia and North Africa (Current Trends in Linguistics,* ed. by T.A. Sebeok, Vol. VI; The Hague/Paris); *MEAH=Miscelánea de Estudios Arabes y Hebraicos; MGWJ=Monatsschrift für Geschichte und Wissenschaft des Judentums; MIO=Mitteilungen des Instituts für Orientforschung; OLP=Orientalia Lovaniensia Periodica; OLZ=Orientalistische Literaturzeitung; OrAn=Oriens Antiquus; OrSu=Orientalia Suecana; OTS=Oudtestamentische Studiën; OYS=Oṣar Yehude Sefarad; PAAJR=Proceedings of the American Academy for Jewish Research; PEFQS=Palestine Exploration Fund Quarterly Statement; PEQ=Palestine Exploration Quarterly; PIASH=Proceedings of the Israel Academy of Science and Humanities; PICSS=Proceedings of the International Conference on Semitic Studies held in Jerusalem, 19–23 July 1965* (Jerusalem); *PSBA=Proceedings of the Society of Biblical Archaeology; P4(...9)WCJS=Proceedings of the Fourth (... Ninth) World Congress of Jewish Studies* (Jerusalem); *RA=Revue d'Assyriologie et d'Archéologie Orientale; RB=Revue Biblique; RBI=Rivista Biblica Italiana; REJ=Revue des Etudes Juives; RENLO=Revue de l'Ecole Nationale des Langues Orientales; RHPR=Revue d'Histoire et de Philosophie Religieuses; RQ=Revue de Qumran; RSF=Rivista di Studi Fenici; RSO=Rivista degli Studi Orientali; ScrHier=Scripta Hierosolymitana; SEL=Studi Epigrafici e Linguistici; Shenaton=Shenaton la-Mikra we-la-Ḥeker ha-Mizraḥ ha-Kadum; SVT=Supplements to Vetus Testamentum; TAJ=Tel-Aviv Journal of Archaeology; TLZ=Theologische Literaturzeitung; TZ=Theologische Zeitschrift; UF=Ugarit-Forschungen; VT=Vetus Testamentum;*

WdO=Die Welt des Orients; WZMLU= Wissenschaftliche Zeitschrift der Martin-Luther-Universität, Halle-Wittenberg, Gesellschafts- und sprachwissenschaftliche Reihe; YMḤSI=Yedi'ot ha-Makhon le-Ḥeker ha-Shirah ha-'Ivrit; ZA=Zeitschrift für Assyriologie und verwandte Gebiete; ZAW=Zeitschrift für die alttestamentliche Wissenschaft; ZDMG=Zeitschrift der Deutschen Morgenländischen Gesellschaft; ZDPV= Zeitschrift des Deutschen Palästina-Vereins; ZNW=Zeitschrift für die neutestamentliche Wissenschaft; ZP=Zeitschrift für Phonetik; ZS=Zeitschrift für Semitistik und verwandte Gebiete.

'*' indicates pages within a separately paginated Hebrew section; 'H.' (at the end of a reference) indicates that the item is written in Hebrew.

Aartun, K., 1967: 'Althebräische Nomina mit konserviertem kurzem Vokal in der Hauptdrucksilbe', *ZDMG* 117, 247–65.

1971: 'Hebräisch "'āni" und "'ānāw"', *BibOr* 28, 125–26.

1974: 'Notizen zur hebräischen Nominalmorphologie', *BibOr* 31, 38–39.

1974–78: *Die Partikeln des Ugaritischen.* 2 vols. Neukirchen-Vluyn.

1975: 'Über die Grundstruktur der Nominalbildungen vom Typus "qaṭṭal"/"qaṭṭōl" im Althebräischen', *JNSL* 4, 1–8.

1981: 'Noch einmal zum Problem der Haupttondehnung beim Nomen im Althebräischen', *ZDMG* 131, 28–41.

Abbadi, S., 1985: 'Ein ammonitisches Siegel aus 'Ammān', *ZDPV* 101, 30–31.

Abbot, W.G.M., 1944–45: 'Did Jesus speak Aramaic?', *ET* 56, 305.

Abel, F.-M., 1911: 'Un mot sur les ostraca de Samarie', *RB* 8, 290–93.

Abramson, G., 1971–72: 'Colloquialisms in the Old Testament', *Semitics* 2, 1–16.

Abramson, S., 1941–43: 'Le-shimmushe ha-lashon ba-shirah ha-Sefardit', *Leshonenu* 11, 54–57.

1943: 'Leshon-RaSaG be-'Essa Meshali', in Y. Fishman (ed.), *Rav Se'adyah Ga'on. Koveṣ torani-mada'i*, Jerusalem, pp. 677–88.

1956–57: 'Mi-leshon ḥakhamim', *Leshonenu* 21, 94–103.

1965: *Bi-lshon kodemim. Meḥkar be-shirat Yisra'el bi-Sfarad.* Jerusalem.

1974: 'On the Hebrew in the Babylonian Talmud', *ANDRL*, II, 9–15. H.

1978–79: 'Makor we-shem ha-po'al', *Leshonenu* 43, 211–16.

Académie des Inscriptions et Belles-Lettres (de Paris), 1881–83: *Corpus inscriptionum Semiticarum*. I. Paris.

1900–33: *Répertoire d'épigraphie sémitique*. 6 vols. Ed. by C. Clermont-Ganneau and J.B. Chabot. Paris.

Ackermann, A., 1893: *Das hermeneutische Element der biblischen Accentuation. Ein Beitrag zur Geschichte der hebräischen Sprache.* Berlin.

Ackroyd, P.R., 1951: 'The Hebrew root "B'Š"', *JTS*, n.s., 2, 31–36.

1953: 'Criteria for the Maccabean dating of Old Testament literature', *VT* 3, 113–32.

1968: 'The meaning of Hebrew "dōr" considered', *JSS* 13, 3–10.

Adar, H., 1965: 'New words in agricultural terminology created during the "Bilu" period'. Doct. diss., Hebrew University, Jerusalem. H.

Adini, U., 1979–80: 'A biblical *hapax legomenon* in Modern Hebrew', *HS* 20–21, 12–16.

Aeshcoly, A.Z., 1937: *L'Hébreu moderne. Leçon inaugurale du cours d'hébreu moderne à l'Ecole Nationale des Langues Orientales Vivantes (20 – XII – 1937).* Paris.

Agmon-Fruchtman (Fruchtman), M., 1981–82: '"Umor 'im 'ahalim": a linguistic study of a phrase appearing in a poem by Dunash ibn Labraṭ', *Leshonenu* 46, 3–8. H.

Agus, I.A., 1974: 'The languages spoken by Ashkenazic Jews in the High Middle Ages', in S.B. Hoenig and L.D. Stitskin (eds.), *Joshua Finkel* Festschrift*: in honor of Joshua Finkel*, New York, pp. 19–28.

Aharoni, Y., 1950–51: 'A new Ammonite inscription', *IEJ* 1, 219–22.

1961: 'Excavations at Ramat Raḥel', *BA* 24, 98–118.

1962: 'The Samaria ostraca–an additional note', *IEJ* 12, 67–69.
1966: 'Hebrew ostraca from Tel Arad', *IEJ* 16, 1–7.
1966a: 'The use of hieratic numerals in Hebrew ostraca and the shekel weights', *BASOR* 184, 13–19.
1968: 'Trial excavations in the "solar shrine" at Lachish. Preliminary report', *IEJ* 18, 157–69.
1968a: 'Arad: its inscriptions and temple', *BA* 31, 2–18.
1968b: 'The Arad ostraca', *Qadmoniot* 1, 101.
1970: 'Three Hebrew ostraca from Arad', *BASOR* 197, 16–42.
1971: 'Khirbet Raddana and its inscription', *IEJ* 21, 130–35.
1973: 'The Hebrew inscriptions', in *Beer-Sheba I. Excavations at Tel Beer-Sheba, 1969–1971 seasons*, Tel-Aviv, pp. 71–78.
1975: *Investigations at Lachish: the sanctuary and the residency (Lachish V).* Tel-Aviv.
1981: *Arad inscriptions*. English ed. by A.F. Rainey. Jerusalem.
Aharoni, Y. and Amiran, R., 1964: 'Excavations at Tel Arad. Preliminary report on the first season, 1962', *IEJ* 14, 131–47.
Aḥituv, S., 1984: *Canaanite toponyms in ancient Egyptian documents.* Leiden.
Ahrens, K., 1910: 'Der Stamm der schwachen Verba in den semitischen Sprachen', *ZDMG* 64, 161–94.
Aistleitner, J., 1954: *Untersuchungen zur Grammatik des Ugaritischen.* Berlin.
1967: *Wörterbuch der ugaritischen Sprache*. 3rd ed. by O. Eissfeldt. Berlin.
Albeck, C., 1971: *Einführung in die Mischna.* Berlin/New York.
1969: *Mavo la-Talmudim.* Tel-Aviv.
Albrecht, C., 1887–88: 'Die Wortstellung im hebräischen Nominalsatze', *ZAW* 7, 218–24; 8, 249–63.
Albrecht, K., 1911: '"Še-" in der Mischnah', *ZAW* 31, 205–17.
1913: *Neuhebräische Grammatik auf Grund der Mishna.* Munich.
Albright, W.F., 1926: 'Notes on early Hebrew and Aramaic epigraphy', *JPOS* 6, 75–102.
1932: 'New light on early Canaanite language and literature', *BASOR* 46, 15–20.
1934: *The vocalization of the Egyptian syllabic orthography.* New Haven.
1936: 'Ostracon C 1101 of Samaria', *PEFQS* 68, 211–15.
1936a: 'From the School in Jerusalem', *BASOR* 63, 36–37.
1938: 'The oldest Hebrew letters: the Lachish ostraca', *BASOR* 70, 11–17.
1939: 'A re-examination of the Lachish letters', *BASOR* 73, 16–21.
1939a: 'An Aramaean magical text in Hebrew from the seventh century B.C.', *BASOR* 76, 5–11.
1941: 'New Egyptian data on Palestine in the patriarchal age', *BASOR* 81, 16–21.
1941a: 'The land of Damascus between 1850 and 1750 B.C.', *BASOR* 83, 30–36.
1943: 'The Gezer calendar', *BASOR* 92, 16–26.
1944: 'The oracles of Balaam', *JBL* 63, 207–33.
1945: 'The Old Testament and the Canaanite language and literature', *CBQ* 7, 5–31.
1948: 'The early alphabetic inscriptions from Sinai and their decipherment', *BASOR* 110, 6–22.
1950: 'The Psalm of Habakkuk', in H.H. Rowley (ed.), *Studies in Old Testament prophecy*, Edinburgh, pp. 1–18.
1950a: 'Some important recent discoveries: alphabetic origins and the Idrimi statue', *BASOR* 118, 11–20.
1950–51: 'A catalogue of early Hebrew lyric poems (Psalm lxviii)', *HUCA* 23, 1–39.
1954: 'Northwest-Semitic names in a list of Egyptian slaves from the eighteenth century B.C.', *JAOS* 74, 222–33.
1955: 'New light on early recensions of the Hebrew Bible', *BASOR* 140, 27–33.
1958: 'An ostracon from Calah and the North-Israelite diaspora', *BASOR* 149, 33–36.
1959: 'Some remarks on the Song of Moses in Deuteronomy xxxii', *VT* 9, 339–46.
1966: *The Proto-Sinaitic inscriptions and their decipherment*. Cambridge, Mass.
1970: 'Some comments on the 'Ammân citadel inscription', *BASOR* 198, 38–40.
Allegro, J.M., 1955: 'Uses of the Semitic demonstrative element "z" in Hebrew', *VT* 5, 309–12.
Allony, N., 1941–43: 'He'arot we-haṣa'ot li-lshon shirat yeme ha-benayim', *Leshonenu* 11, 161–64.
1947: 'Mi-leshono shel Dunash ben Labraṭ', *Leshonenu* 15, 161–72.
1959: 'Mi-shirat Sefarad u-leshonah', *Sinai* 22, 152–69.

1960: 'Mi-shirat Sefarad u-leshonah, ii', *OYS* 3, 15–49.
1963: 'Keta' Mishnah 'im nikkud Ereṣ-Yisra'el', in *Sefer ha-yovel le-Rabbi Ḥanokh Albeck*, Jerusalem, pp. 30–40.
1964: 'Ezehu "ha-nikkud shellanu" be-Maḥzor Vitry?', *BM* 8, 135–45.
1964a: 'Mi-shirat Sefarad u-leshonah, iii', *Sinai* 28, 236–62.
1966: 'Mi-shirat Sefarad u-leshonah, iv', *Sinai* 30, 127–42.
1969: 'Mi-shirat Sefarad u-leshonah, v', *Sinai* 33, 12–35, 155–75.
1973: 'Sefer ha-'Egron ha-'Ivri ke neged ha-"'Arabiyyah"', in B.Z. Luria (ed.), *Zer li'gevurot: the Zalman Shazar jubilee volume ... A collection of studies in Bible, Eretz Israel, Hebrew language and Talmudic literature*, Jerusalem, pp. 465–74.
1973–74: *Kiṭ'e Genizah shel Mishnah, Talmud, u-midrash menukkadim be-nikkud Ereṣ-Yisre'eli.* Jerusalem.
1974: 'Ha-lashon ha-'Ivrit bi-yme ha-benayim'. Typescript, University of Beer-Sheba.
1974a: 'Ha-Kuzari le-R. Yehudah Halevi be-'or ha-"shu'ubiyyah"', *Biṣaron* 65, 105–13.
1975: Mi-leshon yeme ha-benayim (shte millim kashot be-diwan RaŠBaG)', *Sinai* 39, 157–72.
1975a: 'The reaction of Moses ibn Ezra to "'Arabiyya"', *BIJS* 3, 19–40.
1976: 'Mi-shirat RaŠBaG u-leshono', *HUCA* 47, 1–104.
1977: '"Tufinim" ba-lashon ha-medubberet ba-me'ah ha-'ashirit be-Ṭeveryah', *Sinai* 81, 20–26.
1979: 'Hishtakefut ha-mered ba-'Arabiyya be-sifrutenu bi-yme ha-benayim', in C. Rabin, D. Patterson, B.Z. Luria, and Y. Avishur (eds.), *Sefer Meir Wallenstein. Studies in the Bible and the Hebrew language offered to Meir Wallenstein on ... his 75th birthday*, Jerusalem, pp. 80–136.
1980–81: 'Ben Maimon, Ben Asher, Ben Buyaà and the Aleppo Codex', *Tarbiz* 50, 348–70. H.
Allony, N. and Díez Macho, A., 1958: 'Dos manuscritos "palestinenses" más de la Geniza del Cairo', *EstBib* 17, 83–100.
1958a: 'Otros dos manuscritos "palestinenses" de Salmos', *Sefarad* 18, 254–71.
1959: 'A fragment of the Pesikta de Rav Kahana with Palestinian vocalization', *Leshonenu* 23, 57–71. H.
1959a: 'Lista de variantes en la edición de los Mss "palestinenses" T-S 20/58 y 20/52', *EstBib* 18, 293–98.
Alster, G. and Mossel, B.M., 1969: *Hadachlil. Leerboek van het Israëlische Hebreeuws.* Assen.
Altbauer, M., 1947–48: 'Gilgule mashma'ut', *LeshLA* 84.
1953–54: 'Mi-leshon dayyage Yisra'el', *LeshLA* 45–46, 26–32.
1964: 'New negation constructions in Modern Hebrew', in *For Max Weinreich on his seventieth birthday: studies in Jewish languages, literature, and society*, The Hague, pp. 1–5.
Altheim, F. and Stiehl, R., 1959–63: *Die aramäische Sprache unter den Achaimeniden.* I. Frankfurt-am-Main.
1965: *Die Araber in der alten Welt.* II. Berlin.
1966: 'Jesus der Galiläer', in *Die Araber in der alten Welt*, III, Berlin, pp. 74–97.
Altman, A., 1980: 'The original meaning of the name "Amurrû", "ha-Emori"', in G.B. Ṣarfatti, P. Artzi, J.C. Greenfield, and M.Z. Kaddari (eds.), *Studies in Hebrew and Semitic languages dedicated to the memory of Prof. E.Y. Kutscher*, Ramat-Gan, pp. 76–102. H.
Amusin, J.D. and Heltzer, M.L., 1964: 'The inscription from Meṣad Ḥashavyahu. Complaint of a reaper of the seventh century B.C.', *IEJ* 14, 148–60.
Andersen, F.I., 1966: 'Moabite syntax', *Orientalia* 35, 81–120.
1969: 'A short note on construct "k" in Hebrew', *Biblica* 50, 68–69.
1970: 'Biconsonantal byforms of weak Hebrew roots', *ZAW* 82, 270–75.
1970a: *The Hebrew verbless clause in the Pentateuch.* Nashville/New York.
1970b: 'Passive and ergative in Hebrew', in H. Goedicke (ed.), *Near Eastern studies in honor of William Foxwell Albright*, Baltimore/London, pp. 1–15.
1974: *The sentence in Biblical Hebrew.* The Hague.
Andersen, F.I. and Forbes, A.D., 1986: *Spelling in the Hebrew Bible.* Rome.
Anderson, A.A., 1962: 'The use of "ruaḥ" in 1QS, 1QH and 1QM', *JSS* 7, 293–303.

Archer, G.L., 1974: 'The Hebrew of Daniel compared with the Qumran sectarian documents', in J.H. Skilton (ed.), *The law and the prophets: Old Testament studies prepared in honor of Oswald Thompson Allis*, Nutley, pp. 470–84.
Archi, A., 1985: *Testi amministrativi: assegnazioni di tessuti* (Archivi reali di Ebla. Testi; 1). Rome.
Archi, A. and Biga, M.C., 1982: *Testi amministrativi di vario contenuto* (Archivi reali di Ebla. Testi; 3). Rome.
Argyle, A.W., 1955–56: 'Did Jesus speak Greek?', *ET* 67, 92–93.
Ariel, S., 1972: 'The functions of the conjugations in colloquial Israeli Hebrew', *BSOAS* 35, 514–30.
1973: 'The functions of the *binyanim* in Modern Hebrew', *P5WCJS*, IV, 17–30.
Arnaud, D., 1982: 'Les textes cunéiformes suméro-accadiens des campagnes 1979–80 à Ras Shamra-Ougarit', *Syria* 59, 199–220.
1985: *Recherches au pays d'Aštata: Emar VI. Textes sumériens et accadiens*. 3 vols. Paris.
Aro, J., 1964: *Die Vokalisierung des Grundstammes im semitischen Verbum*. Helsinki.
1965: 'Parallels to the Akkadian stative in the West Semitic languages', in H.G. Gueterbock and T. Jacobsen (eds.), *Studies in honor of Benno Landsberger on his 75th Birthday*, Chicago, pp. 407–11.
Aronson, R., 1969: 'The predictability of vowel patterns in the Hebrew verb', *Glossa* 3, 127–45.
Artom, E.S., 1931–32: 'Studi sull'accento e la quantità delle vocali in ebraico', *RSO* 13, 150–64.
1946–47: 'Mivṭa ha-'Ivrit eṣel Yehude 'Iṭalyah', *Leshonenu* 15, 52–61.
Artzi, P., 1968: 'Some unrecognized Syrian Amarna letters', *JNES* 27, 163–71.
Asmussen, J.P., 1961: 'Das iranische Lehnwort "naḫšir" in der Kriegsrolle von Qumran (1QM)', *AcOr* 26, 3–20.
Aufrecht, W.E., 1983: 'A bibliography of Ammonite inscriptions', *Newsletter for Targumic and Cognate Studies*, Supplement 1.
Avigad, N., 1951: 'Some new readings of Hebrew seals', *EI* 1, 32–34.
1953: 'Another "bat le-melekh" inscription', *IEJ* 3, 121–22.
1953a: 'The epitaph of a royal steward from Siloam village', *IEJ* 3, 137–52.
1954: 'Seven ancient Hebrew seals', *BIES* 18, 147–53. H.
1954a: Ancient monuments in the Kidron Valley. Jerusalem.
1955: 'The second tomb inscription of the royal steward', *IEJ* 5, 163–66.
1957: 'A new class of "Yehud" stamps', *IEJ* 7, 146–53.
1959: 'Some notes on the Hebrew inscriptions from Gibeon', *IEJ* 9, 130–33.
1960: 'Two ancient seals', in M. Haran and B.Z. Luria (eds.), *Sefer [N.H.] Ṭur-Sinai ... li-mle'ut lo shiv'im shanah*, Jerusalem, pp. 319–24. H.
1970: 'Ammonite and Moabite seals', in J.A. Sanders (ed.), *Near Eastern archaeology in the twentieth century. Essays in honor of Nelson Glueck*, Garden City, pp. 284–95.
1972: 'Two Hebrew inscriptions on wine-jars', *IEJ* 22, 1–9.
1976: 'The governor of the city', *IEJ* 26, 178–82.
1976a: *Bullae and seals from a post-exilic Judean archive* (*Qedem* 4). Jerusalem.
1977: 'New Moabite and Ammonite seals at the Israel Museum', *EI* 13, *108–10. H.
1977a: 'Two Ammonite seals depicting the *dea nutrix*', *BASOR* 225, 63–66.
1979: 'Hebrew epigraphic sources', in I. Eph'al (ed.), *The age of the monarchies*, I: *Political history* (The world history of the Jewish people, first series; IV), Jerusalem, pp. 20–43.
1986: *Hebrew bullae from the time of Jeremiah*. Jerusalem.
Avinery, I., 1935–36: *Millon ḥiddushe Ḥ.N. Bialik she-bi-khtav we-she-be-'al-peh*. Tel-Aviv.
1940–60: *Heichal Rashi, encyclopaedia containing alphabetically all that Rashi created in the field of language and exegesis*. 4 vols. Tel-Aviv. H.
1946: *The achievements of Modern Hebrew*. Merḥavyah. H.
1964: *Yad ha-lashon: oṣar leshoni be-seder alef-bet shel ha-nose'im*. Tel-Aviv.
Avishur, Y., 1971–72: 'Pairs of synonymous words in the construct state (and in appositional hendiadys) in Biblical Hebrew', *Semitics* 2, 17–81.
1974: 'Pairs of words in biblical literature and their parallels in Semitic literature of the ancient Near East'. Doct. diss., Hebrew University, Jerusalem. H.

1975: 'Word pairs common to Phoenician and Biblical Hebrew', *UF* 7, 13–47.

1976: 'Studies of stylistic features common to the Phoenician inscriptions and the Bible', *UF* 8, 1–22.

1984: *Stylistic studies of word-pairs in biblical and ancient Semitic literatures*. Neukirchen-Vluyn.

Avrunin, A., 1939–40: 'Li-mkorot leshono shel Mendele', *Leshonenu* 10, 159–72.

1953–54: *Meḥkarim bi-lshon Bialik we-YaLaG*. Tel-Aviv

Azar, M., 1971–72: 'A syntactic and semantic approach to verbs governing prepositional phrases', *Leshonenu* 36, 220–27, 282–86. H.

1981: '"ᵃḇāl", "'ællā'" and "'ællā' šæ" in Modern Hebrew', *Leshonenu* 45, 133–48. H.

1983: 'Pseudo-"casus pendens" in the Mishnah', *Leshonenu* 47, 264–71. H.

Bacher, W., 1893: 'The views of Jehuda Halevi concerning the Hebrew language', *Hebraica* 8, 136–49.

1903: 'Der sprachliche Charakter des Mischne Tora', *Jahresbericht der Landesrabbinerschule in Budapest*, 117, 128–29, 283, 290.

1914: 'Zum sprachlichen Charakter des Mischne Tora', in W. Bacher, M. Brann, and D. Simonsen, *Moses ben Maimon. Sein Leben, seine Werke und sein Einfluss. Zur Erinnerung an den siebenhundertsten Todestag des Maimonides herausgegeben*, II, Leipzig, pp. 280–305.

1974: *Die Anfänge der hebräischen Grammatik und Die hebräische Sprachwissenschaft vom 10. bis zum 16. Jahrhundert*. Ed. by L. Blau. Amsterdam.

Bachi, R., 1956: 'A statistical analysis of the revival of Hebrew in Israel', *ScrHier* 3, 179–247.

Bahaṭ, J. and Ron, M., 1959–60: *We-dayyek: tikkune lashon we-shippur ha-signon*. Tel-Aviv.

Bahaṭ, S., 1964: 'The relative clause in Modern Hebrew'. Doct. diss., Hebrew University, Jerusalem. H.

Baker, D., 1980: 'Further examples of the *waw explicativum*', *VT* 30, 129–36.

Baldacci, M., 1981: 'The Ammonite text from Tell Siran and North-West Semitic philology', *VT* 31, 363–68.

Balentine, S.E., 1980: 'A description of the semantic field of Hebrew words for "hide"', *VT* 30, 137–53.

Band, O., 1983: *Hebrew: a language course. Level 2*. New York.

Bandstra, B.L., 1982: 'The syntax of the particle "ky" in Biblical Hebrew and Ugaritic'. Doct. diss., Yale University.

Baneth, D.H., 1935–36: 'On the philosophic terminology of Maimonides', *Tarbiz* 6, 10–40. H.

1939–40: 'R. Yehudah al-Ḥarizi u-sheloshet ha-targumim shel ma'amar Teḥiyyat ha-Metim la-RaMBaM', *Tarbiz* 11, 260–70.

1952: 'Maimonides translating his own writings as compared with his translators', *Tarbiz* 23, 170–91. H.

Banitt, M., 1967: *L'Etude des glossaires bibliques des juifs de France au moyen âge: méthode et application* (*PIASH* 2.10). Jerusalem.

Bar, F., 1936: *Liturgische Dichtungen von Jannai und Samuel*. Bonn.

Bar-Adon, A., 1959: 'Children's Hebrew in Israel'. 2 vols. Doct. diss., Hebrew University, Jerusalem. H.

1966: 'New imperative and jussive formations in contemporary Hebrew', *JAOS* 86, 410–13.

1972–73: 'S.Y. Agnon and the revival of Modern Hebrew', *Texas studies in literature and language* 14, 147–75.

1974: 'Language planning and processes of nativization in the newly revived Hebrew', in *Proceeedings: Association Internationale de Linguistique Appliquée, third congress, Copenhagen, 1972*, Heidelberg, pp. 1–16.

1975: *The rise and decline of a dialect. A study in the revival of Modern Hebrew*. The Hague/Paris.

1986: 'Al terumatah shel ha-'aliyah ha-sheniyyah li-tḥiyat ha-lashon ha-'Ivrit. Dimmuy', *P9WCJS*, Division D, 63–70.

Bar-Adon, P., 1975: 'An early Hebrew inscription in a Judean Desert cave', *IEJ* 25, 226–32.

Bar-Asher, M., 1971: *Mishna codex Parma 'B', Seder Teharot*, Jerualem.

1972–80 (ed.): *Koveṣ ma'amarim bi-lshon ḤaZaL*. 2 vols. Jerusalem.

1976: 'Ṣurot nedirot bi-lshon ha-Tanna'im', *Leshonenu* 41, 83–102.

1980: *The tradition of Mishnaic Hebrew in the communities of Italy (according to Ms. Paris 328–329)*. Jerusalem. H.

1983: 'Nishkaḥot bi-lshon ha-Tanna'im: ben ha-sofer la-nakdan shel Ketav-yad Kaufmann shel ha-Mishnah (berur rishon)', in M. Bar-Asher, A. Dotan, G.B. Ṣarfatti, and D. Téné (eds.), *Hebrew language studies presented to Professor Zeev Ben-Ḥayyim*, Jerusalem, pp. 83–110.
1984: 'Ha-ṭipusim ha-shonim shel leshon ha-Mishnah', *Tarbiz* 53, 187–220.
1984a: 'On vocalization errors in Codex Kaufmann of the Mishna', in *Massorot: studies in language traditions*, I, Jerusalem, pp. 1–17. H.
1985: 'The historical unity of Hebrew and Mishnaic Hebrew research', in *Language studies*, I, Jerusalem, pp. 75–99. H.
1986: 'La langue de la Mishna d'après les traditions des communautés juives d'Italie', *REJ* 145, 267–78.
1987: 'The different traditions of Mishnaic Hebrew', in D.M. Golomb and S.T. Hollis (eds.), *Working with no data. Semitic and Egyptian studies presented to Thomas O. Lambdin*, Winona Lake, pp. 1–38.
Bardowicz, L., 1894: *Studien zur Geschichte der Orthographie des Althebräischen*. Frankfurt-am-Main.
1894a: 'Das allmähliche Überhandnehmen der *Matres Lectionis* im Bibeltexte', *MGWJ* 38, 117–21, 157–67.
Bardtke, H., 1954: *Hebräische Konsonantentexte*. Leipzig.
Barkai, M., 1972: 'Problems in the phonology of Israeli Hebrew'. Doct. diss., University of Illinois.
Barkay, G., 1977: 'A second bulla of a "sar ha-'ir"', *Qadmoniot* 10, 69–71.
1984: 'Excavations on the slope of the Hinnom Valley, Jerusalem', *Qadmoniot* 17, 94–108.
Barnes, O.L., 1965: *A new approach to the problem of the Hebrew tenses and its solution without recourse to waw-consecutive*. Oxford.
Barnett, R.D., 1951: 'Four sculptures from Amman', *ADAJ* 1, 34–36.
1957: *A catalogue of the Nimrud ivories*. London.
Baron, S.W., 1958: *A social and religious history of the Jews*. VII: Hebrew language and letters. 2nd ed. New York.
Barr, J., 1962: The semantics of biblical language. 3rd ed. London.
1966–67: 'St. Jerome's appreciation of Hebrew', *BJRL* 49, 281–302.
1967: 'St. Jerome and the sounds of Hebrew', *JSS* 12, 1–36.
1967a: 'Vocalization and the analysis of Hebrew among the ancient translators', *SVT* 16, 1–11.
1968: *Comparative philology and the text of the Old Testament*. Oxford.
1969: *Biblical words for time*. Rev. ed. London.
1968a: 'The ancient Semitic languages–the conflict between philology and linguistics', *Transactions of the Philological Society*, 37–55.
1970: 'Which language did Jesus speak? Some remarks of a Semitist', *BJRL* 53, 9–29.
1974: 'Etymology and the Old Testament', *OTS* 19, 1–28.
1979: 'Semitic philology and the interpretation of the Old Testament', in G.W. Anderson (ed.), *Tradition and interpretation. Essays by members of the Society for Old Testament Study*, Oxford, pp. 31–64.
Barth, J., 1894 (repr. 1967): *Die Nominalbildung in den semitischen Sprachen*. 2nd ed. Leipzig.
1894a: 'Zur vergleichenden semitischen Grammatik', *ZDMG* 48, 1–21.
1899: 'Die Casusreste im Hebräischen', *ZDMG* 53, 593–99.
1913: *Die Pronominalbildung in den semitischen Sprachen*. Leipzig.
Barthélemy, D., 1978: *Etudes d'histoire du texte de l'Ancien Testament*. Göttingen.
1982–86: *Critique textuelle de l'Ancien Testament*. 2 vols. Freiburg/Göttingen.
Bartlett, J.R., 1969: 'The use of the word "rō'š" as a title in the Old Testament', *VT* 19, 1–10.
Barzilay, I., 1979: 'From purism to expansionism: a chapter in the early history of Modern Hebrew', *JANES* 11, 3–15.
Bauer, H. 1910: *Die Tempora in Semitischen: ihre Entstehung und ihre Ausgestaltung in den Einzelsprachen*. Berlin.
1912: 'Noch einmal die semitischen Zahlwörter', *ZDMG* 65, 267–70.
1924: *Zur Frage der Sprachmischung im Hebräischen. Eine Erwiderung*. Halle.
1930: 'Die hebräischen Eigennamen als sprachliche Erkenntnisquelle', *ZAW* 48, 73–80.

Bauer, H. and Leander, P., 1922 (repr. 1962): *Historische Grammatik der hebräischen Sprache des Alten Testaments*. Halle.
1927 (repr. 1962): *Grammatik des Biblisch-Aramäischen*. Halle.
1929 (repr. 1965): *Kurzgefasste biblisch-aramäische Grammatik*. Halle.
Bauer, T., 1926: *Die Ostkanaanäer. Eine philologisch-historische Untersuchung über die Wanderschicht der sogenannten 'Amoriter' in Babylonien*. Leipzig.
Baumgartner, W., 1953: 'Das hebräische Nominalpräfix "mi-"', *TZ* 9, 154–57.
1959: 'Was wir heute von der hebräischen Sprache und ihrer Geschichte wissen', in *Ausgewählte Aufsätze*, Leiden, pp. 208–39.
Bea, A., 1940: 'Der Zahlenspruch im Hebräischen und Ugaritischen', *Biblica* 21, 196–98.
Becking, B.E.J.H., 1981: 'Zur Interpretation der ammonitischen Inschrift vom Tell Sīrān', *BO* 38, 273–76.
Beeston, A.F.L., 1979: 'Hebrew "šibbolet" and "šobel"', *JSS* 24, 175–79.
Beit-Arieh, I., 1981: 'New discoveries in Mine L at Serabit el-Khadem', *Qadmoniot* 14, 35–37. H.
1981a: 'New studies in Mine L at Serabit el-Khadim', *EI* 15, *63–68. H.
1982: 'New discoveries at Serâbît el-Khâdîm', *BA* 45, 13–18.
1983: 'A First Temple period census document', *PEQ* 115, 105–08.
Beit-Arieh, I. and Cresson, B., 1985: 'An Edomite ostracon from Horvat 'Uza', *TAJ* 12, 96–101.
Beit-Arié, M., 1970: 'Codicologic features as paleographic criteria in medieval Hebrew mss.', *KirSef* 45, 435–46. H.
1979: 'A Hebrew-Latin glossary–a testimony of spoken Hebrew in tenth-century Jerusalem?', *Tarbiz* 48, 274–302. H.
1980: 'Ketav-yad Kaufmann shel ha-Mishnah, moṣa'o u-zemano', in Bar-Asher (ed.) 1972–80, II, pp. 84–92.
van Bekkum, W.J., 1983: 'Observations on stem formations ("binyanim") in rabbinical Hebrew', *OLP* 14, 167–98.
1983a: 'The origins of the infinitive in rabbinical Hebrew', *JSS* 28, 247–72.
Beld, S.T., Hallo, W.W., and Michalowski, P., 1984: *The tablets of Ebla: concordance and bibliography*. Winona Lake.
Ben-Asher, M., 1960: 'Niṣṣul ha-mishkalim be-ḥiddushe ha-'Akademiyyah la-Lashon', *Ba-sha'ar* 3, 38–46.
1965: 'The conditional clause in Modern Hebrew'. Doct. diss., Hebrew University, Jerusalem. H.
1969: *Hitgabbeshut ha-dikduk ha-normaṭivi*. Jerusalem.
1970: 'The use of "me'ašer" in Modern Hebrew', *JSS* 15, 239–45.
1973: *'Iyyunim be-taḥbir ha-'Ivrit he-ḥadashah*. Tel-Aviv.
1978: 'Causative Hif'il verbs with double objects in Biblical Hebrew', *HAR* 2, 11–19.
Bendavid, A., 1951: *Leshon ha-Mikra 'o leshon ḥakhamim?* Tel-Aviv.
1956–57: 'The differences between Ben Asher and Ben Naftali', *Tarbiz* 26, 384–409. H.
1957–58: 'Ḥillufe Ben-Asher u-Ben-Naftali 'al-pi bedikah bi-mkorot kadmonim', *BM* 3, 1–20.
1957–58a: 'The source of the division of vowels into long and short', *Leshonenu* 22, 7–35, 110–36. H.
1958: Review of Murtonen 1958, *KirSef* 33, 482–91.
1967: *Biblical Hebrew and Mishnaic Hebrew*. Tel-Aviv. H.
Ben-Ezra, E., 1941–44 'Ḥiddushe millim shel R. Se'adyah Ga'on', *Horeb* 8, 135–47; 9, 176–85; 10, 295–318.
1962–63: 'Leshono shel R. Se'adyah Ga'on', in Y.L. Maimon (ed.), *Sefer yovel, mugash li-khvod ... Israel Elfenbein ... ba-mele'ut lo sheloshim shenot yeṣirah ba-Torah u-ba-mada'*, Jerusalem, pp. 33–43.
Ben-Ḥayyim, Z., 1938: 'On the study of the Samaritan language', *Tarbiz* 10, 81–89. H.
1944: "Ivrit nosaḥ Shomron', *Leshonenu* 12, 45–60, 115–26.
1948–49: 'Targumim nishkaḥim u-matmihim', *Leshonenu* 16, 156–63.
1952–53: 'Lashon 'attikah bi-mṣi'ut ḥadashah', *LeshLA* 35–37.
1952–53a: 'Torat ha-tenu'ot le-Rav Se'adyah Ga'on', *Leshonenu* 18, 89–96.

1953: 'The form of the suffixal pronouns "-kā", "-tā", "-hā"', in U. Cassuto, J. Klausner, and J. Gutman (eds.), *Sefer Assaf ... li-khvod ... Simḥah Assaf ... li-mlot lo shishim shanah*, Jerusalem, pp. 66–99.

1953a: 'Dikduk bene-'Adam', *Massa* 3, 2–9.

1954: *Studies in the traditions of the Hebrew language*. Madrid/Barcelona.

1954a: 'The Samaritan vowel-system and its graphic representation', *ArOr* 22, 515–30.

1955: 'On the description of Hebrew as it is spoken', *Tarbiz* 24, 337–42. H.

1957–77: *The literary and oral tradition of Hebrew and Aramaic amongst the Samaritans*. 5 vols. Jerusalem. H.

1958: 'The Samaritan tradition and its ties with the linguistic tradition of the Dead Sea Scrolls and with Mishnaic Hebrew', *Leshonenu* 22, 223–45. H.

1958a: 'Traditions in the Hebrew language with special reference to the Dead Sea Scrolls', *ScrHier* 4, 200–14.

1958–59: 'Zu dem Aufsatze "Die Qumran-Rollen und die hebräische Sprachwissenschaft 1948–1958" von Goshen-Gottstein', *RQ* 1, 423–24.

1958–62: 'La tradition samaritaine et sa parenté avec les autres traditions de la langue hébraïque', *Mélanges de philosophie et de litterature juives* 3–5, 89–128.

1963: 'Bi-dvar mekorotehen shel haṭ'amat mille'el be-'Ivrit', in S. Lieberman (ed.), *Sefer Ḥanokh Yalon*, Jerusalem, pp. 150–60.

1967: 'Observations on the Hebrew and Aramaic lexicon from the Samaritan tradition', *SVT* 16, 12–24.

1968: *The contribution of the Samaritan inheritance to research into the history of Hebrew* (*PIASH* 3.6). Jerusalem.

1971: 'Some problems of a grammar of Samaritan Hebrew', *Biblica* 52, 229–52.

1977: '"Zemane" ha-po'al bi-lshon ha-Mikra u-masoret ha-Shomronim ba-hem', in S. Werses, N. Rotenstreich, and C. Shmeruk (eds.), *Sefer Dov Saddan ... bi-mlot lo shiv'im we-ḥamesh shanah*, Tel-Aviv, pp. 66–86.

1978: 'Thoughts on the Hebrew vowel system', in Y. Avishur and J. Blau (eds.), *Studies in Bible and the ancient Near East presented to Samuel E. Loewenstamm on his 70th birthday*, II, Jerusalem, pp. 95–105. H.

1979: 'Mono- and bi-syllabic middle guttural nouns in Samaritan Hebrew', *JANES* 11, 19–29.

1985: 'The historical unity of the Hebrew language and its divisions into periods', in M. Bar-Asher (ed.), *Language studies*, I, Jerusalem, pp. 3–25. H.

1985a: 'Ha-'omnam nistar bi-mkom medabber?', in B.Z. Luria (ed.), *Sefer Avraham Even-Shoshan*, Jerusalem, pp. 93–98.

1988–89: 'Be-shule "Ḥok Philippi"', *Leshonenu* 53, 113–20.

1989: 'Samaritan Hebrew–an evaluation', in A.D. Crown (ed.), *The Samaritans*, Tübingen, pp. 517–30.

Bennet, M., 1966: 'Fouilles d'Umm el-Biyara. Rapport préliminaire', *RB* 73, 372–403.

Bennet, T., 1732: *Hebrew grammar*. 3rd ed. London.

Bensabat Amzalak, M., 1928: *Portuguese Hebrew grammars and grammarians*. Lisbon.

Bentolila, Y., 1984: *Mivṭa'e ha-'Ivrit ha-meshammeshet ba-moshav shel yoṣe'e Maroko ba-Negev: perek be-fonologyah ḥevratit*. Jerusalem.

Ben-Yehuda, E., 1919: *'Ad ematay dibberu 'Ivrit?* New York.

Ben-Zvi, I., 1935: *Sefer ha-Shomronim*. 2nd ed. Tel-Aviv. 1970.

1960: 'The codex of Ben Asher', *Textus* 1, 1–18.

Bergey, R.L., 1983: 'The Book of Esther: its place in the linguistic milieu of post-exilic Biblical Hebrew prose–a study in late Biblical Hebrew'. Doct. diss., Dropsie College.

Berggrün, N., 1970: 'The language spoken by the Jews in the diaspora as a source for the study of Hebrew', *Leshonenu* 34, 165–71. H.

1974: 'Berurim bi-lshon ḥakhamim', in E.Y. Kutscher, S. Liebermann, and M.Z. Kaddari (eds.), *Henoch Yalon memorial volume*, Ramat-Gan, pp. 59–63.

Bergman, B., 1981: *Hebrew: a language course. Level 1*. New York.

Bergsträsser, G., 1909: 'Das hebräische Präfix "ש-"', *ZAW* 29, 40–56.
1918–29 (repr. 1986): *Hebräische Grammatik*. 2 vols. Leipzig.
1923: 'Sprachmischung im Hebräischen', *OLZ* 26, 253–60, 477–81.
1924: 'Ist die tiberiensische Vokalisation eine Rekonstruktion?', *OLZ* 27, 582–86.
1928 (repr. 1977): *Einführung in die semitischen Sprachen*. Munich.
Berman, R., 1974–75: 'Gerundive and derived nominals in Modern Hebrew', *Leshonenu* 39, 99–122, 217–35. H.
Bernheimer, C., 1924: *Paleographia hebraica*. Florence.
Beveridge, W., 1658: *De linguarum orientalium praesertim hebraicae, chaldaicae, syriacae, arabicae et samaritanae praesentia*. London.
Beyer K., 1969: *Althebräische Grammatik. Laut- und Formenlehre*. Göttingen.
1971: 'Althebräische Syntax in Prosa und Poesie, i: Die Schöpfungsgeschichte der Priesterschrift', in G. Jeremias, H.W. Kuhn, and H. Stegemann (eds.), *Tradition und Glaube: das frühe Christentum in seiner Umwelt. Festgabe für Karl Georg Kuhn zum 65. Geburtstag*, Göttingen, pp. 76–96.
Biran, A., 1974: 'Tel Dan', *BA* 37, 26–51.
Birkeland, H., 1940: *Akzent und Vokalismus im Althebräischen*. Oslo.
1954: *The language of Jesus*. Oslo.
Birnbaum, S.A., 1954–71: *The Hebrew scripts*. 2 vols. Leiden.
Black, M., 1956–57: 'The recovery of the language of Jesus', *New Testament studies* 3, 305–13.
1957: 'Die Erforschung der Muttersprache Jesu', *TLZ* 82, 653–68.
Blake, F.R., 1917–53: 'Studies in Semitic grammar', *JAOS* 35, 375–85; 62, 109–18; 65, 111–16; 66, 212–18; 73, 7–16.
1940: 'The development of symbols for the vowels in the alphabets derived from the Phoenician', *JAOS* 60, 391–413.
1944: 'The Hebrew waw conversive', *JBL* 63, 271–95.
1950: 'The apparent interchange between "a" and "i" in Hebrew', *JNES* 9, 76–83.
1951: 'Pretonic vowels in Hebrew', *JNES* 10, 243–55.
1951a: *A resurvey of Hebrew tenses*. Rome.
Blanc, H., 1954: 'The growth of Israeli Hebrew', *Middle Eastern affairs* 5, 385–92.
1954–55: 'La-yesod ha-'Aravi she-ba-dibbur ha-Yisre'eli', *LeshLA* 53, 6–14; 54–55, 27–32; 56, 20–26.
1956: 'Dialect research in Israel', *Orbis* 5, 185–90.
1957: 'Hebrew in Israel: trends and problems', *The Middle East journal* 11, 397–409.
1960: *Intensive spoken Israeli Hebrew*. I, IV. Washington.
1964: 'Israeli Hebrew Texts', in H.B. Rosén (ed.), *Studies in Egyptology and linguistics in honour of H.J. Polotsky*, Jerusalem, pp. 132–52.
1965: 'Some Yiddish influences in Israeli Hebrew', in U. Weinreich (ed.), *The field of Yiddish: studies in language, folklore, and literature*, II, The Hague, pp. 185–201.
1968: 'The Israeli koine as an emergent national standard', in J.A. Fishman, C.A. Ferguson, and J. Das Gupta (eds.), *Language problems of developing nations*, Somerset, N.J., pp. 237–51.
Blau, J., 1953: 'Benoni pa'ul be-hora'ah 'akṭivit', *Leshonenu* 18, 67–81.
1954: 'Zum angeblichen Gebrauch von "'t" vor dem Nominativ', *VT* 4, 7–19.
1956: 'Gibt es ein emphatisches "'ēt" im Bibel-Hebräisch?', *VT* 6, 211–12.
1957: 'Über die "t"-Form des Hif'il im Bibelhebräisch', *VT* 7, 385–88.
1957a: '"O she- bi-lshon ḥakhamim"', *Leshonenu* 21, 7–14.
1959: 'Adverbia als psychologische und grammatische Subjekte/Predikate im Bibel-Hebräisch', *VT* 9, 130–38.
1959a: 'The status of Arabic as used by Jews in the Middle Ages', *JJS* 10, 19–21.
1961: 'Reste des "i-" Imperfekts von "zkr" Qal. Eine lexikographische Studie', *VT* 11, 81–86.
1966: *Yesodot ha-taḥbir*. Jerusalem.
1968: 'Some dificulties in the reconstruction of "Proto-Hebrew" and "Proto-Canaanite"', *BZAW* 103, 29–43.
1968a: 'Bibelhebräische Nomina, die auf Pataḥ-'Ayin enden', *ZDMG* 118, 257–58.

1969: 'Some problems of the formation of the old Semitic languages in the light of Arabic dialects', *PICSS*, 38–44.
1970: *On pseudo-corrections in some Semitic languages*. Jerusalem.
1970a: 'He'arot le-gilgule ha-haṭ'amah ba-'Ivrit ha-kedumah', in S. Abramson and A. Mirsky (eds.), *Sefer Ḥayyim Schirmann: koveṣ meḥkarim*, Jerusalem, pp. 27–38.
1970b: Review of Jenni 1968, *Leshonenu* 34, 228–33. H.
1971: 'Studies in Hebrew verb formation', *HUCA* 42, 133–58.
1971a: 'Hebrew language, biblical', *EJ*, XVI, 1568–83.
1971–72: 'Sentences containing parallel members, and generative grammar', *Leshonenu* 36, 308–20. H.
1973: Der Übergang der bibelhebräischen Verba "(w)y" von Qal im Hif'il im Lichte des Ugaritischen', *UF* 5, 275–77.
1974: 'Studies in Semitic pronouns (including the definite article)', in E.Y. Kutscher, S. Liebermann, and M.Z. Kaddari (eds.), *Henoch Yalon memorial volume*, Ramat-Gan, pp. 17–45. H.
1975: "Al be'ayot bi-tḥum ha-haṭ'amah ba-'Ivrit ha-kedumah', in A. Saltman, M.Z. Kaddari, M. Schwarcz, and M. Adler (eds.), *Baruch Kurzweil memorial volume*, Tel-Aviv, pp. 62–73.
1976: *A grammar of Biblical Hebrew*. Wiesbaden.
1977: '"Weak" phonetic change and the Hebrew śin', *HAR* 1, 67–119.
1978: 'Hebrew and North West Semitic: reflections on the classification of the Semitic languages', *HAR* 2, 21–44.
1978a: 'Hebrew stress shifts, pretonic lengthening, and segolization: possible cases of Aramaic interference in Hebrew syllable structure', *IOS* 8, 91–106.
1979: 'Non-phonetic conditioning of sound change and Biblical Hebrew', *HAR* 3, 7–15.
1979a: 'Some remarks on the prehistory of stress in Biblical Hebrew', *IOS* 9, 49–54.
1979–80: 'Short philological notes on the inscription of Meša'', *Maarav* 2, 143–57.
1980: 'The parallel development of the feminine ending "-at" in Semitic languages', *HUCA* 51, 17–28.
1980–81: 'Stages in the weakening of laryngals/pharyngals in Biblical Hebrew', *Leshonenu* 45, 32–39. H.
1981: 'On pausal lengthening, pausal stress shift, Philippi's law and rule ordering in Biblical Hebrew', *HAR* 5, 1–13.
1982: *On polyphony in Biblical Hebrew* (*PIASH* 6.2). Jerusalem.
1982a: 'Remarks on the development of some pronominal suffixes in Hebrew', *HAR* 6, 61–67.
1983: 'Eine Theorie der Haupttondehnung im Althebräischen', *ZDMG* 133, 24–29.
1983a: 'Are Rabbinical Hebrew forms like "hâyât" archaic?', *Leshonenu* 47, 158–59. H.
1984: *The renaissance of Modern Hebrew and Modern Arabic: parallels and differences in the revival of two Semitic languages*. Berkeley.
1985: 'The influence of Middle Arabic on the Hebrew of Arabic-speaking Jews', in M. Bar-Asher (ed.), *Language studies*, I, Jerusalem, pp. 243–50. H.
Bloch, A., 1963: 'Zur Nachweisbarkeit einer hebräischen Entsprechung der akkadischen Verbalform "iparras"', *ZDMG* 113, 41–50.
Blommerde, A.C.M., 1969: *Northwest Semitic grammar and Job*. Rome.
Boberg, A., 1733: *'Al leshon u-khetav ha-Shomronim sive De lingua et literis Samaritanorum dissertatio philologica*. Uppsala.
1734: *'Al leshon we-Torat ha-Shomronim sive De lingua et Pentateucho Samaritanorum*. Stockholm.
Bobzin, H., 1973: 'Überlegungen zum althebräischen "Tempus" System', *WdO* 7, 141–53.
Bocaccio, J., 1964: 'Hebreo bíblico', in *Enciclopedia de la Biblia*, III, 1115–27.
Boecker, H., 1963: *Redeformen des Rechtslebens im Alten Testament*. Neukirchen-Vluyn.
de Boer, P.A.H, 1948: 'An inquiry into the meaning of the term "mś'"', *OTS* 5, 197–214.
1954: 'Etude sur le sens de la racine "QWH"', *OTS* 10, 225–246.

1962: *Gedenken und Gedächtnis in der Welt des Alten Testaments. Vorlesungen zur Bedeutung der Wurzel* ZKR. Leiden.

Bogaert, M., 1964: 'Les suffixes verbaux non-accusatifs dans le sémitique nord-occidental et particulièrement en hébreu', *Biblica* 45, 220–47.

de Liagre Böhl, F.M.T., 1909: *Die Sprache der Amarna-Briefe mit besonderer Berücksichtigung der Kanaanismen*. Leipzig.

Bojarin, D., 1972–73: 'Reversal of the substantive-attribute order in Aramaic and in Hebrew', *Leshonenu* 37, 113–16. H.

Bolozky, S., 1980: 'Paradigm coherence in Hebrew', *AAL* 7, 104–26.

1984: 'Subject pronouns in colloquial Hebrew', *HS* 25, 126–30.

Bordreuil, P., 1986: *Catalogue des sceaux ouest-sémitiques inscrits de la Bibliothèque Nationale, du Musée du Louvre et du Musée Biblique et Terre Sainte*. Paris.

Bordreuil, P. and Caquot, A., 1979: 'Les textes en cunéiformes alphabétiques découverts en 1977 à Ibn Hani', *Syria* 56, 295–324.

1980: 'Les textes en cunéiformes alphabétiques découverts en 1978 à Ibn Hani', *Syria* 57, 344–73.

Bordreuil, P. and Lemaire, A., 1982: 'Nouveaux sceaux hébreux et araméens', *Semitica* 32, 21–34.

Borée, W., 1930: *Die alten Ortsnamen Palästinas.* Leipzig.

Borger, R., 1967, 'Knudzton, Jörgen Alexander', in *Handbuch der Keilschriftliteratur,* I (Repertorium der sumerischen und akkadischen Texte), Berlin, pp. 237–40.

Bornhäuser, K., 1926: 'Die Bedeutung der sprachlichen Verhältnisse Palästinas zur Zeit Jesu für das Verständnis der Evangelien', *Neue kirchliche Zeitschrift* 37, 187–200.

Bornstein, D.J., 1927: *Einführung in das Hebräisch der Gegenwart. Methodische Texte und Erläuterungen*. Berlin.

Bornstein, Ḥ.Y., 1904: 'Maḥaloket Rav Se'adyah Ga'on u-Ben-Me'ir bi-kvi'at shenot 4672–4674', in *Sefer ha-yovel ... li-khvod Naḥum Sokolow ... me'et ḥaveraw we-re'aw ha-soferim,* Warsaw, pp. 19–189.

Botterweck, G.J., 1952: *Der Triliterismus im Semitischen erläutert an den Wurzeln* GL ,KL, QL. Bonn.

Bowman, J., 1957: 'Contact between Samaritan sects and Qumran?', *VT* 7, 184–89.

1957–58: 'Samaritan studies', *BJRL* 40, 298–327.

1958–59: 'The importance of Samaritan researches', *ALUOS* 1, 43–54.

Bowman, R.A., 1948: 'Arameans, Aramaic and the Bible', *JNES* 7, 65–90.

van den Branden, A., 1958: Le déchiffrement des inscriptions protosinaïtiques', *Al-Machriq*, 361–95.

1962: 'L'origine des alphabets protosinaïtiques, arabes préislamiques et phéniciens', *BibOr* 19, 198–206.

1962a: 'Les inscriptions protosinaïtiques', *OrAn* 1, 197–214.

1969: *Grammaire phénicienne*. Beirut.

1979: 'Nouvel essai du déchiffrement des inscriptions protosinaïtiques', *BeO* 21, 156–251.

Braun, R.L., 1979: 'Chronicles, Ezra, and Nehemiah: theology and literary history', *SVT* 30, 52–64.

Bravmann, M.M., 1951–52: 'Notes on the forms of the imperative in Hebrew and Arabic', *JQR*, n.s., 42, 51–56.

1971: 'The Hebrew perfect forms: "qāṭ^{e}lā", "qāṭ^{e}lū"', *JAOS* 91, 429–30.

Brekelmans, C., 1963: 'Pronominal suffixes in the Hebrew Book of Psalms', *JEOL* 17, 202–06.

Brin, G., 1978–79: 'Linguistic notes to the Temple Scroll', *Leshonenu* 43, 20–23. H.

Brockelmann, C., 1904: 'Zur hebräischen Lautlehre', *ZDMG* 58, 518–25.

1908–13: *Grundriss der vergleichenden Grammatik der semitischen Sprachen*. 2 vols. Berlin.

1916: *Semitische Sprachwissenschaft*. 2nd ed. Berlin/Leipzig.

1940: 'Neuere Theorien zur Geschichte des Akzents und des Vokalismus im Hebräischen und Aramäischen', *ZDMG* 94, 332–71.

1941: 'Zur Syntax der Sprache von Ugarit', *Orientalia* 10, 223–40.

1944: 'Stand und Aufgabe der Semitistik', in R. Hartmann (ed.), *Beiträge zur Arabistik, Semitistik und Islamwissenschaft*, Leipzig, pp. 3–41.

1951: 'Die "Tempora" des Semitischen', *ZP* 5, 133–54.

1954: 'Die kanaanäischen Dialekte mit dem Ugaritischen', in B. Spuler (ed.), *Handbuch der Orientalistik*, III, Leiden, pp. 40–58.

1956: *Hebräische Syntax*. Neukirchen Kreis Moers.

1968: *Syrische Grammatik*. 11th ed. Leipzig.

Brongers, H.A., 1963–64: 'Das Wort "npš" in den Qumranschriften', *RQ* 4, 407–15.

1965: 'Merismus, Synekdoche und Hendiadys in der bibel-hebräischen Sprache', *OTS* 14, 100–14.

1965a: 'Bemerkungen zum Gebrauch des adverbialen "w^{e}'attāh" im Alten Testament (ein lexikologischer Beitrag)', *VT* 15, 289–99.

1973: 'Die Partikel "l^{e}-ma'an" in der biblisch-hebräischen Sprache', *OTS* 18, 84–96.

Brønno, E., 1940: 'Some nominal types in the Septuagint. Contributions to pre-Masoretic Hebrew grammar', *Classica et mediaevalia* 3, 180–213.

1941–42: 'Einige Namentypen der Septuaginta. Zur historischen Grammatik des Hebräisch', *AcOr* 19, 33–64.

1943: *Studien über hebräische Morphologie und Vokalismus auf Grundlage der Mercatischen Fragmente der zweiten Kolumne der Hexapla des Origenes*. Leipzig.

1950: 'Zu den Theorien Paul Kahles von der Entstehung der tiberischen Grammatik', *ZDMG* 100, 521–65.

1956: 'The Isaiah scroll DSIa and the Greek transliterations of Hebrew', *ZDMG* 106, 252–58.

1967: 'The Hebrew laryngals in non-Masoretic traditions', *P4WCJS*, I, 113–15.

1968: 'Samaritan Hebrew and Origen's Secunda', *JSS* 13, 192–201.

1970: *Die Aussprache der hebräischen Laryngale nach Zeugnisse des Hieronymus*. Aarhus.

Brovender, H., 1971: 'Hebrew language, pre-biblical', *EJ*, XVI, 1560–68.

Bruce, F.F., 1944–45: 'Did Jesus speak Aramaic?', *ET* 56, 328.

Bryan, M.A., 1947: *The distribution of the Semitic and Cushitic languages of Africa*. Oxford.

Bucellati, G., 1966: *The Amorites of the Ur III period*. Naples.

Burchard, C., 1959–65: *Bibliographie zu den Handschriften vom Toten Meer*. 2 vols. Berlin.

Burchardt, M., 1909–10: *Die altkanaanäischen Fremdworte und Eigennamen im Ägyptischen*. Leipzig.

Burkitt, F.C., 1922: 'Is Ecclesiastes a translation?', *JTS* 23, 22–28.

Burrows, M., 1949: 'Orthography, morphology and syntax in the St. Mark's Isaiah manuscript', *JBL* 68, 195–212.

Bush, F.W., 1959–60: 'Evidence from Milḥamah and the Masoretic Text for a penultimate accent in Hebrew verbal forms', *RQ* 2, 501–14.

Bynon, J. and T. (eds.), 1975: *Hamito-Semitica. Proceedings of a colloquium held at ... London, ... March 1970*. The Hague/Paris.

Cagni, L. (ed.), 1981: *La lingua di Ebla. Atti del convegno internazionale (Napoli, 21–23 aprile 1980)*. Naples.

1984: *Il bilinguismo a Ebla. Atti del convegno internazionale (Napoli, 19–22 aprile 1982)*. Naples.

Calice, F., 1936: *Grundlagen der ägyptisch-semitischen Wortvergleichung. Eine kritische Diskussion des bisherigen Vergleichsmaterials*. Ed. by H. Balcz. Vienna.

Campbell, E.F., 1964: *The chronology of the Amarna letters*. Baltimore.

Cano, M.J., 1978: 'La poesía báquica y amorosa de Shelomoh ibn Gabirol'. Undergraduate diss., University of Granada.

Cantera, F., 1941: 'Reseña del estado de las cuestiones. Lingüística: a) Gramática y sus problemas; b) Diccionarios y lexicografía', *Sefarad* 1, 167–77.

1942: 'De epigrafía hebraico-española', *Sefarad* 2, 99–112.

1943: 'Lápidas hebraicas del Museo de Toledo', *Sefarad* 3, 107–14.

1943a: 'Nuevas inscripciones hebraicas leonesas', *Sefarad* 3, 329–58

1944: 'Inscripciones hebraicas de Toledo. Nuevo hallazgo epigráfico', *Sefarad* 4, 45–72.

1950: 'Nueva lápida hebraica en Tarragona', *Sefarad* 10, 173–76.

1951: 'Epigrafía hebraica en el Museo Arqueológico de Madrid', *Sefarad* 11, 105–11.

1951a: 'La epigrafía hebraica en Sevilla', *Sefarad* 11, 371–89.

1952: 'Unas palabras más sobre la lápida del médico sevillano R. Shelomoh ben Ya'ish', *Sefarad* 12, 159–60.
1953: 'Sellos hispano-hebreos', *Sefarad* 13, 101–11.
1954: 'Nuevo hallazgo epigráfico en León', *Sefarad* 14, 119–21.
1954a: 'Nuevas inscripciones hebraicas', *Sefarad* 14, 389–91.
1955: 'Nueva inscripción trilingüe tarraconense?', *Sefarad* 15, 151–56.
1955a: 'Hallazgo de nuevas lápidas hebraicas en el Levante español', *Sefarad* 15, 387–94.
Cantera, F. and Millás, J.M, 1956: *Las inscripciones hebraicas de España*. Madrid.
Cantineau, J., 1930–32: *Le nabatéen*. 2 vols. Paris.
1931: 'De la place de l'accent de mot en hébreu et en araméen biblique', *BEOIFD* 1, 81–98.
1932: 'Accadien et sudarabique', *BSLP* 33, 175–204.
1932a: 'Elimination de syllabes brèves en hébreu et en araméen biblique', *BEOIFD* 2, 125–44.
1932–40: 'La langue de Ras-Shamra', *Syria* 13, 164–70; 21, 38–61.
1935: *Grammaire du palmyrénien épigraphique*. Cairo.
1949: 'Racines et schèmes dans les langues sémitiques', in *Actes du XXIe Congrès International des Orientalistes, Paris 23–31 juillet 1948*, Paris, pp. 93–95.
1950: 'La langue de Ras-Shamra', *Semitica* 3, 21–34.
1950a: 'La notion de "schème" et son altération dans diverses langues sémitiques', *Semitica* 3, 73–83.
1950b: 'Essai d'une phonologie de l'hébreu biblique', *BSLP* 46, 82–122.
1951: 'Le consonantisme du sémitique', *Semitica* 4, 79–94.
1955: 'Quelle langue parlait le peuple en Palestine au prémier siècle de notre ère?', *Semitica* 5, 99–101.
Caquot, A., 1960–63: 'L'araméen de Hatra', *GLECS* 9, 87–89.
Caquot, A. and Lemaire, A., 1977: 'Les textes araméens de Deir 'Alla', *Syria* 54, 189–208.
Caquot, A., Sznycer, M., and Herdner, A., 1974: *Textes ougaritiques*. I: *Mythes et légendes*. Paris.
Caquot, A., de Tarragon, J.-M., and Cunchillos, J.L., 1989: *Textes ougaritiques*. II: *Textes religieux, rituels, correspondence*. Paris.
Carmignac, J., 1961–62: 'Notes sur les *pshârîm*', *RQ* 3, 505–38.
1964–66: 'Un aramaïsme biblique et qumrânien: l'infinitif placé après son complément d'objet', *RQ* 5, 503–20.
1967: 'Le sens de la racine "MLḤ" II dans la Bible et à Qumran', in G. Buccellati (ed.), *Studi sull'Oriente e la Bibbia offerti al P. Giovanni Rinaldi*, Genoa, pp. 77–81.
1972–75: 'L'emploi de la négation "'yn" dans la Bible et à Qumrân', *RQ* 8, 407–14.
1977–78: 'Le complément d'agent après un verbe passif dans l'hébreu et l'araméen de Qumrân', *RQ* 9, 409–27.
1985–86: 'L'infinitif absolu chez Ben Sira et à Qumrân', *RQ* 12, 251–62.
Casanowicz, I.M., 1894–96: 'The emphatic particle "l" in the Old Testament', *JAOS* 16, 166–71.
1910: 'Note on some usages of "lāḵēn"', *JAOS* 30, 343–46.
Castellino, G.R., 1962: *The Accadian personal pronouns and verbal system in the light of Semitic and Hamitic*. Leiden.
Catastini, A, 1984: 'Noti di epigrafia ebraica, i–ii', *Henoch* 6, 129–38.
Cathcart, K.J., 1969: '"Trkb qmḥ" in the Arad ostracon and Biblical Hebrew "rekeb", "upper millstone"', *VT* 19, 121–23.
1973: *Nahum in the light of Northwest Semitic*. Rome.
Cavalletti, S., 1957: 'Ebraico biblico ed ebraico mishnico', *Sefarad* 17, 122–29.
Cazelles, H., 1947: 'Note sur l'origine des temps convertis hébreux d'après quelques textes ugaritiques', *RB* 54, 388–93.
1951: 'La mimation nominale en ouest-sémitique', *GLECS* 5, 79–81.
1954–57: 'Un vestige de pseudo-participe en hébreu', *GLECS* 7, 46–48.
1973: 'Le sens du verbe "B'R" en hébreu', *Semitica* 25, 5–10.
Centre National de la Recherche Scientifique, 1974: *La Paléographie hébraïque médiévale*. Colloque international, Paris, 11–13 septembre 1972. Paris.

1974a: *Les Techniques de laboratoire dans l'étude des manuscrits*. Colloque international, Paris, 13–15 septembre 1972. Paris.

Chanoch (Garbell), I., 1930: *Fremdsprachliche Einflüsse in modernen Hebräisch*. Berlin.

Chapira, B., 1914: 'Fragments inédits du Sefer Haggalui de Saadia Gaon', *REJ* 68, 1–15.

Chase, D.A., 1982: 'A note on an inscription from Kuntillet 'Ajrūd', *BASOR* 246, 63–67.

Chayen, M.J., 1971–72: 'The pronunciation of Israeli Hebrew', *Leshonenu* 36, 212–19, 287–300. H.

1973: *The phonetics of Modern Hebrew*. The Hague/Paris.

Chayen, M.J. and Dror, Z., 1976: *Introduction to Hebrew transformational grammar*. Leiden.

Chiesa, B., 1978: *L'Antico Testamento ebraico secondo la tradizione palestinese*. Turin.

1979: *The emergence of Hebrew biblical pointing: the indirect sources*. Frankfurt-am-Main/Cirencester.

Chomsky, W., 1941: 'The history of our vowel-system in Hebrew', *JQR*, n.s., 32, 27–49.

1951–52: 'What was the Jewish vernacular during the Second Commonwealth?', *JQR*, n.s., 42, 193–212.

1962: 'The growth and progress of Modern Hebrew', in M. Ben-Horin, B.D. Weinryb, and S. Zeitlin (eds.), *Studies and essays in honor of Abraham A. Neuman*, Leiden, pp. 106–27.

1967: 'The growth of Hebrew during the Middle Ages', in A.A. Neuman and S. Zeitlin (eds.), *The seventy-fifth anniversary volume of the Jewish quarterly review*, Philadelphia, pp. 121–36.

1969: *Hebrew, the eternal language*. Philadelphia.

1970: 'The ambiguity of the prefixed prepositions "mi-", "l^e-", "b^e-" in the Bible', *JQR*, n.s., 61, 87–89.

1971: 'The pronunciation of the shewa', *JQR*, n.s., 62, 88–94.

Christian, V., 1927: 'Das Wesen der semitischen Tempora', *ZDMG* 81, 232–58.

1953: *Untersuchungen zur Laut- und Formenlehre des Hebräischen*. Vienna.

Chwolson, D.A., 1876: *Die Quiescentes 'H', 'W', 'Y' in der althebräischen Orthographie*. St. Petersburg.

1882 (repr. 1974): *Corpus inscriptionum hebraicarum enthaltend Grabschriften aus der Krim und andere Grab- und Inschriften in alter hebräischer Quadratschrift*. St. Petersburg.

Claassen, W.T., 1971: 'The rôle of /ṣ/ in the North-West Semitic languages', *AION* 31, 285–302.

1971b: 'On a recent proposal as to a distinction between Pi'el and Hiph'il', *JNSL* 1, 3–10.

1972: 'The declarative-estimative Hiph'il', *JNSL* 2, 5–16.

1983: 'Speaker-orientated functions of "kî" in Biblical Hebrew', *JNSL* 11, 29–46.

Clines, D.J.A., 1974: 'The etymology of Hebrew "ṣelem"', *JNSL* 3, 19–25.

Cody, A., 1970: 'A new inscription from Tell al-Rimāḥ and King Jehoash of Israel', *CBQ* 32, 325–40.

Cohen, C., 1936: 'Die Bedeutung der verschiedenen Punktationssysteme für die Aussprache des Hebräischen', *MGWJ* 80, 390–97.

Cohen, C. (Ḥ), 1972: 'Hebrew "tbh": proposed etymologies', *JANES* 4, 36–51.

1982–83: 'Expressing the pronominal object in Mishnaic Hebrew', *Leshonenu* 47, 208–18. H.

Cohen, D., 1968: 'Les langues chamito-sémitiques', in A. Martinet (ed.), *Le Langage* (*Encyclopédie de la Pléiade*, XXV), Paris, pp. 1288–330.

1970: *Dictionnaire de racines sémitiques ou attestées dans les langues sémitiques*. I. The Hague.

Cohen, D. and Zafrani, Ḥ., 1968: *Grammaire de l'hébreu vivant*. Paris.

Cohen, H.R., 1978: *Biblical* hapax legomena *in the light of Accadian and Ugaritic*. Missoula.

Cohen, J., 1912: *Wurzelforschungen zu den hebräischen Synonymen der Ruhe*. Berlin.

Cohen, M., 1924: *Le Système verbal sémitique et l'expression du temps*. Paris.

1947: *Essai comparatif sur le vocabulaire et la phonétique du chamito-sémitique*. Paris.

1952: 'Langues chamito-sémitiques', in A. Meillet and M. Cohen (eds.), *Les Langues du monde*, 2nd ed., I, Paris, pp. 81–181.

1969: 'Vue générale du verbe chamito-sémitique', *PICSS*, 45–48.

Cohen, Menachem, 1983–84: 'The victory of the Ben-Asher text: theory and reality', *Tarbiz* 53, 255–72. H.

Cohen, M.B., 1972: 'The Masoretic accents as a biblical commentary', *JANES* 4, 2–11.

Cohen, N., 1970: '*ZDH* in the Siloam inscription', *BM* 15, 359–60. H.

Cohen, R, 1985: "Les ostraca de Qadesh-Barnéa", *Le Monde de la Bible* 39, 24–25.
Cohen, S., 1982: 'A note on the dual in Biblical Hebrew', *JQR*, n.s., 73, 38–58.
Cole, P., 1976 (ed): *Studies in Modern Hebrew syntax and semantics.* Amsterdam.
Colorni, V., 1964: *L'uso del greco nella liturgia del giudaismo ellenistico.* Milan.
Coogan, M.D., 1976: *West Semitic personal names in the Murašu documents.* Missoula.
Cook, S.A., 1903: 'A pre-Masoretic biblical papyrus', *PSBA* 25, 34–56.
1924: 'Inscribed Hebrew objects from Ophel', *PEFQS* 56, 180–86.
Cooke, G.A., 1903: *A text-book of North-Semitic inscriptions, Moabite, Hebrew, Phoenician, Aramaic, Nabataean, Palmyrene, Jewish.* Oxford.
Cooper, R.L., 1985: 'Language and social stratification among the Jewish population of Israel', in J.A. Fishman (ed.), *Readings in the sociology of Jewish languages*, Leiden, pp. 65–81.
Coote, R.B., 1980: 'The Tell Siran bottle inscription', *BASOR* 240, 93.
Corré, A.S., 1956: 'The Anglo-Sephardic pronunciation of Hebrew', *JJS* 7, 85–90.
Corriente, F., 1969–70 'A survey of spirantization in Semitic and Arabic phonetics', *JQR*, n.s., 60, 147–71.
1971: *Problemática de la pluralidad en semítico. El plural fracto.* Madrid.
Cowley, A.E., 1894–95: 'The Samaritan liturgy and reading of the Law', *JQR* 7, 121–40.
1909: *The Samaritan liturgy.* 2 vols. Oxford.
Craigie, P.C., 1981: 'Ugarit and the Bible: progress and regress in 50 years of literary study', in G.D. Young (ed.), *Ugarit in retrospect. Fifty years of Ugarit and Ugaritic*, Winona Lake, pp. 99–111.
Croatto, J.S., 1966: '"Abrek" "intendant" dans Gén. xli 41, 43', *VT* 16, 113–15.
1971: 'L'article hébreu et les particules emphatiques dans le sémitique de l'ouest', *ArOr* 39, 389–400.
Cross, F.M., 1954: 'The evolution of the Proto-Canaanite alphabet', *BASOR* 134, 15–24.
1956: 'Lachish letter iv', *BASOR* 144, 24–26.
1958: *The ancient library of Qumran and modern biblical studies.* New York.
1961: 'Epigraphic notes on Hebrew documents of the eighth-sixth centuries B.C.', *BASOR* 163, 12–14.
1961a: 'The development of the Jewish scripts', in G.E. Wright (ed.), *The Bible and the ancient Near East. Essays in honor of William Foxwell Albright*, Garden City, pp. 133–202.
1962: 'Epigraphic notes on Hebrew documents of the eighth-sixth centuries B.C., ii: The Murabba'at papyrus and the letter found near Yabneh-Yam', *BASOR* 165, 34–42; 168, 18–23.
1964: 'The history of the biblical text in the light of the discoveries in the Judaean Desert', *HTR* 57, 281–99.
1966: 'The contribution of the Qumran discoveries to the study of the biblical text', *IEJ* 16, 81–95.
1967: 'The origin and early evolution of the alphabet', *EI* 8, 8–24.
1968: 'Jar inscriptions from Shiqmona', *IEJ* 18, 226–33.
1969: 'Epigraphic notes on the 'Ammān citadel inscription', *BASOR* 193, 13–19.
1969a: 'An ostracon from Heshbon', *AUSS* 7, 223–29.
1969b: 'Judean Stamps', *EI* 9, 20–27.
1969c: 'Two notes on Palestinian inscriptions of the Persian age', *BASOR* 193, 19–24.
1969d: 'Papyri of the fourth century B.C. from Daliyeh', in D.N. Freedman and J.C. Greenfield (eds.), *New directions in biblical archaeology*, Garden City, pp. 42–43.
1970: 'The cave inscriptions from Khirbet Beit Lei', in J.A. Sanders (ed.), *Near Eastern archaeology in the twentieth century. Essays in homage to N. Glueck*, Garden City, pp. 299–306.
1971: 'An inscribed jar handle from Raddana', *BASOR* 201, 19–22.
1973: 'Notes on the Ammonite inscription from Tell Sīrān', *BASOR* 212, 12–15.
1973a: 'Heshbon ostracon ii', *AUSS* 11, 126–31.
1975: 'Ammonite ostraca from Heshbon: Heshbon ostraca iv–viii', *AUSS* 13, 1–20.
1976: 'Heshbon ostracon xi', *AUSS* 14, 145–48.
1980: 'Newly found inscription in old Canaanite and early Phoenician scripts', *BASOR* 238, 1–20.
1985: 'A literate soldier: Lachish letter iii', in A. Kort and S. Morschauser (eds.), *Biblical and related studies presented to Samuel Iwry*, Winona Lake, pp. 41–47.

1986: 'An unpublished Ammonite ostracon from Ḥesbān', in L.T. Geraty and L.G. Herr (eds.), *The archaeology of Jordan and other studies*, Berrien Springs, pp. 475–89

Cross, F.M. and Freedman, D.N., 1948: 'The blessings of Moses', *JBL* 67, 191–210.

1951: 'The pronominal suffixes of the third person singular in Phoenician', *JNES* 10, 228–30.

1952: *Early Hebrew orthography: a study of the epigraphic evidence*. Baltimore.

1953: 'A royal song of thanksgiving. II Samuel 22 = Psalm 18', *JBL* 72, 15–34.

1955: 'The Song of Miriam', *JNES* 14, 237–50.

1972: 'Some observations on early Hebrew', *Biblica* 53, 413–20.

Cross, F.M. and Lambdin, T.O., 1960: 'An Ugaritic abecedary and the origins of the Proto-Canaanite alphabet', *BASOR* 160, 21–26.

Cross, F.M. and Talmon, S. (eds.), 1975: *Qumran and the history of the biblical text*. Cambridge, Mass.

Cunchillos, J.L., 1982: 'Bibliographie des textes de Ras Ibn Hani', *UF* 15, 27–32.

1985: 'Las bases de la cultura ugarítica. I: Prehistoria, protohistoria y lengua de Ugarit', *UF* 17, 73–93.

Cuny, A., 1943: *Recherches sur le vocalisme, le consonantisme et la formation des racines en "nostratique", ancêtre de l'indoeuropéen et du chamito-sémitique*. Paris.

1946: *Invitation à l'étude comparative des langues indoeuropéennes et des langues chamito-sémitiques*. Bordeaux.

Dahood, M.J., 1952: 'Canaanite-Phoenician influence in Qohelet', *Biblica* 33, 30–52, 191–221.

1952a: 'The language of Qohelet', *CBQ* 14, 227–32.

1954: 'The language and date of Psalm 48 (47)', *CBQ* 16, 15–19.

1956: 'Enclitic mem and emphatic lamedh in Psalm 85', *Biblica* 37, 338–40.

1957: 'Some Northwest-Semitic words in Job', *Biblica* 38, 306–20.

1959: 'The linguistic position of Ugaritic in the light of recent discoveries', in J. Coppens, A. Descamps, and E. Massaux (eds.), *Sacra pagina. Miscellanea biblica Congressus Internationalis Catholici de Re Biblica*, I, Paris/Gembloux, pp. 267–79.

1962: 'Qohelet and Northwest Semitic philology', *Biblica* 43, 349–65.

1962a: 'Northwest Semitic philology and Job', in J.L. McKenzie (ed.), *The Bible in current Catholic thought*, New York, pp. 55–74.

1963: *Proverbs and Northwest Semitic philology*. Rome.

1963–74: 'Hebrew-Ugaritic lexicography', *Biblica* 44, 289–303; 45, 393–412; 46, 311–32; 47, 403–19; 48, 421–38; 49, 355–69; 50, 337–56; 51, 391–404; 52, 337–56; 53, 386–403; 54, 351–66; 55, 381–93.

1965: *Ugaritic-Hebrew philology. Marginal notes on recent publications*. Rome.

1966: 'Vocative lamedh in the Psalter', *VT* 16, 299–311.

1969: 'Ugaritic-Hebrew syntax and style', *UF* 1, 15–36.

1970: 'The independent personal pronoun in the oblique case in Hebrew', *CBQ* 32, 86–90.

1972: 'A note on third person suffix "-y" in Hebrew', *UF* 4, 163–64.

1979: 'Third person masculine singular with preformative "t-" in Northwest Semitic', *Orientalia* 48, 97–106.

1982: 'Eblaite and Biblical Hebrew', *CBQ* 44, 1–24.

Dahood, M.J. and Penar, T., 1970: 'The grammar of the Psalter', in M.J. Dahood, *Psalms*, III: 100–150, Garden City, pp. 361–456

1972: 'Ugaritic-Hebrew parallel pairs', in L.R. Fisher (ed.), *Ras Shamra parallels. The texts from Ugarit and the Hebrew Bible*, I, Rome, pp. 71–382.

Dajani, R.W., 1967–68: 'The Amman theater fragment', *ADAJ* 12–13, 65–67.

Dalman, G.H. (A.), 1902: *The words of Jesus considered in the light of post-biblical Jewish writings and the Aramaic language*. I: *Introduction and Fundamental ideas*. Edinburgh.

1905 (repr. 1960): *Grammatik des jüdisch-palästinischen Aramäisch*. 2nd ed. Leipzig.

1929: *Jesus-Jeshua. Studies in the Gospels*. London.

1938 (repr. 1987): *Aramäisch-neuhebräisches Handwörterbuch zu Targum, Talmud und Midrasch*. 3rd ed. Göttingen.

Davidson, A.B., 1901 (repr, 1924): *Hebrew syntax*. 3rd ed. Edinburgh.

Davidson, I., 1914: 'Eccentric forms of Hebrew verse', *Jewish Theological Seminary of America students' annual* 1, 81–94.
Davies, G.I., 1991: *Ancient Hebrew inscriptions: corpus and concordance.* Cambridge.
Decroix, J., 1970: 'Les ostraca de Samarie', *Bible et Terre Sainte* 120, 15–17.
Degen, R., 1969: *Altaramäische Grammatik der Inschriften des 10.–8. Jh. v. Chr.* Wiesbaden.
1971: 'Zur neueren hebraistischen Forschung', *WdO* 6, 47–79.
Degen, R., Müller, W.W., and Röllig, W., 1972–1978: *Neue Ephemeris für semitische Epigraphik.* 3 vols. Wiesbaden.
Delavault B. and Lemaire A., 1979: 'Les inscriptions phéniciens de Palestine', *RSF* 7, 1–39.
Delcor, M., 1967: 'Two special meanings of the word "yd" in Biblical Hebrew', *JSS* 12, 230–40.
1974: 'De l'origine de quelques termes relatifs au vin en hébreu biblique et dans les langues voisines', *APCI*, 223–33.
1975: 'Quelques cas de survivances du vocabulaire nomade en hébreu biblique', *VT* 25, 307–22.
Delcor, M. and García Martínez, F., 1982: *Introducción a la literatura esenia de Qumran.* Madrid.
Delekat, L., 1970: 'Ein Bittschriftentwurf eines Sabbatschänders (*KAI* 200)', *Biblica* 51, 453–70.
Demsky, A., 1972: '"Dark wine" from Judah', *IEJ* 22, 233–24.
1977: 'A Proto-Canaanite abecedary dating from the period of the Judges and its implications for the history of the alphabet', *TAJ* 4, 14–27.
Devens, M.S., 1980: 'Oriental Israeli Hebrew: a study in phonetics', *AAL* 7, 128–42.
Dever, W.G., 1969–70: 'Iron Age epigraphic material from the area of Khirbet el-Kôm', *HUCA* 40–41, 139–204.
1971: 'Inscriptions from Khirbet el-Kom', *Qadmoniot* 4, 90–92. H.
Dhorme, E. (P.), 1913–14: 'La langue de Canaan', *RB* 10, 369–93; 11, 37–59, 344–72.
1923: *L'Emploi métaphorique des noms des parties du corps en hébreu et en akkadien.* Paris.
1930: 'L'ancien hébreu dans la vie courante', *RB* 39, 63–73.
1930a: *Langues et écritures sémitiques.* Paris.
1946–48: 'Déchiffrement des inscriptions pseudo-hiéroglyphiques de Byblos', *Syria* 25, 1–35.
Diakonoff, I.M., 1965: *Semito-Hamitic languages. An essay in classification.* Moscow.
1970: 'Problems of root structure in Proto-Semitic', *ArOr* 38, 453–80.
1975: 'On root structure in Proto-Semitic', in J. and T. Bynon (eds.), pp. 133–53.
1984: 'An evaluation of Eblaite', in Fronzaroli (ed.), pp. 1–10.
1990: 'The importance of Ebla for history and linguistics', in C.H. Gordon, G.A. Rendsburg, and N.H. Winter (eds.), *Eblaitica: essays on the Ebla archives and Eblaite language,* II, Winona Lake, pp. 3–29.
Díaz Esteban, F., 1954: 'Notas sobre la Masora', *Sefarad* 14, 316–21.
1958: 'The Sefer Oklah w'Oklah as a source of not registered Bible textual variants', *ZAW* 70, 250–53.
1966: 'El fragmento babilónico Ms. Heb. d 62 fol. 7 de la Bodleyana de Oxford', *Boletín de la Asociación Española de Orientalistas* 2, 89–107.
1966a: 'Los supuestos errores de la Masora', *Sefarad* 26, 3–11.
1968: 'References to Ben Asher and Ben Naftali in the *Massora magna* written in the margins of Ms. Leningrad B19a', *Textus* 6, 62–74.
1970: 'Tensiones en el hebreo contemporáneo', *Sefarad* 30, 366–81.
1975 (ed.): *Sefer 'Oḵlah wᵉ-'oḵlah.* Madrid.
1982, 'La lengua del paraíso', *Anuario de filología* 8, 111–35.
Diem, W., 1974: 'Das Problem von "š" im Althebräischen und die kanaanäische Verschreibung', *ZDMG* 124, 221–52.
1975: 'Gedanken zur Frage der Mimation und Nunation in den semitischen Sprachen', *ZDMG* 125, 239–58.
Diening, F., 1938: *Das Hebräische bei den Samaritanern. Ein Beitrag zur vormasoretischen Grammatik des Hebräischen.* Stuttgart.
Dienstag, J., 1969: Le-yaḥas Maran el mishnat ha-RaMBaM', in I. Raphael (ed.), *Rabbi Yosef Karo: 'iyyunim u-meḥkarim be-mishnat Maran ba'al ha-Shulḥan 'Arukh,* Jerusalem, pp. 156–77.

Dietrich, M., 1968: *Neue palästinisch punktierte Bibelfragmente*. Leiden.

Dietrich, M. and Loretz, O., 1968: 'Untersuchungen zur Schrift- und Lautlehre des Ugaritschen, i: Der ugaritische konsonant "ǵ"' *WdO* 4, 300–15.

1976: *Die Elfenbeininschriften und S-Texte aus Ugarit*. Neukirchen-Vluyn.

Dietrich, M., Loretz, O., Berger, P.R., and Sanmartín, J., 1973: *Ugarit-Bibliographie 1928–1966*. 4 vols. Neukirchen-Vluyn.

Dietrich, M., Loretz, O., and Sanmartín, J., 1976: *Die keilalphabetischen Texte aus Ugarit einschliesslich der keilalphabetischen Texte ausserhalb Ugarits*. I: *Transkription*. Neukirchen-Vluyn.

Dietrich, M., Loretz, O, and Delsman, W.C., 1986: *Ugarit-Bibliographie 1967–71. Titel, Nachträge, Register*. I. Neukirchen-Vluyn.

Díez Macho, A., 1954: 'Tres nuevos mss. "palestinenses"', *EstBib* 13, 247–65.

1954a: 'Descubrimiento de nuevos manuscritos babilónicos', *Sefarad* 14, 216–18.

1954b: 'Un importante manuscrito targúmico en la Biblioteca Vaticana', in *Homenaje a Millás-Vallicrosa*, I, Barcelona, pp. 375–463.

1955: 'Fragmentos de *piyyuṭim* de Yannay en vocalización babilónica', *Sefarad* 15, 287–340.

1956: 'Un manuscrito hebreo protomasorético y nueva teoría acerca de los manuscritos Ben Naftalí', *EstBib* 15, 187–222.

1956a: 'Nuevos manuscritos importantes bíblicos o litúrgicos en hebreo o arameo', *Sefarad* 16, 2–22.

1957: 'Un manuscrito "palestinense" en la Biblioteca Nacional de Estrasburgo', *Sefarad* 17, 11–17.

1957a: 'Valiosos manuscritos bíblicos en la Biblioteca Nacional y Universitaria de Estrasburgo', *EstBib* 16, 83–88.

1957b: 'Nuevos manuscritos bíblicos babilónicos', *EstBib* 16, 235–77.

1957c: 'Un ms. yemení de la Biblia babilónica', *Sefarad* 17, 237–79.

1957d: 'Fragmentos del texto hebreo y arameo del Libro de Números escrito en una muy antigua *megillah* en sistema babilónico', *Sefarad* 17, 1–3.

1957e: 'Importants manuscrits hébreux et araméens aux Etats-Unis', *SVT* 4, 27–46.

1958: 'An Onqelos ms. with Babylonian transliterated vocalization in the Vatican Library', *VT* 8, 113–33.

1958a: 'La cantilación protomasorética del Pentateuco', *EstBib* 17, 223–51.

1959: 'Un espécimen de ms. bíblico babilónico en papel', *Biblica* 40, 171–76.

1959a: 'Un manuscrito babilónico de Onqelos en el que se confunden los timbres vocálicos pataḥ y qameṣ', *Sefarad* 19, 273–82.

1959b: 'Un ms. protobabilónico de los libros poéticos de la Biblia', *EstBib* 18, 235–56.

1960: 'Un ms. de Onqelos de transición del sistema palestinense al prototiberiense', *Estudios eclesiásticos* 34, 461–66.

1960a: 'A new fragment of Isaiah with Babylonian pointing', *Textus* 1, 132–43.

1963: 'Un nuevo ms. "palestinense" del Libro de Jueces entre los fragmentos de la Genizah de la Biblioteca Universitaria de Cambridge (T.S. New Series 281/2)', *Sefarad* 23, 236–51.

1963a: 'A new list of the so-called Ben Naftali manuscripts preceded by an inquiry into the true character of these manuscripts', in D. Winton Thomas and W.D. McHardy (eds.), *Hebrew and Semitic studies presented to Godfrey Rolles Driver*, Oxford, pp. 16–62.

1963b: 'La lengua hablada por Jesucristo', *OrAn* 2, 95–132.

1963c: *La lengua hablada por Jesucristo*. Buenos Aires.

1967: 'Nuevo manuscrito bíblico palestinense procedente de la Geniza del Cairo (T.S. new series 246) de la Biblioteca Universitaria de Cambridge', *Studia papyrológica* 6, 15–25.

1969: 'Manuscritos babilónicos de la Biblia procedentes del Yemen, i–ii', *Augustinianum* 9, 197–234, 427–54.

1970: 'Catálogo de nuevos manuscritos pseudo-Ben Naftalí de la Biblioteca Universitaria de Cambridge', *Augustinianum* 10, 213–40.

1971: 'La vocalización de los manuscritos palestinenses según E.J. Revell', *Augustinianum* 11, 549–64.

1971a: *Manuscritos hebreos y arameos de la Biblia*. Rome.

1972: *El Targum. Introducción a las traducciones aramaicas de la Biblia*. Barcelona.

Díez Macho, A. and Larraya, J.A.G., 1957: 'Ms. 4083, ff. i–ii de la Biblioteca Nacional y Universitaria de Estrasburgo', *EstBib* 16, 383–87.

1960: 'El Ms. 4084, ff. i–ii de la Biblioteca Nacional y Universitaria de Estrasburgo', *EstBib* 19, 74–95.

Díez Macho, A. and Martínez, T.J., 1957: 'Ms. 4083, f. ii de la Biblioteca Nacional y Universitaria de Estrasburgo', *EstBib* 16, 389–91.

1958: 'Ms. 4065, pp. 81–82 de la Biblioteca Universitaria de Estrasburgo', *EstBib* 17, 429–36.

1960: 'Ms. 4065, pp. 83–84 de la Biblioteca Nacional y Universitaria de Estrasburgo', *EstBib* 19, 245–47.

Díez Merino, L., 1973: 'Catálogo de manuscritos bíblicos hebreos y arameos en puntuación babilónica'. Typescript, Jerusalem.

1975: *La Biblia babilónica*. Madrid.

van Dijk, H.J., 1968: *Ezekiel's prophecy on Tyre (Ez. 26,1–28,19). A new approach*. Rome.

1968a: 'A neglected connotation of three Hebrew verbs ["ntn", "śym", "šyt"]', *VT* 18, 16–30.

1969: 'Does third masculine singular "*taqtul" exist in Hebrew?', *VT* 19, 440–47.

Dijkstra, M., 1983: 'Notes on some Proto-Sinaitic inscriptions including an unrecognized inscription of Wadi Rod el-'Aîr', *UF* 15, 33–38.

Di Lella, A.A., 1966: *The Hebrew text of Sirach. A text-critical and historical study*. The Hague.

Dion, P.E., 1974: *La langue de Ya'udi: description et classement de l'ancien parler de Zencirli dans le cadre des langues sémitiques du nord-ouest*. Waterloo.

1975: 'Notes d'épigraphie ammonite', *RB* 82, 24–33.

1978: 'The language spoken in ancient Sam'al', *JNES* 37, 115–18.

Diringer, D., 1934: *Le iscrizione antico-ebraiche palestinesi*. Florence.

1941: 'On ancient Hebrew inscriptions discovered at Tell ed-Duweir (Lachish)', *PEQ* 73, 38–56, 89–106.

1953: 'Early Hebrew inscriptions', in O. Tufnell (ed.), *Lachish (Tell ed Duweir)*, III (The Iron Age), I, London/New York, pp. 331–59.

Diringer, D. and Brock, S.P., 1968: 'Words and meanings in early Hebrew inscriptions', in P.R. Ackroyd and B. Lindars (eds.), *Words and meanings. Essays presented to David Winton Thomas*, Cambridge, pp. 39–46.

Dolgopolsky, A., 1977: 'Emphatic consonants in Semitic', *IOS* 7, 1–13.

1978: 'On phonemic stress in Proto-Semitic', *IOS* 8, 1–12.

Dombrowski, B.W., 1962: 'Some remarks on the Hebrew Hitpa'el and inversative "-t-" in the Semitic languages', *JNES* 21, 220–23.

1966: '"Hyḥd" in 1QS and "to koinón". An instance of early Greek and Jewish synthesis', *HTR* 59, 293–307.

Donald, T., 1964: 'The semantic field of rich and poor in the wisdom literature of Hebrew and Akkadian', *OrAn* 3, 27–41.

Donner, H. and Röllig, W., 1971–76: *Kanaanäische und aramäische Inschriften*. 3rd ed. 3 vols. Wiesbaden.

Dorman, M., Safrai, S., and Stern, M., 1970 (eds.): *In memory of Gedaliahu Alon: essays in Jewish history and philology*, Jerusalem. H.

van Dorssen, J.C.C., 1951: *De derivata van de stam* 'MN *in het Hebreeuwsch van het Oude Testament*. Amsterdam.

Dossin, G., 1934: 'Une nouvelle lettre d'El-Amarna', *RA* 31, 125–36.

Dotan, A., 1965: 'Ha-'omnam ninkad Keter Ḥaleb bi-yde Aharon ben Asher?', *Tarbiz* 34, 136–55.

1967 (ed.): *Sefer Dikduke ha-Ṭe'amim le-Rabbi Aharon ben Mosheh ben Asher*. Jerusalem.

1971: 'Masorah', *EJ*, XVI, 1401–82.

1973 (ed.): *Torah, Nevi'im u-Khetuvim*. Tel-Aviv.

1976: 'Stress position and vowel shift in Phoenician and Punic; Phoenician/Punic-Hebrew linguistic relationship re-examined', *IOS* 6, 71–121.

1981: 'New light on the 'Izbet Ṣarṭah ostracon', *TAJ* 8, 160–72.

1981a: 'The relative chronology of Hebrew vocalization and accentuation', *PAAJR* 48, 87–99.
Dothan, M., 1961: 'An inscribed jar from Azor', *Atiqot* 3, 181–84.
Draper, H.M., 1955–56: 'Did Jesus speak Greek? *ET* 67, 317.
van Drival, E., 1879: *Grammaire comparée des langues sémitiques et de l'égyptien*. 2nd ed. Paris.
Driver, G.R., 1930–35: 'Studies in the vocabulary of the Old Testament, i–viii', *JTS* 31, 275–84; 32, 250–57, 361–66; 33, 38–48; 34, 33–45, 375–85; 35, 330–93; 36, 293–301.
1936: *Problems of the Hebrew verbal system*. Edinburgh.
1936a: 'Supposed Arabisms in the Old Testament', *JBL* 55, 101–20.
1937 'Problems of Semitic grammar', *ZDMG* 91, 343–51.
1944: 'Seals from 'Amman and Petra', *Quarterly, Department of Antiquities in Palestine* 11, 81–82.
1948: 'Gender in Hebrew numbers', *JJS* 1, 90–104.
1951: *The Hebrew scrolls*. London.
1951a: 'Hebrew Scrolls', *JTS*, n.s., 2, 17–30.
1953: 'Hebrew poetic diction', *SVT* 1, 26–39.
1954: *Aramaic documents of the fifth century B.C.* Oxford.
1957: 'Three difficult words in Discipline (iii 3–4; vii 5–6, 11)', *JSS* 2, 247–50.
1965: *The Judaean scrolls. The problem and a solution*. Oxford.
1966: 'Forgotten Hebrew idioms', *ZAW* 78, 1–7.
1967: 'Hebrew homonyms', *SVT* 16, 50–64.
1969: 'Some uses of "QTL" in the Semitic languages', *PICSS*, 49–64.
1970: *Semitic writing from pictograph to alphabet*. 3rd ed. London.
1970a: 'Colloquialisms in the Old Testament', in D. Cohen (ed.), *Mélanges Marcel Cohen: études de linguistique, ethnographie et sciences connexes offertes ... a l'occasion de son 80ème anniversaire*, The Hague, pp. 232–39.
1973: 'Affirmation by exclamatory negation', *JANES* 5, 104–14.
Driver, S.R., 1892 (repr. 1970): *A treatise on the use of the tenses in Hebrew and some other syntactical questions*. 3rd ed. Oxford.
Dukes, L., 1846: *Die Sprache der Mischnah. Lexicographisch und grammatisch betrachtet*. 2 vols. Esslingen.
Dunand, M., 1945: *Byblia grammata. Documents et recherche sur le développement de l'écriture en Phenicie*. Beirut.
Dupont-Sommer, A., 1942–44: 'La tablette cunéiforme araméenne de Warka', *RA* 39, 35–62.
1949: 'Etude du texte phénicien des inscriptions de Karatepe', *Oriens* 2, 121–26.
1949a: *Les Araméens*. Paris.
Dussaud, R., 1925–26: 'Samarie en temps d'Achab', *Syria* 6, 314–38; 7, 9–29.
Ebeling, E., 1910: *Das Verbum der El-Amarna-Briefe*. Leipzig.
Edelmann, R., 1934: *Zur Frühgeschichte des Mahzor. Geniza-Fragmente mit palästinischer Punktation*. Stuttgart.
Edzard, D.O., 1967: 'Die semito-hamitischen Sprachen in neuer Sicht', *RA* 61, 137–49.
1981: *Verwaltungstexte verschiedenen Inhalts* (Archivi reali di Ebla. Testi; 2). Rome.
1984: *Hymnen, Beschwörungen und Verwandtes* (Archivi reali di Ebla. Testi; 5). Rome.
Efros, I., 1926–27: 'Studies in pre-Tibbonian philosophical terminology', *JQR*, n.s., 17, 129–64, 323–68.
1929–30: 'More about Abraham B. Ḥiyya's philosophical terminology', *JQR*, n.s., 20, 113–38.
Eisenbeis, W., 1969: *Die Wurzel* ŠLM *im Alten Testament* (*BZAW* 113). Berlin.
Eisenstadt, S., 1967: *Sefatenu ha-'Ivrit he-ḥayyah*. Tel-Aviv.
Eissfeldt, O., 1965: *The Old Testament: an introduction*. Oxford.
1966: 'Etymologische und archäologische Erklärung alttestamentlicher Worte', *OrAn* 5, 165–76.
Eitan, E. and Ornan, U., 1971: 'Hebrew language, modern period', *EJ*, XVI, 1642–57.
Eitan, I., 1924: *A contribution to biblical lexicography*. New York.
1928–30: 'Hebrew and Semitic particles', *AJSL* 45, 197–211; 46, 22–51.
Elbogen, I., 1913: *Der jüdische Gottesdienst in seiner geschichtlichen Entwicklung*. Leipzig.
Eldar, I., 1978: *The Hebrew language tradition in medieval Ashkenaz*. 2 vols. Jerusalem. H.
1980–81: 'On Ben-Asher and Ben-Naftali', *Leshonenu* 45, 311–13. H.

1983–84: 'The two pronunciations of Tiberian resh', *Leshonenu* 48–49, 22–34. H.
1986: 'Be'ure millim eṭimologiyyim be-farshanut ha-Mikra u-ve-millona'ut ha-'Ivrit bi-yme ha-benayim', *P9WCJS*, Division D, *49–53.
Ellenbogen, M., 1962: *Foreign words in the Old Testament: their origin and etymology*. London.
1969: 'The common pre-historic origin of certain non-synonymous Semitic roots', *Journal of Hellenic studies* 1, 161–66.
1977: 'Linguistic archaeology, semantic interpretation, and the discovery of lost meanings', *P6WCJS*, I, 93–95.
Elliger, K., 1971: 'Der Sinn des hebräischen Wortes "šᵉfi"', *ZAW* 83, 317–29.
Ember, A., 1930: *Egypto-Semitic studies*. Ed. by F. Behnk. Leipzig.
Emerton, J.A., 1970: 'Were Greek transliterations of the Hebrew Old Testament used by Jews before the time of Origen?', *JTS*, n.s., 21, 17–31.
1973: 'The problem of vernacular Hebrew in the first century A.D. and the language of Jesus', *JTS*, n.s., 24, 1–23.
1977: 'The etymology of "hištaḥᵃwāh"', *OTS* 20, 41–55.
Enoch, P., 1965: 'Essai de phonétique comparée de l'hébreu et du français contemporain'. Doct. diss., Université de Franche-Comté, Besançon.
Epstein, I., 1946–47: *Meḥkarim ba-psikhologya shel ha-lashon we-ha-ḥinnukh ha-'Ivri: toldotaw u-fo'al ḥayyaw*. Jerusalem.
Epstein, J.N.,1957: *Introduction to Tannaitic literature: Mishna, Tosephta and halakhic* midrashim. Ed. by E.Z. Melamed. Jerusalem/Tel-Aviv. H.
1962: *Prolegomena ad litteras Amoraiticas, Talmud Babylonicum et Hieroloymitanum*. Ed. by E.Z. Melamed. Jerusalem. H.
1964: *Mavo le-nosaḥ ha-Mishnah*. 2nd ed. Jerusalem.
Ewald, H., 1848: 'Die assyrisch-hebräische punctuation', *Jahrbücher der biblischen Wissenschaft* 1, 160–72.
Eybers, I.H., 1972: 'The root "Ṣ-L" in Hebrew words', *JNSL* 2, 23–36.
Faber, A., 1984: 'Semitic sibilants in Afro-Asiatic context', *JSS* 29, 189–224.
Fabry, H.J., 1975: *Die Wurzel* šûḇ *in der Qumran-Literatur, zur Semantik eines Grundbegriffes*. Cologne.
Fainberg, Y., 1977: 'Linguistic and socio-demographic factors influencing the acceptance of Hebrew neologisms'. Doct. diss., Hebrew University, Jerusalem.
Falk, Z.W., 1960–69: 'Hebrew legal terms', *JSS* 5, 350–54; 12, 241–44; 14, 39–44.
Fassberg, S.E., 1987: 'Supra-linear ' and ^ in Palestinian pointed manuscripts of Hebrew and Aramaic from the Cairo Geniza', in D.M. Golomb and S.T. Hollis (eds.), *Working with no data. Semitic and Egyptian studies presented to Thomas O. Lambdin*, Winona Lake, pp. 75–103.
Federbush, S., 1967: *Ha-lashon ha-'Ivrit be-Yisra'el u-ba-'amim*. Jerusalem.
Fellman, J., 1973: *The revival of a classical language. Eliezer Ben Yehuda and the modern Hebrew language*. The Hague/Paris.
1974–75: 'The consonantal phonemes of Israeli Hebrew', *Abr-Nahrain* 15, 18–19.
1977: 'The linguistic status of Mishnaic Hebrew', *JNSL* 5, 21–22.
1985: 'A sociolinguistic perspective on the history of Hebrew', in J.A. Fishman (ed.), *Readings in the sociology of Jewish languages*, Leiden, pp. 27–34.
Fensham, F.C., 1978: 'The use of the suffix conjugation and the prefix conjugation in a few old Hebrew poems', *JNSL* 6, 9–18.
Fenton, T., 1921–22: 'Light on the history of the Hebrew verb', *JQR*, n.s., 12, 25–32.
Fenton, T.L., 1963: 'The Ugaritic verbal system'. Doct. diss., University of Oxford.
1970: 'The absence of a verbal formation "*yaqattal" from Ugaritic and North-West Semitic', *JSS* 15, 31–41.
1973: 'The Hebrew "tenses" in the light of Ugaritic', *P5WCJS*, IV, 31–39.
1979–80 'Questions connected with attestation of Ugaritic literature in biblical vocabulary', *Leshonenu* 44, 268–80. H.
Fernández Marcos, N., 1979: *Introducción a las versiones griegas de la Biblia*. Madrid.

Ferre, D., 1987: 'Pirqe Arnau de Vilanova'. Doct. diss., University of Granada.
Février, J.G., 1948: 'Remarques sur le calendrier de Gézer', *Semitica* 1, 33–41.
Field, F., 1875: *Origenis Hexaplorum quae supersunt*. 2 vols. Oxford.
Finet, A., 1956: *L'accadien des lettres de Mari*. Brussels.
Fink, F.D., 1980: 'The Hebrew grammar of Maimonides'. Doct. diss., Yale University.
Fischler, B.-Z., 1975: '"B", "K", "P" degushot we-refuyyot she-lo' ke-din ba-'Ivrit ha-Yisre'elit', in U. Ornan and B.-Z. Fischler (eds.), *Rosén memorial volume*, Jerusalem, pp. 86–99.
Fisher, L.R., 1971: *The Claremont Ras Shamra tablets*. Rome.
Fita, F., 1874: *Lápidas hebreas*. Gerona.
Fitzgerald, A., 1972: 'A note on G-stem "yinṣar" forms in the Old Testament', *ZAW* 84, 90–92.
1978: 'The interchange of "l", "n", and "r" in Biblical Hebrew', *JBL* 97, 481–88.
Fitzmyer, J.A., 1967: *The Aramaic inscriptions of Sefire*. Rome.
1970: 'The languages of Palestine in the first century A.D.', *CBQ* 32, 501–31.
1978: Review of Hoftijzer and van der Kooij 1976, *CBQ* 40, 93–95.
1979: *A wandering Aramean: collected Aramaic studies*. Missoula.
1990: *The Dead Sea Scrolls. Major publications and tools for study*. Rev. ed. Atlanta.
Fleisch, H., 1944: *Les Verbes à allongement vocalique interne en sémitique. Etudes de grammaire comparée*. Paris.
1947: *Introduction à l'étude des langues sémitiques. Eléments de bibliographie*. Paris.
Fleischer, E., 1973: *The poems of Shelomo ha-Babli*. Jerusalem.
1975: *Hebrew liturgical poetry in the Middle Ages*. Jerusalem. H.
Fohrer, G., 1968: *Introduction to the Old Testament*. Abingdon.
1968a: 'Twofold aspects of Hebrew words', in P.R. Ackroyd and B. Lindars (eds.), *Words and meanings. Essays presented to David Winton Thomas*, Cambridge, pp. 95–103.
1970: Review of Macuch 1969, *ZAW* 82, 163.
Fontinoy, C, 1961: *Le Duel dans les langues sémitiques*. Paris.
1971: 'Les noms de lieux en "-ayim" dans la Bible', *UF* 3, 33–40.
Foster, F.H., 1932–33: 'Is the Book of Job a translation of an Arabic original?', *AJSL* 49, 21–45.
Fraenkel, G., 1966: 'A structural approach to Israeli Hebrew', *JAOS* 86, 32–38.
Fraenkel, M., 1949: *Handbook of Hebrew slang, with vocabulary*. Jerusalem. H.
1970: *Zur Theorie der Lamed-He-Stämme; gleichzeitig ein Beitrag zur semitisch-indogermanischen Sprachverwandschaft*. Jerusalem.
Frankel, Z., 1841: *Vorstudien zu der Septuaginta*. Leipzig.
Franken, H.J., 1967: 'Texts from the Persian period from Tell Deir 'Allā', *VT* 17, 480–81.
Freedman, D.N., 1960: 'Archaic forms in early Hebrew poetry', *ZAW* 72, 101–07.
1964: 'A second Mesha inscription', *BASOR* 175, 50–51.
1969: 'The orthography of the Arad ostraca', *IEJ* 19, 52–56.
1972: 'Some observations on early Hebrew', *Biblica* 53, 413–20.
1972a: 'The broken construct chain', *Biblica* 53, 534–36.
1980: *Pottery, poetry, and prophecy. Studies in early Hebrew poetry*. Winona Lake.
Frey, J.–B., 1952: *Corpus inscriptionum iudaicarum: recueil des inscriptions juives qui vont du IIIe siècle avant Jésus-Christ au VIIe siècle de notre ère*. II: *Asie-Afrique*. Rome.
Frick, F.S., 1974: 'Another inscribed jar handle from El-Jīb', *BASOR* 213, 46–48.
Friedländer, M., 1894–95: 'A third system of symbols for the Hebrew vowels and accents', *JQR* 7, 564–68.
1896: 'Some fragments of the Hebrew Bible with peculiar abbreviations and peculiar signs for vowels and accents', *PSBA* 18, 86–98.
Friedmann, C.B., 1927: *Zur Geschichte der ältesten Mischna-Überlieferung*. Frankfurt-am-Main.
Friedmann, M., 1896: *Onkelos und Akylas*. Vienna.
Friedrich, J., 1922: 'Der Schwund kurzer Endvokale im Nordwestsemitischen', *ZS* 1, 3–14.
1923: 'Zum Phönizisch-Punischen', *ZS* 2, 1–10.
1949: 'Kanaanäisch und Westsemitisch', *Scientia* 84, 220–23.
1952: 'Semitisch und Hamitisch', *BO* 9, 154–57.

1964: 'Kleinigkeiten zum Phönizischen, Punischen und Numidischen', *ZDMG* 114, 225–31.
1965: 'Zur Stellung des Jaudischen in der nordwestsemitischen Sprachgeschichte', in H.G. Gueterbock and T. Jacobsen (eds.), *Studies in honor of Benno Landsberger on his 75th Birthday*, Chicago, pp. 425–29.
Friedrich, J. and Röllig, W., 1970: *Phönizisch-punische Grammatik*. 2nd ed. Rome.
Fronzaroli, P., 1955: *La fonetica ugaritica*. Rome.
1963: 'Sull elemento vocalico del lessema in semitico', *RSO* 38, 119–27.
1984 (ed.): *Studies in the language of Ebla*. Florence.
Fruchtman (Agmon-Fruchtman) M., 1985: ''Al tevah 'aḥat be-shir shel R. Shelomoh Ibn Gabirol', in Z. Malachi (ed.), *Studies in the work of Shlomo Ibn Gabirol*, Tel-Aviv, pp. 225–29.
Fu'ad, H.A., 1942: 'The Hebrew of the Samaritans', *BFAC*, 55–71.
1946–47: 'Beiträge zur Kenntnis der hebräisch-samaritanischen Sprache', *BFAC*, 1946, 19–37; 1947, 17–84.
Fuentes, M.J., 1980: *Vocabulario fenicio*. Barcelona.
1986: *Corpus de las inscripciones fenicias, púnicas y neopúnicas de España*. Barcelona.
1986a: 'Corpus de las inscripciones fenicias de España', *AuOr* 4, 5–30.
Fulco, W.J., 1978: 'The 'Ammān citadel inscription: a new collation', *BASOR* 230, 29–43.
1979: 'The Amman theater inscription', *JNES* 38, 37–38.
Futato, M., 1978: 'The preposition "beth" in the Hebrew Psalter', *Westminster Theological Journal* 41, 68–81.
Gai, A., 1982: 'The reduction of the tense (and other categories) of the consequent verb in North-West Semitic', *Orientalia* 51, 254–56.
von Gall, A.F., 1918: *Der hebräische Pentateuch der Samaritaner*. Giessen.
Gan, M., 1961–62: 'Ben kodesh le-ḥol', *LeshLA* 125, 67–77.
Garbell (Chanoch), I., 1946: 'Ha-mivṭa ha-'Ivri we-darkhe limmudo', *Leshonenu* 14, 39–47.
1946–47: 'Mivṭa ha-'iṣṣurim ha-'Ivriyyim be-fi Yehude 'Iran', *Leshonenu* 15, 62–74.
1954: 'The pronunciation of Hebrew in medieval Spain', in *Homenaje a Millás-Vallicrosa*, I, Barcelona, pp. 647–96.
1954a: 'Quelques observations sur les phonèmes de l'hébreu biblique et traditionel', *BSLP* 50, 231–43.
1955: 'The pronunciation of Hebrew in Israel', *Le Maître phonétique* 104, 26–29.
1959: 'The phonemic status of the shewa, the ḥªṭéfim and spirantal "begadkefat" in Masoretic Hebrew', *Leshonenu* 23, 152–55. H.
1968: 'Mesorot ha-mivṭa ha-'Ivri shel Yehude 'Asya we-'Afrika la-ḥaṭivotehen', *P4WCJS*, II, 453–54.
Garbini, G., 1930: 'La mimazione e la nunazione nelle lingue semitiche', *RSO* 12, 217–65.
1954–56: 'Note sul "calendario" di Gezer', *AION* 6, 123–30.
1956: *L'aramaico antico*. Rome.
1957: 'La congiunzione semitica "*pa-"', *Biblica* 38, 419–27.
1960: *Il semitico di nord-ovest*. Naples.
1964: 'Il consonantismo dell'ebraico attraverso il tempo', *AION* 14, 165–90.
1965: 'La semitistica: definizioni e prospettive di una disciplina', *AION* 15, 1–15.
1969: 'L'iscrizione di Siloe e gli annali dei re di Giuda', *AION* 19, 261–63.
1970: 'La lingua degli Ammoniti', *AION* 30, 249–58.
1970a: 'Una iscrizione bilingue sabeo-ebraica da Ẓafar', *AION* 30, 153–65.
1971: 'Il tema pronominale "p" in semitico', *AION* 31, 245–48.
1971a: 'The phonetic shift of sibilants in North-Western Semitic in the first millenium B.C.', *JNSL* 1, 32–38.
1972: *Le lingue semitiche. Studi di storia linguistica*. Naples.
1974: 'Ammonite inscriptions', *JSS* 19, 159–68.
1974a: 'Il causativo "hqtl" nel dialetto fenicio di Biblo', *AION* 34, 411–12.
1974b: 'La position du sémitique dans le chamito-sémitique', *APCI*, 21–26.
1977: 'I dialetti del fenicio', *AION* 37, 283–94.
1978: 'Su un'iscrizione di Khirbet el-Kom', *AION* 38, 191–93.

1978a: 'Sull'alfabetario di 'Izbet Ṣarṭah', *OrAn* 17, 287–95.
1979: 'L'iscrizione di Balaam Bar-Beor', *Henoch* 1, 166–88.
1979a: *Storia e problemi dell'epigrafia semitica antica*. Naples.
1981: 'Lingue e "varietà linguistiche" nel semitico nordoccidentale del I millennio a.C.', *AIΩN* 3, 95–111.
1982: 'I sigilli del regno di Israel', *OrAn* 21, 163–76.
1984: 'Dati epigrafici e linguistici sul territorio palestinese fino al VI sec. a.C.', *RBI* 32, 67–83.
Garfunkel, J, 1988: 'The meaning of the word "mpqd" in the Tel 'Ira ostracon', *Leshonenu* 52, 68–74. H.
Garr, W.R., 1985: *Dialect geography of Syria-Palestine 1000–586 B.C.E.* Philadelphia.
1985a: 'On vowel dissimilation in Hebrew', *Biblica* 66, 572–79.
Gaster, M., 1906: 'Massoretisches in Samaritanischen', in C. Bezold (ed.), *Orientalische Studien Theodor Nöldeke zum siebzigsten Geburtstag*, Giessen, pp. 513–36.
1925: *The Samaritans. Their history, doctrines and literature.* London.
Geiger, A., 1845: *Lehr- und Lesebuch zur Sprache der Mischnah.* Breslau.
1857: *Urschrift und Übersetzungen der Bibel*. Breslau.
1863: 'Die hebräische Grammatik bei den Samaritanern', *ZDMG* 17, 718–25.
Gelb, I.J., 1957: *Glossary of Old Akkadian.* Chicago.
1958: 'La lingua degli Amoriti', *Rendiconti dell'Accademia Nazionale dei Lincei*, 8th series, 13, 143–64.
1961: 'The early history of the West Semitic peoples', *JCS* 15, 27–47.
1961a: *Old Akkadian writing and grammar*. Chicago.
1968: 'An Old Babylonian list of Amorites', *JAOS* 88, 39–46.
1969: *Sequential reconstruction of Proto-Akkadian.* Chicago.
1980: *Computer-aided analysis of Amorite*. Chicago.
Geraty, L.T., 1972: 'Third century BC ostraca from Khirbet el-Kom'. Doct. diss., Harvard University.
Gerleman, G., 1948: *Synoptic studies in the Old Testament*. Lund.
1966: 'Bemerkungen zum alttestamentlichen Sprachstil', in W.C. van Unnik and A.S. van der Woude (eds.), *Studia biblica et semitica Theodoro Christiano Vriezen ... dedicata*, Wageningen, pp. 108–14.
1967: '"Heute", "Gestern" und "Morgen" im Hebräischen', *Teologinen Aikakauskirja* 72, 84–89.
1973: 'Die Wurzel "ŠLM"', *ZAW* 85, 1–14.
1974: 'Der Nichtmensch. Erwägungen zur hebräischen Wurzel "NBL"', *VT* 24, 147–58.
1978: 'Das übervolle Mass: ein Versuch mit "ḥæsed"', *VT* 28, 151–64.
Gertner, M., 1962: 'Terms of Scriptural interpretation: a study in Hebrew semantics', *BSOAS* 25, 1–27.
Gesenius, F.H.W., 1815: *De Pentateuchi samaritani origine, indole et auctoritate commentatio philologica-critica*. Halle.
Gevirtz, S., 1957: 'On the etymology of the Phoenician particle "aš"', *JNES* 16, 124–27.
1963: *Patterns in the early poetry of Israel*. Chicago.
1982: 'Formative 'ayin in Biblical Hebrew', *EI* 16, 57–66.
Gibson, A., 1981: *Biblical semantic logic: a preliminary analysis*. New York.
Gibson, J.C.L., 1963–64: 'Hebrew writing as a subject of linguistic investigation', *Glasgow University Oriental Society Transactions* 20, 49–62.
1966: 'Stress and vocalic change in Hebrew: a diachronic study', *Journal of Linguistics* 2, 35–56.
1969: 'On the linguistic analysis of Hebrew writing', *Archivum linguisticum* 17, 131–60.
1971: *Textbook of Syrian Semitic inscriptions*. I: Hebrew and Moabite inscriptions. Oxford.
Giesen, G., 1981: *Die Wurzel* ŠB' *"schwören"*. Bonn.
Ginsberg, H.L., 1935: 'Notes on the Lachish documents', *BJES* 3, 77–86. H.
1936: 'The rebellion and death of Ba'lu', *Orientalia* 5, 161–98.
1936a: Review of Diringer 1934, *ArOr* 8, 145–47.
1938: 'Lachish notes', *BASOR* 71, 24.
1940: 'Lachish ostraca new and old', *BASOR* 80, 10–13.
1940a: Review of Harris 1939, *JBL* 59, 550.
1948: *Studies in Daniel*. New York.

1950: *Studies in Kohelet*. New York.
1952: 'Supplementary studies in Kohelet', *PAAJR* 21, 35–62.
1955: 'The structure and contents of the Book of Kohelet', *SVT* 3, 138–49.
1959: 'The classification of the North-West Semitic languages', in H. Franke (ed.), *Akten des XXIV. Internationalen Orientalistenkongress (München 1957)*, Wiesbaden, pp. 256–57.
1967: 'Lexicographical notes', *SVT* 16, 71–82.
1970: 'The Northwest Semitic languages', in B. Mazar (ed.), *Patriarchs* (The world history of the Jewish people, first series; II), London, pp. 102–24, 270, 293.
1973: 'Ugaritico-Phoenicia', *JANES* 5, 131–47.
Ginsburg, C.D., 1880–1905: *The Massorah. Compiled from manuscripts, alphabetically and lexically arranged*. 4 vols. London.
1897: *Introduction to the Massoretico-critical edition of the Hebrew Bible*. London. Repr. 1966, with a Prolegomenon by H. Orlinsky.
Girón, L., 1976: *Pentateuco hebreo samaritano: Génesis*. Madrid.
Glinert, L., 1982: 'Negative and non-assertive in contemporary Hebrew', *BSOAS* 65, 434–70.
Glück, J.J., 1964–66: 'The verb "PR" in the Bible and in the Qumran literature', *RQ* 5, 123–27.
Glueck, N., 1938: 'The first campaign at Tell el-Kheleifeh (Ezion-Geber)', *BASOR* 71, 3–17.
1941: 'Ostraca from Elath', *BASOR* 82, 3–11.
1967: 'Some Edomite pottery from Tell el-Kheleifeh', *BASOR* 188, 8–38.
1970: 'Tell el-Kheleifeh inscriptions', in H. Goedicke (ed.), *Near Eastern studies in honor of William Foxwell Albright*, Baltimore/London, pp. 225–42.
Gluska, I., 1980–81: 'Nouns of the "maqṭel" pattern in Biblical and Mishnaic Hebrew and their meanings', *Leshonenu* 45, 280–98. H.
1983: 'The gender of "śadeh" in Mishnaic Hebrew', *Bar-Ilan* 20–21, 43–66. H.
Goeseke, H., 1958: 'Die Sprache der semitischen Texte Ugarits und ihre Stellung innerhalb des Semitischen', *WZMLU* 7, 623–52.
Goetze, A., 1938: 'The tenses of Ugaritic', *JAOS* 58, 266–309.
1939: 'Accent and vocalism in Hebrew', *JAOS* 59, 431–59.
1941: 'Is Ugaritic a Canaanite dialect?', *Language* 17, 127–38.
1942: 'The so-called intensive of the Semitic languages', *JAOS* 62, 1–8.
1958: 'The sibilants of Old Babylonian', *RA* 52, 137–49.
1959: 'Amurrite names in Ur III and early Isin texts', *JSS* 4, 193–203.
Goldberg, A., 1962–77: 'Le-ṭiv leshon ha-Mishnah', *Leshonenu* 26, 104–17; 41, 6–20.
Goldenberg, E., 1971: 'Hebrew language, medieval', *EJ*, XVI, 1607–42.
Goldenberg, G. 1971: 'Tautological infinitive', *IOS* 1, 36–85.
1974: 'L'étude du gouragué et la comparaison chamito-sémitique', in *IV Congresso Internazionale di Studi Etiopici (Roma, 10–15 aprile 1972)*, II, Rome, pp. 235–49.
1983: 'Doḥak ha-shir be-torat ha-lashon ha-'Ivrit bi-yme ha-benayim', in M. Bar-Asher, A. Dotan, G.B. Ṣarfatti, and D. Téné (eds.), *Hebrew language studies presented to Professor Zeev Ben-Ḥayyim*, Jerusalem, pp. 117–41.
Goodenough, E.R., 1953–65: *Jewish symbols in the Greco-Roman period*. 12 vols. New York.
Goodwin, D.W., 1969: *Text-restoration methods in contemporary U.S.A. biblical scholarship*. Naples.
Gordis, R., 1936–37: 'Studies in Hebrew roots of contrasted meanings', *JQR*, n.s., 27, 33–58.
1943: 'Notes on the asseverative "kaph" in Ugaritic and Hebrew', *JAOS* 63, 176–78.
1945: 'Studies in the relationship of Biblical and Rabbinic Hebrew', in S. Lieberman *et al.* (eds.), *Louis Ginzberg jubilee volume on ... his seventieth birthday*, New York, pp. 173–99.
1946–47: 'The original language of Qohelet', *JQR*, n.s., 37, 67–84.
1949–50: 'The translation theory of Qohelet re-examined', *JQR*, n.s., 40, 103–16.
1952: 'Kohelet – Hebrew or Aramaic?', *JBL* 71, 93–109.
1955: 'Was Kohelet a Phoenician?', *JBL* 74, 103–14.
Gordon, C.H., 1937: 'Lachish letter iv', *BASOR* 67, 30–32.
1937–38: 'The Aramaic incantation in cuneiform', *AfO* 12, 105–17.
1938: 'Notes on the Lachish letters', *BASOR* 70, 17–18.

1938a: 'The accentual shift in the perfect with waw consecutive', *JBL* 57, 319–25.
1940: 'The cuneiform Aramaic incantation', *Orientalia* 9, 29–38.
1940a: *Ugaritic grammar*. Rome.
1947: 'The new Amarna tablets', *Orientalia* 16, 1–21.
1947a: *Ugaritic handbook*. Rome.
1955: *Ugaritic manual*. Rome.
1955a: 'North Israelite influence on postexilic Hebrew', *IEJ* 5, 85–88.
1957: 'Egypto-Semitica', *RSO* 32, 269–77.
1963: 'Hebrew origins in the light of recent discoveries', in A. Altmann (ed.), *Biblical and other studies*, Cambridge, Mass., pp. 3–14.
1965: *Ugaritic textbook*. Rome.
1970: 'The accidental invention of the phonemic alphabet', *JNES* 29, 193–97.
1990: 'Eblaite and Northwest Semitic', in C.H. Gordon, G.A. Rendsburg, and N.H. Winter (eds.), *Eblaitica: essays on the Ebla archives and Eblaite language*, II, Winona Lake, pp. 127–39.

Görg, M., 1980: 'Ein problematisches Wort ["zdh"] der Siloah-Inschrift', *Biblische Notizen* 11, 21–22.

Goshen-Gottstein (Gottstein), M.H., 1957: 'The Thirteen Principles of Maimonides as translated by Al-Ḥarizi', *Tarbiz* 26, 185–96, 335–36. H.
1958: 'Linguistic structure and tradition in the Qumran documents', *ScrHier* 4, 101–37.
1958a: 'Die Qumran-Rollen und die hebräische Sprachwissenschaft 1948–1958', *RQ* 1, 103–12.
1959: 'Philologische Miszellen zu den Qumrantexten, 3: Der Qumran-Typus "y^{e}qoṭlehu" und das hebräische Verbalsystem', *RQ* 2, 43–51.
1959a: *The Qumran scrolls and their linguistic status. Studies in Hebrew and biblical philology*, I. Jerusalem/Tel-Aviv. H.
1960: 'The authenticity of the Aleppo Codex', *Textus* 1, 17–58.
1960a: *Text and language in Bible and Qumran*. Jerusalem.
1961: 'Le-darke ha-targum we-ha-metargemim bi-yme ha-benayim', *Tarbiz* 30, 385–95.
1962: 'Biblical manuscripts in the United States', *Textus* 2, 28–59.
1963: 'The rise of the Tiberian Bible text', in A. Altmann (ed.), *Biblical and other studies*, Cambridge, Mass., pp. 79–122.
1964: 'Semitic morphological structures. The basic morphological structure of Biblical Hebrew', in H.B. Rosén (ed.), *Studies in Egyptology and linguistics in honour of H.J. Polotsky*, Jerusalem, pp. 104–16.
1967: 'Hebrew biblical manuscripts. Their history and their place in the H.U.B.P. edition', *Biblica* 48, 243–90.
1968: 'The study of Mediaeval Hebrew as influenced by Arabic – achievements and objectives', *P4WCJS*, II, 109–12. H.
1969: 'The system of verbal stems in the classical Semitic languages', *PICSS*, 70–91.
1969a: *Introduction to the lexicography of Modern Hebrew*. Jerusalem/Tel-Aviv. H.
1973: 'Hebrew syntax and the history of the Bible text: a *pesher* in the MT of Isaiah', *Textus* 8, 100–06.
1975 (ed.): *The Book of Isaiah*. 2 vols. Jerusalem.
1976 (ed.): *The Aleppo Codex*. Jerusalem.
1985: 'Problems of Semitic verbal stems: a review', *BibOr* 42, 278–83.

Gottlieb, H., 1971: 'The Hebrew particle "nâ"', *AcOr* 33, 47–54.

Gottstein (Goshen-Gottstein), M.H., 1947: ''Iyyune-lashon 'al yesod targume millot ha-higgayon le-ha-RaMBaM', *Leshonenu* 15, 173–83.
1949: 'Afterthought and the syntax of relative clauses in Biblical Hebrew', *JBL* 68, 35–47.
1951: 'Syntax and vocabulary of medieval Hebrew as influenced by Arabic'. Doct. diss., Hebrew University, Jerusalem. H.
1951a: 'Ha-lashon ha 'Ivrit ha-medubberet ke-nose le-meḥkar', *Leshonenu* 17, 231–40.
1953: 'Studies in the language of the Dead Sea Scrolls', *JJS* 4, 104–07.
1953a: 'Mi-darke ha-targum we-ha-metargemim bi-yme ha-benayim', *Tarbiz* 23, 210–16.
1953–54: 'Balshanut mivnit u-poliṭikah leshonit', *LeshLA* 43, 17–24.

Gowan, D.E., 1971: 'The use of "ya'an" in Biblical Hebrew', *VT* 21, 168–85.

Graetz, H.L., 1844–45: Review of Geiger 1845, *LBdOr* 5, 822–27; 6, 30–31, 54–59, 76–78, 86–90.

Grant, E. and Wright, G.E., 1939: *Ain Shems excavations.* V. Haverford.

Grant, F.C., 1953: 'Modern study of the Jewish liturgy', *ZAW* 65, 59–77.

Gray, L.H., 1934: *Introduction to Semitic comparative linguistics.* New York.

1935–36: 'Observations on the phonology of "begadkefath"', *AJSL* 52, 171–77.

Greenberg, J.H. 1950: 'The patterning of root morphemes in Semitic', *Word* 6, 162–81.

1952: 'The Afro-Asiatic (Hamito-Semitic) present', *JAOS* 72, 1–9.

Greenberg, M., 1956: 'The stabilization of the Hebrew Bible reviewed in the light of the biblical materials from the Judean Desert', *JAOS* 76, 157–67.

1970: Ḫab/piru and Hebrews, in B. Mazar (ed.), *Patriarchs* (The world history of the Jewish people, first series; II), London, pp. 188–200, 279–81, 296.

Greenfield, J.C., 1958–59: 'Lexicographical notes', *HUCA* 29, 203–28; 30, 141–51.

1969: 'Amurrite, Ugaritic and Canaanite', *PICSS*, 92–101.

1969a: 'The "periphrastic imperative" in Aramaic and Hebrew', *IEJ* 19, 199–210.

1977: 'The prepositions "'ad"/"'al" in Aramaic and Hebrew', *BSOAS* 40, 371–72.

1978: 'The dialects of Early Aramaic', *JNES* 37, 93–99.

Greenspahn, F.E., 1980: 'The number and distribution of *hapax legomena* in Biblical Hebrew', *VT* 30, 8–19.

1984: Hapax legomena *in Biblical Hebrew. A study of the phenomenon and its treatment since antiquity with special reference to verbal forms*. Chico.

Griffiths, J.G., 1944–45: 'Did Jesus speak Aramaic?', *ET* 56, 327–28.

Grimme, H., 1896: *Grundzüge der hebräischen Akzent- und Vokallehre.* Freiburg.

1915: 'Die jemenische Aussprache des Hebräischen und Folgerungen daraus für die ältere Sprache', in Gotthold Weil (ed.), *Festschrift Eduard Sachau, zum siebzigsten Geburtstage gewidmet von Freunden und Schulern*, Berlin, pp. 125–42.

Grintz, J.M., 1957: *Sefer Yehudit: Taḥazoret ha-nosaḥ ha-mekori.* Jerusalem.

1958–59: "Ivrit li-lshon ha-sefer we-ha-dibbur bi-yme Bayit Sheni ha-'aḥaronim', *Eshkolot* 3, 125–44.

1960: 'Hebrew as the spoken and written language in the last days of the Second Temple', *JBL* 79, 32–47.

Grøndahl, F., 1967: *Die Personennamen der Texte aus Ugarit.* Rome.

Gross, W., 1974: 'Die Herausführungsformel–zum Verhältnis von Formel und Sprache', *ZAW* 86, 425–53.

1975: 'Das nicht-substantivierte Partizip als Prädikat im Relativsatz hebräisches Prosa', *JNSL* 4, 23–27.

1976: *Verbform und Funktion:* wayyiqṭol *für die Gegenwart? Ein Beitrag zur Syntax poetischer althebräischer Texte.* St. Ottilien.

1981: 'Syntaktische Erscheinungen am Anfang althebräischer Erzählungen: Hintergrund und Vordergrund', *SVT* 32, 131–45.

Guggenheimer, E. and H., 1972–73: 'Notes on the Talmudic vocabulary', *Leshonenu* 37, 105–12. H.

Guidi, I., 1878–79: 'Della sede primitiva dei popoli semitici', *Atti della Real Accademia dei Lincei*, Memorie delle Classi di scienze morali, storiche e filologiche, third series, 3, 566–615.

Guillaume, A., 1965: *Hebrew and Arabic lexicography: a comparative study.* Leiden.

Gulkowitsch, L., 1931: *Die Bildung von Abstraktbegriffen in der hebräischen Sprachgeschichte.* Leipzig.

Gumpertz, Y.F., 1953: *Mivṭa'e sefatenu*. Jerusalem.

Gundry, R.H., 1964: 'The language milieu of first-century Palestine: its bearing on the authenticity of the Gospel tradition', *JBL* 83, 404–08.

Gutman, D., 1973: 'The phonology of Massoretic Hebrew', *HCL* 7, 1–52.

Gwilliam, G.H., 1890–91: 'The vernacular of Palestine in the time of Our Lord and the remains of it in St. Mark', *ET* 2, 133–34.

Hackett, J.A., 1980: 'Studies in the plaster text from Tell Deir 'Allā'. Doct. diss., Harvard University.

1984: *The Balaam text from Deir 'Allā*. Chico.

1984a: 'The dialect of the plaster text from Tell Deir 'Allā', *Orientalia* 53, 57–65.

1986: 'Some observations on the Balaam tradition at Deir 'Allā', *BA* 49, 216–22.

Hadas-Lebel, M., 1981: *Histoire de la langue hébraïque, des origines à l'époque de la Mishna*. 3rd ed. Paris.

Hadley, J.M., 1987: 'The Khirbet el-Qôm inscription', *VT* 37, 50–62.

1987a: 'Some drawings and inscriptions on two pithoi from Kuntillet 'Ajrud', *VT* 37, 180–211.

Halévy, J., 1901: 'L'origine de la transcription du texte hébreu en caractères grecs dans les Hexaples d'Origène', *JA* 9, 335–41.

Halkin, A.S., 1963: 'The medieval Jewish attitude toward Hebrew', in A. Altmann (ed)., *Biblical and other studies*, Cambridge, Mass., pp. 233–48.

1972–73: 'Mosheh ibn 'Ezra' u-leshon ha-shir', *Molad* 5, 316–21.

Hallo, W.W. and Tadmor, Ḥ., 1977: 'A lawsuit from Hazor', *IEJ* 27, 1–11.

Hammershaimb, E., 1941: *Das Verbum im Dialekt von Ras Schamra*. Copenhagen.

1963: 'On the so-called *infinitivus absolutus* in Hebrew', in D. Winton Thomas and W.D. McHardy (eds.), *Hebrew and Semitic studies presented to Godfrey Rolles Driver*, Oxford, pp. 85–94.

1977: 'De aramaiske indskrifter fra udgravningene Deir 'Allā', *Dansk teologisk tidskrift* 40, 217–42.

Haneman, G., 1974: 'Uniformization and differentiation in the history of two Hebrew verbs', *ANDRL*, II, 24–30. H.

1974a: 'Le-masoret ha-ketiv shel Ketav-yad Parmah ha-menukkad (Ketav-yad Romi 66)', in E.Y. Kutscher, S. Liebermann, and M.Z. Kaddari (eds.), *Henoch Yalon memorial volume*, Ramat-Gan, pp. 84–98.

1976: "Al millat-ha-yaḥas "ben" ba-Mishnah u-ba-Mikra', *Leshonenu* 40, 33–53.

1980: *A morphology of Mishnaic Hebrew according to the tradition of the Parma Manuscript (De Rossi 138)*. Tel-Aviv. H.

Haramati, S., 1971: 'A basic word list for the training of Hebrew readers in the diaspora', in S. Kodesh (ed.), *Kamrat memorial volume: essays on the teaching of Hebrew as a second language*, Jerusalem, pp. 62–97.

Harkavy, A. and Strack, H.L., 1875: *Catalog der hebräischen Bibelhandschriften der Kaiserlichen Öffentlichen Bibliothek in St. Petersburg*. St. Petersburg.

Harper, R.F., 1909: *Assyrian and Babylonian literature*. New York.

Harris, Z.S., 1936: *A grammar of the Phoenician language*. New Haven.

1939: *Development of the Canaanite dialects. An investigation in linguistic history*. New Haven.

1941: 'Linguistic structure of Hebrew', *JAOS* 61, 143–67.

1948: 'Componential analysis of a Hebrew paradigm', *Language* 24, 87–91.

1954: 'Transfer grammar', *IJAL* 20, 259–70.

Hartmann, A.T., 1825–26: *Thesauri linguae hebraicae e Mischna augendi*. 3 vols. Rostock.

Hartom, E.S., 1950–51: "Al be'ayat ha-neginah shel he-'avar ha-mehuppakh le-'atid be-'Ivrit', *Leshonenu* 17, 88–89.

Harviainen, T., 1977: *On the vocalism of the closed unstressed syllables in Hebrew*. Helsinki.

Har-Zahab, Z., 1930: *Leshon dorenu. Ma'amre bikkoret 'al ha-tofa'ot ha-shonot she-nitgalu be-'esrot ha-shanim ha-'aḥaronot be-haḥaya'at ha-lashon ha-'Ivrit u-she'ar ma'amarim be-'inyene ha-lashon*. Tel-Aviv.

Hazan, E., 1980: 'Poetic elements in the liturgical poetry of Yehuda Halevi'. Doct. diss., Hebrew University, Jerusalem. H.

Hayon, Y., 1972: 'Having and being in Modern Hebrew', *HCL* 5, 10–23.

1973: *Relativization in Hebrew: a transformational approach*. The Hague.

Hecker, K., 1982: 'Das Arabische im Rahmen der semitischen Sprachen', in W. Fischer (ed.), *Grundriss der arabischen Philologie*, I: *Sprachwissenschaft*, Wiesbaden, pp. 6–15.

van der Heide, A., 1974: 'A biblical fragment with Palestinian-Tiberian ("pseudo-Ben Naftali") punctuation in the Leyden University Library', *Le Muséon* 87, 415–23.

Heidenheim, M., 1884–96: *Bibliotheca samaritana*. 3 vols. Leipzig/Weimar.

Heinemann, J., 1963–64: *Ha-tefillah bi-tkufat ha-Tanna'im we-ha-'Amora'im.* Jerusalem.
Helck, W., 1962: *Die Beziehungen Ägyptens zu Vorderasien im 3. und 2. Jahrtausend v. Chr.* Wiesbaden.
Held, M., 1962: 'The "yqtl"-"qtl" ("qtl"-"yqtl") sequences of identical verbs in Biblical Hebrew and in Ugaritic', in M. Ben-Horin, B.D. Weinryb, and S. Zeitlin (eds.), *Studies and essays in honor of Abraham A. Neuman*, Leiden, pp. 281–90.
1965: 'The action-result (factitive-passive) sequence of identical verbs in Biblical Hebrew and Ugaritic', *JBL* 84, 272–82.
1968: 'The root "ZBL"/"SBL" in Akkadian, Ugaritic and Biblical Hebrew', *JAOS* 88, 90–96.
1970–71: 'Studies in biblical homonyms in the light of Akkadian', *JANES* 3, 47–55.
1973: 'Pits and pitfalls in Akkadian and Biblical Hebrew', *JANES* 5, 173–90.
1974: 'Hebrew "ma'gal": a study in lexical parallelism', *JANES* 6, 107–16.
1979: 'On terms for deportation in the Old Babylonian royal inscriptions with special reference to Yahdunlim', *JANES* 11, 53–62.
Heltzer, M.L., 1976: 'Zu einer neuen ammonitischen Siegelinschrift', *UF* 8, 441–42.
Herdner, A., 1963: *Corpus de tablettes en cunéiformes alphabétiques découvertes à Ras Shamra-Ugarit de 1929 à 1939.* Paris.
Herr, L.G., 1978: *The scripts of ancient Northwest Semitic seals.* Missoula.
Hestrin, R. and Dayagi (Dayagi-Mendeles), M., 1974: 'A seal impression of a servant of King Hezekiah', *IEJ* 24, 27–29.
Hestrin, R. and Dayagi-Mendeles (Dayagi), M., 1978–79: *Ḥotamot mi-yeme Bayit Rishon.* Jerusalem.
Hestrin, R., Israeli, Y., Meshorer, Y., and Eitan, A., 1973: *Inscriptions reveal. Documents from the time of the Bible, the Mishna and the Talmud.* Israel Museum catalogue; 100. 2nd rev. ed. Jerusalem.
Hetzron, R., 1967: 'Agaw numerals and incongruence in Semitic', *JSS* 12, 169–97.
1969: 'The evidence for perfect "*y'aqtul" and jusive "*yaqt'ul" in Proto-Semitic', *JSS* 14, 1–21.
1969–70: 'Third person singular pronoun suffixes in Proto-Semitic (with a theory on the connective vowels in Tiberian Hebrew)', *OrSu* 18, 101–27.
1974: 'La division des langues sémitiques', *APCI*, 181–94.
Hill, A.E., 1981: 'The Book of Malachi: its place in post-exilic chronology linguistically reconsidered'. Doct. diss., University of Michigan.
Hill, D., 1967: *Greek words and Hebrew meanings. Studies in the semantics of soteriological terms.* Cambridge.
Hillel, F., 1891: *Die Nominalbildung in der Mischna.* Frankfurt-am-Main.
Hilliger, J.W., 1679: *Summarium linguae aramaeae, i.e., chaldaeo-syro-samaritanae.* Wittenberg.
Hodge, C.T., 1969: 'Afroasiatic pronoun problems', *IJAL* 35, 366–76.
1970: 'Afroasiatic. An overview', *LSWANA*, 237–54.
Hoffman, Y., 1982: 'The root "QRB" as a legal term', *JNSL* 10, 67–73.
1986: 'Leshono shel ha-makor ha-Kohani u-she'elat zeman ḥibburo', in M.A. Friedman and M. Gil (eds.), *Te'uda IV: studies in Judaica*, Tel-Aviv, pp. 13–22.
Hoftijzer, J., 1963: 'La *nota accusativi* "'t" en phénicien', *Le Muséon* 76, 195–200.
1965: 'Remarks concerning the use of the particle "'t" in Classical Hebrew', *OTS* 14, 1–99.
1973: 'The nominal clause reconsidered', *VT* 23, 446–510.
1981: *A search for method: a study in the syntactic use of the* h locale *in Classical Hebrew.* Leiden.
1985: *The function and use of the imperfect forms with* nun paragogicum *in Classical Hebrew.* Assen.
Hoftijzer, J. and van der Kooij, G., 1976: *Aramaic texts from Deir 'Alla.* Leiden.
1991 (eds.): *The Balaam text from Deir 'Alla re-evaluated. Proceedings of the international symposium held at Leiden 21–24 August 1989.* Leiden.
Holladay, W.L., 1958: *The root* šûbh *in the Old Testament with particular reference to its usages in covenantal texts.* Leiden.
Holm-Nielsen, S., 1960: *Hodayot – psalms from Qumran.* Aarhus.
Hommel, E., 1917: *Untersuchungen zur hebräischen Lautlehre.* I. Leipzig.

Honeyman, A.M., 1948: 'Phoenician inscriptions from Karatepe', *Le Muséon* 61, 43–57.
1953: 'The syntax of the Gezer calendar', *JRAS*, 53–58.
Honnorat, M., 1933: *Démonstration de la parenté des langues indoeuropéennes et sémitiques.* Paris.
1933a: *Démonstration de la parenté de la langue chinoise avec les langues japhétiques, sémitiques et chamitiques.* Paris.
Horn, S.H., 1967–68: 'The Amman citadel inscription', *ADAJ* 12–13, 81–83.
1969: 'The Ammān citadel inscription', *BASOR* 193, 2–13.
Horowitz, E., 1960: *How the Hebrew language grew.* New York.
Hospers, J.H., 1966: 'A hundred years of Semitic comparative linguistics', in W.C. van Unnik and A.S. van der Woude (eds.), *Studia biblica et semitica Theodoro Christiano Vriezen ... dedicata*, Wageningen, pp. 138–51.
1973 (ed.): *A basic bibliography for the study of the Semitic languages.* I. Leiden.
Hruby, K., 1964: 'La survivance de la langue hébraïque pendant la période post-exilienne', *Travaux de l'Institut Catholique [de Paris]* 10, 109–20.
Huesman, J., 1956: 'Finite uses of the infinitive absolute', *Biblica* 37, 271–95.
1956a: 'The infinitive absolute and the waw + perfect problem', *Biblica* 37, 410–34.
Huffmon, H.B., 1965: *Amorite personal names in the Mari texts.* Baltimore.
Hughes, J.A., 1970: 'Another look at the Hebrew tenses', *JNES* 29, 12–24.
Hulst, A.R., 1960: *Old Testament translation problems.* Leiden.
Hummel, H.D., 1957: 'Enclitic "mem" in early Northwest Semitic, especially Hebrew', *JBL* 76, 85–107.
Hurvitz, A., 1964–66: 'Observations on the language of the third apocryphal psalm from Qumran', *RQ* 5, 225–32.
1967: 'The language and date of Psalm 151 from Qumran', *EI* 8, *82–87. H.
1967a: 'The usage of "šš" and "bwṣ" in the Bible and its implications for the date of P', *HTR* 60, 117–21.
1968: 'The chronological significance of "Aramaisms" in Biblical Hebrew', *IEJ* 18, 234–40.
1972: *The transition period in Biblical Hebrew. A study in post-exilic Hebrew and its implications for the dating of Psalms.* Jerusalem. H.
1972a: *Leshono shel Ben Sira.* Jerusalem.
1974: 'The evidence of language in dating the Priestly Code', *RB* 81, 24–56.
1974a: 'The date of the prose-tale of Job linguistically reconsidered', *HTR* 67, 17–34.
1975: 'Leshono shel sippur-ha-misgeret be-Sefer Iyov u-mekomah be-toldot ha-'Ivrit ha-Mikra'it', *BM* 20, 457–72.
1976 ''Al shelifat ha-na'al she-bi-Mgillat Rut', *Shenaton* 1, 45–49.
1982: *A linguistic study of the relationship between the Priestly source and the Book of Ezekiel.* Paris.
1983: 'The language of the Priestly source and its historical setting – the case for an early date', *P8WCJS*, Division A, 83–94.
Hurwitz, S.T.H., 1913: *Root-determinatives in Semitic speech. A contribution to Semitic philology.* New York.
Idelsohn, A.Z., 1913: 'Die gegenwärtige Aussprache des Hebräischen bei Juden und Samaritanern', *MGWJ* 57, 527–45, 697–721.
1917: *Phonographierte Gesänge und Ausspracheproben des Hebräischen der jemenitischen, persischen und syrischen Juden.* Vienna.
Ilani, N., 1982: 'Harḥavat kevuṣot ha-beḥirah shel pe'alim mikra'im bi-lshon yamenu', *HCL* 19, *5–17.
Israel, F., 1975: 'L'"olio da toeletta" negli ostraca di Samaria', *RSO* 49, 17–20.
1977: 'Un nuovo sigillo ammonita?', *BeO* 19, 167–70.
1979: 'The language of the Ammonites', *OLP* 10, 143–59.
1979a: 'Miscellanea idumea', *RBI* 27, 171–203.
1979b: 'Un'ulteriore attestazione dell'evoluzione fonetica "ā" > "ō" nel semitico di nord-ovest', *RSF* 7, 159–61.
1984: 'Classificazione tipologica delle inscrizioni ebraiche antiche', *RBI* 32, 48–69.
1986: 'Observations on Northwest Semitic seals', *Orientalia* 55, 70–77.

1987: 'Les sceaux ammonites', *Syria* 64, 141–46.

Isserlin, B.S.J., 1972: 'Epigraphically attested Judean Hebrew, and "upper class" and "popular" speech variants in Judea during the 8th–6th centuries B.C.', *Australian journal of biblical archaeology* 2, 197–203.

Jabotinsky, Z., 1930: *Ha-mivṭa ha-'Ivri*. Tel-Aviv.

Jackson, K.P., 1983: *The Ammonite language of the Iron Age*. Chico.

Janssens, G., 1957: 'Contribution au déchiffrement des inscriptions pseudo-hiéroglyphiques de Byblos', *La Nouvelle Clio* 7–8, 361–77.

1982: *Studies in Hebrew historical linguistics based on Origen's Secunda*. Leuven.

Japhet, S., 1967: 'Ḥillufe shorashim ba-po'al ba-eksim ha-makbilim be-Sefer Divre ha-Yamim', *Leshonenu* 31, 165–79, 261–79.

1968: 'The supposed common authorship of Chronicles and Ezra-Nehemia', *VT* 18, 330–71.

Jaros, K., 1982: *Hundert Inschriften aus Kanaan und Israel*. Freiburg.

Jastrow, M., 1886–1903 (repr. 1989): *A dictionary of the Targumim, the Talmud Babli and Yerushalmi, and the midrashic literature*. 2 vols. London/New York.

Jean, C.-F., 1946: 'Notes sur l'amorite des lettres de Mari', *L'Ethnographie* 38, 33–38.

1950: 'Les noms propres de personnes dans les lettres de Mari et dans les plus anciens textes du Pentateuque', in A. Parroth (ed.), *Studia Mariana*, Leiden, pp. 63–98.

Jean, C.-F. and Hoftijzer, J., 1965: *Dictionnaire des inscriptions sémitiques de l'ouest*. Leiden.

Jellicoe, S., 1968: *The Septuagint and modern study*. Oxford.

Jenni, E., 1967: 'Faktitiv und Kausativ von "'BD" "zugrunde gehen"', *SVT* 16, 143–57.

1968: *Das hebräische Pi'el*. Zurich.

1971: '"Wollen" und "nicht wollen" im Hebräischen', in *Hommages à André Dupont-Sommer*, Paris, pp. 202–07.

1972: 'Zur Verwendung von "'attā" "jetzt" im Alten Testament', *TZ* 28, 5–12.

1973: 'Zur Funktion der reflexiv-passiven Stammformen im Biblisch-Hebräisch', *P5WCJS*, IV, 61–70.

Jepsen, A., 1958: '"Pardes"', *ZDPV* 74, 665–68.

1969: 'Kleine Bemerkungen zu drei westsemitischen Inschriften', *MIO* 15, 2–4.

Jirku, A., 1953: 'Zum *Infinitivus absolutus* im Ugaritischen', *JKF* 3, 111–15.

1957: 'Eine "Af'el"-Form im Ugaritischen?', *AfO* 111, 129–30.

1963: 'Der Buchstabe Ghain im Ugaritischen', *ZDMG* 113, 481–82.

1970: 'Die Umschrift ugaritischer Laryngale durch den akkadischen Buchstaben "ú"', *ArOr* 38, 129–30.

Johnson, B., 1979: *Hebräisches Perfekt und Imperfekt mit vorangehenden* wᵉ-. Lund.

Jongeling, B., 1958–59: 'Les formes "qṭwl" dans l'hébreu des manuscrits de Qumrân', *RQ* 1, 483–94.

1971: *A classified bibliography of the finds in the Desert of Judah 1958–1969*. Leiden.

1973: 'Qumran, Murabba'at, Masada, etc.', in Hospers (ed.), pp. 214–65.

1973a: 'La particule "raq"', *OTS* 18, 97–107.

Joüon, P., 1937: 'Parallèles palmyréniens à l'infinitif du type "bo'ᵃḵah" (Gn. 10, 19 etc.)', *Biblica* 18, 334–36.

Kaddari, M.Z., 1964–65: 'Sadot semanṭiyyim bi-lshon ha-megillot ha-genuzot', *Leshonenu* 29, 226–37.

1964–65a: ''Al herkeve shem-to'ar ba-'Ivrit shel yamenu', *LeshLA* 159–60, 195–206.

1964–66: 'The Root "TKN" in the Qumran texts', *RQ* 5, 219–24.

1967–68: 'Ha-tikbolet ha-mikra'it mi-beḥinah semanṭit', *Leshonenu* 32, 37–45.

1968: *Semantic fields in the language of the Dead Sea Scrolls*. Jerusalem. H.

1970: *The medieval heritage of Modern Hebrew usage*. Tel-Aviv. H.

1972: 'Grammatical notes on Saul Lieberman's Tosefta Kifshutah (Zera'im)', *ANDRL*, I, 163–73. H.

1973: 'Problems in Biblical Hebrew syntax', *P5WCJS*, IV, 232–33, 274–75.

1974: '"Mah le-" + N(oun) P(hrase) preceeding clauses in Mishnaic Hebrew', *ANDRL*, II, 85–95. H.

1976: 'Masav ha-meḥkar ba-'Ivrit ha-Yisre'elit bi-tḥum ha-taḥbir we-ha-millona'ut', *Bar-Ilan* 13, 341–54.

1977–78: 'Nitpa'al ke-benoni ba-lashon ha-rabbanit (ha-Š u-T) – mah ṭivo?', *Leshonenu* 42, 190–202.

1978: ''Iyyun be-toledot ha-lashon ha-'Ivrit ha-modernit', *Bikkoret u-farshanut* 11–12, 5–17.

1978–79: ''Al ha-po'al "HYH" bi-lshon ha-Mikra', *Bar-Ilan* 16–17, 112–25.

1981: 'Homonymy and polysemy of Nitpa'el forms in the language of the *responsa* literature', *Bar-Ilan* 18–19, 233–47. H.

1982: 'Yaḥas ha-wittur bi-lshon ha-Mikra', in B. Uffenheimer (ed.), *Te'uda II: Bible studies* in memoriam *Joshua M. Grintz*, Tel-Aviv, pp. 325–48.

Kahle, P.E., 1898: *Textkritische und lexikalische Bemerkungen zum samaritanischen Pentateuchtargum*. Leipzig.

1901: 'Beiträge zur Geschichte der hebräischen Punktation', *ZAW* 21, 273–317.

1901a: 'Zur Geschichte der hebräischen Akzente', *ZDMG* 55, 167–194.

1902: *Der masoretische Text des Alten Testaments nach der Überlieferung der babylonischen Juden*. Leipzig.

1913: *Masoreten des Ostens*. Leipzig.

1921: 'Die überlieferte Aussprache des Hebräischen und die Punktation der Masoreten', *ZAW* 39, 230–39. Repr. in *Opera minora*, Leiden (1956), pp. 38–47.

1922: 'Die masoretische Überlieferung des hebräischen Bibeltextes', in Bauer and Leander, pp. 71–162.

1925: 'Die Punktation der Masoreten', *BZAW* 41, 167–72.

1927–30: *Masoreten des Westens*. 2 vols. Stuttgart.

1928: 'Die hebräischen Bibelhandschriften aus Babylonien', *ZAW* 46, 113–37.

1937: 'Index codicum Veteris Testamenti babylonicorum', in R. Kittel and P.E. Kahle, *Biblia hebraica*, 3rd ed., Stuttgart, pp. xxx–xxxiii.

1950: 'Zur Aussprache des Hebräischen bei den Samaritanern', in W. Baumgartner, O. Eissfeldt, K. Elliger, and L. Rost (eds.), *Festschrift Alfred Bertholet zum 80. Geburtstag*, Tübingen, pp. 281–86. Repr. in *Opera minora*, Leiden (1956), pp. 180–86.

1951: 'The Hebrew Ben Asher Bible manuscripts', *VT* 1, 161–67.

1958: 'Das palästinische Pentateuchtargum und das zur Zeit Jesu gesprochene Aramäisch', *ZNW* 49, 100–116.

1959: *The Cairo Geniza*. 2nd ed. Oxford.

1960: 'Die Aussprache des Hebräischen in Palästina vor der Zeit der tiberischen Masoreten', *VT* 10, 375–85.

1960a: 'Das zur Zeit Jesu gesprochene Aramäisch: Erwiderung', *ZNW* 51, 55.

1961: 'Hebreo premasorético', *Sefarad* 21, 240–50.

1961a: *Der hebräische Bibeltext seit Franz Delitzsch*. Stuttgart.

1962: Pre-Massoretic Hebrew', *Textus* 2, 1–7.

Kamhi, D.J., 1971: 'The gentilitial adjective in Hebrew', *JRAS*, 2–8.

1971a: 'The term "tō'ar" in Hebrew and its status as a grammatical category', *BSOAS* 34, 256–72.

1973: 'The root "ḤLQ" in the Bible', *VT* 23, 235–39.

Karmiel, Y., 1969–70: 'Metaphors in Mapu's writings', *Leshonenu* 34, 306–08. H.

Katz, E., 1967: *Die Bedeutung des* hapax legomenon *der Qumraner Handschriften* HUAHA. Bratislava.

Kaufman, I.T., 1966: 'The Samaria ostraca. A study in ancient Hebrew palaeography'. 2 vols. Doct. diss., Harvard University.

Kaufman, S.A., 1980: 'The Aramaic texts from Deir 'Allā', *BASOR* 239, 71–74

Kautzsch, E., 1902: *Die Aramaismen im Alten Testament*. I: Lexicalischer Teil. Halle.

Keller, C., 1683: *Philologicarum lucubrationum sylloge, hoc est, Praecipuarum linguarum orientis*. Jena.

1705: *Horae samaritanae, hoc est, Excerpta Pentateuchi samaritanae versionis*. 2nd ed. Jena/Frankfurt-am-Main.

Kelso, J., 1948: *The ceramic vocabulary of the Old Testament*. New Haven.

Kena'ani, J., 1930–31: *Millon konkordanṣyoni li-lshon ha-piyyuṭim*. Jerusalem.

1932–33: 'Ḥiddushe lashon bi-tkufat ha-Haskalah', *Leshonenu* 5, 59–72.
Kenyon, K.M., 1966: *Amorites and Canaanites*. London.
Kesterson, J.C., 1984: 'Tense usage and verbal syntax in selected Qumran documents'. Doct. diss., University of Washington, D.C.
Kienast, B., 1960: 'Das Punktualthema "*japrus" und seine Modi', *Orientalia* 29, 151–67.
Kippenberg, H.G., 1971: *Garizim und Synagoge*. Berlin/New York.
Kirchheim, R., 1851: *Karme Shomeron. Introductio in librum talmudicum de Samaritanis*. Frankfurt-am-Main.
Klar, B.M., 1951: 'Le-toledot ha-mivṭa ha-'Ivri bi-yme ha-benayim', *Leshonenu* 17, 72–75.
1953–54: *Meḥkarim we-'iyyunim ba-lashon, ba-shirah, u-ba-sifrut*. Tel Aviv.
Klarberg, H., 1970–71: 'Stress patterns in spoken Israeli Hebrew', *Abr-Nahrain* 10, 129–33.
Klatzkin, J., 1928–33: *Thesaurus philosophicus linguae hebraicae*. 4 vols. Berlin.
Klausner, J., 1938: *Dikduk kaṣar shel ha-'Ivrit ha-ḥadashah*. 2nd ed. Tel-Aviv.
1939: *Eli'ezer ben-Yehudah: toledotaw u-mif'al ḥayyaw*. Tel-Aviv.
1949: *Ha-lashon ha-'Ivrit lashon ḥayyah*. Tel-Aviv.
1957: *Ha-'Ivrit he-ḥadashah u-ve'ayoteha*. Tel-Aviv.
Klopfenstein, M.A., 1972: *Scham und Schande nach dem Alten Testament. Eine begriffsgeschichtliche Untersuchung zu den hebräischen Wurzeln* bôš, klm *und* ḥpr. Zurich.
Klostermann, E., 1896: 'Die Mailänder Fragmente der Hexapla', *ZAW* 16, 334–37.
Knudtzon, J.A., 1907–15: *Die El-Amarna Tafeln*. 2 vols. Leipzig.
Kober, M., 1929: *Zum Machsor Jannai*. Frankfurt-am-Main.
Kochavi, M., 1977: 'An ostracon of the period of the Judges from 'Izbet Ṣarṭah', *TAJ* 4, 1–13.
1978: *Aphek-Antipatris 1974–1977. The inscriptions*. Tel-Aviv.
Kogut, S., 1969–70: 'Does the form "q^{e}ṭol" = "qoṭel" exist in the Bible?', *Leshonenu* 34, 20–25. H.
1984: 'The language of Sefer Ḥasidim, its linguistic background and methods of research', in I. Twersky (ed.), *Studies in medieval Jewish history and literature*, II, Cambridge, pp. 95–108.
Köhler, L., 1952–53: 'Syntactica, i–iv', *VT* 2, 374–77; 3, 84–87, 188–89, 299–305.
Kohn, S., 1865: *De Pentateucho samaritano eiusque cum versionibus antiquis nexu. Dissertatio inauguralis*. Leipzig.
1876: *Zur Sprache, Literatur und Dogmatik der Samaritaner*. Leipzig.
König, F.E., 1874: *Gedanke, Laut und Akzent als die drei Factoren der Sprachbildung comparativ und physiologisch am Hebräischen dargestellt*. Weimar.
1897: *Syntax der hebräischen Sprache*. Leipzig.
1902: 'Zur Syntax der Zahlwörter im Alten Testament', *AJSL* 18, 129–48.
1913: 'Über den Lautwert des hebräischen 'Ain', *ZDMG* 87, 65–66.
Könnecke, C., 1885: *Die Behandlung der hebräischen Namen in der Septuaginta*. Stargard.
Kopelovitch, Z., 1984: '"'^{a}ḇāl" and "'ællā'" conjunctions in Modern Hebrew', *HS* 25, 132–40.
Kopf, L., 1976: *Studies in Arabic and Hebrew lexicography*. Ed. by M.H. Goshen-Gottstein. Jerusalem.
Körner, J., 1969: 'Die Bedeutung der Wurzel "BR'" im Alten Testament', *OLZ* 64, 533–40.
Koskinen, K., 1964: 'Kompatibilität in den dreikonsonantigen hebräischen Wurzeln', *ZDMG* 114, 16–58.
Kosmala, H., 1965: 'The three nets of Belial. A study in the terminology of Qumran and the New Testament', *ASTI* 4, 91–113.
1969: 'The term "geber" in the Old Testament and in the Scrolls', *SVT* 17, 159–69.
Kraeling, G., 1953: *The Brooklyn Museum Aramaic papyri. New documents of the fifth century B.C. from the Jewish colony at Elephantine*. New Haven.
Krahmalkov, C.R., 1969: 'The Amorite enclitic particle "ta/i"', *JSS* 14, 201–04.
1970: 'Studies in Phoenician and Punic grammar', *JSS* 15, 181–88.
1970a: 'The enclitic particle "ta/i" in Hebrew', *JBL* 89, 218–19.
1976: 'An Ammonite lyric poem', *BASOR* 223, 55–57.
1979: 'On the third feminine singular of the perfect in Phoenician-Punic', *JSS* 24, 25–28.
Krauss, S., 1898–1900: *Griechische und lateinische Lehnwörter im Talmud, Midrasch und Targum*. 2 vols. Berlin.

1907: 'Die Kaufmann'sche Mischnah-Handschrift', *MGWJ* 15, 54–66, 142–63, 323–33, 445–61.
Kropat, A., 1909: *Die Syntax des Autors der Chronik verglichen mit der seiner Quellen. Ein Beitrag zur historischen Syntax des Hebräischen* (*BZAW* 16). Giessen.
Kuhnigk, W., 1974: *Nordwest-semitische Studien zum Hoseabuch*. Rome.
Kuhr, E., 1929: *Die Ausdrucksmittel der konjunktionslosen Hypotaxe in der ältesten hebräischen Prosa*. Leipzig.
Kuryłowicz, J., 1949: 'Le système verbal du sémitique', *BSLP* 45, 47–56.
1957–58: 'Esquisse d'une théorie de l'apophonie en sémitique', *BSLP* 53, 1–38.
1962: *L'Apophonie en sémitique*. The Hague.
1972: *Studies in Semitic grammar and metrics*. Wrocław.
1973: 'Verbal aspect in Semitic', *Orientalia* 42, 114–20.
Kustár, P., 1972: *Aspekt im Hebräischen*. Basle.
Kutsch, E., 1970: 'Sehen und bestimmen. Die Etymologie von "b^{e}rit"', in A. Kuschke and E. Kutsch (eds.), *Archäologie und Altes Testament. Festschrift für Kurt Galling z. 8. Jan. 1970*, Tübingen, pp. 165–78.
Kutscher, E.Y., 1949–52: 'Studies in Galilean Aramaic', *Tarbiz* 21, 192–205; 22, 53–63, 185–192; 23, 36–60. Repr. in 1977, pp. *169–225. H.
1952: 'Bavu'a shel ha-lashon ha-'Ivrit bi-yme ha-Bayit ha-Sheni', *Haaretz*, 28 September; 17, 31 October.
1956: 'Inscriptions from Jerusalem of the First Temple period', in M. Avi-Yonah (ed.), *Sefer Yerushalayim*, I, Jerusalem, pp. 349–50. Repr. in 1977, pp. *10–26. H.
1956a: 'Hebrew and Aramaic inscriptions from Jerusalem of the Second Temple period', in M. Avi-Yonah (ed.), *Sefer Yerushalayim*, I, Jerusalem, pp. 349–50. Repr. in 1977, pp. *27–35. H.
1956b: 'Leshon ḥakhamim, mah ṭivah?', *Haaretz*, 22 June; 29 July.
1956c: 'Modern Hebrew and "Israeli" Hebrew', *Conservative Judaism* 10.3, 28–45.
1957: 'The language of the "Genesis Apocryphon": a preliminary study', *ScrHier* 4, 1–35. Repr. in 1977, pp. 3–36.
1960: 'Das zur Zeit Jesu gesprochene Aramäisch', *ZNW* 5, 146–54.
1961: *Millim we-toledotehen*. Jerusalem.
1961a: '"Mḥwz" = "harbour" in the Dead Sea Scrolls', *BIES* 25, 161–62. H.
1961–62: 'The Hebrew and Aramaic letters of Bar Koseba and his contemporaries', *Leshonenu* 25, 117–33; 26, 7–23. Repr. in 1977, pp. *36–70. H.
1963: 'Mishnaic Hebrew', in S. Lieberman (ed.), *Sefer Ḥanokh Yalon*, Jerusalem, pp. 246–80. Repr. in 1977, pp. *73–107. H.
1963–64: 'Aramaic calque in Hebrew', *Tarbiz* 33, 118–30. Repr. in 1977, pp. *394–406. H.
1964: 'Mišnisches Hebräisch', *Rocznik orientalistyczny* 28, 35–48.
1964–65: Review of Garbini 1960, *Leshonenu* 29, 47–58, 115–28. Repr. in 1977, pp. *279–90. H.
1965: 'Contemporary studies in North-Western Semitic', *JSS* 10, 21–51.
1966: Yemenite Hebrew and ancient pronunciation', *JSS* 11, 217–25.
1967: 'Mittelhebräisch und Jüdisch-Aramäisch im neuen Köhler-Baumgartner', *SVT* 16, 158–175. Repr. in 1977, pp. 156–73.
1967a: 'Ha-hashpa'at ha-Yawanit 'al ha-lashon ha-'Ivrit', *Maḥanayim* 112, 54–57.
1969: 'Articulation of the vowels "u", "i" in [Greek and Latin] transcriptions of Biblical Hebrew, in Galilean Aramaic and in Mishnaic Hebrew', in E.Z. Melamed (ed.), *Sefer zikkaron le-Benjamin de Vries*, Jerusalem, pp. 218–51. Repr. in 1977, pp. *135–68. H.
1969a: 'Studies in the grammar of Mishnaic Hebrew according to Ms. Kaufmann', in M.Z. Kaddari (ed.), *Sefer Bar-Ilan le-mada'e ha-ruaḥ we-ha-ḥevrah*, X.2, pp. 51–77. Repr. in 1977, pp. *108–34. H.
1969b: 'Words and their history', *Ariel* 25, 64–74.
1970: 'Aramaic', *EJ*, III, 259–87.
1970a: 'Aramaic', *LSWANA*, 347–412. Repr. in 1977, pp. 90–155.
1971: 'Hebrew language, the Dead Sea Scrolls', *EJ*, XVI, 1583–90.
1971a: 'Hebrew language, Mishnaic', *EJ*, XVI, 1590–1607.

1972: 'The present state of research into Mishnaic Hebrew (especially lexicography) and its tasks', *ANDRL*, I, 3–28. H.

1972a: 'Some problems of the lexicography of Mishnaic Hebrew and its comparisons with Biblical Hebrew', *ANDRL*, I, 29–82. H.

1972b: 'Addenda to the lexicographical section', *ANDRL*, I, 83–94. H.

1972c: 'Trivia', *ANDRL*, I, 5–105. H.

1974: *The language and linguistic background of the complete Isaiah Scroll (1QIsa[a])*. Leiden.

1977: *Hebrew and Aramaic studies*. Ed. by Z. Ben-Ḥayyim, A. Dotan, and G.B. Ṣarfatti. Jerusalem.

1982: *A history of the Hebrew language*. Ed. by R. Kutscher. Jerusalem.

Kutscher, R., 1972: 'A new inscription from 'Amman', *Qadmoniot* 5, 27–28. H.

Labuschagne, C.J., 1966: 'The emphasizing particle "gam" and its connotations', in W.C. van Unnik and A.S. van der Woude (eds.), *Studia biblica et semitica Theodoro Christiano Vriezen ... dedicata*, Wageningen, pp. 193–203.

1966a: '"Teraphim" – a new proposal for its etymology', *VT* 16, 115–17.

1973: 'The particles "hen" and "hinneh"', *OTS* 18, 1–14.

Lacau, P., 1970: *Les Noms des parties du corps en égyptien et en sémitique*. Paris.

de Lagarde, P., 1889: *Übersicht über die im Aramäischen, Arabischen und Hebräischen übliche Bildung der Nomina*. Göttingen.

Lambdin, T.O., 1953: 'Egyptian loan-words in the Old Testament', *JAOS* 73, 145–155.

1970: 'The junctural origin of the West Semitic definite article', in H. Goedicke (ed.), *Near Eastern studies in honor of William Foxwell Albright*, Baltimore/London, pp. 315–33.

Lambert, M., 1892: 'Remarques sur le pluriel des noms en hébreu', *REJ* 25, 99–111.

1893: 'Le vav conversif', *REJ* 26, 47–62.

1897: 'De la formation des racines trilitères fortes', in G.A. Kohut (ed.), *Semitic studies in memory of ... Alexander Kohut*, Berlin, pp. 354–62.

1897a: 'La trilitéralité des racines med. gem. et med. u', *REJ* 34, 203–12.

Lancellotti, A., 1983: 'Il vocalismo ebraico', *FrancLA* 33, 15–52.

Landau, J., 1822: *Geist und Sprache der Hebräer nach dem zweiten Tempelbau*. Prague.

Landau, R., 1967: 'The bound phrase in contemporary Hebrew: its character, sources and developmental trends'. Doct. diss., Bar-Ilan University. H.

Lande, I., 1949: *Formelhafte Wendungen der Umgangssprache im Alten Testament*. Leiden.

Landersdorfer, S., 1916: *Sumerisches Sprachgut im Alten Testament: eine biblisch-lexikalische Studie*. Leipzig.

Landes, G.M., 1962: 'Ammon, Ammonites', in *Interpreter's dictionary of the Bible*, I, New York, pp. 108–14.

Landsberger, B., 1926: 'Prinzipienfragen der semitischen, speziell der hebräischen, Grammatik', *OLZ* 29, 967–76.

1938: 'Die Gestalt der semitischen Wurzel', in *Atti del XIX Congresso Internazionale degli Orientalisti. Roma ... 1935*, Rome, pp. 450–52.

1954: 'Assyrische Königsliste und "dunkles Zeitalter"', *JCS* 8, 31–45, 47–73.

1967: 'Akkadisch-hebräische Wortgleichungen', *SVT* 16, 176–204.

de Langhe, R., 1948: 'Documents et témoignages nouveaux concernant l'origine et l'évolution de l'alphabet phénicien', *BibOr* 5, 73–83.

Lapide, P., 1972–75: 'Insights from Qumran into the languages of Jesus', *RQ* 8, 483–501.

Lapp, P.N., 1970: 'The Tell Deir 'Allā challenge to Palestinian archaeology', *VT* 20, 243–56.

Laroche, E., 1968: *Glossaire de la langue hourrite*. Paris.

LaSor, W.S., 1956: 'Secondary opening of syllables originally closed with gutturals', *JNES* 15, 246–50.

1958: *Bibliography of the Dead Sea Scrolls 1948–1957*. Pasadena.

Lavi, A., 1979: 'A comparative study of Al-Ḥariri's *maqamat* and their Hebrew translation by Al-Ḥarizi'. Doct. diss., University of Michigan.

Leahy, T.W., 1957: 'A study of the language of the Essene Manual of Discipline'. Doct. diss., Johns Hopkins University.

1960: 'Studies in the syntax of 1QS', *Biblica* 41, 135–57.

Leander, P., 1920: 'Einige hebräische Lautgesetze chronologisch geordnet', *ZDMG* 74, 61–77.
1928: *Laut- und Formenlehre des Ägyptisch-Aramäischen.* Gothenberg.
1936: 'Bemerkungen zur palästinischen Überlieferung des Hebräischen', *ZAW* 54, 91–99.
van Leeuwen, C., 1973: 'Die Partikel "'im"', *OTS* 18, 15–48.
Lehman, M.R., 1964–66: 'Identification of the Copper Scroll based on its technical terms', *RQ* 5, 97–105.
Lek'iašvili, A., 1971: 'Über die Kasusflexion in den semitischen Sprachen', *ZP* 24, 76–90.
Lemaire, A., 1973: 'L'ostracon "Ramat Négeb" et la topographie historique du Négeb', *Semitica* 23, 11–25.
1976: 'Prières en temps de crise: les inscriptions de Khirbet Beit Lei', *RB* 83, 558–68.
1977: 'Les inscriptions de Khirbet el-Qôm et l'ashérah de YHWH', *RB* 84, 595–608.
1977a: *Inscriptions hébraïques*. I: *Les Ostraca*. Paris.
1978: 'Les ostraca paléo-hébraïques des fouilles de l'Ophel', *Levant* 10, 156–61.
1979–84: 'La langue de l'inscription sur plâtre de Deir 'Alla', *GLECS* 24–28, 317–40.
1980: 'Notes d'épigraphie nord-ouest sémitique', *Semitica* 30, 17–32.
1981: "Classification des estampilles royales judéennes", *EI* 15, 54–60.
1981a: 'Une inscription paléo-hébraïque sur grenade en ivoire', *RB* 88, 236–39.
1984: 'Date et origine des inscriptions hébraïques et phéniciennes de Kuntillet 'Ajrud', *SEL* 1, 131–43.
1984a: 'Probable head of priestly scepter from Solomon's Temple surfaces in Jerusalem: inscription containing name of God incised on ivory pomegranate', *Biblical Archaeology Review* 10, 24–29.
1985: 'Les inscriptions de Deir 'Alla et la littérature araméenne antique', *Comptes Rendus de l'Académie des Inscriptions et Belles-Lettres*, 270–85.
1988: 'Recherches actuelles sur les sceaux nord-ouest sémitiques', *VT* 38, 220–30.
Lemaire, A. and Vernus, P., 1980: 'Les ostraca paléo-hébreux de Qadesh-Barnéa', *Orientalia* 49, 341–45.
1983: 'L'ostracon paléo-hébreu n° 6 de Tell Qudeirat (Qadesh-Barnéa)', in M. Görg (ed.), *Fontes atque pontes. Eine Festgabe für Hellmut Brunner*, Wiesbaden, pp. 302–26.
Leslau, W., 1943: 'South-East Semitic (Ethiopic and South-Arabic)', *JAOS* 63, 4–14.
1958: *Ethiopic and South Arabic contributions to the Hebrew lexicon*. Berkeley/Los Angeles.
1959: 'The position of Ethiopic in Semitic – Akkadian and Ethiopic', in H. Franke (ed.), *Akten des XXIV. Internationalen Orientalistenkongress (München 1957)*, Wiesbaden, pp. 251–53.
1962: 'Semitic and Egyptian comparisons', *JNES* 21, 44–49.
1969: *Hebrew cognates in Amharic*. Wiesbaden.
Levenston, E.A., 1965: 'The translation paradigm: a technique of contrastive syntax', *International review of applied linguistics in language teaching* 3, 221–25.
1966: 'A scale-category description of the syntax of Israeli Hebrew'. Doct. diss., University of London.
1966a: 'A classification of language differences', *International review of applied linguistics in language teaching* 4, 199–206.
1967–68: 'The structure of the Hebrew clause', *Leshonenu* 32, 389–98. H.
Levi della Vida, G., 1961 (ed.): *Linguistica semitica: presente e futuro*. Rome.
1968: 'The Shiloaḥ inscription reconsidered', *BZAW* 103, 162–66.
Levias, C., 1898–99: 'The Palestinian vocalization', *AJSL* 15, 157–64.
Levin, I., 1962: '"Zᵉmān" we-"tēḇēl" be-shirat ha-ḥol ha-'Ivrit bi-Sfarad (bi-yme ha-benayim)', *OYS* 5, 68–79.
1986: *Mystical trends in the poetry of Solomon ibn Gabirol*. Lod. H.
Levin, S., 1971: *The Indo-European and Semitic languages: an exposition of structural similarities related to accent, chiefly in Greek, Sanscrit, and Hebrew*. New York.
1973: 'The accentual system of Hebrew in comparison with the ancient Indo-European languages', *P5WCJS*, IV, 71–77.
1981: 'The correspondence between Hebrew and Arabic pausal verb-forms', *ZDMG* 131, 229–33.

Levine, B.A., 1969: 'Notes on a Hebrew ostracon from Arad', *IEJ* 19, 49–51.
1981: 'The Deir 'Allā plaster inscriptions', *JAOS* 101, 195–205.
1983: 'Late language in the Priestly source: some literary and historical observations', in *P8WCJS*, Division A, 69–82.
Levy, J., 1924: *Wörterbuch über die* Talmudim *und* Midraschim. 2nd ed. Berlin/Vienna.
Levy, K., 1936: *Zur masoretischen Grammatik.* Stuttgart.
Levy, R., 1964: *Trésor de la langue des juifs français au moyen age.* Austin.
Lewin, B.M., 1932: 'Essa Meshali le-Rav Se'adyah Ga'on', *Tarbiz* 3, 147–60.
1943: 'Essa Meshali', in Y. Fishman (ed.), *Rav Se'adyah Ga'on. Koveṣ torani-mada'i*, Jerusalem, pp. 501–676.
Lexa, F., 1922: *Comment se révèlent les rapports entre les langues hamitiques, sémitiques et la langue égyptienne dans la grammaire des pronoms personnels, des verbes et dans les numéraux cardinaux 1–9*. Prague.
Licht, J., 1956–57: The term "gwrl" in the Dead Sea Scrolls', *BM* 1, 90–99. H.
Lidzbarski, M., 1898: *Handbuch der nordsemitischen Epigraphik nebst ausgewählte Inschriften.* 2 vols. Weimar.
1902–15: *Ephemeris für semitische Epigraphik.* 3 vols. Giessen.
1907: *Kanaanäische Inschriften (moabitisch, althebräisch, phönizisch, punisch).* Giessen.
Lidzbarski, M., Gray, G.B., and Pilcher, E.J., 1909: 'An old Hebrew calendar-inscription from Gezer', *PEFQS* 41, 26–34.
Lieberman, S., 1939: 'Ḥazzanut Yannai', *Sinai* 2, 221–50.
1942: *Greek in Jewish Palestine.* New York.
1950: *Hellenism in Jewish Palestine.* New York.
Lipiński, E., 1969: 'Trois hébraïsmes oubliés ou méconnus', *RSO* 44, 83–101.
1974: 'From Karatepe to Pyrgi. Middle Phoenician miscellanea', *RSF* 2, 45–61.
1980: 'Notes lexicographiques et stylistiques sur le Livre de Job', *FolOr* 21, 65–82.
Lipschütz, E.M., 1920: *Vom lebendigen Hebräisch: ein sprachgeschichtlicher Versuch.* Berlin.
Lipschütz, L., 1935: *Der Bibeltext der tiberischen Masoretenschulen: Ben Asher – Ben Naftali. Eine Abhandlung des Mischael ben Uzziel veröffentlicht und untersucht*. Bonn.
1962: 'Kitāb al-Khilaf. Mishael Ben Uzziel's treatise on the differences between Ben Asher and Ben Naftali', *Textus* 2, *1–58. H.
1964: 'Kitāb al-Khilaf, the Book of the Ḥillufim', *Textus* 4, 1–29.
Lisowsky, G., 1940: *Die Transkription der hebräischen Eigennamen des Pentateuch in der LXX*. Basle.
Livny, I.J., 1957: *Lashon ke-hilkhatah, perakim be-taḥbir u-ve-signon*. Jerusalem.
Loewenstamm, S.E., 1971: 'Grenzgebiete ugaritischer Sprach-und Stilvergleichung: Hebräisch des Zweitens Tempels, Mittelhebräisch, Griechisch', *UF* 3, 93–100.
1973–74: 'On the predicative use of the suffix joined to a subject-noun in Hebrew and Ugaritic', *Leshonenu* 38, 147–48. H.
Löhr, M., 1894: 'Der Sprach-Gebrauch des Buches der Klagelieder', *ZAW* 14, 31–50.
Loprieno, A., 1980: *The sequential forms in Late Egyptian and Biblical Hebrew: a parallel development of verbal systems.* Malibu.
Loretz, O., 1960: 'Die hebräische Nominalform "qattāl"', *Biblica* 41, 411–16.
1977: 'Die ammonitische Inschrift von Tell Siran', *UF* 9, 169–71.
1984: *Habiru-Hebräer. Eine sozio-linguistische Studie über die Herkunft des Gentiliziums* 'ibrî *vom Apellativum* ḫabiru (*BZAW* 160). Berlin/New York.
Loss, N.M., 1970: 'Il discorso indiretto nell'ebraico biblico', *RBI* 18, 195–202.
Löw, L., 1870–71: *Graphische Requisiten und Erzeugnisse bei den Juden*. Leipzig.
Löwinger, D.S., 1960: 'The Aleppo Codex and the Ben Asher tradition', *Textus* 1, 59–111.
1961: 'Remnants of a Hebrew dialect in 1QIsa[a]', in C. Rabin and Y. Yadin (eds.), *Essays on the Dead Sea Scrolls in memory of E.L. Sukenik*. Jerusalem, pp. 141–61. H.
1968–69 (ed.): 'Keter Aram Ṣovah o Dikduke ha-Ṭe'amim: mahadurah ḥadashah shel Dikduke Ṭe'amim', *Tarbiz* 38, 186–204.
1970 (ed.): *Torah, Nevi'im, u-Khetuvim, Ketav-yad Leningrad B19a.* Jerusalem.

1971 (ed.): *Torah, Nevi'im, u-Khetuvim, Ketav-yad Kahir*. Jerusalem.
Löwisohn, S., 1812: *Bet ha-'osef*. Prague.
Lundin, A.G., 1987: 'Ugaritic writing and the origin of the Semitic consonantal alphabet', *AuOr* 5, 91–99.
Luzzatto, S.D., 1846–47: 'Über die Sprache der Mischnah', *LBdOr* 7, 829–32; 8, 1–5, 46–48, 55–57.
Maag, V., 1953: 'Morphologie des hebräischen Narrativs', *ZAW* 65, 86–88.
Macalister, R.A.S., 1912: *The excavation of Gezer 1902–1905 and 1907–1909*. 2 vols. London.
McCarter, P.K., 1980: 'The Balaam texts from Deir 'Allā: the first combination', *BASOR* 239, 49–60.
McCarter, P.K. and Coote, R.B., 1973: 'The spatula inscription from Byblos', *BASOR* 212, 16–21.
McCarthy, C., 1981: *The* tiqqune sopherim *and other theological corrections in the Masoretic Text of the Old Testament*. Freiburg.
MacDonald, J., 1964 'The particle "'t" in Classical Hebrew: some new data on its use with the nominative', *VT* 14, 264–75.
1966: 'New thoughts on a biliteral origin for the Semitic verb', *ALUOS* 5, 63–85.
1975: 'Some distinctive characteristics of Israelite spoken Hebrew', *BO* 32, 162–75.
McFall, L., 1982: *The enigma of the Hebrew verbal system*. Sheffield.
Macuch, R., 1965: *Handbook of classical and modern Mandaic*. Berlin.
1969: *Grammatik des samaritanischen Hebräisch*. Berlin.
1970: 'Der liquide Apikal und die apikale Liquide des samaritanischen Hebräisch', in R. Stiehl and H.E. Stier (eds.), *Beiträge zur alten Geschichte und deren Nachleben*, II, Berlin, pp. 164–75.
1973: 'Zur Grammatik des samaritanischen Hebräisch', *ArOr* 41, 192–211.
1989: 'Samaritan Hebrew, Samaritan Aramaic', in A.D. Crown (ed.), *The Samaritans*, Tübingen, pp. 531–84.
Maisler (Mazar), B., 1948: 'The historical background of the Samaria ostraca', *JPOS* 22, 117–33.
1950–51: 'The excavations at Tell Qasîle: preliminary report', *IEJ* 1, 61–76, 125–40, 194–218.
1951: 'Two Hebrew ostraca from Tell Qasîle', *JNES* 10, 265–67.
Malamat, A., 1970: 'Northern Canaan and the Mari texts', in J.A. Sanders (ed.), *Near Eastern archaeology in the twentieth century. Essays in homage to N. Glueck*, Garden City, pp. 164–77.
Malone, J.L., 1971: 'Wave theory, rule ordering, and Hebrew-Aramaic segolation', *JAOS* 91, 44–66.
1972: 'A Hebrew flip-flop rule and its historical origins', *Lingua* 30, 422–48.
1979: 'Textually deviant forms as evidence for phonological analysis: a service of philology to linguistics', *JANES* 2, 37–40.
Mandel, G., 1981: 'She'elah Nikhbadah and the revival of Hebrew', in E. Silberschlag (ed.), *Eliezer Ben-Yehuda, a symposium in Oxford*, Oxford, pp. 25–29.
Mann, Y., 1932: 'Ha-ḥibbur ha-piyyuṭi 'Essa Meshali le-Rav Se'adyah Ga'on', *Tarbiz* 3, 380–92.
Mannes, S., 1899: *Über den Einfluss des Aramäischen auf den Wortschatz der Mischna*. I. Berlin.
Mansoor, M., 1958: 'Some linguistic aspects of the Qumran texts', *JSS* 3, 40–54.
Mansour, J., 1959–60: ''Al haṭ'amat mille'el ba-'Ivrit ha-medubberet', *LeshLA* 106–07, 99–105.
1965–66: ''Al yiddu'o shel ha-ṣeruf "shemo shel shem" be-khitve S.Y. Agnon', *Leshonenu* 30, 113–35.
1968: *''Iyyunim bi-lshono shel S.Y. Agnon*. Tel-Aviv.
Marcel, J.J., 1819: *Leçons de langue samaritaine données au Collège Royal de France*. Paris.
Marcus, D., 1968: 'The three alephs in Ugaritic', *JANES* 1, 50–60.
1969: 'Studies in Ugaritic grammar, i', *JANES* 2, 55–62.
1969a: 'The stative and the waw consecutive', *JANES* 2, 37–40.
1970–71: 'The Qal passive in Ugaritic', *JANES* 3, 102–111.
Margain, J., 1973: 'Le "-ah de direction" en hébreu', *GLECS* 14, 1–17.
1973a: '"Yakhol" et l'expression de la modalité "pouvoir"', *GLECS* 14, 47–64.
1976: '"'Abhâl" et l'expression de l'adversatif en hébreu ancien', *GLECS* 15, 17–38.
1976a: *Essais de sémantique sur l'hébreu ancien. Monèmes fonctionnels et autonomes. Modalités*. Paris.
Margaliot, E., 1958–59: 'Li-sh'elat sefat ha-dibbur bi-zman Bayit Sheni u-bi-tkufat ha-Mishnah we-ha-Talmud', *Leshonenu* 23, 49–54.

1960: ''Ivrit la-dibbur', *Leshonenu* 24, 238–41.

1962–63. ''Ivrit wa-'Aramit ba-Talmud u-ba-midrash', *Leshonenu* 27–28, 20–33.

1970: 'Ha-yeḥasim she-ben ha-'Ivrit ha-Talmudit we-ha-'Ivrit shel yamenu', in S. Abramsky (ed.), *Sefer Shemu'el Yeivin: meḥkarim ba-Mikra, arkhe'ologyah, lashon, we-toledot Yisra'el mugashim lo be-hagi'o le-sevah*, Jerusalem, pp. 440–59.

Margalit, B, 1989: 'Some observations on the inscriptions and drawings from Khirbet el-Qôm', *VT* 39, 371–75.

Margalith, O., 1983: '"Keleb": homonym or metaphor?', *VT* 33, 491–95.

Margoliouth, G., 1893: 'The supralinear punctuation, its origin, the different stages of its development and its relation to other Semitic systems of punctuation', *PSBA* 15, 164–205.

Margolis, M.L., 1909–10: 'The pronunciation of the šᵉwa' according to the Hexaplaric material', *AJSL* 26, 62–70.

1925–26: 'Transliterations in the Greek Old Testament', *JQR*, n.s., 16, 117–25.

Martin, M., 1957: 'The use of second person singular suffixes in 1QIsa[a]', *Le Muséon* 70, 127–44.

1958: *The scribal character of the Dead Sea Scrolls*. 2 vols. Leuven.

1961: 'A preliminary report after re-examination of the Byblian inscriptions', *Orientalia* 30, 46–78.

1962: 'Revision and reclassification of the Proto-Byblian signs', *Orientalia* 31, 250–71, 339–83.

Martinet, A., 1953: 'Remarques sur le consonantisme sémitique', *BSLP* 49, 67–78.

Martínez, E.R., 1967: *Hebrew-Ugaritic index to the writings of Mitchell J. Dahood*. Rome.

Maschler, H., 1966: 'Ways of expressing modality in Modern Hebrew'. Doct. diss., Hebrew University, Jerusalem. H.

Masclef, F., 1743: *Grammatica Hebraica*. 2nd ed. Paris.

Masson, E., 1967: *Recherches sur les plus anciens emprunts sémitiques en grec*. Paris.

Masson, M., 1967–69: 'La composition en hébreu israélien', *GLECS* 12–13, 106–30.

1968: 'La dérivation dénominale en hébreu israélien'. Doct. diss., University of Paris.

1973: 'À propos de l'origin du suffix "-nik" en hébreu israélien', *GLECS* 14, 79–87.

1974: 'Remarques sur les diminutifs en hébreu israélien', *APCI*, 256–79.

1976: *Les Mots nouveaux en hébreu moderne*. Paris.

1976a: 'Remarques sur l'exploitation selective des schemes classiques en hébreu israélien', *GLECS* 15, 47–54.

1976b: 'Notes sur les adjectifs en "CaCiC" de l'hébreu israélien', *GLECS* 15, 111–15.

1989: *Langue et idéologie: les mots étrangers en hébreu moderne*. Paris.

Matmon-Cohen, Y., 1935–38: 'Ha-'Ivrit aḥare galut Bavel', *Leshonenu* 6, 172–88; 7, 136–44, 257–65; 8, 15–20, 122–30; 9, 65–75.

Mayer, L.A., 1964: *Bibliography of the Samaritans*. Ed. by D. Broadribb. Leiden.

Mayer, M.L., 1960: 'Ricerche sul problema dei rapporti fra lingue indoeuropee e lingue semitiche', *Acme* 13, 77–100.

Mazar, A., 1973: 'Excavations at Tell Qasîle, 1971–72', *IEJ* 23, 65–71.

Mazar (Maisler), B., 1970: 'The inscription on the floor of the synagogue in En-Gedi. Preliminary survey', *Tarbiz* 40, 18–23. H.

Mazar (Maisler), B. and Rabin, C., 1970: 'Mesha'', *EB*, IV, 921–29.

Mazars, P., 1968: 'Sens et usage de l'Hitpael', *Divinitas* 12, 353–64.

Medan, M., 1951: 'Millonam ha-mikra'i shel ḥakhame-Yisra'el bi-Sfarad', *Leshonenu* 17, 110–14.

1969: 'The Academy of the Hebrew Language', *Ariel* 25, 40–47.

Meek, T.J., 1930–31: 'The co-ordinate adverbial clause in Hebrew', *AJSL* 47, 51–52.

1940: 'The Hebrew accusative of time and place', *JAOS* 60, 224–33.

1941: 'Again the accusative of time in Amos 1:1', *JAOS* 61, 190–91.

1945: 'The syntax of the sentence in Hebrew', *JBL* 64, 1–13.

1955–56: 'Result and purpose clauses in Hebrew', *JQR*, n.s., 46, 40–43.

Mehlmann, I., Rosén, H.B., and Shaked, J., 1960: *A foundation word list of Hebrew*. Jerusalem. H.

Meillet, A., 1921 (repr. 1958): *Linguistique historique et linguistique générale*. I. Paris.

Meinhof, C., 1912: *Die Sprachen der Hamiten*. Hamburg.

Mejía, J., 1963: 'El lamed enfático en nuevos textos del Antiguo Testamento', *EstBib* 22, 179–90.

Melamed, E.Z., 1982–83: 'Taboos in Mishnaic Hebrew', *Leshonenu* 47, 3–16. H.
de Menasce, J.P., 1956: 'Iranien "naxčir"', *VT* 6, 213–14.
Mercati, G., 1895–96: 'D'un palimpsesto Ambrosiano contenente i Salmi esaplari', *Atti della Real Accademia delle Scienze di Torino* 31, 655–76.
1947: 'Il problema della IIa colonna dell'Esaplo', *Biblica* 28, 173–215.
1959: *Psalterii Hexapli reliquiae*. I. Rome.
Meshel, Z., 1977: 'Kuntilat 'Ajrud, 1975–1976', *IEJ* 27, 52–53.
1978: *Kuntillet 'Ajrud. A religious center from the time of the Judaean monarchy on the border of Sinai*. Jerusalem.
Meshel, Z. and Meyers, C., 1976: 'The name of God in the Wilderness of Zin', *BA* 39, 6–10.
Metmann, L., 1904: *Die hebräische Sprache ... seit Abschluss des Kanons*. Jerusalem.
Mettinger, T.N.D., 1971: 'The nominal pattern "qᵉtullā" in Biblical Hebrew', *JSS* 16, 2–14.
1974: 'The Hebrew verbal system: a survey of recent research', *ASTI* 9, 64–84.
Meyer, A., 1896: *Jesu Muttersprache*. Leipzig.
Meyer, R., 1950: 'Zur Sprache von 'Ain Feschcha', *TLZ* 75, 721–26.
1951: 'Probleme der hebräischen Grammatik', *ZAW* 63, 221–35.
1953: 'Zur Geschichte des hebräischen Verbums', *VT* 3, 225–35.
1953–54: 'Die Bedeutung der linearen Punktuation für die hebräische Sprachgeschichte', *Wissenschaftliche Zeitschrift der Karl-Marx-Universität, Leipzig*, Gesellschafts- und sprachwissenschaftliche Reihe, 3, 85–94.
1957: 'Sprache und Schriftzeichen des A.T.', in K. Galling (ed.), *Die Religion in Geschichte und Gegenwart: Handwörterbuch für Theologie und Religionswissenschaft*, 3rd rev. ed., I, Tübingen, pp. 1126–30.
1957a: 'Das Problem der Dialektmischung in den hebräischen Texten von Chirbet Qumran', *VT* 7, 139–48.
1957b: Review of Birkeland 1954, *OLZ* 52, 47–50.
1958: 'Bemerkungen zu den hebräischen Aussprachetraditionen von Chirbet Qumrān', *ZAW* 70, 39–48.
1960: 'Das hebräische Verbalsystem im Lichte der gegenwärtigen Forschung', *SVT* 7, 309–17.
1961: 'A. Sperber neueste Studien über das masoretische Hebräisch', *VT* 11, 475–86.
1961a: 'Spuren eines westsemitischen Präsens-Futur in den Texten von Chirbet Qumran', *BZAW* 77, 118–28.
1964: 'Aspekt und Tempus im althebräischen Verbalsystem', *OLZ* 59, 117–26.
1966–72: *Hebräische Grammatik*. 3rd rev. ed. 4 vols. Berlin.
Michaud, H., 1957: 'Les ostraca de Lakiš conservés à Londres', *Syria* 34, 39–60.
Michel, D., 1960: *Tempora und Satzstellung in den Psalmen*. Bonn.
1977: *Grundlegung einer hebräischen Syntax*. I. Neukirchen-Vluyn.
Milgrom, J., 1970: *Studies in Levitical terminology*. I. Berkeley/Los Angeles.
1978: 'The Temple Scroll', *BA* 41, 105–20.
Milik, J.T., 1953: 'Une lettre de Siméon Bar Kokheba', *RB* 60, 276–94.
1956: 'The copper document from Cave III, Qumran', *BA* 19, 60–64.
1957: *Dieci anni di scoperte nel deserto di Giuda*. Rome.
1957a: 'Deux documents inédits du désert de Juda', *Biblica* 38, 245–68.
1961: 'Textes hébreux et araméens', in P. Benoit, J.T. Milik, and R. de Vaux, *Les grottes de Murabba'ât* (Discoveries in the Judaean Desert; 2), Oxford, pp. 65–205.
1962: 'Commentaire et texte [du Rouleau de Cuivre]', in M. Baillet, J.T. Milik, and R. de Vaux, *Les "petites grottes" de Qumrân* (Discoveries in the Judaean Desert; 3), Oxford, pp. 201–302.
Milik, J.T. and Cross, F.M., 1954: 'Inscribed javelin heads from the period of the Judges: a recent discovery in Palestine', *BASOR* 134, 5–14.
Millard, A.R., 1962: 'Alphabetic inscriptions on ivories from Nimrud', *Iraq* 24, 41.
Millás, J.M., 1931: *D'epigrafia hebráico-catalana*. Barcelona.
1945: 'Epigrafía hebraico-española', *Sefarad* 5, 285–302.
1955: 'Un nuevo fragmento de lápida hebraica en Barcelona', *Sefarad* 15, 169–70.

1961: 'Un antiguo glosario hispanohebraico con transcripciones pretiberienses', *Sefarad* 21, 219–39.
Miller, C.H., 1970: 'The infinitive construct in the lawbooks of the Old Testament: a statistical study', *CBQ* 32, 222–26.
Miller, P.D., 1979: 'Vocative lamed in the Psalter: a reconsideration', *UF* 11, 617–38.
1981: 'Psalms and inscriptions', *SVT* 32, 311–32.
Mirkin, R., 1957–58: ''Al shalosh tofa'ot morfologiyyot ba-'Ivrit ha-ḥadashah', *LeshLA* 92, 286–93.
1961–62: '"i" + shemot ha-pe'ulah ba-'Ivrit ha-sifrutit ha-ḥadashah', *Leshonenu* 26, 217–19.
1967–68: 'Mishkal "mefu'al"', *Leshonenu* 32, 140–52.
Mirsky, A., 1952–53: 'Li-fshutah shel leshon shirat yeme ha-benayim', *Leshonenu* 18, 97–103.
1961: *Itzhak ibn Khalfun. Poems*. Jerusalem. H.
1965: *Reshit ha-piyyuṭ*. Jerusalem.
1965–66: 'The roots of the language of the *piyyuṭ*', *Leshonenu* 30, 296–304. H.
1977 (ed.): *Yosse ben Yosse. Poems*. Jerusalem. H.
1985: *The origin of forms of early Hebrew poetry*. 2nd ed. Jerusalem. H.
Mishor, M., 1979–80: 'Le-habba'at ha-modaliyyut bi-lshon ḥakhamim', *Leshonenu* 44, 76–79.
1983: 'The tense system in Tannaitic Hebrew'. Doct. diss., Hebrew University, Jerusalem. H.
1983a: 'Ha-zeman ba-mashlim ha-pesuki bi-lshon ha-Tanna'im', in M. Bar-Asher, A. Dotan, G.B. Ṣarfatti, and D. Téné (eds.), *Hebrew language studies presented to Professor Zeev Ben-Ḥayyim*, Jerusalem, pp. 407–18.
Mitchell, T.C., 1969: 'The meaning of the noun "ḥtn" in the Old Testament', *VT* 19, 93–112.
Mittwoch, E., 1943: 'Some observations on the language of the prayers, the benedictions and the Mishnah', in I. Epstein, E. Levine, and C. Roth (eds.), *Essays in honour of J.H. Hertz*, London, pp. 325–30.
Möller, H., 1906: *Semitisch und Indogermanisch*. I. Copenhagen.
1911: *Vergleichendes indogermanisch-semitisches Wörterbuch*. Göttingen.
Mommsen, H., Perlman, I, and Yellin, J., 1984: 'The provenience of the "lmlk" jars', *IEJ* 34, 89–113.
Montgomery, J.A., 1907 (repr. 1968): *The Samaritans, the earliest Jewish sect. Their history, theology and literature*. Philadelphia.
de Moor, J.C., 1957: 'Lexical remarks concerning "yaḥad" and "yaḥdaw"', *VT* 7, 350–55.
Morag, S., 1954: 'The independent pronouns of the third person masculine and feminine in the Dead Sea Scrolls', *EI* 3, *166–69. H.
1955–57: 'The shewa in the traditional Yemenite pronunciation of Hebrew', *Leshonenu* 20, 10–29, 112–34; 21, 104–16. H.
1956–57: 'Le-meḥkar mesorot ha-'edot bi-lshon ḥakhamim', *Tarbiz* 26, 4–16.
1956–57a: 'The Pa'el and Nithpa'el verbal systems', *Tarbiz* 26, 349–56. H.
1957–58: 'More on the subject of Pa'el and Nithpa'el', *Tarbiz* 27, 556. H.
1959: 'The vocalization of Codex Reuchlinianus: is the "pre-Masoretic" Bible pre-Masoretic?', *JSS* 4, 216–37.
1959a: 'Planned and unplanned development in Modern Hebrew', *Lingua* 8, 247–63.
1959b: 'Mēšaʿ: a study of certain features of Old Hebrew dialects', *EI* 5, 138–44. H.
1960: 'The seven double letters "bgd kprt"', in M. Haran and B.Z. Luria (eds.), *Sefer [N.H.] Ṭur-Sinai ... li-mle'ut lo shiv'im shanah*, Jerusalem, pp. 207–42. H.
1963: *The Hebrew language tradition of the Yemenite Jews*. Jerusalem. H.
1966–67: ''Ad ematay dibberu 'Ivrit?', *LeshLA* 67–68, 3–10.
1968: 'Nikkud', *EB*, V, 837–57.
1969: 'Uniformity and diversity in a language: dialects and forms of speech in Modern Hebrew', in A. Graur (ed.), *Actes du 10ᵉ Congrès International des Linguistes, Bucarest, 28 août–2 septembre 1967*, Bucharest, pp. 639–44.
1969a: 'Oral tradition and dialects. Toward a methodology for evaluating the evidence of an oral tradition', *PICSS*, 180–89.
1969b: 'Oral tradition as a source of linguistic information', in J. Puhvel (ed.), *Substance and structure of language*, Berkeley/Los Angeles, pp. 127–46.

1970 (ed.): *The Mishnah tractates Neziqin, Qodashin, Teharoth. Codex Jerusalem Heb. 4° 1336.* Jerusalem.
1971: 'Pronunciations of Hebrew', *EJ*, XIII, 1120–45.
1972: *The vocalization systems of Arabic, Hebrew and Aramaic.* 2nd ed. The Hague.
1972a: 'Ha-masoret ha-Ṭavranit shel leshon ha-Mikra: homogeniyyut we-heṭerogeniyyut', *Perakim* 2, 105–44.
1972b: 'Some notes on the vowel system of spoken Hebrew', *Leshonenu* 37, 205–14. H.
1973: *The Book of Daniel. A Babylonian-Yemenite manuscript*. Jerusalem. H.
1973a: 'Semi-mobile šᵉwa', *P5WCJS*, IV, 173–81, 294–95.
1973–74: 'Some aspects of the methodology and terminology of the early Massoretes', *Leshonenu* 38, 49–77. H.
1974: 'On the historical validity of the vocalization of the Hebrew Bible', *JAOS* 94, 307–15.
1974a: 'On some terms of the Babylonian Massora', *MasSt* 1, 67–77.
1978: ''Iyyunim bi-yḥase mashma'ut', *EI* 14, *137–47.
1979: 'Some notes on "muṣawwitāt" in mediaeval Hebrew and Arabic literature', *JANES* 11, 85–90.
1980: 'Ben mizraḥ le-ma'arav. Le-parashat mesiratah shel ha-'Ivrit bi-yme ha-benayim', *P6WCJS*, Division D, 141–56.
1980a: ''Al lashon we-'esteṭikah we-ha-'Ivrit bat zemanenu', *Molad* 250, 81–90.
1980–81: '"Layers of antiquity" – some linguistic observations on the oracles of Balaam', *Tarbiz* 50, 1–24. H.
1982: 'Some notes on Šelomo Almoli's contributions to the linguistic science of Hebrew', in J.A. Emerton and S.C. Reif (eds.), *Interpreting the Hebrew Bible. Essays in honour of E.I.J. Rosenthal*, Cambridge, pp. 157–69.
1983: 'Motivation and methodology in reforming writing systems: on the emergence of the vocalization systems of Hebrew', in S. Hattori and K. Inoue (eds.), *Proceedings of the XIIIth International Congress of Linguists, August 29-September 4, 1982, Tokyo*, Tokyo, pp. 1094–97.
1983a: 'The Yemenite tradition of the Bible: the transition period', in E. Fernández Tejero (ed.), *Estudios Masoréticos (V Congreso de la IOMS) dedicados a Harry M. Orlinsky*, Madrid, pp. 137–149.
1983–84: 'On semantic and lexical features in the language of Hosea', *Tarbiz* 63, 489–511. H.
1985: 'The beginnings of Hebrew: some semantic considerations', in M. Bar-Asher (ed.), *Language studies*, I, Jerusalem, pp. 177–96. H.
1985a: 'Ha-'Ivrit ke-lashon 'illit shel tarbut. Tahalikh gibbush u-mesirah bi-yme ha-benayim be-'arṣot ha-Yam ha-Tikhon', *Pe'amim* 23, 9–21.
1986: 'Latent masorah', *Sefarad* 46, 333–44.
1988: 'Qumran Hebrew: some typological observations', *VT* 38, 148–64.
1988a (ed.): *Studies in contemporary Hebrew.* Jerusalem. H.
1990: 'Modern Hebrew: some sociolinguistic aspects', *Cathedra* 56, 70–92.
1991: 'The Tiberian tradition of Hebrew in the communities of Spain: the first period', in M.H. Goshen-Gottstein, S. Morag, and S. Kogut (eds.), *Studies on Hebrew and other Semitic languages presented to Prof. C. Rabin on the occasion of his seventy-fifth birthday*, Jerusalem, pp. 203–30. H.
1992: 'Las comunidades judías de España y las tradiciones vivas del idioma hebreo', in H. Beinart (ed.), *Moreshet Sefarad*, Jerusalem, pp. 109–19.
Morag, S. and Sapan, R., 1966–67: 'Mi-leshon ha-dayyagim we-yorede ha-yam be-Yisra'el', *Leshonenu* 31, 289–98.
Moran, W.L., 1950: 'A syntactical study of the dialect of Byblos as reflected in the Amarna tablets'. Doct. diss., Johns Hopkins University.
1951: 'New evidence on Canaanite "taqtulu(na)"', *JCS* 5, 33–35.
1957: 'Mari notes on the Execration Texts', *Orientalia* 26, 339–45.
1960: 'Early Canaanite "yaqtula"', *Orientalia* 29, 1–19.

1961: 'The Hebrew language in its Northwest Semitic background', in G.E. Wright (ed.), *The Bible and the ancient Near East. Essays in honor of William Foxwell Albright*, Garden City, pp. 54–72.

1964: '"*taqtul" – third masculine singular?', *Biblica* 45, 80–82.

1975: 'The Syrian scribe of the Jerusalem Amarna letters', in H. Goedicke and J.J.M. Roberts (eds.), *Unity and diversity: essays in the history, literature, and religion of the ancient near east*, Baltimore/London, pp. 146–66.

Mordell, P., 1928–29: 'The discovery of a vowel point system based on the Sephardic pronunciation', *JQR*, n.s., 19, 479–88.

1933–34: 'The beginning and development of Hebrew punctuation', *JQR*, n.s., 24, 137–49.

Moreshet, M., 1966–67: 'The predicate preceding a compound subject in the biblical language', *Leshonenu* 31, 215–60. H.

1966–67a: 'Gilgule mashma'ut shel nivim we-shel ṣerufe lashon she-mekoram ba-Mikra', *LeshLA* 178–79.

1972: 'New and revived verbs in the *baraitot* of the Babylonian Talmud', *ANDRL*, I, 117–62. H.

1974: 'Further studies of the language of the Hebrew *baraitot* in the Babylonian and Palestinian Talmudim', *ANDRL*, II, 31–73. H.

1974a: 'Ha-baraitot ha-'Ivriyyot ba-Bavli 'enan leshon ḥakhamim', in E.Y. Kutscher, S. Liebermann, and M.Z. Kaddari (eds.), *Henoch Yalon memorial volume*, Ramat-Gan, pp. 275–314.

1976: 'Hif'il le-lo' hevdel min ha-Qal bi-lshon ḤaZaL (be-hashwa'ah li-lshon ha-Mikra)', *Bar-Ilan* 13, 249–81.

1980: *A lexicon of the new verbs in Tannaitic Hebrew*. Ramat-Gan. H.

1980a: 'On the Nuf'al stem in Post-Biblical Hebrew', in G.B. Ṣarfatti, P. Artzi, J.C. Greenfield, and M.Z. Kaddari (eds.), *Studies in Hebrew and Semitic languages dedicated to the memory of Prof. E.Y. Kutscher*, Ramat-Gan, pp. 126–39. H.

1981: 'Po'lel/Hitpo'lel in Mishnaic Hebrew and Aramaic dialects', *Bar-Ilan* 18–19, 248–69. H.

Morin, J., 1657: *Opuscula hebraeo-samaritana*. Paris.

Moscati, S., 1947: 'Il biconsonantismo nelle lingue semitiche', *Biblica* 28, 113–35.

1951: *L'epigrafia ebraica antica, 1935–1950*. Rome.

1954: *Il sistema consonantico delle lingue semitiche*. Rome.

1954a: 'The plural in Semitic', in D. Sinor (ed.), *Proceedings of the Twenty-Third International Congress of Orientalists, Cambridge, 21st–28th August 1954*, London, pp. 112–14.

1954b: *Preistoria e storia del consonantismo ebraico antico*. Rome.

1956: 'Il semitico di nord-ovest', in *Studi orientalistici in onore di Giorgio Levi della Vida*, II, Rome, pp. 202–21.

1956a: 'Sulla posizione linguistica del semitico nordoccidentale', *RSO* 31, 229–34.

1957: *Ancient Semitic civilisations*. London.

1957a: 'The Semites: a linguistic, ethnic and racial problem', *CBQ* 19, 421–34.

1958: *Le antiche divinitá semitiche*. Rome.

1960: 'Sulla riconstruzione del proto-semitico', *RSO* 35, 1–10.

1969 (ed.): *An introduction to the comparative grammar of the Semitic languages. Phonology and morphology*. 2nd ed. Wiesbaden.

Mowinckel, S., 1961: 'The verb "śiaḥ" and the nouns "śiaḥ", "śiḥā"', *Studia theologica* 15, 1–10.

Muilenburg, J., 1961: The linguistic and rhetorical usage of the particle "kî" in the Old Testament', *HUCA* 32, 135–60.

Mulder, M.J., 1973: 'Die Partikel "ya'an"', *OTS* 18, 49–83.

Müller, H.-P., 1969: 'Die hebräische Wurzel "ŚYḤ"', *VT* 19, 361–71.

1970: 'Notizen zu althebräischen Inschriften, i', *UF* 2, 229–42.

1971: 'Die Wurzeln "'YQ", "Y'Q", "'WQ"', *VT* 21, 556–64.

1978: 'Einige alttestamentliche Probleme zur aramäischen Inschrift von Dēr 'Allā', *ZDPV* 94, 56–67.

1982: 'Die aramäische Inschrift von Deir 'Allā' und die älteren Bileamsprüche', *ZAW* 94, 214–44.

1983: 'Zur Geschichte des hebräischen Verbs: Diachronie der Konjugationsthemen', *BZ*, n.s., 27, 34–57.
1984: 'Ebla und das althebräische Verbalsystem', *Biblica* 65, 145–67.
1984a: 'Neue Erwägungen zum eblaitischen Verbalsystem', in L. Cagni (ed.), pp. 167–204.
1984b: 'Wie alt ist das jungsemitische Perfekt? Zum semitisch-ägyptischen Sprachvergleich', in W. Helck, H. Altermüller, and D. Wildung (eds.), *Studien zur altägyptischen Kultur*, Hamburg, pp. 365–79.
1984c: 'Die Konjugation von Nomina im Althebräischen', *ZAW* 96, 245–63.
1985: 'Ergativelemente im akkadischen und althebräischen Verbalsystem', *Biblica* 66, 385–417.
Müller, W.W., 1975: 'Beiträge zur hamito-semitischen Wortvergleichung', in J. and T. Bynon (eds.), pp. 63–74.
Muntner, S., 1949: *Rabbi Shabbetai Donnolo*. Jerusalem H.
1971: 'Donnolo, Shabbetai', *EJ*, VI, 168–69.
Muraoka, T., 1969: *Emphasis in Biblical Hebrew*. Oxford.
1975: 'The *nun energicum* and the prefix conjugation in Biblical Hebrew', *AJBI* 1, 63–72.
1985: *Emphatic words and structures in Biblical Hebrew*. Jerusalem/Leiden.
Murphy, R.E., 1952: 'A fragment of an early Moabite inscription from Dibon', *BASOR* 125, 20–23.
1958: '"Šaḥat" in the Qumran literature', *Biblica* 39, 61–66.
1958a: '"Yeṣer" in the Qumran literature', *Biblica* 39, 334–44.
1959: '"Bśr" in the Qumran literature', in J. Coppens, A. Descamps, and E. Massaux (eds.), *Sacra pagina. Miscellanea biblica Congressus Internationalis Catholici de Re Biblica*, I, Paris/Gembloux, pp. 60–76.
1961: '"GBR" and "gbwrh" in the Qumran writings', in H. Gross and F. Mussner (eds.), *Lex tua veritas. Festschrift für Hubert Junker zur Vollendung des siebzigsten Lebensjahres am 8. August 1961*, Trier, pp. 137–43.
Murtonen, A., 1958: *Materials for a non-Masoretic Hebrew grammar*. I: Liturgical texts and psalm fragments provided with the so-called Palestinian punctuation. Helsinki.
1959: 'On the influence of the development of vocalization upon the form system in Samaritan Hebrew', in H. Franke (ed.), *Akten des XXIV. Internationalen Orientalistenkongress (München 1957)*, Wiesbaden, pp. 257–59.
1960–64: *Materials for a non-Masoretic Hebrew grammar*. II: An etymological vocabulary to the Samaritan Pentateuch; III: A grammar of the Samaritan dialect of Hebrew. Helsinki.
1961–62: 'Spoken Hebrew from the tenth century A.D.', *Abr-Nahrain* 3, 45–49.
1963–64: 'A historico-philological survey of the main Dead Sea Scrolls and related documents', *Abr-Nahrain* 4, 56–95.
1964: *Broken plurals: origin and development of the system*. Leiden.
1964a: 'Hebreo palestino, Gramática del', in *Enciclopedia de la Biblia*, III, pp. 1131–36.
1966: 'The Semitic sibilants', *JSS* 11, 135–95.
1967: *Early Semitic. A diachronic inquiry into the relationship of Ethiopic to the other so-called South-East Semitic languages*. Leiden.
1968: 'The pre-historic development of the Hebrew verbal system', *P4WCJS*, II, 29–33.
1968a: 'Prolegomena to a comparative description of non-Masoretic Hebrew dialects and traditions', *BZAW* 103, 180–87.
1973–74: 'On the interpretation of the *matres lectionis* in Biblical Hebrew', *Abr-Nahrain* 14, 66–121.
1974: 'Hebrew, Harari and Somali statistically compared', *APCI*, 68–75.
1981–82: 'Methodological preliminaries to a study of Greek (and Latin) transcriptions of Hebrew', *Abr-Nahrain* 20, 60–73.
1986: *Hebrew in its West Semitic setting*. I: A comparative lexicon. A: Proper names. Leiden.
Nahir, M, 1946–47: *'Ikkere torat ha-mishpaṭ*. Haifa.
1978: 'Normativism and educated speech in modern Hebrew', *International journal of the sociology of language* 18, 49–67.

Nathan, Ḥ., 1984: 'Did Mishnaic Hebrew lose the distinction between the pronominal suffixes of the third person feminine singular and plural?', in M. Bar-Asher (ed.), *Massorot: studies in language traditions*, I, Jerusalem, pp. 121–34. H.

Navarro, A., 1976: *Biblia babilónica. Proverbios. Edición crítica según manuscritos hebreos de puntuación babilónica*. Madrid.

Naveh, J., 1960: 'A Hebrew letter from the seventh century B.C.', *IEJ* 10, 129–39.

1961: 'A Hebrew letter from Meṣad Ḥashavyahu', *BIES* 25, 119–28. H.

1962: 'More Hebrew inscriptions from Meṣad Ḥashavyahu', *IEJ* 12, 27–32.

1963: 'Old Hebrew inscriptions in a burial cave', *IEJ* 13, 74–92.

1964: 'Some notes on the reading of the Meṣad Ḥashavyahu letter', *IEJ* 14, 158–59.

1966: 'The scripts of two ostraca from Elath', *BASOR* 183, 27–30.

1967: 'The date of the Deir 'Allā inscription in Aramaic script', *IEJ* 17, 256–58.

1970: 'The ossuary inscriptions from Giv'at ha-Mivtar', *IEJ* 20, 33–37.

1971: 'Hebrew texts in Aramaic script in the Persian period', *BASOR* 203, 27–32.

1971a: 'Alphabet, Hebrew', *EJ*, I, 674–89.

1973: 'Word division in West Semitic writing', *IEJ* 23, 206–08.

1978: *'Al pesefas we-'even. Ha-ketuvot ha-'Aramiyyot we-ha-'Ivriyyot mi-bate ha-keneset ha-'attikim*. Jerusalem.

1978a: 'Some considerations on the ostracon from 'Izbet Ṣarṭah', *IEJ* 28, 31–35.

1980: 'The ostracon from Nimrud: an Ammonite namelist', *Maarav* 2, 163–71.

1981 (ed.): *Likkutei* Tarbiz. *A Jewish epigraphy reader*. Jerusalem. H.

1981a: 'Ancient synagogue inscriptions', in L.I. Levine (ed.), *Ancient synagogues revealed*, Jerusalem, pp. 133–39.

1982: *Early history of the alphabet. An introduction to West Semitic epigraphy and palaeography*. Jerusalem/Leiden.

1982a: 'A fragment of an ancient Hebrew inscription from the Ophel', *IEJ* 32, 195–98.

Naveh, J. and Greenfield, J.C., 1984: 'Hebrew and Aramaic in the Persian period', in W.D. Davies and L. Finkelstein (eds.), *The Cambridge history of Judaism*, I, Cambridge, pp. 115–29.

Nebe, G.-W., 1972–75: 'Lexikalische Bemerkungen zu "'wšwn" "Fundament, Tiefe" in 4Q 184, Prov. 7, 9 und 20, 20', *RQ* 8, 97–104.

1972–75a: 'Der Gebrauch der sogenannten *Nota accusativi* "'et" in Damaskusschrift xv 5, 9 und 12', *RQ* 8, 257–64.

1972–75b: '"'br" in 4Q 186', *RQ* 8, 265–67.

Nepper-Christensen, P., 1958: *Das Matthäusevangelium, ein judenchristliches Evangelium?* Aarhus.

Nestle, E., 1913: '"Mil'el" und "milra"', *ZAW* 33, 73–75.

Netan'el, E., 1972: 'Leshono shel Ketav-yad Anṭonin 262'. Master's diss., Hebrew University, Jerusalem.

Neubauer, A., 1894–95: 'The Hebrew Bible in shorthand writing', *JQR* 7, 361–64.

Netzer, N., 1983: 'Mishnaic Hebrew in the works of medieval Hebrew grammarians'. Doct. diss., Hebrew University, Jerusalem. H.

Neusner, J., 1964–66 '"Ḥbr" and "n'mn"', *RQ* 5, 119–22.

1973 (ed.): *The modern study of the Mishnah*. Leiden.

Niccacci, A, 1990: *The syntax of the verb in Classical Hebrew prose*. Sheffield.

Nichols, G.J., 1858: *A grammar of the Samaritan language with extracts and vocabulary*. London.

Nir, R., 1967: 'Hebrew idioms and their place in the linguistic education of the secondary-school pupil in Israel'. Doct. diss., Hebrew University, Jerusalem. H.

1975: 'The survival of obsolete Hebrew words in idiomatic expressions', *AAL* 2, 11–17.

1980: 'The semantic structure of nominal compounds in Modern Hebrew', *BSOAS* 43, 185–96.

Nöldeke, T., 1862: 'Über einige samaritanisch-arabische Schriften die hebräische Sprache betreffend', *Göttinger gelehrte Nachträge*, 337–52, 385–416.

1868: 'Über die Aussprache des Hebräischen bei den Samaritanern', *Göttinger gelehrte Nachträge*, 485–504.

1870: *Die Inschrift des Königs Mesa von Moab (9. Jahrhundert vor Christus)*. Kiel.

1875 (repr. 1964): *Mandäische Grammatik*. Halle.

1899: *Die semitischen Sprachen*. 2nd ed. Leipzig.

1903: Review of Kautzsch 1902, *ZDMG* 57, 412–20.

1904: *Beiträge zur semitischen Sprachwissenschaft*. Strasbourg.

1910: *Neue Beiträge zur semitischen Sprachwissenschaft*. Strasbourg.

1912: 'Inkonsequenzen in der hebräischen Punktation', *ZA* 26, 1–15.

Noth, M., 1928 (repr. 1980): *Die israelitischen Personennamen im Rahmen der gemeinsemitischen Namengebung*. Stuttgart.

Nötscher, F., 1953: 'Zum emphatischen Lamed', *VT* 3, 372–80.

Novel, A., 1958–59: 'Loan-translations from Yiddish in Rabbinical Hebrew', *Leshonenu* 23, 172–84, 216–69. H.

Nyberg, H.S., 1920: 'Wortbildungen mit Präfixen in den semitischen Sprachen', *Le Monde oriental* 14, 177–288.

1931: 'Ein iranisches Wort im Buche Daniel', *Le monde oriental* 25, 178–204.

O'Callaghan, R.T., 1949: 'The great Phoenician portal inscription from Karatepe', *Orientalia* 18, 173–205.

1949a: 'The Phoenician inscription on the king's statue at Karatepe', *CBQ* 11, 233–48.

1954: 'Echoes of Canaanite literature in the Psalms', *VT* 4, 164–76.

O'Connor, M., 1987: 'The poetic inscription from Khirbet el-Qôm', *VT* 37, 224–29.

Oded, B., 1971: 'Egyptian references to the Edomite deity Qaus', *AUSS* 9, 47–50.

Ogden, G.S., 1971: 'Time, and the verb "HYH" in O.T. prose', *VT* 21, 451–69.

Olinder, G., 1934: *Zur Terminologie der semitischen Lautähnlichkeiten*. Lund.

del Olmo, G., 1984: *Interpretación de la mitología cananea. Estudios de semántica ugarítica*. Valencia.

1986: 'Fenicio y Ugarítico: correlación lingüística', *AuOr* 4, 31–49.

del Olmo, G. and Aubet, M.E. (eds.), 1986: *Los fenicios en la península ibérica*. Sabadell.

Oppenheim, A.L., 1967: *Letters from Mesopotamia*. Chicago/London.

Orlinsky, H.M., 1947: *Notes on the Qal infinitive construct and the verbal noun in Biblical Hebrew*. New Haven.

Ormann, G., 1934: *Das Sündenbekenntnis des Versöhnungstages*. Frankfurt-am-Main.

Ornan, U., 1958–59: 'Nittuaḥ mekhani we-hora'at ha-taḥbir', *Leshonenu* 23, 243–58.

1964: 'The Tiberian vocalisation system and the principles of linguistics', *JJS* 15, 109–23.

1964a: 'The nominal phrase in Modern Hebrew with special reference to the prose of C.N. Bialik'. Doct. diss., Hebrew University, Jerusalem. H.

1965: *Taḥbir ha-'Ivrit ha-ḥadashah, 'arekhah le-fi harṣa'ot S. Bittermann*. Jerusalem.

1967–68: 'Ka-zeh we-kha-zot', *Leshonenu* 32, 46–52.

1967–68a: 'Pirke yiḥud', *Ma'alot* 6, 46–59.

1971: 'Hebrew grammar', *EJ*, VIII, 77–175.

1973: 'Order rules and the so-called phonologization of ancient allophones in Israeli Hebrew', in L. Heilmann (ed.), *Proceedings of the Eleventh International Congress of Linguists, Bologna-Florence, Aug. 28-Sept. 2, 1972*, II, Bologna, pp. 1023–36.

1986: 'Hebrew in Palestine', *JSS* 29, 225–54.

Ott, H., 1967: 'Um die Muttersprache Jesu: Forschungen seit Gustaf Dalman', *Novum Testamentum* 9, 1–25.

Ouellette, J., 1980: 'An unnoticed device for expressing the future in Middle Hebrew', *HAR* 4, 127–29.

Pagis, D., 1976: *Change and tradition in the secular poetry: Spain and Italy*. Jerusalem. H.

Palache, J.L., 1959: *Semantic notes on the Hebrew lexicon*. Leiden.

Palmaitis, L., 1971: 'The first ancient Ammonite inscription from the I millennium B.C.', *Vestnik drevnej istorii* 118, 119–26. In Russian.

Pardee, D., 1978: 'The judicial plea from Meṣad Ḥashavyahu (Yavneh-Yam): a new philological study', *Maarav* 1, 33–66.

1978a: 'Letters from Tel Arad', *UF* 10, 289–336.

1982: *Handbook of ancient Hebrew letters*. Chico.

Parfitt, T.V., 1972: 'The use of Hebrew in Palestine 1800–1882', *JSS* 17, 237–52.

van Dyke Parunak, H., 1975: 'A semantic survey of "NḤM"', *Biblica* 56, 512–32.
1978: 'The orthography of the Arad ostraca', *BASOR* 230, 25–31.
Patai, R., 1953–54: 'The phonology of "Sabra" Hebrew', *JQR*, n.s., 44, 51–54.
Patterson, D., 1962: 'Some linguistic aspects of the nineteenth-century Hebrew novel', *JSS* 7, 309–24.
1981: 'Revival of literature and revival of language', in E. Silberschlag (ed.), *Eliezer Ben-Yehuda, a symposium in Oxford*, Oxford, pp. 13–24.
Patton, J.H., 1944: *Canaanite parallels in the Book of Psalms*. Baltimore.
Peladah, N., 1958–59: 'Shekhiḥut ha-hagayim be-'Ivrit', *Leshonenu* 23, 235–42.
Pelli, M., 1974: 'The attitude of the first *maśkilim* to the Hebrew language', *BIJS* 2, 83–97.
Penar, T., 1967: '"Lamedh vocativi", exempla biblico hebraica', *Verbum domini* 45, 32–46.
1975: *Northwest Semitic philology and the Hebrew fragments of Ben Sira*. Rome.
Penna, A., 1978: 'Scrittura e pronunzia dell'ebraico secondo S. Girolamo', *RBI* 26, 275–99.
Pennacchietti, F.A., 1968: *Studi sui pronomi determinativi semitici*. Naples.
Percikowitsch, (Pereṣ) A., 1932: *Al-Ḥarizi als Übersetzer der Makamen Al-Ḥariris*. Munich.
Pereṣ, I., 1943: *Taḥbir ha-lashon ha-'Ivrit*. Tel-Aviv.
1961–62: 'Le-darke ha-hadgashah ba-'Ivrit ha-ḥadashah', *Leshonenu* 26, 118–24.
1967: *Mishpaṭ ha-zikkah ba-lashon ha-'Ivrit le-khol tekufoteha*. Tel-Aviv.
1968: 'Shemidut shel shem peraṭi we-to'ar kavod', *P4WCJS*, II, 129–33.
Pérez Castro, F., 1948: 'Problemas de las fuentes de conocimiento del hebreo premasorético', *Sefarad* 8, 145–87.
1951–52: 'Los manuscritos del Mar Muerto', *Sefarad* 11, 115–53; 12, 167–97.
1953: 'El Séfer Abisha'. El antiguo y célebre rollo del Pentateuco samaritano de Nablus puede por fin ser objeto de investigación textual', *Sefarad* 13, 119–29.
1955: 'Bemerkungen zu zwei verschiedenen Entwicklungsstufen in der Überlieferung des hebräischen Bibeltextes', *ZDMG* 105, 45–46.
1955a: 'Corregido y correcto. El Ms. B19a de Leningrado frente al Ms. Or. 4445 (Londres) y al Códice de Profetas de El Cairo', *Sefarad* 15, 3–30.
1956: 'Ben Asher – Ben Naftalí? Números 13–15 en cinco manuscritos a la luz de Mišael ben 'Uzziel', in *Homenaje a Millás-Vallicrosa*, II, Barcelona, pp. 141–48.
1959 (ed.): *Séfer Abša'*. Madrid.
1961: 'Fragmento inédito del Séfer Abiša'', *Sefarad* 21, 3–8.
1963: 'La *masora* del Códice de Profetas de El Cairo', *Sefarad* 23, 227–35.
1965: 'Estudios masoréticos', *Sefarad* 25, 289–317.
1970: 'Fragmentos de códices del Antiguo Testamento hebreo en el Archivo Histórico Nacional, i', *Sefarad* 30, 251–88.
1979–88 (ed.): *El Codice de Profetas de El Cairo*. I: *Josué-Jueces* (1980); II: *Samuel* (1983); III: *Reyes* (1984); IV: *Isaías* (1986); V: *Jeremías* (1987); VI: *Ezequiel* (1988); VII: *Profetas menores* (1979). Madrid.
Pérez Castro, F. and Azcárraga, M.J., 1968: 'The edition of the Kitāb al-Khilaf of Mišael ben 'Uzziel', *BZAW* 103, 188–200.
Petermann, J.H., 1868: *Versuch einer hebräischen Formenlehre nach der Aussprache der heutigen Samaritaner nebst einer darnach gebildeten Transkription der Genesis*. Leipzig.
1873: *Brevis linguae samaritanae grammatica, litteratura, chrestomathia cum glossario*. Berlin.
Petermann, J.H. and Vollers, K., 1872–91: *Pentateuchus samaritanus ad fidem librorum manuscriptorum apud nablusianos repertorum*. Berlin.
Petráček, K., 1956: 'Die Phonologie und ihre Verwendung in der Semitistik', *ArOr* 24, 631–34.
1960–64: 'Die innere Flexion in den semitischen Sprachen', *ArOr* 28, 547–606; 29, 513–45; 30, 361–408; 31, 577–624; 32, 185–222.
1974: 'À propos des limites du chamito-sémitique: les systèmes phonologiques des langues chamito-sémitiques et des langues du Sahara central', *APCI*, 27–29.
1984: 'Les catégories flexionnelles en Eblaite', in Fronzaroli (ed.), pp. 25–57.
Pettinato, G., 1975: 'Testi cuneiformi del 3. millennio in paleo-cananeo rinvenuti nella campagna di scavi 1974 a Tell Mardikh-Ebla, *Orientalia* 44, 361–74.

1981: *The archives of Ebla: an empire inscribed in clay*. Garden City.
Pfeiffer, R.H., 1926: 'Edomitic wisdom', *ZAW* 44, 13–25.
Philippi, F.W.M., 1871: *Wesen und Ursprung des* Status constructus *im Hebräischen*. Weimar.
1878: 'Das Zahlwort "zwei" im Semitischen', *ZDMG* 32, 21–98.
Pinner, E.M., 1845: *Prospectus der Odessaer Gesellschaft für Geschichte und Altherthumer gehörenden ältesten hebräischen und rabbinischen Manuscripte*. Odessa.
Pinsker, S., 1863: *Mavo 'el ha-nikkud ha-'Ashuri 'o ha-Bavli*. Vienna.
du Plessis, S.J., 1971: 'Aspects of morphological peculiarities of the language of Qoheleth', in I.H. Eybers (ed.), *De fructu oris sui. Essays in honour of Adrianus van Selms*, Leiden, pp. 164–80.
Plessner, M., 1931: 'Modernes Hebräisch', *OLZ* 34, 803–08.
van der Ploeg, J., 1957: 'L'usage du parfait et de l'imparfait comme moyen de datation dans le commentaire d'Habacuc', in *Les Manuscrits de la Mer Morte. Colloque de Strasbourg, 25–27 mai 1955*, Paris, pp. 25–35.
Podolsky, B., 1981: 'Stress as a morphological factor in Modern Hebrew', *Leshonenu* 45, 155–56. H.
Poebel, A., 1932: *Das appositionnell bestimmte Pronomen der 1. Pers. Sing. in den westsemitischen Inschriften und im Alten Testament*. Chicago.
1939: 'The antepenult stressing of Old Hebrew and its influence on the shaping of the vowels', *AJSL* 56, 225–30.
1939a: 'Penult stressing replacing ultimate stressing in pre-exilic Hebrew', *AJSL* 56, 384–87.
Polotsky, H.J., 1964: 'Semitics', in E.A. Speiser (ed.), *At the dawn of civilization* (The world history of the Jewish people, first series; I), London, pp. 99–111, 357–58.
Polzin, R., 1976: *Late Biblical Hebrew. Toward an historical typology of Biblical Hebrew prose*. Missoula.
Porat, A., 1936: 'Darke ha-leksikografyah le-sifrut ha-Haskalah', *Leshonenu* 7, 537.
Porath, E., 1938: *Mishnaic Hebrew as vocalized in the early manuscripts of the Babylonian Jews*. Jerusalem. H.
Posener, G., 1940: *Princes et pays d'Asie et de Nubie*. Brussels.
Poznanski, S., 1895: *Mose b. Samuel Hakkohen ibn Chiquitilla nebst den Fragmenten seiner Schriften*. Leipzig.
1912: 'Aus Mose ibn Chiquitilla's arabischen Psalmenkommentar', *ZA* 26, 38–60.
1916: 'Hebräisch-arabische Sprachvergleichung bei Yehuda ibn Bal'am', *ZDMG* 70, 449–76.
Praetorius, F., 1897: *Über den rückweichenden Accent im Hebräischen*. Halle.
1899: 'Über das babylonische Vokalisationssystem des Hebräischen', *ZDMG* 53, 181–96.
1901: *Über die Herkunft der hebräischen Accente*. Berlin.
Pretzl, O., 1932: 'Die Aussprache des Hebräischen nach der zweiten Kolumne der Hexapla des Origenes', *BZ* 20, 4–22.
Priebatsch, H.Y., 1977: 'Die amoritische Sprache Palästinas in ihren Beziehungen zu Mari und Syrien', *UF* 9, 249–58.
Prignaud, J., 1970: 'Notes d'épigraphie hébraïque', *RB* 77, 50–67.
Prijs, J., 1964: 'Ein "Waw der Bekräftigung"?', *BZ*, n.s., 8, 105–09.
Prijs, L., 1950: *Die grammatikalische Terminologie des Abraham ibn Ezra*. Basle.
1967: 'Ergänzungen zum talmudisch-aramäischen Wörterbuch', *ZDMG* 117, 266–86.
Pritchard, J.B., 1956: *Hebrew inscriptions and stamps from Gibeon*. Philadelphia.
Puech, E., 1971: 'Sur la racine "ŠLḤ" en hébreu et en araméen', *Semitica* 21, 5–19.
1974: 'L'inscription du Tunnel de Siloé', *RB* 81, 196–214.
1985: 'L'inscription de la statue d'Amman et la paléographie ammonite', *RB* 92, 5–24.
1986: 'Origine de l'alphabet. Documents en alphabet linéaire et cunéiforme du IIe millénaire', *RB* 93, 161–213.
1986a: Review of Hackett 1984, *RB* 93, 285–86.
Puech, E. and Rofé, A., 1973: 'L'inscription de la citadelle d'Amman', *RB* 80, 531–46.
Purvis, J.D., 1968: *The Samaritan Pentateuch and the origin of the Samaritan sect*. Cambridge, Mass.
Qimron, E., 1970–71: 'The Psalms Scroll of Qumran–a linguistic study', *Leshonenu* 35, 99–116. H.

1977: 'Nitpa'al benoni', *Leshonenu* 41, 144–57.
1977–78: 'Leshonah shel Megillat ha-Mikdash', *Leshonenu* 42, 83–98.
1978: 'Li-lshon Bet Sheni be-Sefer Tehillim', *BM* 23, 139–50.
1980: 'Leshono shel Sefer Yonah', *BM* 25, 181–82.
1980a: 'The vocabulary of the Temple Scroll', *Shenaton* 4, 239–61. H.
1986: *The Hebrew of the Dead Sea Scrolls*. Atlanta.
1988: 'The origins of the Nuf'al conjugation', *Leshonenu* 52, 178–79. H.

Qimron, E. and Strugnell, J., 1985: 'An unpublished halakhic letter from Qumran', *Israel Museum journal* 4, 9–12.

Qisṭar, M., 1982–83: 'Be-shule Sefer Ben Sira', *Leshonenu* 47, 125–46.

Rabin, C., 1938: 'Prolegomena to a phonetic description of Palestinian colloquial Hebrew'. Doct. diss., University of London.
1940: 'La chute de l'oclusive glottale en hébreu parlé et l'évolution d'une nouvelle classe de voyelles', *GLECS* 3, 77–79.
1943: 'Saadya Gaon's Hebrew prose style', in E.I.J. Rosenthal (ed.), *Saadya studies*, Manchester, pp. 127–38.
1943a: 'The development of the syntax of postbiblical Hebrew'. Doct. diss., University of Oxford.
1945: 'R. Abraham bar Ḥiyya u-teḥiyyat ha-'Ivrit ba-me'ah ha-XI', *Meṣudah* 3–4, 158–70.
1948: 'Archaic vocalisation in some Biblical Hebrew names', *JJS* 1, 22–26.
1948a: *Everyday Hebrew*. Rev. ed. London.
1957–58: 'Le-ḥeker ha-'Ivrit ha-sifrutit ha-ḥadashah', *Leshonenu* 22, 246–57.
1958: 'The historical background of Qumran Hebrew', *ScrHier* 4, 144–61.
1958a: *The revival of Hebrew*. Jerusalem.
1958b: 'Language revival: colloquialism or purism', *Jewish frontier*, Supplement, 11–15.
1959–60: 'Leshon ha-tefillot', *Maḥanayim* 40, 45–50.
1960: 'The Hebrew development of Proto-Semitic "ā"', *Tarbiz* 30, 99–111. H.
1960a: 'Ha-tenu'ot ha-keṭanot ba-'Ivrit ha-Ṭavranit', in M. Haran and B.Z. Luria (eds.), *Sefer [N.H.] Ṭur-Sinai ... li-mle'ut lo shiv'im shanah*, Jerusalem, pp. 169–206.
1961: 'Ḥiyyutah shel ha-'Ivrit bi-yme ha-benayim', *LeshLA* 123, 14–18.
1962: 'Millim bodedot', *EB*, IV, 1066–1070.
1962a: 'Millim zarot', *EB*, IV, 1070–1080.
1963: 'The origin of the subdivisions of Semitic', in D. Winton Thomas and W.D. McHardy (eds.), *Hebrew and Semitic studies presented to Godfrey Rolles Driver*, Oxford, pp. 104–15.
1963a: 'Hittite words in Hebrew', *Orientalia* 32, 113–39.
1963–64: *Taḥbir leshon ha-Mikra*. Jerusalem.
1963–66: 'Un phénomène d'alternance stylistique des constructions indéfinies en hébreu biblique', *GLECS* 10, 34–35.
1963–66a: 'L'argot des étudiants en hébreu moderne', *GLECS* 10, 60–63.
1967: 'Three Hebrew terms from the realm of social psychology', *SVT* 16, 219–30.
1967a: *Goremim soṣiologiyyim be-toledot ha-lashon ha-'Ivrit*. New York.
1967–68: 'The vocalization of the third singular perfect of Pi'el in Tiberian Hebrew', *Leshonenu* 32, 12–26. H.
1968: '"l-" with imperative (Gen. xxiii)', *JSS* 13, 113–24.
1968a: 'Towards a descriptive semantics of Biblical Hebrew', in *Proceedings of the Twenty-Sixth International Congress of Orientalists, 1964*, New Delhi, pp. 51–52.
1968b: 'The tense and mood system of the Hebrew of Sepher Ḥasidim', *P4WCJS*, II, 113–16. H.
1969: 'The structure of the Semitic system of case endings', *PICSS*, 190–204.
1969a: 'The nature and origin of the Šaf'el in Hebrew and Aramaic', *EI* 9, *148–58. H.
1969b: 'The revival of the Hebrew language', *Ariel* 25, 25–34.
1970: 'Hebrew', *LSWANA*, 304–46.
1971: 'Semitic languages', *EJ*, XIV, 1149–57.
1971a: ''Ivrit', *EB*, VI, 51–73.

1971b: 'The language revival and the changes in the status and character of Hebrew', *Orot* 10, 61–77.
1973: *A short history of the Hebrew language*. Jerusalem.
1973a: 'Hebrew "baddîm" "power"', *JSS* 18, 57–58.
1974: 'On enlarging the basis of Hebrew etymology', *HA* 15, 25–28.
1975: 'Lexicostatistics and the internal divisions of Semitic', in J. and T. Bynon (eds.), pp. 85–102.
1976: 'Hebrew and Aramaic in the first century', in S. Safrai and M. Stern (eds.), *The Jewish people in the first century*, II, Assen/Amsterdam, pp. 1007–39.
1979: 'The emergence of Classical Hebrew', in A. Malamat (ed.), *The age of the monarchies*, II: *Culture and society* (The world history of the Jewish people, first series; V), Jerusalem, pp. 71–78.
1979a: 'Hebrew and Arabic in medieval Jewish philosophy', in S. Stein and R. Loewe (eds.), *Studies in Jewish religious and intellectual history presented to Alexander Altmann on the occasion of his seventieth birthday*, Alabama, pp. 235–45.
1979–80: 'Meh hayetah teḥiyyat ha-lashon?', in A. Even-Shoshan (ed.), *The book of [Shalom] Sivan*, Jerusalem, pp. 125–40.
1982: 'Safot Shemiyyot', *EB*, VIII, 337–86.
1985: 'The periodization of the Hebrew language', in M. Bar-Asher (ed.), *Language studies*, I, Jerusalem, pp. 27–35. H.
1985a: 'Biblical and Mishnaic elements in contemporary Hebrew', in M. Bar-Asher (ed.), *Language studies*, I, Jerusalem, pp. 273–85. H.
1986: 'Language revival and language death', in J.A. Fishman, A. Tabouret-Keller, M. Clyne, B. Krishnamurti, and M. Abdulaziz (eds.), *The Fergusonian impact: in honor of Charles A. Ferguson on the occasion of his 65th birthday*, II, The Hague, Paris, pp. 543–54.
Rabinovitz, Z.M., 1985: *The liturgical poems of Rabbi Yannai according to the triennial cycle of the Pentateuch and the holidays. Critical edition with introductions and commentary*. Jerusalem. H.
Rabinowitz, I., 1961: 'The Qumran authors' "spr hhgw/y"', *JNES* 20, 109–14.
1962: '"Be opened" = "effatha" (Mark 7, 34): did Jesus speak Hebrew?', *ZNW* 53, 229–38.
1971: 'The Qumran Hebrew original of Ben Sira's concluding acrostic on Wisdom', *HUCA* 42, 173–84.
1971a: '"Effatha" (Mark vii 34): certainly Hebrew, not Aramaic', *JSS* 16, 151–56.
Rabinowitz, S., 1947: *Sefer ha-mishkalim*. New York.
Radday, Y., 1970: 'Two computerized statistical-linguistic tests concerning the unity of Isaiah', *JBL* 89, 319–24.
Rahtjen, B.D., 1961: 'A note concerning the form of the Gezer tablet', *PEQ* 93, 70–72.
Rahmani, L.Y., 1971: 'Silver coins of the fourth century B.C. from Tel Gamma', *IEJ* 21, 158–60.
Rainey, A.F., 1962: 'Administration in Ugarit and the Samaria ostraca', *IEJ* 12, 62–63.
1966: 'Private seal-impressions: a note on semantics', *IEJ* 16, 187–90.
1967: 'The Samaria ostraca in the light of fresh evidence', *PEQ* 99, 32–41.
1970: 'Semantic parallels to the Samaria ostraca', *PEQ* 102, 45–51.
1971: 'A Hebrew "receipt" from Arad', *BASOR* 202, 23–29.
1971a: 'Verbal forms with infixed "-t" in the West Semitic El-Amarna letters', *IOS* 1, 86–102.
1972: 'The word "day" in Ugaritic and Hebrew', *Leshonenu* 36, 186–89. H.
1973: 'Reflections on the suffix conjugation in West Semitized Amarna tablets', *UF* 5, 235–62.
1975: 'Morphology and the prefix-tenses of West Semitized El-'Amarna tablets', *UF* 7, 395–426.
1977: 'Three additional Hebrew ostraca from Tel Arad', *TAJ* 4, 97–102.
1978: *El -Amarna tablets 359–379*. Supplement to J.A. Knudtzon, *Die El-Amarna-Taffeln*. Neukirchen-Vluyn.
1982: 'Wine from the royal vineyard', *BASOR* 245, 57–62.
Ratzaby, Y., 1956–57: ''Iyyune lashon be-shirat Sefarad', *Leshonenu* 21, 22–32.
1959: ''Iyyune lashon be-fiyyuṭe R. Mosheh ben 'Ezra'', *LeshLA* 10, 9–16.
1965: ''Iyyunim be-shire R. Yehudah Halevy', *OYS* 8, 11–16. H.

1967: 'The language of Rabbi Shmuel Hannagid's Ben Mishle', *Bar-Ilan* 4–5, 160–80. H.

1968: 'Arabic influences on Hebrew literature of the Spanish period', *Bar-Ilan* 6, 314–38. H.

1969: ''Iyyune lashon be-shirat ha-tekufah ha-Sefardit', *LeshLA* 20, 67–75, 164–69.

1970: 'Religious elements in profane use in Arab and Spanish-Jewry poetry', *Bar-Ilan* 7–8, 178–203. H.

1972: 'The drinking-songs of Samuel ha-Nagid', *Bar-Ilan* 10, 423–74. H.

1972–73: 'On the Mishnaic language tradition in Spanish Hebrew poetry', *Leshonenu* 37, 311–12. H.

1973: 'Ancient pronunciations in the tradition of Hebrew rhyme', *Bar-Ilan* 11, 267–87. H.

1985: ''Iyyune lashon be-sifrut yeme ha-benayim', in B.Z. Luria (ed.), *Sefer Avraham Even-Shoshan*, Jerusalem, pp. 267–88.

Ravis, C., 1648–50: *A discourse of the oriental tongues together with a general grammar for the ready attaining of the Hebrew, Samaritan, Chaldaic, Syriac, Arabic and Ethiopic tongues.* London.

Reckendorf, H., 1897: 'Zur Karakteristik der semitischen Sprachen', in *Actes du dixième Congrès International des Orientalistes. Session de Genève, 1894*, III.2, Leiden, pp. 3–9.

1911: 'Der Bau der semitischen Zahlwörter', *ZDMG* 65, 550–59.

Reed, W.L. and Winnett, F.V., 1963: 'A fragment of an early Moabite inscription from Kerak', *BASOR* 172, 1–9.

Rehm, M., 1937: *Textkritische Untersuchungen zu den Parallelstellen der Samuel-Königsbücher und der Chronik*. Münster.

Reifenberg, A., 1952: *Ancient Hebrew seals*. London.

Reinisch, L., 1909: *Das persönliche Fürwort und die Verbalflexion in den chamito-semitischen Sprachen*. Vienna.

Reisner, G.A., Fisher, C.S. and Lyon, D.G., 1924: *Harvard excavations at Samaria, 1908–1910*. 2 vols. Cambridge, Mass.

Renan, E., 1855: *Histoire générale et système comparé des langues sémitiques*. Paris.

Rendsburg, G., 1980: Evidence for a spoken Hebrew in biblical times'. Doct. diss., New York University.

1980a: 'Late Biblical Hebrew and the date of "P"', *JANES* 12, 65–80.

1982: 'Dual personal pronouns and dual verbs in Hebrew', *JQR*, n.s., 73, 38–58.

Revell, E.J., 1961–62: 'The order of the elements in the verbal statement clause in 1Q Serek', *RQ* 3, 559–69.

1962: 'A structural analysis of the grammar of the Manual of Discipline'. Doct. diss., University of Toronto.

1964–66: 'Clause structure in the prose documents of Qumran Cave 1', *RQ* 5, 3–22.

1969: 'A new biblical fragment with Palestinian vocalization', *Textus* 7, 59–75.

1970: 'Studies in the Palestinian vocalization of Hebrew', in J.W. Wevers and D.B. Redford (eds.), *Essays on the ancient Semitic world*, Toronto, pp. 51–100.

1970a: *Hebrew texts with Palestinian vocalization*. Toronto.

1971: 'The oldest evidence for the Hebrew accent system', *BJRL* 54, 214–22.

1972: 'The placing of the accent signs in biblical texts with Palestinian pointing', in J.W. Wevers and D.B. Redford (eds.), *Studies on the ancient Palestinian world presented to Professor F.V. Winnett*, Toronto, pp. 34–45.

1973: 'A new subsystem of "Tibero-Palestinian" pointing', *P5WCJS*, IV, 91–107.

1974: 'The relation of the Palestinian to the Tiberian *masora*', *MasSt* 1, 87–97.

1976: 'Biblical punctuation and chant in the Second Temple period', *Journal for the study of Judaism in the Persian, Hellenistic, and Roman periods* 7, 181–98.

1977: *Biblical texts with Palestinian pointing and their accents*. Missoula.

1980: 'Pausal forms in Biblical Hebrew: their function, origin and significance', *JSS* 25, 60–80.

1984: 'Stress and the waw "consecutive" in Biblical Hebrew', *JAOS* 104, 437–44.

Richardson, H.N., 1968: 'A stamped handle from Khirbet Yarmuk', *BASOR* 192, 12–16.

Richter, A, 1925: *Das Neuhebräische in babylonischer Überlieferung*. I: *Handschriften und Akzente*. Giessen.

Rieger, E., 1935: *Oṣar millot ha-yesod shel ha-lashon ha-'Ivrit ha-shimmushit. Meḥkar be-'Ivrit. Tokhnit limmudim.* Jerusalem.
1953: *Modern Hebrew.* New York.
Riesener, I., 1979: *Der Stamm 'BD im Alten Testament* (*BZAW* 149). Berlin/New York.
Rin, S., 1961: '"-e" as an absolute plural ending', *BZ*, n.s., 5, 255–58.
Rinaldi, G., 1962–63: 'La particella "wbkn" in 1QSa 1, 11', *FrancLA* 13, 101–09.
Ringgren, H., 1977: 'Bileam och inskriften från Deir 'Allā', *Religion och Bibel* 36, 85–89.
Ritter, H. and Schaade, A., 1959: 'The pronunciation of Hebrew by the Samaritans as recorded at Nāblus in 1917', ed. by A. Murtonen, in Kahle, pp. 318–35.
Rivkai, I., 1938: *'Al sefat yeladenu ba-'Areṣ.* Tel-Aviv.
Roberts, A., 1877: 'That Christ spoke Greek', *The expositor,* first series, 6, 81–96, 161–76, 285–99, 367–83.
1878: 'That Christ spoke Greek–a reply', *The expositor,* first series, 7, 278–95.
Roberts, B.J., 1948: 'The evidence of the Tiberian Masoretic Text', *JTS* 49, 8–16.
Roberts, J.J.M., 1972: *The earliest Semitic pantheon.* Baltimore/London.
Robertson, D., 1969: 'The morphemes "-Y" ("-ī") and "-W" ("-ō") in Biblical Hebrew', *VT* 19, 211–23.
Robertson, J., 1758: *Grammatica linguae hebraeae ... de antiquitate quadrati et samaritani characteris.* Edinburgh.
Rofé, A., 1979: *The Book of Balaam (Numbers 22:2–24:25).* Jerusalem. H.
Röllig, W., 1974: 'Alte und neue Elfenbeininschriften', in Degen, W.W. Müller, and Röllig 1972–78, II, pp. 37–64.
van Rooy, H.F., 1986: 'Conditional sentences in Biblical Hebrew', *P9WCJS*, Division D, 9–16.
Rosén, H.B., 1949–50: 'Ḥiddushe lashon she-lo' mi-da'at', *LeshLA* 11, 17–20.
1952: 'Remarques descriptives sur le parler hébreu-israélien moderne', *GLECS* 6, 4–7.
1953: 'Remarques au sujet de la phonologie de l'hébreu biblique', *RB* 60, 30–40.
1953–54: *Siḥot 'al lashon we-hisṭoryah.* Tel-Aviv.
1954–55: 'Dikduk ha-'Ivrit ha-Yisre'elit', *Tarbiz* 24, 234–37.
1955: *Ha-'Ivrit shellanu: demutah be-'or shiṭṭot ha-balshanut.* Tel-Aviv.
1956: 'Aspect and tense in Biblical Hebrew (the status of the so-called "conversive wāw")', in *Sefer A. Biram,* II, Jerusalem, pp. 205–18. H.
1957: 'Sur quelques catégories à expression adnominale en hébreu-israélien', *BSLP* 53, 316–44.
1958: 'L'hébreu-israélien', *REJ*, n.s., 17, 59–90.
1959: 'Zur Vorgeschichte des Relativsatzes im Nordwestsemitischen', *ArOr* 27, 186–98.
1961: 'A marginal note on Biblical Hebrew phonology', *JNES* 20, 124–26.
1961a: 'Syntactical notes on Israeli Hebrew: determination, indetermination and the definite article', *JAOS* 81, 21–26.
1963: 'Palestinian *koinē* in rabbinic illustration', *JSS* 8, 55–72.
1963–66: 'Composition adjectivale et adjectifs composés en hébreu-israélien', *GLECS* 10, 126–35.
1969: *A textbook of Israeli Hebrew.* 2nd ed. Chicago/London.
1969a: 'Israel language policy, language teaching and linguistics', *Ariel* 25, 92–111.
1974: 'La position descriptive et comparative des formes contextuelles en hébreu', *APCI*, 246–55.
1977: *'Ivrit ṭovah.* 3rd ed. Tel-Aviv.
1977a: *Contemporary Hebrew.* The Hague/Paris.
1979: *L'Hébreu et ses rapports avec le monde classique. Essai d'évaluation culturelle.* Paris.
1985: 'Outlines of a history of Hebrew verbal tenses', in M. Bar-Asher (ed.), *Language studies,* I, Jerusalem, pp. 287–93. H.
1986: *La nature de l'hébreu médieval.* Tel-Aviv.
Rosenbaum, J. and Seger, J.D., 1986: 'Three unpublished ostraca from Gezer', *BASOR* 264, 51–60.
Rosenberg, J., 1901: *Lehrbuch der samaritanischen Sprache und Literatur.* Vienna.
Rosenthal, D., 1981: 'Mishnat 'Avodah Zarah. Mahadurah bikortit u-mavo'. Doct. diss., Hebrew University, Jerusalem.
Rosenthal, F., 1936: *Die Sprache der palmyrenischen Inschriften und ihre Stellung innerhalb des Aramäischen.* Leipzig.
1939 (repr. 1964): *Die aramäistische Forschung seit Th. Nöldeke's Veröffentlichungen.* Leiden.

1963: *A grammar of Biblical Aramaic*. 2nd ed. Wiesbaden.
1967: *An Aramaic handbook*. 4 vols. Wiesbaden.
Rössler, O., 1950: 'Verbalbau und Verbalflexion in den semito-hamitischen Sprachen', *ZDMG* 100, 461–514.
1951: 'Akkadisches und libysches Verbum', *Orientalia* 20, 101–07, 366–73.
1952: 'Der semitische Charakter der lybischen Sprache', *ZA* 50, 121–50.
1961: 'Eine bisher unbekannte Tempusform im Althebräischen', *ZDMG* 111, 445–51.
1962: 'Die Präfixconjugation Qal der Verba Iae Nûn im Althebräischen und das Problem der sogenannten Tempora', *ZAW* 74, 125–40.
1964: 'Lybisch – Hamitisch – Semitisch', *Oriens* 17, 199–216.
Rost, L., 1971: *Einleitung in die alttestamentlichen Apokryphen und Pseudepigraphen einschliesslich der grossen Qumran-Handschriften*. Heidelberg.
Roth, N., 1983: 'Jewish reactions to the 'Arabiyya and the renaissance of Hebrew in Spain', *JSS* 28, 62–84.
Rottenberg, M., 1967–68: 'The implicit construct phrase in the Bible', *Leshonenu* 32, 347–58. H.
Rowley, H.H., 1932: 'The bilingual problem of Daniel', *ZAW* 50, 256–68.
1933: 'Early Aramaic dialects and the Book of Daniel', *JRAS*, 777–805.
Rubinstein, A., 1952: 'A finite verb continued by an infinitive absolute in Biblical Hebrew', *VT* 2, 362–67.
1953: 'Notes on the use of the tenses in the variant readings of the Isaiah Scroll', *VT* 3, 92–95.
1955: 'Singularities in consecutive-tense constructions in the Isaiah Scroll', *VT* 5, 180–88.
1956: 'Conditional constructions in the Isaiah Scroll (DSIa)', *VT* 6, 69–79.
1957: 'Notes on some syntactical irregularities in Text B of the Zadokite Documents', *VT* 7, 356–61.
1963: 'The anomalous perfect with waw-conjunctive in Biblical Hebrew', *Biblica* 44, 62–69.
Rubinstein, E., 1965: 'The compound nominal clause in Modern Hebrew'. Doct. diss., Hebrew University, Jerusalem. H.
1968: *Ha-mishpaṭ ha-shemani*. Merḥavyah.
1970: *Ha-ṣeruf ha-po'oli*. Merḥavyah.
1970a: 'Sentence modifiers and verb modifiers and their position in the sentence', *Leshonenu* 35, 60–74. H.
1973–74: '"Šalaḥ" and "šillaḥ": a syntactic and semantic study in Biblical Hebrew', *Leshonenu* 38, 11–32. H.
1975: 'Double causation in a sentence: a syntactic-semantic study in Biblical Hebrew', *IOS* 5, 32–44.
1977: 'The verb "ṣiwwāh": a study in the syntax of Biblical Hebrew', *P6WCJS*, I, 207–12.
Rudolph, W., 1966: 'Eigentümlichkeiten der Sprache Hoseas', in W.C. van Unnik and A.S. van der Woude (eds.), *Studia biblica et semitica Theodoro Christiano Vriezen ... dedicata*, Wageningen, pp. 313–17.
Rüger, H.P., 1963: 'Ein neues Genesis-Fragment mit komplizierter babylonischer Punktation aus der Kairo-Geniza', *VT* 13, 235–37.
1966: 'Ein Fragment der bisher ältesten datierten hebräischen Bibelhandschriften mit babylonischen Punktation', *VT* 16, 65–73.
1970: *Text und Textform im hebräischen Sirach. Untersuchungen zur Textgeschichte und Textkritik der hebräischen Sirachfragmente aus der Kairoer Geniza*. Berlin.
Ruiz, G., 1975: 'Lamed y bet enfáticos y lamed vocativo en Deuteroisaías', in L. Alvarez and E.J. Alonso (eds.), *Homenaje a Juan Prado. Miscelanea de estudios bíblicos y hebraicos*, Madrid, pp. 147–61.
Rundgren, F., 1955: *Über Bildungen mit* š- *und* n- t- *Demonstrativen im Semitischen*. Uppsala.
1959: *Intensiv und Aspektkorrelation: Studien zur äthiopischen und akkadischen Verbalstammbildung*. Uppsala/Wiesbaden.
1961: *Das althebräische Verbum. Abriss der Aspektlehre*. Stockholm.
1963: *Erneuerung des Verbalaspekts im Semitischen. Funktionell-diachronische Studien zur semitischen Verblehre*. Uppsala.

Russell, J.K., 1955–56: 'Did Jesus speak Greek?', *ET* 67, 246.

Růžička, R., 1908: 'Über die Existenz des Ghains in Hebräischen', *ZA* 21, 293–340.

1909: 'Konsonantische Dissimilation in den semitischen Sprachen', *BA* 6, 4.

Ryder, S.A., 1974: *The D-stem in Western Semitic*. The Hague/Paris.

Sabottka, L., 1972: *Zephanja*. Rome.

Sachs, H., 1897: *Die Partikeln der Mischna*. Berlin.

Sadaqa, A. & R., 1962–66: *Jewish and Samaritan version of the Pentateuch*. 5 vols. Tel-Aviv.

Sadka, Y., n.d.: *Taḥbir ha-mishpaṭ le-'or te'oryot ḥadashot*. Jerusalem.

1981: *Ha-taḥbir ha-'Ivrit be-yamenu*. Jerusalem.

Sáenz-Badillos, A., 1974: Review of M. Fraenkel 1970, *Sefarad* 34, 128–29.

1975: 'Semitistas' in *Gran Enciclopedia Rialp*, XXI, pp. 171–72.

1975a: 'El hebreo del s. II d.C. a la luz de las transcripciones griegas de Aquila, Símmaco y Teodoción', *Sefarad* 35, 107–30.

1976: 'En torno al Maḥberet de Menaḥem ben Saruq', *MEAH* 25.2, 11–50.

1980: 'El 'Anaq, poema lingüístico de Shelomoh ibn Gabirol', *MEAH* 29.2, 5–29.

1982: 'Linguistical components in Dunash ben Labraṭ's Teshuvot', *P8WCJS*, Division D, 1–5.

1985: 'Leshono shel Menaḥem ben Saruq', in Berit 'Ivrit 'Olamit, *Kenes Paris. Ve Congrès Européen d'Etudes Hébraïques, octobre 1982*, Jerusalem, pp. 69–75.

St. John, R., 1952: *Tongue of the prophets*. New York.

Sanday, W., 1878: 'The language spoken in Palestine at the time of Our Lord', *The Expositor*, first series, 7, 81–99.

1878: 'Did Christ speak Greek? – a rejoinder', *The Expositor*, first series, 7, 368–88.

Sanders, J.A., 1967: 'Palestine manuscripts 1947–1967', *JBL* 86, 431–40.

Sanmartín, J., 1971: 'Notizen zur ugaritischen Orthographie', *UF* 3, 173–80.

Sapan, R., 1963: *Darke ha-slang*. Jerusalem.

1965: *Millon ha-slang ha-Yisre'eli*. Jerusalem.

Sappir, J., 1866–74 (repr. 1969): *Even Sappir*. 2 vols. Lyck.

Sarauw, C., 1939: *Über Akzent und Silbenbildung*. Copenhagen.

Ṣarfatti, G.B, 1958–60: 'Munaḥe ha-matemaṭikah shel Mishnat ha-Middot', *Leshonenu* 23, 136–71; 24, 73–94.

1964–66: ''Iyyunim ba-semanṭikah shel leshon ḤaZaL u-bi-drashotehen', *Leshonenu* 29, 238–44; 30, 29–40.

1968: *Mathematical terminology in the Hebrew scientific literature of the Middle Ages*. Jerusalem. H.

1971–72: '"btkn 'ṣlm" – a riddle of the Copper Scroll', *Leshonenu* 36, 106–11. H.

1979–80: 'Ha-tafkid ha-prosodi shel he ha-yedi'ah bi-lshon ḥakhamim', *Leshonenu* 44, 185–201.

1980: "Al odot ha-yadua' shel ṣerufe ha-semikhut ha-kevulim bi-lshon ḥakhamim', in G.B. Ṣarfatti, P. Artzi, J.C. Greenfield, and M.Z. Kaddari (eds.), *Studies in Hebrew and Semitic languages dedicated to the memory of Prof. E.Y. Kutscher*, Ramat-Gan, pp. 140–54.

1982: 'Hebrew inscriptions of the First Temple period: a survey and some linguistic comments', *Maarav* 3, 55–83.

1983: 'Masoret leshon ḥakhamim – masoret shel "lashon sifrutit ḥayah"', in M. Bar-Asher, A. Dotan, G.B. Ṣarfatti, and D. Téné (eds.), *Hebrew language studies presented to Professor Zeev Ben-Ḥayyim*, Jerusalem, pp. 451–58.

1984: 'L'uso dell'articolo determinativo in espressioni del tipo "keneset ha-gedolah"', *Annuario di studi ebraici* 10, 219–28.

1985: 'Ṣimmude millim be-seder kavua' bi-lishon ḥakhamim', in B.Z. Luria (ed.), *Sefer Avraham Even-Shoshan*, Jerusalem, pp. 301–13.

Sarna, N.M., 1959: 'The interchange of the prepositions "beth" and "min" in Biblical Hebrew', *JBL* 78, 310–16.

1963: 'The mythological background of Job 18', *JBL* 82, 315–18.

Sasson, V., 1979: 'The 'Ammān citadel inscription as an oracle promising divine protection: philological and literary comments', *PEQ* 111, 117–25.

1979a: 'Studies in the lexicon and linguistic usage of early Hebrew inscriptions'. Doct. diss., New York University.
1982: 'The meaning of "whbst" in the Arad inscription', *ZAW* 94, 105–11.
1984: 'A matter to be put right ...', *JNSL* 12, 115–20.
Saur, G., 1974: 'Die Ugaritistik und die Psalmenforschung', *UF* 6, 401–06.
Sawyer, J.F.A., 1967: 'Root-meanings in Hebrew', *JSS* 12, 37–50.
1972: *Semantics in biblical research. New methods of defining Hebrew words for salvation.* London.
1973: 'Hebrew words for the resurrection of the dead', *VT* 23, 218–34.
1975: 'A historical description of the Hebrew root "YŠ"' in J. and T. Bynon (eds.), pp. 75–84.
Saydon, P.P., 1959: *The use of the tenses in Deutero-Isaiah.* Rome.
1962: 'The conative imperfect in Hebrew', *VT* 12, 124–26.
1964: 'Meanings and uses of the particle "'t"', *VT* 14, 192–210.
Schaeder, H.H., 1930: *Iranische Beiträge*. I. Halle.
1930a: *Esra der Schreiber*. Tübingen.
Schaeffer, C.F.A., 1939: *The cuneiform texts of Ras Shamra-Ugarit.* Schweich Lectures, 1936. London.
Schatzmiller, Y., 1983: 'Terminologie politique en hébreu médiéval: jalons pour un glossaire', *REJ* 142, 133–40.
Schechter, S., 1902: 'Saadyana, i–iii', *JQR* 14, 37–63, 197–249, 449–516.
1903: *Saadyana: Genizah fragments of writings of R. Saadya Gaon and others*. Cambridge.
Scheftelowitz, J., 1901: *Arisches im Alten Testament.* Berlin.
Schick, C., 1880: 'Phoenician inscription in the Pool of Siloam', *PEFQS* 12, 238–39.
Schiffman, L., 1980: 'The Temple Scroll in literary and philological perspective', in W. Green (ed.), *Approaches to ancient Judaism*, II, Chico, pp. 143–55.
Schirmann, Ḥ. (J.), 1930: *Die hebräische Übersetzung der Maqamen des Hariri.* Frankfurt-am-Main.
1953: 'Hebrew liturgical poetry and Christian hymnology', *JQR*, n.s., 44, 123–61.
1954: *Ha-shirah ha-'Ivrit bi-Sfarad u-be-Provence*. Jerusalem.
1954a: 'The function of the Hebrew poet in mediaeval Spain', *Jewish social studies* 16, 235–52.
1965–66: *New Hebrew poems from the Genizah.* Jerusalem. H.
1979: *Studies in the history of Hebrew poetry and drama.* Jerusalem. H.
Schlatter, A., 1913 (repr. 1970): *Die hebräischen Namen bei Josephus.* Gütersloh.
Schmelz, U.O. and Bachi, R., 1972–73: 'Hebrew as the everyday language of the Jews in Israel. A statistical appraisal', *Leshonenu* 37, 50–68, 187–201. H.
Schmelczer, M., 1965: 'The poetic work of Isaac ibn Giyat'. Doct. diss., Jewish Theological Seminary of America, New York. H.
Schmuttermayr, G., 1971: 'Ambivalenz und Aspektdifferenz. Bemerkungen zu den hebräischen Präpositionen "b^e-", "l^e-" und "min"', *BZ*, n.s., 15, 29–51.
Schneider, M.B., 1930: 'Yaḥas ha-dikduk ha-Mishnati la-dikduk ha-mikra'i', *Leshonenu* 3, 15–28.
1935–36: 'Ha-lashon ha-'Ivrit ha-sifrutit', *Leshonenu* 6, 301–26; 7, 52–73.
Scholem, G., 1971: 'Zohar', *EJ*, XVI, 1193–1215.
Schoors, A., 1971: 'Literary phrases', in L.R. Fisher (ed.), *Ras Shamra parallels. The texts from Ugarit and the Hebrew Bible*, I, Rome, pp. 1–70.
Schramm, G.M., 1957: 'A reconstruction of the Biblical Hebrew waw consecutive', *General linguistics* 3, 1–8.
1964: *The graphemes of Tiberian Hebrew.* Berkeley.
1967: 'The correspondence of distinctive oppositions in distantly related languages', in *To honor Roman Jakobson: essays on the occasion of his seventieth birthday*, III, The Hague/Paris, pp. 1769–74.
Schreiden, J., 1957: 'Observations sur la prononciation antique de l'hébreu', *Le Muséon* 70, 349–52.
1959: 'Les caractéristiques linguistiques de l'hébreu qumranien et leur inférence sur le problème historique', *Le Muséon* 72, 153–57.
Schreiner, M., 1886: 'Zur Geschichte der Aussprache des Hebräischen', *ZAW* 6, 213–59.
Schulthess, F., 1917: *Das Problem der Sprache Jesu*. Zurich.

Schürmann, H., 1958: 'Die Sprache des Christus', *BZ*, n.s., 2, 54–84.

Schwab, M.M., 1898: *Transcription de mots grecs et latins en hébreu aux premiers siècles de J.C.* Paris.

Schwarzwald, O.R., 1973–74: 'Roots, patterns and the morpheme structure [in Modern Hebrew]', *Leshonenu* 38, 131–37. H.

1975–76: 'Concrete and abstract approaches in the analysis of "bgdkpt-bkp" in Hebrew', *Leshonenu* 40, 211–32. H.

1980: 'Parallel processes in Mishnaic and Modern Hebrew', in G.B. Ṣarfatti, P. Artzi, J.C. Greenfield, and M.Z. Kaddari (eds.), *Studies in Hebrew and Semitic languages dedicated to the memory of Prof. E.Y. Kutscher*, Ramat-Gan, pp. 174–88. H.

1981: 'The pronunciation of 'ayin in the East-Ladino-speaking communities', *Leshonenu* 46, 72–75. H.

1981a: 'Frequency factors as determinants in the *binyanim* meanings', *HS* 22, 131–37.

1981b: 'Grammaticality in Modern Hebrew', *Middle East studies* 13, 11–19.

1984: 'Markedness relations in the pronunciation of the prefixed particles in Modern Hebrew', *AAL* 9.2, 1–14.

Segal, J.B., 1957: 'An Aramaic ostracon from Nimrud', *Iraq* 19, 139–45.

1962: '"Yrḥ" in the Gezer "calendar"', *JSS* 7, 212–21.

Segal, M.H. (Z.), 1908–09: 'Mishnaic Hebrew and its relation to Biblical Hebrew and to Aramaic', *JQR* 20, 647–737.

1910: 'Hebrew in the period of the Second Temple', *International Journal of Apocrypha* 11, 79–82.

1927: *A grammar of Mishnaic Hebrew*. Oxford.

1928: *Yesode ha-fonetikah ha-'Ivrit*. Jerusalem.

1936: *Dikduk leshon ha-Mishnah*. Tel-Aviv.

1936a: 'Meḥkarim ba-lashon', *Leshonenu* 7, 100–20.

1958: *Sefer Ben Sira ha-shalem*. 2nd rev. ed. Jerusalem.

Segert, S., 1957: 'Aramäische Studien, ii: Zur Verbreitung des Aramäischen in Palästina zur Zeit Jesu', *ArOr* 25, 21–37.

1960: 'Considerations on Semitic comparative lexicography', *ArOr* 28, 470–87.

1961: 'Die Sprache der moabitischen Königsinschrift', *ArOr* 29, 197–267.

1963: 'Die Sprachenfragen in der Qumran-Gemeinschaft', in H. Bardtke (ed.), *Qumran-Probleme: Vorträge des Leipziger Symposiums über Qumran-Probleme vom 9. bis 14. Oktober 1961*, Berlin, pp. 315–39.

1964: 'Zur Schrift und Orthographie der altaramäischen Stelen von Sfire', *ArOr* 32, 110–26.

1965: 'Aspekte des althebräischen Aspektsystems', *ArOr* 33, 93–104.

1968: 'Recent progress in Ugaritology', *ArOr* 36, 443–67.

1968a: 'Bedeutung der Handschriftenfunde am Toten Meer für die Aramaistik', in S. Wagner (ed.), *Bibel und Qumran. Beiträge zur Erforschung der Beziehungen zwischen Bibel- und Qumranwissenschaft. Hans Bardtke zum 22.9.1966*, Berlin, pp. 183–87.

1969: 'Versbau und Sprachbau in der althebräischen Poesie', *MIO* 15, 312–21.

1969a: 'Hebrew Bible and Semitic comparative lexicography', *SVT* 17, 204–11.

1975: *Altaramäische Grammatik*. Leipzig.

1976: *A grammar of Phoenician and Punic*. Munich.

1983: 'The last sign of the Ugaritic alphabet', *UF* 15, 201–18.

1984: *A basic grammar of the Ugaritic language*. Berkeley/Los Angeles.

Sekine, M., 1940–41: 'Das Wesen des althebräischen Verbalausdrucks', *ZAW* 58, 133–41.

1963: 'Erwägungen zur hebräischen Zeitauffassung', *SVT* 9, 66–82.

1973: 'The subdivisions of the North-West Semitic languages', *JSS* 18, 205–21.

van Selms, A., 1970: 'Some reflections on the formation of the feminine in Semitic Languages', in H. Goedicke (ed.), *Near Eastern studies in honor of William Foxwell Albright*, Baltimore/London, pp. 421–31.

1971–72: 'Motivated interrogative sentences in Biblical Hebrew', *Semitics* 2, 143–49.

1975: 'Some remarks on the 'Ammān citadel inscription', *BibOr* 32, 5–8.

Sethe, K., 1926: *Die Ächtung feindlicher Fürsten, Völker und Dinge auf altägyptischen Tongefässscherben des mittleren Reiches*. Berlin.

Sevenster, J.N., 1968: *Do you know Greek? How much Greek could the first Jewish Christians have known?* Leiden.

Sgherrì, G., 1974: 'A proposito di Origine e la lingua ebraica', *Augustinianum* 14, 223–57.

Shapiro, M. and Shvika, Y., 1963–64: 'Nittuaḥ mekhanografi shel ha-morfologyah ha-'Ivrit', *Leshonenu* 27–28, 354–72.

Sharvit, S., 1966–67: ''Iyyunim be-millonah shel Megillat ha-Neḥoshet', *BM* 12, 127–35.

1974: 'Studies in the lexicography and grammar of Mishnaic Hebrew based on the *Introductions* of J.N. Epstein', *ANDRL*, II, pp. 112–24.

1980: 'Ma'arekhet ha-zemanim bi-lshon ha-Mishnah', in G.B. Ṣarfatti, P. Artzi, J.C. Greenfield, and M.Z. Kaddari (eds.), *Studies in Hebrew and Semitic languages dedicated to the memory of Prof. E.Y. Kutscher*, Ramat-Gan, pp. 110–25.

1981: 'The crystallization of Mishnaic Hebrew research', *Bar-Ilan* 18–19, 221–32. H.

1989: 'Gutturals in Rabbinic Hebrew', in M.Z. Kaddari and S. Sharvit (eds.), *Studies in the Hebrew language and the Talmudic literature dedicated to the memory of Dr. Menaḥem Moreshet*, Ramat-Gan, pp. 225–43.

Shea, W.H., 1977: 'The date and significance of the Samaria ostraca', *IEJ* 27, 16–27.

1977a: 'Ostracon ii from Heshbon', *AUSS* 15, 217–22.

1978: 'The Siran inscription: Amminadab's drinking song', *PEQ* 110, 107–12.

1979: 'Milkom as the architect of Rabbath-Ammon's natural defences in the Amman citadel inscription', *PEQ* 111, 17–25.

1981: 'The Amman citadel inscription again', *PEQ* 113, 105–10.

Sheehan, J.F.X., 1970: 'Conversive waw and accentual shift', *Biblica* 51, 545–48.

1971: 'Egypto-Semitic elucidation of the waw conversive', *Biblica* 52, 39–43.

Sherman, M.E., 1966: 'Systems of Hebrew and Aramaic orthography: an epigraphic history of the use of *matres lectionis* in non-biblical texts to *circa* A.D. 135'. Doct. diss., Harvard University.

Shiloh, Y., 1984: *Excavations at the City of David*. I: 1978–1982 (*Qedem* 19). Jerusalem.

1985: 'A hoard of Hebrew bullae from the City of David', *EI* 18, 73–87.

1986: 'A group of Hebrew bullae from the City of David', *IEJ* 36, 16–18.

Shiloh, Y. and Tarler, D., 1986: 'Bullae from the City of David. A hoard of seal impressions from the Israelite period', *BA* 49, 197–209.

Shivtiel, I., 1937–39: 'Mesorot ha-Temanim be-dikduk leshon ḥakhamim', in Yalon (ed.), I, pp. 8–15; II, pp. 61–69.

1963: 'Yemenite traditions relating to the grammar of the language of the Mishnah', in S. Lieberman (ed.), *Sefer Ḥanokh Yalon*, Jerusalem, pp. 338–59. H.

Shur, S., 1979: 'Language innovation and socio-political setting: the case of Modern Hebrew', *HCL* 15, 4–13.

Siedl, S.H., 1971: *Gedanken zum Tempussystem im Hebräischen und Akkadischen*. Wiesbaden.

Siegel, J.P., 1971: 'The employment of palaeo-Hebrew characters for the divine names at Qumran in the light of Tannaitic sources', *HUCA* 42, 159–72.

1972: 'The scribes of Qumran. Studies in the early history of Jewish scribal customs, with special reference to the Qumran biblical scrolls and to the Tannaitic traditions of Massekhet Soferim'. Doct. diss., Brandeis University.

1974: 'An orthographic convention of 1QIsa[a] and the origin of two Masoretic anomalies', *MasSt* 1, 99–110.

Siegfried, C., 1884: 'Die Aussprache des Hebräischen bei Hieronymus', *ZAW* 4, 34–83.

1897: 'Beiträge zur Lehre von den zusammengesetzten Satze im Neuhebräischen', in G.A. Kohut (ed.), *Semitic studies in memory of Rev. Dr. Alexander Kohut*, Berlin, pp. 543–56.

Siegfried, C. and Strack, H.L., 1884: *Lehrbuch der neuhebräischen Sprache und Literatur*. 2 vols. Karlsruhe/Leipzig.

Sievers, E., 1901: *Studien zur hebräischen Metrik*. I: Untersuchungen. Leipzig.

Silbermann, L.H., 1961–62: 'Unriddling the riddle. A study in the structure and language of the Habakkuk Pesher', *RQ* 3, 323–64.

Silva, M., 1983: *Biblical words and their meanings: an introduction to lexical semantics*. Grand Rapids.

Silverman, M.H., 1970: 'Hebrew name-types in the Elephantine documents', *Orientalia* 39, 465–91.

1973: 'Syntactic notes on the waw-consecutive', in H.A. Hoffner (ed.), *Orient and occident. Essays presented to Cyrus H. Gordon on the occasion of his sixty-fifth birthday*, Neukirchen-Vluyn, pp. 167–76.

Simon, H., 1970: *Lehrbuch der modernen hebräischen Sprache*. Munich.

Simons, J., 1937: *Handbook for the study of Egyptian topographical lists relating to western Asia*. Leiden.

Sirat, C., 1968: 'La paléographie hébraïque', *P4WCJS*, II, 173–74.

Sirat, R.S., 1966: 'Evolution sémantique de la racine "TQ" en hébreu', *RENLO* 3, 35–62.

1968–69: 'Brèves remarques sur l'évolution de la langue poétique en hébreu', *RENLO* 5, 27–48.

1974: 'Y a-t-il un élément "'ain-resh" commun à plusiers racines hébraïques?', *APCI*, 234–45.

Sister, M., 1937: *Probleme der Aussprache des Hebräischen*. Berlin.

Sivan, D., 1982: 'On the grammar and orthography of the Ammonite findings', *UF* 14, 219–34.

1983: 'Terumat ha-ṭeksṭim ha-'Akadiyyim me-'Ugarit le-ḥeker ha-'Ugaritit u-ba-'akifin le-ḥeker ha-'Ivrit ha-mikra'it, *Leshonenu* 47, 165–86.

1984: *Grammatical analysis and glossary of the Northwest Semitic vocables in Akkadian texts of the 15th–13th C.B.C. from Canaan and Syria*. Neukirchen-Vluyn.

Sivan, R., 1964–65: 'Ṣurot u-megammot be-ḥiddushe ha-lashon ha-'Ivrit bi-tkufat teḥiyyatah'. Doct. diss., Hebrew University, Jerusalem.

1968: *'Al ḥiddushe millim*. Jerusalem.

1969: 'Ben Yehudah and the revival of the Hebrew speech', *Ariel* 25, 35–39.

Skoss, S.L., 1942: 'A study on inflection in Hebrew from Saadia Gaon's grammatical work Kutub al-Lugah', *JQR*, n.s., 33, 171–212.

1952: 'A study of the Hebrew vowels from Saadia Gaon's grammatical work Kutub al-Lugah', *JQR*, n.s., 42, 283–317.

Snaith, N.H., 1962: 'The Ben Asher text', *Textus* 2, 8–13.

Snijders, L.A., 1953: *The meaning of* zār *in the Old Testament*. Leiden.

Sobelman, H., 1961: 'The Proto-Byblian inscriptions: a fresh approach', *JSS* 6, 226–45.

von Soden, W., 1952: *Grundriss der akkadischen Grammatik*. Rome.

1959: 'Tempus und Modus im Semitischen', in *Akten des XXIV. Internationalen Orientalistenkongress (München 1957)*, Wiesbaden, pp. 263–65.

1960: 'Zur Einteilung der semitischen Sprachen', *Wiener Zeitschrift für die Kunde des Morgenlandes* 56, 177–91.

1965: 'Zur Methode der semitisch-hamitischen Sprachvergleichung', *JSS* 10, 159–77.

1965–81: *Akkadisches Handwörterbuch*. 3 vols. Wiesbaden.

1968: '"N" als Wurzelaugment im Semitischen', *WZMLU* 17, 175–84.

1969a: 'Zur Herkunft von hebr. "'ebjōn" "arm"', *MIO* 15, 322–26.

1969b: 'Akkadisch "ḫâšum" I "sich sorgen" und hebräisch "ḥūš" II', *UF* 1, 197.

1974: Review of S. Levin 1971, *OLZ* 69, 126–31.

1984: 'Sprachfamilien und Einzelsprachen im Altsemitischen: Akkadisch und Eblaitisch', in Fronzaroli (ed.), pp. 11–24.

1985: *Einführung in die Altorientalistik*. Darmstadt.

Soggin, J.A., 1965: 'Tracce di antichi causativi in "š-" realizzati come radici autonome in ebraico biblico', *AION* 15, 17–30.

1968: 'Akkadisch "TAR berîti" und hebräisch "krt bryt"', *VT* 18, 210–15.

1972: '"KLH" – "KLL": osservazioni sull'uso di due radici in ebraico biblico', *AION* 32, 366–71.

1981: 'Bemerkungen zum Deboralied, Richter Kap. 5', *TLZ* 106, 625–39.

Soisalon-Soininen, I., 1972: 'Der *Infinitivus constructus* mit "l" im Hebräischen', *VT* 22, 82–90.

Sokolof, M., 1969: 'Ha-'Ivrit shel Bereshit Rabbah Ketav-yad Vatican 30', *Leshonenu* 33, 25–42, 135–49, 270–79.

Solá-Solé, J.M., 1953: 'Una tendencia lingüística en el manuscrito de Isaías (DSIa) de Khirbet Qumran', *Sefarad* 13, 61–71.
1961: *L'Infinitif sémitique*. Paris.
Spanier, A., 1927: *Die massoretischen Akzente*. Berlin.
1929: 'Über Reste der palästinischen Vokalization in Gebetsbüchern', *MGWJ* 73, 472–75.
Speiser, E.A., 1925–34: 'The pronunciation of Hebrew according to the transliterations in the Hexapla', *JQR*, n.s., 16, 343–83; 23, 233–65; 24, 9–46.
1936: 'Studies in Semitic formatives', *JAOS* 56, 22–46.
1942: 'The shibboleth incident (Judges 12:6)', *BASOR* 85, 10–13.
1952: 'The "elative" in West-Semitic and Akkadian', *JCS* 6, 81–92.
1954: 'The terminative-adverbial in Canaanite-Ugaritic and Akkadian', *IEJ* 4, 108–15.
1955: 'The durative Hithpa'el: a "tan"-form', *JAOS* 75, 118–21.
Sperber, A., 1929: 'Das Alphabet der Septuaginta-Vorlage', *OLZ* 32, 533–40.
1937–38: 'Hebrew based upon Greek and Latin transliterations', *HUCA* 12–13, 103–274.
1939: 'Hebrew based upon biblical passages in parallel transmission', *HUCA* 14, 153–249.
1941: 'Hebrew phonology', *HUCA* 16, 415–82.
1942–43: 'Problems of the Massora', *HUCA* 17, 293–394.
1956–59: *Corpus codicum hebraicorum medii aevi*. I: *Codex Reuchlinianus*; II: *The pre-Massoretic Bible*. Copenhagen.
1959: *A grammar of Masoretic Hebrew. A general introduction to the pre-Masoretic Bible*. Copenhagen.
1966: *A historical grammar of Biblical Hebrew*. Leiden.
1970: *The Hebrew Bible with pre-Masoretic vocalization. The Prophets*. Leiden.
Sperber, D., 1965: 'An early meaning of the word "šapud"', *REJ* 124, 179–84.
1974: 'Etymological studies in Rabbinic Hebrew', *ANDRL*, II, 102–111. H.
1975: 'Studies in Greek and Latin loan-words in rabbinic literature', *Scripta classica israelica* 2, 163–74.
1977–79: 'Greek and Latin words in rabbinic literature. Prolegomena to a new dictionary of classical words in rabbinic literature', *Bar-Ilan* 14–15, 9–60; 16–17, 9–30.
1982: *Essays on Greek and Latin in the Mishnah, Talmud and midrashic literature*. Jerusalem. H.
1984: *A dictionary of Greek and Latin legal terms in rabbinic literature*. Ramat-Gan.
1986: *Nautica talmudica*. Ramat-Gan.
Sperling, D., 1970–71: '"ḤGR" I and "ḤGR" II', *JANES* 3, 121–28.
1972: 'Akkdian "egerrû" and Hebrew "bt qwl"', *JANES* 4, 62–74.
1973: 'Late Hebrew "ḥzr" and Akkadian "saḫāru"', *JANES* 5, 397–404.
Spiegel, S., 1930 (repr. 1962): *Hebrew reborn*. Cleveland.
1963: 'Mi-leshon payyeṭanim', *Ha-do'ar* 42, 397–400.
1974: 'On medieval Hebrew poetry', in L. Finkelstein (ed.), *The Jews: their religion and culture*, II, 4th ed., New York, pp. 82–120.
Spitaler, A., 1938: *Grammatik des neuaramäischen Dialekts von Ma'lula*. Leipzig.
Spuler, B., 1954: 'Der semitische Sprachtypus', in *Handbuch der Orientalistik*, III, Leiden, pp. 3–25.
Stamm, J.J., 1965: 'Hebräische Ersatznamen', in H.G. Güterbock and T. Jacobsen (eds.), *Studies in honor of Benno Landsberger on his 75th Birthday*, Chicago, pp. 413–24.
1967: 'Hebräische Frauennamen', *SVT* 16, 301–39.
Staples, W.E., 1939: 'The second column of Origen's Hexapla', *JAOS* 59, 71–80.
Stefaniak, L.W., 1969: 'Old Hebrew inscriptions from Tel Arad', *FolOr* 11, 267–77.
Stein, S., 1888: *Das Verbum der Mischnahsprache*. Berlin.
Steiner, R.C, 1977: *The case for fricative laterals in Proto-Semitic*. New Haven.
1979: 'From Proto-Hebrew to Mishnaic Hebrew: the history of "-āḵ" and "-āh"', *HAR* 3, 157–74.
1982: *Affricated ṣade in the Semitic languages*. New York.
Steinschneider, M., 1893 (repr. 1956): *Die hebräischen Übersetzungen des Mittelalters und die Juden als Dolmetscher*. Berlin.
1897: *Vorlesungen über die Kunde hebräischer Handschriften*. Leipzig.

Stöhr, H., 1796: *Theoria et praxis linguarum sacrarum*. Vienna.
Strack, H.L., 1875: 'Die biblischen und die massoretischen Handschriften zu Tschufut-Kale in der Krim', *Zeitschrift für die gesammte lutherische Theologie und Kirche* 36, 585–624.
1876: *Prophetarum Posteriorum Codex Babylonicus Petropolitanus*. St. Petersburg.
1921: *Grammatik des Biblisch-Aramäischen*. 6th ed. Munich.
Strauss, D., 1900: *Sprachliche Studien in den hebräischen Sirach-Fragmenten*. Zurich.
Striedl, H., 1937: 'Untersuchungen zur Syntax und Stilistik des hebräischen Buches Esther', *ZAW* 55, 73–108.
Suder, R.W., 1984: *Hebrew inscriptions. A classified bibliography*. London/Toronto.
Sukenik, E.L., 1936: 'Note on a fragment of an Israelite stele found at Samaria', *PEFQS* 68, 156.
Sukenik (Yadin), Y., 1946–47: 'The Ophel ostracon', *BJES* 13, 115–18. H.
Sutcliffe, E.F., 1948: 'St. Jerome's pronunciation of Hebrew', *Biblica* 29, 112–25.
1955: 'A note on "'al", "l^e-", and "from"', *VT* 5, 436–39.
Suzuki, Y., 1982: 'A Hebrew ostracon from Meṣad Ḥashavyahu. A form-critical re-investigation', *AJBI* 8, 3–49.
Swiggers, P., 1981: 'The word "šibbolet" in Jud. xii 6', *JSS* 26, 205–07.
1982: 'The Moabite inscription of El-Kerak', *AION* 42, 521–25.
1984: 'Remarques sur la distinction des catégories nominale et verbale dans les langues sémitiques', *OLZ* 79, 325–27.
Sznycer, M., 1967: *Les passages puniques en transcription latine dans le Poenulus de Plaute*. Paris.
Talmon, S., 1951: 'The Samaritan Pentateuch', *JJS* 2, 144–50.
1959–60: 'Maḥzor ha-berakhot shel kat midbar Yehudah', *Tarbiz* 29, 1–20.
1963: 'The Gezer calendar and the seasonal cycle of ancient Canaan', *JAOS* 83, 177–87.
1964: 'The new Hebrew letter from the seventh century B.C. in historical perspective', *BASOR* 176, 29–38.
1970: 'The Old Testament text', in P.R. Ackroyd and C.F. Evans (eds.), *The Cambridge history of the Bible*, I, Cambridge, pp. 159–99.
Talshir, D., 1988: 'A reinvestigation of the linguistic relationship between Chronicles and Ezra-Nehemiah', *VT* 38, 165–93.
Targarona, J., 1986: 'Poemas de Se'adyah ibn Danan. Edición, traducción y notas', *Sefarad* 46, 449–61.
Taylor, R.O.P., 1944–45: 'Did Jesus speak Aramaic?', *ET* 56, 95–97.
Teicher, J.L., 1950–51: 'The Ben Asher manuscripts', *JJS* 2, 17–25.
Teixidor, J., 1986: *Bulletin d'épigraphie sémitique 1964–1980*. Paris.
Telegdi, S., 1935: 'Essai sur la phonétique des emprunts iraniens en araméen talmudique', *JA* 226, 177–256.
Téné, D., 1961: *La Phonologie de l'hébreu contemporain selon l'usage d'un unilingue*. Paris.
1961–62: 'Ha-meshekh ha-nimdad shel ha-tenu'ot be-'Ivrit', *Leshonenu* 26, 220–68.
1967–68: 'Is the Hebrew root content-structured?', *Leshonenu* 32, 173–207. H.
1968: 'L'hébreu contemporain', in A. Martinet (ed.), *Le Langage* (*Encyclopédie de la Pléiade*, XXV), Paris, pp. 975–1002.
1969: 'L'articulation du signifié de monème en hébreu contemporain', *Word* 25, 289–320.
1969a: 'Israeli Hebrew', *Ariel* 25, 48–63.
1971: 'Linguistic literature, Hebrew', *EJ*, XVI, 1352–90.
Thacker, T.W., 1954: *The relationship of the Semitic and the Egyptian verbal system*. Oxford.
Theis, J., 1912: *Sumerisches im Alten Testament*. Trier.
Thompson, H.O., 1973: 'The excavation of Tell Siran (1972)', *ADAJ* 18, 5–13.
Thompson, H.O. and Zayadine, F., 1974: 'The works of Amminadab', *BA* 37, 13–19.
Thorion, Y., 1982–84: 'Die Sprache der Tempelrolle und die Chronikbücher', *RQ* 11, 423–26.
1982–84a: 'Neue Bemerkungen über die Sprache der Qumran-Literatur', *RQ* 11, 579–82.
1984: *Studien zur klassischen hebräischen Syntax*. Berlin.
1985–86: 'Die Syntax der Präposition "b" in der Qumranliteratur', *RQ* 12, 17–64.
1985–86a: 'Beiträge zur Erforschung der Sprache der Kupfer-Rolle', *RQ* 12, 163–76.

Thorion-Vardi (Vardi), T., 1982–84: 'Die adversativen Konjunktionen in der Qumran-Literatur', *RQ* 11, 571–78.
1985–86: 'The use of the tenses in the Zadokite Documents', *RQ* 12, 65–88.
Throntveit, M.A., 1982: 'Linguistic analysis and the question of authorship in Chronicles, Ezra, and Nehemiah', *VT* 32, 201–16.
Thureau-Dangin, F., 1922: 'Nouvelles lettres d'El Amarna', *RA* 19, 91–108.
Tobin, Y., 1986: 'Aspectual markers in Modern Hebrew', *P9WCJS*, Division D, 53–60.
Toll, T., 1972: 'Die Wurzel "PRṢ" im Hebräischen', *OrSu* 21, 73–86.
Tomback, R.S., 1978: *A comparative lexicon of the Phoenician and Punic languages*. Missoula.
Torczyner, H. (Ṭur-Sinai, N.H.), 1916: *Entstehung des semitischen Sprachtypus*. I. Vienna.
1939: 'The Siloam inscription, the Gezer calendar and the Ophel ostracon', *BJES* 7, 4–6. H.
1946–47: 'A new interpretation of the Gezer calendar', *BJES* 13, 1–7. H.
1947: 'A Hebrew incantation against night-demons from biblical times', *JNES* 6, 18–29.
Torczyner, H. (Ṭur-Sinai, N.H.), Harding, L., Lewis, A., and Starkey, J.L., 1938: *Lachish I. The Lachish letters*. Oxford.
Torres, A., 1982: '"Aspecto verbal" y "tiempo" en la conjugación hebrea, a la luz de la reciente investigación, i', *MEAH* 31.2, 1–29.
Torrey, C.C., 1948–49: 'The question of the original language of Kohelet', *JQR*, n.s., 39, 151–60.
1950: 'The Hebrew of the Geniza Sirach', in S. Lieberman (ed.), *Alexander Marx jubilee volume on ... his seventieth birthday*, New York, pp. 585–602.
Ṭovi, Y., 1972–73: 'About the tradition of Mishnaic and Talmudic Hebrew in medieval Hebrew poetry', *Leshonenu* 37, 137–55. H.
1982: 'The liturgical poems of Rav Sa'adia Gaon. Critical edition [of the *yoṣerot*] with a general introduction to his poetic work'. Doct. diss., Hebrew University, Jerusalem. H.
Tromp, N.J., 1969: *Primitive conceptions of death and the nether world in the Old Testament*. Rome.
Tsevat, M., 1955: *A study of the language of the biblical Psalms*. Philadelphia.
Tubielewicz, W., 1956: 'Vom Einfluss europäischer Sprachen auf die Gestaltung des modernen Hebräisch', *Rocznik orientalistyczny* 20, 337–51.
Tucker, A.N., 1967: '"Fringe" Cushitic: an experiment in typological comparison', *BSOAS* 30, 655–80.
Tufnell, O., 1953: *Lachish III (Tell ed Duweir). The Iron Age*. Oxford.
Turner, W., 1876: 'The tenses of the Hebrew verb', in *Studies biblical and oriental*, Edinburgh, pp. 338–407.
Ṭur-Sinai, N.H. (Torczyner, H.), 1951–52: 'Some ideas on the place of Ugaritic among the Semitic languages', *Tarbiz* 23, 143–45. H.
1952: 'Modern Hebrew and its problems', *Civilisations* 2, 33–40.
1954–59: *Ha-lashon we-ha-sefer*. 3 vols. Jerusalem.
1960: *The revival of the Hebrew language*. Jerusalem.
Tyloch, W., 1980: 'Quelques remarques sur l'hébreu contemporain', *FolOr* 21, 175–77.
Tzori, N., 1961: 'A Hebrew ostracon from Beth-Shean', *BIES* 25, 145–46. H.
Uhlemann, F., 1837: *Institutiones linguae samaritanae*. Leipzig.
Ullendorff, E., 1956: 'The contribution of South Semitic to Hebrew lexicography', *VT* 6, 190–98.
1957: 'Modern Hebrew as a subject of linguistic investigation', *JSS* 2, 251–63.
1958: 'What is a Semitic language?: a problem of linguistic identification', *Orientalia* 27, 66–75.
1961: 'Comparative Semitics', in Levi della Vida (ed.), pp. 13–32.
1962: 'The knowledge of languages in the Old Testament', *BJRL* 44, 455–65.
1970: 'Comparative Semitics', *LSWANA*, 261–73.
1970a: Review of Macuch 1969, BSOAS 33, 689–70.
1971: 'Is Biblical Hebrew a language?', *BSOAS* 34, 241–55.
Ussishkin, D., 1968–69: 'On the short inscription from the tomb of "...yahu who is over the house"', *Leshonenu* 33, 297–303. H.
1969: 'On the shorter inscription from the "tomb of the royal steward"', *BASOR* 196, 16–22.
1978: 'Excavations at Tel Lachish, 1973–1977. Preliminary report', *TAJ* 5, 1–97.
1983: "Excavations at Tel Lachish, 1978–1983. Second preliminary report", *TAJ* 10, 97–175.

Vannutelli, P., 1931–34: *Libri synoptici Veteris Testamenti.* 2 vols. Rome.
Vardi (Thorion-Vardi), T., 1967: 'The concessive clause in Modern Hebrew'. Doct. diss., Hebrew University, Jerusalem.
Vattioni, F., 1969: 'I sigilli ebraici', *Biblica* 50, 357–88.
1971: 'I sigilli ebraici, ii', *Augustinianum* 11, 447–54.
1978: 'I sigilli ebraici, iii', *AION* 38, 227–54.
de Vaux, R., 1939: 'Les ostraca de Lachish', *RB* 48, 181–206.
1953: 'Quelques textes hébreux de Murabba'at', *RB* 60, 268–75.
Vawter, B., 1955: 'The Canaanite background of Genesis 49', *CBQ* 17, 1–18.
Veenhof, K.R., 1965: 'Nieuwe Palestijnse inscripties', *Phoenix* 11, 243–60.
1972: 'De Amman citadel inscriptie', *Phoenix* 18, 170–79.
1973: 'Een Ammonietische inscriptie', *Phoenix* 19, 299–300.
Vergote, J., 1974: 'Le rapport de l'égyptien avec les langues sémitiques: quelques aspects du problème', *APCI*, 49–54.
1975: 'La position intermédiaire de l'ancien égyptien entre l'hébreu et l'arabe', in J. and T. Bynon (eds.), pp. 193–99.
Vermes, G., 1982: *The Dead Sea Scrolls: Qumran in perspective.* 2nd ed. London.
1987: *The Dead Sea Scrolls in English.* 3rd ed. Sheffield.
Verreet, E., 1984–85: 'Beobachtungen zum ugaritischen Verbalsystem, i–ii', *UF* 16, 307–21; 17, 319–44.
Vincent, P., 1909: 'Un calendrier agricole israélite', *RB* 6, 243–69.
Virolleaud, C., 1931: 'Le déchiffrement des tablettes alphabétiques de Ras-Shamra', *Syria* 12, 15–23.
Vycichl, W., 1960: 'Gedanken zur ägyptisch-semitischen Sprachverwandtschaft', *Le Muséon* 73, 173–76.
Vogt, E., 1971: 'Zur Geschichte der hebräischen Sprache', *Biblica* 52, 72–78.
de Vries S.J., 1964–66: 'The syntax of tenses and interpretation in the Hodayoth', *RQ* 5, 375–414.
1965: 'Consecutive constructions in the 1Q sectarian scrolls', in I.T. Naamani (ed.), *Doron. Hebraic studies (essays in honor of Professor Abraham I. Katsh)*, New York, pp. 75–87.
Vriezen, T.C., 1961: 'Einige Notizen zur Übersetzung des Bindewortes "kī"', *BZAW* 77, 266–73.
Vriezen, T.C. and Hospers, J.H., 1951: *Palestine inscriptions.* Leiden.
Wächter, L., 1971: 'Reste von Šaf'el-Bildungen im Hebräischen', *ZAW* 83, 380–89.
Wagner, M., 1966: *Die lexikalischen und grammatikalischen Aramaismen im alttestamentlichen Hebräisch* (*BZAW* 96). Berlin.
1967: 'Beiträge zur Aramaismenfrage im alttestamentlichen Hebräisch', *SVT* 16, 355–71.
Wagner, S., 1968: '"YD"' in den Lobliedern von Qumran', in *Bibel und Qumran. Beiträge zur Erforschung der Beziehungen zwischen Bibel- und Qumranwissenschaft. Hans Bardtke zum 22.9.1966*, Berlin, pp. 232–52.
Wagner, V., 1968: 'Umfang und Inhalt der "mōt" – "jūmat" Reihe', *OLZ* 63, 325–28.
Waldman, N.M., 1973: 'Akkadian loanwords and parallels in Mishnaic Hebrew'. Doct. diss., Gratz College, Philadelphia.
1989: *The recent study of Hebrew: a survey of the literature with selected bibliography.* Cincinnati.
Walker, N., 1955: 'Concerning the function of "'ēth"', *VT* 5, 314–15.
Wallenstein, M., 1959: 'Some aspects of the vocabulary and morphology of the Hymns Scroll with special reference to the interpretation of related obscure passages', *VT* 9, 101–07.
Waltke, B.K., 1965: 'Prolegomena to the Samaritan Pentateuch'. Doct. diss., Harvard University.
Waltke, B.K. and O'Connor, M., 1990: *An introduction to Biblical Hebrew syntax.* Winona Lake.
Wambacq, B.N., 1959: 'Les prières de Baruch (i 15–v 19) et de Daniel (ix 5–19)', *Biblica* 40, 463–75.
Wartsky, I., 1970: *Leshon ha-midrashim.* Jerusalem.
Watson, W.G.E., 1969: 'Shared consonants in Northwest Semitic', *Biblica* 50, 525–33.
1972: 'Archaic elements in the language of Chronicles', *Biblica* 53, 191–207.
Watta, J.W., 1951 (repr. 1964): *A survey of syntax in the Hebrew Old Testament.* Nashville.
Wechter, P., 1964: *Ibn Barun's Arabic works on Hebrew grammar and lexicography.* Philadelphia.
Weerts, J., 1906: 'Über die babylonisch punktierte Handschrift Nr. 1546 der II. Firkowitschen Sammlung (Codex Tschufut-Kale Nr. 3)', *ZAW* 26, 49–84.

Wehmeyer, G., 1970: *Der Segen im Alten Testament. Eine semasiologische Untersuchung der Wurzel* BRK. Basle.

van der Weiden, W.A., 1970: *Le Livre des Proverbes: notes philologiques*. Rome.

Weil, G.E., 1961–62: 'Un fragment de Okhlah palestinienne', *ALUOS* 3, 68–80.

1963: 'Quatre fragments de la Massorah Magna babylonienne', *Textus* 3, 74–120.

1963a: 'La Bible de l'Université Hébraïque de Jérusalem', *RHPR* 43, 193–99.

1971: Massorah Gedolah *juxta Codicem Leningradensem B19a*. I: Catalogi. Rome.

1972: 'La massorah', *REJ* 131, 5–104.

1979: 'Trilitéralité fonctionelle ou bilitéralité fondamentale des racines verbales hébraïques: un essai d'analyse quantifiée', *RHPR* 59, 281–311.

Weiman, R.W., 1950: *Native and foreign elements in a language: a study in general linguistics applied to Modern Hebrew*. Philadelphia.

Weinberg, W., 1965: 'Special bibliography: spoken Israel Hebrew', *HA* 10, 18–32.

1966: 'Spoken Israeli Hebrew: trends in the departure from classical phonology', *JSS* 11, 40–68.

1969–70: 'Transliteration and transcription of Hebrew', *HUCA* 40–41, 1–32.

1971–72: 'The new publication of the "Rules for the unpointed scripts", *Leshonenu* 36, 203–11. H.

1973: 'Benötigt: eine Grammatik des gesprochenen Hebräisch', in W. Dietrich and H. Schreckenberg (eds.), *Festgabe für Karl Heinrich Rengstorf zum 70. Geburtstag*, II, Leiden, pp. 389–413.

1974: 'Biblical grammar/Israeli grammar: accepted and unacceptable changes', *HA* 15, 32–41.

1975–80: 'The history of Hebrew *plene* spelling', *HUCA* 46, 457–87; 47, 237–80; 48, 301–33; 49, 311–38; 50, 289–317.

1985: 'Observations about the pronunciation of Hebrew in rabbinic sources', *HUCA* 56, 117–43.

Weinfeld, M., 1981–82: 'The Balaam oracle and the Deir 'Allā inscription', *Shenaton* 5–6, 141–47.

1984: 'Kuntillet 'Ajrud inscriptions and their significance', *SEL* 1, 121–30.

Weingreen, J., 1954: 'The construct-genitive relation in Hebrew syntax', *VT* 4, 50–59.

Weinreich, M., 1954: 'Prehistory and early history of Yiddish', in U. Weinreich (ed.), *The field of Yiddish: studies in language, folklore, and literature*, II, The Hague, pp. 73–101.

1963–64: 'The origin of the Ashkenazic pronunciation with reference to related problems of Yiddish and Askenazic Hebrew', *Leshonenu* 27–28, 131–47, 230–51, 318–19. H.

Weinreich, U., 1953: *Languages in contact*. New York.

Weippert, H. and M., 1982: 'Die "Bileam"-Inschrift von Tell Dēr 'Allā', ZDPV 98, 75–103.

Weippert, M., 1964–66: 'Archäologischer Jahresbericht', *ZDPV* 80, 169–72; 82, 328–30.

1971: 'Edom. Studien und Materialien zur Geschichte der Edomiter auf Grund schriftlicher und archäologischer Quellen'. Inauguration-Dissertation, Eberhard-Karls-Universität, Tübingen.

Weisberg, D., 1968: 'Some observations on late Babylonian texts and rabbinic literature', *HUCA* 39, 71–80.

Weiss, J.H., 1867: *Mishpaṭ leshon ha-Mishnah*. Vienna.

Weiss, R., 1965–66: 'Bibliyyografyah shel ha-Shomronim', *Tarbiz* 35, 400–03.

Welten, P., 1969: *Die Königs-Stempel*. Wiesbaden.

Wensinck, A.J., 1909: *Het oudste Arameesch*. Utrecht.

Wernberg-Møller, P., 1957: 'Pronouns and suffixes in the Scrolls and the Masoretic Text', *JBL* 76, 44–49.

1958: '"Pleonastic" waw in Classical Hebrew', *JSS* 3, 321–26.

1958a: 'Studies in the defective spellings in the Isaiah-Scroll of St. Mark's Monastery', *JSS* 3, 244–64.

1959: 'Observations on the Hebrew participle', *ZAW* 71, 54–67.

1959–60: 'The noun of the "qṭwl" class in the Massoretic Text', *RQ* 2, 448–50.

Werner, A., 1979: 'Leshono shel Sefer Yonah ke-midah li-kvi'at zeman ḥibburo', *BM* 24, 396–405.

Werner, F., 1983: *Die Wortbildung der hebräischen Adjektiva*. Wiesbaden.

Wertheimer, Y., 1975–76: 'On "'omnam" and its compounds as concessive particles', *Leshonenu* 40, 233–49. H.

Wevers, J.W., 1961: 'Semitic bound structures', *Canadian journal of linguistics* 7, 9–14.

1970: 'Ḥeth in Classical Hebrew', in J.W. Wevers and D.B. Redford (eds.), *Essays on the ancient Semitic world*, Toronto, pp. 101–12.
Wexler, P., 1990: *The schizoid nature of Modern Hebrew: a Slavic language in search of a Semitic past*. Wiesbaden.
Wheeler, S.B., 1970–71: 'The infixed "-t-" in Biblical Hebrew', *JANES* 3, 21–31.
Whitaker, R.E., 1971: *A concordance to the Ugaritic literature*. Cambridge, Mass.
Whitley, C.F., 1972: 'Some functions of the Hebrew particles "beth" and "lamedh"', *JQR*, n.s., 72, 199–206.
1972a: 'The positive force of the Hebrew particle "bal"', *ZAW* 84, 213–19.
1974: 'Has the particle "šām" an asseverative force?', *Biblica* 55, 394–98.
1975: 'Some aspects of Hebrew poetic diction', *UF* 7, 493–502.
1975a: 'The Hebrew emphatic particle "l^{e}-" with pronominal suffixs, *JQR*, n.s., 65, 225–28.
Wickes, W., 1970: *Two treatises on the accentuation of the Old Testament*. With a Prolegomenon by A. Dotan. New York.
Wiesenberg, E.J., 1976: 'Rabbinic Hebrew as an aid in the study of Biblical Hebrew, illustrated in the exposition of the rare words "rḥt" and "mzrh"', *HUCA* 47, 143–80.
Wilch, J.R., 1969: *Time and event. An exegetical study of the use of* 'eth *in the Old Testament*. Leiden.
Wildberger, H., 1967: '"Glauben": Erwägungen zu "h'myn"', *SVT* 16, 372–86.
Wilensky, M., 1978: *Meḥkarim be-lashon u-ve-sifrut*. Ed. by S. Abramson, Jerusalem.
Williams, R.J., 1967: *Hebrew syntax: an outline*. Toronto.
1970: 'The passive Qal theme in Hebrew', in J.W. Wevers and D.B. Redford (eds.), *Essays on the ancient Semitic world*, Toronto, pp. 43–50.
Williamson, H.G.M., 1977: *Israel in the Books of Chronicles*. Cambridge, pp. 37–59.
Wilson, R.M., 1956–57: 'Did Jesus speak Greek?', *ET* 68, 121–22.
Winton Thomas, D., 1938: 'The language of the Old Testament', in H. Wheeler Robinson (ed.), *Record and revelation*, Oxford, pp. 374–402.
1939: *The recovery of the ancient Hebrew language*. Cambridge.
1953: 'A consideration of some unusual ways of expressing the superlative in Hebrew', *VT* 3, 209–24.
1956: 'The use of "neṣaḥ" as a superlative in Hebrew', *JSS* 1, 106–09.
1968: 'Some further remarks on unusual ways of expressing the superlative in Hebrew', *VT* 18, 120–24.
1974: Review of Macuch 1969, in P.R. Ackroyd (ed.), *Bible bibliography 1967–1973: Old Testament. The Book Lists of the Society for Old Testament Study 1967–73*, Oxford, pp. 273–74.
Wiseman, D.J., 1953: *The Alalakh tablets*. London.
Woolley, C.L., 1955: *Alalakh. An account of the excavations at Tell Atchana in the Hatary, 1937–1949*. Oxford.
van der Woude, A.S., 1964: 'Das hebräische *Pronomen demonstrativum* als hinweisende Interjektion', *JEOL* 18, 307–13.
Wright, W., 1890: *Lectures on the comparative grammar of the Semitic languages*. Cambridge.
Wunderlich, C., 1978: 'An outline of the grammar of selected Hebrew ostraca from Arad'. Doct. diss., Harvard University.
Würthwein, E., 1979: *The text of the Old Testament: an introduction to the Biblia Hebraica*. Grand Rapids.
Wutz, F.X., 1925: 'Ist der hebräische Urtext wieder erreichbar?', *ZAW* 43, 115–19.
1925–53: *Die Transkriptionen von der Septuaginta bis zu Hieronymus*. 2 vols. Stuttgart.
1933: 'Abweichende Vokalisationsüberlieferung im hebräischen Text', *BZ* 21, 9–21.
1937: *Systematische Wege von der Septuaginta zum hebräischen Urtext*. Stuttgart.
Xella, P., 1981: *I testi rituali di Ugarit*. I: Testi. Rome.
Yadin (Sukenik), Y., 1959: 'Recipients or owners: a note on the Samaria ostraca', *IEJ* 9, 184–87.
1960: *Hazor II. An account of the second season of excavations*. Jerusalem.
1961: 'Ancient Judaean weights and the date of the Samaria ostraca', *ScrHier* 3, 9–25.
1961a: 'The expedition to the Judean Desert 1960. Expedition D', *IEJ* 11, 36–52.

1962: 'A further note on the Samaria ostraca', *IEJ* 12, 64–66.
1965: *The Ben Sira Scroll from Masada*. Jerusalem.
1968: 'A further note on the lamed in the Samaria ostraca', *IEJ* 18, 50–51.
1983: *The Temple Scroll*. 3 vols. Jerusalem.

Yahalom, Y., 1969–70: 'The Palestinian vocalization in Ḣedwata's *kedushtot* and the language tradition it reflects', *Leshonenu* 34, 25–60. H.
1974: 'The syntax of the ancient *piyyuṭ* (including Yannai) as a basis for its style'. Doct. diss., Hebrew University, Jerusalem. H.
1977: 'Rishme tarbut Yawan ba-piyyuṭ ha-'Ivri ha-kadum', *P6WCJS*, III, 203–13.
1978: *Kiṭ'e ha-Genizah shel piyyuṭe Yannay*. Jerusalem.
1980–81: 'Ha-pasiv ba-piyyuṭ: leshon ha-shir u-leshon ha-prozah u-binyane ha-po'al', *Leshonenu* 45, 17–31.
1981: '"Aṣ koṣeṣ" (gishot we-'emdot bi-sh'elot signon ha-piyyuṭ u-leshono)', *Jerusalem studies in Hebrew literature* 1, 167–81.
1985: *Poetic language in the early* piyyuṭ. Jerusalem. H.
1988: 'Ha-nikkud ha-'Ereṣ-Yisre'eli – ha-meḥkar we-hesegaw', *Leshonenu* 52, 112–43.

Yahuda, A.S., 1933: *The language of the Pentateuch in its relation to Egyptian*. I. London.

Yalon, Ḥ., 1937–39 (ed.): *Kunṭeresim le-'inyene ha-lashon ha-'Ivrit*. 2 vols. Jerusalem.
1959–60: 'Nimmukim le-mishnayot menukkadot', *Leshonenu* 24, 15–39, 157–66, 253.
1960–61: 'Mishnahs and their pointing', *Sinai* 48, 89–105. H.
1960–61a: 'Versions and forms of language in various Mishnahs', *Sinai* 48, 254–60. H.
1963–64: *Mavo le-nikkud ha-Mishnah*. Jerusalem.
1963–64a: 'The kameṣ in Babylonian phonetics and in Yemen', *Tarbiz* 33, 97–108. H.
1964–65: 'He'arot we-tikkunim', *Leshonenu* 29, 59–62.
1966–67: 'Linguistic notes to Yannay's *piyyuṭim*', *Leshonenu* 31, 118–22. H.
1967: *Studies in the Dead Sea Scrolls. Philological essays 1949–1952*. Jerusalem. H.
1967–68: 'Gleanings on Mishnaic Hebrew', *Tarbiz* 37, 133–34. H.
1971: *Pirke lashon*. Jerusalem.

Yannay, I., 1973–74: 'Multiradical verbs in the Hebrew language', *Leshonenu* 38, 118–30. H.

Yarden, D., 1958–62: 'Mi-millono ha-mikra'i shel R. Shemu'el ha-Nagid', *LeshLA* 87, 135–49; 90, 215–25; 129, 174–78.
1964: 'Mi-millono ha-mikra'i shel R. Shemu'el ha-Nagid', *Biṣaron* 29, 188–91.
1966: *Diwan Shemu'el ha-Nagid: Ben Tehillim*. Jerusalem.
1967–75: 'Mi-leshono shel R. Shelomoh ibn Gabirol', *LeshLA* 19, 218–20; 20, 12–16; 21, 28–36; 26, 233–36.
1977–79: *The liturgical poetry of Rabbi Solomon ibn Gabirol*. 2 vols. Jerusalem. H.
1986: 'Mi-millono ha-mikra'i shel Rabbi Shelomoh ibn Gabirol', *Sinai* 50, 97–98.

Yassine, K. and Teixidor, J., 1986: 'Ammonite and Aramaic inscriptions from Tell El-Mazār in Jordan', *BASOR* 264, 45–50.

Yeivin, I., 1959–60: 'A biblical fragment with Tiberian non-Masoretic vocalization', *Tarbiz* 29, 345–56. H.
1962: 'A Babylonian fragment of the Bible in the abbreviated system', *Textus* 2, 120–39.
1962a: 'Biblical fragments from Yemen written on vellum', *KirSef* 37, 267–71. H.
1963: 'A Palestinian fragment of *hafṭaroth* and other mss. with mixed pointing', *Textus* 3, 121–27.
1964: 'New Babylonian-Yemenite Bible-fragments in the Jewish National Library', *KirSef* 39, 563–72. H.
1965: 'Babylonian-Yemenite Bible-fragments from the collection of Mr. Yehudah Levi Naḥum, Ḥolon', *KirSef* 40, 560–68. H.
1968: 'The Babylonian vocalization and the linguistic tradition it reflects'. Typescript, Jerusalem. H.
1968a: *The Aleppo Codex of the Bible. A study of its vocalization and accentuation*. Jerusalem. H.
1972: 'Mivḥar kitve-yad be-nikkud Bavli'. Typescript, Jerusalem.
1972a: 'Ṣurot "yqṭwlnw", "yqwṭlnw" bi-Mgillot Yehudah le-'or masoret ha-nikkud ha-Bavli', in B. Uffenheimer (ed.), *Ha-Mikra we-toledot Yisra'el*, Tel-Aviv, pp. 256–76.
1974 (ed.): *Osef kiṭ'e ha-Genizah shel ha-Mishnah be-nikkud Bavli*. Jerusalem.

1978: 'The dageshed alephs in the Bible', in Y. Avishur and J. Blau (eds.), *Studies in Bible and the ancient Near East presented to Samuel E. Loewenstamm on his 70th birthday*, II, Jerusalem, pp. 223–27. H.
1979–80: 'Millim 'aḥadot we-nikkudan be-masoret ha-lashon ha-Bavlit', *LeshLA* 31, 148–55.
1980: *Introduction to the Tiberian Masorah.* Trans. and ed. by E.J. Revell. Missoula.
1980a: 'Nikkude millim we-ṣurotehen be-kitve-yad we-terumatan la-millon we-la-dikduk', *P6WCJS*, Division D, 215–22.
1981–82: 'The *ga'yot* and their function', *Leshonenu* 46, 39–56. H.
1985: *The Hebrew language tradition as reflected in the Babylonian vocalization.* 2 vols. Jerusalem. H.
Yeivin, S., 1969: 'Ostracon A1/382 from Hazor and its implications', *EI* 9, *86–87. H.
Yellin, D., 1905: *Ha-mivṭa we-ha-ketiv be-'Ivrit*. Jerusalem.
1923: 'Ben-Yehudah and the revival of the Hebrew language', *JPOS* 3, 93–109.
1925–26: 'Ben Kohelet of Samuel ha-Nagid', *JQR*, n.s., 16, 267–78.
1935–36: 'Mosheh ben 'Ezra' we-shirato', *Tarbiz* 7, 319–34.
1975: *Hebrew poetry in Spain*. Jerusalem. H.
Yitshaki, Y., 1969–71: 'The Hebrew authors of the *Haskala*: their views on the Hebrew language', *Leshonenu* 34, 287–305; 35, 39–59. H.
Yo'eli, M., 1953–54: *Taḥbir 'Ivri*. Tel-Aviv.
Young, G.D., 1951–52: 'The present status of Ugaritic studies', *JKF* 2, 225–45.
1956: *Concordance of Ugaritic*. Rome.
Zaborski, A., 1969: 'Root determinatives and the problem of biconsonantal roots in Semitic', *FolOr* 11, 307–13.
1971: 'Biconsonantal verbal roots in Semitic', *Zeszyty naukowe Uniwersitetu Jagiellońskiego* 269, 51–98.
Zadok, R., 1978: '[Review of M.D. Coogan] West Semitic personal names in the Murašû documents [Missoula, 1976]', *BASOR* 231, 73–78.
1982: 'Remarks on the inscriptions of "HD YS'Y" from Tall Fakhariya', *TAJ* 9, 117–29.
Zafrani, Ḥ., 1963–66: 'La lecture traditionnelle de l'hébreu chez les juifs arabophones de Tiznit (Maroc)', *GLECS* 10, 29–31.
Zayadine, F. and Thompson, H.O., 1973: 'The Ammonite inscription from Tell Siran', *Berytus* 22, 115–40.
1973a: 'The Tell Siran inscription', *BASOR* 212, 5–11.
Zeidmann, Y.A., 1943: 'Signon Mishneh Torah la-RaMBaM', *Sinai* 6, 428–38; 7, 96–101.
1955: ''Al leshono shel ha-RaMBaM', *LeshLA* 6, 3–10.
Zeldner, E., 1966: 'And it's all in Hebrew', *Modern language journal* 40, 71–75.
Zevit, Z., 1980: Matres lectionis *in ancient Hebrew epigraphs*. Cambridge, Mass.
1984: 'The Khirbet el-Qôm inscription mentioning a goddess', *BASOR* 255, 39–47.
Zimmerli, W., 1971: '"Ḥsd" im Schriftum von Qumran', in *Hommages à André Dupont-Sommer*, Paris, pp. 439–49.
Zimmermann, F., 1938: 'The Aramaic origin of Daniel viii–xiii', *JBL* 57, 255–72.
1939: 'Some verses in Daniel in the light of a translation hypothesis', *JBL* 58, 349–54.
1948–49: 'The Aramaic provenance of Qohelet', *JQR*, n.s., 39, 17–45.
1949–50: 'The question of Hebrew in Qohelet', *JQR*, n.s., 40, 79–102.
1951–52: 'Chronicles as a partially translated book', *JQR*, n.s., 42, 265–82, 387–412.
1960–61: 'Hebrew translation in Daniel', *JQR*, n.s., 51, 198–208.
Zimmern, H., 1917: *Akkadische Fremdwörter als Beweis für babylonischen Kultureinfluss.* 2nd ed. Leipzig.
Zuber, B., 1986: *Das Tempussystem des biblischen Hebräisch. Eine Untersuchung am Text.* Berlin/New York.
Zucker, M., 1964: 'Berurim be-'Essa Meshali le-Rav Se'adyah Ga'on', *Tarbiz* 33, 40–57.
Zulay, M, 1933: *Zur Liturgie der babylonischen Juden. Geniza Texte herausgegeben, übersetzt und bearbeitet sowie auf ihre Punktation hinuntersucht*. Stuttgart.

1936: 'Meḥkare Yannay', *YMḤSI* 2, 213–391.
1942–43: 'Nishkaḥot bi-lshon ha-payyeṭanim', *'Inyene lashon* 1, 1–6; 2, 1–4.
1943: 'Leshon payyeṭanim', *Moznayim* 16, 217–23.
1944: 'Li-dmutah shel leshon ha-payyeṭanim', *Melilah* 1, 69–80.
1945–46: ''Iyyune lashon be-fiyyuṭe Yannay', *YMḤSI* 6, 161–248.
1964: *Ha-'askolah ha payyeṭanit shel Rav Se'adyah Ga'on*. Jerusalem.
Zuntz, G., 1956: 'Greek words in the Talmud', *JSS* 1, 129–40.
Zunz, L., 1865: *Literaturgeschichte der synagogalen Poesie*. Berlin.
1920: *Die synagogale Poesie des Mittelalters*. 2nd ed. Frankfurt-am-Main.
Zurawel, T., 1984: 'The Qal conjugation in Samaritan Hebrew', in M. Bar-Asher (ed.), *Massorot: studies in language traditions*, I, Jerusalem, pp. 135–51. H.

Index

John 1 n.
John Hyrcanus 147
Jonah 122–23
Joseph ha-Qostandini 106
Josephus 1, 77 n.
Jubilees 127
Judah Halevi 221, 225, 226–27, 230, 240, 242

kabbalah, mysticism 224, 245, 262, 266
Kerak 42
ketiv 67, 74, 95, 110
Khirbet Beit Lei 64
Khirbet el-Meshash 64 n.
Khirbet el-Qom 63
Khirbet Raddana 64 n.
kinah 223
Kitāb al-Ḫulaf (Mishael b. 'Uzziel) 106, see also '*ḥillufim*'
Kitāb al-Muḥāḍara wal-Muḏākara (Moses ibn Ezra) 225, 226 nn., 240 n.
Kitāb al-Tawṭi'a (Abū Isḥāq Shams al-Ḥukamā') 150
Koheleth 115, 124–25
koinē 170, 275, 282, see also '*lingua franca*'
Koran 15, 205
kotvanim 77
Kuntillet 'Ajrud 63, 67

Lachish 17, 41, 63, 65, 67, 68
Lampronti, I. 267
langue mélangée 164, see also '*Mischsprache*'
Late Biblical Hebrew 112–29, see also names of post-exilic books of the Bible, etc.
 overall linguistic features 129
 historical background 112–14
Latin 16, 38, see also 'transcriptions, Greek and Latin'
 connexions with Hebrew
  Mediaeval and Modern 204, 245, 252, 263–64, 271
  Qumran and Rabbinic 146, 167, 168, 180, 188, 199, 201
lavlarim 77
Lebensohn, A.D. 268
Lehr- und Lesebuch zur Sprache der Mischnah (Geiger, A.) 162
Leshon Benei 'Adam (Blanc, H.) 276
Leshon ha-Mikra 'o Leshon Ḥakhamim? (Bendavid, A.) 273
Lexicon Heptaglotton (Castell, E.) 5
Libyan, Libyco-Berber 4, 26
Liḥyan 15
lingua franca 9, 15, 270, see also '*koinē*'

The literary and oral tradition of Hebrew and Aramaic (Ben-Ḥayyim, Z.) 152
loan-translations, see also under 'Arabic' (for Mediaeval Hebrew)
 Aramaic, in Late Biblical and Rabbinic Hebrew 121, 122, 201
 European, in Modern Hebrew 286
 German, in Mediaeval and Modern Hebrew 265–66, 268
 Greek, in Qumran and Rabbinic Hebrew 146, 201
 Italian, in Mediaeval Hebrew 264
 Latin, in Qumran Hebrew 146
 Romance, in Mediaeval Hebrew 243
loanwords, see also under 'Arabic' (for Mediaeval Hebrew)
 Akkadian, in Rabbinic Hebrew 199, 201
 Arabic, in Modern Hebrew 270–71, 280
 Aramaic
  in Modern Hebrew 271
  in Qumran Hebrew 146
  in Rabbinic Hebrew 173, 199, 200–01
 English, in Modern Hebrew 280
 Greek
  in Late Biblical and Rabbinic Hebrew 115, 188, 199, 201
  in Mediaeval and Modern Hebrew 211, 256, 265, 271
 Italian, in Mediaeval Hebrew 265
 Latin
  in Mediaeval and Modern Hebrew 264, 271
  in Rabbinic Hebrew 188, 199, 201
 Persian
  in Late Biblical and Qumran Hebrew 115, 146
  in Rabbinic Hebrew 199, 201
 Semitic
  in Biblical Hebrew 75
  in Greek 28
 Yiddish, in Modern Hebrew 280
LXX, see '*Septuagint*'

ma'amad 224
Maggid (journal) 267
Maḥberet (Menaḥem b. Saruq) 246–49
Maḥzor Vitry 86
Maimonides 107, 162, 205, 208, 261, 263
Manual of Discipline (1QS) 130
manuscripts and codices
 Babylonian 95–100
 Palestinian 90
 Palestino-Tiberian 92–93